CURRENT ISSUES IN URBAN ECONOMICS

CURRENT ISSUES IN URBAN ECONOMICS

**EDITED BY PETER MIESZKOWSKI
AND MAHLON STRASZHEIM**

*THE JOHNS HOPKINS UNIVERSITY PRESS
BALTIMORE AND LONDON*

Manufactured in the United States of America

The Johns Hopkins University Press, Baltimore, Maryland 21218
The Johns Hopkins Press Ltd., London

Library of Congress Catalog Number 78–14947
ISBN 0–8018–2109–6
ISBN 0–8018–2184–3 (pbk.)

Library of Congress Cataloging in Publication data will be found on the last printed page of this book.

CONTENTS

TABLES

PREFACE

Nearly twenty years ago, the Committee on Urban Economics was formed to stimulate research in urban economics. With support by the Ford Foundation and Resources for the Future, a series of conferences were sponsored to disseminate research in the field. In 1968 CUE published a lengthy conference volume, *Issues in Urban Economics,* intended to summarize the field of urban economics, to suggest research initiatives, and to stimulate further scholarly effort.

During CUE's existence urban economics had developed considerably. A considerable variety of outlets for research publication and various sources of funding for urban specialists now exist. In 1976, Dick Netzer as the Chairperson of CUE asked us to organize and edit a follow-up volume to *Issues in Urban Economics,* which would culminate CUE's activities. This volume has a similar motivation to the first: to assess the state of urban economics and its theoretical foundations, to outline outstanding research questions, and to summarize major policy issues.

A conference on initial drafts of most of the papers was held in early May 1977, in Columbus, Ohio, under the sponsorship of the Academy of Contemporary Problems, where each paper was formally discussed.

In planning the volume, we attempted a comprehensive review of all of the major issues in urban economics. Authors were asked to review current literature as well as to highlight major unresolved research questions. In some instances we have included papers in new topics that we felt unusually timely, important to the future development of the field, or important because of the relevant complementary research in other branches of economics. The choice of papers and the general subject of each paper reflect to some extent the choices and research biases of the editors and the authors respectively.

We shall not attempt to provide a detailed contrast between this volume and *Issues in Urban Economics,* nor shall we provide summaries of the sixteen papers. The major differences between the two volumes reflect the differences in research emphasis in urban economics between 1968 and the present. A number of topics that appear only in the current volume reflect the recent developments in the field.

The most striking difference between the two volumes is that in *Current Issues in Urban Economics* relatively little space is devoted to interurban or regional economics. The paper by Mieszkowski on regional development trends, Rosen's paper on the measurements of the quality of life in different cities, and Smith-Welch's paper on interregional wage differentials are the only papers that explicitly deal with systems of cities.

The limited attention devoted to regional economics in this volume reflects the development of urban economics in the last decade. Regional economics has historically been concerned with location theory, interregional migration and factor mobility, and interregional transportation. Many of the theoretical issues of interest have been central to the field of international trade; the relationships between these two branches of economics is apparent in the paper by Mieszkowski.

As population shifts in the postwar period have resulted in an increasing share of the population residing within urban areas, research in regional economics has increasingly tended to focus on growth differentials among metropolitan areas. Environmental and resource implications of alternative regional growth patterns have also been emphasized. However, analysis of growth patterns in regional economics continues to be plagued by severe data problems; migration data are very incomplete except for census years and virtually no data exist on interregional movements of capital. Data on regional labor markets are available and analyzed in the Smith-Welch paper, but little empirical data exist for modeling the causes of regional development processes in the absence of better data on interregional capital flows.

In contrast, a very considerable research effort has been devoted in urban economics to theoretical and empirical modeling of intrametropolitan development and the structure of urban areas. This has been facilitated by a very substantial data base. Among the most important theoretical developments is the work of Mills and Muth that extends and elaborates the earlier work by Alonso on moncentric models of urban areas. A rapidly growing literature that uses analytic models has emerged and is reviewed by William Wheaton. Another key theoretical issue important to the analysis of urban form and residential choice is the influence of public goods. Henderson reviews the extensive work on the Tiebout model and related issues of fiscal capitalization. The papers of Henderson and Wheaton also deal with the question of optimal city size and the optimal allocation of population between cities.

An alternative theoretical approach to urban economics treats space in urban areas as a set of neighborhoods with irregular boundaries, often created by racial composition, jurisdictional boundaries, or the composition of housing stocks. Housing markets are modeled as a stock adjustment process. Quigley reviews the econometric models of housing markets under these general assumptions. Analysis of market clearing and the evolution of submarkets in such an approach is a general equilibrium problem of considerable complexity, typically requiring large-scale computer simulation models. Ingram surveys this literature.

The transport sector plays a critical role in all of the models of urban spatial structure. The role of externalities is important in the analysis of urban transport systems. The papers by Mohring and Straszheim consider how congestion and other externalities affect the comparative costs of alternative modes.

The literature on housing markets is the most extensive portion of the empirical literature on urban spatial structure. The papers by Quigley and Yinger review the housing market literature and the special attention devoted to the role of race in urban housing markets. A separate paper by John Weicher is devoted to housing policy.

Another characteristic of urban economics research is its orientation toward public policy. Research into the nature of the public sector within urban areas and the consequences of a wide variety of public sector actions has accounted for an increasing share of research in urban economics in recent years. Papers by Henderson, Inman, Oakland, Mills, Rubinfeld, and Clotfelter deal primarily with the local public sector. Considerable attention has been devoted to the analysis of the conditions for efficiency and capitalization, which Henderson surveys. The papers by Mills and Rubinfeld analyze zoning, property rights, and equity—issues that are likely to become increasingly important to the field. Papers by Clotfelter on busing and Oakland on the financial plight of central cities consider how selected policy instruments might affect metropolitan development patterns. Together with Inman's review of the literature of public choice and fiscal federalism as it applies to urban areas, and supporting empirical evidence on public sector decision-making, these several papers review virtually all the major issues of the public sector as it impacts on urban areas.

Many topics were omitted from this volume, often because of the length constraint. Urban economics now has an extensive and well-defined body of literature in a very wide range of subtopics. There is no paper on comparative (European or third-world) urban problems and policies. Urban crime, environmental policy, and energy issues are not covered.

A lengthy research agenda describing what remains to be accomplished in urban economics cannot be attempted here. Many of the unsettled issues emerge in the papers. Among the most prominent issues not covered in this volume is the relative importance of different factors in employment location and decentralization patterns within metropolitan areas, which deserves far more research. Principally because of data problems, little research has been conducted on employment locations or urban labor markets in recent years. Effective use of the censuses of employment is plagued by disclosure rules. The basis for the decline of the northern regions of the country relative to warmer southern and western regions is little understood.

This is a volume that reflects the research progress that has taken place in the last ten years. We appreciate the effort made by all the authors to capture the state of the field in their papers. We hope it will be of interest to undergraduate and graduate students in economics and other social sciences and to policy-makers involved with urban planning and problems.

PETER MIESZKOWSKI AND MAHLON STRASZHEIM

I

METROPOLITAN DEVELOPMENT TRENDS AND WELFARE IMPLICATIONS

1

RECENT TRENDS IN URBAN AND REGIONAL DEVELOPMENT

PETER MIESZKOWSKI

INTRODUCTION

This chapter describes the broad patterns of urban and regional development in the United States in the postwar period. Interregional migration, regional shifts in employment, and changes in regional income differentials receive primary emphasis. That interregional trends deserve increasing attention in urban economics derives from several facts. The most important is that as different regions in the United States have become increasingly integrated, the fortunes and development of different regions and cities have become increasingly closely interrelated. For example, in the past, lagging Southern development induced many unskilled Southerners to migrate to the industrial cities of the North. The large increase in the minority population of Northern cities, especially of central cities, and the large increase in the dependent population of these areas created problems for those cities. More recently, Southern and Western development has occurred at the expense of the North. Cities in the North are facing various problems because of the out-migration of capital, deteriorating tax bases, and slow economic growth.

The theoretical arguments that growth rates among cities are interrelated are also quite persuasive. Henderson's work (1974) on economies of scale implies a system of cities must exist. Polinsky and Rubenfeld (1977) and Courant and Rubenfeld (1978) have also focused on an intermetropolitan perspective. They have shown, for example, that if a particular city intro-

Peter Mieszkowski is a professor of economics at the University of Houston.

I would like to thank Mahlon Straszheim for his excellent comments on previous drafts of this chapter and for his editorial assistance, which greatly improved the organization of this chapter. The comments of Irving Hoch, Dick Netzer and Lou Stern are also gratefully acknowledged.

duces a new transportation network, the resulting migration of labor and capital will result in the benefits of the investment being diffused throughout the system of cities.

Regional issues have also assumed greater importance in recent discussions of national urban policy. The particular formulas to be used for the distribution of revenue sharing funds have always been debated, with regional or geographic implications of various formulas central to the debate. The recent shifts in regional growth have also fostered a debate about the regional dimensions of federal policies and the need for a national growth policy. As economic conditions in the North have deteriorated relative to those of the South throughout the 1970s, Northern politicians have increasingly laid stress on the importance of the federal taxation and expenditure process in draining resources away from the North. Some analysts attempt to characterize the North as a declining region that is in need, and worthy of fiscal aid. Much of the urban policy discussion has recently revolved around whether Northern central cities should be subsidized in a "targeted manner." Public employment job programs and Comprehensive Employment Training Act (CETA) job training has also had a heavy regional focus. An important regional dimension has been added to federal policy discussions.

1. TRENDS IN REGIONAL DEVELOPMENT

The rapid urbanization of the United States and the shifts of population out of agricultural and rural areas into metropolitan areas have slowed down and probably reversed in the 1970s. In 1950 the total farm population was 23 million. The most dramatic decrease in the farm population occurred in the South where the farm population fell from 11.9 million in 1950 to 3.8 million in 1970. National farm employment has stabilized at about 3.3 million in the mid 1970s. The farm population has become so small relative to the total population that a future decline cannot be expected—given the food shortages throughout the world and the strong comparative advantage of the United States in the production of food.

The annual growth rate of population of metropolitan counties relative to nonmetropolitan areas was over three times higher (1.3/.4) during the 1960s. During the 1970s the relative growth rates had reversed in favor of nonmetropolitan counties (.8/1.2). However, in 1975, 73 percent of the U.S. population of 213 million lived in metropolitan counties. The farm population is only 9 million of the total population of nonmetropolitan areas, which is alternatively estimated to number between 57 and 58 million in 1975 by Deavers (1977) and Morrison (1977), so roughly 23 percent of the nation's population is nonfarm, nonmetropolitan.

Deavers estimates that over 50 percent of the nonmetropolitan population resides in counties that are not adjacent to metropolitan counties and the recent population growth for the adjacent counties is somewhat higher than nonadjacent counties. The attachment of this population to metropolitan areas may be quite weak. Morrison estimates that at most 4 million of the nonmetropolitan population of 57 million commute to Standard Metropolitan Statistical Areas (SMSAs). However, a fair proportion of nonmetropolitan growth is probably a spillover from metropolitan areas, as currently defined by the Census Bureau.

It is too early to tell whether the more rapid increase in nonmetropolitan population in recent years represents a significant disenchantment with big city life and a preference for small New England towns, the Catskills, Pocanos, Ozarks, and the Texas hill country. These communities have always been attractive and data in Haren (1977) that indicates that 40 percent of employment increases between 1970 and 1977 occurred in nonmetropolitan counties is strong evidence of the vitality of these areas and their potential as recreational and retirement centers and their importance as mining communities.

The slowdown in metropolitan growth has been accompanied by very slow growth of the largest metropolitan areas. During the 1950s the population of SMSAs that exceed 3 million grew at twice the rate of national population change. During the 1960s they grew at the national average, about 10 percent. In the 1970s the population of these areas has remained roughly unchanged, while the nation's population has been growing at 1 percent a year. For example, during 1970–74 the population of the New York SMSA declined by .34 million, Los Angeles lost .12 million persons, and Chicago, Detroit, and Philadelphia lost small percentages of population; the population of San Francisco grew by less than 1 percent in the four years. Also, a number of other large SMSAs located in the North lost population. In contrast, a number of Southern and Western SMSAs (other than Los Angeles and San Francisco) have been growing very rapidly in recent years.

The most striking trend in regional development is the more rapid growth of the South and the West (the "Sunbelt") relative to the older, colder regions of the Northeast and Midwest. Although the populations of the South and the West have been growing at rates above the national average since 1950, there has been a significant acceleration in the rates of population growth and employment of these two regions relative to the Northeast and North Central regions. Between 1970 and 1976 the growth of population in the South and the West was almost double the national average of 5.9 percent. During the same period the population growth of the middle Atlantic states was .3 percent, and the population of New York State fell by about 1 percent.

As birth and death rates do not vary a great deal between regions, interregional migration must be a key element in explaining differences in

TABLE 1.1. Net Migration of Whites (in Thousands), 1950–75

Region	1950–60	1960–70	1970–75
United States	2685	2284	0
Northeast	−206	−519	−1278
North Central	−679	−1272	−1143
South	52	1806	1815
West	3518	2269	606

SOURCE: U.S. Bureau of the Census, Statistical Abstracts of the United States, 1966 (table 35) and 1975 (table 30), and Current Population Reports, Series P–20, No. 292.

population growth. It is well known that the decline of employment opportunities in Southern agriculture caused a substantial out-migration during the 1950s and 1960s. The migration of blacks from the South is most striking: it involved some 2.8 million people during this 20-year period, who moved primarily to the North. Since 1970 this migration has stopped and reversed. Between 1970 and 1975, one hundred and fourteen thousand blacks migrated from the North, 90 percent of them to the West.

The migration of whites from the North to the West and to the South has been substantial. Table 1.1 indicates that out-migration of whites from the North accelerated in the 1970s. Migration information from current population reports is not comparable to census data, which includes information on immigrants. The construction of a time series of *total* migrants from population surveys shows a marked acceleration in net out-migration from the Northeast. During 1971–76 an average of 260 thousand persons a year migrated out of the Northeast, i.e., four times the annual rate during 1954–70.

In contrast, the trend of out-migration from the North Central region is much less definite and seems to be more closely correlated with the business cycle than the out-migration from the Northeast. The levels of out-migration from the North Central region during the 1975 recession are about the same as during the 1958 recession. Although out-migration from both Northern regions accelerates during recessions, a reading of the time-series evidence suggests that North Central economic activity (population levels) are quite sensitive to cyclical variations.

Table 1.2 presents information on rates of growth in nonagricultural employment by major census regions for five-year intervals beginning in 1940 through 1970 and from 1970 to the middle of 1977. The last point is a rate-of-change figure over a seven-year interval. This is not an ideal measure of employment opportunities by state or region, as the relative importance of agricultural employment varies by region, but it is quite good, especially for the most recent time period.

Although the data is presented in aggregate form by region, I shall

TABLE 1.2. Percent Change in Nonagricultural Employment by Major Census Regions for Selected Periods, 1940–77

Region	1945	1950	1955	1960	1965	1970	1977
United States	24.7%	12.0%	12.0%	6.6%	12.0%	17.0%	16.0%
Northeast	14.0	7.5	6.1	4.2	8.2	13.5	9.0
Mid-Atlantic	16.8	9.1	6.0	3.3	6.5	11.2	0.4
East North Central	22.9	14.3	10.9	1.2	10.6	13.3	11.3
West North Central	22.6	15.6	9.3	6.4	10.3	15.9	18.8
South Atlantic	24.6	14.3	14.9	12.9	18.5	23.6	22.5
East South Central	29.9	12.6	13.3	8.4	17.4	18.1	27.0
West South Central	34.5	18.3	16.7	9.8	15.6	21.2	32.2
Mountain	24.6	23.1	20.5	21.6	16.1	22.5	42.2
Pacific	51.8	6.9	23.0	21.4	17.5	20.1	26.2

SOURCE: Bureau of Labor Statistics Bulletin 1370-12 and Employment and Earnings, October 1977.

NOTE: Percentage change shown for period is calculated as a percentage of that period relative to employment five years earlier.

make reference to intraregional differences and to specific states. The general conclusions that emerge from table 1.2 are as follows:

1. The relative growth trends that have been observed in the 1970s are of longstanding duration. In general, the Southern states (South Atlantic, East–South Central, West–South Central) have been growing well above the national average throughout the post-war period. The measure of nonagricultural employment biases the interpretation of the trends of regional relative development, since a larger part of Southern growth in nonagricultural employment has been a shift from agricultural activity. In the 1970s all states in the South grew well above the national average, with a number (among them Florida and Texas) growing at double the national rate.

2. The rapid growth of the Pacific states is well known, but growth there, particularly in California, has slowed during the 1970s to slightly below the national average.

3. The growth of the lightly populated Mountain states has been especially rapid in the 1970s. This growth is related in part to mineral production. After a long decline, there has also been a revival of mining in West Virginia.

4. The West–North Central region, which comprises the Plains states of Iowa, Nebraska, Kansas, Minnesota and others, has grown at a rate close to the national average; during the 1970s a number of states in this region have grown at rates well above the national average.

5. The performance of the Midwest (East–North Central) has been

reasonably strong in the post-war period. In particular, Wisconsin has performed at or above national rates. The performance of such large industrial
states as Illinois, Michigan, Ohio, and Indiana is more mixed. Over the
post-war period these states grew at rates between two-thirds to three-
quarters of the national average. The performance of these states has been
especially weak during periods of recession (note the 1955–60 period and
the 1970s). Despite the slow recovery of this region from the 1974 recession, my speculation is that employment in the Midwest will grow at the
national average under conditions of full employment. The fortunes of the
Mid-West—with heavy specialization in capital goods and automobiles—
is most vulnerable to cyclical variations.

6. The performance of the New England and Middle Atlantic states is
weak, though recent trends are mixed. Employment change in such small
states as Vermont, Maine, and New Hampshire has been rapid in recent
years and confirms the strong growth of nonmetropolitan areas. Although
weak in the 1970s, New Jersey and Connecticut grew at the national
average throughout the post-war period.

7. The remaining states are Pennsylvania, Massachusetts, and New
York. Massachusetts and Rhode Island have grown slowly during the last
thirty years. Employment in manufacturing has declined in Massachusetts—
some of this activity has moved to New Hampshire—but the growth of
service employment, especially in Boston, has maintained the economic
base of the state. Employment in that state has grown and continues to
grow at a rate roughly one-half the national average. Pennsylvania has a
similar but weaker record, especially during the period 1955–60 when
absolute employment fell in Pennsylvania. The real disaster area in the
Northeast is New York, which, like Massachusetts, grew at roughly one-
half the national average until 1970. Between 1970 and mid 1977 employment in the nation grew by 17 percent, but employment in New York
State fell by 10 percent. Although the rest of the nation is recovering from
the 1974 recession, employment in New York continues to fall in absolute
terms.

There is really nothing very new about rapid Southern development: it
simply was not noted or its magnitude was not recognized until the last
five years or so. There has been no such shock as an energy crisis or a
major recession to explain the decline of the North. Although recessions,
especially prolonged ones, are especially detrimental to the long-term
development of the North, my interpretation is that the comparative advantages of the North have been gradually eaten away by incremental
movements of capital and population to the West and the South. This
process has accelerated in recent years because the development of the
South relative to the North has become more apparent.

In addition, there is the very weak performance of New York State and
New York City. The decline of the Northeast is largely the decline of New

York State. Although the economic malaise of this state is general, with cities such as Buffalo declining, most of the state's recent economic losses are concentrated in the New York metropolitan area. For example, from 1970 to mid 1977 nonagricultural employment in New York State fell by 299 thousand and the decrease in manufacturing employment was 243 thousand for the New York metropolitan area, and for New York City the losses were 555 thousand (total employment) and 234 thousand (manufacturing employment).

Explaining the economic decline of New York City is a major research task and here I can only provide a few fragmentary speculations.

Although the most dramatic employment decline in New York has been concentrated during the recession-prone 1970s and is general across industry groups, durable and nondurable manufacturing, wholesaling, retail trade, and so forth, I believe that the causative factors are of longstanding duration. Decentralization within the New York metropolitan region has been going on throughout this century (Hoover and Vernon, 1959; Vernon, 1960). Vernon, speculating about the future of New York, noted that the city's fate is determined not by glamour industries—broadcasting, theatres —but by national-market manufacturing. Vernon also noted that although New York is *not* a high-wage city, the concentration of low-wage industries in the region renders its wages high relative to competing cities. For example, the hourly wages for apparel workers in New York City are currently 40 percent higher than in North Carolina; in 1950 the differential was 70 percent. In printing, New York wages are currently 15 percent higher than in Los Angeles, and on average, municipal workers in New York City are paid about 15 percent more than employees of other cities with populations of more than one million. Vernon indicated that high wage disadvantages, cost disadvantages related to congestion, and high transportation costs are weighed against the positive agglomeration economies associated with New York.

The simplest and most general explanation—it is almost tautological— of New York's decline is that the disadvantages have overtaken the advantages. In terms of its industrial structure, New York is highly vulnerable to competition with low-wage states and foreign countries. Bob Leone (1974) showed that in the early 1970s firm relocations were much less important in explaining central-city manufacturing job losses than was the poor health of the companies that remained in the city.

The well-publicized fiscal crisis is probably more a symptom of the economic decline of New York than a direct cause of that decline. However, New York has been most generous with respect to income maintenance, higher education, medical services to the poor, and so on. The city could afford these public expenditures when it was economically dominant, but as the advantages of the city have eroded, the rents that financed the redistributions have declined and—despite the fact that a great deal of the increased public spending in New York has been financed by federal funds (Gramlich, 1976)—the city is currently in severe difficulty.

2. INTRAMETROPOLITAN TRENDS

It is well known that intrametropolitan decentralization has been going on for some time. Some of the documentation was presented by Kain (1968) who studied employment and population growth for the forty largest SMSAs between 1948 and 1963 and found that these cities have lost manufacturing jobs absolutely since 1954 and wholesaling and retailing jobs declined after 1958. Over the same periods employment growth in the metropolitan ring grew steadily. For the cities studied by Kain (1950 central-city boundaries) the suburban ring's share of SMSA manufacturing employment went up from 33 percent in 1948 to 52 percent in 1963, and its share of population went up from 36 percent to 54 percent in the same time span. Over the same period the suburbs' share of retailing employment went up 25 percent to 45 percent. Data presented by Mills (1972) for ninety SMSAs for 1948 and 1963 confirms these trends.

The same trends have continued since 1963 through 1973. Data collated by Seymour Sacks (1977) for the major cities in the four principal regions of the country is presented in table 1.3. His data indicate that central cities in the East and Midwest have continued to lose population and manufacturing employment since 1963 and have grown very slowly, if at all. Metropolitan growth has been more rapid in the South and the West—especially in the South—and confirms the more rapid growth of this region. Differences in the patterns of growth by region is partly due to annexation of land by central cities, which is a practice more prevalent in the South and West. The importance of annexation is illustrated by tables 1.4 and 1.5.

The information on annexations for the Midwest is somewhat misleading: most of the annexations in this region have occurred in two cities,

TABLE 1.3. Mean Population and Employment in Manufacturing Selected SMSAs by Region (in Thousands)

| Region | Population | | | | | | Manufacturing Employment | | | |
| | 1960 | | 1970 | | 1973 | | 1963 | | 1972 | |
	City	Ring	City	Ring	City	Ring	City	Ring	City	Ring
East	902	941	884	1156	851	1184	114	99	92	107
Midwest	599	595	589	747	558	799	91	65	85	85
South	332	232	397	300	408	326	27	12	53	54
West	479	546	554	753	562	797	45	48	45	58

TABLE 1.4. Change in Population of Central Cities Through Annexation, by Region, 1960–70 (Percent Change in Central-city Population)

Region	With Annexation	Without Annexation
Northeast	−1.9	−2.1
Midwest	−0.3	−4.6
South	11.2	3.2
West	18.0	9.9
Total	5.3	0.5

SOURCE: Table A, U.S. Bureau of the Census, Census of Population and Housing: 1970. General Demographic Trends for Metropolitan Areas, 1960 to 1970, Final Report PHC-(2)–1 United States. (Washington, D.C.: U.S. Government Printing Office, 1971.)

TABLE 1.5. Central-City Acreage for Selected Central Cities, 1960, 1970 (in Thousands of Acres—Average)

Region	1960	1973
East	38.40	38.77
Midwest	46.63	68.79
South	64.43	129.77
West	54.29	85.59

SOURCE: Trends in Metropolitan America, Advisory Commission on Intergovernmental Relations (ACIR), Information Report No. M–108. February 1977. Washington, D.C.

Indianapolis and Kansas City. The boundaries for the other major central cities (Chicago, Detroit, St. Louis, Cincinnati, and Cleveland) have been fixed for about thirty-five years.

Although I shall make no systematic attempt to contrast central-city and metropolitan growth by region, it is important to stress the more robust, often very rapid, recent development of Southern and Western metropolitan areas. Because of more metropolitan development, central cities in these regions have also fared better with respect to population growth and employment than the typical central city in the East and Midwest. Yet the decentralization process of metropolitan areas has also taken place in the South and the West. As noted, part of this decentralization is masked by the process of annexation and by averaging in the extremely rapid growth of Houston, Phoenix, and San Diego.

However, central cities such as Birmingham, Miami, Atlanta, Louisville,

Dallas, New Orleans, Los Angeles, and San Francisco that have relatively fixed boundaries are all presently losing population or are growing very slowly relative to metropolitan growth.

For a summary of central-city decline I will draw on a table in Campbell (1977). Between 1960 and 1970 the net out-migration of population from all central cities average 350 thousand people a year. Between 1970 and 1975 the annual rate of out-migration increased by a factor of four to an annual figure of 1.4 million. Between 1970 and 1975, 5.9 million persons moved from the cities to the suburbs and 1.1 million moved from cities to nonmetropolitan areas. These figures indicate a dramatic acceleration in the population decline of central cities during the 1970s and seem to confirm the more pessimistic forecasts regarding the future of those cities.

One of the difficulties of determining the relative importance of different factors that influence intrametropolitan decentralization is the need to control for the overall growth of a metropolitan area. When population and employment in some metropolitan areas are constant, the time pattern of decentralization is obvious.

If suburbanization is to be explained by contemporary phenomenon— such as the widespread use of the automobile, the interstate highway system, or to the postwar inflow of minority groups into central cities—it is necessary to demonstrate *that decentralization has accelerated in the postwar period.*

In an attempt to compare past and pre–World War II decentralization, a number of authors (Mills, 1972; Muth, 1969) have estimated urban growth and density functions. Mills estimated density functions in eighteen metropolitan areas for the postwar years 1948, 1954, 1958, and 1963 for population and for employment in manufacturing trade and services. In general, for most cities both the intercept and the slope of the gradient function decreased over time; thus both a decrease in density at the center and a decrease in the gradient were shown. For example, the average gradient for population was .58 in 1948 and .38 in 1963.

The more interesting, though because of data limitations, more questionable results are the gradient functions estimated for the prewar period that go as far back as 1880 for a small number of metropolitan areas. The main conclusion that Mills reached is that there is surprisingly little variation over time in the rate at which metropolitan areas have decentralized. The average rate of annual decrease in the density gradient for the period 1880–1963 is .011, for 1948–54 the change is .017, for 1954–58 .012, and for 1958–63 .008. This evidence calls into question the proposition that suburbanization is essentially a postwar phenomenon and should be explained primarily in terms of technological and social phenomenon of this period. Although current conditions—such as racial strife—and fiscal considerations bear on contemporaneous location decisions, they are not, according to his view, the central factor underlying the decentralization

TABLE 1.6. Mean Population for a Sample of Central-City Areas by Race (in Thousands)

Region	1960		1970	
	White	Black	White	Black
East	736	162	646	228
Midwest	480	116	428	155
South	253	78	290	102
West	415	38	458	58

process. According to Mills, the more basic factors are real-income changes that influence the demand for housing and land, transportation technology and technological change that bears on the relative cost of dense (i.e., tall) building relative to less dense residential and industrial development. To the best of my knowledge, density gradients have not been estimated for the period 1963–72, and so I am unable to compare the last ten years with the earlier postwar period.

There is some question of how much weight can be placed on Mills' estimates for the period before 1940, since the Census Bureau did not provide tract data and Mills' estimates before that period are two-point estimates. Harrison and Kain (1974) present a set of estimates of historical densities that conflict sharply with those of Mills for the earlier periods.

From Sacks (1977) we see that between 1960 and 1970 blacks became increasingly concentrated in central cities, and the black proportion of central-city populations increased significantly. In the East and the Midwest the pattern throughout the sixties is clear cut—the whites moved out of central cities and the blacks moved in. In the South and the West, where central cities are growing more rapidly, the pattern is not as strong, but the percentage of blacks in central cities is increasing. By 1970 Atlanta, Gary, Newark, and Washington had majority black populations, and in Baltimore, Birmingham, Detroit, New Orleans, Richmond, St. Louis, and Savannah blacks constituted 40 percent or more of its population. In central-city populations, over 30 percent black is the rule rather than the exception; in 1970 the black populations of New York City and Chicago were 1.7 and 1.1 million, respectively. Furthermore, for some cities percentage black significantly underrepresents the concentration of minority population, as the largest U.S. cities and a number of cities in the Southwest have Hispanic concentrations. In 1970 the Hispanics in New York City, Los Angeles, and Chicago numbered 1.3, 0.5, and 0.25 million, respectively.

Since 1940 there has been a significant interregional redistribution of population by race. In 1940, 77 percent of the black population lived in the South. By 1974 this figure had fallen to 53 percent. Blacks were also becoming increasingly concentrated in metropolitan areas—between 1960 and 1974 the percentage of blacks residing in these areas went up from

TABLE 1.7. Ratio of Regional per Capita Income to U.S. per Capita, 1880–1975

Region	1880	1900	1920	1930	1940	1950	1960	1970	1975
Northeast	141	134	124	129	121	106	109	108	103.3
Mid-Atlantic	141	139	134	140	124	116	116	113	108.4
East North Central	102	106	108	111	112	112	107	105	103.7
West North Central	90	97	87	82	84	94	93	95	98.0
South Atlantic	45	45	59	56	69	74	77	86	93.4
East South Central	51	49	52	48	55	63	67	74	79.2
West South Central	60	61	72	61	70	81	83	85	90.6
Mountain	168	139	100	83	92	96	95	90	93.1
Pacific	204	163	135	130	138	121	118	110	110.5

SOURCE: Historical Statistics of the United States to 1970 and Survey of Current Business, May 1977.

68 percent to 76 percent, and the percentage of black central-city residents went up from 53 percent to 58 percent. So the rate of suburbanization of blacks is very slight, their proportion rising from 15 percent to 17 percent between 1960 and 1974.

3. INTERREGIONAL INCOME DIFFERENCES

Closely related to the significant development of the Western states and of the South is a narrowing of per capita income among regions.

Table 1.7 presents ratios of per capita personal income by region over the last 100 years. The convergence towards the national mean is quite impressive. The nominal income differences between regions may significantly overstate real differences, the construction of cost-of-living indices by city and by state has indicated. Prices are higher in the North and in the West relative to the South.

Part of the nominal income differences relates to city size. Irving Hoch (1972, 1977, and 1976) has shown that both the nominal wage and the cost of living increase with city size. And since the North is more urbanized than the South and the typical Northerner lives in a larger city than the typical Southerner, nominal-income differences will overstate real-income differences. In addition, Hoch's work shows a residual 7.5 percent regional differential *net* of city size considerations.

Coelha and Gholi (1971) argued for the end of the North-South real wage differential. They used data for metropolitan areas and cost-of-living indices by cities and found that the real wage is slightly higher (2.5 percent) for a sample of Southern cities relative to a sample of Northern cities. One can confirm these results in a gross way using 1975 personal income per capita data. After cost-of-living adjustment, per capita incomes are: $5174 for Houston; $4856 for Dallas; $5219 for Atlanta; $4828 for

New York; $4299 for Buffalo; $4233 for Boston; $4280 for Philadelphia. This is obviously an incomplete list, but it is rather startling to conclude that per capita real income is 20 percent higher in Atlanta and Houston than in Boston and Buffalo, though this difference may be due in part to market-basket differences not corrected for in the cost-of-living adjustment. The cost of living is calculated on the basis of how much nominal *before-tax* income a family of a general income level would have to spend on a particular basket of goods. As taxes and public services are higher in the North, the cost-of-living difference will be exaggerated by a greater reliance on public service provision there. Also, as older Northern cities are larger and denser, housing prices will be higher because of high land prices. Yet no account is taken of shorter commuting distances. Housing in Houston and Atlanta may be relatively cheap, but travel distances and travel time are long.

Table 1.8 presents absolute nominal per capita income by region, deflated by a regional cost-of-living index constructed by Williamson (1977). The cost-of-living index is for 1970, and so the deflation is less than ideal, though the cost of living for various metropolitan areas shows that there has not been much, if any, change in relative cost by region during the 1970s. But the index is biased, and the real income of rapid-growth areas appear higher than they actually are.

The picture that emerges from table 1.8's data is roughly consistent with the city data. Real income across broad regional groups is quite narrow, though the Pacific states are about 10 percent higher than the national average and the East South Central states (Kentucky, Tennessee, Alabama, and Mississippi) are about 15 percent below.

If there is any generalization that can be made it is that intraregional income differentials are larger than interregional differences. This is especially true of the diverse South Atlantic region, which includes Mary-

TABLE 1.8. Personal Income per Capita, by Region, 1975

Region	Money	Deflated Real	Northeast = 100
United States	$5903		
Northeast	6098	6098	100.0
Mid-Atlantic	6398	6218	102.0
East North Central	6121	6383	104.7
West North Central	5788	6138	100.7
South Atlantic	5510	6042	99.1
East South Central	4676	5284	86.7
West South Central	5347	6097	100.0
Mountain	5416	5695	93.4
Pacific	6526	6659	109.2

SOURCE: Survey of Current Business, April 1976 and May 1977; and Williamson (1977).

land and Florida with deflated per capita incomes of $6878 and $6488, respectively, and states such as South Carolina ($5720) and West Virginia ($5265). Texas ($6480) is well above the other states in the South West Central. Texas now has a real per capita income on a par with a typical Northern state, though states that border it and the East South Central region are well below Texas on a per capita income basis. Another point is that real income in California, the dominant Pacific state, is about 10 percent higher (bearing in mind that cost of living is measured as of 1970) than in the typical Eastern state. It is now more meaningful to talk of poor South and affluent South, or poor Southerners and rich Southerners, rather than of the rich North and the poor South. Despite the convergence in per capita income by state, nominal wages are still somewhat higher in the North relative to the South.

Hoch (1976b) has used detailed and well-defined occupational groupings to analyze the relationship between city size and wage rate. Hoch found that wage rates increase with city size by about 9 percent per order of magnitude of population; thus a city of a million will pay 9 percent more than one of one hundred thousand. These wage differences reflect supply and demand factors—workers demand more to live in large cities, and because of agglomeration economies, employers are able to pay this premium.

In addition, Hoch found a pure regional wage differential for all occupations of about 7.5 percent between the South and the rest of the country. The negative wage differential for the South was stronger for blue-collar than for white-collar occupations; it is about 17.5 percent for low-paid blue collar and only 3.5 percent for high-paid white collar, taking a regional cost-of-living differential of about 10 percent. This implies a higher real wage for white-collar workers in the South and a lower real wage for unskilled workers in the South and possibly explains the long-term migration of blacks to the North and of whites from the North to the South.

Goldfarb and Yezer (1976) used the same data as Hoch and reached similar conclusions for the occupational differences. But when they distinguished between Northeast, North Central, and West and make the city size variable and nonlinear, they found that the regional differences between North, East, and South are smaller and weaker for skilled blue collar differentials than between South, North Central, and West. Yet on the basis of their results, typical patterns of wage differences for blue-collar occupations are 10–15 percent between the South and the rest of the country and for some occupations the differentials are much larger.

One very common impression is that the poor are increasingly concentrated in the central cities of the North. In Table 1.9 I present a breakdown of persons classified as poor in March 1976 by race, family type, region, and centrality location, which brings out a number of points. First, in the

TABLE 1.9. Persons Classified as Poor by Type of Household and Race (in Thousands), March 1976

	North and West				South			
	White		Black		White		Black	
	Male	Female	Male	Female	Male	Female	Male	Female
Total								
Population	104,563	11,175	6350	3481	45,521	4402	7658	4099
Total Poor	5554	3347	588	1757	3668	1230	1777	2412
Metropolitan	3184	2463	535	1648	1259	689	688	1396
Central City	1440	1210	429	1441	525	377	449	1112

SOURCE: Current Population Reports: P-20, No. 311, August 1977.

North and the West poor blacks are concentrated in the central cities of metropolitan areas. Poor whites are much more dispersed both with respect to metro-nonmetro location and with respect to central-city-suburban locations. The same sort of pattern exists for the South, though it is not nearly as strong and a larger proportion of whites and blacks classified as poor reside in nonmetropolitan areas.

The incidence of poverty between regions is quite different. The South, with roughly 30 percent of the population, is home to 45 percent of the poor population. A large part of the regional difference in poverty incidence is explained by the incidence of poverty among black households. In the South, 36 percent of all blacks are poor, whereas in the North and the West, only 23 percent of blacks are poor. So although the number of poor blacks resident in the South has fallen significantly from 7.5 to 4.2 million between 1959 and 1976, a significant number of poor blacks continue to reside in that region. From the Census publication, Low-Income Areas in Large Cities (1974), it is apparent that the incidence of poverty among minority group populations is significantly higher in the South than in the North.[1] Also, contrary to the impression given by press reports that black unemployment is concentrated in the ghettos of New York, Chicago, and Detroit, this problem is in fact national in scope.

Unpublished census data compiled by Campbell (1977) shows that there is no systematic relationship between region and absolute black unemployment, and if anything the black-white unemployment ratio is higher in the South than in the North. The same point applies to black teenage unemployment. The intraregional differences are much larger than the interregional differences. In 1976 some of the highest black teenage unemployment rates were in Southern cities—such as Atlanta and Dallas-Fort Worth—and while the unemployment rate for black teenagers is relatively low in Houston at 26.7 percent, it is not significantly different than Cleveland's rate of 28.6 percent.

4. GENERAL EXPLANATIONS
OF INTERREGIONAL EMPLOYMENT SHIFTS

One obvious importance of wage differences among regions is that they influence plant location decisions and the interregional migration of labor. However, before I discuss the evidence for the classical adjustment mechanism between regions, I would like to begin with a few historical considerations and general ("taste") factors that bear on interregional shifts.

One possible explanation for why it has taken the South so long to catch up is the importance of European immigrants in the late nineteenth and early twentieth century. During the period 1900–15, close to 1 million immigrants a year entered the United States, primarily from Europe. This flow, which was cut in half during the 1920s, dropped to a trickle in the 1930s, and was about three hundred thousand a year after World War II, is currently about one-half million people a year. Most of the immigrants in the early 1900s settled in the Northeast and North Central regions. From 1900 until 1910, twice as many immigrants settled in Massachusetts than did in the whole South, and although settlement of immigrants in the West was at a rate twice as large as in the South, it seems correct to a first order approximation to say that most of the immigrants settled in the Northeast and North Central regions during the first quarter of this century. Large ethnic communities formed in virtually all large Northern and Midwestern cities. In the early part of this century the immigrants were very important, from a supply and demand standpoint, to the rapid growth of industry in the Northern urban areas.

In effect, the immigrants offset the decline of Northern population growth that resulted from the significant out-migration of native born whites to the West that goes back well into the nineteenth century. Their presence encouraged the migration of the native born to the West and, through competition for jobs and housing, inhibited the in-migration of Southern blacks. The absolute and relative decrease in immigration from Europe in the postwar period might well be an important factor in the relative decline of the North during the last twenty-five to thirty years. The decrease in immigration by cutting the supply of unskilled labor in the North facilitated the migration of unskilled blacks from the South to the North during this period and accelerated the development of the low-wage (cost) Southern region.

The migration of Southern whites to the West during the depression probably contributed to the phenomenal growth of the Pacific states during the 1940–45 period. World War II appears to have triggered the rapid postwar development of the Pacific states and of such major Sunbelt states as Texas and Florida.

In addition to the historical shocks, a number of technological or taste considerations have been presented to explain population and employment movements to the West and, more recently, to the South.

One set of considerations is the influence of climate and the availability of recreational facilities—sun, sea, and so forth. The migration of large number of retirees to Florida, California, Arizona, and other coastal areas is well known. There is some evidence in the work of Hoch (1976a) and Rosen (precipitation, in this volume) that climatic extremes—extreme cold, and humidity—have a positive effect on real wages. Hoch calculated the optimal summer temperature to be around seventy-four degrees (fahrenheit). This suggests that climate may have been significant in the growth of California and that without the large-scale introduction of air conditioning during the last twenty years or so the development of the South would have proceeded at a slower rate. As a resident of Houston, I cannot imagine living there without air conditioning any more than I can imagine living in Montreal without heat.

General increases in real income have also probably operated to decentralize the population from the established population centers. Part of this decentralization relates to earlier retirement and a great emphasis on leisure time and recreation, though it has not been established that the North is at a great disadvantage regarding these amenities. Increased income has provided the wealth that finances movement and acquires information on options.

The dismantling of the most blatant forms of racism in the South during the last fifteen years is impressive, and the improvement in race relations has operated not only to stem the outflow of blacks from the South but also to facilitate the recruitment of Northern whites in national labor markets.

Another set of factors that are difficult to appraise quantitatively are various technological improvements in transportation and communication. Cheap automobile transportation has increased the effective labor force in less populated areas and has allowed the establishment of plants in low-wage Southern areas. Goods can be trucked cheaply and quickly to large population centers in the North from low-cost production points. This has weakened the comparative advantage of large Northern cities. The introduction of jet travel has weakened the site relationship between managerial control and production functions. The improvement of telephone technology and other innovations in telecommunications have also diminished the importance of location in the older, established regions of the country. Urban economists—such as W. Thompson—have developed a diffusion theory of regional development in which technological and production innovations are introduced in established urban centers and diffused to lower-wage areas as the processes become more routinized. To the extent that research and development is primarily performed by multibranch corporations, rather than by the inventive genius who sets up the industry in his place of residence, the diffusion process has become more rapid and the relationships between the locations of innovation and production is being weakened. Industry and the different functions of a firm have become more "foot-lose," and factor cost (wages) is now more important than communication and transportation cost in plant location decisions.

5. COST CONSIDERATIONS IN INTERREGIONAL SHIFTS

Although I predict that a decrease in transportation and communication costs will increase the importance of other cost factors, especially wage costs, in the location decision, the role of wage costs in determining the relative growth of employment and income of regions is an unsettled issue.

In the standard aggregative neoclassical model of growth (Borts and Stein, 1964) capital should flow from high-wage to low-wage regions in order to equalize the rate of return, and low-wage regions should experience the highest rates of capital and wage growth. Borts and Stein tested these propositions against state data for the periods 1918–29, 1929–48, and 1948–53 and found that the explanatory power of their model is quite weak. They adopted a number of ad hoc explanations to rationalize their findings: the shifts of population to high-wage regions induced capital formation in housing and services; the demand for exports of high-wage regions was buoyant during the periods analysed (this is essentially an industrial composition explanation).

In extending the simple neoclassical model to explore relative employment growth in different states, Borts and Stein stressed labor supply and intersectoral shifts. Their basic proposition is that differences in employment growth in manufacturing by state will depend on the growth of the labor supply. If a state has a large manufacturing sector relative to other forms of employment, then it will be at a disadvantage with respect to further development. As migration occurs from low-wage to high-wage states it is not obvious that low wages will enhance growth in non-agricultural employment. On the one hand capital is attracted to low-wage states, on the other hand labor is migrating out of low-wage states. Borts and Stein found no significant relationship between a state's wage level and its rate of employment change.

Although I am not aware of any attempts to update the Bort-Stein work, I conjecture that relationships between wages and net investment and wage level and employment change will be stronger for more recent periods. Borts and Stein laid emphasis on the size of a state's agricultural sector as a factor in determining manufacturing employment growth, which is important in explaining the recent past in the light of the rapid growth of manufacturing employment in the South and in the Plains states.

Nevertheless, a clear-cut empirical relationship between wage levels and employment change by state or metropolitan area has not been established.

Certain pair-wise comparisons of states do not fit well into this explanation. For example, nominal wages in Texas manufacturing are only 10 percent lower than those in New York and are about equal to those in Massachusetts, yet manufacturing employment in Texas has been growing very rapidly while declining significantly in the two Northeastern states.

David Birch (1977) has tabulated employment change between 1960 and 1970 and wage levels for about 315 economic areas and found that many of the slowest growing areas have low wage rates. This suggests that there are factors other than wages that bear on firm location and the relative success of firms at different locations.

Birch has also compiled evidence on other costs and found (1) That residential land costs are about 20 percent lower in the South relative to the North and 70 percent lower relative to the West; farm land is also distinctly cheaper in the South than in other parts of the country. (2) Bank loan interest rates do not vary appreciably across regions, though short-term credit is about 5 percent cheaper in New York City than in the rest of the nation and long-term credit is about 10 percent cheaper in Northeastern cities other than New York. (3) With respect to rail transportation, the Southeast has an advantage as the least expensive region to ship to and from; in contrast, the Pacific and Mountain states are remote and expensive to ship to and from. (4) With respect to trucking, the Southeast and the Southwest have an advantage over other regions except the Northeast, which is on a par with the South. On a cost per vehicle mile, costs are about 32 percent less in the South than in the Midwest and 56 percent less than on the Pacific Coast.

A factor that has received considerable attention in recent years is the increasing cost of energy. Some writers (Miernyk, 1977; McDonald, 1977) believe that the present and future shortage of energy will tend to accelerate the movement of industry to the South and the West. Irving Hoch (1977), though tending to be in agreement with this view, is more guarded and tentative with respect to the quantitative significance of energy-related employment shifts.

Hoch's paper has interesting data from which it is possible to piece together information on regional differences in the cost of energy in 1972. In table 1.10 I present price indices on the cost of energy by region for 1972. These indices represent average prices actually paid.

The relative prices per BTU reveal a remarkable similarity in the cost of energy for household use across regions. Contrary to expectation, there is no advantage to household use for the South and, in fact, the South Atlantic region is the high-cost region. For business use the picture is very different. The East South Central region and the West South Central region (Texas, Louisiana, Oklahoma, and Arkansas) have an advantage relative to the rest of the country, especially relative to the Northeast.

The explanation for these interregional differences lies in the heavy

TABLE 1.10. Indices of Average Prices Paid for Energy, 1972, by Region

Region	Household Use All Sources	Business Use All Sources	Relative Price of Natural Gas	Electricity
Northeast	103	149	288	141
Mid-Atlantic	100	124	183	133
East North Central	92	103	132	105
West North Central	94	106	98	117
South Atlantic	116	115	127	99
East South Central	106	90	89	67
West South Central	101	64	50	86
Mountain	98	98	81	91
Pacific	98	101	104	80
United States	100	100	100	100

business use of natural gas in the Southwest and the low price of natural gas in this region relative to other regions. In table 1.11 I reproduce some of the data put together by Hoch on energy consumption by region. From that table we can infer that the South West Central region was a very heavy user of energy and that the difference between regions results from the heavy industrial use of cheap natural gas in the Southwest.

The heavy industrial use of natural gas in the Southwest is explained in part by the low price in that region, which in turn is related to heavy business use. Natural gas was sold to businesses at lower prices with the provision that the supply would be interrupted in the event of a shortage. The lower prices also reflect lower transportation (pipeline) costs.

Until the recent price increase of natural gas, this source of energy was cheaper by a factor of three (per Btu) relative to petroleum. The question arises, Why industry in the North did not make more use of gas as an energy source in the early part of the postwar period? Although there is no easy explanation of this puzzle, my colleague Henry Steele tells me that the

TABLE 1.11. Consumption of Energy in Million Btu per Capita, 1972 (by Region)

Region	Total All Sources	Household Use All Sources	Natural Gas All Uses
New England	270.1	116.0	22.3
Mid-Atlantic	291.2	103.2	50.7
East North Central	369.6	112.5	105.5
West North Central	336.8	104.4	131.5
South Atlantic	299.8	82.4	50.7
East South Central	385.8	85.1	92.6
West South Central	565.4	88.6	375.1
Mountain	403.6	95.5	148.4
Pacific	322.9	86.9	98.5
United States	351.5	97.8	40.2

natural gas was sold to utility companies in the North and North Central regions that did not encourage natural gas use by industry and preferred to reserve the gas for household use. Lobbying by the coal interests also discouraged the conversion of industry to natural gas. In contrast, industry in the Southwest dealt directly with the gas producers and often located close to the fields, incurring small transportation costs and frequently gaining very favorable long-term contracts for the then abundant natural gas reserves.[2]

The general picture that emerges is that throughout the postwar period, industry in the Southwest was favored by very low energy prices relative to the rest of the country. There is little question that the rapid development of the petrochemical industry in Texas was in part due to the availability of cheap energy. This development has continued in recent years, even after the unregulated intrastate price rose to 40 percent above the regulated price on "new" interstate gas. Producers preferred to settle in the states where they were assured of a supply from new discoveries.

In addition to the advantage of the natural gas producing states, table 1.10 reveals the advantage of the Tennessee Valley Authority (TVA), which contributes greatly to keeping the price of electricity in the East South Central region at 33 percent less than the national average.

It is hard to predict the future fate of relative energy prices by region. The announced policy of the Carter administration is to encourage a shift to the use of coal and to discourage prospecting for new oil and natural gas deposits. This shift will enhance the development of the Mountain states as producers. Coal reserves are fairly wide-spread throughout the country, with large deposits in the Midwest and Appalachia, so the differential regional impact of the shift to coal may not be very large. Environmental problems associated with the use of coal will be more severe in the more densely populated North.

In general, the Southwest will lose much of its past advantages both as a producing region and as a consuming region. The price of natural gas will probably be uniform across the country, exclusive of transportation costs, and the cheap price of natural gas will no longer lure industry to the Southwest. The price of electricity will increase more rapidly in the Southwest as that region converts from natural gas to alternative sources of electrical power.[3]

To conclude this section on the role of cost as the determinant of regional decentralization and the shift to the Sunbelt, I suggest that the combination of low wage, land, transportation, and energy costs has played a significant role in the development of the South relative to the North. The evidence on some of the relative costs by regions is somewhat fragmentary and there is the problem of controlling for labor quality, but the South appears to have advantages in the relative costs of all factor inputs.

In contrast, the cost-advantage explanation of present regional shifts does not fit the rapid development of the West. The Pacific Coast, especially California, is a high-wage area, which because of its relative isolation from the rest of the country, is subject to high transportation costs. I suggest that a plentiful resource base (broadly defined) and a favorable export base enables this region to overcome its high nominal costs.

6. TOWARDS AN ECLECTIC THEORY OF REGIONAL DEVELOPMENT

It is clear from the work of Borts and Stein and from the evidence of the success of the Pacific Coast—a high-cost region—that the simple, stark, neoclassical model may be of low predictive value in explaining trends in regional employment. Low-wage regions may continue to stagnate while some high-wage regions continue to develop very rapidly. To improve its predictive power and to increase its revelance, the simple market-adjustment model must be modified and extended, which can be done in a number of directions.

One method is to introduce economies of scale and agglomeration in production and consumption. This has been done in a neoclassical framework for cities (Henderson, 1974) and for regions (Flatters et. al., 1974). The basic implication of this work is that over a range an increase in the population or labor force need not decrease the utility or real income, which will in fact increase. Over a range of population, perhaps quite large, a process of cumulative causation stressed by anti-neoclassical writers (Kaldor, 1970) will occur.

A second modification of the simple neoclassical theory is a recognition that labor may not be homogeneous and equally productive; low wages may persist in a region if the labor is inherently nonproductive. On the other hand, the most productive (educated) labor may be drawn to the high-wage industries or regions.

A third extension is to recognize demand or export base considerations (industrial mix) that will partly explain the demand for labor in a region or city. This consideration (demand) was used by Bort and Stein to rationalize the quick growth of high-wage regions. There are also supply or migration considerations that will draw labor to a high-wage region.

My main objective in this section of the chapter is to combine some of the above factors and to sketch a model that will allow for both supply and demand factors, readily admit economies of scale, and in contrast to the primitive export-base model, allow for price and wage considerations and for changes in the industrial base of a region.

This section borrows heavily from the recent work of Dornbusch, Fisher, and Samuelson (1977) on Ricardian trade models, and is also heavily influenced by the "dual" nature of regional adjustment in the United States, where a high-cost (wage) and a low-cost region are growing most rapidly relative to the older, established industrial areas of the Northeast. In effect, we need a minimum of three regions to stylize trends in the United States, Northeast, South and West.

To consider Northeast-West adjustments first, assume that the South does not exist and that the East is settled and developed first. The West, richly endowed in natural resources—sea, forest, land (irrigated)—is underpopulated. In the simplest terms, the resource-to-population endowment in the West is high relative to the East, and the nominal and real wage is considerably higher in the West than in the East. But the West is isolated and relatively poor in the quantity and quality of social capital (broadly defined), education and cultural facilities, churches, and family relations. Distance and high transportation costs act as a barrier to migration and the real-wage differential persists over a very long period (it still remains today).

Because of its limited population, the West is initially a small region and will tend to be highly specialized in production. This is an implication of the reworking of Ricardo by Dornbusch et al., in which they assume that each country can produce and will wish to consume an indefinitely large number of commodities. So for the simple case, where labor is the only input explicitly recognized, the comparative advantage, as determined by the average products of labor in different activities, is a continuum. Productivities vary across the two regions because of differences in natural resource endowments, variations in technical knowledge, or varying amounts of private or social capital.

In the Ricardian model, in which there is a continuum of commodities, the key link between the factor prices in the two regions is the relative labor productivity for the marginal or "limbo" commodities, i.e., the tradeables that are produced by both regions. This marginal commodity will change as the relative sizes of the two regions change through migration.

While the West is very small it will produce nothing but a small range of commodities (e.g., forest products) in which it has the greatest comparative advantage. In addition, a small range of home goods or nontradeables (services) are produced. Other commodities are imported and are expensive, in large measure because labor is in limited supply and is very expensive.

One of the results of this model, which was proved by Dornbusch et al., is that as population shifts from one region to another the region that is expanding in population will become less specialized in its production structure—will be pushed down on its scale of comparative advantage. The reason for this result is quite straight forward. The new labor has to be absorbed, and because of the demand assumption, some of it will produce services. The supply of exports from the declining region will decrease so that expanding regions will produce some of the commodities previously imported.

The model is supply oriented in that the production structure of each region is determined by the size of the available labor force. The model also predicts the observed phenomenon that as such industries as agriculture decline because of low-income elasticities of demand, the growth of non-agricultural employment will be more rapid in the region with the relatively large agricultural sector. More generally, as a region develops and its population grows its production structure will become broader and more diversified. Although an increase in the population will tend to decrease the real wage in the expanding region, this decrease will be moderated by the development of import-competing industries that generate savings on transportation costs.

When applied to regions, the simplified Ricardian model of trade can be interpreted as an export base model: an increase in the demand for its exports will tend to increase the real wage of the region and stimulate its growth. However, in contrast to the simple export base model there is no fixed mechanistic relationship between growth in export demand and change in total employment. Changes in total employment will depend on the labor force adjustment that acts through shifts from low-productivity sectors (agriculture) and immigration.

The model allows for the development of import-competing industries that grow as a result of technical change (change in labor productivity) or migration of labor. With appropriate elaborations that can only be sketched here, the importance of the home-goods industry as a basis for the development of a region can be put into proper perspective. It is noteworthy that Buchanan (1950, 1952), in explaining the lagging development of the South in the fifties, stressed the region's underdeveloped public sector and the high tax prices (after controlling for the quality of these facilities) that skilled labor and capital had to pay relative to the prices that prevailed in the industrial North. Although our characterization of the development process of the South and the West is somewhat different, there is the common feature that as both regions develop—the West by attracting capital and labor and the South by urbanizing and industrializing—the quantity and quality of collectively consumed nontraded goods have increased. For many publicly or privately financed jointly consumed goods produced and consumed in the region, there may exist minimum scale requirements such that many services will not be produced at low levels of population and income, or the quality of the services produced will be low. Consequently, as population grows the real income of the region will improve through the appearance of a wider range of home goods. If the minimum scale can be reached and the goods or services appear, economies of scale may further decrease the price and increase consumption of (and employment in) these goods.

Another interesting implication of this model is that the benefits of improved transportation between regions will tend to accrue dispropor-tionately to smaller regions, as determined by cost conditions in the East. When the East becomes imperfectly specialized in some commodities the absolute benefits to each region from transportation improvement will be the same. The West, which exports (imports) a large share of its product, will gain more relative to its income from transportation improvements and these improvements will tend to stimulate the development of the smaller, less populated regions.

On this point it is interesting to compare the cost-of living-indices found in table 1.12 (Williamson, 1977) for the period 1920–1970.

Although one cannot precisely explain the decrease in the cost of living in the less developed regions relative to the Northeast, the data are con-sistent with the notion that development and population growth lead to decreases in the cost of living. Part of the decrease in the more peripheral regions is due to a decrease in transportation costs.

In attempting to characterize the historical development of the West and the immigration to the Pacific Coast I have stressed two factors: the high resource-to-labor ratio in this region, which results in higher real wages; and the "filling in" of the region through immigration, which leads to a broadening of the industrial structure, the improvement of local amenities through the introduction of more and better local services (economies of scale in consumption), and a decrease in the relative cost of living that maintains the real-income differential between West and East even when the nominal wage or per capita income in the West is falling. This combina-tion of factors has served to sustain the rapid development of the West over a very long time, even in the face of such disammenities as congestion,

TABLE 1.12. Relative Cost of Living by Region, 1920, 1970

Region	1920	1970
New England	100.0	100.0
Mid-Atlantic	101.3	102.9
East North Central	96.1	95.9
West North Central	98.8	94.3
South Atlantic	99.5	91.2
East South Central	97.2	88.5
West South Central	94.6	87.7
Mountain	117.6	95.1
Pacific	103.1	98.0
California	103.1	95.9

pollution, and shortages (e.g., water). Although the development of agriculture in California paralleled the industrial development of the Western
region, the intersectoral shift of population from agriculture is not, as North
(1955) has argued, an essential part of the explanation of this region's
development.

The export-base aspects emphasized by North definitely have a place in
the characterization that we have presented. Yet the mechanistic export-
base model is incomplete, especially since it makes no allowance for
changes in relative prices and in the industrial srtucture away from the
conventional exports of the region. Finally, in the modified comparative-
cost model of trade, population movement (migration) plays an essential
role as jobs do follow people; it is clear that agglomeration considerations
or economies of scale, although they complicate the more conventional
adjustment mechanism, complement the modified model rather than replace
or negate classical cost considerations.

Whereas the regional adjustment between East and West is primarily
one that took place through the migration of labor from a relatively low-
wage region (East) to a high real-income area (West), the North-South
adjustment over the last thirty-five years took a somewhat different form.
At the beginning of the period (1940), the South was very undeveloped
and unindustrialized relative to the North; the South was richly endowed
with unskilled labor and poorly endowed with skilled labor and capital.

Since 1940 two main adjustment processes have occurred: the out-
migration of unskilled labor from the South to the North, and to a lesser
extent to the West; and the rapid development of Southern industry, especially manufacturing. In table 1.2 I have documented the rapid development
of Southern nonagricultural employment since 1940. As noted earlier,
this process has been constant since 1940 in most of the Southern states,
and some Southern states (Arkansas and Alabama) that lagged (relatively)
in the immediate postwar period have grown rapidly in the last ten to
fifteen years.

The population shift from low productivity agriculture has been
dramatic. In 1940, 40 percent of the Southern population was in agriculture;
for the entire nation this was 23 percent. By 1970 the proportion of the
farm population in the South and in the nation had fallen to 6 percent and
4.8 percent, respectively.

This rapid agricultural shift, the migration of Southern unskilled workers
to the North, and the development of Southern industry have lead to a
significant convergence in per capita incomes between South and North.
During the post–World War II period nominal per capita income in the
South increased at roughly double the rate of increase in the North.

Another point of the convergence between North and South is the relative proportion of manufacturing employment: in 1947, 73.3 percent of
the nation's manufacturing employment was in the North with 19 percent

located in the South; in 1973 the percentages were 59.9 and 27.5 respectively.

This convergence in per capita income and nonagricultural employment strongly suggests that a classic adjustment mechanism—low wages and an abundance of labor in the South and higher costs in the North—is at work. Other analysts may wish to place different emphases on these adjustments —wage levels as an inducement to the more rapid growth of investment and employment in the South, intersectoral shifts of employment and a very elastic supply of labor to Southern manufacturing and related employment —but whatever the emphasis, the explanation is supply (cost) oriented and explains interregional shifts in neoclassical terms.

Industrial mix or economic-base considerations do not seem to play a significant role in explaining interregional shifts. At a somewhat general level it can be noted that national employment in such traditionally Southern industries as tobacco, textile mill products, and apparel has fallen by about 230 thousand from 1947 until 1976. However, in lumber and furniture, two other industries in which the South is specialized, employment has remained constant, nationally, at about 1.1 million over the same period.

Other industries that are typically associated with the South are tourism and retirement (especially in Florida), petroleum products and chemicals (on the Gulf Coast), and defense related industries. Without denying the importance of these industries, I am inclined to stress the broad, general nature of Southern industry, and the shift of manufacturing employment from the North to the South.

What is impressive about the recent economic development of the South is the broad, general nature of employment growth in Southern manufacturing. In virtually all the Southern states, employment in durable goods manufacturing has been more rapid than employment in nondurable goods, especially in Florida and Texas. The South now has a substantial employment base in such diverse industries as fabricated metals, machinery, chemicals, and transportation equipment. In general, the old stereotype of the South as the producer of a few labor intensive products such as textiles and furniture no longer applies. This is not to say that the South has not done very well in its traditional products. Since 1947, New York State has lost about three hundred thousand jobs in textile mill products and apparel; over the same period, North Carolina increased employment by one hundred thousand in these industries, and employment has increased substantially throughout the South in textiles.

The broadening of the industrial base in the South can be explained in part by increases in population and income (demand). The general explanation here is very similar to the one given earlier for Western development. As employment and income in a region increase, it pays to transfer technology to the expanding region to save on transportation costs and to

take advantage of lower wages. An example of decentralization is automobile assembly. Although the production of the automobile parts continues to be concentrated in Michigan and Ohio, General Motors has six
assembly plants in the South, five of which are not unionized.

I have not carried out a systematic analysis between employment growth
or investment by region and relative wage, transportation, land, and energy
costs, and I have noted that the Borts-Stein work provides weak support for
the hypothesis that low-cost regions (states) grow more rapidly than high-
cost areas. However, I believe that there are strong a priori reasons for
stressing relative costs in the explanation of North-South adjustments.

7. THE FEDERAL GOVERNMENT AND THE REGIONAL SHIFT

Relative cost differentials among regions are also important to the explanation of recent trends in the regional patterns of purchases of (primarily
defense) goods and services by the federal government. The post-Vietnam
cut-back in defense expenditures has been felt disapportionately in the
Northern states, as strict cost minimizing procurement by the Department
of Defense has lead to a more rapid closing of higher-cost facilities in the
Northern states (Petersen and Mueller, 1977).

The question of defense procurement and the regional location of defense
contractors and military bases is central to the broader question of whether
federal tax and expenditure policies have played a major role in stimulating
the shift to economic activity to the South and the West. This issue, which
is an important element in the so-called new sectionalism, is being used by
Northern political coalitions to attempt to change grant formulas so as to
increase the North's share in federal grant funding. A recent article in the
National Journal (1976), a publication widely read by official Washington,
maintained that present federal tax expenditures cause a massive flow
of wealth—$40 billion for fiscal year 1975—from the North to the South
and the West. Although I cannot do justice to all of the issues in the fiscal-
flow controversy, I believe in general that it represents a misplaced emphasis in regional trends.

In large measure, the "deficit" incurred by the higher-income regions
in their allotment of federal dollars is the result of a mildly progressive
federal tax system. In recent years about one-half of the federal tax receipts
have been collected from the federal income tax, the payroll tax that
finances social security and the corporate profits tax constitute the bulk of
the rest. Deficits are ignored in this discussion and it is assumed that the
burden of debt finance is proportional to tax payment. In 1975 about 55
percent of all personal income accrued to persons residing in the Northeast, the North Central region, and the Plains states. The North, broadly
defined in this way, had just over one-half of the nation's population—107

million out of 213 million—and about 55 percent of the federal income tax was collected from Northern residents.

From information in a recently completed Yale dissertation (Catsambas, 1977), I calculate that in 1972 the residents of the North paid about 56 percent of the social security tax and the corporate tax (the latter allocated regionally on the basis of dividends). Consequently, it is primarily the relative affluence of the Northern states that leads to "deficits" on federal accounts. For a federal budget of $400 billion that is distributed on a per capita basis on the expenditure side, the North will incur a "deficit" of $40 billion, in the sense that taxes collected in the North will exceed expenditures in the North by $40 billion.

In part, however, the higher taxes in the North result from higher nominal wages. It is highly unlikely for practical considerations that the federal tax system will ever be indexed by regional cost of living and as discussed earlier, there are reasons for believing that estimates of differences in regional cost of living are biased upwards. However, the progressive nature of the federal tax system and the denomination of various exemptions and deductions in nominal terms imposes a larger inequitable real burden on high wage, Northern residents of high-cost areas.

Under a proportional tax system there is little basis for making cost-of-living adjustments on equity grounds. Under such a system, residents of different regions will pay the same *real* tax burden. But even under tax proportionality a case can be made on efficiency grounds for admitting cost-of-living adjustment in federal tax liability. I cannot go into this issue except to note that social or national efficiency requires that *before* tax, income-wage levels should be equated to such real differences as transportation costs or diseconomies of scale in urban sizes.

Another main explanation for the disadvantage of the North is the change in its share of federal spending, especially for defense. Since 1961 the defense budget in constant (1976) dollars has fallen from $105 billion to $94 billion in 1975, a sharp fall from the Vietnam peak (1968) of $144 billion. The pattern that appears from table 1.13 is that the North has been losing its share of contracts and military related salaries. The trend is definitely towards the West in both contracts and personnel.[4]

The advantage of the South relative to the North is in defense bases, not in contracts. On a per capita basis, defense contracts in 1975 were actually higher in the North than in the South. Another aspect of the expenditure pattern is that the Vietnam build-up was felt primarily in the North and South; the South received most of the incremental build-up in personnel. In fact, the relative decline in salaries between 1967 and 1975 has been larger in the South than in the North.

Petersen and Mueller (1977) reported that in fiscal 1978 only 10 percent of 780 million dollars worth of military construction will take place in the North.

TABLE 1.13. Federal Expenditures by Region—Defense-Related Activity

Region	Population in 1975	Defense Contracts in Billions			
		1961	1965	1967	1975
North (including Plains States)	107.1	10.6	11.1	18.9	16.4
South (including Capital region)	68.1	4.2	5.5	10.2	9.6
West (Pacific plus Mountain)	37.8	7.3	6.7	8.3	11.3
Total	213.0	22.1	23.3	37.4	37.3

	Defense Payrolls (Military and Direct-hire Civilians)			
	1961	1965	1967	1975
North	3.87	4.25	4.31	5.83
South	4.63	6.52	8.97	10.81
West	3.15	3.79	4.11	10.00
Total	11.65	14.56	17.34	26.62

SOURCE: Calculated from Statistical Abstracts of the United States, 1964 (table 344), 1968 (table 361), and 1976 (table 527).

Although the tax side of the budget and the pattern of defense expenditures work against the Northern states, the remaining components of the federal budget are neutral across broad regional groupings, *but there are significant differences for individual states within regions.* The trend of per capita federal grants to state and local governments has also been running strongly in favor of the mature Northern states, and given recent formula changes, this advantage promises to improve in the future. Petersen and Mueller utilized data found in Brown (1976) to show that between 1970 and 1976 grants to state and local governments increased from $104 per capita to $275 per capita for the mature industrial states and have gone from $127 per capita to $250 per capita for the sunbelt states. The typical sunbelt state currently receives per capita about 91 percent of what a Northern state receives.

Recently the adoption of antirecessionary revenue sharing and community development grants have significantly tilted towards the older, Northern sections of the country that have been losing population. For community development, the age of the housing stock and the degree of population loss are for the first time factors in determining entitlements.

Some Northern states such as Ohio and Indiana receive relatively little in grants; they are high-income areas with relatively small poverty populations, they are not particularly generous in their poverty programs, and because of general fiscal conservatism, are not aggressive in seeking out grants that require matching state and local funds. Thus conservative New Hampshire receives 40 percent less in grants than neighboring Vermont, and such conservative states as Florida, Ohio, and Texas receive 70 percent less (on a per capita basis) than more generous states (such as New York) or needy states (such as Mississippi) that make greater fiscal efforts.

One of the difficulties in appraising whether some states or regions are favored by federal programs is knowing how different programs should be weighed or compared. National policy dictates that taxes should be raised in line with the ability to pay or according to income or wage-tax base. Presumably this will remain a fundamental principle of national tax policy and is hardly the basis for increased aid to a high-income, declining state such as New York.

In large part, federal tax dollars are used to buy national public goods such as national defense—more affluent individuals should pay a disproportionate share of the tax burden. It is hard to see how the pattern of defense expenditures can be neutral with respect to region; political pressure has unquestionably played a role in the concentration of defense installations in the South and the West. Comparative cost factors—the availability and cost of land, open space, water—and climate work to discourage the location of defense-related activity in the North. The federal government does not control the location of defense contractors, and the most successful of these firms are not located in the North. The fundamental difference between defense expenditures and transfers to individuals or to government is that in exchange for the defense, a good or service is produced. The difficulty with justifying transfers to states on the grounds that they are not receiving their fair share of defense expenditures is that there is no meaning to fair shares of defense spending any more than there is a meaning to fair share of automobile production or wheat production. Of course, if all regions are identical with respect to comparative advantage in defense production and the siting of defense installations, the political element becomes more important and a neutral policy with respect to defense procurement is called for. Otherwise, the development of some regions may be unfairly promoted at the expense of others.[5]

This does not mean that cost or efficiency considerations should not be compromised in expenditure policy if unemployment is concentrated in certain regions and classical market processes are inoperative or work very slowly. Reduced to the simplest possible terms, the high-wage North cannot maintain its previous advantages relative to the rest of the country. Workers are being laid off, yet wages are rigid downwards and migration does not work quickly enough. Then, indeed, the shadow price of unemployed labor in the North may be quite low, especially if significant transfer payments are made in the face of a prolonged period of unemployment. Assume that the real wage of the typical worker is 1.20 in the North and 1.00 in the

South. If the workers in the South are fully employed while significant unemployment exists in the North, an argument can be made for incurring the
higher costs in the North so as to increase employment there. Although the
cost of the same product will be 20 percent higher in the North, the increase
in the social product will be $1.20 higher than if the worker had been
otherwise unemployed. This argument is based on very special assumptions:
if the contract has been let to the South and unemployed Northern workers
migrate in response to the improved employment opportunities in the South,
taxpayers will save 20 percent and national unemployment will decline by
the same amount. The placement of contracts with high-cost producers in
high-unemployment areas is a form of subsidy to the high-cost areas and
protects the status quo with respect to wage levels and employment. To the
extent that cost (wage) factors are important in explaining the decline of
the North, the policymaker is faced with a rather unusual situation in which
the region in decline is the high-wage region and the subsidies that are
meant to deal with stagnation and outmigration do not help a low-income
population. The subsidies are instead meant to preserve the advantages of
the high-income industrial areas whose comparative advantage is being
eroded by the competition of a developing, previously backward, region
and a high-income region (the West) that continues to attract people and
businesses despite unprecedented growth during the last thirty years. Of
course, parallel between this form of interregional competition and the
calls for protection from low-cost foreign competition that it evokes from
Northern politicians is quite apparent. The only difference is that the
desired protection would come at the expense of United States nationals
rather than at the expense of foreign residents.

To conclude this section, I would like to restate the basic position that I
have tried to develop. Although I recognize that no simple explanation or
category of explanations is fully consistent with all of the facts, my main
emphasis in understanding the more rapid development of the South relative
to the North in the post–World War II period is the very basic consideration of comparative or differential costs.

CONCLUSION

I have devoted relatively little space to speculation on the factors that
are important in intrametropolitan decentralization. Mills, Muth, and other
urban theorists have stressed the role of the demand for cheap land and
new housing in suburbanization. In this volume, Oakland analyzes the fiscal
plight of central cities, and Clotfelter deals with school desegregation. Both
factors are prominent in general discussions of intrametropolitan decentralization. The technological changes that have promoted decentralization
have been set out by Meyer, Kain, and Whol (1965).[6] There is a growing

awareness of the interaction between employment and residential decentralization.

Oakland's chapter concludes that the solution to central-city fiscal problems should not take the form of help to cities per se but should be selectively targeted. Somewhat in contrast, one of my principal conclusions is that a federal policy that is "targeted" towards the poverty population in large Northern cities—on the grounds that this is where most of the need is—would be far from effective. A disproportionate number of the poor continue to reside in the South, and policy that is aimed at helping the poor according to need rather than location will necessarily result in a transfer of resources to the South (Golladay and Haveman, 1977).

Although a case can be made for federal aid going to cities throughout the nation, where the poor are concentrated, the case for help going to the North is very weak. As indicated above it has certainly not been demonstrated that Northern states are short-changed with regard to federal transfers or direct federal expenditures, and the "deficits" that some prominent Northern senators constantly allude to are not very meaningful in a economy that operates on principles of comparative advantage and cost minimization.

I have attempted to argue that the relative decline of the North is primarily due to a classical adjustment mechanism. One of the problems the North faces is that since 1950 the nominal wage structure in different parts of the country has remained relatively constant. So when nominal wage increases are weakly related to employment changes or unemployment, the high-wage regions of the North and Midwest face a real dilemma. How can they continue to hold onto their industrial base in the face of a cost disadvantage and pressure from increased international and interregional competition? As employment in the high-wage states declines, workers that remain employed protect their relative real-income position and the high rate of nominal wage increase leads to a further readjustment of capital at the margin that in turn erodes the employment base. In the absence of wage deflation in the North or relative wage inflation in the South, interregional shifts will continue unabated.

NOTES

1. These conclusions need to be tempered a bit by virtue of the cost-of-living differences between regions. Poverty measures account for rural-urban differences but not for regional differences in the cost of living. So Southern poverty will be overstated relative to Northern poverty.

2. Dick Netzer in commenting on a first draft of this chapter has drawn my attention to the whole web of regulation in explaining the "puzzle" of why more natural gas was not sold in the North. Federal Power Commission regulations lead to the dumping of gas at low prices locally rather than introducing it into interstate commerce and becoming *permanently* subject to Federal Power Commission regulations. Also the pipeline charges imposed by the Interstate Commerce Commission affected

investment decisions in pipelines and lead to severe constraints on the capacity to deliver gas to the North.

3. These changes are important in the light of the recent unpublished findings of D. Carlton (1978) that energy cost is an important factor in the determination of plant location of manufacturing firms.

4. Recent unpublished work by M. Homer (1978) brings out the shortcomings of Community Services Administration data on primary contractor in military procurement. For 1975, this data source indicates that 29.2 percent of procurement is from firms located in the South. However, from a recent census survey that better reflects actual work done, because of inclusion of subcontracting, the South's share drops to 19.6 percent, whereas the estimate of the Northeast's share changes from 23.1 percent to 26.2 percent, for the West the change is from 31.0 percent to 34.1 percent, and for the North-Central region the increase is from 23.1 to 26.2 percent.

5. In commenting on this section, Dick Netzer pointed out to me that in addition to Congressional politics, there is also the personal locational preferences of military bureaucrats who are disproportionately from the South. Also there is the retrospective thinking about "fighting the last war." The right place for training for a war in the South Pacific may be the South. But it is not clear that this is also true of training for combat in Northwest Europe or for the training of crews of all-weather combat aircraft. Finally, Netzer points out that "low-wage locations may not be low-cost ones. Admiral Rickover has denounced the Newport News shipyards more intensively than the Groton or Puget Sound shipyards."

6. The factors listed by these authors include: the increasing use of automobiles and trucks as means of transportation and containerization that allow workers to commute to suburban locations and free firms from the necessity of locating at rail heads and close to water transportation; increasing real wages that put a premium on a continuous process or automatic material-handling basis and make manufacturing a more land-intensive activity; electronic data processing that decreases the demand for large numbers of semiskilled clerks who rely on public transportation; in central areas, the jet age has changed the nature of intercity travel and partially shifted hotels and related activities to sites around airports; changes in entertainment technology (T.V.), which have decentralized entertainment away from large, centrally located movie houses and music halls.

REFERENCES

Beale, Calvin L. 1975. "The Revival of Population Growth in Non-Metropolitan America," *U.S. Department of Agriculture,* ERS-605, June, pp. 3–8.

Birch, David L. 1977. "Regional Differences in Factor Costs: Labor, Land Capital and Transportation." Presented at the L.B.J. School of Public Affairs, University of Texas, Austin, September 24.

Borts, George H., and Stern, Jerome L. 1964. *Economic Growth in a Free Market.* Columbia University Press: New York.

Brown, George D. 1976. "The Relative Importance of Federal Grant-in-Aid Formulas in an Overall Agenda for the Northeast." Prepared for the Federal Domestic Outlays Working Group.

Buchanan, James M. 1950. "Federalism and Fiscal Equity." *American Economic Review* 40 (September): 583–99.

————. 1952. "Federal Grants and Resource Allocation." *Journal of Political Economy* 60 (June): 208–17.

Campbell, Alan K. 1977. "Intra- and Interregional Changes in Population and Economic Activity." Presented at the L.B.J. School of Public Affairs, University of Texas, Austin. September 24.

Carlton, Dennis W. 1978. "Why New Firms Locate Where They Do." Presented at the Conference on Inter-regional Growth in the American Economy, sponsored by the Committee on Urban Public Economics. Baltimore, May 5–6.

Catsambas, Athanassios F. 1977. "The Regional Distribution of Federal Tax and Expenditures: A Study in the Theory and Estimation of Fiscal Incidence." Ph.D. Diss. Yale University.

Coelha, Philip, and Gholi, M. A. 1971. "The End of the North-South Wage Differential." *American Economic Review* 61 (December): 932–37.

Deavers, Kenneth L. 1977. "Rural Conditions and Regional Differences." Presented at the L.B.J. School of Public Affairs, University of Texas, Austin, September 24.

Dornbusch, R.; Fischer, S.; and Samuelson, P. A. 1977. "Comparative Advantage, Trade, and Payments in a Ricardian Model with a Continuum of Goods." *American Economic Review* 67 (December): 838–39.

Flatters, F.; Henderson V.; and Mieszkowski, P. 1974. "Public Goods, Efficiency and Regional Fiscal Equalization." *Journal of Public Economics* 3 (May): 99–112.

Golladay, Frederick L., and Haveman, Robert H. 1977. *The Economic Impacts of Tax-Transfer Policy.* New York: Academic Press.

Golfarb, Robert S., and Yezer, Anthony M. J. 1976. "Evaluating Alternative Theories of Intercity and Interregional Wage Differentials." *Journal of Regional Science* 16 (December): 345–65.

Gramlich, Edward M. 1976. "The New York Fiscal Crisis: What Happened and What is to Be Done." *American Economic Review* 66 (May): 415–29.

Haren, C. C. 1977. "Where the Jobs Are." *Farm Index* 16 (August): 20–21.

Harrison, David, Jr., and Kain, John F. 1974. "Cumulative Urban Growth and Urban Density Functions." *Journal of Urban Economics* 1 (January): 61–98.

Havemann, Joel; Stanfield, Rochelle L.; and Pierce, Neal R. 1976. "Federal Spending: The North's Loss Is the Sunbelt's Gain." *National Journal,* June 26, pp. 878–91.

Henderson, J. V. 1974. "The Sizes and Types of Cities." *American Economic Review* 64 (September): 640–56.

Hoch, Irving. 1972. "Urban Scale and Environmental Quality." In Commission on Population Growth and the American Future, Research Reports, Vol. 3, *Population Resources and the Environment,* R. G. Ridker, ed., pp. 235–84.

———. 1974. "Factors in Urban Crime." *Journal of Urban Economics* 1 (April): 184–229.

———. 1976a. "Climate, Wages and Urban Scale." In *Urban Costs of Climate Modification.* Edited by T. A. Ferrar. New York: John Wiley.

———. 1976b. "City Size Effects, Trends and Policies." *Science* 193 (September): 856–63.

———. 1977a. "Variations in the Quality of Urban Life Among Cities and Regions." In *Public Economics and the Quality of Life,* pp. 28–65. Edited by L. Wingo and A. Evans. Baltimore: Johns Hopkins University Press.

———. 1977b. "The Role of Energy in Regional Distribution of Economic Activity." Presented at the L.B.J. School of Public Affairs, University of Texas, Austin, September 24.

Holmer, Martin. 1978. "Preliminary Analysis of the Regional Economic Effects of Federal Procurement." Presented at the Conference on Inter-regional Growth in the American Economy, sponsored by the Committee on Urban Public Economics. Baltimore, May 5–6.

Hoover, E. M., and Vernon, R. 1959. *Anatomy of a Metropolis*. Cambridge, Mass.: Harvard University Press.

Jusenius, C. L., and Ledebur, L. C. 1976. "A Myth in the Making: The Southern Economic Challenge and Northern Economic Decline." Office of Economic Research, Economic Development Administration, U.S. Department of Commerce. November.

Kain, John F. 1968. "The Distribution and Movement of Jobs and Industry." In *The Metropolitan Enigma*, pp. 1–43. Edited by James Q. Wilson. Cambridge, Mass.: Harvard University Press.

Kaldor, Nicholas. 1970. "The Case for Regional Policies." *Scottish Journal of Political Economy* 17: 337–47.

Leone, Robert A. *The Location of Manufacturing Activity in the New York Metropolitan Area*. New York: National Bureau of Economic Research.

McDonald, Steven. 1977. Quoted in "Energy Shortage Is Said to Pose Lasting Threat to North." *New York Times*, 1 February, p. 18.

Meyer, John; Kain, John F.; and Wohl, Martin. 1965. *The Urban Transportation Problem*. Cambridge, Mass.: Harvard University Press.

Miernyk, W. H. 1977. "Rising Energy Prices and Regional Economic Development." *Growth and Change* (July): 2–7.

Mills, Edwin S. 1972. *Studies in the Structure of the Urban Economy*. Baltimore: Johns Hopkins Press.

Morrison, Peter A. 1977. "Current Demographic Change in Regions of the United States." Presented at the L.B.J. School of Public Affairs, University of Texas, Austin, September 24.

Muth, Richard. 1969. *Cities and Housing*. Chicago: University of Chicago Press.

North, Douglas C. 1955. "Location Theory and Regional Economic Growth." *Journal of Political Economy* 63 (June): 243–58.

Peterson, George E., and Muller, Thomas. 1977. "The Regional Impact of Federal Tax and Spending Policies." Presented at the L.B.J. School of Public Affairs, University of Texas, Austin, September 24.

Polinsky, A. Mitchell, and Rubinfeld, Daniel L. 1977. "Property Values and the Benefits of Environmental Improvements: Theory and Measurement." In *Public Economics and Quality of Life*, pp. 154–80. Edited by Lowdon Wingo and Alan Evans. Baltimore: Johns Hopkins Press.

Courant, Paul N., and Rubenfeld, Daniel L. 1975. "On the Measurement of Benefits In An Urban Context: Some General Equilibrium Issues." Working Paper No. 114, National Bureau of Economics Research, Cambridge, Mass. November. Forthcoming in *Journal of Urban Economics*, 1978, vol. 5.

Sacks, Seymour. 1977. *Trends in Metropolitan America*. Advisory Commission of Intergovernmental Relations M-108, Washington, February.

Thompson, Wilbur R. 1965. *A Preface to Urban Economics*. Baltimore: Johns Hopkins Press.

U.S. Bureau of the Census. 1974. *Low Income Areas In Large Cities*. Special

Subjects Studies of the 1970 Census, C 3.223/10.970, Vol. 2, Part 9B. Washington, D.C.

Vaughan, Roger J. 1976. "The Impact of Federal Policies on Urban Economic Development." Manuscript dated May.

Vernon, Raymond. 1976. *Metropolis 1985*. Cambridge, Mass.: Harvard University Press.

Williamson, Jeffrey G. 1977. "Unbalanced Growth, Inequality and Regional Development: Some Lessons from American History." Presented at the L.B.J. School of Public Affairs, University of Texas, Austin, September 24.

2

RACE DIFFERENCES IN EARNINGS: A SURVEY AND NEW EVIDENCE

JAMES P. SMITH AND FINIS WELCH

INTRODUCTION

Controversy has always surrounded analyses of trends in income differences by race. This follows in part from the uneven historical progress toward racial equality, as the prediction based on the experience of one decade have been negated by the reality of the next. While we believe that the broad sweep of American history suggests a steady but slow narrowing in racial income differences, there have clearly been reversals of this process. Even if one agrees on the direction of movement, sharp disputes exist concerning the root causes of change. Many have argued that a reduction in racial discrimination, partly induced by governmental pressure, has been the prime mover in raising the income of minorities. Others have contended that the basic underlying causal factors rest in the convergence in income-producing characteristics of blacks and whites as reflected in schooling levels and quality, regional location, and job experience. In this chapter we attempt to provide additional evidence on this subject using eight large microdata sets that span the time interval 1967–74.

This chapter has a two-fold purpose. In an earlier paper,[1] we analyzed changes in black-white male incomes between 1960 and 1970 based on the decennial U.S. Census. We argued on the basis of our work that that decade witnessed a significant improvement in the relative economic position of blacks. Our first objective is to update our previous research to determine if the momentum of the last decade has continued unabated into the mid-

James P. Smith is senior economist, The Rand Corporation; Finis Welch is professor of economics, University of California at Los Angeles, and senior economist, The Rand Corporation.

Comments offered by Eric Hanushek and Peter Mieskowski were extremely helpful. Jon Duringer, Iva MacLennan, and Dan Shapiro provided excellent research assistance. This research was funded by a grant from NSF.

1970s. To address the question, we use data from the 1968–75 Current Population Surveys. Our second goal is to explore in greater detail the role of regional characteristics in the improved status of black males. In our research based on the Census data, we found that geographical location had the largest and most favorable effect of the factors we examined in explaining the convergence in male wages by race over the decade. The rising black-white wage ratios in the South and North Central regions were the key geographical variables, with the South by far the most important.

This paper is organized in two parts. In the first section, we present an overview of the literature on black-white wage differentials. In addition to summarizing recent changes in these income ratios, we assess the more popular explanations for the narrowing of wage differences by race. The second part contains our new evidence for recent changes in income ratios by race, and we outline the methodology employed in using the Current Population Surveys and discuss in detail our empirical findings in explaining wage trends for the recent period.

1. OVERVIEW

This section summarizes the recent history of black-white wage ratios and reviews the principal competing hypotheses that have emerged to explain the partial elimination of race differences in wages. In lieu of an exhaustive survey of the literature, we have selected a few studies, relying heavily on our own past research, which have highlighted the central controversies.

The major explanations for the narrowing racial wage differences can be placed in five general categories. The first emphasizes convergence in black and white income-producing characteristics. As blacks and whites become increasingly congruent in such attributes as education, increases in black-white wage ratios should follow. A related hypothesis involves relative cohort or "vintage" improvement among blacks, i.e., enhancement in the perceived quality of these income-producing characteristics. The central idea is that relative to whites, more recent black cohorts begin their job experiences with larger initial stocks of human capital than cohorts of blacks already in the market. Skill distributions are seen as relatively constant within cohorts, and convergence is accomplished as increasingly more racially similar cohorts enter labor markets while other, less similar ones exit (retire). Because education is an important determinant of earnings, and changes in school quality are more easily indexed, most research on this subject has concentrated on educational quality. The third category involves the impact of migration. The geographical distribution of people differs significantly by race, and there is substantial between-region dispersion in black-white wage ratios. Historically, migration of blacks from the South to the North was the primary factor, but more recently, increasing urbanization of the black South has assumed an important role. The fourth category involves the effects of government affirmative action and reductions in labor market discrimination. Finally, business cycle variations can account for short-run changes in the relative economic status of blacks; traditionally, blacks have suffered relative to whites during business contractions, and observed changes in wages may, at least over short periods of time, be attributable to business cycles.

We begin with a brief description of the historical trends in black-white wage ratios with an emphasis on regional differences.

Recent Trends in Black-White Male Wage Ratios

Table 2.1 presents wage ratios for selected years from 1947 to 1975 separately for all wage and salary workers and for those employed full time. Although the post–World War II era is characterized by a definite upward drift in the relative income of blacks, there were sharp cyclic swings. There was a slight increase in black-white income ratios in the late forties and early fifties continuing a process that apparently operated throughout the forties.[2] In the late fifties there occurred a deterioration in relative black male income that ended in the early sixties. The relative wage of blacks began to climb after 1963 and experienced a steady rise until 1970. We analyzed this expansion in our work with the censuses. The CPS data clearly indicate that this trend has continued into the mid-1970s.[3] Since this

TABLE 2.1. Ratios for Median Male Wage and Income, by Race, for Selected Years, 1947–75

	Wage and Salary Earnings[a]	
Year	All Workers $\left(\dfrac{\text{black males}^{\text{b}}}{\text{white males}}\right)$	Full-time Workers $\left(\dfrac{\text{black males}}{\text{white males}}\right)$
1947	.543	.640[c]
1951	.616	
1955	.588	.635
1959	.580	.612
1963	.568	.654
1967	.639	.675
1969	.666	.694
1973	.695	.719
1974	.709	.736
1975	.734	.769

SOURCE: Current Population Reports.
[a] Data are for all individuals fourteen years old and over.
[b] "Black" refers to Negro and other non-Caucasian races.
[c] Data refer to 1946 Urban and Rural Nonfarm.

decade was characterized by a recession in which wages of blacks and low-skill workers typically decline relative to the average, the published CPS data for the seventies suggest that the factors at work raising black relative wages during the sixties have continued uninterrupted. Comparisons among full-time earners are useful in providing a partial control of business cycle fluctuations in employment at the expense of introducing potential censoring problems into this restricted sample. Full-time earnings ratios have risen more rapidly than those of all earners combined. In the last decade, racial earning ratios for all workers and full-time workers have diverged, especially among the younger entrants. This suggests the possibility that income distribution among blacks is becoming more unequal,[4] with fully employed blacks experiencing large gains without this improvement filtering down to the most economically disadvantaged blacks. Mean income ratios may conceal the fact that segments of the black community may not be sharing in these recent economic advances.

In table 2.2, nonwhite-white income ratios are listed for the four census regions.[5] Some care must be exercised in interpreting time series statistics of regional wage differentials. In addition to differential growth in real income across regions, these ratios may be altered substantially by migration. The characteristics of migrants relative to those in place of origin and destination can create the illusion of differential trends among regions. The historically large outmigration of blacks from the South to the other census regions suggests that this problem may be serious in this context. Simple summary statistics of mean wages by region cannot discriminate between changes caused by differential regional growth and those that result primarily from between-region migration. With this in mind, table 2.2 describes the following patterns in racial incomes by region.

The only regions that exhibit any uniform trend in the black-white income ratios are those we identified in our census work—the North Central and the South. The most dramatic changes have clearly occurred in the South. There has been a strong, persistent rise in income ratios in the South resulting in a narrowing of racial wage differentials among regions. How-

TABLE 2.2. Nonwhite/White Income Ratios, by Region

Year	Northeast	North Central	South	West	Overall United States
1956	.730	.768	.423	.764	.523
1958	.735	.768	.391	.726	.498
1961	.732	.716	.376	.778	.517
1963	.716	.742	.427	.791	.521
1967	.745	.841	.495	.772	.588
1969	.762	.824	.539	.691	.590
1973	.769	.803	.560	.758	.629
1974	.719	.811	.546	.744	.634

ever, in spite of this rapid improvement the Southern income ratio still remains substantially below that of other regions.[6]

When the sample is stratified into regions and age groups, wage gains in the South exist in all age groups, with the greatest improvement registered among the younger workers. There is no question that black males are at least equal participants with whites in the recent economic resurgence in the South.

Converging Characteristics and the Role of Education

The most straightforward explanation for the improved economic status of black males is that in terms of characteristics producing higher wages, blacks and whites are simply becoming more alike. While this increased similarity is reflected in many characteristics, the economic literature gives special attention to education. In this century we have seen a remarkable convergence in the income-producing characteristics of black and white males. This is documented effectively in table 2.3, which lists years of schooling completed by years of labor market entry from 1930 to 1970. Comparisons between races at point of entry into the labor market are used because they are more sensitive indicators of cohort changes than comparisons of educational distribution of all workers. In 1930 the average black new labor force entrant had credentials quite different from his white competitor: the typical black male began his work career with 3.7 fewer years of formal schooling; almost 80 percent of these blacks had a grade school diploma or less and only 3 percent had any postsecondary schooling. As successive cohorts entered the labor force over the last forty years, the competitive disadvantage of blacks has continuously narrowed. By 1970, 1.2 years of schooling separated black and white males at the times of their initial labor force experience. Furthermore, only 10 percent of these new

TABLE 2.3. Years of School Completed at Estimated Time of Labor Market Entry

| | Year of Labor Market Entry | | | | |
	1930	1940	1950	1960	1970
Mean years schooling of blacks	5.9	8.0	9.9	11.1	11.4
Mean years schooling of whites	9.6	11.1	12.0	12.6	12.6
Proportion of blacks with fewer than 9 years of schooling	0.78%	0.58%	0.31%	0.15%	0.11%
Proportion of whites with fewer than 9 years of schooling	0.42%	0.22%	0.15%	0.10%	0.07%
Proportion of blacks with more than 12 years of schooling	0.03%	0.07%	0.13%	0.19%	0.19%
Proportion of whites with more than 12 years of schooling	0.08%	0.20%	0.32%	0.37%	0.38%

black workers had fewer than 9 years of schooling and almost a fifth of them had some postsecondary education. There is no question that in terms of measurable nominal characteristics associated with earnings, black and white males are becoming increasingly congruent. It should not be surprising that they also appear increasingly similar regarding monetary rewards offered by the market.

In our work using the 1960 and 1970 census, we were able to test for black-white differences in the returns to education as well as the presence of structural shifts over the decade. Initial studies based on the 1960 census by Hanoch, Thurow, and others painted a consistent picture of low returns to schooling for blacks. Later work based principally on the Survey of Economic Opportunity (see Leonard Weiss and Jeffery Williamson, 1972; Welch, 1973) estimated black educational coefficients that were as large or larger than those obtained for whites in 1960. This raised the possibility of a strong structural shift during the decade in the effectiveness of black schooling. Because we had pooled estimates based on both the 1960 and 1970 census, we were able to directly test for black-white differences in the return to schooling and the existence of structural shifts. Our estimates are reported in table 2.4. For grade school, the returns for blacks were lower than for whites. In contrast, the marginal returns to postsecondary schooling were actually higher for blacks than for whites. If school systems were not an effective means of increasing black incomes, it is clear that the problem

TABLE 2.4. Estimated Schooling Coefficients by Race and Years of Labor Market Experience

Years of Experience	White Male	Black Male	White Male	Black Male
Elementary and Secondary School				
	1970		1960	
1–5	.138	.092	.149	.099
6–10	.108	.093	.096	.070
11–15	.067	.053	.062	.044
16–20	.061	.045	.064	.043
21–30	.058	.030	.059	.032
31–40	.047	.028	.053	.023
College				
1–5	.123	.162	.098	.132
6–10	.088	.010	.080	.084
11–15	.090	.097	.079	.075
16–20	.088	.088	.068	.055
21–30	.076	.085	.072	.060
31–40	.074	.075	.049	.048

SOURCE: Smith-Welch (1977).
NOTE: The schooling coefficients can be read as the fractional increase in income associated with an extra year of schooling.

was at the elementary and secondary level. There was little trend in the income benefits from grade school for either race between 1960 and 1970, but higher wage benefits to college occurred in 1970. There is some evidence as well that wage benefits from college grew more during the decade for blacks than for whites. This may reflect the shift of black students from Southern Negro colleges to the presumably higher quality Northern colleges.

The converging educational distributions by race in conjunction with the evidence that, at least among new workers, the income benefits from schools are comparable for blacks to those received by whites indicates that education has played an important role in raising the relative income of blacks. Despite this past record there is a question of the future potential for schooling to achieve additional wage improvements for blacks. In section 2 of this chapter, we present new estimates of the returns to schooling by race for each year between 1967 and 1974.

COHORT IMPROVEMENT. The chief proponent of the vintage hypothesis that converging income ratios reflect relative improvement of more recent black cohorts is Finis Welch. The bulk of Welch's evidence is that the improved quality of new generations of black workers reflects schooling quality. The evidence he accumulated refers to measures of changing attributes of black schools during this century. The current, and in many cases valid, criticism of the quality of contemporary black education tends to make us forget that the situation historically was much worse. In terms of nominal characteristics of schools, Welch (1974) collected data that tell a clear story of improving relative quality of black schools. A sample of his supporting data is reported in table 2.5. The change that may have been

TABLE 2.5. Comparisons of Twentieth-century Trends in Characteristics between Segregated Negro Schools, Southern White Schools, and All U.S. Schools, 1899–1954

Year	Average Days Attended per Pupil Enrolled		Pupils Enrolled per Classroom Teacher		Ratio of Enrollment in First & Second Grades	
	Negro schools	All schools	Negro schools	All schools	Negro schools	All schools
1899–1900	57	69[a]	56.7	42.5[a]	1.37	1.14[a]
1908–9	71	88	56.4	39.9[a]	1.45	1.49[a]
1919–20	80	121	56.0	31.8	1.96	1.64
1929–30	97	143	43.7	30.0	2.35	1.48
1939–40	126	152	45.3	29.0	2.03	1.29
1949–50	148	158	33.6	27.5	1.62	1.20
1953–54	151	159	32.9	27.9	1.45	1.25

[a] Southern white schools only.

of greatest importance in terms of learning acquired is the convergence of school-term length between blacks and whites. In 1920 black youths attended school three quarters of a year less than white students. By 1954, the year of the Supreme Court desegregation decision, there were no real black-white differences in days attended. In 1920 Negro teachers had one and three quarters as many pupils as the national average. By 1954 this difference had been substantially reduced. In examining the data on black schools, the most striking dimension cited by Welch is the extraordinarily high ratio of first to second graders.[7] Welch contends that between 1920 and 1940 Negro students averaged about two years to complete the first grade. Retention rates that average 100 percent would hardly seem to be indicative of high-quality education; rather, they suggest low quality coupled with inflexible standards. But note in table 2.5 that between 1940 and 1954 the implicit retention rates in Southern Negro schools converged towards the national norm. It has always been difficult to link attributes of schools to measures of school achievement. It is, indeed, possible that some of the measures offered—days attended, pupil-teacher ratios, retention rates, schooling expenditures per student, teacher quality—have had little impact on achievement. However, the consistent picture of simultaneous convergence in all these dimensions makes the case for improving relative quality of black schools plausible.

Although the bulk of the evidence on vintage concerns schooling quality, other dimensions may be equally important; the evidence cited on trends in black educational levels is particularly relevant.

The persistent effects of past educational levels affect the market performance of present generations through family background. Even as current educational levels by race converge, the weight of the past will be a factor depressing relative wages of blacks. However, in terms of tracking changes over time, the history of generational improvement will contribute to the convergence between races. Blacks not only have higher educational level relative to whites than their fathers did, but their fathers also had more education relative to whites than *their* parents did.

MIGRATION. The third factor contributing to the rising relative economic position of blacks relates to changing geographical distribution by race. Table 2.6 lists the distribution of blacks and whites living in the four census regions from 1900 to 1970 and the proportion of individuals located in urban areas. The salient migratory event is, of course, the large exodus of blacks from the South. In 1900 almost 90 percent of blacks were located in the South. In a process beginning in 1910 and accelerating after the Second World War, blacks left the South and relocated in the urban North. By 1970 the proportion of blacks in the South had declined by approximately one-half. The earliest black migration was to the Northeastern and North Central regions, but more recently, blacks as well as whites have moved into the Western region. An equally striking development is the increasing urbanization of the black South.[8] While practically all Northern blacks are in urban areas, blacks traditionally resided in rural sections of the South. In 1900 less than 20 percent of black Southerners lived in urban areas; by 1970 the proportion had risen to almost 70 percent. The chapter in American history during which one could correctly employ the dichotomy of the Northern black as urban and the Southern black as rural is rapidly coming to a close. The Southern-rural to Northern-urban migration of blacks has partly been superseded by the move of Southern blacks to the economically vibrant and growing Southern cities.

The short (eight-year) period covered by CPS data for individuals limits the extent to which migration trends can be traced. The most important recent development is the continuing black urbanization in the South. Between 1968 and 1975, the fraction of black Southerners living in Standard Metropolitan Statistical Areas increased from .524 to .606. Among white Southerners, a similar but less pronounced shift occurred as the proportion living in SMSAs rose from .549 to .591. The distinction between the races lies in the tendency for urban blacks to live in central cities of SMSAs (over 70 percent), while approximately 45 percent of white Southerners in SMSAs are in central cities. Within the South, the propor-

TABLE 2.6. Regional Distribution of Blacks and Whites

	Northeast		North Central		South		West	
Year	Whites	Blacks	Whites	Blacks	Whites	Blacks	Whites	Blacks
A. Distribution by Race within Region								
1970	.249	.192	.291	.202	.284	.530	.177	.075
1960	.261	.160	.302	.183	.274	.599	.163	.058
1950	.277	.134	.312	.148	.273	.680	.138	.038
1940	.292	.106	.329	.110	.268	.770	.113	.013
1930	.305	.096	.341	.106	.254	.787	.099	.010
1920	.305	.065	.350	.076	.255	.852	.090	.008
1910	.310	.049	.358	.055	.251	.890	.080	.005
1900	.311	.044	.386	.056	.247	.897	.058	.003
B. Proportion Urban by Race by Region								
1970	.787	.966	.693	.955	.639	.673	.826	.861
1960	.791	.952	.668	.939	.586	.582	.776	.788
1950	.787	.936	.626	.912	.489	.476	.697	.716
1940	.761	.897	.573	.850	.368	.363	.508	.518
1930	.771	.887	.569	.834	.347	.325	.596	.504
1920	.757	.862	.516	.787	.292	.251	.530	.426
1910	.722	.809	.447	.662	.232	.211	.492	.395
1900	.669	.705	.382	.582	.185	.171	.412	.321

SOURCE: U.S. Bureau of the Census.

tion of whites in central cities declined slightly from 1967, while the corresponding proportion of blacks increased from .399 to .443 percent.

In the light of the considerable between-region dispersion in racial income ratios (documented in tables 2.2 and 2.3), the substantial redistribution of population by race during the twentieth century suggests that location variables had the potential to explain a significant part of the more rapid rise in black wages. Area of residence can account for an improvement in the relative economic status of blacks for two reasons. The direct effect of relocation results from black migration from regions (the South) with low relative black-white wages into regions where the black wage disadvantage is smaller (the North). Since racial wage ratios have risen more rapidly in the South, where blacks are more heavily represented, the second flows from converging racial income differences between regions.

The existing empirical evidence indicates that location was, in fact, the most consistent cause of rising black-white wage ratios up to 1970. James Gwartney (1970) reports that migration was the principal reason for the rise in racial income ratios between 1940 and 1960. This was a consequence of the black migration from the South to the North, and more importantly, the more rapid increases in relative wages in the South. Gwartney estimates that relative wages rose by 21.7 percent in the South and by 16.2 percent in the North and the West between 1940 and 1960. Furthermore, the change in the regional composition of people during this time span increased the nonwhite-white income ratio by 3.1 percent. In our work with the census data, we measured the effect of location between 1960 and 1970; geographical residence had the largest and most favorable effect of all the factors we examined in that research. The locational effects were dominated by changed earnings ratios within regions, with migration per se being of secondary importance.

In spite of the historical importance of migration in accounting for rising relative black wages, the potential for migration movements to explain more recent changes in black-white wage ratios is open to question.

THE ROLE OF GOVERNMENT.   Perhaps the most common explanation of the recent rise in black-white wage ratios is the alleged positive effect of governmental pressure commonly known as "affirmative action." Title VII of the 1964 Civil Rights Act forbids both employment and wage discrimination on the basis of race. The Civil Rights Act created the Equal Employment Opportunity Commission (EEOC) to monitor employers' compliance with the provisions of the act; although the initial powers of the EEOC were limited, since 1972 the Commission has had the power to initiate litigation. The Office of Federal Contract Compliance (OFCC) was established in 1965 to administer an executive order forbidding discrimination by government contractors. The existing empirical evidence on the effects of this legislation has indicated conflicting and mixed results. These studies have taken a variety of forms, but the most numerous have been individual or case studies of firms affected by either EEOC or OFCC. A second group is based on time-series analysis of trends in black-white wage ratios. Finally, cross-sectional studies usually embedded in a larger context have attempted to test for the impact of affirmative action. The vast number of studies preclude any extensive survey so we will have to content ourselves with a broad-brush approach.[9]

Because they do not deal with economy-wide effects, the case studies of EEOC and OFCC are the least useful in determining aggregate effects on black-white wage ratios. Butler and Heckman, in their survey of the existing research, cite the work of Andrea Beller (1974) as the most sophisticated of the microstudies of EEOC. She concluded that the enforcement of the wage and employment provisions of the 1964 Civil Rights Act appear to have a slight positive economy-wide impact on relative employment and no (or possibly a negative) impact on relative wages. The OFCC studies are of questionable value because they deal only with relative-employment effects and contain no information on relative-wage effects. Butler and Heckman conclude that the evidence suggests small but positive short- and long-run effects on employment and possible negative effects on relative occupational position.[10]

The most influential of the time-series studies was conducted by Richard Freeman.[11] With time-series data for the years 1947–71, Freeman regressed the black-white income ratios on a time trend, deviations from GNP as a proxy for cyclic variation, relative education of blacks, and a variable measuring cumulative EEOC expenditures. The latter variable was used as an index of federal antidiscrimination programs and had a statistically significant positive coefficient. On the basis of this evidence, Freeman concluded that affirmative action pressures had shifted the time-series pattern of relative wages toward blacks. His work is consistent with that of Vroman, and together they are the principal evidence in support of strong positive effects of affirmative action. (In fact, Vroman only showed that the timing of relative-wage growth was consistent with that of the government's affirmative action emphasis and Freeman's work.)

Their work is open to a number of criticisms. The ability of limited time-series data to detect the effect of affirmative action and, more importantly, to discriminate among alternative hypotheses is questionable. There was a dramatic increase between 1965 and 1966 in black-white wage ratios, which is often used as evidence that the immediately preceding civil rights laws played a large causative role in the recent improvement in the earnings of blacks. Variables, such as Freeman's cumulative EEOC-expenditure series, that also changed rapidly during this period will undoubtedly capture the sharp break at the time in the time-series pattern. However, year-to-year changes in this series are often quite irregular. For example, there are two other points (1951–52 and 1958–59) where the increase in the black-white ratio is almost as large as the 1965–66 change; in these periods there was, of course, no comparable legislation.

In their excellent critique of the Freeman study, Butler and Heckman cast serious doubts on his conclusions. They argue that one cause of the recent rise in relative black wages results from a supply-side phenomenon— the declining labor-force participation rates of prime-aged black males. They attribute this decline to the expansion of the welfare system, which has increased nonmarket opportunities for low-income individuals, and for blacks in particular. Since it is reasonable to suppose that the lowest-wage blacks will leave the market first, Butler and Heckman contend that some of this recent rise is merely a statistical artifact—the consequence of censoring out low-wage blacks resulting in a reported rise in the black-white wage ratios of remaining participants. Butler and Heckman replicated Freeman's time-series analysis and also included a variable measuring the predicted relative labor force participation rates of black males. Not only does their new variable have the expected negative effect, but alongside it Freeman's accumulative EEOC-expenditure variable is statistically insignificant. The Butler-Heckman study, added to our general skepticism concerning the usefulness of time-series data, convinces us that Freeman's inference about strong affirmative action effects is not warranted on the basis of this evidence alone.[12]

Many cross-sectional studies (Link, 1975; Weiss-Williamson, 1975; Haworth, Gwartney, and Haworth, 1975) have also assigned a major part of the improvement in relative black-white income to the effects of government antidiscriminatory legislation. Unfortunately, the standard empirical practice was to deduce the impact of the government as a component of the residual—all changes in black-white wage ratios not accounted for by other explanatory variables. Since these residuals measure aggregate ignorance and could proxy any neglected factor, more direct tests of affirmative action are required before any confidence can be placed in this conclusion. In our research based on the 1960 and 1970 censuses, we attempted to test the role of government in the rise in black-white wage ratios over that decade.[13] We argued that the implied threat of pressures on government contractors for affirmative action gave us our best observation of effects of this legislation. The only method at our disposal with the censuses was an indirect one—to focus on workers most susceptible to governmental influence. We identified workers by the degree of their contact with the government: government employees, workers in industries regulated by the government, and workers in industries that sell a large part of their product to the government. If affirmative action was an important causal factor, its impact should have been strongest on employment and wage trends in these industries. Our empirical research indicated, however, that the largest gains in black-white wage ratios between 1960 and 1970 occurred in those industries least vulnerable to federal or local government influence—i.e., the private sector. We concluded that the effects of affirmative action during the sixties was probably small.

Whatever the causes of the racial trends before 1970, it is conceivable that more weight must be assigned to the role of government for recent changes. There is evidence of expansion in the budgets of the government agencies responsible for enforcing antidiscrimination legislation. Moreover, it is alleged that a series of court decisions imposing severe financial penalties on firms for noncompliance with affirmative action goals have added sharp teeth to government. In section 2 we update our earlier analysis to evaluate the possibility of more recent impact of affirmative action.

THE IMPACT OF BUSINESS CYCLES.   The years since 1969 have generally been characterized by a business-cycle contraction and by rising unemployment rates. There is abundant historical evidence that wages of blacks decline relative to those of whites during cyclic downswings, so that more stable business conditions could have produced a more rapid increase in black-white wage ratios than was observed over this period. To investigate the influence of cyclic conditions on racial earnings ratios we regressed, for the time span 1948–69, the log of the black-white earnings ratio on a quadratic time trend and the unemployment rate of prime-aged males. This regression was used to predict racial earning ratios for the 1970–74 period under two assumptions. (The regression is reported in table 2.7). The first, graphed as the broken line in figure 2.1, uses the actual unemployment rates for these years. The second (the dotted line in figure 2.1) assumes that the unemployment rate remained at its 1969 level. Comparing these predicted ratios to the actual trend indicates that business cycle conditions did partly depress the increase in black-white relative wages. Using the 1969 unemployment rate, the predicted earnings ratio increased by .058 percentage points while the actual ratio rose by .043.

TABLE 2.7. Time Series Regression on Black/White Income Ratios

Time Period Covered	Independent Variables					
	Time	Time Squared	Unemployment Rate	Unemployment Rate Time	Constant	R^2
1948–69	−.0087 (−1.450)	.0005 (−1.95)	−.0308 (−3.960)		−.4972 (−14.871)	.733
1948–74	−.0155 (3.25)	.0007 (5.39)	−.0403 (3.23)	.0011 (1.22)	−.4536 (8.96)	.863

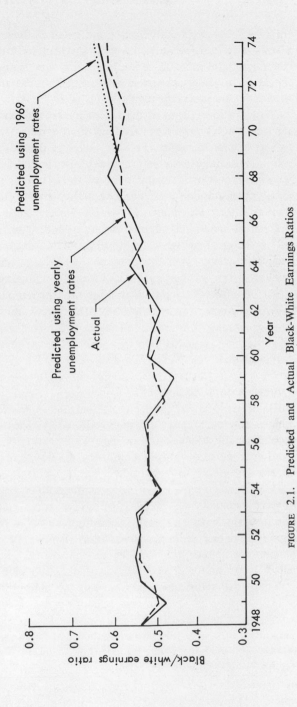

FIGURE 2.1. Predicted and Actual Black-White Earnings Ratios

If business-cycle conditions improve over the remainder of this decade, black-white male wage ratios should rise more rapidly for the rest of the seventies than they did in the last five years. This rise could easily match the large advances experienced during the 1960s. Figure 2.1 also shows that, using the actual unemployment rates for this recent period, the actual earnings ratio was not as depressed by recent business cycle conditions as our regressions predicted. We hypothesize that the types of factor leading to the secular increase in black wages (increased quantity and quality of schooling) have probably made black males less vulnerable to cyclic vagaries than was historically the case. As blacks become more like whites in the characteristics that produce higher earnings, it is reasonable to suppose that they will likewise resemble whites more closely in their reaction to business-cycle fluctuations. As a simple test of this hypothesis, table 2.7 lists a second regression on the black-white earnings ratio that includes a time interaction with the unemployment rate. Although this interactive variable is only marginally significant, results indicate that the negative effect of business cycles on relative black earnings, as indexed by unemployment rates, may be losing severity over time.

2. ANALYSIS OF THE CPS FILES

Framework for Analysis

In this section we describe the methodology employed for investigating recent trends in black-white male wage ratios. Our samples are derived from eight Current Population Surveys for the years 1968–75. In each year, separate samples were extracted for black and white males between the ages of fourteen and sixty-five.[14] The dependent variable is the ($1n$) weekly wage computed by dividing earnings by weeks worked. The explanatory variables fall into five classes: schooling, regional residence, market experience, direct and indirect government employment, and a set of estimated probabilities controlling for non-full-time work. These variables were interacted in a number of ways that are described below.

There are two variables for years of schooling completed. The first ranges from zero to twelve and indicates years of elementary and secondary schooling. The second measures years of postsecondary schooling. If a person reports a positive number of years of college, the grade school variable is set equal to twelve. This "spline" function is linearly segmented to permit slope coefficients to differ between the first twelve years of schooling and succeeding years, but the segments are constrained to join at twelve years. Because the returns to schooling are characterized in cross-sectional data sets by a significant interaction with labor market experience, we interacted both schooling variables with a linearly segmented experience measure—the first ten years of market experience and experience defined as post-ten-year market experience.

Geographic location includes binary variables indicating residence for the North Central and West regions and for three subregions in the South—the South Atlantic, East South Central, and West South Central. The omitted (base) class is the Northeastern region. Residence in each region was interacted with market experience to determine whether experience profiles of earnings differed among regions. Dummy variables were included if the individual resides in a Standard Metropolitan Statistical Area or within a central city of the SMSA, so the omitted class refers to residents of nonmetropolitan areas. In order to capture differences between the South and the rest of the United States more finely, the SMSA dummy was interacted with region of residence in the South and the non-South, and the Southern SMSA was interacted with labor-market experience.

A number of variables were added to indicate whether the individual is a federal, state, or local government employee or works in an industry that is government regulated (federal or state). For those who work neither for a government nor in government-regulated industry, two additional variables are incorporated. One represents purchases by the federal government as a fraction of value added originating in the industry; the other is similarly defined for purchases by state and local governments. With these variables, we attempt to identify wage effects of governmental efforts to enforce anti-discriminatory legislation. Because it is alleged that discrimination is more intense in the South and that government pressure against it has been more vigorous there, we have interacted the set of government variables with residence in the South and the non-South.

Most cross-sectional data sets, including the Current Population Surveys and the census, do not contain direct measures of labor-market experience. The definition of experience we employed in previous research was

$$Exp = Age - EAge$$

where EAge is age at entry into the labor force, supplied from a table as a function of schooling.[15] This definition of market experience has a number of defects. Since it is constructed from a rigid link between schooling and age, it is impossible to estimate separate parameters for accumulated market experience and cohort effects of either year of labor-market entry or year of birth. Even if this measure were based on an accurate estimate of the mean age of labor-market entry for each schooling class, there exists a distribution of entry ages about that expected mean. For younger, more recent entrants into the labor force, the expected age of entry should be computed as the expected value of the entry age distribution truncated at the current age of the worker. For example, a twenty-year-old high school graduate who is working has an expected entry age clearly less than the mean age for all high school graduates (age 20), since he was (relative to his peers) an early participant in the labor force.[16]

Our problem was to construct a complete distribution of entry ages for school-completion levels and cohorts. In an unpublished paper, Gould and Welch (1976) used data from the 1940, 1950, 1960, and 1970 censuses to estimate densities of school age completion by schooling level and birth cohort.[17] Because it is relatively common for individuals to begin their work careers before final completion of schooling, these schooling completion densities represent only the first stage in estimating entry age distributions. The Coleman-Rossi data of 1589 males thirty to forty years old in 1969 provide retrospective life histories of respondents including information on age at taking first full-time job and age at school completion. This data was used to obtain a functional relationship between entry age and school completion age in order to map the schooling-age distributions into entry-age distributions. Thus, for each age, schooling, and cohort class, we can compute expected age of entry conditional upon current work. For a person with characteristics X, observed to be working at any age α, the expected entry age is

$$E(EAge \mid EAge < \alpha; X) = \frac{\int_0^\alpha y f_x(y) dy}{\int_0^\alpha f_x(y) dy}.$$

Our estimated entry ages have some desirable properties. First, they allow for vintage effects, since entry age varies with cohort. There is evidence that age at school completion has declined secularly, so that for any schooling level more recent cohorts have entered the labor market earlier than older cohorts. To illustrate, we estimate that a typical high school graduate of the mid-1960s completed his education two years younger than a high school graduate at the turn of the century. Second, we have not imposed an identical entry age distribution on black and white males. Welch (1974) has reported that retardation rates in the early decades of the twentieth century were considerably higher among blacks; many black children spent more than one year completing a grade. Therefore, among similarly aged and schooled blacks and whites, black men would have less labor-market experience. Our estimated entry-age distributions reflect this racial difference, with blacks having higher entry ages than whites among older cohorts. Black-white entry ages have recently converged to the point that among young cohorts there is no evidence of any racial differences.[18]

One problem encountered in using successive cross-sectional data sets is that sample characteristics may vary across the years. As business conditions deteriorated over the 1967–74 period, the proportion of people with zero earnings and the fraction involved in part-time work increased. It is likely that the lowest-wage earners leave the market first, so that the observed mean-wage rates of the remaining participants depend in part on the extent of market withdrawal as well as the mean wage of the participants relative to those who left the labor force. Since we have confined our analysis to individuals with positive earnings, the possibility exists that our black-white comparisons could be contaminated by differential censoring across these years. To control for this source of bias, we estimated a set of probabilities relating to non-full-time work—the probability of zero earnings; the probability of part-year, part-time work; the probability of full-year, part-time work; and the probability of part-year, full-time work.[19] We computed the probability of each individual in our sample being in each of these four categories and included these predicted probabilities as regressors.

The original number of parameters to be estimated for each race was 352 (44 parameters in each of eight years). Since some coefficients were insignificant in all years or remained stable over time, this completely free form of allowing the full set of 352 parameters was clearly too general. The strategy we followed was an iterative one. We initially estimated for each race the 44 parameters in each year.[20] Based on these estimates, we imposed a number of constraints—deleting variables that were insignificant in each year and combining variables that did not differ significantly.[21, 22] Finally, for coefficients that were stable over the years, we constrained the parameter to be the same in all years.[23] We then reestimated the model, separating by race, with all eight years of data pooled. By imposing these constraints, we reduced to 183 the number of parameters to be estimated. While this process of sequential hypothesis testing has obvious pitfalls, it seemed preferable in that we obtained more efficient estimates for the remaining variables. Estimates and standard errors of the separate regressions for white and black males are available in a report issued by the Rand Corporation.[24] In the following section, we have organized the presentation of our empirical findings around three variables of interest—schooling, geographical location, and government.

Empirical Results with CPS Data

SCHOOLING. In table 2.8, the schooling coefficients for white males are evaluated at selected years of market experience. For each segment of the schooling spline, two sets of coefficients are presented. In the first panel (*A*), coefficients refer to a regression that does not include the three variables predicting the probability of part-time work and zero earnings, whereas table 2.8*B* lists schooling coefficients when these probabilities are included

TABLE 2.8. Schooling Coefficients for White Males

	Elementary and High School					College				
	Years of Market Experience					Years of Market Experience				
Year	0	10	20	30	40	0	10	20	30	40
					A					
1967	.019	.098	.079	.059	.040	.141	.064	.064	.064	.065
1968	.021	.105	.082	.059	.036	.148	.056	.058	.059	.061
1969	.023	.111	.085	.060	.035	.164	.051	.059	.066	.074
1970	.026	.107	.082	.057	.032	.151	.061	.063	.066	.069
1971	.039	.113	.085	.057	.028	.153	.060	.063	.066	.069
1972	.044	.111	.083	.056	.028	.120	.064	.063	.063	.062
1973	.062	.122	.091	.060	.030	.118	.060	.058	.057	.055
1974	.069	.126	.094	.062	.029	.115	.054	.057	.059	.062
					B					
1967	.035	.073	.064	.056	.047	.044	.086	.083	.079	.076
1968	.038	.079	.067	.056	.045	.050	.079	.076	.073	.070
1969	.045	.081	.069	.056	.044	.046	.078	.078	.078	.078
1970	.042	.077	.064	.052	.039	.043	.087	.083	.080	.076
1971	.046	.080	.064	.048	.032	.057	.083	.081	.078	.076
1972	.054	.083	.067	.050	.034	.033	.084	.079	.074	.069
1973	.066	.094	.074	.053	.032	.044	.078	.072	.067	.061
1974	.065	.095	.074	.053	.031	.045	.071	.071	.071	.070

NOTE: Section A reports the regression results when the probabilities of part-time work and zero earnings are not included. Section B shows the schooling coefficients with these probabilities included as regressors.

as regressors.[25] These variables measure the probability of obtaining full-time jobs and also serve as a partial control for business cycles. The schooling coefficients are obviously sensitive to these controls for part-time work. The standard skill specificity models of Oi and Rosen (1962; 1968) demonstrate that the brunt of business-cycle adjustments will fall on hours rather than employment, as firms endeavor to retain commitments from their previous investments in skilled labor. This substitution of hours for employment variation in adapting to cyclic downturns should be more important for skilled labor, and it is evident from table 2.8 that the college segment of the education spline is most sensitive to the inclusion of these variables.

Concentrating initially on table 2.8A, the percentage of increase in earnings from college at the point of entry into the labor market is quite high but declines quickly over the first ten years of market experience. After this point, however, the wage premiums to college are relatively stable for the remainder of the life cycle. In contrast, the elementary school coefficients rise rapidly during the initial ten years in the labor force and then fall significantly over the rest of the work career. Controlling for the probability of part-time work (table 2.8B), the life-cycle patterns for the elementary and secondary school segment maintain the same general shape, although both the initial rise and ensuing fall in coefficients over the life cycle are less acute. However, this control for hours worked results in a reversal in the initial decline in the college coefficients that now parallel the rising trend exhibited in the elementary and high school segment.

To understand these patterns, it is important to distinguish between the two segments of the experience variable and the separation of the wage and hours effects illustrated in table 2.8A and 2.8B. The purpose of segmenting the experience variable at ten years was to capture the difference between two distinct stages of the work career. The first stage, which we identify with the first ten years in the labor force, represents a period of considerable investment in a job, whereas throughout the second stage such investment behavior is less important. The difference between tables 2.8A and 2.8B represents that part of the return to schooling that can be attributed to higher hours worked and more stable jobs.[26]

For post-ten-year market experience, we interpret the declining coefficients for elementary and high school and the stable pattern for college as evidence that the skills of low-skill labor are more vulnerable to obsolescence than those of skilled labor. During the first ten years in the labor market, a large component of the gains from college attendance results from the more rapid acquisition of full-time jobs with longer working hours. This is clearly concentrated at the beginning of the work career, as the differences among schooling groups due to longer working hours quickly evaporate. This differential in achievement of full-time jobs by education level partly explains the rapid decline in the college coefficients over the first ten years of experience in table 2.8A. In table 2.8B, where this job characteristic is held constant, the college and elementary and secondary school coefficients both rise during the early part of a worker's life cycle. This divergence in wage experience profiles for all schooling classes in table 2.8B is consistent with complementarity between schooling and job investments. If such complementarity exists, more schooled workers will initially have proportionately lower observed earnings as they finance their human capital investment with foregone earnings. As they recoup the returns on their investment, the experience profiles of earnings by schooling levels will diverge and produce rising schooling coefficients.

Turning to the changes observed over this time period, the following trends emerge. First, there appears to be a shift upward in the wages of high school graduates relative to the wages of those with less education. In table 2.8A, the college coefficients peak in 1969 and drift slowly downward thereafter. This decline has received much recent attention, especially in the work of Richard Freeman (1975). He argues that two factors have resulted in a severe drop in income gains from having attended college since 1969. On the demand side, there was a relative decline in demand for skilled labor resulting from low secular growth rates for skilled intensive industries. On the supply side, this period witnessed the entry into the labor market of the relatively highly skilled postwar baby boom cohorts. While the trend for college graduates in table 2.8*A* appears consistent with Freeman's view, a number of other patterns cast doubt on his interpretation. First, the smaller coefficients after 1969 are almost completely concentrated at the beginning of the work career. There is almost no time-series trend for those with more than ten years of experience. If Freeman's argument based on a permanent structural change was valid, we would expect that some of these deleterious effects would have affected the more experienced workers. While the substitution between skilled labor arrayed by years of labor-market experience is not perfect, we would be surprised if a permanent alteration in the demand and supply structure for skilled versus unskilled labor would be completely absorbed by new entrants.

The second argument against Freeman's interpretation lies in the expected impact of business-cycle conditions on the demand for skilled labor. Coincident with the entry of the baby boom cohorts, the economy entered a recessionary period. While conventional economic analysis indicates that unskilled labor will suffer relative to skilled labor during recessions, it is important to distinguish between skilled labor already working and new skilled entrants into the labor market. During recessions, firms have an incentive to hoard their existing stock of skilled labor. While firms are in the process of hoarding skilled labor, it follows that they will not be simultaneously hiring new highly skilled entrants. With this in mind, note that when the probabilities of full-time employment are held constant, there is little secular pattern to the college coefficients. Thus, most of the recent problems for college graduates are due to increased difficulty in obtaining full-time jobs with long working hours. This is what one would expect from purely business-cycle phenomena.

The schooling coefficients for black males are listed in table 2.9. Because of the smaller size of the black samples, there is more instability in the estimated schooling parameters for blacks. Individual year exceptions to regularity make us less confident in formulating hypotheses concerning the impact of schooling on the future income prospects of blacks. Since many patterns in table 2.9 are similar to those reported for whites, it is unnecessary to detail them again. In particular, the black elementary and high school segment has the inverted "V" life-cycle shape observed among whites. Apparently, a significant component of the initial gains from college completion for blacks is also a consequence of longer working hours and more stable jobs. This part of the reward for college completion once again dissipates rapidly over the first ten years of market experience. Finally, for the post-ten-year segment of the experience variable, the black college coefficients are relatively stable, while those estimated for elementary and secondary schooling decline throughout.

Although these similarities exist between black and white males, there

TABLE 2.9. Schooling Coefficients for Black Males

	Elementary and High School					College				
	Years of Market Experience					Years of Market Experience				
Year	0	10	20	30	40	0	10	20	30	40
					A					
1967	.039	.067	.049	.031	.013	.071	.072	.069	.067	.064
1968	.012	.064	.045	.026	.006	.115	.093	.081	.069	.056
1969	.021	.066	.049	.032	.015	.136	.059	.063	.066	.070
1970	.016	.064	.047	.029	.012	.243	.060	.064	.068	.072
1971	.030	.085	.055	.025	−.004	.233	.029	.050	.071	.093
1972	.058	.098	.068	.037	.006	.179	.072	.059	.046	.032
1973	.082	.101	.067	.033	.000	.108	.076	.064	.053	.041
1974	.029	.090	.058	.026	−.005	.124	.085	.057	.029	.002
					B					
1967	.039	.048	.037	.026	.015	.010	.099	.092	.084	.077
1968	.016	.044	.032	.019	.007	.057	.111	.096	.081	.066
1969	.023	.042	.034	.027	.019	.045	.080	.080	.079	.079
1970	.017	.042	.033	.024	.015	.164	.080	.077	.075	.073
1971	.034	.060	.040	.021	.001	.146	.053	.068	.082	.096
1972	.051	.072	.053	.034	.014	.122	.085	.070	.054	.038
1973	.069	.083	.056	.028	.001	.074	.089	.074	.059	.044
1974	.034	.078	.051	.025	−.001	.074	.105	.072	.039	.005

NOTE: Section *A* reports the regression results when the probabilities of part-time work and zero earnings are not included. Section *B* shows the schooling coefficients with these probabilities included as regressors.

are some significant differences. For elementary and secondary schools, tables 2.9*A* and 2.9*B* show lower schooling coefficients for black males. The racial disparity increases over the first experience segment and remains at 3 to 5 percent (depending on the control for hours worked) for the remainder of the life cycle. If school systems are not an effective mechanism for increasing black incomes, it is clear that the problem lies at the elementary and secondary levels. On a more optimistic note, there may be some evidence based on the CPS files that this black-white difference may be decreasing. Unfortunately, the small time-span covered by our data, combined with the instability in black schooling coefficients, makes this a tentative finding at best. The marginal returns to postsecondary schooling are actually higher for blacks, particularly in the early years of market experience. For more experienced workers, the white college coefficients are as large as and may even exceed those of blacks. Two factors may explain these racial differences at the college level. First, since the end of the Second World War, increasing numbers of blacks have attended racially mixed Northern colleges (probably of higher quality). The second argument relates to the likely impact of government affirmative action pressures. If this pressure is strongest where blacks have traditionally been scarce (skilled jobs), firms may well pay a premium to attract recent black college graduates. Table 2.9 indicates that there was an upward shift in the returns to college for blacks that was most acute at the initial point of labor-market entry and highest at the turn of the decade. Also note that, in contrast to the trend for whites, the evidence is that black college coefficients rose (although not uniformly) over this period.

GEOGRAPHICAL RESIDENCE.   After controlling for education, job experience, and degree of government employment, we estimate large wage differentials among regions. Identifying the underlying cause of these wage differentials is a complex empirical problem that does not lie within the scope of this chapter; some of these differentials simply reflect cost-of-living differences between regions or compensating payments for the relative attractiveness or undesirability of locational attributes (e.g., climate, crime rate, population density). Given the magnitude of the differential we estimate, it is more likely that they proxy unobserved indices of skill. We have not undertaken the task of decomposing these regional wage differentials into their component parts. Our less ambitious goal is to measure how much of the change in black-white wages over time can be attributed to the different racial-regional structure of wages and population densities. As wages between regions change over time, whatever their underlying cause, we can measure the impact of such changes on the aggregate black-white wage ratio.

Regional differences in wages are small between the Northeast, North Central, and West relative to those that exist between the South and the rest of the country (see table 2.10). Wages for white males are 4.9 percent higher in the North Central than in the base Northeastern region, while

TABLE 2.10. Non-Southern Regional Variables

Region	White Males	Black Males
North Central	.0489	.0956
West 1967	.0351	.0653
West 1968	.0167[a]	.0667
West 1969	.0250[a]	.0637[a]
West 1970	.0125[a]	−.0023[a]
West 1971	.0080[a]	.0535[a]
West 1972	−.0059[a]	−.0334[a]
West 1973	−.0128[a]	.0461
West 1974	−.0080	−.0756
Northern SMSA	.1586	.1280
Northern Central City	−.0752	−.0605

[a] indicates coefficient not significantly different from zero.

North Central black males earn 9.6 percent more than blacks living in the Northeast. The wage differential is even smaller in the West, with whites receiving at most 2 to 4 percent higher wages (than Northeastern whites) and blacks 4 to 6 percent higher wages (than Northeastern blacks). The small wage differential enjoyed by whites and blacks in 1967 had essentially disappeared by 1974. This is consistent with the report of our earlier study that the wage premium in the West declined between 1960 and 1970. Finally, for Northern SMSA residents, we estimate a 16 percent wage differential for whites and a 13 percent differential for blacks. These differentials should be decreased by 7.5 percent and 6.1 percent, respectively, for whites and blacks who live in the central cities of these urban areas.[27]

In table 2.11, the Southern wage coefficients are evaluated at selected years of labor-market experience.[28] Because we found in preliminary testing that the coefficients did not differ significantly between the South Atlantic and West South Central regions, these two areas were combined. There

TABLE 2.11. Southern Regional-Experience Interaction

		A. Whites							
		Non-SMSA				SMSA[a]			
		Years of Market Experience				Years of Market Experience			
	Year	0	10	20	30	0	10	20	30
South Atlantic	1967	.034	−.013	−.060	−.107	.109	.115	.120	.125
and West	1970	.048	−.006	−.060	−.114	.128	.124	.120	.116
South Central	1972	.013	−.024	−.061	−.098	.133	.126	.120	.113
	1974	.071	.010	−.050	−.110	.136	.121	.106	.090
East South	1967	−.004	−.066	−.128	−.190	.071	.062	.052	.043
Central	1970	−.002	−.063	−.124	−.186	.079	.067	.056	.045
	1972	.046	−.028	−.101	−.175	.166	.122	.079	.036
	1974	.079	.017	−.046	−.108	.145	.128	.110	.092

		B. Blacks							
		Non-SMSA				SMSA[a]			
		Years of Market Experience				Years of Market Experience			
	Year	0	10	20	30	0	10	20	30
South Atlantic	1967	−.274	−.308	−.343	−.378	−.063	−.094	−.126	−.157
and West	1970	−.090	−.203	−.317	−.431	−.029	−.063	−.097	−.131
South Central	1972	−.018	−.129	−.240	−.351	−.013	−.034	−.055	−.070
	1974	−.047	−.159	−.271	−.382	.002	−.044	−.090	−.131
East South	1967	−.425	−.439	−.454	−.469	−.214	−.225	−.237	−.248
Central	1970	−.210	−.293	−.326	−.459	−.150	−.153	−.156	−.158
	1972	−.213	−.275	−.337	−.399	−.208	−.180	−.152	−.125
	1974	−.155	−.251	−.348	−.445	−.104	−.136	−.168	−.199

[a] For central-city residents in the SMSA, a constant differential of −.056 percent should be subtracted from these numbers.

were, however, important wage differences between urban and nonurban
residents in the South, and the table lists separately the wage reductions
(relative to the Northeast) for nonresidents and residents of Southern
SMSAs.

For young white male workers, wages in both Southern regions are comparable to those received in the rest of the United States. Presumably as a
consequence of the economic resurgence in the South, there has been a
secular rise in wages of young Southern whites since 1967; by the end of
the period, market opportunities for whites actually exceeded those available elsewhere. Because wages increase with market experience at a somewhat slower rate in the South, white males with thirty years of labor force
experience receive wages 10 to 18 percent below those of their Northern
counterparts. This rise in wages of young blacks suggests that strong vintage
effects exist in that region. Young black Southern males appear to be quite
different in terms of marketable skills from their predecessors.

In contrast to these relatively small white wage differential, we estimate
large wage difference for black males within the South and between the
South and the North. In addition to the general improvement for Southern
blacks, there has been a reduction in wage inequality within the South
among the new cohorts of black workers. In 1967, black wages were
approximately 15 percent lower in the East South Central region than in
the combined South Atlantic and West South Central regions. By 1974,
however, this differential for young workers had declined to about 8 percent. The interregional wage trends for blacks are even larger. Wage
differentials in 1967 were 20 to 30 percent lower than those for whites in
the nonurban South Atlantic and West South Central sections, and over 35
percent lower in the nonurban East South Central area. These wage differentials are considerably smaller in the urban areas of the South, with black-
white wage differentials of approximately 15 to 25 percent. A comparison
of wage experience profiles for blacks also illustrates important urban-rural
differences in the South. The jobs with little career growth possibilities for
blacks are located in the rural sections of the South. Estimated wage-
experience profiles are similar in the urban South to those in the rest of
the country, but for most years wages in the rural South increased much
less than the national average for workers with experience. The most dramatic change over this period is the decline of 20 to 30 percent in the wage
coefficient for young black Southern workers. For workers with thirty years
of market experience, there is no evidence of any secular change. New
black Southern workers differ significantly from their predecessors and
apparently will face wage and career prospects that differ significantly from
those previously experienced in the South.

Our estimates indicate that on net these locational variables predict a
3.2 percent rise in black-white wages—a gain dominated by changes within
the South. The combined Northern variables would have decreased black-

white wages by approximately 0.5 percent. The improvement for blacks within the South is due principally to changes in the South Atlantic and West South Central areas that produced a 4.5 percent rise in relative black wages; the East South Central region accounted for approximately 0.3 of a percent of the increased wage ratio. The negative effect of the experience interactions in the two Southern regions reflect the strong vintage effects in the South. Because younger black workers have gained the most over this period, cross-sectional experience wage profiles had become less steep in the South by 1974. Somewhat surprisingly, the urban South variables were relatively unimportant, reflecting the fact that the major black gains occurred in the nonurban South. The predictions are dominated by changing geographical location and especially convergence in racial wage differentials between 1967 and 1974. Converging black-white wage ratios within the South are about twice as important as the relocation of blacks across regions. The total impact of geographical relocation accounted for approximately one-third of the predicted wage increase, and is due in large part to the movement of blacks into SMSAs and into the South Atlantic region. The convergence in black-white Southern wages raised relative wages by 2.11 percent, with the South Atlantic and West South Central playing the major role.

GOVERNMENT AND AFFIRMATIVE ACTION.   The difficult empirical problem in assessing the impact of affirmative action involves obtaining direct tests of the probable impact of discrimination and the success of government efforts to combat it. Admittedly, the method we have selected is indirect. We have included variables measuring wage premiums in industries that, at least at first blush, seem most susceptible to government pressures. The most direct is, of course, employment by the government itself. We have divided government employment into employees of the federal government and employees of state and local governments. The second level measures employment in industries regulated by either the federal or state and local governments. The final set of variables indicates the fraction of an industry's sales to either the federal or state and local governments. An examination of the employment patterns by race and trends in wages and employment in these industries can be used to detect past discriminatory practices in hiring and to track recent changes in such behavior.

One controversial issue relates to the relative historical roles of the private and public sectors in discriminatory hiring. In particular, we are interested in regional differences between the North and the South (where discrimination is allegedly more intense) in public and private sector behavior. Employment by race in these industries is reported in table 2.12. For direct government employment, strong differences exist between the North and the South. In the North, the federal government is intensive in

TABLE 2.12. Relative Black-White Employment Intensity in Direct and Indirect Government Employment

Direct	Year		Indirect	Year	
	1967	1974		1967	1974
Northern federal employees	2.14	2.29	% of product sold to federal government in North		.903
				.827	
Southern federal employees	.748	1.01	% of product sold to federal government in South		.925
				.738	
Northern state and local employees	.892	1.26	% of product sold to state and local government in North	.835	.880
Southern state and local employees	.444	.475	% of product sold to state and local government in South	1.10	.936
			regulated by federal government in North	.714	.727
			regulated by federal government in South	.586	.696

hiring black workers. Relative to their population sizes, two blacks are hired as Northern federal employees for every white hired. In the South, however, approximately 0.8 of a black worker is employed for every white worker. While state and local governments in either region are less likely than the federal government to hire blacks, the racial difference between the North and South is similar to that observed for federal government employment.

Table 2.12 cannot, of course, be viewed as conclusive evidence of a history of discriminatory practices in Southern public sector employment; skill distributions of blacks and whites differ between regions, and the basic question involves hiring practices relative to skill requirements.

The racial wage differentials in these industries are large and typically favor blacks. While this is what one would expect from affirmative action, black-white wage ratios in these sectors have generally declined over this period. The wages of federal government employees have increased since 1967, but at a more rapid rate for whites. These wage differentials, combined with the employment patterns, can be used to predict the effect of government variables on the recent trend in black-white wage ratios. Our results indicate that these government variables would have predicted a *decrease* in the black-white wage ratio between 1967 and 1974 of three-quarters of a percent. The direct effect of employment changes—the increased relative representation of blacks in direct and indirect government sectors—was favorable toward blacks, but the magnitude of this change was quite small in raising black incomes (approximately 0.14 of a percent). This employment trend was more than offset by the increase in the wages of whites relative to blacks in these industries over the period. Thus, the rise in black-white wage ratios has occurred primarily in the more private sectors of the private economy and not in those industries most susceptible to affirmative action pressures.[29] Our test should not be interpreted as proof that affirmative action has had no effect. The hiring and wage practices of some individual firms and industries may have been radically altered by these programs. Our results do suggest, however, that the effect of government on the aggregate black-white wage ratio is quite small and that the popular notion that these recent changes are being driven by government pressure has little empirical support.

COHORT AND LIFE-CYCLE COMPARISONS: EVIDENCE FOR THE VINTAGE HYPOTHESIS. One feature common to all cross-sectional studies of black-white earnings differences is that younger blacks fare better in comparison to whites than do their older counterparts. This is consistent with extreme life-cycle or cohort views that have very different implications for the future course of black-white differentials. Early theories of labor-market discrimination tended toward a life-cycle explanation, holding that over-the-career black earnings increase less rapidly than whites'. These theories of "secondary" labor markets view labor markets as stratified; some are less upwardly mobile than others. The extreme life-cycle view offers no basis for predictions of future patterns of wage differentials. The cohort view, on the other hand, does provide a basis for projection if the future course of differences among cohorts conforms to the past. From the cohort viewpoint, each individual in a cross-section is a member of a distinct cohort at one point in his life-cycle path. More rapid black improvement in schooling quality or home environment over time could have led to increases in the relative initial human capital stock of successive generations of black workers. In the cohort view, the observed cross-sectional decline in relative black-white wages with experience simply reflects the lesser work experience of members of newer cohorts. A single cross-section is incapable of separating the life-cycle and cohort hypotheses. By comparing cross-sections at different points in time, the potential of distinguishing life-cycle and cohort effects is established. If vintage effects reflect secular change, either through rising relative quality of black labor or declining front-end discrimination, then younger, more recent cohorts of blacks would fare better in comparison to whites than did older cohorts.

Because we use eight successive cross-sections, our ability to distinguish cohort and life-cycle effects is enhanced in this study. Most previous studies

TABLE 2.13. Comparisons of Cross-sectional and Life-Cycle Black-White Wage Ratios

Year	Years of Experience				
		Schooling = 16 years			
1967	x	.834	.806	.779	.760
1968	$x + 1$	.885	.858	.829	.804
1969	$x + 2$	.846	.807	.774	.758
1970	$x + 3$	.908	.864	.818	.781
1971	$x + 4$	.892	.843	.798	.769
1972	$x + 5$	.984	.912	.842	.791
1973	$x + 6$	.879	.855	.824	.792
1974	$x + 7$	.880	.853	.810	.758
		Schooling = 12 years			
1967	x	.853	.817	.781	.755
1968	$x + 1$	.779	.764	.747	.734
1969	$x + 2$	.807	.772	.744	.731
1970	$x + 3$	.768	.752	.738	.731
1971	$x + 4$	.852	.809	.771	.746
1972	$x + 5$	.865	.829	.799	.783
1973	$x + 6$	.809	.799	.785	.769
1974	$x + 7$	.765	.768	.763	.747
		Schooling = 8 years			
1967	x	.892	.860	.830	.803
1968	$x + 1$	.863	.850	.837	.826
1969	$x + 2$	.914	.870	.833	.814
1970	$x + 3$	.859	.837	.817	.804
1971	$x + 4$	.913	.871	.834	.812
1972	$x + 5$	.876	.844	.819	.808
1973	$x + 6$	.798	.799	.799	.797
1974	$x + 7$	.794	.807	.813	.807

that have compared cross-sections, including our own, have used only two data sets. For any cohort in 1967, we can contrast actual life-cycle wage paths experienced through 1974 to those that we would have predicted from our cross-sectional data. Such comparisons are made in table 2.13. For individuals with one, five, ten, or fifteen years of market experience in 1967, we have tracked the predicted career profiles of wages of blacks relative to whites. Reading across a row in this table, the predicted life-cycle, black-white wage ratios from the individual cross-section for each schooling class are given. Reading down a column, we follow an individual cohort through its life-cycle experience. The cross-sectional patterns uniformly predict declining black-white wage ratios with years of market experience; this gave credence to the secondary labor-market view for blacks. But note that the within-cohort trends indicate that, if anything, black-white wage ratios have increased over the life cycle, especially for more schooled workers. Therefore, the weight of the evidence supports cohort improvement and not the life-cycle view. Younger blacks fare better not because they are young, but because they are not similar to whites, and the evidence here is that whatever advantage they enjoy will not be diminished as they age.

CONCLUSION

In this chapter, we have analyzed causes of the recent convergence in black-white earnings ratios. Between 1968 and 1975, black male wages rose at a more rapid rate than those of whites, continuing a process that began during the 1960s. Our research was based on eight Current Population Surveys that spanned this time interval. We found, in general, that the variables that accounted for the rise observed between 1960 and 1970 were also the principal causal factors in explaining the more recent improvement in the economic status of black males. Increased congruency in black-white income-producing characteristics, such as education and region of residence, played the dominant role in explaining the recent trend. Black educational levels have been converging relative to whites' throughout the twentieth century, and this process continued between 1968 and 1975.

The main migration trends were the greater urbanization of the black South, as well as the movement of blacks from low-wage to high-wage areas within the South and, to a lesser extent, from the South to the North. However, more important than migration per se was the narrowing of between-region racial wage differentials. Historically, the South was characterized by the lowest relative black wages. While this is still the case, black-white wage ratios have risen more rapidly in the South than elsewhere; since black males are more heavily represented in the Southern regions, they gain the most from wage increases in that area. Moreover, this improvement was concentrated among younger black Southern workers. This suggests that the career prospects of blacks in the "new" South are likely to be far different from the typical historical experiences of black Southerners.

Confirming a conclusion we reached in our research for the decade of the sixties, government pressure through affirmative action programs was a relatively minor contributor to rising relative wages of blacks.

We have also addressed the controversial question of the validity of the vintage and life-cycle views of the black labor market. The life-cycle view is the basis of the secondary labor-market hypothesis that claims that blacks have been relegated to dead-end jobs with little career wage-growth potential. The more optimistic vintage hypothesis is that newer cohorts of blacks relative to their white counterparts start their careers with higher initial stocks of marketable human capital than their black predecessors already in the labor market. The preponderance of evidence from our work rejects the secondary labor-market view and tends to favor the vintage hypothesis.

NOTES

1. See Smith and Welch (1977).

2. See Gwartney (1970) for an analysis of the 1940s using 1940 and 1950 Census Bureau data.

3. This is especially true when one looks at earnings rather than at income ratios and is more dramatic for full-time workers than all wage earners.

4. For some evidence that inequality among black earnings has increased compared to those of whites between 1960 and 1970, see Smith and Welch (in press).

5. More than 90 percent of all "nonwhites" in the United States are blacks.

6. Among full-time earners there is evidence of an increase for blacks in all four regions, although the South and North Central still have the largest increases.

7. If all students complete at least the second grade, and if there is no growth in total enrollment (Southern Negro school enrollment has grown at annual rates of less than 1 percent per decade in this century), then the ratio of enrollment of first to second graders is the time required to complete the first grade relative to the time required to complete the second.

8. This is partly due to the accelerating urbanization of the South, in general, as well as to the movement of black and white Southerners from rural to urban areas.

9. For two excellent reviews of the affirmative action literature that go well beyond our simple survey, see Butler-Heckman (1977) and Flanagan (1976).

10. Another class of studies has concentrated on studying the actual mechanics of enforcement by the two agencies. The mechanics include funding and staffing levels and length of time of litigation. This evidence leads to skepticism that these agencies have had much impact. See Wallace (1975).

11. See Freeman (1973).

12. The Butler-Heckman point should not be overstated. It is unlikely that recent changes in relative wages of blacks are due exclusively to censoring phenomena. As a crude check on this source of bias, we present income ratios for all workers and for nonrecipients of welfare and unemployment benefits. This table illustrates the significant expansion in the number of men receiving either welfare or unemployment payments during the last decade, although the increase appears as large among whites as among blacks.

Year	Income		Earnings		Proportions Receiving Welfare and Unemployment	
	All	Nonrecipients of welfare and unemployment	All	Nonrecipients of welfare and unemployment	Black	White
1967	.571	.567	.574	.575	.114	.097
1968	.611	.617	.614	.632	.134	.108
1969	.591	.597	.594	.610	.143	.121
1970	.595	.594	.596	.606	.168	.157
1971	.602	.604	.605	.616	.167	.164
1972	.620	.619	.622	.631	.161	.155
1973	.615	.615	.617	.626	.159	.136
1974	.626	.626	.623	.638	.199	.174

Yet, for all income recipients and for those not receiving welfare and unemployment, income ratios are not very different. We view this as circumstantial evidence that not all these recent gains flow from the expansion in the welfare system.

13. See Smith-Welch (1977).

14. Sample sizes range from 2281 to 2700 blacks and 24,449 to 26,888 for whites. The following restrictions were imposed for sample eligibility: positive earnings and weeks worked, computed weekly wages in excess of $10, civilians who were not self-employed and who were working without pay, and part-year workers who were not in school and who had not retired.

15. The table, produced by Hanoch (1965), is:

Schooling Level	0–7	8	9–11	12	13–15	16	17+
EAge	14	16	18	20	23	25	28

16. For older workers this is not a serious problem. Their current age typically exceeds the highest entry age in the distribution, so that there is no issue of truncation.

17. See Gould and Welch, 1977, for a detailed description of the technique used to compute these densities.

18. To illustrate, for the 1897 cohort of high school completers, we estimate that the entry age was 20.47 years for whites and 22.35 for blacks; for the 1970 cohort, we estimate an identical entry age of 18.50 for black and whites males.

19. "Part-year" meaning fewer than forty weeks per year; part-time is defined as working fewer than thirty-five hours per week.

20. Even at this level, we engaged in some experimentation of the functional form to be specified; for example, we tried alternative forms of the schooling experience and regional experience interactions.

21. The deleted variables were the experience and regional experience interaction in the West and North Central region.

22. We combined the South Atlantic and West South Central region, and the estimated probability of part-time, part-year and part-time, full-year work.

23. The following variables were constrained to have the same parameters in each year: North Central; North and South Central City; Northern SMSA; Southern and Northern state and local employment; industries regulated by state and local governments in the South; percentage of value added to federal government in South. For the following variables, we constrained adjacent years to have identical parameters: Southern and Northern federal government employment; Southeast and Northern industries regulated by federal government; Northern industries regulated by state and local governments; percentage of product sold to federal government in North; percentage sold to state and local governments in the North and in the South; and the probability of part-time work and full-time, past-year work.

24. See "Race Differences in Earnings: Survey and New Evidence," Rand P-2295-NSF, March 1978.

25. The three probabilities are the probability of (1) full-time, part-year work; (2) part-time work; (3) zero earnings.

26. Neither the coefficients listed in table 2.8A nor those in table 10B are the "true" returns to schooling. For an analysis of this problem, see Lindsay (1971).

27. Since these wage differentials for urban Northern residence did not vary over our sample, we constrained the coefficients to be the same for all years.

28. These wage coefficients are relative to the wage level of the Northeast at the relevant level of labor market experience.

29. This finding confirms results we reported for the period 1960–70; see Smith-Welch (1977).

REFERENCES

Ashenfelter, O., and Heckman, James J. 1977. "Measuring the Effect of Anti-discrimination Programs." In *Evaluating the Labor Market Effects of Social Programs.* Edited by Orley Aschenfelter and James Blum. Princeton: Princeton University Press.

Becker, G. 1971. *Economics of Discriminations.* 2d ed. Chicago: University of Chicago Press.

Beller, A. H. 1977. "The Effects of Title VII of the Civil Rights Act of 1964 on the Economic Position of Minorities." Ph.D. diss., Columbia University.

Burman, George. 1973. "The Economics of Discrimination: the Impact of Public Policy." Ph.D. diss., University of Chicago.

Butler, Richard, and Heckman, James. 1977. "The Impact of the Government in the Labor Market Status of Black Americans: A Critical Review of the Literature and Some New Evidence."

Flanagan, Robert J. 1976. "Actual versus Potential Impact of Government Antidiscrimination Programs." *Industrial Labor Relations Review* 29, no. 4: 486–507.

Freeman, Richard. 1973. "Changes in the Labor Market of Black Americans, 1948–1972." In *Brookings Papers,* vol. 1: 67–120. Washington, D.C.: Brookings Institution.

———. 1975. "The Declining Economic Value of Higher Education and the American Social System." Harvard Institute of Economic Research discussion paper no. 421. Cambridge, Mass.

Gould, William, and Welch, Finis. 1977. "Imputing Labor Market Experience."

Gwartney, James. 1970. "Changes in the Non-White/White Income Ratio— 1939–67. *American Economic Review* 60 (December): 872–83.

Hanoch, Giora. 1965. "Personal Earnings and Investments in Schooling." Ph.D. diss., University of Chicago.

Haworth, J.; Gwartney, J.; and Haworth, C. 1975. "Earnings, Productivity, and Changes in Employment Discrimination During the 1960s." *American Economic Review* 65 (March): 158–68.

Heckman, James, and Wolpin, Kenneth. 1976. "Does the Contract Compliance Program Work? An Analysis of Chicago Data." *Industrial and Labor Relations Review* 29 (July): 544–64.

Lindsay, Cotton, M. 1971. "Measuring Human Capital Returns." *Journal of Political Economy* (November/December): 1195–215.

Link, C. 1975. "Black Education, Earnings, and Interregional Migration: A Comment and Some New Evidence. *American Economic Review* 65 (March): 236–40.

Oi, Walter. 1962. "Labor as a Quasi-Fixed Factor." *Journal of Political Economy* 70 (October: 538–55.

Rosen, Sherwin. 1968. "Short-run Employment Variation of Class-1 Railroads in the United States, 1947–1963." *Econometrica* 36 (July/October): 511–29.

———. 1979. "Wage-Based Indices of Urban Quality of Life." In *Current Issues in Urban Economics.* Edited by Peter Mieszkowski and Mahlon Straszheim. Baltimore: Johns Hopkins University Press.

Smith, J. P., and Welch, F. 1977. "Black-White Male Wage Ratios: 1960–1970." *American Economic Review,* (June): 323–38.

———. In press. "Inequality: Race Differences in the Distribution of Earnings." *International Economic Review.*

Thurow, Lester. 1969. *Poverty and Discrimination.* Washington, D.C.: Brookings Institution.

Vroman, Wayne. 1974. "Changes in Black Workers' Relative Earnings: Evidence from the 1960s." In *Patterns of Racial Discrimination*. Edited by G. M. Furstenberg. Lexington, Mass.: Lexington Books.

Wallace, Phyllis A. 1975. "A Decade of Policy Development in Equal Opportunities in Employment and Housing." Massachusetts Institute of Technology paper no. 767–75.

Weiss, L., and Williamson, J. G. 1972. "Black Education, Earnings and Interregional Migration: Some New Evidence." *American Economic Review* 62 (June): 372–83.

————. 1975. "Black Education, Earnings and Interregional Migration: Even Newer Evidence." *American Economic Review* 65 (March): 241–44.

Welch, F. 1967. "Labor Market Discrimination: An Interpretation of Income Differences in the Rural South." *Journal of Political Economy* 75 (June): 225–40.

————. 1973. "Black-White Returns to Schooling." *American Economic Review* 63 (December): 893–907.

————. 1974. "Education and Racial Discrimination." In *Discrimination in Labor Markets*. Edited by O. Ashenfelter and A. Rees. Princeton: Princeton University Press.

3

WAGE-BASED INDEXES OF URBAN QUALITY OF LIFE

SHERWIN ROSEN

INTRODUCTION

This paper explores some possibilities for imputing an index of the "quality of life" among metropolitan areas from wage data. The observations from which such an index might be inferred are the nonmarketable attributes (amenities and disamenities) offered by different cities and the real wage rates that otherwise identical workers must be paid in order to live and work in them. The implicit prices of the attributes are the raw material for the quality of life index, as in the construction of quantity index. This quantity index computed on a city-by-city basis can be used to rank cities by quality of life. Aggregate computations provide an overall adjustment to GNP for changes in the value of urban disamenities and amenities over time. And the implicit price weights themselves often are useful for cost-benefit analysis, as in the evaluation of crime reduction and pollution control programs.

The conceptual basis for the proposed method of imputing urban quality of life is related to the theory of local public goods (Tiebout; Stigler). Think of the attributes of cities—including such things as air and water pollution, crime, climate, and crowding—as tied features of locational choice. From an individual's point of view, the attributes are fixed for each city but vary among cities (of course, there is considerable variation among different neighborhoods in a major metropolitan area, but ignore these for the moment). Then the observed combinations of attributes, wage rates, and costs of living must satisfy an equilibrium condition reminiscent

I am indebted to Robert Goldfarb, Peter Mieszkowski, and Mahlon Straszheim for their helpful comments on the first draft; to Jennifer Roback and David Salant for their excellent research assistance; and to the National Science Foundation for financial support.

of a "voting with your feet" criterion; each household's locational choice maximizes its welfare and no family can be made better off by moving to another city. The relevant equilibrium concept is a stable distribution of households among the cities. One can think of this as an allocation, or more descriptively as an assignment of households to cities. The prices corresponding to the observed attribute-wage cost-of-living nexus embedded in the assignment arises from a kind of implicit market mechanism to which standard economic theory can be applied.

For example, sufficiently universal preferences for attributes imply that a set of equalizing money wage and cost-of-living differences will be observed among cities. Those cities exhibiting negatively valued attributes such as high crime rates and extensive pollution must also offer higher wages and lower prices of housing services to induce workers to locate there. Conversely, cities embodying the more preferred attributes will offer lower wage rates and higher site values as in-migration increases the labor supply in those locations relative to the demand for it and also increases the demand for living space. The differences in wages and living costs between cities with different attributes are in fact the prices that signal the proper assignments by choking off demand for preferred locations and impelling people to live in less desirable places because it is cheaper to do so. As I have detailed elsewhere (Rosen), it is possible to analyze markets of this sort as a generalized location problem in the space of attributes rather than on the geographical map, on the working hypothesis that the units to which assignments are made can be decomposed into a finite set of measurable attributes. For any empirical application it is necessary that the number of attributes are of small enough dimension to be manageable. Some results on the feasibility of finding such a set from extant data follow and some preliminary estimates of the attribute gradients are presented.

1. THE LITERATURE

The methods employed here have been used often for many related issues. Price-attribute regression studies of physical goods can be used to compute quality indexes, and there are well-known applications to housing and other durable goods (King and Mieszkowski; Griliches). In a very similar vein to the work reported below, several investigators have attempted to infer the implicit value of pollution from its effects on property values (Rubinfeld), and there have been several direct tests of the local public goods model, which relates local taxes and public expenditure to site values (Oates). In the labor market, these methods have been applied to the market for risky jobs, to impute values of life for cost-benefit analysis (Thaler and Rosen; Smith; Viscusi); to the market for teachers, to impute market discrimination coefficients and tastes for discrimination (Antos and

Rosen); to compute quality adjustments for medical practitioners (Feldman); and to impute values of reserve stocks of unemployed workers (Hall).

In spite of its relevance and newsworthiness, literature specifically on value imputations of urban amenities and disamenities is not lengthy. Practically all studies employ regression methods, in which wage rates are related to attributes of cities and to other factors that influence wages, such as education and age.[1] The regression coefficients on the attributes have the dimensionality of prices (dollars per unit of each attribute) and might as well be labeled as such. These estimated prices serve as the value weights in the construction of the quantity index of urban amenities and disamenities on a per-household basis. The next section, where I summarize some previous results, discusses several conceptual issues underlying the construction of such indexes.

Virtually all existing studies have been based on aggregate cross section data (intercity averages). The main sources are the Census of Population and Bureau of Labor Statistics area wage surveys.

Studies Based on Census Data

Perhaps the best-known study is by Nordhaus and Tobin, who embedded it in a much broader study of the measurement of economic welfare. This work is notable for laying out many conceptual issues, but apropos of a pioneering effort, each separate imputation hardly exhausted all available data sources and methods. On balance, Nordhaus and Tobin impute net disamenities to urbanization based on cross-county regressions in five states from the 1960 census. Average income in the county is the dependent variable and measures of population, population density, and percentage urbanized are used as proxies for urban attributes. Average education, percentage nonwhite, and aspects of the age distribution in each county are used to control for other sources of wage variation. They found that urban disamenities subtracted about $35 billion from GNP in 1965, which illustrates the practical importance of the problem.

Meyer and Leone reworked these estimates using average observations across thirty-nine Standard Metropolitan Statistical Areas. Here the dependent variable is median family income in the SMSA deflated for intercity differences in cost of living. They also include a more extensive list of attribute indicators as regressors, including measures of climate, public goods, pollution, and public safety, as well as demographic indicators such as percentage nonwhite, median education, etc. They report some sensitivity of imputations to the empirical specification of city attributes. However, their preferred estimate still implies negative net values to urbanization, though only half as large as those found by Nordhaus and Tobin.

The most complete study using Census Bureau data is by Getz and Huang, who also used averages across thirty-nine SMSAs for 1970. Real median earnings were used as the dependent variable and the regressions were computed separately for one-digit occupational classifications. To measures of pollution, crime, and climate, Getz and Huang added measures of average commuting time and of consumption opportunities related to leisure activities. The latter is represented by the first principal component on such variables as number of restaurants, commercial sports, skating rinks, zoos, symphony orchestras, and so forth. As expected, opportunity amenities reduce the real wage and commuting time increases it. Instead of entering population size per se in these regressions, an interesting two-step procedure was employed. In the second step, several of the amenity measures are statistically related to population size. The constructed consumption opportunity variable was found to be nonlinearly related to population. From these estimates it is possible to compute the city size that minimizes real wages, a value that is associated with the "optimum" city size. Two local minima are found, one at a population of about 40,000 and the other at 7.5 million, suggesting a trade-off between commutation costs and consumption opportunities. However, as will be implicit in the next section, the concept of *the* optimal city size is fraught with difficulty when there are differences in preferences in the population.

Studies Based on Area Wage Surveys

The Bureau of Labor Statistics periodically publishes wage information for selected occupations in metropolitan areas. As distinct from census data, no personal, economic, or demographic information is available from these surveys. However, the BLS occupational classifications may be sufficiently narrow that examining intercity differences within occupations may adequately control for other factors affecting wage rates. A study by Izreali used BLS data and was one of the first to estimate a wage-amenities function. This study is notable for outlining the fundamental empirical procedures used by virtually all subsequent investigators. It includes a list of regressors similar to Meyer and Leone's, and with similar results, including sensitivity of the estimates to specification. A more recent study by Goldfarb and Yezer also has used this data and is differentiated from other work by its emphasis on some of the demand forces that help determine intercity wage differences. Although demand influences prove difficult to isolate with these data, Goldfarb and Yezer do find substantially different patterns of intercity wage variation between different occupations, particularly between white- and blue-collar jobs. Occupational differences have been found by all other investigators who have analyzed these data.

The most extensive work with area wage surveys has been done in a series of studies by Hoch, who adopts a two-stage methodology that is almost the reverse of Getz and Huang's. First, the effects of city size and region on nominal wage rates are established (Hoch [1977]), which follows a long line of research in labor economics (Fuchs). The second stage is devoted to examining the role of differences in cost of living and disamenity considerations in explaining these effects. Cost of living is found to account for anywhere from one-third to one-half of nominal wage differences. Moreover, cost of living may account for almost all of the North-South nominal wage differential universally found in wage studies. In addition, Hoch has examined the effects of climate and temperature in explaining the remaining differences and has obtained significant results in the expected direction, though climate alone accounts for only a small fraction of real wage differentials. He also presents fragmentary results on other disamenities such as pollution.

In distinction to these studies, I present below some preliminary results based on micro data from Census Current Population Surveys. A virtue of using micro data for studying wage variations is that it allows much better control for personal characteristics of workers that are known to affect earnings than is possible with aggregate data. Moreover, these personal characteristics may well be correlated with locational attributes, because workers with higher earning capacity may choose to spend some of their earnings by living in more amenable cities.

The next section presents a simple model of assignment of households to locations that motivates the nature of most empirical work in this field and helps point out its limitations. Two issues are particularly important. First, since individuals have different tastes, some very subtle index number problems arise that are akin to the problem of international cost-of-living comparisons. The result is that quantity indexes derived from regression weights are likely to be biased measures of the "quality of life," though the nature of the biases are predictable; this issue does not seem to be well known in this connection. Second, a rudimentary analysis of the role of production in sustaining wage differentials is presented. These issues are thoroughly complicated and have not yet been completely analyzed. A simple example illustrates their importance. Many of the papers cited above contain a working hypothesis that disamenities are, on balance, associated with urbanization, by way of increases in crime, crowding, and pollution. Yet the secular trend of increasing urbanization in the United States (at least until recently) is a salient fact of our economic history. If urbanization is truly associated with attributes that are negatively valued, this observation cannot be explained unless the productivity augmenting effects of urbanization are at least as great as the negatively valued by-products associated with them. This is another way of saying that prices are the result of both supply and demand. And while it is true that the factors underlying the supply of labor to alternative locations are crucial to the construction of quality-of-life indexes, wage differentials must be supported and sustained by demand factors as well. I also raise, but do not resolve, the related issue of the extent to which equilibrium assignments are signaled by location-specific prices (costs of living), by nominal wages, or by both.

2. A CONCEPTUAL FRAMEWORK

The principal problem in computing an index of city attributes lies in finding an appropriate set of value weights. In this work, implicit price weights are estimated by regressing real wages on indicators of amenities and dis-amenities after controlling for personal differences (such as education and race) that also affect wage rates. As noted above, the estimated regression coefficients on city attributes clearly have the dimensionality of prices. A question remains regarding the limitations imposed by such a procedure, and to answer it, a theory of price determination in such markets is required. This section sketches a simple model that illustrates a few of the essential features of the assignment problem and the price mechanism. The model is incomplete but is presented to illustrate the index number problem. Consequently, production decisions are treated in the simplest possible manner in order to focus on the supply decisions of workers. Location decisions of firms have yet to be completely analyzed.

Households are viewed as self-producers of a consumption good, and the amenity attributes of the location of production may or may not affect productivity. The productive capacity of each household is assumed to be exogenously determined. There are three types of goods: a consumption good, which the household produces, consumes, and perhaps sells in the product market; the land that it occupies in its chosen location (used as shorthand for housing services); and the amenity values jointly consumed with location. For simplicity, individuals are assumed to reside in the location at which production takes place. The assumptions of self production and fixed productive capacity fix the nominal wage in each location independently of who locates there and put the main burden of assignment on the prices of location-specific factors. That is, the prices of land signal the proper assignments by way of their effects on the cost of living in each locality, with nominal wages per se playing a secondary role. However, since it is the real wage—the money wage divided by the cost of living—that is instrumental in the assignment and not each component separately, this is a useful simplification at this stage. It remains an open and interesting problem to ascertain a precise decomposition of the separate roles of money wage rates and costs of living in determining market equilibrium location patterns; a determination must await a more complete specification, including the role of agglomeration economies, location decisions of firms, and the demand for labor.

Index locations by an n-vector s, where s_i represents measured attributes of location (city) i. Consider the geographical map as a grid with M possible locations, each of which has a fixed and immutable vector s associated with it. Assume that M is very large. The land available in each city is fixed and denoted by $Y_i = Y(s_i)$. There are N households (with N much larger than M) to be allocated over the M cities. The ownership of land is predetermined and household j is endowed with an ownership vector $y_j(s)$, some or all of whose elements may be zero. Of course, $\sum\limits_{j}^{N} y_j(s) = Y(s)$.

Each household has a quasi-concave utility function for consumption goods, living space, and amenities: $u = U(x,y,s)$, where x is the consumption good, y is the amount of space occupied (a proxy for housing services), and s is amenities tied to locational choice. Let $r(s)$ and $w(s)$ denote rental price of land and productive capacity (in terms of ability to produce x) of the household at location s. Typically, r depends on s because amenities affect relative demands for land in various locations. If s only affects utility and not productivity, then $w'(s) = 0$ and the household's goods production is the same in all locations. But productivity effects of attributes may render $w'(s)$ nonzero. For example, good climate may affect productivity directly by making workers healthier, but it may also reduce measured market productivity if it induces workers to supply less time to market activities. For another example, pollution is productive from the private point of view, since controlling polluting by-products is expensive; on the other hand, pollution reduces the healthiness of the labor force and therewith productivity.

Choosing the price of x as numeraire, the budget constraint is

$$x + r(s)y(s) = w(s) + \sum_{j} r_j(s)y_j(s) = w(s) + z. \tag{1}$$

Market income from labor and nonlabor sources is allocated between consumption goods and land. Evidently, total income includes psychic income from the consumption of amenities in addition to market income.

A bid-rent gradient approach to maximizing U subject to the budget clearly reveals the structure of the solution and the limits of imputations from market data. For this it is necessary to study the indirect utility function conditional on s, since it defines the whole family of bid-rent functions. The gradients of such functions are readily interpreted as marginal willingness to pay (compensating variations) for amenities and can be related to observed data.

Choose an arbitrary value of s and maximize U with respect to x and y, subject to the budget (1) in that location. The familiar marginal conditions for this problem are

$$U_x = U_y/r = \lambda \tag{2}$$

where λ is the marginal utility of money at location s. Equation (2) requires that land and goods be consumed at each location in such proportions that their marginal rate of substitution equals their relative price. Solve (1) and (2) jointly to obtain demand functions for goods and land conditional on location s:

$$x = g(r, w+z, s) \tag{3}$$

$$y = f(r, w+z, s). \tag{4}$$

Finally, substitute (3) and (4) into $U(\cdot)$ to obtain the indirect utility function

$$u = U(g(r, w+z, s), f(r, w+z, s), s) = V(r, w, z, s). \tag{5}$$

Equation (5) implicitly defines bid-rent for land and labor as functions of s and u. Furthermore, the optimal location is found by maximizing (5) with respect to s subject to the *market* restrictions $r \geq r(s)$ and $w \leq w(s)$.[2]

Before examining that solution, it is useful to investigate some properties of (5). The total differential is

$$\begin{aligned} du &= (U_x g_r + U_y f_r)dr + (U_x g_w + U_y f_w)dw + (U_x g_s + U_y f_s \\ &\quad + U_s)ds \\ &= \lambda[(g_r + rf_r)dr + (g_w + rf_w)dw + (g_s + rf_s + U_s/U_x)ds] \\ &= \lambda[-ydr + dw + (U_s/U_x)ds] \end{aligned} \tag{6}$$

where the second equality follows from (2) and the third equality from (1), (3), and (4). Imposing the market restriction $w = w(s)$, elementary manipulations of (6) yield

$$du/\lambda = (w + z)\left\{(-ry/w + z)\frac{dr}{r} + \left[w/w + z)\,(w's/w)\right.\right.$$

$$\left.\left. + (x/w + z)\left(\frac{sU_s}{xU_x}\right)\right]\frac{ds}{s}\right\}. \tag{7}$$

Define $\theta = ry/w+z$ as the expenditure share for land, κ as the proportion of total market income accounted for by earnings, $\epsilon = dln\ w/dln\ s$ as the marginal productivity effect of amenities on earnings in elasticity terms, and $\eta = sU_s/xU_x$ as the relative valuation of amenities in terms of consumption goods. Then (7) becomes

$$du/(w + z)\lambda = -\theta dln\ r + (\kappa\epsilon + (1 - \theta)\ \eta)dln\ s. \tag{8}$$

Adding $\theta dln\ w - \theta\epsilon\ (=0)$ to the right-hand side of (8) yields an equivalent expression in terms of the real wage (w/r):

$$du/(w+z)\lambda = \theta dln\ w/r + [(\kappa-\theta)\epsilon + (l-\theta)\eta]dln\ s. \tag{9}$$

Bid-rent functions show willingness to pay for amenities at constant values of u. Setting $du = 0$, (8) gives the bid-rent gradient for land:

$$\frac{dln\ r}{dln\ s} = (\kappa\epsilon + (l-\theta)\eta)/\theta. \tag{10}$$

Equivalently, (9) gives the acceptance-wage gradient for labor:

$$\frac{dln\ w/r}{dln\ s} = -[(\kappa-\theta)\epsilon + (l-\theta)\eta]/\theta. \tag{11}$$

In both cases the gradient functions are neatly decomposed into weighted sums of a real productivity effect, ϵ, and a pure taste effect, η. For example, if here is no productivity effect ($\epsilon=0$) and s^k measures a positive amenity ($\eta > 0$), the bid-land-rent function must be positively inclined and the acceptance real wage function must be negatively inclined. If there is no taste effect ($\eta=0$), but a positive productivity effect ($\epsilon > 0$), then the bid-land-rent function is positively inclined and the acceptance wage function is negatively inclined so long as earnings account for a sufficiently large share of total income. Of course, all kinds of intermediate cases are possible; for example, pollution may increase private productivity on balance even though there is distaste associated with it. Then the clean air gradients may be either positive or negative, depending on which effect dominates.

The optimal choice of location may be analyzed with either the bid-rent function or the acceptance-wage function. The latter approach is taken here, since the observed market relationship between real wages and amenities is estimated below.[3] Figure 3.1 depicts the solution graphically. The curves labeled $\xi(s\ ;u)$ are the acceptance-wage functions for a household, the derivatives of which are given by (11). These give the locus of amenities and real wages that leave the household equally well off. Equivalently, they show the amounts of real earnings the household is willing to accept for amenities at a given level of utility when it plans to purchase the optimal amount of space and consumption goods in each city. Since greater real earnings unambiguously increases utility, the "direction of indifference" is positive and utility must be increasing along any ray through the origin ($u_2 > u_1 > u_0$). As drawn, I have assumed that s offers positive amenity values that outweigh negative direct productivity effects, if any, so that

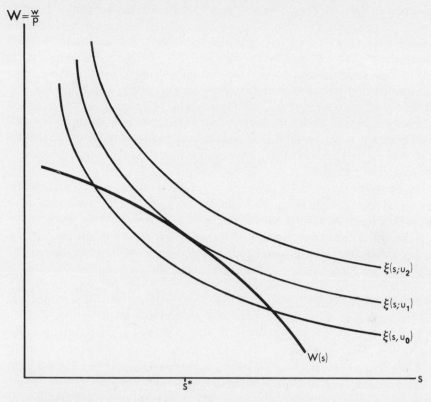

$W = \frac{w}{P}$

$\xi(s; u_2)$

$\xi(s; u_1)$

$\xi(s, u_0)$

$W(s)$

s^*

s

FIGURE 3.1

equation (11) is negative and the household willingly accepts a smaller real wage for larger amenities. Of course, it would prefer to have very large values of s at very high wages, but such opportunities are not available. It can receive no more than the amounts indicated by the curve labeled $W(s)$, which gives the market determined opportunities available to it. $W(s)$ is the function estimated in the empirical work. All points above $W(s)$ are not feasible. Hence the maximum utility level is achieved by choosing a value of s at which the offer-wage function is tangent to the market opportunities function. At that point the incremental amount the family is willing to pay for additional amenities in terms of wage reductions equals the incremental amount it has to pay to get them.

The optimal choice s^* shown in figure 3.1 is implemented by finding a particular city offering those values. Obviously, families with steeper acceptance-wage schedules choose to live in a city with greater amenities because they are willing to pay more for amenities and in fact do so by accepting lower real wages. The converse applies to families with flatter reservation price schedules. It is clear that these kinds of variation in optimum choices are caused by whatever factors shift the subjective reservation price schedule and can arise because of differences in taste among families (represented by different utility functions), differences in personal productivity (different production functions), or because of income effects due to differences in wealth (represented above by z). For example, if all households had the same underlying utility function, one would observe stratification of people according to wealth. However, once taste differences are admitted, then the precise nature of the assignment in the overall market depends on the pattern of covariances between tastes for amenities and wealth, and statements about stratification become more difficult, if not impossible to make.

To complete the model it is necessary to establish an overall equilibrium among all locations. In equilibrium, prices are such that all agents act as in figure 3.1 and no one has any incentive to move. That is, there is an equilibrium distribution of people assigned to cities. As mentioned above, in this model the main burden of market equilibrium adjustments must be borne by the markets for land. The equilibrium is established by finding the pattern of rentals that equates the demand and supply for space in each location. Without going into the details of existence of equilibrium, it is nonetheless clear that if $W(s)$ is the equilibrium gradient function in figure 3.1, then the typical agent located at s^* in figure 3.1 must behave in the manner depicted there.[4]

Some simple properties of equilibrium are easy to establish in particular cases. Suppose that all people are unanimous in their assessments of city attributes in the sense that the slopes of their acceptance wage functions for each component of s have the same sign, though the particular amounts they are willing to pay may differ among them. Then the sign of $W'(s)$ observed in the market must be the same as the sign of individual acceptance wage functions. The level of the market-clearing function $W(s)$ depends on the total amount of space available in the preferred locations. Also, if the most amenable city is large enough and the amenities are sufficiently highly valued by everyone, then all families might be found in one location and the other cities are not viable. However, if the amount of land available in the most preferred location is smaller than that, the real wage there must be bid down so that individuals whose tastes are less intense for the things that location has to offer rationally choose to live in a less desirable city with larger real wages. Therefore the cities that are not viable must be those offering the least desirable values of s.

Now suppose that people are not unanimous in the sense defined above— some people may prefer a colder climate because they like the change of seasons, whereas others prefer warmer weather all year around—then $\xi(s \; ; u)$ may be negatively inclined for some and positively inclined for others. Hence, in equilibrium, W' may be either positive or negative, depending on the intensity of each group's preferences, the relative numbers of people in each group, and the relative amount of space available in each location. For example, W' may be zero, in which case nothing can be observed about preferences and the notion of willingness to pay that underlies the construction of an index number from observing $W(s)$ alone.

The literature summarized above and the empirical work reported below presents estimates of $W(s)$ across several cities in the United States. The derivatives of this function have the interpretation of prices and serve as the prices used to construct the quality-of-life index. The model shows how they measure value at the margin, just like all prices. Yet the second example above suggests some limitations of the method that should not pass unnoticed. In fact, the difficulty is even more general than that example suggests and exists even when the direction of preferences is unanimous.

A simple example in which there are two cities and two types of household is shown in figure 3.2. Label families with larger acceptance wage gradients A, and those with smaller gradients B. City 1 offers s_1 and city 2 offers s_2. If both cities coexist, there are four possible cases to consider. Panel a depicts a case where both groups have exactly the same tastes. In this case the observed real wage difference $W_2 - W_1$ is an equalizing difference for all agents and is an ideal index of their true valuation of the incremental amenities offered in city 2. However, panel b shows a case of differential preferences and a possible equilibrium in which only people of type A live in city 2, and only those of type B live in city 1. Here the observed wage difference is not ideal at all, since it overestimates valuations for the Bs (otherwise some would have chosen to live in city 2), while it undervalues the preferences of the As (otherwise some would be found in city 1). Panel c shows a case where the Bs live in both places but the As are concentrated in city 2. Here the observed price difference is a good index for members of group B, but is an underestimate for members of group A. Essentially the opposite is true in panel d.

We know that index numbers automatically imply corresponding utility functions that may or may not be true—the index-number problem. The same must be true of quality-of-life or similar index numbers obtained from price-attribute information. Indeed, the method effectively imputes an acceptance-wage function for the "representative person" in the market that is exactly equivalent to the functional form of the estimated wage-attributes surface. Figure 3.2 shows that this is correct only when all people have similar tastes. Otherwise the index applies only to those at the margin of indifference, as an panels c and d, and is automatically biased, though in predictable ways, for the rest of the population. Standard index-number theory assumes that marginal subjective valuations of goods are equal to observed prices and therefore are equated across all agents in the market, whether or not people have similar preferences. But it is the tie-in feature of the consumption of amenities and location that breaks that equality for index numbers based on the above constructs: figure 3.1 shows that the

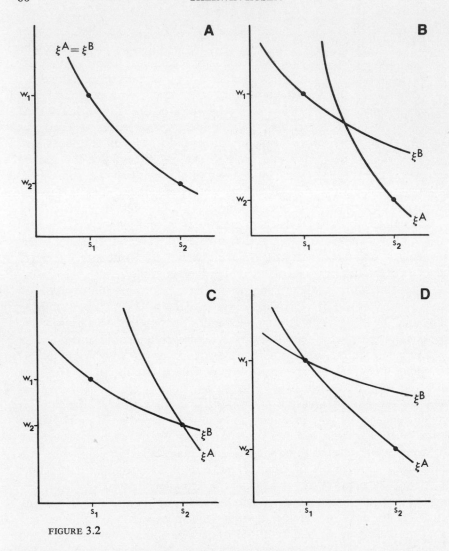

FIGURE 3.2

marginal prices obtained by evaluating the observed gradient at any point in the s-space is correct only for people who chose to live there; figure 3.2 shows that many people are off that particular margin, since the observed price difference is not equalizing for them. Therein lies the difference between the standard index number problem and a hedonic index-number problem, and this limitation must be borne in mind in evaluating such indexes.

One final qualification is necessary before turning to the results. I have discussed the theory in terms of equilibrium constructs. But relationships between real wages and amenities always can be observed whether or not there is overall market equilibrium. In this sense the statistical estimates merely attempt to describe systematically the information that households must have to make rational decisions. Observed mobility among cities need not reflect disequilibrium phenomena entirely since some individuals, particularly the young, are endowed with locations that may not be optimal for them. Furthermore, changing technologies and tastes may also impel systematic movements among cities and corresponding movements in the wage-amenities function. Yet it seems rash to assume away any disequilibrium problems; the construction above suggests a way of coping with them empirically. Consider the real wage-amenities regression across cities as the average opportunities available to people. If a particular city exhibits a deviation below the regression line that persists for some time, then there is either a specification error, which some omitted, unobserved amenity may account for, or the city offers a "worse deal" than some others with similar amenities, and net out-migration should be observed. Conversely, if a city exhibits a positive deviation that persists for some time, it should attract people and grow in size if there is a disequilibrium in the market and no omitted disamenity that might otherwise cause it to persist. Finally, if these deviations arise from genuine disequilibrium phenomena, the forces of attraction or repulsion act as a self-correcting servomechanism that drives the system toward equilibrium.

3. DATA AND ESTIMATES

Sources and Methods

This section presents preliminary estimates of the determinants of intercity wage differentials using microdata on individuals. The data are from the *Current Population Survey* (*CPS*), which is the only systematic source of individual economic and demographic information that also gives geographical location of respondents at the SMSA detail. Relaxation of data disclosure rules only recently has allowed the Bureau of the Census to make SMSA information available for public use. Although selected SMSA identification of CPS respondents is available for the annual surveys from 1967 to 1975, the estimates below are based on 1970 data only and must be viewed as tentative and preliminary—they are meant mainly to illustrate some of the issues raised above.

The theory suggested that estimation of value weights for quality-of-life imputations can be obtained by fitting a statistical relationship between market prices and objective indexes of amenities and disamenities offered by alternative cities, the estimation of $W(s)$ conditioned on personal earning capacity. I have used the real wage—the money wage deflated by a cost-of-living index in the city of residence at the time of the *CPS* survey—for this purpose. The cost-of-living deflator is meant to capture some of the location-specific factors discussed in section 2 above, though the extent to which amenities are reflected in wages or are capitalized in the values of location-specific factors that influence living costs cannot be examined by using the ratio. Any resolution of this decomposition requires introducing locational decisions of firms and some aspects of intercity trade. In such a theory, goods that are produced and traded among cities and nontraded goods, such as services that are consumed only in the locale of their production, must be distinguished. The precise decomposition of the effects of attributes on location-specific prices, such as those of land, and on wage rates is related to questions of factor price equalization in international trade theory. It is obvious that there is an important interaction between equalizing differences in wage rates and in cost of living; any equalizing differences in wage rates must feed back into the cost-of-living index because they also alter the price of an important factor in the production of nontraded goods, which in turn affects living costs. Examining the ratio of wages to prices finesses this important problem without resolving it.

Attempting to explain wage variation brings into play a set of influences other than location that determines a person's productivity and earning capacity and that accounts for interpersonal variation in wage rates. It is precisely at this point that microdata are superior to data used in previous studies. The factors determining personal earning capacity have been well studied, and the *CPS* data are reasonably rich in statistical indicators of them.

The model to be estimated is of the form

$$(W/P)_{ij} = F(E_{ij}, S_j, e_{ij}), \tag{12}$$

where subscript i refers to individuals and j to cities. W_{ij} is the wage of person i in city j; P_{ij} is an index of the cost of living in city j for families with characteristics similar to those of the person in question; E_{ij} is a vector of personal productivity variables such as education and work experience that have demonstrable effects on earning power; S_j is the vector of city attributes believed to be relevant for location choice and observed equalizing wage differences; and e_{ij} is a usual disturbance term. Thus, the empirical specification is the wage equation often studied by labor economists augmented by costs of living and characteristics of the cities in which people live.

The 1970 *CPS* identified nineteen major SMSAs, and cost-of-living data are available for all of them.[5] The cities are listed in table 3.2 (note that they are large cities).[6] In addition, the sample was restricted to males who were out of school and who reported earnings in 1969. There were 8,968 such persons. The intercity cost-of-living information was constructed from published data on urban family budgets put together by the BLS (in *Bulletins*). Three separate budgets based on low, medium, and high total expenditure are distinguished in these data. Since it is known that expenditure patterns vary with family circumstances, one of the three cost-of-living indexes can be assigned to each person in the sample because *CPS* reports total family income and family size. This is another virtue of these data compared with macro observations. My reading of BLS adjustments for family size suggested smaller official imputations of economies of scale for family size than seemed reasonable. A somewhat greater allowance for scale economies than that of the official method has been employed.

Table 3.1 shows the results of wage regressions typically performed on this kind of data. The dependent variable in column 1 is the logarithm of total earnings from all sources (wages and salaries plus self-employment income) in the year prior to the survey; city effects are not included. Since it is known that a major determinant of annual earnings is the amount of time worked during the year, the log of weeks worked in that year has been entered as a regressor. Dummies for full-time employment and for whether or not the person usually works fewer than thirty-five hours per week have been entered for this reason, and also to take account of the possibility that jobs requiring full-time employment pay different hourly wages than part-time jobs. The only other slightly unusual variables in the table are two dummies for whether the person experienced no stretch of unemployment during the year or one stretch of unemployment (normalized on more than one stretch), since there is some speculation in the literature that unemployment may proxy an unobserved person-specific factor that affects wages. Whether or not that is true, these two variables were statistically insignificant in all trials. This list of personal variables was included in all regressions.

The other variables have the same order effects as are usually found, even though the sample is restricted to people in large cities. Whites, heads of families, married men, veterans, and full-time workers earn more than their opposites. Self-employed workers earn less than private wage and salary workers and government workers after controlling for hours worked, major industry, and occupation. The effects of work experience show a familiar concave pattern and the effects of schooling are much the same as in other data. The latter is true in spite of entering major industry and occupation of primary employment in the regression, and there is a presumption that a major affect of schooling on earnings is to increase occupational and industrial mobility. Of course, some mobility remains within these broad aggregates. Nonetheless, controlling for them is expected to reduce the magnitude of the schooling coefficient. However, since unbiased estimates of rates of return to schooling and experience are of no particular interest in this study, it seems desirable to distinguish among major occupations and industries for two reasons. First, the unionization status of individuals is not known for this sample but is known to have important effects on earnings. Second, there are a great many nonpecuniary factors

TABLE 3.1. Estimated Personal Characteristic Effects: Least Squares Estimates

Dichotomous Variables	Dependent Variable		
	Log W	Log W/P	Log W/P
White	.194*	.186*	.150*
Family head	.170*	.168*	.160*
Married	.089*	.098*	.085*
Veteran	.056*	.061*	.050*
Full-time	.600*	.594*	.597*
0–35 hours/wk.	−.137*	−.147*	−.142*
Pvt. W/S	.164*	.159*	.160*
Govmnt.	.119*	.113*	.125*
Unemp. spell 0	.041	.050	.050
Unemp. spell 1	−.072	−.069	−.068
Sales occ.	−.202*	−.203*	−.198*
Crafts	−.160*	−.159*	−.157*
Operatives	−.268*	−.264*	−.263*
Laborer	−.274*	−.271*	−.270*
Service occs.	−.308*	−.307*	−.302*
Durable goods	−.076*	−.073*	−.086*
Nondurables	−.106*	−.123*	−.105*
Transport	−.077*	−.093*	−.074*
Trade	−.170*	−.182*	−.165*
Other service	−.193*	−.210*	−.186*
Pub. admin.	−.049	−.067	−.039
Continuous Variables			
Schooling	.049*	.048*	.048*
Experience	.015*	.014*	.015*
(Exp.)^2	−.0002*	−.0002*	−.0002*
Log weeks worked	.840*	.837*	.835*
R^2	.325	.323	.337
City attributes in regression	No	No	Yes

NOTES: * denotes that t-statistic exceeds 2. It is four or five times that magnitude for most personal effects variables, as might be expected with such large samples.

In the first two regressions, the list of regressors is exhaustive, apart from the usual constant term. The third regression contains a full specification of city attribute indicators as well.

Regressions where log P is entered as an independent variable are much the same as those shown here.

tied to industries and occupations that are common across cities and that are presumed to affect wage rates. While the use of dummies on one-digit occupational and industry classes admittedly is a crude proxy for such factors, I feel that some control of this sort is better than none at all.[7]

Column 2 of the table shows the regression coefficients when $\log(W/P)_{ij}$ is used as the dependent variable instead of $\log W_{ij}$. It is remarkable that the estimates are almost identical with those found in column 1. That is, although omission of living costs in wage regressions seemingly amounts

TABLE 3.2. Estimated City Effects: Least Squares Estimates

City	Dependent Variable	
	Log W	Log W/P
Los Angeles	.018	.104*
Chicago	.049*	.139*
Philadelphia	—.067*	.041*
Detroit	.106*	.236*
San Francisco	—.011	.035
Boston	—.108*	—.100
Pittsburgh	—.072*	.089*
St. Louis	—.061	.071*
Washington, D.C.	.010	.102*
Cleveland	.060	.157*
Baltimore	—.108*	.024
Newark	—.108	—.016
Minneapolis	—.035	.076*
Buffalo	—.052	.015
Houston	—.003	.213*
Milwaukee	.046	.109*
Paterson-Clifton-Passaic	—.024	—.031
Dallas	—.027	.166*
New York	. . .	. . .
F-Statistic	4.1	7.0

NOTE: * indicates t-statistic exceeds 2; however, these are sensitive to the normalization. The appropriate test is the significance of these variables as a group, for which the F-statistic shown is relevant. Both regressions include all variables listed in table 3.1; the estimated personal effects are similar to those shown in the table.

to a specification error, little bias on the effects of the usual variables of interest results from ignoring it. This strong conclusion must be qualified by the fact that my sample contains only persons living in large cities. The results may not hold up for the population at large, since differences in cost of living undoubtedly are smaller in this sample than among all cities and nonurban places in the United States—unfortunately, data are not available to test the broader hypothesis. Finally, column 3 shows the comparable results when all city attribute indicators are included in the regression. While the above theory suggests that high-earning individuals might be attracted to the more amenable cities, spending some of their high earning capacity on amenities and thus exhibiting smaller pecuniary wage rates, these results show that there is no substantial bias of this type either. However, this conclusion, too, must be qualified for the sample selection of large cities.

As preparation for estimating the implicit prices of city attributes, table 3.2 shows estimates of the entire population of city effects, obtained by including dummy variables for each city as well as all the personal variables of table 3.1. These coefficients estimate mean percentage differences from the normalized city (New York) given personal differences, and in a very general sense constitute the data to be explained by intercity differences in attributes. Thus, if there were no significant city effects, there would be nothing to impute to amenities in these data. When the log of earnings unadjusted for living costs is used as a dependent variable, the estimated city effects are weaker than when real earnings are used, though in both specifications city effects as a whole are statistically significant.[8] I conclude that both nominal wages and the cost of living are factors in a worker's choice of city.

I distinguish five major groups of city attributes: pollution, climate, crime, crowding, and market conditions. Unfortunately, statistical indicators of these attributes are SMSA averages and do not pertain to the precise location within the SMSA in which individuals live, a problem common to all other studies. This would be less of a problem if the cost-of-living index made the proper adjustments for intracity differences in living costs; however, CPS does indicate whether each person lives in the central city or in the suburbs. Also, the indicators that are available may not be bad approximations of the kind of information that people have in making their choices.

Many measures proxying each of the major groupings are available. For pollution there are general measures of suspended particulates and details on nitrates and oxides, inversions, and so on. There are also good engineering measures of water pollution and noise. For climate a plethora of indexes is available, including temperature during different seasons, sunshine, and precipitation. For both climate and pollution, measures of variance during the year also are available. Crime statistics come from FBI reports and detail types and seriousness of criminal activity (I simply note the well-known suburban bias in these data without further comment). Population density and measures of traffic and car registrations are obvious candidates for the effects of crowding. Finally, market conditions are proxied by general unemployment experience in the city, the concentration of industry there (e.g., the large role of automobile production in Detroit or of aircraft manufacture in Seattle), and the general growth of the city. It would be easy to extend this list to incorporate such things as consumption opportunities and commutation costs. As will be clear in the discussion, several of these aspects may be proxied in part by such variables as density and population size.[9]

An examination of the many available city attribute indicators in published sources reveals an important and possibly limiting empirical difficulty in implementing the methods of section 2; there are far too many variables to be used in any statistical analysis. For example, it is easy to think of twenty or more measures of various aspects of climate, and there is no convenient index of climate (as there is for noise). If there were sufficient statistical independence among indicators, the regression weights themselves would form a basis for constructing a proper index of climate. The same would hold true of pollution and the other attributes.[10] However, preliminary experimentation reveals too much interdependence to make this feasible. Substantial collinearity problems arise when more than six or seven indicators of various types are included in the regression. Hence, there is a statistical issue of "data reduction."

An extreme solution to the data reduction problem is to include only a few measures with which many of the omitted factors are correlated. Then, of course, the regression coefficients cannot be interpreted as the marginal effects of the included variables alone; rather, they represent an amalgam of all factors with which the included variables are correlated. An example is Nordhaus and Tobin's estimate previously discussed, wherein only measures of population size, density, and urbanization are included as regressors, all of which proxy crime, pollution, crowding, and so on. Although the separate effect of each underlying factor is not identified, one may not do too badly in the construction of an overall index number if the correlation patterns of included and excluded indicators are sufficiently stable. However, one would hope to do better, because such stability is not guaranteed and because implicit valuations of each underlying factor have independent interest.

Another common approach is "principal components." I pursued on about fifty of Liu's variables in the hope that the component weights could be interpreted. Principal components in this context is an ad hoc method, since the weights are obtained from a purely mechanical algorithm unrelated to relative valuations. Indeed, it is not clear that one can do a proper data reduction on this basis, since the importance of the components for wages and prices need not be in the same order as they are in accounting for overall variance, e.g., a trivial component may have a large effect on prices. In any case, my attempts along these lines were discouraging. The components did not decompose along the lines of the major groupings. Moreover, no meaningful reduction of dimension was achieved since a great many components were required to account for as little as 75 percent of the variance. Finally, indicators germane to selected groupings, such as all measures relating to climate, were put through mini-principal component analyses, again with meaningless results.

The final compromise was some limited experimentation with alternative combinations of variables. A summary of results showing estimated signs of effects and an indication of the magnitude of the associated t-statistic (the latter surely not meant as a rigorous statistical test given the procedure) is given in table 3.3. Each column of the table represents a single regression in which the presence of a $+$ or $-$ indicates that the variable was entered in the equation. Reading across rows gives a rough and ready indication of robustness to alternative specifications. The signs of the effects for pollution, climate, market conditions, and to a lesser extent,

TABLE 3.3. Summary of Regression Results. Each column gives sign of regression coefficient for the corresponding variable. Complete vector of personal characteristics in each regression.

Independent Variables	Regression Number																															
	1	2	3	4	5	6	7	8	9	10	11	12	13	14	15	16	17	18	19	20	21	22	23	24	25	26	27	28	29	30	31	32
Pollution																																
Particulates	+*	+*	+*	+*	+*	+	+*	+*	+*	+*	+*	+*	+*	+*	+*	+*	+*	+*	+*	+	+	+*	+*	+*	+*	+*	+*	+*	+*	+*	+*	+*
Sulfur dioxide			−*	−	+	+	+*	+	+*	+	+*	+	+	+*	+	+*	+*	−*	−	+	+	+*	+*	+*	+*	+*	+*	+*	+*	−*	+*	+*
Inversion days							+*	+*	+*																						−*	
Water pollution							−	+	−																−*							−
Climate																																
No. Rainy days	+*	+*	+	+*	+*	+*				+*	+*	+*	+*	+	+*	+*	+*	+*	+*	+*	+*	+*	+*	+*	+*	+*	+	+*	+*	+*	+	+*
No. Sunny days	−	−	+	+*	−	−	−*	−*	−*	+*				+*	+*	−	−	+	+*	−	−					+*				−*		+*
No. Days 90° F+ temperature	−	−	+	+*	−	−	+*	+*	+*					+*	+*	−	−	+	+*	−	−	+*				+*						
Crime																																
Total crime rate	+*	+*	+	−	+*	+*	+*	+*	+*	+	−	+*	+*	+	−	+	+	+	+	+*	−	+*	+	+	+	+	+	−*	+	−	+	−*
Crowding																																
Population density	−*	−*		−*	−*	−*		−*	−*			−*	−*			−*	−*	−	−	−	−				−*			−	−	+			
Population size																	+*	−	−	+*	+*	−*	−*	−*	−*			+*	+*	+*	+*	
Live in Central City	−*	−*	−*	−*		−*			−*	−*	−*	−*	−*	−		−*	−*	−*	−	−*	−*	−*	−*	−*	+*			−*		−*	−*	−*
Market conditions																																
Unemployment rate		+		+*		+					+*	+*			+*		+		+*		+		+*	+	−*	+	+*	+*	+	+*	+*	+*
Population growth											+*	+*				+*						+*	+*		−*		+*	+*	+*	+*	+*	+*

NOTE: * indicates that *t*-statistic is 2 or greater. A blank entry signifies that that variable did not appear in regression.

crime, largely go in the expected direction, though multicollinearity obviously takes its toll when a large number of indicators within each major grouping are entered at once.

Interpretation of Results

At any early stage of the experimentation, I decided to concentrate attention on city attributes that reflected actual outcomes rather than instruments. For example, it is conceivable to think of city services (for example, the number of police officers per capita) as city attributes. However, it is not the police per se, but rather the amount of crime people are exposed to that matters. The effects of the police department should be reflected in the cost of living through tax rates. Furthermore, it is known that the city attributes are interrelated to some extent and are not endogenous to location patterns in the overall market. For an example of the former, pollution and city size tend to create "heat islands" that affect temperature and climatic conditions in cities; as an example of the latter, attractive locations create in-migration that in turn affects crowding. These interesting issues have been ignored here because I am attempting to estimate the trade-off facing individuals who rationally consider existing attributes as fixed and beyond their control, though decisions by all agents in the market affect observed attributes as in all competitive markets.

The model of section 2 made a distinction between pure consumption and pure production effects of amenities on real wage rates. However, there may be some other effects in the estimates that are related to discussions of "productive consumption" or "regrettable necessities" in the national income accounting literature (Juster). Examples are expenditures on locks and guard dogs in high crime areas and home heating expenditures in the North. It will take us too far afield to discuss these issues formally, but a simple example illustrates how these effects are reflected in the regression coefficients. The crux of the matter is that the cost-of-living index (within each expenditure class) is a fixed weighted index of the same market basket in all cities. In principle, prices, and not the content of the goods in the market basket, vary across cities.[11] Home fuel expenditure is a good example; the same quantities are used in both Northern and Southern city cost-of-living indexes in spite of the lower fuel consumption in the South. Two effects are present. First, the nominal wage may be higher in the North than in the South to compensate for the greater fuel expenditure. Of course, these larger wages must be supported by some other productivity effect in the North. Second, the price of site values may tend to be higher in the South, other things being equal, because the savings on fuel bills are capitalized in land values. In this case the price of housing in the cost-of-living index is greater in the South, and a fixed weighted index would indicate a

larger cost of living in the South. In either case, or in some combination
of the two, the measured *real wage* is greater in the North than in the
South. But since the North and South are characterized by clearcut climatic
differences, the estimated temperature gradient in the wage-amenities regression reflects differences in fuel expenditure as well as factors previously
discussed. Examples for other factors such as pollution, crime, and crowding are easily constructed.

Given these qualifications, the major findings are as follows:

POLLUTION INDICATORS. *Particulates* refers to a measure of mean suspended particles. With its close relative, the number of inversion days, it
has consistently positive effects on real wages across cities. On the other
hand, the effects of sulphur dioxide and water pollution are hardly robust;
the former often exhibits a negative effect. Many other possible measures,
such as nitrates, remain to be tried. However, of the variables listed in the
table, a case can be made that particulates closely proxy the kind of information available to most people, and its consistently positive effect on real
wages supports the conceptual framework.

CLIMATE INDICATORS. Again, only a limited set of measures have been
tried. The presence of rain has a consistently positive effect on real wages,
similar to the effect of particulates. Sunny days have a consistently negative
effect on real wages. Both are in accordance with a priori expectations.
However, as with some of the other measures of pollution, a measure of
extreme temperature exhibits far less consistent effects, though in most cases
it shows positive effects when its t-value is large.

CRIME. The FBI's unweighted total crime rate has been used, without
separate examination of its major components by type or seriousness of
crime. The results are not quite as robust as for some of the climate and
pollution measures, but nonetheless go mainly in the expected positive
direction. Note also that the crime rate in the SMSA may be an error-
ridden measure of exposure to criminal activity depending on precise location within the area, as discussed previously.

MARKET CONDITIONS. The unemployment rate has two opposing effects.
On the one hand it may reflect temporary slackness in the labor market;
then low demand for labor results in corresponding temporary deviations
from the regression line. On the other hand, insofar as intercity differences
in unemployment rates are more permanent attributes, they call forth a true
equalizing difference, requiring positive wage premiums in high unemployment cities to compensate for less average time employed there (Hall).
Evidently the equalizing difference effect dominates in these data, since
consistently positive effects are observed in all specifications, confirming

Hall's results. The population growth rate (between the 1960 and 1970 censuses) surely indexes temporary fluctuations in the demand for labor relative to its supply and exerts a corresponding positive effect on real wages.

CROWDING. The variables listed under this heading admit the most ambiguous interpretation in terms of the theory of equalizing differences because they proxy many things. The variable "live in central city" is not a city effect at all. Rather, it is a person effect (a zero-one dummy applicable to each person in the sample) and has been included because most of the other city variables do not distinguish between suburban and non-suburban locations within SMSAs. Of the many possible effects captured by his variable, its consistent negative sign suggests that it indexes an unmeasured productivity effect between the average person living within the confines of the city itself and the average person living in the suburbs.

The estimated effects of density and sheer size are more interesting. The most striking result shown in table 3.3 is the negative effect of population density on real wages. (The measure reported refers to density in the central city—negative effects are consistently observed when overall density in the SMSA is used instead.) The negative effects of density are so strong that when population size is entered without a density index, its effect is negative, too. However, when both population size and density are entered together, population has a positive effect and density a negative effect. While the positive effect of city size is consistent with the results of Nordhaus and Tobin, the negative effect of density is in marked contrast to their estimates.

These results call for more discussion. Several factors arise naturally in this connection, including transaction costs, real productivity effects, and economies of scale.

The theory sketched in section 2 showed how the measured effects of amenities in real wage equations reflect both taste and productivity effects. Consider, for example, the positive estimated effects of unemployment. Firms must be willing to pay the costs of maintaining a "reserve army of the unemployed" in order for such effects to be observed. That unemployment calls forth positive wage premiums is evidence that the productivity effects of maintaining a pool of labor to meet fluctuating demand is positive and at least as great as its cost. This, of course, does not imply that social and private costs are equal.

A corresponding argument might apply to the positive effect of population in the presence of scale economies. Sheer size is conducive to greater specialization and division of labor and is certainly a real productivity effect that increases market income and output. However, if this effect applied uniformly to all production activities with no other factors at work, then all industry would be concentrated in extremely large cities. But there may

be the equivalent of taste offsets, too. If there is a distaste for the imper-
sonality of living in large places, the productivity gains from scale economies must be sufficient to offset it. Similarly, living in a large SMSA undoubtedly increases transportation costs, since the average journey to work
is greater in such places and the time-cost components never appear in
cost-of-living data. This cost, too, must be more than offset by the gains
from specialization to interpret the positivity of the population size effect.

The negative effect of density is somewhat more puzzling. Yet comparable logic applies. For a city of a given population size, greater density
creates a tendency to reduce transaction costs in two important senses: it
reduces commutation costs; and density supports a whole range of consumption activities that simply are not available in more sparsely populated
areas because those markets are too thinly traded. The matching of consumption tastes to a larger spectrum of goods availabilities in densely populated areas results in greater utility of consumption and represents a truly
higher standard of living. Moreover, these factors are not adequately captured in the cost-of-living index. For example, the official budgets take no
account of the availability of some goods in many cities.[12] As the final
link in the argument, the factors that enter the reservation price gradient of
labor with respect to density are the sum of a positive effect due to a
possible distaste for crowding and a negative unmeasured cost of living
effect detailed above. The negativity of the population density coefficient
suggests that the cost of living effect outweighs the pure crowding-distaste
effect. In sum, this result suggests that no disamenity imputation should be
made for density per se, except insofar as it is associated with more crime
and pollution.

CONCLUSION

Table 3.4 presents a sample of numerical results underlying table 3.3. Since
the magnitude of the regression coefficients shown there depends on the
units of measure of the variable, the means and standard deviations of the
city-attribute indicators used are shown at the foot of the table. A more
convenient summary of the numerical estimates is contained in table 3.5.

The first column gives the range of point estimates found in table 3.4.
The second column shows the standard deviation of the variable in question. The third column is the product of the low and high estimates of the
effect of a one standard deviation change in the attribute on the percentage
change in the wage. For example, the figures .017–.050 for particulates
indicate a wage premium ranging from 1.7 percent to 5.7 percent for each
standard deviation increase (thirty-eight units in this case) in suspended
particles in the atmosphere. To put these percentage differences in perspective, the geometric mean annual earnings of the workers in this sample is

TABLE 3.4. Selected Regression Results, City Attributes Regression Coefficients

City Attributes	Regression Number (corresponds to table 3.2)								
	10	11	7	27	28	25	24	17	29
Particulates	.106E-2*	.681E-3*	.897E-3*	.150E-2*	.110E-2*	.692E-3*	.602E-3*	.553E-3*	.921E-3*
Inversion days			.102E-1*						
Water pollution			-.868E-3						
Rainy days	.122E-2*	.286E-2*		.406E-3	.225E-2*	.230E-2*	.272E-2*	.295E-2*	.174E-2*
Sunny days			-.962E-2*						
Days temp 90° F+			-.239E-2*						
Total crime rate	.107E-4	-.521E-5	.316E-4*	.270E-5	-.170E-4	.120E-4	.614E-5	.926E-5	.492E-5
Unemployment rate		.457E-1*			.539E-1*		.149E-1	.950E-2	.195*
Growth rate				.479*	.533*				
Population density						-.110E-4*	-.998E-5*	-.112E-4*	-.899E-5*
Population						.966E-8*	.899E-8*	.967E-8*	.104E-7*
Live in central city	-.943E-1*	-.908E-1*	-.823E-1*	-.910E-1*	-.863E-1*	-.960E-1*	-.950E-1*	-.950E-1*	-.864E-1*

Variable	Mean	Std. Dev.
Particulates	113.44	32.82
Inversion days	29.59	5.56
Water pollution	11.80	11.84
Rainy days	29.53	16.72
Sunny days	59.98	60.52

Variable	Mean	Std. Dev.
Days temp. 90° F+	24.83	15.49
Crime rate	3939.30	1129.28
Unempl. rate	4.23	1.10
Pop. den.	13367.93	6844.58
Population	547382.00	3763091.00
ln real wage	9.09349	.65176

NOTE: E means appropriate power of 10. * indicates t-statistic of 2 or greater.

TABLE 3.5. Summary of Results

	Point Estimates		Standard Deviation	Percentage Effect	
	low	high		low	high
Particulates	.00055	– .0015	38	.017	– .057
Rainy days	.0004	– .0030	17	.0068–	.051
Crime	—.0000052	–+.000032	1100	—.0057–	.035
Unemployment	.0095	– .054	1.1	.010	– .059
Population density	—.000011	——.000009	6800	—.063	——.075
Population	.9 x 10⁻⁸ –	.1 x 10⁻⁸	3760000	.036	– .038

approximately $9000, so that a one percentage point effect amounts to about ninety dollars per annum and a five percentage point effect amounts to $450 per annum. The many qualifications underlying these estimates have been amplified at length above. However, it bears repeating that I view these results as very tentative and preliminary. Nevertheless, they are not unreasonable estimates compared with the results of other investigators using different data and methods.

It is clear that the qualitative results of both the estimates presented here and the studies reviewed in section 1 support the conceptual framework of analysis based on the theory of equalizing differences. However, the point estimates are not sufficiently robust to make definitive city-by-city comparisons of the quality of life or specific aggregate time-series urban disamenity corrections to GNP at the present time.

Merely to illustrate a potential use of these estimates, I have computed the average quality-of-life rankings arising from the estimates above. The regression weights are multiplied by observed attributes and summed to obtain a score for each city. The cities are then ranked from lowest to highest score and placed in rough quartiles in table 3.6. Also shown are extreme values of attributes for each city (as proportions of standard deviation units of each variable) that weigh most heavily in that city's score. By and large, the cities in the first quartile exhibit less pollution, better climate, and lower crime rates, whereas cities in the fourth quartile have the opposite characteristics. But there are exceptions. San Francisco has a high crime rate but is not marked down much for it because crime receives a fairly low weight in my index. Similarly, Chicago has a relatively low crime rate but is not marked up for the same reason. The cities in the middle ranks tend to weight more heavily on density and population size than those at either extreme. Five cities are unranked: the rankings of Houston and Dallas are markedly altered by changes in the specifications, particularly the effects of density. These are the least densely populated cities in the sample and rank as very amenable cities when density is not included in the specification, but very disamenable cities when density is included, density having a marked negative weight in the index. Paterson-

TABLE 3.6. Provisional Quality of Life Rankings, by Quartile, and Extreme Attributes, by City

Quartile and City	Extreme Values—Standard Deviation Units				
	Particulates	Rain	Crime	Density	Size
First					
San Francisco	−3/2	−2	+1		−1
Philadelphia	−1		−5/4		
Washington, D.C.					
Boston		−1			
Second					
Milwaukee			−3/2		−1
Minneapolis	−1			−1	−1
Los Angeles		−2	+5/4	−1	
Third					
Buffalo			−5/4		−1
St. Louis		+1			−1
Pittsburgh			−2		−1
Baltimore	+1				
Fourth					
Chicago	+5/4	+1	−1		
Detroit	+5/4		+1		
Cleveland	+3		−1		−1
Unranked					
Houston		+5/2		−3/2	−1
Dallas		+1		−3/2	
Paterson-Clifton-Passaic*	−3/2		−5/4		−1
New York*			+1	+2	+3/2
Newark*					−1

NOTE: Numerical values refer to the approximate values of the attributes as deviations from means measured as ratios to standard deviation of the variable; e.g., +3 means that the value of that attribute for a city was three standard deviations above the mean value for all cities. A minus sign means that the value exhibited for that variable was below the mean for all cities. Only extreme values are shown.

* The same price index was used for all these cities.

Clifton-Passaic, New York, and Newark are not ranked because, as already noted, a single price index had to be used for all three cities. However, their computed scores would place New York and Newark in the middle ranks: New York because of its extremely high density, which my quantity index weights very strongly; and Newark because it has few extreme values of any measured characteristic one way or the other. Paterson-Clifton-Passaic comes out in the first quartile because of its low measured pollution values and low crime rates.

Although there are some surprises in these ranks, let the reader recall that they represent average valuations of the "representative person" in the sample, and differences in tastes necessarily alter the weights given to each component. Table 3.6 is not meant to be definitive but only illustrates one possible use of this kind of estimate. Perhaps further study and more extensive samples will narrow some of the imprecision in this work.

NOTES

1. Other methods are possible: Liu uses an ad hoc weighting scheme on as many as seventy indicators, and the Social Indicators method employs survey research and direct questioning of residents.

2. It is conceptually simple to include location choices within cities in the formal analysis by examining subgradients within cities and intracity attributes (e.g., rent-distance trade-offs). The analysis is similar to the above, but requires an additional step. It is more difficult to incorporate them in empirical work. See below.

3. Continuity assumptions are made for expositional convenience and, if taken literally, require that the number of cities constitute a dense set. The virtue of this assumption is that it allows the use of marginal analysis. Without it, some equilibrium conditions in the text must be regarded as approximations; the analysis is not much affected in any case. See figure 3.2 for the discrete case.

4. I have abstracted from costs of moving in this outline of the theory, though such factors also can be incorporated into the bid-rent approach. In the absence of transaction costs the market equilibrium price-attributes, function is independent of initial location. The main difficulty posed by moving costs is that the resulting market equilibrium definitely is not independent of the initial distribution of the population.

5. The same cost-of-living index is used for New York, Newark, and Clifton-Paterson-Passaic because BLS does not report separate indexes for each. I have retained all three, since the number of identified cities in the 1970 CPS is small. Another strategy would be to combine them into one super SMSA. Neither approach seems satisfactory, since housing costs are likely to be smaller in Clifton-Paterson-Passaic than in the other two cities, and I suspect that the measured real wage assigned to people living there is too small on that account. Many more cities are identified in later CPS surveys and this should be less of a problem.

6. Though there are only nineteen SMSAs in the sample, almost one-third of the total population of the United States lives in them. Hence the sample is not quite as selective as it appears on the surface. In view of the selectivity in these markets discussed in section 2, it may make sense to stratify samples by city size.

7. Given the exploratory nature of this exercise, no interactions with occupation have been estimated, though prior studies have found them.

8. These regressions include all personal effects listed in table 3.1 as regressors, in addition to the city dummies. The F-statistic listed in the table tests the hypothesis that city effects are not present in addition to the personal effects. The critical value of F is 1.95 (at the .99 level) and the null hypothesis is rejected.

9. The main sources of my amenities data are published Census Bureau volumes and Liu. Liu does give many indicators of consumption opportunities, such as number of parks, major league teams, etc., so that it is possible to construct a variable similar to that used by Getz and Huang. Because of reservations about principal components analysis in this context, I have not constructed such a variable; city size and density will pick up some of the indicators of consumption opportunities. See below.

10. Of course the number of indicators cannot exceed the number of cities, no matter how many individuals there are in the sample. The question has arisen whether the city effects shown in table 3.2 are linear combinations of the estimated implicit prices of attributes. That would be true if the amenities were orthogonal to all personal, socioeconomic variables in table 3.1, in which case the estimates in

table 3.2 could be used as the data to be explained by amenity indicators. However, in general (and certainly in these data), that two step procedure is invalid because the orthoganality requirement has not been met. In any event, the city effects in table 3.2 include random factors as well as systematic parts due to differential amenities and disamenities, and for this reason they are not appropriate estimates of an overall quantity index in and of themselves.

11. This is not strictly true in the BLS data. For example, it is known that pork and poultry receive higher weight in Southern food budgets, while beef gets higher weight in Northern budgets. These adjustments reflect differential expenditure patterns and belong, not in a standard cost of living index, but possibly in a constant utility index. It is possible to reweight BLS figures, but I have not done so.

12. It is not only the existence of entertainment facilities and the like that are relevant. Large and densely populated cities support more product variety of all types, including a greater range of qualities of food, clothing, and other standard budget items.

REFERENCES

Antos, J., and Rosen, S. 1975. "Discrimination in the Market for Teachers." *Journal of Econometrics* 3: 123–50.

Feldman, R. 1975. "The Market for Physicians' Services." Ph.D. thesis, University of Rochester.

Fuchs, V. 1967. "Differentials in Hourly Earnings by Region and City Size, 1959." NBER Occasional Paper 101.

Getz, M., and Huang, Y. C. 1975. "Consumer Revealed Preference for City Size." Vanderbilt University.

Goldfarb, R. S., and Yezer, A. M. J. 1976. "Evaluating Alternative Theories of Intercity and Interregional Wage Differentials." *Journal of Regional Science,* vol. 16, no. 3.

Griliches, Z., ed. 1971. *Price Indexes and Quality Change.* Cambridge, Mass.: Harvard University Press.

Hall, R. 1972. "Why Is the Unemployment Rate So High at Full Employment?" *Brookings Economic Papers.*

Hoch, I. 1977. "Climate, Wages and the Quality of Life." In *Public Economics and the Quality of Life,* pp. 28–65. Edited by Lowden Wingo and Alan Evans. Baltimore: Johns Hopkins University Press.

———. 1976. "City Size Effects, Trends and Policies." *Science.*

———. 1974. "Inter-Urban Differences in the Quality of Life." In *Transport and the Urban Environment,* Edited by J. Rothenberg and R. Heggie. New York: Macmillan.

Izraeli, O. 1973. "Differentials in Nominal Income and Prices between Cities." Ph.D. dissertation, University of Chicago.

Juster, F. T. 1973. "A Framework for the Measurement of Economic and Social Performance." In *The Measurement of Economic and Social Performance,* Edited by M. Moss. New York: Columbia University Press.

King, T., and Mieszkowski, P. 1973. "Racial Discrimination, Segregation and the Price of Housing." *Journal of Political Economy*

Meyer, J. R., and Leone, R. A. 1977. "The Urban Disamenity Revisited." In *Public Economics and the Quality of Life,* pp. 66–91. Edited by Lowden Wingo and Alan Evans. Baltimore: Johns Hopkins University Press.

Nordhaus, W., and Tobin, J. 1972. "Is Growth Obsolete?" In *Economic Growth*. New York: National Bureau of Economic Research.

Oates, W. E. 1969. "The Effects of Property Taxes and Property Values: An Empirical Study of Tax Capitalization and the Tiebout Hypothesis." *Journal of Political Economy* 77: 957–71.

Rosen, S. 1974. "Hedonic Prices and Implicit Markets." *Journal of Political Economy* 825: 34–53.

Rubinfeld, D. 1977. "Market Approaches to the Measurement of the Benefit of Air Pollution Abatement." University of Michigan, Ann Arbor.

Stigler, G. 1957. "The Tenable Range of Functions of Local Government." *Joint Economic Committee Symposium*. Washington, D.C.: U.S. Government Printing Office.

Thaler, R., and Rosen, S. 1975. "The Value of Saving a Life: Evidence from the Labor Market." In *Household Production and Consumption*, pp. 265–98. Edited by N. Terleckyj. New York: Columbia University Press.

Tiebout, C. M. 1956. "The Pure Theory of Local Expenditures." *Journal of Political Economy*, vol. 64.

U.S. Department of Labor. Bureau of Labor Statistics. *Three Standards of Living for an Urban Family of Four Persons*. Bulletin No. 1570-5.

————. *Three Budgets for an Urban Family of Four Persons, 1969–70*. Supplement to Bulletin No. 1570-5.

U.S. Environmental Protection Agency. 1975. *Quality of Life Indicators in U.S. Metropolitan Areas, 1970*, by B. C. Liu. Washington, D.C.: U.S. Government Printing Office.

U.S. Department of Labor. Office of Evaluation. 1973. "Compensating Wage Differentials and Hazardous Work," by R. S. Smith. Washington, D.C.: Government Printing Office.

Viscusi, W. K. 1978. "Wealth Effects and Earnings Premiums for Job Hazards." *Review of Economics and Statistics*. (Forthcoming.)

II

MODELS OF LOCATION
AND SPATIAL INTERACTION

4

MONOCENTRIC MODELS OF URBAN LAND USE: CONTRIBUTIONS AND CRITICISMS

WILLIAM C. WHEATON

INTRODUCTION

The family of so-called monocentric city models represents a distinct and unique branch of microeconomics. Each model expands the theory of consumer or producer behavior to incorporate space consumption and locational preference. The added spatial dimension complicates traditional theory, for it creates a nonconvexity in the consumption set. Firms or households must locate in one and only one location, and two such households cannot occupy the same location. To treat this problem in as simple a manner as possible, all monocentric models are based on a common set of three assumptions.

First, it is assumed that at least one member of every household is engaged in productive work, and that all such activity occurs at a single point in space. Residences and work places must, therefore, be separated—a fact that introduces costly commuting.

Second, within the neoclassical framework, a household utility function is assumed in which the consumption of space is a positive argument. Given a constrained budget, utility maximization results in a situation in which space consumption must be traded against commuting cost. Density patterns evolve solely as a consequence of this trade-off.

Third, it is assumed that the consumption of space does not involve the use of capital that is either rigid or immobile. Past land use, therefore, plays no role in determining present or future density.

It is essential to emphasize at the outset that all these assumptions are highly unrealistic; urban structure in almost every society departs from at least one of them. Housing capital is rigid in all but nomadic cultures, and while some cities may have a dominant pattern of central employment, locational decision-making is rarely based solely on a trade-off between

space and commuting costs. Consequently, one should not expect the monocentric models to produce especially accurate representations of modern
cities. While the models' utility in forecasting urban growth for policy
analysis is limited, they still serve an important educational function: they
increase the understanding by planners and economists of how urban spatial
markets operate. Even if the assumptions and outcome of the models seem
unrealistic, the clarity of their simple structure has created a new awareness of spatial equilibrium and of the role of transportation.

In this chapter, the monocentric city models are reviewed and then
critically evaluated with respect to their three basic assumptions. Section 1
presents the simplest model, developed by Von Thunen and generalized by
Alonso, and explores some of the results produced by that model. Section 2
describes the Mills-Muth variant of the original model, amended to include
housing considerations, but still retaining the assumption of mobile capital.
Section 3 explores the very important extension of the model, to accommodate the simultaneous relationship between transportation and density. Section 4 discusses the normative theory of "optimal" monocentric cities, and
how those cities compare with the equilibrium models of previous sections.
Finally, section 5 looks at the recurrent three assumptions; it is suggested
that the relaxation of any one of them will create mathematical difficulties
that demand more complicated simulation approaches to urban modeling.
Loss of generality and mathematical elegance is the price of realism.

1.

The original concept of a monocentric city was developed by Von Thunen
(1826; Lösch, 1967) just over 150 years ago. Von Thunen was concerned
with the arrangement of different agricultural land uses around a common
market center. He theorized that the pattern emerged was the result of
the different shipping costs for each crop and the intensity with which it
was grown. Many years later, Alonso (1964) substantially generalized the
agricultural model by incorporating neoclassical production and consumption decisions; thus improved, it was applied to the problem of urban land
use.

In the simplest version of the neoclassical model, N workers are assumed
to be employed at a central site of production. Each worker earns an income, y, which can be spent on space or land, q, other goods including
food, clothing, and housing, x, and the cost of commuting distance t to
work, $k(t)$. The price of land is $R(t)$, which depends on location and is
to be determined in equilibrium. The cost of commuting is exogenous, as
is the unitary price of x that serves as the numeraire. Each worker's household has a common utility function, in which x and q enter as positive
arguments and t enters as a negative one, to account for the time or nui-

sance (as opposed to cost) of commuting. At a particular distance from work, t, the traditional maximization of consumer utility, equation (1), subject to budgetary constraint, equation (2), yields equation (2) plus the marginal condition, equation (3).

$$u(x,q,t), \tag{1}$$

$$y = R(t)q + x + k(t), \tag{2}$$

$$\frac{\partial u}{\partial q} \Big/ \frac{\partial u}{\partial x} = R(t). \tag{3}$$

The choice of location involves maximizing consumer utility with respect to t, subject to budgetary constraint. This yields:

$$\frac{\partial u}{\partial t} \Big/ \frac{\partial u}{\partial x} = q \frac{\partial R}{\partial t} + \frac{dk}{dt}. \tag{4}$$

Households select that location where the marginal rate of substitution between distance and other goods equals the ratio of the money costs of such a change.

This partial equilibrium immediately raises the problem of competing demands. With identical individuals, the solution to equations (2), (3), and (4) will yield the same chosen site for each—clearly an impossible situation. In a general equilibrium, households must live at different distances to work, and yet at each location the conditions of equation (4) will have to hold. To determine a rent profile that satisfies this condition, (4) may be rewritten as equation (5). Since equations (2) and (3) determine x and q as functions of t and R, (5) is a straightforward differential equation of R in t.

$$\frac{dR}{dt} = \left[\frac{\partial u}{\partial t} \Big/ \frac{\partial u}{\partial x} - \frac{dk}{dt} \right] \Big/ q \tag{5}$$

While equation (5) defines rent variation over space so that consumers are equally satisfied, an actual rent gradient requires a constant of integration. This constant is found by balancing the aggregate supply and demand for land with two additional equations.

In the first equation, the rent profile determined by (5) competes with the rent from a nonurban, or alternative to urban use, s. The supply of land available for urban use, therefore, reaches from the city center to a distance b, where urban rent equals this "opportunity cost":

$$R(b) = s. \tag{6}$$

The urban rent profile also generates a pattern of demanded land consumption through equations (2) and (3). Given these land demands, the total number of households needed to fill the space from city center to urban border must just equal the population to be housed, N. In a plain, with a uniform transportation system, this condition is:

$$2\pi \int_0^b t/q \, dt = N. \tag{7}$$

Thus, equations (2), (3), and (5) determine q and R as functions of a constant of integration and equations (6) and (7) simultaneously determine that constant and the border of urbanization, b.

In his original work, Alonso developed a parallel, or dual, method of deriving these results that sheds considerable light on the meaning of the constant of integration. Adopting the perspective of the landlord, Alonso suggested that land use emerges from a competitive auction. Mindful of their resources, consumers bid for sites; they are careful not to bid so much for one area that it would yield less net utility than would their offers for other sites. Given a common level of utility, u^o, households will offer for each site the maximum their budget will allow:

$$R(t) = \frac{y - x - k(t)}{q}. \tag{8}$$

The land market auction will thus extract the greatest household bid in equation (8), subject to the constraint that such offers yield the uniform and equilibrium level of welfare, u^o. This constraint is expressed in equation (9), and not surprisingly, the result of the constrained maximization is the original marginal efficiency condition, equation (3).

$$u^o = u(x, q, t) \tag{9}$$

In the Alonso rent-maximization approach, then, equations (3), (8), and (9) are used to determine x, q, and the offered bid-rent, $R(t)$—all as functions of t and u^o. This compares with utility maximization, where equations (2) and (5) are combined with equation (3) to determine the same variables, as functions of t and the constant of integration. Not surprisingly, the constant is simply a monotone transform of the equilibrium level of utility, and both are determined by the same pair of equilibrium conditions, equations (6) and (7).

The simultaneous solution of these equilibrium conditions represents the so-called closed city model. In that model, population is exogenous and the level of welfare is determined to meet the resulting demand for space. It is sometimes argued that mobility between cities may be sufficient to make these assumptions unwarranted. The alternative is the so-called open city, in which the level of utility is taken as exogenous. In the latter model, the equilibrium conditions, equations (6) and (7), are used sequentially to determine first the population and then the size of city that sustains this level of welfare. This chapter takes the view that the open city model is generally unrealistic in developed economies. If all households must essentially work in urban areas, then a level of utility must eventually be determined endogenously, perhaps for a system of cities. A truly exogenous level of utility is found only in less-developed countries, where an extensive agricultural sector provides ample opportunity for an alternative subsistence.

In either case, the model is mainly descriptive in nature. To be useful, the model should yield empirical tests or theorems that are at least insightful if not valid. The major attempt to produce such theorems from the model is contained in a recent paper by Wheaton (1974).

In the closed city model there are four parameters: income, y, transportation costs, k, rural rent, s, and population size, N. Given these parameters, the equilibrium conditions determine the solution to rent and density patterns, $R(t)$, $1/q(t)$, as well as the level of utility, u^o, and the urban border, b. Using quite general mathematics, Wheaton's paper determines the sign of all elements in the 4×4 matrix of comparative static derivatives. The results are:

$$\frac{du^o}{dN} < 0 , \quad \frac{du^o}{sd} < 0 , \quad \frac{du^o}{dk} < 0 , \quad \frac{du^o}{dy} > 0$$

$$\frac{db}{dN} > 0 , \quad \frac{db}{ds} < 0 , \quad \frac{db}{dk} < 0 , \quad \frac{db}{dy} > 0$$

$$\frac{dR(t)}{dN} > 0 , \frac{dR(t)}{ds} > 0 , \frac{dR(o)}{dk} > 0 , \frac{dR(o)}{dy} < 0 \tag{10}$$

$$\frac{dq(t)}{dN} < 0 , \frac{dq(t)}{ds} < 0 , \frac{dq(o)}{dk} < 0 , \frac{dq(o)}{dy} > 0$$

A similar matrix was obtained for the open city model, and while neither matrix produced results that were very surprising, the theorems are essential for testing the model. Do larger cities have higher central rents? Are wealthier cities more decentralized? Do cities with better transportation systems have lower rents? Unfortunately, empirical tests of these propositions, and hence of the basic assumptions of the model, have never been satisfactorily carried out.

As long as all households are assumed to be identical, very few additional results can be derived from the basic model. It is natural, therefore, that several authors began exploring more general models in which there were classes of locators. Beckman (1969) devised the simplest of these generalizations: all households have identical utility functions, but not equal incomes. In fact, the population to be located in his closed city has the income distribution

$$n(y) = Ay^{-\alpha} \qquad y > y^\circ \tag{11}$$

where:

$$n = \text{number of people with income} \geqq y$$
$$y_o = \text{minimum income}$$
$$n(y_o) = N.$$

In Beckman's generalization of the Alonso model two spatial gradients must be determined: rent, $R(t)$, and the spatial pattern of income, $y(t)$. At each location t, given the rent and income of consumers locating there, utility maximization through equations (2) and (3) still determines the consumption of x and q as functions of y and R. To determine the spatial gradients of these latter, a system of two differential equations are solved. The first of these is simply equation (5), whereas the second follows from a location specific balance between land supply and demand. As distance changes by one unit, income varies by $\dfrac{dy}{dt}$, and the number of households within this range is $\dfrac{dn}{dy}$. Given their space consumption q, the absolute value of the product of these terms must equal land supply, $2\pi t$. The resulting condition is equation (13).

$$\frac{dR}{dt} = \left[\frac{\partial u}{\partial t} \bigg/ \frac{\partial u}{\partial x} - \frac{dk}{dt}\right] \bigg/ q \tag{12}$$

$$\left|\frac{dy}{dt}\right| = 2\pi t \bigg/ \frac{dn}{dy} q \tag{13}$$

Thus the conditions of equations (2) and (3) determine q and x as functions of R and y, while equations (12) and (13) are solved as a system of differential equations to determine R and y jointly as functions of t. With such a system there will be two constants of integration. The first serves to set the overall rent level and may be interpreted as the level of utility achieved by the poorest household in the city. Like the city boundary, it is determined by the equilibrium condition of equations (6) and (7). The second constant must set the absolute spatial pattern of income; equation (13) merely describes the rate at which income increases or decreases with distance. Beckman's resolution of this issue was incomplete. Although his actual model used a Pareto distribution of income and a logarithmic utility function, he could not characterize the general solution for these forms. Instead, he "presented" a particular set of functions that satisfied all of the conditions. With these conditions, the final constant of integration was determined so that income at the center, $y(o)$, was the minimum, y^o. Of course, this led to a spatial pattern in which income increased with distance from the city center. In a follow-up article, Montesano (1972) proved that all solutions to a model with logarithmic utility require that income increase from the center, with $y(o)$ equal to y^o.

Although both of these papers were very important contributions, neither adequately clarified why income increases rather than decreases with commuting distance. Alonso, in his original treatment, shed more light on this phenomena with the bid-rent approach. In a somewhat more general model, there were any number of households, each with a unique utility function and level of income. Using equations (3), (8), and (9), a bid-rent and a corresponding space consumption gradient are determined for each household. Naturally, these gradients are functions of commuting distance and of the level of welfare that each particular household assumes.

If it is remembered that market clearing with the bid-rent approach adopts the perspective of the landlord who is auctioning his land, it clearly follows that the location pattern depends on which household has the highest bid for each particular site. If a particular household bids the most for many sites, then, according to Alonso, it has accepted a needlessly low level of welfare in computing its bid-rent gradient. The household should bid less for all sites (raising its utility) until it captures just as much land as it needs. Similarly, a household that finds itself without the highest bid at any site must tighten its belt, offering more at all locations, until it finally commands just the quantity of land it demands.

Consider for the moment a situation in which there are m groups of households, each with N_i, $i = l, m$, members. Each group has a common income and a common utility function, and hence a common level of welfare, u_i^o $i = l, m$. The bid-rent and land consumption functions for each group, determined by equations (3), (8), and (9), may be represented as

$$R_i(u_i{}^o, t) \qquad i = l, m \tag{14}$$

$$q_i(u_i{}^o, t).$$

With these, the solution to the general location problem requires that m utility levels be determined by the following m equilibrium conditions:

$$\int_{\epsilon_i} 2\pi\, t/q_i\, dt = N_i \qquad i = l, m$$

$$\epsilon_i = \{t: \text{such that } R_i \geq R_j, j \neq i\}.$$

(15)

In the monocentric city model, the question of who locates centrally, as opposed to peripherally, depends on the steepness with which consumer bid rents decline over distance. In the simple case of two households with linear bid rents it is clear that if each must outbid the other for some land, then the household with the steeper bid gradient will outbid the other for central locations. Of course, bid rents are rarely linear, and for many household groups there may not be a simple and monotonic locational solution. If one household's bid gradient is fairly linear, and another's is quite convex, it is probable that those with the linear bid will locate at an intermediate distance. The other households with a convex bid gradient, will locate both in the most central and peripheral locations.

The slope of a bid gradient with respect to distance can be determined by differentiating equation (8) and its constraint, (9), with respect to t. Applying the envelope theorem, it follows that this derivative, $\dfrac{dR}{dt}$, is the same as the marginal location condition (equation [5]). Returning to the question of income and location, Alonso examined this derivative and argued as follows: As income increases, both the value of time, $\dfrac{\partial u}{\partial t} / \dfrac{\partial u}{\partial x}$ and the consumption of space, q, will also increase. The former tends to steepen bid slopes, whereas the latter flattens them. If the consumption of space increases significantly more than the value of time, wealthier households would have flatter bid gradients and would locate peripherally; with the magnitudes reversed, the rich would tend to live centrally.

An empirical answer to the question of how bid gradients for the rich and the poor compare is an important test of the models' ability to explain location patterns. In a recent paper, Wheaton (1977) estimated utility functions for American consumers of different ages, family sizes, and incomes. Using computed values for time and space consumption, equilibrium location patterns were obtained for a monocentric city. Young households and those with few children had a low preference for space and a high disutility for commuting, giving them a clearly dominant position in bidding for central locations. Between income levels, however, there was surprisingly little difference. To be sure, as income increased, values for time and space consumption rose, but they increased in an exactly offsetting manner. Thus, the bid gradients of low-, middle-, and upper-income households all looked quite similar. This was sufficiently true that differences between income groups were statistically insignificant. Therefore, the tendency for wealthy Americans to live further from the city cannot be adequately explained by the simple decision-making of the Von Thunen-Alonso model.

Despite serious doubts about the validity of the model, there have been several attempts to utilize it as a tool in analyzing contemporary policy issues. For example, Polinsky and Shavell (1975) expanded the model to investigate the impact of air pollution on the urban form. They sought to determine whether aggregate changes in land rents that might accompany improved air quality accurately reflected the resulting benefits. They concluded first that rent changes would occur only if there was a differential improvement in pollution over space, and second that as the land market reached a new equilibrium, aggregate rent change did not necessarily capture total benefits.

This brings up the important issue of how land rents in general are disposed of within the model. At present, the rents are not used for anything and presumably accrue to an absentee landlord. If the monocentric model is supposed to represent a prototypical city within a national economy, however, it is more reasonable to expect that rents will be shared by households. In the simple model, with a single consumer, this is accomplished by a seventh equilibrium condition:

$$y = y_o + 1/N \, 2\pi \int_0^b (R-s)t \, dt. \tag{16}$$

In equation (14) income is redefined so as to come both from an exogenous "wage" source, y^o, and an equal share of the net rental payments that accrue from urbanization. Of course, this closure somewhat complicates the model. Although the basic system of equations [1] through [7] can often be solved analytically, the inclusion of equation (16) usually necessitates numerical methods. Rent and consumer welfare are first obtained as a function of income and then the latter is adjusted based on rent payments. The conversion of solution algorithms never seems to be a problem (Solow, 1973).

Using this expanded model, Wheaton (1977) recently investigated another problem in policy-making—the benefits of a reduction in travel cost, which presumably occur as a result of greater highway investment. Wheaton sought to determine if the present method of measuring only the cost savings to users captures all the consumer surplus. A reduction in travel cost within the more general model would not only benefit users directly but, by adjusting aggregate rents, could also alter their income. Changing rent would also affect land consumption, and so secondary consumer surplus may be gained or lost in the land market as well. To capture all of these effects, Wheaton determined the general equilibrium income compensation necessary to offset the reduction in transportation costs.

The magnitude of this compensation is:

$$\frac{dy}{dk}_{\text{income constant}} = \left[\frac{dy}{dk} + \frac{du}{dy}\frac{dR}{dk}/N\right] \Big/ \left[\frac{du}{dy} + \frac{du}{dy}\frac{dR}{dy}/N\right]. \quad (17)$$

In equation (17) all of the derivatives are constructed from those in the comparative static matrix (equation [10]). The two derivatives $\frac{dR}{dk}$ and $\frac{dR}{dy}$ are similarly the general equilibrium change in rent in response to travel cost and income changes. Evaluating all of these terms in some detail, Wheaton showed that equation (17) reduces to the change in consumer surplus under the derived demand curve for travel. Thus, the general equilibrium benefits of highway investment need only consider the direct benefits to users; changing land rent can be ignored in benefit calculations.

There have been a number of additional articles (such as Yameda [1972]), but most of them have involved clarifications or discussions of the model rather than true extensions or applications. In retrospect, one might say that the dominant value of the model has been as a descriptive, educational device; it exemplifies the application of traditional microeconomics to spatial decisions, and the creation, by transportation, of a so-called hedonic market for urban land.

2.

While Alonso was expanding the Von Thunen model to consider land consumption by households, Muth (1968) and, later, Mills (1972) were trying to expand it to incorporate housing. The result is a model that has considerable pedagogical value, although in retrospect it appears mathematically equivalent to Alonso's version.

In the Muth-Mills variation, consumer utility depends on the consumption of other goods, x, and on an aggregate commodity called "housing," h. In addition to commuting cost, consumers face a unit price for x and a price, $P(t)$, for housing. Housing is produced from capital inputs, c, and land, q. The price of the former is exogenous and equal to r, whereas land rent, $R(t)$, will be determined, like the price of housing, endogenously to vary over space. Given the budget constraint (equation [18]), households maximize their utility (equation [19]), which results in the marginal condition of equation (20). Producers, on the other hand, maximize profits from the production function shown in equation (21), which results in the marginal conditions of equations (22) and (23).

$$y = x + P(t)h + k(t) \tag{18}$$

$$u(x, h) \tag{19}$$

$$\frac{\partial u}{\partial h} \Big/ \frac{\partial u}{\partial x} = P(t) \tag{20}$$

$$h = f(c, q) \tag{21}$$

$$P(t) \frac{df}{dc} = r \tag{22}$$

$$P(t) \frac{df}{dq} = R(t) \tag{23}$$

Given the price of housing at any location t, the equations above are solved for x, h, c, q, and land rent, $R(t)$. The price of housing is determined by a locational marginal condition, in which increased commuting cost is balanced against housing expenditure savings rather than land, as in the Alonso model.

$$h \frac{dP}{dt} + \frac{dk}{dt} = 0 \tag{24}$$

The solution to differential equation (24) provides the price gradient of housing once a constant of integration is obtained. Both this constant and the size of the city are determined by the same equilibrium conditions used by Alonso: equations (6) and (7).

Mathematically, the Mills-Muth approach is effectively no different than Alonso's. Equations (18) through (24) are actually equivalent to a reduced form model in which consumers directly select land consumption and housing capital from the composite utility function:

$$u(x, f[c, q]). \tag{25}$$

The addition of housing capital as a variable that consumers may select does not adequately address the role that such capital plays in urban land use. Since households consume c in any amount, anywhere, and at any time, it is equivalent to food and clothing and behaves just as x does. Housing capital is mainly an appendage that does not really change the model's mathematical character.

While the Mills-Muth approach may be mathematically equivalent to Alonso's, there is an important conceptual difference. In Alonso's model, the direct household preference for land determines residential density; in the Muth-Mills model, consumers have no direct preference for land, and residential density is determined by the technical characteristics of a production function for housing. It is clear that in the case of single-family housing consumer preference plays a dominant role in determining density. Therefore, the Alonso model more accurately describes the process of residential density formation. However, in the case of nonresidential uses— or even of high-density apartments—production possibilities between land and capital probably do play an important role. For such uses, Muth's model is the more realistic one. Clearly there are merits to each approach, and actual land use is undoubtedly the result of both demand and production characteristics.

In summary, the work of Mills and Muth forms an interesting introduction of housing capital and producer decisions into the model. However, it fails to capture the essence of housing capital—that which distinguishes it from other ordinary goods. Once built, housing capital yields a flow of services that provide an opportunity cost against new construction. This cost, in conjunction with the long life of housing, makes housing a highly rigid and immobile form of capital. Without accounting for this feature, the incorporation of housing into a monocentric city model is of mostly descriptive value.

3.

The models discussed so far have recognized only part of the relationship between land use and transportation. While the friction of space gives rise to a density pattern, the location of residences may in turn influence the cost of travel. It is well recognized that the character of highway transportation results in congestion externalities (Mohring, 1970). The extent of these externalities depends jointly on the size of the highway facilities and the magnitude of their usage. In a monocentric city, where all commuting is done radially to the center, the shape of the density gradient will affect the volume of traffic passing each point. Unless investment in transportation facilities is sufficient to insure free-flow travel, travel cost and residential density must be determined simultaneously. Mills (1972) and Solow (1972) are the two writers who have investigated this relationship to date, and both have made important contributions to the model by incorporating the influence of congestion.

The consumer model used by Mills and Solow is essentially the same as that in section 2. Households maximize a utility function that depends on other goods, x, and space consumption, q, given the budget constraint, equation (26). The result at each location is the marginal condition, equation (27), while the choice of location involves the familiar differential equation (28).

$$y = R(t)q + x + K(t) \tag{26}$$

$$\frac{\partial u}{\partial q} \bigg/ \frac{\partial u}{\partial x} = R(t) \tag{27}$$

$$\frac{dR}{dt}q + \frac{dK}{dt} = 0 \tag{28}$$

The cost of travel in this model, $K(t)$, is distinguished from that in other sections because it incorporates the value of time costs in addition to direct money expenses. Therefore, the total cost of traveling a unit mile, $\frac{dK}{dt}$, will depend on traffic flow or speed and hence on the supply of transportation facilities and the volume of traffic at location t. The supply of transportation facilities is presumed to be proportional to the amount of land devoted thereto. In a monocentric city, a fraction of land at each location, $w(t)$, is exogenously set aside for highways. The volume of traffic, $v(t)$, passing through these facilities at a particular point depends on the number of commuters who live beyond that location.

$$v(t) = 2\pi \int_t^b z/q \, dz \tag{29}$$

The cost per mile of travel, therefore, is expressed in the function:

$$\frac{dK}{dt} = G[v(t), w(t)] \tag{30}$$

where $\frac{dG}{dv} \geq 0, \frac{dG}{dw} \leq 0$.

Equations (26) and (27) determine q and x as functions of R and K. Equations (29), (30), and (27) form a system of two differential equations that are solved for $R(t)$ and $K(t)$. Of course, if the G function is simply a constant, then the entire model reduces to that of section 1.

The system of differential equations (28), (29), and (30) requires two constants of integration for a final solution. To determine these, plus the size of the city, b, the following three conditions are added:

$$2\pi \int_0^b [1 - w(t)] \, t/q \, dt = N \tag{31}$$

$$R(b) = s \tag{32}$$

$$K(o) = k^o. \tag{33}$$

Equation (31) is a variant of (5), modified to account for the portion of land withdrawn from the residential market for use in transportation. Equation (32) is obvious and (33) insures that travel costs at the CBD equal a predetermined amount (usually zero).

Despite the conceptual simplicity of this model, it is virtually impossible to solve it analytically for given utility and G functions. Both Mills (1972) and Solow (1973) eventually used numerical analysis to determine the solution in specific cases.

Mills was mainly interested in the sensitivity of the model to various parameters. In particular, he questioned whether the historical flattening of American density gradients was due to expanded transportation facilities, rising income and population, or shifts in relative prices. Comparing solutions with different parameter values, Mills did suggest that urban density and rents were somewhat insensitive to expanded highway facilities. The suburbanization of American land, he concluded, is due more to rising income and strong housing demand.

Solow (1973), Robson (1976), and Oron, Pines, and Sheshinski (1973) on the other hand all addressed the planning problem of pricing and investment in urban highway capacity. Including congestion and time cost in the model renders the supply of transportation capacity an explicit parameter—subject to policy choice. In addition, it is also possible to incorporate a commuting toll into the model—one that varies with location to capture the appropriate social costs of congestion. Most of this research does not develop new theoretical conclusions regarding highway pricing or investment, but simply rephrases well-known results in a spatial context and examines the impact of such policies on land-use patterns.

As is well documented in the traditional public finance literature, highway congestion creates an external cost—one that should be priced for true economic efficiency. When priced, the appropriate level of highway capacity is determined by a straightforward application of cost-benefit principles. In the absence of tolls, however, a "second best" solution is called for and simple cost-benefit investment rules are not optimal (Mohring, 1970). Solow (1973) and then Robson (1976) both re-derived this latter result within a spatial framework. Solow assumed that $w(t)$ is a linear function and then sought the optimal values of its parameters with respect to the equilibrium level of consumer utility. The resulting optimal highway capacity was evaluated by cost-benefit analysis. Benefits appear to always exceed cost at the optimum, so that traditional investment rules lead to overinvestment in highways.

Robson generalized this result and proved that following cost-benefit investment procedures leads to a larger than optimal road at each and every location. Excessive highway capacity thus reduces travel cost, and so leads to less dense urban land use. Robson's paper clearly suggests that highway planning based on cost-benefit principles—in the absence of congestion tolls—can lead to unoptimally sprawled development.

Contemporary with these efforts, Oran, Pines, and Sheshinski reiterated the necessity for charging congestion tolls, given whatever pattern of highway capacity exists. Not surprisingly, they found that optimal tolls should equal the marginal social cost of road usage. Within the context of their particular spatial model, this turned out to be proportional to the number of households living beyond each location. Charging such a toll at each location would obviously increase transport cost and contract land development. Despite the resulting higher density, consumers are able to achieve higher equilibrium utility levels when the toll money is redistributed.

The logical outcome of these determinations is the development of a spatial model in which tolls and investment are jointly optimized. The results, however, would certainly be consistent with traditional theory; if, and only if, appropriate congestion tolls are in effect, then optimal highway capacity is determined by the simple equality of marginal benefits with marginal costs.

4.

The final version of the monocentric city model involves an interesting application of the theory of optimal control. Control theory is most frequently used in dynamic systems where an integral expression over time must be maximized by selecting the optimal trajectory or time path of some variable. If "time" is replaced by "distance," the application to spatial design becomes apparent—maximize the aggregate welfare of city inhabitants by selecting the appropriate spatial gradients or trajectories for density and the consumption of other goods.

This approach was first conceived by Mirrlees (1972), who used a fairly simple model to develop its basic conclusions. To illustrate these results in a form comparable to the previous models, consumer utility is assumed to arise from the consumption of other goods, x, and space, q. Given an urban density gradient $1/q$, the aggregate sum of individual utilities in the city is:

$$2\pi \int u(x, q) t/q \, dt \, . \tag{34}$$

Expression (31) constitutes a simple welfare function, and while there are a vast array of alternative forms that might be used (Dixit, 1973), this one is generally believed to be both equalitarian (all individuals have equal weights) and responsive to individual preferences. It is the only one used by Mirrlees and a number of subsequent authors.

To keep things simple for the moment, it is assumed that transportation involves no time congestion, only a monetary cost to travel, $k(t)$. Aggregate expenditures on travel and other goods must, of course, add up to some finite amount of urban resources, Y. This constraint, together with one on population, serve as limits on resource allocation.

$$2\pi \int xt/q \, dt + 2\pi \int k(t)t/q \, dt = Y \tag{35}$$

$$2\pi \int t/q \, dt = N \tag{36}$$

The stage is now set for the ultimate planning problem: given N consumers with preferences as described, and an aggregate quantity of resources to be spent on other goods and travel, design a city and a spatial pattern of consumption that maximize the sum of utility levels. The solution is two gradients—$x(t)$, $q(t)$—that must obey certain conditions. In the optimal control literature, Euler's rules are frequently used to elucidate the character of the solution.

Using Euler's results, Mirrlees showed that at each location t, the optimal gradients $x(t)$ and $q(t)$ must obey the following conditions:

$$\frac{\partial u}{\partial x} = \lambda \text{ (a constant)}; \tag{37}$$

$$u - \frac{\partial u}{\partial q} q - \lambda x = \mu \text{ (a constant)}. \tag{38}$$

Since (37) and (38) hold at all locations, they may be differentiated by t to yield the conditions:

$$U_{xx} \frac{dx}{dt} + U_{qq} \frac{dq}{dt} = 0 \; ; \tag{39}$$

$$q \left[U_{qq} \frac{dq}{dt} + U_{qx} \frac{dx}{dt} \right] + \lambda \frac{dk}{dt} = 0 \; . \tag{40}$$

These are solved for:

$$\frac{dq}{dt} = \frac{-\lambda}{q} \frac{dk}{dt} \left[\frac{U_{xx}}{U_{xx}U_{qq} - U_{xq}^2} \right] \geq 0; \tag{41}$$

$$\frac{dx}{dt} = \frac{-\lambda}{q} \frac{dk}{dt} \left[\frac{U_{xq}}{U_{xx}U_{qq} - U_{xq}^2} \right] \gtrless 0. \tag{42}$$

The inequality in equation (41) follows from the convexity of utility, which insures the negativity of the expression within brackets. However, the sign of $\frac{dx}{dt}$ cannot be determined unambiguously. In the optimal city, therefore, space consumption will always increase with distance, while consumption of x may either increase or decrease. A result that continuously intrigues theorists is that the net effect of $\frac{dq}{dt}$ and $\frac{dx}{dt}$ does not necessarily yield equal utility at all locations. In fact:

$$\frac{du}{dt} = \frac{\partial u}{\partial q}\frac{dq}{dt} + \frac{\partial u}{\partial x}\frac{dx}{dt}$$

$$= \frac{-\lambda}{q}\frac{dk}{dt}\,[U_{xq}\,U_x + U_{xx}\,U_q]/[U_{xx}\,U_{qq} - U_{xq}{}^2] \gtreqless 0\,. \qquad (43)$$

This result was first seen to be highly counterintuitive. If the welfare function gives equal weight to all individuals, why should the optimum town necessitate different levels of utility at different locations (and hence for different individuals)? The problem can also be examined in the competitive market realization of the optimal city. Mirrlees showed that it is possible to devise a price gradient for space and to divide aggregate resource Y into an income distribution, such that the resulting equilibrium city exactly matches the optimum. The necessary income distribution, however, will not be uniform unless a strict equality holds in equation (43).

Recent work on optimal monocentric cities has expanded the model considerably. Dixit (1973) and Riley (1973), for example, included congestion cost and an aggregate productive activity at the center of the city. The fact that continues to puzzle researchers, however, is the unequal utility levels despite the equal weights in the welfare function. Even when the welfare function is changed to penalize inequality, unequal utility frequently occurs in the optimum solution (Dixit, 1973). Only in the extreme case of the so-called Rawlsian welfare function is equality guaranteed under certain conditions.

There have been several explanations offered for the paradox of unequal treatment for equals. Mirrlees suspected that the friction of space might create some form of implicit externality. In contrast, Levhari, Oron, and Pines (1972) suggested that the inequality results from the inherent nonconvexity of locational choice. Consumers must select only one location—they cannot partially reside in many. Another, fairly controversial, opinion occurs in an unpublished paper by Varaiya, Schweizer, and Hartwick (1975). Recalling the basics of welfare economics, these authors demonstrated that the maximum solution to the sum of individual utilities does not always yield equal utility in any economy. Using a simple two-person, nonspatial model, they demonstrated that for many monotonic transformations of a utility function, equals should not be treated equally. Although this may be true, the class of cardinal utility functions which exhibit diminishing marginal utility normally does produce equal treatment of equals. This is not the case in the Mirrlees model—a fact that supports the explanation based on the inherent nonconvexity of locational choice.

Questions such as the preceding pose a problem for the optimal city approach. One of the foundations of neoclassical economics is that utility need only be ordinal. There are an infinite number of monotonic transformations of any particular utility function, all of which yield identical demand curves. If each in turn may yield a different solution to the welfare maximization problem, which is to be chosen? Without a normative or empirical foundation upon which to guide the selection of either a welfare function or a particular cardinal utility index, the solution to any welfare maximization problem is somewhat arbitrary. Of course, this is not a problem in equilibrium models, where monotonic transformations of the utility function leave the rent and density pattern unchanged.

CONCLUSION

Taken as a group, monocentric city models have three characteristics in common: they assume that all employment is centrally located; they assume that locational choice depends only on commuting cost and space consumption; and they assume that all housing capital is fluid and mobile.

These assumptions illustrate an important problem in any scientific research: models that are simple enough to yield general, deductive conclusions frequently require overly restrictive assumptions. The monocentric city models are an excellent case-in-point. On the one hand, the assumptions are essential for mathematical tractibility; without them, solutions to the models become less general in character, and noticeably more difficult to obtain. On the other hand, the assumptions are sufficiently unrealistic that doubts are raised about their usefulness. Each assumption eliminates an important and essential feature of urban structure. These features are often the core of many current urban policy issues.

The central location of employment is perhaps the most widely criticized assumption of the monocentric models; there are few cities with even a majority of employment located in a central business district. Service employment is widely spread around most regions, and there has been recent decentralization of office and industrial establishments as well (Meyer, Kain, and Wohl, 1965). Evidence even suggests that the employment distribution of many nineteenth-century cities was less centralized than had been supposed (Moses, 1962).

In an effort to justify the concept of an employment center, Von Thunen,

Alonso, and later, Solow (1973) extended the monocentric city model to incorporate the location of firms. Firms are presumed to have a bid gradient for industrial space that declines with distance from a central transportation terminal to which all shipping is done. If bids of firms decline more rapidly than those of households, a central business district will emerge from a competitive solution to the land market.

Although this situation may depict the structure of early agricultural cities, over the last century the availability of transportation has been continually decentralizing. Railroad spur lines and urban highways years ago made the central business district obsolete for the purpose of product shipping (Meyer, Kain, and Wohl, 1965). Clearly, the Von Thunen model of employment location is largely irrelevant to modern cities.

More recent studies of industrial location have emphasized the role of spatial markets and the supply of labor (Kemper, 1974). Both factors suggest that the location of households and firms is closely interdependent. In the case of retail and service establishments, the availability of a local spatial market is of singular importance. With the decentralization of residences in recent years, such markets have moved to the suburbs, as has a large share of service employment (Harrison, 1974). In the case of firms that "export" their product, local markets are irrelevant; access to a diverse labor supply becomes important, and only if a firm's workforce is spatially diffused will a central location be optimal. A concentrated distribution of labor easily makes a decentralized site more attractive (Moses, 1962).

If the problem is only one of mutual dependence, it should be possible to model a region as a system of monocentric subcities, each with an employment center and a surrounding workforce. A consideration such as agglomeration economies would presumably explain the number of subcenters and the degree of employment decentralization (Mills and Lav, 1964). Interestingly, in such a model, greater decentralization (more and smaller subcenters) leads to less aggregate commuting. This may contradict one's intuitive feelings about such cities as Los Angeles, but enough data is available to resolve the issue empirically. But even such a multi-monocentric model does not address the growing tendency toward two-worker households and the large amount of travel for purposes other than commuting to work (Meyer, Kain, and Wohl, 1965). These considerations suggest that many consumers use a concept of accessability more general than simply to the subcenter of their own employment.

The trouble with all these generalizations is that they hopelessly complicate the elegant simplicity of the original model. With multiple centers, workplaces, or trip purposes, transportation cost bears a discontinuous and highly complicated relationship to euclidean space. The only recourse is to develop models in which space is approximated by discrete parcels or cells. As the chapter by Ingram in this volume makes clear, such models tend to be costly and unwieldy.

The second assumption of the monocentric models is that locational choice depends on income, the preference for space, and the disutility of commuting. As section 1 indicates, there is little empirical support for the proposition that these factors alone explain the spatial pattern of residences in American cities. As an alternative, a second and entirely separate body of literature has evolved that emphasizes the role of spatial externalities and the differential provision of public services (Tiebout, 1956). The importance of these factors is well documented by studies that reveal the influence of neighborhood composition, crime, and school quality on location and the price of housing capital (Bradford and Kelejian, 1973). It is interesting that there has to date been no attempt to reconcile these different theories or to incorporate them into a single monocentric model.

The apparent incompatibility of these approaches is largely a result of the different mathematical requirements inherent in their perspectives. The monocentric models rely on a continuous representation of space, where the concept of travel cost can be easily determined. Theories that emphasize externalities and public goods, however, destroy this simplicity. The very concept of a political jurisdiction divides space into discrete parcels, and the external cost arising between such parcels is not simply linear. As a result, monocentric models have ignored external and fiscal factors, and theories that have considered these influences have failed to recognize the spatial relationship between jurisdictions. Perhaps the most important problem raised by the consideration together of spatial and external factors is co-location. The site selection of different households becomes interrelated rather than solely dependent on a set of exogenous variables. This generates market equilibria that depend on an initial location pattern, a fact that creates both normative and mathematical difficulties. Any models that attempt to consider both theories jointly will necessarily involve simulation solutions, the cost of which will be high, both in computer time and in loss of generality.

The final assumption of the monocentric models is that in the long run all capital is mobile. Presumably, the structure of a city in which capital is built gradually will, in the limit, closely resemble that of a city in which capital is put in place all at once. In general, this simply is not the case. A model in which capital stocks influence future flows need not have a steady state, much less one that is identical to a purely static solution. Since housing is the most rigid form of capital, urban land development is inherently an evolutionary process.

There has been some recent work on urban growth that suggests the possibility of incorporating rigid capital within the monocentric framework. Equally important, this work verifies that the urban structure that evolves from growth models may look quite different from that obtained in a static equilibrium solution. Harrison and Kain (1974) developed a model in which present urban density is a combination of those density gradients that emerge from past market solutions. While an important insight, this ignores the frequent profitability of replacing even rigid capital. Proceeding from this point, Anas (in press) describes the conditions under which urban growth occurs through demolition or conversion, as opposed to new development. But neither of these papers describes the market equilibrium that results as consumers in each period bid alternatively for existing housing or development on new land. With increasing urban population, new households are first accommodated on vacant land at the fringe; as demand builds and the city expands, the land rent for more central sites exceeds that for the capital structures already there. At this point, conversion or demolition and new construction occurs. Such a growth pattern contrasts sharply with the comparatively static predictions of Mills (1972) and Wheaton (1974). With rigid capital, the city should expand more rapidly at the fringe, and the urban rent profile should be more convex. History is an important determinant of urban structure, one that the current generation of models has ignored.

If the monocentric city models contain a lesson, it is that spatial relationships substantially complicate microeconomics' simple analytics. Even without externalities and rigid capital, the hedonic character of locational choice requires the assumption of monocentric employment for mathematical modeling. Once capital is immobile, and locational preferences are interdependent, mathematical methods become inadequate and simulation is necessary to obtain solutions. Perhaps it is time to recognize the inherent limitations of general mathematics and direct more attention toward an expanded simulation methodology.

REFERENCES

Alonso, William. 1964. *Location and Land Use*. Cambridge, Mass.: Harvard University Press.

Anas, Alex. 1976. "Short Run Dynamics in the Urban Housing Market." In *Essays in Mathematical Land Use Theory*. Edited by Anas and Dendrinos. Lexington, Mass.: Lexington Books.

Beckman, M. J. 1969. "On the Distribution of Urban Rent and Residential Density." *Journal of Economic Theory* 1: 60–67.

Bradford, D., and Kelejian, H. 1973. "An Econometric Model of the Flight to the Suburbs." *Journal of Political Economy* (May).

Dixit, A. 1973. "The Optimum Factory Town." *Bell Journal of Economics and Management Science* 4 (2): 637–51.

Harrison, B. 1974. *Employment and Economic Development*. Washington, D.C.: Urban Institute.

Harrison, D., and Kain, J. 1974. "Cumulative Urban Growth and Urban Density Functions." *Journal of Urban Economics* 1: 68–69.

Kemper, Peter. 1974. "Manufacturing Location and Production Requirements. New Haven: Yale University.

Levhari, D.; Oron, Y.; and Pines, D. 1972. "In Favor of Lottery in Cases of Non-Convexity." Center for Urban and Regional Studies, Tel-Aviv, paper no. 10.

Meyer, J.; Kain, J.; and Wohl, M. 1965. *The Urban Transportation Problem.* Cambridge, Mass.: Harvard University Press.

Mills, E. S. 1972. *Studies in the Structure of the Urban Economy.* Baltimore: Johns Hopkins University Press.

Mills, E. S., and Lav, M. 1964. "A Model of Market Areas with Free Entry." *Journal of Political Economy* (June): pp. 278–88.

Mirrlees, J. 1972. "The Optimum Town." *Swedish Journal of Economics* 74 no. 1: 114–35.

Mohring, H. 1970. "The Peak Load Problem with Increasing Returns and Prizing Constraints." *American Economic Review* 60 (September): pp. 693–705.

Montesano, A. 1972. "A Restatement of Beckman's Model on the Distribution of Urban Rent and Residential Density." *Journal of Economic Theory,* 4 no. 2: 329–54.

Moses, Leon. 1962. "Towards a Theory of Intra-Urban Wage Differentials and their Influence on Travel Patterns." Regional Science Association. *Papers and Proceedings* 9.

Moses, L., and Fales, R. 1972. "Land Use Theory and the Spatial Structure of the Nineteenth-Century City." Regional Science Association. *Papers and Proceedings.* 28: 49–80.

Muth, R. 1968. *Cities and Housing.* Chicago: University of Chicago Press.

Oron, Y.; Pines, D.; and Sheshinski, E. 1973. "Optimum vs. Equilibrium Land Use Pattern and Congestion Toll." *Bell Journal* (Autumn).

Polinsky, M., and Shavell, S. 1975. "The Air Pollution and Property Value Debate." *Review of Economics and Statistics* 57: 100–4.

Riley, J. G. 1973. "Gammaville: An Optimal Town." *Journal of Economic Theory.*

Robson, A. 1976. "Cost Benefit Analysis and the Use of Urban Land for Transportation." *Journal of Urban Economics* 3: 180–91.

Solow, R. M. 1973. "On Equilibrium Models of Urban Location." In *Essays in Modern Economics.* Edited by J. M. Parkin. London: Logmans.

———. 1972. "Congestion, Density and the Use of Land in Transportation." *Swedish Journal of Economics* 74: 161–73.

———. 1973. "Congestion Costs and the Use of Land for Streets." *Bell Journal of Economics and Management Science* 602–18.

Sweeney, J. L. 1974. "Quality, Commodity Hierarchies and Housing Markets." *Econometrica,* vol. 42, no. 1.

Tiebout, C. 1956. "A Pure Theory of Local Expenditure." *Journal of Political Economy* (October).

Varaiya, P. Schweizer, Urs.; and Jartwick, J. 1975. "On Inequality in the 'Optimum' Town." Cambridge, Mass.: Massachusetts Institute of Technology.

Von Thunen. 1826. *Der Isolierte Staat in Beziehung auf Landwirtschaft und Nationalökonomie.* Hamburg.

Wheaton, William. 1974. "A Comparative Static Analysis of Urban Spatial Structure." *Journal of Economic Theory* 9 no. 2: 223–37.

————.1977. "Income and Urban Residence." *American Economic Review* (September).

————. 1977. "Residential Decentralization, Land Rents and the Benefits of Urban Transportation Investment." *American Economic Review* (March).

Yamada, H. 1972. "On the Theory of Residential Location." Regional Science Association. *Papers and Proceedings* 29.

5

SIMULATION AND ECONOMETRIC
APPROACHES TO MODELING URBAN AREAS

GREGORY K. INGRAM

INTRODUCTION

The development and use of computer based models has grown rapidly over the past twenty years owing to the proliferation of computers and the accompanying nearly thousandfold decline in the real cost of their services. In this period numerous computer models have been designed to analyze urban problems and simulate the process of urban development. Early generation urban development models were usually components of transportation planning exercises that forecast future levels of employment and residential activity in a particular target year for each of several hundred zones of a metropolitan area. The techniques used in these early models included trend extrapolation, gravity models, and linear programming procedures, and their orientation was to long run equilibrium solutions. The models' behavioral content was usually not compelling, and few were well documented.[1] During recent years, the emphasis of urban development models has shifted from the comprehensive approach required for transport planning to a narrower focus on residential location and housing market behavior. Recent models give less importance to spatial disaggregation and much more to representing economic behavior and modeling market outcomes.

This chapter summarizes recent progress in urban modeling by reviewing four urban development models that have been created or refined during the past few years. The first is the Disaggregated Residential Allocation Model (DRAM). A refinement of the Lowry model, DRAM is representa-

Gregory K. Ingram is an associate professor in the Department of Economics, Harvard University and is currently on leave as an economist at the International Bank for Reconstruction and Development.

I wish to thank Mahlon Straszheim and Peter Mieszkowski for editorial advice, Marcia Fernald for editorial assistance, and Ofelia Miranda for manuscript preparation.

tive of urban development models now available for use in transportation planning exercises—it focuses on residential location and is spatially disaggregated. The second model, designed by Engle, Rothenberg, and others (E/R model), is a spatially disaggregated, simultaneous equation model of ten-year changes in the housing market; it represents both residential locations and housing supply activity. The third model, the Urban Institute Housing Model (UI model), simulates both the demand and supply sides of the housing market over a ten-year period, but is spatially more aggregate than the E/R model. Finally, the National Bureau of Economic Research (NBER) Urban Simulation Model projects annual changes in an urban housing market; less spatially disaggregated than transport planning models, it also represents both the demand and supply sides of the housing market. These four models have very different structures and present a wide range of alternative approaches to modeling urban development patterns.

1. COMPUTER MODELS VS. ANALYTICAL APPROACHES

Although computer based models are widely employed to represent and analyze urban phenomena, they have several deficiencies relative to traditional analytical approaches. Perhaps their most serious drawback is that they produce particular rather than general solutions, which means that a large number of specific solutions may be required to gain the same information contained in the general solution of an analytic model. In this respect, computer models are likely to be more expensive than analytic models. Higher cost also stems from model construction, the need for more input data, and more complicated or extensive parameter estimation. Moreover, because the structure of computer models is often more complex than that of analytical models, computer model results may be less transparent or understandable than those of the analytical models.

Given these deficiencies, why are computer models widely used in urban economics? Because many problems or models that are not analytically tractable can be solved with computer based procedures. Often, a model must be simplified in important respects to make it amenable to analytical solution; the critical issue is then whether the idealized analytically tractable model is sufficiently similar to the original model for the analytical solution to carry over. In urban economics, analytical models typically require the following simplifying assumptions:

1. *Monocentric location of economic activity.* Virtually all analytical models of urban development assume that employment and other economic activity is concentrated at a single point at the center of the urban area or located symmetrically about that center. The crucial implication of this assumption is that the city becomes radially symmetrical; two-dimensional space can be represented by one dimension, distance from the center.

2. *Independence of location choices.* Most analytical models determine location choice for a household or firm as a function of travel cost and land or building price. Households or firms are assumed not to be influenced by the location choices of other households or firms.

3. *Absence of non-market produced goods.* Analytical models of residential location typically exclude any reference to local public goods as attributes of housing services or location.

4. *Long-run equilibrium on the supply side.* Analytical models assume that the existing stock of capital in housing, transportation, firms, etc., is quite malleable relative to the time horizon for which the model is used.

The principal advantage of computer based models of urban development is that they allow the relaxation of these four assumptions. The assumption of monocentricity is avoided in virtually all computer based models. Furthermore, its relaxation calls for a true two-dimensional representation of space, which nearly always requires numerical rather than analytical solution. Since allowing interdependent location choices can produce multiple or unstable solutions, interdependency is typically incorporated into computer based models along with transaction costs or durable capital stocks, either of which will usually produce fairly stable outcomes with interdependence and allow some measure of path-dependence in model solutions. Computer based models of urban development are beginning to introduce proxies for local public goods as a locational attribute, but they are still some distance from incorporating an endogenous local public sector. The typical current approach is to proxy local public goods with a variable we will call "neighborhood quality," defined as a function of household and/or housing attributes in each location. Much more progress has been made in relaxing the final assumption, that capital stocks are in long-run equilibrium. Several computer based models have incorporated representations of the supply side of the housing market that allow for supply adjustments that reflect the constraints that durable stocks of capital place on supply responses.

Incorporating any one of these changes in a complete analytical model of urban development is very difficult; incorporating more than one is nearly impossible. The choice of assumptions can therefore determine the modes of solution available to represent a theory of urban development, and computer based techniques are often the only feasible way to model complex behavior or to represent a particular urban area.

2. OVERVIEW OF FOUR MODELS

Before describing each model individually, it might be useful to compare their general characteristics. One way of doing this is to review each

TABLE 5.1. Treatment of Major Simplifying Assumptions by the Four Models

Simplifying Assumption	Model			
	DRAM	E/R	UI	NBER
Monocentric symmetry	No; location described by travel times to many workplace zones	No; location described by two accessibility measures	No; location described by average worktrip travel time	No; location described by travel times to many workplace zones
Independence of location choices	No; choice a function of zones' income composition	No; choice a function of zones' racial composition, percent on welfare	No; choice a function of zones' racial composition, average zone rents	No; choice a function of racial composition, neighborhood quality measure
Absence of non-market produced public goods	Yes	No; proxied by exogenous pupil-teacher ratio, effective tax rate	No; proxied by endogenous average zone rent	No; proxied by endogenous neighborhood quality measure
Long-run equilibrium; no explicit supply side	Nearly; lacks supply side but implicitly assumes existing units are infinitely durable	No; includes structure types; models construction, conversion, demolition	No; models supply change in existing units and new construction; homogeneous housing services used rather than structure types	No; includes structure types; models construction, conversion, operation of existing units

model's treatment of the four major assumptions made by the analytic models. A summary is presented in table 5.1.

Although the assumption of monocentric symmetry is relaxed by all four, only two models—DRAM and NBER—use workplace-specific travel time to characterize the relative position of residence zones. The E/R and UI models use average travel time or accessibility to describe zone location, an approach that essentially treats space as one-dimensional. All four models also make an attempt to allow interdependence of location choices: DRAM makes location choice dependent on zonal income level, whereas the other three models introduce both racial composition and a measure of socioeconomic status. Three of the models incorporate a location descriptor that can be viewed as a proxy for the level of local public services. The E/R model uses an output variable (pupil/teacher ratio) and a price variable (effective tax rate) to describe these services, but both variables are exogenous. The NBER and UI models proxy public services with an endogenous measure of each zone's "quality," but DRAM uses only its zonal income composition measure. An explicit representation of supply activities, including new construction and transformations of existing units, is included in the E/R, UI, and NBER models. DRAM simulates only the demand side, but its representation of housing assumes that the density of existing units cannot be changed. In this respect it is essentially a "putty-clay" model of housing, whereas the other three models could be characterized as having "putty-malleable clay" representations.

Each model represents locations, households, and housing over time. Comparing the dimensions, shown in table 5.2, used to represent these variables is another way of differentiating the four models. Differences in spatial disaggregation are quite dramatic across the four models, ranging from the 4 to 6 zones used in the UI model to the 108 residence zone by 108 workplace zone representation used in DRAM. The E/R model, like the UI model, omits the explicit representation of workplaces and uses workplace accessibility to represent employment locations. The NBER model takes yet another course with relatively few explicit workplaces and numerous residence zones. Differences in the representation of space reveal the different orientations of these models. DRAM is intended for transport

TABLE 5.2. Basic Dimensions and Typology of the Four Models

Item	Model			
	DRAM	E/R	UI	NBER
Residence zones	108	89	4–6	200
Workplace zones	108	......	......	20
Household classes:				
Income	4	3	Continuous	6 or continuous
Race	......	......	2	2
Lifecycle	......	......	2	8
Housing descriptors	Density	3 structure types; average size; average age; average number of bathrooms	Quantity of housing services (continuous)	10 structure types; 5 neighborhood types; quantity of structure services (continuous)
Time interval represented	Variable	Decadal	Decadal	Annual

planning exercises, and thus produces a highly disaggregated matrix of worktrips. The NBER model, designed to analyze housing market behavior, includes some workplace disaggregation because its architects felt that workplace location has a large impact on housing choice. However, the worktrip table it produces would be less useful for transport planning. The E/R and UI models do not produce any explicit worktrip distributions; they are primarily concerned with housing. In short, the dimensional trade-offs that are made across models reflect different objectives and an overall constraint on model size.

Of course, comparing the dimensions used to describe households and dwelling units can be somewhat difficult because of differences in model structure—the UI and NBER models are both microanalytic and therefore store data for individual sample households, whereas DRAM and the E/R model are aggregate and use matrix storage. Table 5.2 shows, for example, that income is continuous in the UI model; it can thus have a different value for each household, or up to forty-five values. On the other hand, the UI model uses a limited set of integer values for race and life cycle, so these dimensions are readily comparable to those in DRAM and the E/R model. With this warning in mind, it appears that DRAM represents households and dwelling units with the least detail, and that dimensional richness increases from left to right across table 5.2.

Finally, both the E/R and NBER models use structure type to describe housing in terms of the number of units per building (e.g., single-family or multi-family), although in the NBER model structure type also encompasses lot size and unit size. The only model whose time interval per cycle is readily variable, DRAM can be run on an annual basis to represent incremental growth, or operated to produce a target year projection in one step. The E/R and UI models are calibrated with census data and therefore represent ten years per modeling cycle, whereas the NBER model has a one year modeling period.

A final way of summarizing the structures of the four models is to characterize the basic process of urban development in terms of a household's choice of a set of workplace and residential attributes. Let us denote households as H, residential location as I, workplaces as J, dwelling unit types or quantities of housing services as K, and occupations or industries as L. From a household's point of view, the urban development problem can be expressed as choosing a combination of I, J, K, and L that maximizes utility. A planner attempts to shape urban development by affecting employment location decisions that determine J and L, and by influencing the supply side of the housing market that alters available combinations of K and I.

Many of the major differences in the four models are reflected in how the models represent household choices. DRAM assigns households that have a workplace to a residence zone [$(H,J) \rightarrow I$]. The E/R model assigns households to residence zones [$H \rightarrow I$]. The UI model simultaneously represents a household's choice of dwelling unit and location [$H \rightarrow (K,I)$]. The NBER model employs a hierarchical choice framework by assigning a household with an occupation or industry affiliation first to a workplace; second, to a dwelling unit type; and third, to a residence zone [$(H,L) \rightarrow J;$ $(H,L,J) \rightarrow K; (H,L,J,K) \rightarrow I$].

Three of the four models have households pick only one workplace or residence attribute altogether, or else one workplace or residence attribute at a time; only the UI model attempts to represent the choice of two attributes simultaneously, and this is accomplished by keeping the model's dimensions at a modest level. A second feature of existing models that is highlighted by the synopsis of household choices is that they pay very little attention to the labor market—the household's choice of J and L. The NBER model incorporates some elements of a spatial labor market, but the topic has not been seriously addressed in urban development models.

DRAM: Disaggregated Residential Allocation Model

Developed by Stephen Putman, DRAM is a descendant of the allocation model designed by Ira Lowry for Pittsburgh.[2] The Lowry model has spawned a host of residential allocation models that have been widely employed both in the United States and abroad.[3] Relative to other Lowry derivatives, the major changes in DRAM are in the formulation and calibration of the residential allocation equations.[4] The allocation procedures used in the original Lowry model can be written as

$$T_{ij} = P_{ij} \cdot E_j, \text{ or as} \tag{1}$$

$$N_i = g\sum_j P_{ij} \cdot E_j, \tag{2}$$

where E_j is employment at j; P_{ij} is the proportion of workers at j living at i; T_{ij} are worktrips from i to j; N_i is the population living at i; and g is a scaling parameter. In the Lowry formulation, P_{ij} was a gravity expression of the form

$$P_{ij} = (C_{ij})^{-1.33R}, \tag{3}$$

where C_{ij} was the airline distance from zone i to j, and R was the number of residence zones at distance C_{ij}. Three major improvements have been made. First, travel time, travel cost, or both have replaced distance as the impedance between i and j. Second, several versions of the model assign increments of each zone's employment over time instead of assigning all activity in one step. And third, the gravity distribution expression (i.e., equation [3]) has been expanded to include measures of the opportunities available in zone i, so that the expression for P_{ij} takes the form

$$P_{ij} = f(C_{ij}) \cdot O_i, \tag{4}$$

where O_i is a measure of opportunities at i. Several partial attempts have been made to estimate equation (4). These have usually involved fitting T_{ij} to some $f(C_{ij})$ or regressing N_i on measures of O_i. However, in DRAM the parameters for $f(C_{ij})$ and O_i are estimated jointly as

$$\frac{T_{ij}}{E_j} = \frac{f(C_{ij}) \cdot O_i}{\sum_i f(C_{ij}) \cdot O_i}, \tag{5}$$

where $f(C_{ij})$ is formulated as Tanner's function,

$$f(C_{ij}) = C_{ij}{}^a \cdot e^{-b \cdot C_{ij}}, \tag{6}$$

and C_{ij} are interzonal travel times. The expression for the opportunities at zone i is

$$O_i = S_{1,i}{}^{B1} \cdot S_{2,i}{}^{B2} \cdot S_{3,i}{}^{B3} \cdot S_{4,i}{}^{B4} \cdot \text{VAC}_i{}^{B5} \cdot \text{PDEV}_i{}^{B6} \cdot \text{DEN}_i{}^{B7}, \tag{7}$$

where $S_{k,i}$ is the proportion of households of income class k in zone i; VAC_i is land available for development in zone i; PDEV_i is the percentage of developable land in zone i that is developed; and DEN_i is the residential density in zone i. VAC times DEN is hypothesized to be a measure of the zone's unused capacity, and PDEV is a proxy for transaction or search costs. In this formulation households are divided into four income classes; equation (5) is estimated separately for each class, using an iterative gradient search procedure. Following their estimation, the equations can be used to forecast residential distributions.

DRAM's employment allocation procedure relies on an approach very similar to that used in the original Lowry model. Essentially a spatial generalization of economic base theory, this approach divides employment into two categories: a basic sector composed of export industries or site-oriented industries whose location decisions are independent of the locations of other economic actors in the region; and a retail sector composed of establishments whose location choices are sensitive to the distribution of population because they deal principally with local residents. The location of basic sector employment was assigned exogenously in early versions of the Lowry model, and retail sector employment is a function of accessibility to households, employment, and other zonal characteristics. This approach has been somewhat improved, e.g., DRAM uses a set of equations to allocate basic employment as a function of site characteristics, and it is perhaps the most successful available technique for representing interdependencies between employment and residential locations.

The type of distribution function shown in equations (5) through (7) has a number of difficulties when used to allocate households to residences or employment to workplaces. First, the equations are often estimated in average share form—i.e., T_{ij}/E_j is the dependent variable—and then applied in incremental allocation models where marginal shares—i.e., $\Delta T_{ij}/\Delta E_j$—are distributed. The assumption that marginal shares equal average shares can lead to cross-section bias in forecasts, a common problem with land-use allocation models of this type.[5]

Second, although, many theoretical models of residential choice and much empirical evidence suggest that prices play a major role in a household's choice of residential location, price variables are notably absent as components of the zonal opportunity measure. The allocation equations are at best reduced form equations with respect to price variables, and will no longer be valid if those variables change; at worst they are merely descriptions of market outcomes. A variety of procedures could be used to investigate the magnitude of possible biases due to excluded price and travel cost variables. For example, since central-city workers face different travel costs and housing prices than suburban workers, separate distribution equations could be estimated for different workplaces, and differences in coefficients could be related to the travel cost and housing price differences. Until allocation functions incorporate economic behavior, their forecasting use must be suspect.

A third shortcoming of the allocation equations is that they omit other than price variables. Income is often included in these equations, but other household characteristics—significant determinants of housing consumption and residential location, such as race, lifecycle, and family size—are absent. A somewhat less serious problem with the specification is that zones that presently lack any residential activity (PDEV=0; DEN=0) will never receive any households. This is a really extreme manifestation of the cross-section bias problem mentioned earlier.

Finally, DRAM lacks any representation of supply side activity and essentially assumes that proper supplies will be forthcoming when needed. The lack of a supply side, in conjunction with the omission of price variables, implies that additional units in each zone will be provided at current (constant) prices, a situation that approximates long-run equilibrium for supply. At the same time, conversion activity is apparently excluded, because a full zone (VAC=0) cannot receive additional households. The omission of structural conversion is consistent with the assumption of infinitely durable dwelling units.

Data and estimation requirements of this model are fairly large, considering its simple multiple equation structure. To estimate the model in average share form requires a detailed inventory of worktrips and employment by location. Such data can be obtained from the Census Bureau, as a special cross-tabulation, or collected in a household survey. To estimate the model in marginal share form requires a worktrip and employment inventory at two points in time. Many cities now have two origin and destination surveys, but zonal compatibility problems often prevent estimation of the model in marginal form. The actual estimation procedure—use of a gradient search algorithm—undoubtedly calls for special expertise; however, such algorithms should be readily available to potential users.

Engle/Rothenberg Model

The Engle/Rothenberg (E/R) model has been under development since the early 1970s and was conceived as a comprehensive multi-stage model of urban development relating the distribution of households and changes in housing stocks to employment changes.[6] Only the household location and housing components of the model have advanced sufficiently to be described here.[7]

This model consists of a set of household allocation equations (the demand side) and a set of dwelling unit provision equations (the supply side) estimated from Census data for the Boston metropolitan area. A set of eighty-nine zones, consisting of fourteen subareas for Boston and one zone for each of seventy-five surrounding cities and towns, were used. The estimated model is based on changes in zonal characteristics between 1960 and 1970.

The demand formulation used in the E/R model can be viewed as an extension of the allocation equations used in DRAM and the Lowry models. The approach essentially consists of combining a form of the dependent variable of equation (2) with an enlarged list of "opportunity" variables as sketched in equation (4). The new opportunity variables or residence zone descriptors include dwelling unit and other zonal characteristics, as well as measures of zonal prices or search costs, in order to overcome many of the objections to the specification of opportunities used in DRAM and similar allocation models. Although it increases the number of zonal characteristics, the E/R model replaces interzonal travel cost and zonal employment measurement with indexes of employment and highway accessibility. As a result, the demand side of the E/R model is basically a regression of relative zonal population shares on relative zonal characteristics. These share equations are estimated separately for each of three income classes, which continues the parallel with the DRAM equations.

Table 5.3 displays the dependent variable and the five categories of independent variables. The dependent and independent variables are first defined as ratios with respect to the Standard Metropolitan Statistical Area (SMSA) average of each variable and then formulated as decadal differences ($\Delta X_i/X$), so that the estimated coefficients are elasticities. Preliminary estimates of the equations produced reasonable sign patterns and a value for R^2 of between 0.4 and 0.5.

The specification of zonal characteristics used in the E/R model is an improvement over those used in DRAM; the inclusion of price terms is

TABLE 5.3. Variables Used in the E/R Demand Allocation Equations

Category	Variable
Structure and land	ST_1 = Percentage of zone's units with 7+ rooms ST_2 = Percentage of 1960 units built before 1930 ST_3 = Percentage of zone's units with more than one bathroom ST_4 = Population density
Social environment	SO_1 = Percentage nonwhite of zone's population SO_2 = Percentage of zone's population on welfare SO_3 = FBI crime rate
Local goods	LG_1 = Pupil/teacher ratio in high school LG_2 = Effective property tax rate
Potential access	AC_1^y = Job Access$_i^y$ = $\sum_{j=1}^{89} E_j^y \cdot C_{ij}$, where C_{ij} are travel times and E_j^y is zone j's share of SMSA employment for income class y AC_2 = Highway availability
Price	P_1 = Housing price index for zone P_2 = Zonal housing vacancy rate
Dependent variable	H^y = Number of households of income class y in zone

particularly noteworthy. However, the demand allocation portion suffers from many of DRAM's other shortcomings; for example, the stratification of allocation equations by income is useful, but additional stratification would improve the model, because other household characteristics (e.g., race, lifecycle) also influence locational choices and housing consumption. The use of average zonal characteristics to summarize zonal attributes is appropriate for variables measuring accessibility, local goods, and the social environment, but questionable for structure and land characteristics. The first three variables are either local public goods or display relatively little intrazonal variation, whereas structure characteristics can vary a great deal within a zone. For example, a zone with half three-room apartments and half seven-room houses would have the same value for ST_1 as a zone with half six-room and half seven-room houses. The demand equations are estimated using a two-stage least squares technique in which the endogenous variables are the four "structure and land" variables, percentage nonwhite, percentage on welfare, and the housing price index. It is likely that the two "local goods" variables should also be treated as endogenous in this system; specifying them as exogenous may introduce a simultaneous equation bias. The use of zonal averages in the demand side of the E/R model emphasizes the choice of residential location.

The supply side of the E/R model has a somewhat more complicated specification than the demand side, because it includes both new construction and the conversion of existing units. Moreover, the estimates of additional units supplied in each zone are projected for each of three structure types: single-family structures, small multi-family structures (two to four units), and large multi-family structures (five or more units). Separate conversion equations are estimated for each structure type in much the same way that the demand equations are estimated for each income class, but the new construction equations employ a two-step procedure instead of a simple structure type stratification. A single equation is first estimated to predict the proportional change, accounted for by new construction, in the total number of units by zone; additional equations are then estimated to predict the share of each structure type in a zone's new units.

The aggregate supply function for new units is derived from a theoretical construct that assumes: (1) housing is produced from land and nonland with constant returns to scale; (2) a competitive industry produces housing; and (3) zonal land prices are inversely related to the percentage of zonal land that is vacant. This results in a supply equation in which the proportional change in amount of housing produced $\left(\dfrac{\Delta Q}{Q}\right)$ is a function of the change in housing prices $\left(\dfrac{\Delta P}{P}\right)$ and the proportion of land that is vacant $\left(\dfrac{V}{T}\right)$. To these variables are added: (1) a second measure of land prices, the changes in land devoted to nonresidential use $\left(\dfrac{\Delta NR}{T}\right)$; (2) a second measure of housing prices, the change in the vacancy rate $\left(\dfrac{\Delta VR}{VR}\right)$; and (3) a zoning variable, the fraction of zonal land that is vacant but not subject to minimum lot sizes over 25,000 square feet (OPEN). The aggregate supply function is of the form

$$\frac{\Delta Q}{Q} = B_0 + B_1 \cdot \frac{V}{T} \cdot \frac{\Delta P}{P} + B_2 \cdot \frac{\Delta NR}{T} + B_3 \cdot \frac{\Delta VR}{VR} + B_4 \text{ OPEN}, \quad (8)$$

and the proportion of base year units added by new construction during the decade is used as $\dfrac{\Delta Q}{Q}$. R^2 for this equation is 0.44.

The aggregate increase in dwelling units forecast by equation (8) is next allocated to structure types by two equations that predict the share of new single-family and large multi-family units; small multi-family units are forecast as a residual. Structure type shares are a function of proportions of land in a zone that are: (1) restricted to a 25,000 square foot minimum lot size; (2) served by sewers; and (3) vacant. These equations have plausible sign patterns, and their R^2 values are all nearly 0.8.

The conversion equations for each structure type use the decadal change in the number of units not due to new construction as the dependent variable. Independent variables describe the existing stock (the number of units built before 1930; the number of deteriorating units; the number of public housing units) and the prices or demand pressures (proportional price change; vacancy rate; change in vacancy rate; new construction) in each zone. Higher prices seem to promote conversions to single-family units, whereas increased vacancy rates seem to reflect a conversion to apartments. Deteriorating units are apparently prime candidates for removal, and the presence of old units has a mixed impact on conversion. The explanatory power of the conversion equations is high: their R^2 values are all over 0.9.

The six equations used to represent new construction and conversion activity in each zone have plausible, if somewhat ad hoc, specifications and perform fairly well, considering the aggregate level of data used. However, one potential specification problem lurks in the new construction equation ([8]), which assumes that output, Q, is measured as units of housing services. Equation (8) is only used to represent increases in Q that result from new construction, and $\Delta Q/Q$ is proxied by $\Delta N/N$, the proportional increase in all units attributable to new construction. The problem is that new units can be of different structure types and can therefore embody different amounts of added housing services. The specification of equation (8) thus assumes that a new efficiency apartment increases Q by the same proportion as a new single-family house in the same zone. The potential impact of this assumption can be analyzed by first writing the true model as

$$\frac{\Delta Q}{Q} = BX + u, \tag{9}$$

and by characterizing the assumption that $\Delta N/N$ proxies $\Delta Q/Q$ as

$$\frac{\Delta Q}{Q} = \frac{\Delta N}{N} + v. \tag{10}$$

Substitution of $\Delta N/N$ for $\Delta Q/Q$ in equation (9) yields the equation to be estimated:

$$\frac{\Delta N}{N} = BX + u - v. \tag{11}$$

Estimates of B will be unbiased if v is independent of X. I hypothesize that $\Delta N/N$ underestimates $\Delta Q/Q$ in zones where single-family houses are being constructed, and overestimates $\Delta Q/Q$ in zones where apartments are being constructed. If this is true, then v is likely to be correlated with one or more of the X's, and the coefficients will be biased. Weighting structure types differentially or stratifying the new construction equation by structure type are possible remedies to this problem.

A second problem with the supply side of the E/R model is that changes in the number of units are also the only measure of conversion activity. A large portion of the investment in existing dwelling units is devoted to upgrading the quality of existing units, rather than to altering their structure type; but very little provision is made for quality change on either the supply or the demand side of the E/R model. Moreover, the price index used in the model is based on repeated sales of dwelling units in each zone but has no measure of quality change. If some zones are being upgraded and others downgraded, the price index includes both price and quality changes and is actually an expenditure index.

When the supply side is considered in conjunction with the demand side, it becomes apparent that the overall E/R model is incomplete: the demand side produces a zonal allocation of households by income class; the supply side produces a zonal allocation of dwelling units by structure type. The unfinished step is the assignment within zones of household income classes to structure types. This omission clearly indicates that the E/R model is primarily a spatial allocation model that treats each housing market zone as an independent submarket; it also raises a number of accounting and specification questions about the model. For example, what prevents the number of households allocated to a zone from exceeding the number of units supplied? Should the vacancy rate be respecified so that low vacancy rates have a large deterrent effect on demand? In its present form, the model is more an econometric description of decennial development changes than a structural representation of development behavior.

In discussing the demand side of the E/R model, several parallels were drawn to DRAM, but the correspondence is obviously not complete. DRAM is intended to be a projective model, and values for its independent variables are relatively easy to forecast. The E/R model is not really a projective model, because the future values of many of its independent variables—such as prices, racial mix, and welfare enrollments—are not readily available, nor could they be regarded as exogenous.

Although most of the data required for estimation of the E/R model are derived from the decennial Census, some additional information on employment location and interzonal travel times is required. The parameter estimates are obtained with two-stage least squares, a technique familiar to econometricians and widely available in software packages. Since neither its data requirements nor its estimation procedures are as demanding as DRAM's, the E/R model should be easily transferable to other metropolitan areas.

Urban Institute Model

The Urban Institute (UI) model is a decided departure from the allocation-over-space approach characterized by the previous two models.[8] It attempts to represent a household's choice of both location and dwelling unit jointly in a market clearing context that may be envisioned as a form of Walrasian auction with re-contracting that continues until no further beneficial trades can be made. It is evident from table 5.2 that the UI model has relatively little spatial detail, and it emphasizes housing much more than spatial location. To a large extent the model's compact dimensions are related to its solution algorithm, which does not fare well as the dimensions of the model are increased.

The UI model represents a household's demand for housing by means of a utility function instead of a demand curve. The utility of the household depends on its income; the quantity of housing it consumes; the price of housing relative to other goods; and three zonal characteristics that can be called accessibility, neighborhood quality, and racial composition. The model is microanalytic and represents individual households, each with its own utility function. Households can differ by income and are categorized into one of two racial groups and one of two life cycle categories. Certain of the utility function parameters vary across the four race-lifecycle categories; none vary with income. The utility level household i would obtain from dwelling unit j in zone k can be summarized as

$$U_{ijk} = H_{ij} \cdot X_{ij} \cdot ZA_{ik} \cdot ZN_k \cdot ZR_{ik} , \tag{12}$$

where H_{ij} is a measure of housing services; X_{ij}, a measure of other goods; ZA_{ik}, a measure of zonal accessibility; ZN_k, a measure of neighborhood quality; and ZR_{ik}, a measure of racial composition. The two measures of housing and other goods have similar specifications:

$$H_{ij} = (Q_j - \gamma_1 \alpha_i Y_i/P_n)^{\alpha_i}, \tag{13}$$

$$X_{ij} = [(Y_i - P_jQ_j) - \gamma_1(1 - \alpha_i) Y_i]^{1-\alpha_i}. \tag{14}$$

In these expressions, Y_i is household "model income," Q_j is the quantity of housing services, P_j the price of housing services, P_n the price per unit of housing services in a new unit, and α_i and γ_1 are parameters. These two specifications collapse to the Cobb-Douglas form when γ_1 equals zero, and the portion of each expression containing γ_1 can be interpreted as a minimum required level of housing and other goods. The γ_1 parameter is a measure of the substitutability of housing for other goods, and a zero value indicates great substitutability; this parameter is constant for all households. The α_i parameter indicates the budget share spent on housing and has a different value for each race-lifecycle category. The basic Cobb-Douglas form used in equation (13) implies that the price elasticity of housing is -1 and the income elasticity is $+1$. In order to reduce the income elasticity of expenditure, household model income is defined as

$$Y_i = YA_i{}^{.6}\overline{Y}{}^{.4},$$ (14)

where YA_i is the household's actual income and $\overline{Y}$ is average household income. Equation (14) implies that the elasticity of household model income with respect to actual income is 0.6, and this value is also the actual income elasticity of demand for housing.

The zonal accessibility measure is a function of T_k, the zone's average round trip travel time in hours per month, and it is

$$ZA_{ik} = (200 - T_k)^{.5+\alpha_i-\alpha_1},$$ (15)

where α_1 is the value of α_i for white, nonelderly households and 200 represents the number of leisure hours per month that might be available for travel. Hence $(200 - T_k)$ is a measure of net leisure time. The neighborhood quality measure is

$$ZN_k = \frac{\overline{NR_k}}{\overline{\overline{NR}}}^{.01\gamma_2},$$ (16)

where $\overline{NR_k}$ is the average net rent per unit of housing services (net rent = price paid, less the cost of operating inputs) in zone k, $\overline{NR}$ is the average net rent over the modeled area, and γ_2 is a parameter that is constant for all households. The racial composition term is

$$ZR_{ik} = R_{ik} + [(1000/100 \, \gamma_3 + 1)],$$ (17)

where R_{ik} is the proportion of households in zone k of the same race as household i, and γ^3 is a parameter that is constant for all households. Given these specifications of the utility function, a total of seven parameters must be estimated to complete the demand side of the model. Moreover, two of the zonal characteristics, ZN and ZR, will be endogenous since their values vary as households change locations within the model.

The supply side of the model is somewhat simpler than the demand side in that it has only two parameters to be estimated. The supply side is based on a production function for housing services from existing units of the form

$$Q_j{}^1 = \left[B_1 + \left(2B_2 \frac{X_j}{Q_j{}^0} \right)^{1/2} \right] Q_j{}^0,$$ (18)

where Q_j^1 is the quantity of housing services produced by unit j at the end of the decade; Q_j^0 is the quantity produced at the beginning of the decade; X_j is additional capital inputs; and B_1 and B_2 are supply parameters. If no capital is added to a unit over the decade, the new quantity will be B_1 times the old, so $1 - B_1$ is a decadal depreciation rate. Equation (18) also implies that the addition of capital to an existing unit is subject to decreasing returns. Furthermore, since the production function does not include operating inputs, it is apparently impossible to substitute operating inputs for capital. Hence, the production function is fixed coefficients in terms of operating inputs and capital stock with decreasing returns to increments in capital stocks.

The marginal cost or supply function that is derived from the production function is

$$Q_j^1 = \left[B_1 + \frac{2}{3} B_2 \left(\frac{P_j - P_0}{P_C} \right) \right] Q_j^0 , \qquad (19)$$

where P_j is the marginal cost per unit of housing services; P_0 is the cost of operating inputs per unit of housing services; and P_C is the capital rental cost per unit of housing services for a newly constructed dwelling unit. Both P_C and P_0 are independent of Q. If no funds are spent on capital during the decade, the marginal cost of producing housing services with an existing unit is P_0, and it is again apparent (by setting $P_j = P_0$) that B_1 will be a survival rate for Q_j^0. Differentiating Q_j^1 with respect to P_j yields

$$\frac{2}{3} \frac{B_2 Q_0}{P_C} ,$$

which indicates that B_2 determines both the slope of the marginal cost curve and the price elasticity of supply. In addition to providing supply curves for existing units, the UI model has a sector that constructs new housing units with a constant returns to scale technology costing P_n per unit of housing services, and $P_n = P_0 + P_C$. Since new units are available at P_n, existing units will not typically operate if marginal cost exceeds P_n. Furthermore, P_0 is the minimum level of marginal cost for an existing unit, so the marginal cost and price observed for an existing unit will usually lie between P_0 and P_n.

The combination of supply curves and utility functions can be explained most easily with the aid of figure 5.1 and figure 5.2. The household utility function is illustrated in figure 5.1 as an indifference curve labeled U_o; the two price lines correspond to P_n, the price of new units, and P_o, the operating cost or minimum marginal cost of producing housing services with an existing unit. Figure 5.2 also contains the two price lines and the indifference curve, U_o. Since U_o is tangent to price line P_n in figure 5.1, it is

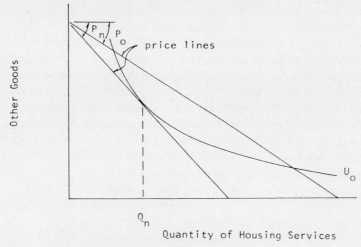

FIGURE 5.1   Household Choice in Quantity Space

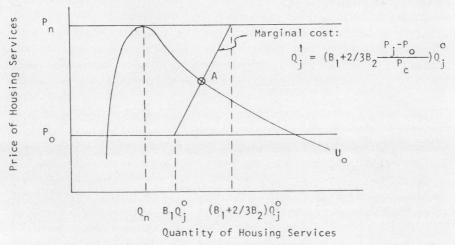

FIGURE 5.2   Household Choice in Price-Quantity Space

also tangent to price line P_n in figure 5.2, and Q_n represents the quantity of housing services a household would consume if it purchased a new dwelling unit. The solution algorithm works by first setting prices of all existing units at P_n, so that nearly all households will choose new units. The price of each existing unit is then lowered until the unit is preferred by a household, or until its price reaches P_o and no household chooses it. Prices are adjusted to maximize profits and households are assigned to units that maximize utility. In figure 5.2, these rules lead to the household's selection of an existing unit at the price-quantity combination labeled A. In the actual market-clearing algorithm, all households relocate during a model run, and an iterative search process produces an equilibrium. The algorithm produces multiple solutions that are treated in two ways. First, the rule that landlords maximize profits, and the procedure that prices are reduced from high levels are hypothesized to yield a unique outcome when there may be several possible market-clearing solutions. And second, when endogenous zonal attributes ZN and ZR produce multiple outcomes, the outcome closest to the original situation will be selected. For example, if many alternative racial combinations among zones are feasible, the solution having the least proportional change in racial composition relative to the base period is selected. The iterative solution procedure for forty households costs about $120 for computer time, but cost and solution difficulties increase significantly when more households or zones are added.

To set up the model, household and dwelling unit distributions are required, and the seven demand and two supply parameters must be estimated. Generating distributions of model households is fairly straightforward, since census data provide substantial amounts of information about households including income, race, and lifecycle. Households are first organized into race and lifecycle categories and sorted by income. Each category is then divided into several income intervals. Average interval incomes are used for each model household within the race and lifecycle categories. To obtain thirty model households in a typical metropolitan area with 600,000 households, each interval must contain roughly 20,000 households.

Obtaining distributions of dwelling units by the level of housing services produced is less straightforward, because housing services are unobservable and must be estimated. Since the initial distribution of model dwelling units by level of housing services is an important determinant of the model's parameters, a summary of its estimation follows. Census data provide information on housing expenditures, or price times quantity, so the determination of quantities requires that a price index be estimated for each of the model's zones. Using the Census public-use tapes, a hedonic index can be estimated for all dwelling units in metropolitan areas within the modeled city's state. This index incorporates unit characteristics plus two variables—the race of the occupant and a dummy variable for central-city location—as proxies for neighborhood quality. After the equation is estimated, the average value for each dwelling unit characteristic is calculated for each model zone. These average zonal values, plus the city-wide average for the neighborhood quality variables, are inserted into the estimated index and the predicted ($\hat{\bar{R}}_k$), as well as actual ($\tilde{\bar{R}}_k$), average rents are calculated for each zone. Then the actual value is divided by the predicted value to calculate relative price indexes for each zone:

$$P_k = \tilde{R}_k / \hat{R}_k . \tag{20}$$

Housing expenditures in each zone are transformed into quantities of housing services by means of these indexes. Dwelling units in each zone are sorted by rental value and divided into intervals; the average rent in each interval is calculated and divided by the price index to yield the model dwelling unit's quantity of housing services.

The possibility of misspecifying the underlying hedonic price index raises serious difficulties for this technique of formulating base period values for quantities of housing services. Suppose that the correctly specified hedonic price index is

$$R = B_0 + B_1 X_1 + B_3 X_3 + e. \tag{21}$$

In this case, the price index that is calculated will be (where single bars indicate zonal averages)

$$P_k = \frac{\overline{B_0 + B_1 X_1 + B_3 X_3 + e}}{B_0 + B_1 \overline{X} + B_3 \overline{\overline{X}}_3} , \tag{22}$$

and the price index will measure the average zonal effect of the error term plus the variation in X_3 relative to the city-wide average (indicated by two bars) value of X_3, where X_3 measures neighborhood effects. Hence, the price index is in effect a quantity index for neighborhood effects.

Let us set X_3 aside for the moment and consider what happens when X_1 is not the only measure of a unit's characteristics, and X_2 is a second omitted unit characteristic.[9] In this case, the true model is

$$R = B_0 + B_1 X_1 + B_2 X_2 + e, \tag{23}$$

but we mistakenly estimate

$$R = \mathcal{B}_0 + \mathcal{B}_1 X_1 + u. \tag{24}$$

We can determine the values of our estimated coefficients by doing the auxiliary regression

$$X_2 = b_0 + b_1 X_1 , \tag{25}$$

and solving to get

$$\mathcal{B}_0 = B_0 + B_2 b_0; \quad \mathcal{B}_1 = B_1 + B_2 b_1 . \tag{26}$$

Equation (24) is estimated over all metropolitan areas in a state; we will denote statewide averages for variables with three bars. Hence, we can transpose equation (25) and obtain

$$b_0 = \bar{\bar{\bar{X}}}_2 - b_1 \bar{\bar{\bar{X}}}_1 \ . \tag{27}$$

By substituting equations (27) and (26) into equation (24), we can formulate a new price index in parallel with equation (22), for this misspecified case, as

$$P_k = \frac{\overline{B_0 + B_1 X_1 + B_2 X_2 + e}}{B_0 + B_1 \bar{X}_1 + B_2 \bar{\bar{X}}_2 + b_1 B_2 \ (\bar{X}_1 - \bar{\bar{\bar{X}}}_1)} \ , \tag{28}$$

where one bar still indicates zonal averages. In this misspecified case, equation (28) reveals that P_k will have elements of a quantity index for unit characteristics. This is most evident when the value of b_1 is zero, for then P_k will indicate how the zonal average of X_2 differs from the statewide average of X_2, where X_2 is the omitted unit characteristic. This somewhat tedious exercise demonstrates that the price index interpretation of the calculation described by equation (20) is fairly sensitive to specification error, and that the "price index" obtained is likely to contain elements of a quantity index of both unit characteristics and neighborhood effects. Base period quantities of housing services in each zone will therefore be biased if the basic hedonic price index is misspecified. Since the Census public-use tapes do not include all relevant housing characteristics, some misspecification is probable.

Given the base period values for households and dwelling units, obtaining values for the nine major model parameters is the next step in model calibrations. Four of the model's parameters, the α_i's, can be estimated directly, because they are essentially rent-income ratios. The three gamma values and the two supply parameters are not amenable to direct estimation and result from calibration runs with the model. The gamma values are determined by running the model to assign model households to the model dwelling units in the base period. For this calibration, the quantities of housing services are fixed at their base period values by setting $B_1=1$ and $B_2=0$ in the supply equations. The model is then operated to produce results for alternative values of the gammas. Since quantities of housing services are fixed and average housing prices are used as a calibration criteria, the price indexes described above play a key role in determining the model's parameters.

Given values for the gammas, the two remaining supply side parameters are determined in an analogous fashion. The model is run from the base period (1960) to the end of the decade (1970), with varying values of B_1 and B_2. A problem akin to multicollinearity is encountered in estimating

B_1 and B_2; the calibration runs do not differentiate well among values of the two parameters that produce a constant value for $B_1 + \frac{2}{3} B_2$. An examination of figure 5.2 reveals that the calibration procedure can determine the point where a unit's supply curve intersects the P_n price line, but it cannot accurately determine the slope of the supply curve. The inability to distinguish combinations of B_1 and B_2 is troublesome, for changing their values alters the existing units' elasticity of supply and has a significant impact on model results.

The entire calibration procedure of the UI model is fairly straightforward, but it is subject to several reservations. First, the price indexes play a major role in establishing base period values for the level of housing services produced by model dwelling units. Housing service levels in turn play an important role in the calibration of the gamma parameters, as do the price indexes themselves, yet the indexes and housing service levels may well be misspecified because of the limited set of dwelling unit characteristics available in the Census public-use tapes. Second, the calibration procedures themselves have some inconsistencies. For example, both prices and quantities are empirically determined for the base period units, but during calibration of the gamma parameters the quantities are fixed and the prices are allowed to vary. The estimation of the hedonic and zonal price index is implicitly based on an assumption that long-run equilibrium holds, but the gamma calibration procedure contradicts this assumption. Another inconsistency inherent in the two-stage calibration procedure is that supply side parameters are conditional on a set of gamma parameters that are in turn conditional on yet another set of supply side parameters. It would seem to be relatively simple to iterate across the calibration procedures, or to calibrate all five parameters at once, so that the parameter values were consistent with one another. A final problem is the calibration procedure's fundamental dependence on overall model structure. Consider, for example, the contrast between the estimates of the α_i parameters and the supply parameters. The former are rent-income ratios, and their values are independent of model specification, the form of the utility function, and so forth. The B_1 and B_2 parameter values, on the other hand, depend on the details of the market clearing algorithm and the entire model specification. Given the collinearity problem between B_1 and B_2, it would seem advisable to develop independent estimates of $1-B_1$, the ten-year depreciation rate of dwelling units, from nonmodel sources.

Beyond calibration problems, there are three shortcomings evident in the overall structure of the UI model. First, the model's market clearing algorithm is costly to use and its properties are not well understood. Moreover, the capacity of the solution algorithm places severe constraints on the number of households and zones that the model can accommodate. Second, the supply, or marginal cost, curve is used to determine prices in a way that is inconsistent with the usual theoretical result that entrepreneurs set their prices at the point where marginal cost equals marginal revenue. In the UI model, a unit's price of housing services (or average revenue) is set equal to the marginal cost of providing the services, and marginal revenue plays no role in the determination of output.[10] Changing this feature of the model may be fairly difficult and require changes in the market clearing algorithm. Finally, the temporal discreteness of the model makes it inappropriate for analyses in which short-run policy impacts may be important. The time period used in the model can be shortened to less than ten years, but using the model for periods as short as one year would weaken its utility because of its strong equilibrium orientation (all households are relocated each period, etc.).

Despite these shortcomings, the UI model has several strengths, not the least of which is its extensive reliance on decennial Census data. Except for the average zonal travel times, nearly all of the data used in the UI model are Census based. The model is therefore readily transferable from one city to another and may be calibrated using a special set of software. Thus far, the model has been calibrated to over half a dozen U.S. cities. The UI model also deals jointly with a household's choice of dwelling and location; this simultaneous treatment is perhaps its most significant accomplishment. Although the model's policy uses have to date focused on the evaluation of housing allowance programs, it is well suited for the analysis of other financial programs; however, its spatial aggregation renders it less useful for traditional planning problems.

NBER Urban Simulation Model

The basic objective of the NBER model—like the UI model—is to represent a household's choice of both dwelling unit and location within an urban housing market.[11] One major structural difference, however, is that in the UI model households are represented as making this choice simultaneously, whereas in the NBER model the choice is represented sequentially. The substantial savings in computation cost resulting from a sequential representation of the dwelling unit-location choice enables the NBER model to have extensive dimensional detail: nearly 200 residential zones and 20 workzones, a spatial disaggregation approaching that of DRAM.

The NBER model is microanalytic; its current version stores data for 70,000 to 85,000 individual households and dwelling units. Each observation is processed by the model during each model period. Such a large sample of households is processed each period to avoid the small-numbers problem that occurs when very few households choose particular types of dwelling units or locate in particular zones.

Relocating only a portion of all households each period is a second major structural difference of the NBER model. The incremental adjustment process incorporated in the NBER model adds stability when household locations aggregate to produce externalities—such as zonal neighborhood quality or racial composition—and it allows the model's adjustment path to have a larger impact on model outcome. However, allowing only a fraction of the households to move each period requires that the model include more households, so that moving behavior is reasonably representative. In the one-year model period, 12,000 to 18,000 households participate in the housing market. The number of participating households must exceed a minimum level to avoid the small-numbers problem. Accordingly, the sample size employed by the model is related to the model's number of zones, number of housing types, and time period represented.

In addition to the characteristics in table 5.2, the NBER model maintains records of each head of household's labor-force status, industry, occupation, and housing tenure (own or rent). These latter characteristics can affect employment changes, decisions to relocate, and the choice of tenure, but they are not determinants of location or dwelling unit choice. In its representation of dwelling units, the NBER model uses zonal characteristics similar to those in the UI model (neighborhood quality; racial composition and distance from the nearest ghetto; general accessibility). The dwelling units representation could be described as a combination of the approaches used in the UI and E/R models. The first major dwelling unit dimension is structure type, which defines the number of units in a building (single-family; small multi-family; large multi-family), the size of the unit in number of bedrooms (three categories for single-family; two for each multi-family structure type), and two lot size categories for single-family units (one-eighth and three-eighths of an acre). The ten structure types embody the general configuration of the unit, and major investment is required to change a unit from one structure type to another. The second major dwelling unit dimension—structure services—could be characterized as the quality level produced by the unit. This dimension is relatively easy to change through incremental investment or by altering the unit's level of operating inputs; therefore, it is not an essential determinent of a household's residential choice. Neighborhood quality takes one of five values and is based on a zone's average level of structure services. The major characteristics desired by households in the NBER model are structure type and neighborhood quality, which together define fifty different housing bundle types.

The demand side of the NBER model represents changes in demographic characteristics including household size, income level, and age of the head of household. Changes in the age of the head of household are straightforward; every year the head becomes a year older. Changes in household size and income level are based on two sets of cumulative transition probabilities and a random number draw. The household size transition probabilities are derived from restrospective interview data, and the income level transition probabilities reflect data available on age-earning profiles. The demand side also includes a rudimentary job change submodel that uses a simple search procedure to locate a new job for a head of household, whose decision to leave a job is a function of changes in employment levels by workplace and occupation, as well as job separation rates that vary by industry, occupation, and race. Cumulative job separation probabilities combine these two factors, and random number draws are used to determine whether each head of household keeps his job in a given period. Those who have lost their jobs search for new ones, first in their old work zone; then in workzones between their residence and the CBD; and finally in all other workzones.

The probability that a household moves during the period varies only with the head of household's age, current housing tenure, change in family size, and change in employment; neighborhood variables are omitted. Moving households are then augmented by new households and immigrants to satisfy exogenous population targets. All households seeking housing are placed on a demand list, and all vacant units are placed on an available units list, to be used by the model's supply side.

The 12,000 to 18,000 households on the demand list are then assigned to one of the fifty housing bundles (ten structure types multiplied by five neighborhood qualities) included in the model. This assignment is carried out with a set of demand equations estimated using data from the modeled metropolitan area. A separate demand equation for each of ninety-six household classes (six income categories times eight lifecycle categories times 2 races) predicts the probability that a household of class H and workplace J will choose a housing bundle type K. The general form of the demand equations is

$$\text{PROB}(K \mid H, J) = f\{A(H, K)$$
$$+ B(H) \cdot \text{MGP}(K, H, J) + C(H) \cdot [\log \text{AVAIL}(K)]\}, \quad (29)$$

where $\text{PROB}(K|H,J)$ is the probability that K will be chosen given H and J; MGP is the minimum gross price of unit K for a household of type H working at J; AVAIL is the total number of vacant available units of type K in the modeled area; A, B, and C are estimated parameters; and f represents the multinomial logit specification. Letting f symbolize the expression within the braces in equation (29), the multinomial form would be

$$\text{PROB}(K \mid H, J) = \frac{e^f}{\sum_k e^f}. \quad (30)$$

The minimum gross price, MGP, in the demand equation is derived from a numerical approximation of the household's optimal location for bundle K, as predicted by a traditional travel cost-location rent trade-off model.[12] The total cost or gross price of type K housing in residence zone I to a household of type H working in zone J is the sum of (1) the market price of a type K unit in zone I; (2) the travel cost from I to J for household H in terms of out-of-pocket costs, travel time, and nonwork travel cost for zone I; and (3) the discrimination cost incurred by black households. Discrimination costs thus influence the choice of unit, as well as the choice of location. The household characteristics that influence gross prices are income (travel time is valued at four-tenths of the hourly wage) and race (blacks are assumed to encounter a discrimination markup that varies with zone I's racial composition and its distance from a major ghetto). The AVAIL variable in equation (29) can be interpreted as a price proxy, much in the way vacancy rates are used in the demand equations of the E/R model.

The NBER model calculates a gross price for each zone and selects the minimum gross price for use in the demand equations for house type. In fact, the location that defines this minimum price is not used in the NBER model at this point; only the bundle type chosen is recorded. The household's location choice is explicitly determined only in the market clearing step of the model.

Before moving to the supply side of the model, two aspects of the demand side deserve comment. First, the representation of the household's decision to move could obviously be enriched in this version of the model through the implementation of some form of a stock adjustment mechanism. For example, the demand equations could be used to predict the household's current most-likely-choice of structure type and neighborhood quality. If this most-likely-choice was quite different from its current unit, the household would become a moving household. This procedure could be costly to implement but might provide a better prediction of movers. It should be emphasized that in this model, moving households play a key role since their demands influence the marginal changes in housing stocks over time. Experiments with the model have shown that changes in the composition of moving households have a significant effect on model outcomes. Second, the use of *minimum* gross prices in the demand equations might produce shocks or cyclical behavior if the minimum prices exhibit high variability over time. More experience is required with other specifications of this term in the demand equations to assess the problem's potential severity.

Because supply activity in the NBER model is largely determined by the expected profitability of new construction and conversion, the model must first project expected rents for future periods. This is done with a naive trend extrapolation based on rents for the past four periods; expected rents are discounted to yield present values of revenue for each housing bundle in each neighborhood. Demand targets for each housing bundle are also forecast as a function of rent level and changes in population and income. Present market prices of dwelling units and land are calculated by the model; new construction and conversion costs are an exogenous input. With these price and cost data, the model calculates and ranks the expected profitability of all possible new construction and conversion activity; then supply activities are carried out, starting with the most profitable, until the demand targets are satisfied. Vacant land and available vacant units are used as inputs and thereby act as constraints on supply activities.

Supply activities may require more than one period to complete, so the list of currently available units is updated to reflect new structures initiated in previous periods. Upgrading or investment activities that do not change the structure type of units are also represented in the supply side of the NBER model, and their extent is also influenced by expected profitability. Available vacant units that result from supply activity are described by structure type, location, and inventories of several types of capital stocks that are used to produce structure services—the quality dimension of housing.

Although this matrix of available units by bundle type and location resembles the supply side results of the E/R model, the NBER model's demand equations assign households to bundle types, rather than households to locations. The task remaining for the market-clearing portion of the NBER model is the assignment of households to locations within each bundle type.

This allocation is performed separately for each of the fifty bundle types by a linear programming algorithm of the Hitchcock, or transportation, type. The objective function minimizes total travel and discrimination cost for households in each bundle type. The algorithm also generates shadow prices for each zone and bundle type that are used to revise market prices for the next period. To form location rents, the shadow prices are averaged with past-period shadow prices by means of a set of exponentially decreasing weights.[13] Market prices are calculated by adding supply costs to these location rents. These endogeneously calculated market prices are then used in the next period as determinants of household demand and market supply activity. This use of endogenously calculated prices over a sequence of periods is perhaps the most distinctive feature of the NBER model.

When households have been assigned to specific units in particular residence zones, supply activity involving the production of structure services is carried out. A particular household's demand for structure services is compared with the dwelling unit's marginal cost of supplying those services, and investment or disinvestment in capital stocks that supply structure services is undertaken.

The result of the demand, supply, and market-clearing portions of the NBER model are: (1) new assignment of households to dwelling units by location; (2) investment and disinvestment in existing units; (3) construction of new units; and (4) projections of housing prices by structure type and location for the next period. Although the model is dimensionally large, it is not prohibitively expensive to operate. Annual simulations for a decade cost from $160 to $340, or from 1.3 to 3.0 times the cost of executing the UI for a decade. Solving the linear programming problems each year accounts for roughly thirty percent of the total execution cost.

Some difficulties with the NBER model structure or specification have already been mentioned; they will now be reviewed. Sequential, rather than simultaneous, representation of a household's choice of structure type and location is obviously a simplification at variance with reality. Households can in fact trade off location attributes for dwelling unit characteristics, and it would be useful to represent this in the model. Moreover, separation of dwelling unit choices from location choices in the NBER model can result in more households selecting a bundle type than can be accommodated by the current stock of available units. When demand exceeds supply for a bundle type, prices are raised and the nonlocated households immediately become movers in the subsequent period. It would be more realistic if those households re-entered the market in the current period. However, experiments have shown that allowing nonlocated households to choose another bundle type (by iterating over the demand side) is very expensive.

A second weakness of the NBER model is its use of calibration rather than estimation to produce values for such parameters as the discrimination markups used to calculate gross prices and to allocate households to locations. The discrimination markups result from a series of experiments with the market or spatial allocation submodel; those markups that best reproduced the spatial distributions of blacks and whites in Pittsburgh and Chicago were selected for use in the model. The expectational framework used to project future rents for the supply side calculations also results from calibration, as does the set of exponentially declining weights used to combine current and past-period shadow prices to form location rents. The calibration procedures that determine each of these parameter values are not well documented. Moreover, as pointed out in regard to the UI model, calibration procedures depend on the specification of the overall model.

The linear programming procedure used in the market-clearing section of the NBER model has several strengths: solution algorithms are very efficient; the solutions produced have well-known properties; and the shadow prices have useful interpretations. In earlier versions of the model, the linear programming model minimized travel cost, and the shadow prices were interpreted as location rents. In the current version, however, the matrix of costs to be minimized includes discrimination markups and other elements in addition to travel cost. Hence, interpretations of the shadow prices may have to be altered to reflect these non–travel costs. Experience with the current version of the NBER model also suggests that the programming assignments tend to locate high-income households too close to their workplaces. The model's authors speculate that this probably occurs because the lot sizes of single-family houses do not vary enough in the model. Demand for large lots is very income elastic; high-income households that locate far from their workplaces often do so in order to purchase a large lot. Since the model's largest single-family lot is three-eighths of an acre, additional large-lot size categories may be necessary to produce more accurate location choices for high-income households.

The properties of the ranking procedure used to determine the location and extent of new construction and conversions are not well understood. The representation of these activities seems to call for a large linear programming problem that maximizes profits over all supply activities. The ranking procedure employed corresponds to a technique that is often used to determine the first feasible solutions in linear program solution algorithms. It is unknown how close this solution is to one that maximizes profits.

A final difficulty in the NBER model relates to the empirical support for the supply of dwelling quality. Although more is known now than ever before about supply side relationships, the magnitude of many supply side parameters is still imprecise. For example, the elasticity of substitution between operating inputs and capital stocks used in the production of services from existing units is not known very accurately. Similarly, the extent to which existing units suffer from decreasing returns to scale in the production of housing services is also subject to debate. The results obtained from most housing market models are inclined to be quite sensitive to these two parameters.

The NBER model may well be the most difficult of the four models surveyed to set up for a new city. The demand equation parameters have been estimated using a household survey, in combination with decennial Census data; many of the transition probabilities used in the demand side of the model are based on special data sets, although some are estimated from Census data; the data used to specify the start-up list of households and dwelling units are derived from Census data. In general, the NBER model has increased its reliance on Census data, which is a widely available and standardized data set that allows for a model's relatively easy transferral from one urban area to another.

There is some uncertainty about the cost of transferring the NBER model to other metropolitan areas, because many of its parameters will probably not have to be recalibrated for each new city. For example, the transition probabilities used to represent demographic change probably do not differ widely across cities. To date, the NBER model has been used to represent the Pittsburgh and Chicago housing markets; these two model versions have many parameters in common, and the demand equations have been only partially reestimated, using Census data, for Chicago. Although the NBER model has been used almost solely to analyze the impact of housing allowance programs, its policy applications could include many other housing market, employment location, and transport/land-use issues.

3. MODEL EVALUATION AND VALIDATION

This review of four urban development models has focused on their structure and specification and avoided comparisons of their relative validity. Model validation is often raised with respect to simulation models, because their structure is frequently more realistic than those of other approaches. The complexity that accompanies the greater realism of such models obscures their limitations and makes it difficult to know intuitively which results to attend and which to ignore. Furthermore, the general model description probably reveals little about the model's workings; the term *simulation model* can apply to almost any set of mathematical manipulations.

The complexity and difficulty of intuitively comprehending computer based models would be less problematic if ample detailed reviews and critiques of them were available—few critical analyses were produced during the early years of computer based urban development models, and there is still relatively little activity in this area. The literature on models tends toward taxonomy rather than critical review. Peer review, the traditional mechanism of quality control used in research, has tended to break down when applied to computer based urban models because the cost of learning precisely how someone else's model works is extremely high. This high cost of review has produced what is essentially a market failure, and relatively few comprehensive reviews of urban development models are available. For some other applications of computer based models, however, the cost of peer review is not always high. For example, persons constructing quarterly macroeconomic models all typically use the same data and are attempting to do the same thing—forecast economic aggregates for the next several quarters. Given this commonality of data and purpose, it is relatively easy for the designer of one macro-model to review another. In the field of urban development, however, models have typically been based on non–comparable data sets for particular cities, and their objectives often differ; experience with one model, therefore, has not always developed the expertise that could be used to evaluate another. In addition, for many early computer based urban development models documentation was nonexistent, and computer listings were proprietary. Detailed reviews were thus virtually impossible; modelers could not learn from one another's mistakes; and knowledge did not cumulate. The situation has improved dramatically in terms of the documentation for more recent models, which are beginning to incorporate more common objectives and to use Census data that is comparable though from different cities.

In reviewing or evaluating a model our concern should be to determine which results do and which do not deserve to be taken seriously, and not whether the model has passed through a particular validation ritual. Particular attention should be paid to the model's general specification in relation to theory; its key simplifications, given its objectives; and the determination of model parameters. Models that are transferable from one site to another are more readily checked for reproducibility in terms of parameter estimates and results. This is important, for reproducibility is a prime prerequisite of good science.

4. ISSUES IN MODEL DEVELOPMENT

The four models reviewed above have different objectives and structures, yet they share common omissions and shortcomings in their attempt to represent urban development. Some of these shortcomings may prove very difficult to overcome, or require skills not possessed by persons generally involved in modeling efforts at this time; others either require special data sets or more attention than they have received. This section briefly summarizes several issues that should be addressed in future model development.

Operation of the Local Public Sector

The above review of four urban development models indicates that none of them attempts to represent the operation of the local public sector. The E/R model makes taxes and output of public goods exogenous, whereas the UI and NBER models use measures of neighborhood quality as reduced-form proxies for the level of local public goods. Our understanding of the determinants of local public good demand and supply may recommend this simple approach, but it would be useful to introduce a representation of local public good demand—such as a median voter model—into a dynamic model of urban development. This general issue warrants exploration because a great deal of empirical and theoretical work suggests that local public services are important determinants of residential location and housing price. Local public services, like housing services, are a bundle of heterogeneous attributes that different households are inclined to value differently. Accordingly, systematic differences in the composition of public service bundles across residential locations may have an impact on residential location that is impossible to capture with a single neighborhood quality variable. It is possible that the demand for some components of local public services are highly correlated with the demands for some components of the housing bundle,[14] but much empirical work would be required to substantiate the hypothesis. In the meantime, the local public sector constitutes an important omitted variable in most computer based urban development models.

Supply Side of the Housing Market

The supply side of the housing market has received less attention than the demand side in empirical work. Long-run analyses of demand often assume that housing is produced with a constant returns to scale technology, an assumption that is probably realistic for new construction. Existing units are long-lived, however, and have an important bearing on housing production over years and even decades. Until recently, relatively little empirical work has been done on the supply characteristics of existing units,[15] and some of the supply parameters used in models of urban development are specified exogenously rather than estimated. Studies being carried out in connection with HUD's housing allowance experiments are increasing our understanding of the production functions of existing units, but more empirical work is required to determine the elasticity of substitution among inputs and the existence of decreasing returns to scale in existing units. Unfortunately, estimates of the elasticity of substitution among inputs to existing units typically assume that the existing units have constant returns to scale.[16] The substitution elasticity determines the shape of the short-run marginal cost or supply curve for existing units, whereas the returns to scale factor determines the shape of the long-run marginal cost or supply curve for existing units. It is difficult to overstate the significance of these parameters in models of urban development, yet we still know less than we should about their values.

Determinants of Employment Location

The location of employment is explicitly represented in only two of the four models reviewed here, but changes in employment location will have a great impact on model forecasts. Fairly accurate projections of jobs by workplace can be made for population-serving employment, but that category only encompasses about 20 percent of all jobs. The other 80 percent, including regional service and export employment, have location determinants that are poorly understood. The result is that our forecasts of urban development or analyses of policy impacts are typically conditional on exogenous forecasts of employment location. Most of the research on employment location carried out over the past ten years deals primarily with manufacturing employment, and even less is known about the location determinants of service employment.[17] Developing accurate models of employment location will probably require substantial additional research.

Metropolitan Land Markets

Despite the slight attention it has received relative to the market for housing, the land market plays a key integrating role in models of urban development. The land market is the major intermediary between competing
residential and nonresidential uses. More theoretical and empirical analyses
of the determinants of the demand, supply, and price of land are required
to demonstrate how efficiently land markets work in metropolitan areas,
and how well they perform their allocative function. For example, we currently know relatively little about the role played by land speculators.

CONCLUSION

The foregoing topics represent the major substantial areas in which existing
computer based models of urban development are deficient. Other areas
could doubtless be added, but these four deserve priority for research or
model development: research findings in each area could be adapted into
existing models and could improve significantly our ability to analyze
policies that affect patterns of urban development. It is not surprising that
a review of urban models concludes with a list of future research needs;
attempts to construct consistent representations of urban development
quickly reveal major gaps in our knowledge. One significant side benefit of
urban models has been their helpfulness in structuring research programs
in urban economics.

NOTES

1. See Brown et al. (1972), for a synopsis of six planning models, and Ohls and
Hutchinson (1974), for a summary of twelve reviews of urban development models.
2. Lowry (1964).
3. For a summary of Lowry model derivatives, see Goldner (1971), and Batty
(1972).
4. The description here is based on Putman (1976).
5. See Brown et al. (1972), for a discussion of this problem. DRAM's author was
well aware of this problem, but data limitations forced the estimation of an average
share model.
6. Engle et al. (1972) and Engle (1974a and 1974b).
7. The discussion here is based on Bradbury et al. (1977).
8. This discussion is based mainly on de Leeuw and Struyk (1975).
9. X_3 is omitted here merely to simplify the equations.
10. I am indebted to Raymond Struyk and Larry Ozanne for this point. Of course,
setting price equal to marginal cost is appropriate for owner occupants.
11. The discussion in this section is based on Kain, Apgar, and Ginn (1976).
An earlier version is described in Ingram, Kain, and Ginn (1972).
12. See, for example, Kain and Ingram (1974).
13. These weights are derived from an adaptive expectations model.
14. See Straszheim (1977), for an exposition of this approach.

15. Recent studies include Ozanne and Struyk (1976), and Ingram, Leonard, and Schafer (1976).
16. This is true in Ingram et al. (1976) and in Peter Rydell (1975).
17. For example, see Hamer (1975), Leone (1974), Schmenner (1973), and Struyk and James (1975).

REFERENCES

Batty, M. 1972. "Recent Developments in Land Use Modeling: A Review of British Research." *Urban Studies* 9: 151–77.

Bradbury, K.; Engle, R.; Levine, O.; and Rothenberg, J. 1977. "Simultaneous Estimation of the Supply and Demand for Household Location in a Multizonal Metropolitan Area." In *Residential Location and Urban Housing Markets.* Cambridge, Mass.: Ballinger. Edited by G. K. Ingram.

Brown, H. J.; Ginn, J. R.; James, F. J.; and Straszheim, M. R. 1972. *Empirical Models of Urban Land Use.* New York: Columbia University Press.

de Leeuw, F., and Struyk, R. 1975. *The Web of Urban Housing.* Washington, D.C.: Urban Institute.

Engle, R. F. 1972. "An Econometric Simulation Model of Intra-Metropolitan Housing Location: Housing, Business, Transportation, and Local Government." *American Economic Review* 62 (May): 87–97.

———. 1974*a*. "Disequilibrium Model of Regional Investment." *Journal of Regional Science* 14: 367–76.

———. 1974*b*. "Issues in the Specification of an Econometric Model of Urban Growth." *Journal of Urban Economics* 1: 250–67.

Fromm, G.; Hamilton, W. L.; and Hamilton, D. E. 1974. *Federally Supported Mathematical Models: Survey and Analysis.* Final Report under National Science Foundation Contract NSF-C-804. Washington, D.C.: U.S. Government Printing Office, June.

Goldner, W. 1971. "The Lowry Model Heritage." *Journal of the American Institute of Planners* 37: 100–110.

Hamer, A. M. 1975. *Industrial Exodus from the Central City.* Lexington, Mass.: D. C. Heath.

Ingram, G. K.; Kain, J. F.; and Ginn, J. R. 1972. *The Detroit Prototype of the NBER Urban Simulation Model.* New York: Columbia University Press.

Ingram, G. K.; Leonard, H. B.; and Schafer, R. 1976. "Simulation of the Market Effects of Housing Allowances." Vol. 3: "Development of the Supply Sector of the NBER Model." Final Report Prepared for the U.S. Department of Housing and Urban Development.

Kain, J. F., and Ingram, G. K. 1974. "The NBER Urban Simulation Model as a Theory of Urban Spatial Structure." In *Urban and Social Economics in Market and Planned Economies.* New York: Praeger. Edited by A. Brown, J. Licari, and E. Neuberger.

Kain, J. F.; Apgar, W. C., Jr.; and Ginn, J. R. 1976. "Simulation of the Market Effects of Housing Allowances." Vol. 1: "Description of the NBER Urban Simulation Model." Final Report Prepared for the U.S. Department of Housing and Urban Development, August.

Koopmans, T. C. and Beckman, M. 1957. "Assignment Problems and the Location of Economic Activities." *Econometrica* 25: 53–76.

Leone, R. A. 1974. *Location of Manufacturing in the New York Metropolitan Area.* New York: National Bureau of Economic Research.

Lowry, I. S. 1964. *A Model of Metropolis.* Santa Monica, Calif.: RAND, RM-4035-RC.

Mills, E., and MacKinnon, J. 1973. "Notes on the New Urban Economics." *Bell Journal of Economics and Management Science* 4: 593–601.

Nelson, Richard R., and Winter, Sidney G. 1977. "Simulation of Schumpeterian Competition." *American Economic Review* 67: 271–76.

Ohls, James C., and Hutchinson, Peter. 1974. "Models in Urban Development." In *A Guide to Models in Government Planning and Operations.* Report Prepared for the U.S. Environmental Protection Agency, August.

Orcutt, G. H.; Greenberger, M.; Korbel, J.; and Rivlin, A. M. 1961. *Microanalysis of Socioeconomic Systems.* New York: Harper and Row.

Ozanne, L., and Struyk, R. 1976. *Housing from the Existing Stock.* Washington, D.C.: Urban Institute Paper 221-CO.

Putman, S. H. 1976. *Laboratory Testing of Predictive Models.* Final Report under National Science Foundation Contract NSF-GI-38978; available as U.S. Department of Transportation Report P5010.

Rydell, C. Peter. 1975. "Rental Housing in Site I, Characteristics of Capital Stock at Baseline." Santa Monica, Calif.: RAND, WN-8978-HUD.

Schelling, T. C. 1969. "Models of Segregation." *American Economic Review* 59: 488–93.

Schmenner, R. 1973. "City Taxes and Industry Location." Ph.D. diss., Yale University.

Straszheim, Mahlon. 1977. "Interdependencies between Public Sector Decisions and the Urban Housing Market." In *Residential Location and Urban Housing Markets.* Cambridge, Mass.: Ballinger. Edited by G. K. Ingram.

Struyk, R., and James, F. 1975. *Intra-metropolitan Industrial Location.* Lexington, Mass.: D. C. Heath.

Tiebout, C. M. 1956. "A Pure Theory of Local Expenditures." *Journal of Political Economy* 64 (October): 416–22.

6

THE BENEFITS OF RESERVED BUS LANES, MASS TRANSIT SUBSIDIES, AND MARGINAL COST PRICING IN ALLEVIATING TRAFFIC CONGESTION

HERBERT MOHRING

INTRODUCTION

Laments are common about the quality of urban transportation services, particularly as regards the extreme levels of peak hour congestion often experienced. Among the techniques that have been proposed to alleviate this congestion are marginal cost pricing of street capacity, mass transit subsidies, and preferential access to freeway and street capacity for mass transit vehicles. This study provides rough quantifications of the benefits derivable from the application, singly and in combination, of these techniques.

Regarding the ameliorative techniques studied, the procedures currently employed to price the services of urban street and expressway capacity confer a substantial subsidy to automobile travel, particularly during peak hours. The basic toll (gasoline and some other user taxes) paid by users of urban road capacity falls far short of the cost that each peak hour traveler's contribution to traffic congestion imposes on other travelers. Many economists have espoused a solution to this problem that is simple in concept: eliminate the subsidy to automobile travel by imposing tolls that fully reflect the costs auto trips impose on other travelers.

Whether because of technological or political problems, pricing solutions

Herbert Mohring is a professor of economics at the University of Minnesota.

Financial support for this research was provided by the University of Toronto-York University Joint Program in Transportation. I am indebted to Donald Dewees and Helen Tauchen for helpful advice and to Tauchen and Sampson Chan for computer assistance.

to traffic congestion have rarely been adopted. Indeed, Singapore so far remains unique among major cities in having put into effect the equivalent of peak hour auto tolls. Far more common are subsidies to existing mass transit services and the construction of new mass transit facilities, in the full expectation that their revenues will fall far short of their costs. In addition, techniques for giving buses preferential access to arterial capacity are growing in importance. These techniques include providing buses and, in some cases, car pools with reserved street and expressway lanes and expressway access ramps, as well as proposals for electronic systems that would give bus drivers control over traffic signals.

This study provides rough quantifications of the benefits of these procedures for ameliorating traffic congestion by developing five quite complicated but still highly simplified models of travel behavior along an urban traffic artery. Numerical results are obtained by solving these models for reasonably realistic alternative values of the several parameters they contain. The five models have several common ingredients. In all of them, along each mile of a one-way street, N people per hour desire to begin trips, each M miles in length. Each traveler faces the same fare for a bus trip and the same, higher, dollar cost for auto travel. Travelers differ, however, in the amount they are willing to pay to save travel time. Each traveler chooses the travel mode that provides him with the lower "full price" of a trip, i.e., with the lower sum of dollar outlay plus value of required travel time. Each model determines the amount of bus service and the number of bus (and hence auto) travelers that minimize *total* travel costs.[1] These total costs include not only those incurred in providing the services of buses and autos but also the total value to travelers of the time their trips require.

In model 1, the number of bus travelers, N_b, is arbitrarily specified and the level of bus service that minimizes total costs is determined. Model 2 determines the cost minimizing modal split, N_b/N, and service levels. Model 3 adds the possibility of preferential treatment for buses; specifically, it allows for restricting a fraction, η, of the street for use only by buses, with the remainder of the street being employed only by autos. In models 4 and 5, auto tolls are fixed arbitrarily and the deficit that may be incurred in providing bus service is less than would be necessary to achieve a modal split that minimizes total costs. These last two models differ in that 5 allows for reserved bus lanes, whereas 4 does not.

Section 1 provides a formal development of the models; section 2 describes the numerical values of their solutions when their parameters are assigned values that were more or less realistic in the Twin Cities Metropolitan Area during 1974. The number of variables and parameters contained in models 1 through 5 is bewilderingly large. Appendix A therefore lists and defines them and indicates the values assigned to them in the empirical analysis. Appendix B details the rationales underlying the assignment of parameter values.

1. THE STEADY STATE TRAFFIC ARTERY MODELS

The models that generate the numerical results described in section 2 are quite complex. In addition, transportation differs from the commodities normally considered in economic analyses in an important respect. If it costs one manufacturer 20¢ to produce a widget, and another $10.00, the high-cost producer will soon go out of business. But suppose that a millionaire wishes to make a trip. Although he attaches a far higher value to his time than does an unemployed ditchdigger, he cannot employ the ditchdigger to perform the service for him. These considerations suggest the desirability of introducing with a simple example that both provides an overview of the models that follow and suggests important elements of similarity between transportation and more commonly considered commodities.

Suppose, then, that N people per hour desire to travel between two points and that two physically separate modes, f for fast and s for slow, are available. The time it takes is the only cost of travel. On mode i ($i = f, s$), time per trip equals $f_i(N_i, K_i)$ where N_i and K_i are respectively the actual and the maximum possible hourly rates of travel by the mode. Travelers differ in the values they attach to their travel time. Specifically, ranking travelers in ascending order of time values, $v(x)$ is the amount traveler x would be willing to pay to save an hour of travel time. If travelers are divided between the two modes so that those with time values of $v(N_s)$ or less use the slow mode with the remainder traveling on the fast mode, total short-run travel costs can be approximated by

$$C_{SR} = t_s \int_0^{N_s} v(x) \, dx + t_f \int_{N_s}^N v(x) \, dx . \tag{1}$$

Since $N_s + N_f = N, dN_f/dN_s = -1$. This being the case, differentiating with respect to N_s and rearranging terms yields

$$(t_s - t_f) v(N_s) = \frac{\partial t_f}{\partial N_f} \int_{N_s}^N v(x) \, dx - \frac{\partial t_s}{\partial N_s} \int_0^{N_s} v(x) \, dx$$

$$= N_f \, V_f \, \partial t_f/\partial N_f - N_s \, V_s \, \partial t_s/\partial N_s \tag{2}$$

as the first order condition for achieving a cost-minimizing modal split, i.e., a cost-minimizing allocation of travelers between the two modes. In equation (2), V_i denotes the average value of travel time for all mode i travelers.

The left-hand side of equation (2) equals the difference between the direct costs to traveler N_s of trips on the two modes. The right-hand side equals the difference between the costs an additional trip would impose on all other users of the two modes. The market would achieve such a cost minimizing modal split if a toll of $N_i V_i \, \partial t_i / \partial N_i$ is imposed on *each* mode i traveler. With such tolls in effect, anyone who values his time at less than $v(N_s)$ would find the sum of the time and money costs of a slow mode trip to be less than that of a fast mode trip. The reverse would be true of someone with a travel time value greater than $v(N_s)$. Finally, traveler N_s himself would have no preferred mode.

In the long run, travel costs can be altered by adjusting slow and fast mode capacities and by shifting travelers between the two modes. Suppose that the hourly cost of a unit of mode i capacity is P_i, an amount that is independent of the mode's total capacity, then long-run total costs can be written:

$$C_{LR} = C_{SR} + P_s K_s + P_f K_f \tag{3}$$

where C_{SR} is given by equation (1). Differentiating with respect to K_i yields

$$- N_i V_i \, \partial t_i / \partial K_i = P_i . \tag{4}$$

In words, mode i capacity should be adjusted to equate the hourly cost of a unit of this capacity with the value of the time savings that unit would afford mode i travelers.

Assume, in addition, that travel time per trip on mode i takes the form $t_i(N_i, K_i) = t_i(N_i/K_i)$. This assumption, together with that underlying equation (3), serves to make both modes subject to constant returns to scale. A doubling of both travel volume, N_i, and the resources devoted to capacity, $P_i K_i$, leaves travel time per trip unchanged and hence doubles total travel time inputs. Given this special form for the travel time function, $\partial t_i / \partial K_i$ can be written $t_i' N_i / K_i^2$. Substituting this expression in equation (4) and multiplying by K_i yields

$$N_i^2 V_i t_i' / K_i = P_i K_i \tag{5}$$

as an alternative way of writing the first order condition for achieving a cost minimizing level of capacity for mode i. Similarly, $\partial t_i / \partial N_i = t_i' / K_i$. Again, $T_i = N_i V_i \, \partial t_i / \partial N_i$ is the efficient toll for a mode i trip. Substituting the alternative way of writing $\partial t_i / \partial N_i$ into the expression for an efficient toll and multiplying by N_i yields

$$N_i^2 V_i t_i' / K_i = N_i T_i . \tag{6}$$

The right-hand side of this expression equals total toll collections from mode i travelers; its left-hand side is identical to the left-hand side of equation (5).

Thus, if providing both services involves constant returns to scale, coupling marginal cost tolls with capacity levels that minimize long-run costs would result in toll revenues for each mode just sufficient to cover its capital costs. But this situation is no different from that for any other constant-returns-to-scale activity. Given constant returns to scale, marginal cost prices just cover total costs in long-run equilibrium. In this respect, the only difference between mode i and a more commonly considered commodity lies in the nature of the price charged. The money price of a standard commodity covers both wages paid to variable inputs and rent for the fixed capital used in production. The "price" of a mode i trip also covers both types of input, but only the rent to fixed capital is paid in cash. The variable input, travel time, is provided directly by each traveler.

All of the models from which the numerical results of section 2 derive are elaborations on this simple two-mode model. All have the following common features: N people per hour begin and N people per hour terminate trips along each mile of an urban one-way street. N is independent of the "full" (i.e., cash plus value of time) cost of either a bus or an auto trip; full cost serves only to determine which mode a traveler takes. Trip origins and destinations are uniformly distributed along the street.[2] Each trip is M miles long and must be taken by either auto or bus. The total resource costs of providing service to those who travel along the artery includes bus company and auto operating costs, the value to travelers of the time they spend aboard buses and in autos, and for bus travelers, the values of walking and waiting time. Expressions for these costs can most easily be developed in terms of those whose trips originate in any given one-mile segment of the artery.

Automobile operating costs are $C_a(t_a) = H_0 + H_1 \ln t_a$ dollars per vehicle mile where t_a is the number of hours required for an auto to travel one mile. The costs of each auto trip are shared by a passengers. Total vehicle operating costs for the N_a auto travelers who originate in a one mile stretch of the artery are $N_a(M C_a + g)/a$ where g is a fixed cost that is independent of trip length. Two factors enter into the determination of g: such parking charges as may be imposed; the opportunity cost of the vehicle itself.

Traveler i values an hour spent aboard a bus or in an automobile at V_i dollars. Total auto travel time costs are $N_a \bar{V}_a M t_a$ where $\bar{V}_a$ is the average over all auto travelers of the value of an hour's travel time. A similar expression, $N_b \bar{V}_b M t_b$, applies to the time in transit costs of bus travelers. Travelers are numbered in ascending order of travel time values. These values are uniformly distributed over the range $0 \leq V_i \leq V_N$.

Most bus travelers neither live nor have destinations on the traffic arteries traversed by the buses they use. Rather, a typical bus rider must walk to the route from his origin and from the route to his destination. To account for this, h minutes are added to the remaining time costs of each bus trip. Once a traveler reaches the artery, he must walk to the nearest bus stop. If there are Y uniformly spaced bus stops per mile, if origins and destinations are uniformly distributed between stops, and if the average length of a bus passenger's wait at a stop is a fraction, β, of the headway between buses, $1/\chi$, then it can be shown[3] that total walking and waiting costs are

$$\alpha \bar{V}_b t_w = \alpha \bar{V}_b (\beta/\chi + 1/2\gamma Y + h)$$

where γ is walking speed, and α is the ratio of the value of walking and waiting time, t_w, to the value of time in transit, $\bar{V}_b$.

In models 1, 2, and 4, buses and autos are assumed to distribute themselves uniformly across the width of the artery. In these models, travel time per auto trip mile is a function of the artery's volume/capacity ratio. Specifically,[4]

$$t_a = t_0 + t_1 [(b\chi + MN_a/a)/K]^c. \tag{7}$$

In this expression, t_0, t_1, and c are parameters and b is a bus's auto congestion equivalent. That is, an additional bus is assumed to slow traffic by the same amount as would b autos. MN_a enters this expression because any given point on the road is passed by auto travelers who originated in each of the M miles preceding that point.

Travel time per bus trip has two components. First, when not engaged in stopping and starting maneuvers, a bus is assumed to travel at the same speed as an auto, i.e., to require t_a minutes per mile. In addition, in each route mile, N_b travelers board and N_b leave χ buses at Y or fewer stops. Hence, $\mu = 2N_b/\chi Y$ is the average number of passengers that board or leave any one bus at any one stop. Suppose that bus travelers make their decisions as to when to travel independently. It then follows that the number of passengers boarding at any given stop is Poisson distributed with mean μ and that the time required for a bus to travel a mile is[5]

$$t_b = t_a + 2N_b\epsilon/\chi + \delta Y[1 - e^{-\mu}] \tag{8}$$

where ϵ is the time required to board or unload a passenger once a bus has stopped, and δ is the amount by which the time required to traverse a route segment is increased by each stopping and starting maneuver.

Models 3 and 5 allow for the possibility of reserved bus lanes. That is, they allow for the possibility of reserving a segment of the artery for the use of buses only. The mechanics involved in this restriction are simple and, unfortunately, unrealistic: a fraction, η, of the artery's total capacity is allocated to buses while the remaining capacity, $(1 - \eta)K$, is allocated to autos. The value of η selected need not comprise an integral number of the artery's lanes. With reserved bus lanes, the time required for an auto trip is

$$t_a = t_0 + t_1 [MN_a/a(1 - \eta)K]^c \tag{9}$$

while, in the expression for t_b given by equation (8), t_a is replaced by

$$t_b{}^* = t_0 + t_1 [b\chi/\eta K]^c. \tag{10}$$

Whether traveler i takes trips by auto or bus depends on which has the lower full price. His auto and bus full prices are respectively

$$P_{ai} = M(V_it_a + (F_a + C_a)/a) + g/a \qquad (11)$$

and

$$P_{bi} = F_b + MV_it_b + \alpha V_it_w. \qquad (12)$$

In these expressions, F_a is the toll per mile charged for auto trips and F_b is the fare charged for a bus trip. The value of an hour of travel time is the only component of the full price of a trip that differs from traveler to traveler. Therefore, if an auto trip has a lower full price for traveler i, it will also have a lower full price for all travelers with numbers greater than i. Similarly, if a bus trip has a lower full price for traveler j, it will also have a lower full price for travelers with numbers less than j.

Summing these cost components gives the total time and money cost per hour of the trips taken by the residents of a one mile segment of the traffic artery:

$$Z = B\chi t_b + N_a(MC_a + g)/a + N_a\bar{V}_aMt_a$$
$$+ N_b\bar{V}_bMt_b + \alpha N_b\bar{V}_b (1/2\gamma Y + \beta/\chi + h), \qquad (13)$$

where B is the cost of providing an hour of bus service. This basic cost function is common to each of the five models from which the numerical results described in section 2 are derived.

Model 1

In this model, the basic question asked is, How sensitive are total travel costs to the modal split N_b/N? *Some* combination of auto toll and bus fare exists that would achieve *any* arbitrarily specified modal split. Taking for granted the alternative combinations of toll and fare necessary to make equation (11) exceed equation (12) for a fraction, N_b/N, of the travelers, the model determines the level of bus service that minimizes total travel time plus vehicle operating costs *given* N_b/N and the remaining parameters of the system—N, B, M, Y, and so forth.

Model 2

This model involves the same basic cost assumptions as does model 1. It determines the cost minimizing modal split and service levels. That is, it finds those values of χ and N_b (and hence of $N_a = N - N_b$) that satisfy $\partial Z/\partial N_b = \partial Z/\partial \chi = 0$. No useful purpose would be served by reproducing these partial derivatives. They are quite messy and do not yield explicit relationships for the cost minimizing values of χ and N_b. These roots must be determined by iterative techniques.

Model 2 also computes marginal cost bus fares and bus and auto tolls (i.e., charges equal to the time and money costs that any one bus or auto trip imposes on the bus operator and on other travelers), the value of the marginal product of street capacity (i.e., the amount by which an increment to street capacity would reduce total costs), full prices for representative travelers, the subsidy to bus operations required to minimize total costs, and other money and time magnitudes of interest. It is to be hoped that the principles involved in computing most of these numbers are self-evident, but additional words are in order on the marginal cost tolls and fares and the value of the marginal product of arterial capacity.

The marginal cost toll for an auto traveler can be inferred by asking what the addition of one auto traveler would add to total costs. That is, the marginal cost toll can be inferred by differentiating total cost, equation (13), with respect to N_a *while ignoring the equality of* N_b *and* $N - N_a$. This derivative can be written:

$$\partial Z/\partial N_a = [M(\bar{V}_a t_a + C_a/a) + g/a]$$
$$+ N_a M(\bar{V}_a + C_a'/a)\partial t_a/\partial N_a$$
$$+ (B\chi + N_b \bar{V}_b M)\partial t_b/\partial N_a, \tag{14}$$

where, from equations (7) and (8),

$$\partial t_a/\partial N_a = \partial t_b/\partial N_a = ct_1[(b\chi + MN_a/a)/K]^{c-1} M/aK.$$

The bracketed expression in the first line of equation (14) is the cost borne by a traveler himself. It is the value to him of the time his trip requires plus his share, $1/a$, of the cost of operating a vehicle. The second line of the equation is the cost his trip imposes on the remaining auto travelers by increasing the time and vehicle operating costs of their trips, whereas the third line is the costs he imposes on the bus operator and on bus travelers.[6]

Similar considerations apply to the marginal cost bus fare. Differentiating equation (13) with respect to N_b (again ignoring that $N_a = N - N_b$) and relying on equation (8) to evaluate $\partial t_b/\partial N_b$ yields:

$$\partial Z/\partial N_b = [\bar{V}_b(Mt_b + \alpha(1/2\gamma Y + \beta/\chi))]$$
$$+ 2(B + N_b \bar{V}_b M/\chi)(\epsilon + \delta e^{-\mu}) . \tag{15}$$

As with the auto traveler toll, the bracketed expression in the first line of equation (15) is the resource cost borne by the traveler—the value of the time he spends walking to and from bus stops, waiting for a bus, and traveling on the bus. The second line in this equation is the marginal cost fare. It reflects the costs an additional traveler imposes on the bus company and on the passengers already aboard the bus on which he travels. In this expression, $e^{-\mu}$ is the probability that a stop would *not* have been made in the absence of the additional traveler. Therefore, $A = 2(\epsilon + \delta e^{-\mu})$ is the average amount of time required to serve an additional traveler. Since there is an average of MN_b/χ passengers already aboard the bus, serving him imposes a cost of $A\bar{V}_b MN_b/\chi$ on them. AB is the cost to the bus company of the additional bus hours required to keep headways unchanged.[7]

In real world bus operations, an additional passenger *would* affect road congestion even if the bus company responded to his trip by increasing the hours of bus service to keep headways unchanged; a stopped bus serves as a barrier to the vehicles behind it in a traffic stream, slowing them down. A more realistic model would take into account the congestion-increasing effects of bus loading and unloading maneuvers, since the models involved in this study do not do so, they understate to some degree the marginal cost of bus trips and hence marginal cost fares.

The scheduling of an additional bus on a traffic artery adds to the level of congestion, thereby slowing automobiles and other buses. In scheduling decisions, the bus company would likely take into full account the effects on its operations of changing the number of hours of bus service but might ignore the effects of these changes on the cost of auto trips. If so, efficiency would dictate imposing a toll on the bus company to reflect these latter costs. In computing subsidies and bus operating costs in section 2, however, this toll is ignored—the bus system is assumed to take into account the effects of its scheduling on auto travelers as well as on itself and its patrons.

In normal operation, buses use less street capacity per passenger than do automobiles. This is why the calculations in section 2 reveal that diversion of travelers from autos to buses would yield dramatic cost savings on heavily congested arteries. With information on the costs of road capacity, it would be possible to determine whether such savings result from the efficiency of buses in long-run equilibrium or from the existence of a short-run equilibrium in which road capacity is suboptimum. In principle, this issue could be dealt with by adding a road capacity cost function to equation (13) and solving for the cost minimizing value of K as well as those of N_b and χ. Unfortunately, it seems impossible to capture the costs of providing arterial streets of alternative widths and hence capacities in a simple general function. However, by determining the value of the marginal product of road capacity, some light is shed on the subject. It can be computed by evaluating $\partial Z/\partial K$, i.e., the amount by which an additional unit of capacity would reduce the time and vehicle operating costs of N trips given system parameter values (including an arbitrarily specified capacity level) and the optimizing values of N_b, χ, and in models 3 and 5, of η.

Capacity levels are fixed in the section 2 calculations by specifying alternative values of MN/K. A value of MN/K can be interpreted as the traffic artery's volume/capacity ratio if all trips are taken in one passenger automobiles. Thus, with 400 five-mile trips originating hourly in each mile,

$MN = 5 \times 400 = 2,000$ individuals an hour would pass each point along the artery. An MN/K value of two would then imply that the artery has 1,000 capacity units—a little less than the capacity of two ten-foot lanes on a one-way street with green signals 50 percent of the time.

Model 3

This model differs from models 1 and 2 only in that it allows a fraction, η, of the artery's total capacity to be reserved for buses, with the remaining capacity, $(1 - \eta)K$, allocated to automobiles. With reserved bus lanes, equation (13) still provides an expression for total costs. The only difference between model 3 and the preceding models in this respect is in the expressions for t_a and t_b. With reserved bus lanes, the time per mile for an auto trip is given by equation (9) rather than equation (7), whereas travel time per mile by bus is determined by substituting equation (10) for t_a in equation (8).

To allow reserved bus lanes is, in effect, to allow the division of an artery into two separate rights-of-way and to permit allocation of the artery's total capacity so as to equalize the value of its marginal product on these two rights-of-way. The numerical analysis in section 2 reveals that equality of the marginal products of capacity invariably calls for a lower volume/ capacity ratio on the bus than on the auto right-of-way.

Model 4

The provision of bus service involves economies of scale: suppose that a bus company responds to a doubling of demand along a route by doubling the number of buses serving that route. If the resulting increase in traffic congestion is ignored, the average number of passengers per mile served by each bus and hence average travel time per trip, and bus company costs per passenger served would be unchanged. However, doubling service would cut headways between buses in half, thereby cutting waiting time costs per passenger in half. Actually, as the numerical calculations described in section 2 suggest, costs could be further cut by responding to a demand increase with a less than proportionate increase in bus service.

Because of these scale economies, if cost-minimizing values of N_b, χ, and η are established in models 2 and 3 and marginal cost fares are charged for bus trips, the revenues generated are typically insufficient to cover total bus operating costs.[8] Cost minimization coupled with marginal cost fares would therefore require subsidized bus service.

In addition, for the ratios of trip volume to arterial capacity that seem typical of urban areas during morning and afternoon rush hours, models

2 and 3 typically yield marginal cost auto tolls far higher than the roughly two cents per mile implied by gasoline and other excise taxes imposed on auto travel in North American cities. Therefore, if existing "tolls" on auto travel are taken to be incapable of alteration, truly astronomical subsidies for buses would be required to achieve a modal split that would minimize the total resource costs of trips.

These considerations suggest the desirability of adding two sorts of pricing constraints to the models: that wrong (i.e., inefficiently low) tolls are, for whatever the reasons, charged for auto travel; and that bus operations must either break even or, more realistically, incur deficits less than those that would be required to minimize total travel costs. These constraints can most easily be handled by allowing the toll for auto trips to be specified arbitrarily and by requiring fare revenues from the bus operation to equal bus operating costs minus an arbitrarily specifiable allowable deficit.

With the system specified in this fashion, its control variables can be regarded as F_b, the bus fare plus χ and N_b. However, those in control of the system do not have complete freedom to specify these variables. Rather, a constraint implicit in models 1–3 must be explicitly taken into account: N_b individuals will travel by bus only if the individual with the N_b^{th} highest travel time value—call him traveler m (for marginal or middle)—is indifferent between trips on the two modes because he is confronted by the same full price for auto and bus trips. This is, χ, N_b, and F_b must be chosen subject to the constraint that

$$G(N_b, \chi, F_b) = F_a + (MC_a + g)/a + V_m M t_a$$
$$- [V_m(\alpha/2\gamma Y + \alpha\beta/\chi + \alpha h + M t_b) + F_b] = 0$$
$$(16)$$

where V_m is individual m's travel time value and F_a is the arbitrarily specified toll for an auto trip.

Incorporating the "bus deficit" and "indifference of traveler m" constraints into the system leads to the objective of minimizing

$$Z^{**} = Z + \lambda_1[F_b N_b + D - B\chi t_b] + \lambda_2 G(N_b, \chi, F_b) \qquad (17)$$

where Z is given by equation (13) and D is the bus system's allowable deficit per mile-hour. A second variant of equation (13) is also studied, the "free bus" constraint. It involves setting the bus fare in equation (13) equal to zero and minimizing

$$Z^{***} = Z + \lambda G(N_b, \chi, 0). \qquad (18)$$

As with models 2 and 3, little would be served by displaying the first order conditions for minimizing Z^{**} and Z^{***}; they are extremely messy and do not yield explicit solutions for the cost minimizing values of the system variables.

Model 5

This model differs from model 4 in the same way that model 3 differs from model 2. That is, model 4 involves the assumption that autos and buses are uniformly distributed across the artery while model 5 allows for reserved bus lanes. Analogous to the situation with models 2 and 3, equations (17) and (18) are the expressions to be minimized in model 5 and in model 4. The two models differ only in their expressions for auto and bus travel time and in that optimization in model 5 is with respect to η as well as χ, N_b, and F_b.

2. THE BENEFIT/COST IMPLICATIONS OF THE STEADY STATE MODELS

Pseudoempirical analysis of the models described in section 1 has been undertaken for the parameter value combinations indicated in Appendix A. The travel time plus vehicle operating costs per trip shown in tables 6.1 and 6.2 reflect the cost-minimizing level of bus service given the modal split (i.e., the ratio of bus to total travelers) and other parameter values shown.

Tables 6.1 and 6.2 reveal that the scale economies associated with bus operation yield only modest reductions in system costs with increases in the scale of the system. Naturally enough, the cost-minimizing modal split declines with reductions in MN/K, the volume/capacity ratio that would prevail if all trips were taken in single-occupant automobiles. With MN/K equal to two, cost minimization would call for about 75 percent of all trips to be taken by bus while, depending on system scale, modal splits in the 10–20 percent range would be called for with an MN/K value of 0.5. With high M/K values, the provision of an optimum level of bus service would reduce system costs to substantially below the levels that would result with only automobile travel; however, with low MN/K values, the benefits of bus service are modest. With MN/K equal to 0.5, an optimum level of bus service would result in costs 1 to 6 percent less than those with only auto travel while, with MN/K equal to 0.25, all-auto and optimum-bus operations lead to virtually identical costs.

Tables 6.3 and 6.4 deal with the potential benefits of reserved bus lanes when marginal cost auto tolls and bus fares are charged and when auto tolls are restricted to those implicit in current gasoline taxes and deficit constraints are imposed on bus operations. The parameter values leading to table 6.3 are those that seem most representative of peak-hour travel; off-peak values underlie table 6.4.

Perhaps the most important generalization suggested by these tables and their counterparts for all of the other parameter value combinations tested

TABLE 6.1. Cost per Trip as a Function of Modal Split, Congestion Level, and Travel Demand with Peak-cost Conditions

Travel Rate (N)	Alternative Modal Splits (model 1)						Optimum Modal Split (model 2)		
	0	25%	50%	75%	100%	Cost/Trip	Percent	VMP of Capacity (¢/mi-hr)	Auto Toll (¢/mile)
Congestion Level: $MN/K = 2$									
100	$8.05	$4.86	$3.17	$2.67	$2.96	$2.67	76.0%	40.9¢	77.1¢
400	8.05	4.65	2.88	2.41	2.77	2.41	73.9	34.8	68.7
1600	8.05	4.56	2.77	2.32	2.72	2.32	72.9	33.0	66.0
Congestion Level: $MN/K = 1$									
100	2.44	1.97	1.93	2.25	2.83	1.90	39.6	21.1	40.1
400	2.44	1.87	1.79	2.11	2.70	1.77	41.6	17.4	35.2
1600	2.44	1.82	1.73	2.06	2.66	1.71	42.0	16.1	33.5
Congestion Level: $MN/K = 0.5$									
100	1.40	1.42	1.67	2.14	2.79	1.38	10.7	4.3	11.9
400	1.40	1.36	1.58	2.03	2.67	1.34	16.5	3.5	10.4
1600	1.40	1.33	1.54	1.99	2.64	1.32	18.5	3.2	9.8
Congestion Level: $MN/K = 0.25$									
100	1.22	1.32	1.63	2.11	2.78	1.22	0.0	0.5	2.3
400	1.22	1.27	1.54	2.01	2.67	1.21	7.6	0.4	2.0
1600	1.22	1.24	1.51	1.98	2.64	1.20	10.5	0.3	1.9

NOTE: 5-mile trips, 8 bus stops per mile, medium travel time exponents, no reserved bus lane, 1.25 passengers per auto. Optimization assumes the imposition of marginal cost auto tolls and bus fares.

TABLE 6.2. Cost per Trip as a Function of Modal Split, Congestion Level, Travel Demand, and Trip Length

Trip Length Miles (M)	Alternative Modal Splits (model 1)					Optimum Modal Split (model 2)			
	0	25%	50%	75%	100%	Cost/Trip	Percent	VMP of Capacity (¢/mi-hr)	Auto Toll (¢/mile)
				$N = 400$, $MN/K = 2$, Peak Costs					
2.5	$4.17	$2.59	$1.83	$1.75	$2.16	$1.72	65.6%	69.6¢	44.1¢
5	8.05	4.65	2.88	2.41	2.77	2.41	73.9	34.8	68.7
10	15.79	8.76	4.98	3.68	3.81	3.62	83.3	17.2	106.8
				$N = 200$, $MN/K = 1$, Off-Peak Costs					
2.5	0.80	0.80	1.04	1.48	2.11	0.77	12.1	29.3	48.8
5	1.60	1.39	1.54	1.98	2.63	1.39	26.3	19.1	38.9
10	3.21	2.57	2.53	2.90	3.57	2.49	39.2	11.9	27.6

NOTE: 8 bus stops per mile, medium travel time exponents, no reserved bus lanes. Optimization assumes the imposition of marginal cost auto tolls and bus fares.

TABLE 6.3. Comparison of System Operation With and Without Reserved Bus Lanes under Different Pricing and Financial Constraints: Base Peak-hour Case

Constraints	Cost per Trip		Bus Fare		Bus Operating Cost/Passenger		Buses per Hour	
	Without	With	Without	With	Without	With	Without	With
Marginal cost	$2.41	$2.34	27.1¢	25.9¢	21.8¢	18.3¢	25.3	22.1
Zero fare	4.56	2.71	0.0	0.0	102.8	31.1	23.3	43.0
Subsidy: 100%	3.91	2.70	−55.3	−10.5	39.6	24.8	10.2	28.3
75%	4.23	2.73	−38.5	0.4	41.6	26.1	8.8	31.3
50%	4.64	2.76	−18.8	12.2	44.0	28.3	7.2	37.2
25%	5.25	2.77	6.5	29.2	46.9	34.6	5.2	74.6
0	6.57	2.77	52.1	34.6	52.1	34.6	2.2	74.6

Constraints	Modal Split		Bus Share of Capacity		Volume/Capacity Reserved Lanes		"Marginal" Benefit/Subsidy Dollar	
	Without	With	Without	With	Auto	Bus	Without	With
Marginal cost	73.9%	71.0%	17.5%	21.2%	58.8%	36.4%		
Zero fare	31.4	69.4	6.9	44.9	88.8	33.5		
Subsidy: 100%	34.0	61.2	3.3	29.7	88.3	33.4	$3.88	$0.61
75%	30.3	62.9	2.7	33.8	89.7	32.4	5.13	0.56
50%	25.8	67.0	2.1	42.1	91.2	30.9	7.50	0.24
25%	20.0	100.0	1.4	100.0	—	26.1	16.36	0.00
0	9.5	100.0	0.5	100.0	—	26.1		

NOTE: $MN/K = 2$, $N = 400$, 5-mile trips, 8 stops per mile, 1.25 passengers per auto, peak period costs. "With" figures derived from models 3 and 5; "without" figures from models 2 and 4.

TABLE 6.4. Comparison of System Operation With and Without Reserved Bus Lanes under Different Pricing and Financial Constraints: Base Off-peak Case

Constraints	Cost per Trip		Bus Fare		Bus Operating Cost/Passenger		Buses per Hour	
	Without	With	Without	With	Without	With	Without	With
Marginal cost	$1.39	$1.39	12.5¢	12.5¢	20.9¢	19.1¢	6.0	5.9
Zero fare	1.53	1.52	0.0	0.0	48.4	39.7	4.2	4.6
Subsidy: 100%	1.50	1.50	−21.2	−17.7	28.1	24.2	2.1	2.4
75%	1.52	1.51	−15.7	−12.4	28.7	24.6	1.8	2.1
50%	1.54	1.53	− 9.2	− 6.1	29.6	25.2	1.4	1.7
25%	1.56	1.55	− 1.0	1.9	30.7	26.0	0.9	1.2
0	1.60	1.60	—	—	—	—	0	0

Constraints	Modal Split		Bus Share of Capacity		Volume/Capacity with Reserved Lanes		"Marginal" Benefit/Subsidy Dollar	
	Without	With	Without	With	Auto	Bus	Without	With
Marginal cost	26.3%	26.7%	4.1%	4.9%	51.4%	42.1%		
Zero fare	7.6	8.7	2.4	3.3	62.9	48.6		
Subsidy: 100%	7.5	8.2	1.2	1.9	62.4	43.8	$1.58	$1.67
75%	6.3	7.0	1.0	1.7	63.1	43.6	1.97	2.09
50%	4.8	5.5	0.8	1.4	63.9	43.1	2.65	2.84
25%	1.5	1.8	0.5	1.0	64.9	42.0	4.51	5.36
0	0	0	0	0	66.7	—		

NOTE: $MN/K = 1$, $N = 200$, 5-mile trips, 8 stops per mile, 1.5 passengers per auto, off-peak costs. "With" figures derived from models 3 and 5; "without" figures from models 2 and 4.

is: if marginal cost bus fares and auto tolls could be charged, reserved bus lanes would be of little value. If the road use optimizer could do so, he would allocate arterial capacity to provide lower volume/capacity ratios for buses than for autos. An optimum allocation of this sort would result in modest cost reductions—3 or 4 percent under peak conditions and a percent or so in off-peak periods. But achieving the optimum volume/ capacity ratios would, in general, require nonintegral numbers of bus lanes —a clear impossibility. If consideration had been restricted to integral numbers of bus lanes, their provision would rarely have reduced total costs, again given marginal cost auto tolls and bus fares.

This finding is subject to a very important qualification: as tables 6.1 and 6.2 indicate, under all but the least congested travel conditions considered, the auto tolls required to achieve an efficient allocation of trips between buses and automobiles are far higher than those implicit in gasoline taxes and other auto user charges. A proposal to levy the tolls of 10 to 75 cents per vehicle mile listed in table 6.1 for MN/K ratios of 0.5 or more would certainly generate overwhelming opposition. With auto tolls approximating those currently charged, reserved bus lanes appear to have considerable merit, at least during periods of high traffic flow.

If the demand for trips is totally inelastic, an efficient allocation of resources could, *in principle,* be achieved by matching differences between actual and marginal cost auto tolls with the corresponding differences between actual and marginal cost bus fares. "In principle" is stressed for two reasons. The magnitude of the required subsidy to bus travel would impose an intolerable fiscal burden. The calculations underlying table 6.3 yield a marginal cost toll of $2.75 for a five-mile person-trip by auto in the absence of reserved bus lanes. The charge for the same trip implied by current gasoline taxes is about 6.25 cents. Imposing such a constraint on auto tolls therefore implies that a bribe of $2.42 per five-mile trip would be required to achieve an efficient modal split under the conditions on which table 6.3 is based. The corresponding operating subsidy works out to $779 per mile-hour of peak period bus service. Furthermore, subsidies of this magnitude would generate considerable additional bus travel even if the "genuine demand" for trips is totally inelastic. Waiting and travel time per bus trip amount to thirty-three minutes under optimum conditions without reserved lanes (table 6.3). At $2.42 a trip, bus travel would therefore provide earnings of about $4.40 an hour.

A proposal to institute negative bus fares would probably be met with as much enthusiasm as a proposal to increase auto tolls to seventy or more cents a vehicle mile. About the most that could be hoped for would be the institution of free bus service. Under table 6.3 conditions, minimizing total resource costs subject to the zero bus fare and gasoline tax auto toll constraints would result in average resource costs per trip of $4.56 in the absence of reserved lanes—89 percent greater than the costs achievable with marginal cost tolls and fares. If these pricing constraints are accompanied by allocating 44.9 percent of arterial capacity to buses, however, minimum total resource costs work out to $2.71 per trip—only 16 and 12 percent greater than the costs attainable respectively with and without reserved bus lanes when marginal cost tolls and fares are imposed.

With 44.9 percent of road space allocated to buses, the value of the marginal product of a unit of capacity (VMP of K) is $1.39 per hour on the auto side of the artery but only 13.5 cents per hour on the bus side. Reallocating road space from buses to autos would therefore reduce total costs *if* it could be accomplished without altering the modal split; unfortunately, reallocation could not be accomplished in this fashion. Shifting road capacity from bus to auto lanes would respectively lower and increase auto and bus travel times, thereby inducing a shift from bus to auto travel. This shift in patronage would increase total costs more than the move toward more nearly equal values of the marginal products of capacity would reduce them.

A general principle appears to underlie this phenomenon: the full price of a trip by any mode involves both cash and in-kind components. Suppose that the cash component of a trip price must, for whatever reasons, be less than would be called for by marginal cost pricing and that the demand for trips is not totally inelastic. Then (constrained) efficiency would call for allocating less transportation capacity to these trips than would be required to minimize the sum of the capacity and in-kind costs of the equilibrium number of trips. Under these circumstances, the benefits that additional capacity would confer by lowering the costs borne by present travelers would be more than offset by the costs imposed by the additional travel that increased capacity would evoke.[9]

The operating cost subsidies required under table 6.3 conditions to minimize resource costs subject to the zero bus fare and gasoline tax auto toll constraints are $129 per mile-hour of bus service without reserved bus lanes and $86 with them. While considerably lower than the deficits that would be required to match auto toll and bus fare reductions, these subsidies are still substantial. The deficit constraint models were designed both to test the resource cost implications of more realistic subsidy levels and to explore the consequences of giving the bus operation greater flexibility in spending subsidy dollars, for example, by allowing it to charge a positive fare and thereby to provide more service than would be possible with a zero fare.

In the absence of reserved bus lanes, subsidy reductions would result in substantial cost increases. Thus, table 6.3 indicates that the increase in total trip costs that would result from lowering the bus operating subsidy from $97 to $65 per mile-hour (i.e., from 75 to 50 percent of the value required to minimize costs subject to the zero-fare and gas tax-toll constraints) works out to a "marginal" benefit per subsidy dollar of $5.13. It should be noted that cost minimization subject to deficit and auto toll constraints requires negative bus tolls when relatively large subsidies are possible; these calculations therefore understate attainable average trip costs and overstate marginal subsidy benefits to some degree if, as seems reasonable, negative bus fares are deemed impractical.

Subsidy restrictions are much less costly when reserved lanes are permitted. Cutting the bus operation's allowable deficit from the value associated with the zero fare, gas tax-toll optimum to half that amount leads to only a five-cent—2 percent—increase in average trip costs. Complete elimination of subsidies adds only an additional penny to the average cost of a trip although to minimize costs in the absence of bus subsidies requires the surprising and politically implausible condition that 100 percent of arterial capacity be devoted to buses, i.e., that auto travel be completely eliminated.

The differences between the results reported in tables 6.3 and 6.4 stem in part from differences in assumptions about travel rate (N), auto occupancy, and vehicle operating costs. The major source of these differences in results is the difference in assumed MN/K values, i.e., differences in the assumed arterial volume/capacity ratio that would prevail if all trips were taken in single-occupant automobiles. Regardless of the specific combinations of other system parameters that were incorporated in the computer runs, all of those for which MN/K was set equal to two revealed substantial benefits for reserved bus lanes when pricing constraints were imposed. Reserved lanes yielded minor benefits in all of the runs that assumed MN/K to be less than or equal to one. Furthermore, regardless of whether reserved lanes are allowed, the provision of bus service itself yields only modest benefits when MN/K is assumed to be less than or equal to one and when pricing constraints are imposed. Thus, under table 6.4 conditions, going from the zero fare, gas tax-toll optimum to all-automobile travel increases costs by only 4 to 5 percent and saves subsidies of $7.40 per mile-hour of bus operations without reserved lanes, and of $6.89 with them. Indeed, if all of the remaining parameter values in table 6.4 are held fixed while MN/K is set equal to 0.5, marginal cost pricing leads to a minimum average cost per trip of 97.15 cents and requires a bus operating subsidy of $1.26 per mile-hour both with and without reserved bus lanes. Eliminating bus service increases the average cost of a trip only to 97.34 cents.

To summarize briefly, when values of MN/K are substantial—one or two—provision of an optimum level of bus service lowers urban travel costs substantially below those for all-auto travel. With low MN/K values, however, bus service provides modest benefits. Similarly, with high MN/K values, reserved bus lanes substantially ameliorate the inefficiencies that result from the present practice of imposing automobile tolls that are substantially lower than those required for marginal cost pricing. With low MN/K values, however, reserved lanes are of little value.

These findings suggest important questions. Are high MN/K values (and hence large benefits attributed to bus service and reserved lanes) consistent with an efficient allocation of resources to urban transportation? Or might high MN/K values result from short-run equilibria with inefficiently low levels of urban street capacity? The answers to these questions largely depend on just how costly additional urban arterial capacity is. Arterial expansion costs vary so substantially with the uses to which abutting sites are put that drawing general conclusions on this score is impossible. Still, some rough calculations suggest the orders of magnitude that are involved.

Appendix B indicates that an MN/K value of two seems roughly characteristic of peak-hour, main-direction trip rates in St. Paul and Minneapolis. During off-peak hours (more accurately, early evening and daytime between peak hours) and in the reverse direction during peak hours, MN/K is about equal to one. Under optimum conditions with no reserved lanes, table 6.2 indicates that the hourly value of the marginal product of a unit of capacity (i.e., a strip about 0.02 of an inch wide and one mile long) is about 35 and 19 cents for five-mile trips when MN/K respectively equals two (with peak parameters) and one (with off-peak parameters). Similarly, with gas tax auto tolls, zero bus fares, and reserved lanes, the VMP of K is 83 cents under base peak-period conditions. With the same pricing constraints, base off-peak parameters, and no reserved lanes, the VMP of K is 33 cents. Assuming three peak, main direction and nine "off-peak" hours per weekday, five days per week and fifty-two weeks per year, yields $720 and $1,420 as annual values of the marginal product of capacity under these alternative operating assumptions.

A ten-foot lane on an urban arterial street has a "basic capacity" of about 625 vehicles per hour if signals are green 50 percent of the time.[10] Annual alternative gross benefits of (625 × $720 =) $450,000 and (625 × $1,420 =) $888,000 from adding a ten-foot lane to one mile of an existing artery are indicated.[11] The first column of Table 6.5 lists the present values of these gross benefits under alternative assumptions about interest rates and project lives. Data cited in Appendix B suggest that during 1975 in Minneapolis, the construction and maintenance costs for such an addition would respectively be about $270,000 (given a bare site) and $1,700 a year. Deducting the present values of these costs[12] from the present values of gross benefits and making the indicated conversions yields table 6.5's final two columns.

Whichever of these numbers seems most appropriate can be interpreted as the approximate cost of acquiring and clearing the land needed to expand an artery, above which its expansion would *not* be called for. Even in the absence of a careful examination of urban land values, these implied site values seem very large. It is therefore tempting to conclude that concrete should be poured. But qualifications are in order that leave the matter in doubt.

TABLE 6.5. Present Value of an Added Ten-foot Urban Arterial Street Lane and Implied Site Value for Existing Capacity to Be Optimal

		Benefit Present Value/10' Lane ($1000)	Implied Site Value ($/ft²)	Implied Site Value ($1000/acre)
		Marginal Cost Pricing		
25-year life	6%	$5800	$104	$4500
	12%	3500	61	2700
Infinite life	6%	7500	136	5900
	12%	3800	67	2900
		Zero Bus Fares, Gas Tax Auto Tolls		
25-year life	6%	$11400	$210	$9200
	12%	7000	127	5500
Infinite life	6%	14800	275	12000
	12%	7400	135	5900

The "marginal cost pricing" values in table 6.5 arise from a system with very high auto tolls. If tolls approaching 10 to 70 cents per auto mile were imposed, auto occupancy rates would almost certainly increase from the 1.25—1.5 values that currently characterize urban travel. Higher occupancy rates mean that fewer autos would be required to handle any given number of auto trips; hence lower congestion, congestion tolls, and values of the marginal product of capacity. No data exist, unfortunately, from which the elasticity of the auto occupancy rate with respect to auto tolls can be inferred. It therefore remains an open question whether it would be desirable to pour more concrete if a regime of marginal cost prices could be established.

The auto tolls implicit in table 6.5's price-constrained results provide no incentive for increased auto occupancy rates. Here, however, a qualification is in order related to the earlier rationalization for the striking differences that model 5 yields between the values of the marginal product of highway capacity in auto and bus lanes. Contrary to the assumption underlying the entire analysis of this study, the demand for urban travel is not totally inelastic. More concrete would lead to faster travel and more trips. The cash components of the full prices of both auto and bus trips are too low in the analysis underlying the bottom half of table 6.5. This being the case, (constrained) efficiency dictates that the in-kind component of trip prices result from capacity levels for which the VMP of K exceeds its cost. I have conducted only a limited examination of the magnitude of the gaps between the VMP of K and its cost, which are dictated by dollar components of trip prices that are too low.[13] This examination indicates the required gaps to be not nearly as great as those suggested by table 6.5. In addition, although constrained optimum volume/capacity ratios are, indeed, greater than the optimum ratios associated with marginal cost pricing, constrained optimum capacity is also greater than optimum capacity in the examples with which I have worked. If this finding can be extended to the models at hand, it would not necessarily follow that capacity expansion would be undesirable under the more realistic pricing constraints incorporated in models 4 and 5, even if it could be assumed that the adjustments in vehicle occupancy and travel rates that would result from the imposition of marginal cost auto tolls and bus fares would make capacity expansion undesirable. However, this analysis can hardly be regarded as definitive.

Before concluding, it seems worthwhile to examine briefly the way in which changes in system parameters other than MN/K affect the optimizing attributes of system operation. The time a bus traveler spends walking to and from bus stops and waiting for a bus to arrive can be viewed as a fixed input to his trips, i.e., one that is independent of its length if service frequency is held fixed. The greater the length of his trip, the greater is the number of miles over which this fixed input is averaged and hence the lower is the ratio of a bus trip's full price to the full price of an auto trip for any given traveler. If only for this reason, the cost minimizing modal split increases with length of trip. Under peak cost conditions without reserved bus lanes, for example, efficiency would dictate having 65.4, 74.6, and 83.3 percent of all travelers use buses for 2.5-, 5-, and 10-mile trips. The ratio of the marginal cost bus fare to the average cost of providing bus service also increases with trip length. Again under peak cost conditions without reserved bus lanes, marginal cost fares would be 14.3, 27.1, and 66.2 cents while operating costs would be 17.3, 21.8, and 40.2 cents per passenger with respective trip lengths of 2.5, 5, and 10 miles.

Stop spacing has opposing effects for the average bus traveler. On the one hand, the closer stops are to each other, the smaller is the distance he must walk. On the other hand, closer stop spacing implies greater travel time per mile. Time in transit accounts for a larger share of total travel time for long than for short trips. A systematic relationship therefore exists among stop spacings, trip lengths, and travel costs. For 2.5 mile trips, four and eight allowable stops per mile yield almost exactly the same average cost per trip. For longer trips, however, allowing four stops per mile yields distinctly lower costs than does allowing eight or sixteen stops.

Although published evidence on the subject is scanty, it seems plausible to suppose that the relationship between travel time and the volume/capacity ratio on an arterial street varies from artery to artery. Specifically, in comparison to a two-way street on which little effort has been expended to sequence signals so as to improve traffic flow, it seems plausible to suppose that a one-way street with carefully sequenced signals would exhibit both greater speed at all volume/capacity ratios and less dependence of speed on the volume/capacity ratio except at high values of this ratio. That is, on a graph with travel time on the vertical axis and the volume/capacity ratio on the horizontal, the one-way street relationship would lie below that for two-way streets and be more concave from above.

The results described in tables 6.1–4 apply to traffic arteries with attributes intermediate between those of a carefully signaled one-way street and a carelessly signaled two-way street. Analyses using alternative travel time-volume/capacity relationships suggest that the returns to careful traffic engineering are substantial. Under peak conditions with marginal cost tolls and fares, trip costs on carelessly signaled two-way streets and carefully signaled one-way streets are respectively about 10 percent greater and 10 percent less than those under the conditions dealt with in table 6.1–4. Under off-peak conditions and with pricing constraints in effect, the percentage differences are even greater.

If—a big if—the numerical results summarized in this section can be accepted at face value, they have policy implications that are in some respects surprising and in some disturbing. First, the increasingly common practice of giving mass transit vehicles preferential access to urban road capacity has much to commend it, at least under the traffic and pricing conditions that prevail during peak hours in most North American cities. While marginal cost pricing, the economist's almost automatic prescription for any problem, could do even better, reserved bus lanes appear capable of substantially reducing current peak period travel costs. Given the results of the reserved lane models, it also seems reasonable to expect substantial cost savings from existing and proposed techniques for giving buses preferential access to expressway ramps and control over traffic signals.[14]

But whether preferential bus access is a long- or a short-run second-best solution for traffic congestion remains open to debate. The road use conditions that promise significant benefits from preferential access also suggest that road expansion might yield substantial benefits. While my results on this score are hardly conclusive, they are consistent with the conclusion (one I find repugnant) that pouring more concrete is at least part of the answer to urban traffic congestion in both the first- and the second-best long runs.

If pouring concrete is, indeed, part of the long-run best answer, then whether buses are an efficient mode of urban transportation is open to serious question. Under the base off-peak period conditions studied in this paper—conditions that might well prevail during the *peak* period if a benefit maximizing expansion of capacity were to take place—providing buses in the absence of marginal cost pricing yields average trip costs only marginally below those afforded by an all-auto system. And for lesser congestion levels, a system with buses appears only marginally superior to an all-auto system, even with marginal cost pricing.

APPENDIX A
GLOSSARY OF SYMBOLS AND SUMMARY
OF PARAMETER VALUES USED IN MODELS 1–5

a Occupants per automobile: 1.5 off-peak, 1.25 peak

$A \equiv 2(\epsilon + \delta e^{-\mu})$ The average delay to a bus from boarding and discharging a passenger

b The number of automobiles that impose the same traffic congestion burden as one bus: 3.5

B Bus operating cost per hour: \$19 off-peak, \$25 peak

$C_a \equiv H_0 + H_1 \ln t_a$ Automobile operating costs per mile: $0.3576 + 0.0895 \ln t_a$

D Allowable bus system operating deficit per mile-hour

F_a Toll per auto traveler for an M-mile trip: optimized in models 2 and 3; 1¢ off-peak, 1.25¢ peak in models 4 and 5

F_b Fare per bus traveler for an M-mile trip

g Fixed cost of automobile trip: 0 off-peak, 30¢ per traveler peak

h Time required for bus traveler to walk to and from artery along which buses run: 4.8 minutes

K Capacity of artery in vehicles per hour: $MN/K = 1$ off-peak, 2 peak with sensitivity tests for 0.25 and 0.5

M Trip length: 5 miles, with sensitivity tests for 2.5 and 10 miles

N Total trips originating per mile-hour: 200 off-peak, 400 peak, with sensitivity tests for 100, 800, 1600

N_a Auto trips originating per mile-hour

N_b Bus trips originating per mile-hour

P_{ai} Full price of auto trip to traveler i

P_{bi} Full price of bus trip to traveler i

$t_a \equiv t_0 + t_1 (\text{Volume}/K)^c$ Time required for auto to travel one mile: $t_0 = 2.2$, $t_1 = 5.8$, $c = 2.7$, with sensitivity tests for $t_0 = 2$, $t_1 = 4$, $c = 3$ and $t_0 = 2.4$, $t_1 = 7.6$, $c = 2.5$

t_b Time required for bus to travel one mile

t_b^* Bus travel time per mile on reserved lane

t_w when not engaged in stopping and starting maneuvers

t_w Average time spent walking to and from bus stops and waiting for service

$\bar{V}_a$ Average travel time value of auto travelers

$\bar{V}_b$ Average travel time value of bus travelers

V_i Travel time value of traveler i, $i = 1, \cdots N$: $0 \leq V_i \leq \$7$

X Bus hours of service

Y Number of evenly spaced bus stops per mile: 8 with sensitivity tests for 4, 16

Z Total system costs

α Ratio of walking and waiting time value to time in transit value for bus travelers: 3

β Expected fraction of bus headway spent waiting for bus service: one-half

γ Walking speed: 3 miles per hour

δ Time required for a bus's stopping and starting maneuver: 18 seconds

ϵ Time required to embus or debus a passenger once a bus has stopped: 1.8 seconds

η Fraction of street capacity allocated to buses

μ Number of passengers embusing or debusing at an average bus stop

χ Buses per hour passing each point on a route

APPENDIX B
DERIVATION OF COST AND RELATED PARAMETERS

Values of several parameters were taken without change from an earlier study of mine on bus route optimization.[15] These are: the time required for a passenger to embus or debus (ϵ) and for a bus to decelerate, open its doors at a bus stop, close them, and accelerate (δ); the ratio of the value of walking and waiting time to that of time in transit for bus passengers (α); the fraction of the headway between buses that the average passenger waits for service (β); and average walking speed (γ).

Auto Travel Time-Volume/Capacity Relationship

The relationship used, $t = t_0 + t_1 (W/K)^c$ where W represents traffic volume, was suggested by Solow and Vickrey.[16] Empirical studies of city street traffic flows yield contradictory implications for the values of this relationship's parameters. With the aid (but not necessarily the full approval) of Matthew Huber of the University of Minnesota's Department of Civil and Mineral Engineering, I therefore settled on parameter values for a hypothetical one-way street with carefully sequenced signals that imply speeds of 10, 20, and 30 miles per hour at volume/capacity ratios of 1, 0.63, and 0 respectively. The parameter values adopted for a carelessly signalled two-way street imply speeds of 6, 15.5, and 25 miles per hour at volume/capacity ratios of 1, 0.5, and 0 respectively.

The Auto Equivalent of a Bus's Congestion Contribution (b)

The *Highway Capacity Manual* (p. 83) indicates that one bus has an effect on the capacity of a city street intersection equivalent to that of 3 to 5 autos. This statistic was the basis for the 3.5 autos per bus value used in the computer runs. It should be added, however, that later evidence suggests that a bus's auto congestion equivalent may be considerably higher than 3.5 under the conditions with which this study is primarily concerned.[17]

Travel Time Value Distribution

Studies by Beesley and Lisco[18] suggest that travelers with incomes in excess of $10,000 a year (mid-1960s prices) were willing to pay about 50 percent of their hourly income to save travel time. For individuals with incomes of less than $10,000 a year, the ratio of travel time value to income, V/I, was proportional to income. That is, $V/I = aI$, or $V = aI^2$. Using the Bureau of Labor Statistics Consumer Price Index to inflate the income levels in these studies, and applying the Beesley-Lisco formulas to Census Bureau family income data for 1974,[19] yields an estimated mean value of travel time for the U.S. population of $3.35, with a standard deviation of $3.20. A desire for algebraic tractability led to working with a uniform distribution of travel time values. If such a distribution is to have the population mean and standard deviation estimated for 1974, it must unfortunately have a negative lower bound. The lower bound of the distribution used was therefore set equal to zero and the upper bound to $7.00 so as approximately to preserve the estimated population mean.

Auto Operating Costs

The expression used derived from experimentation with relationships developed by Winfrey from late-1960s data on the effects on vehicle operating costs of running speed, frequency and duration of stops, and the like.[20] His cost figures were adjusted by a factor of 1.5 to account roughly for subsequent price increases.

Auto Toll Implied by Gasoline Taxes (F_a in models 4 and 5)

The values used derive from gasoline mileage data presented by Liston and Sherrer[21] and an estimate that federal and state gasoline taxes average 13 cents a gallon in the United States.

Auto Trip Fixed Costs (g)

An analysis by Lisco indicates that household commuting decisions take into account the opportunity costs of their vehicles[22]—the value to other household members of the trips they might have taken if the car had not been driven to work. Half the daily fixed costs of ownership derived from the Liston and Sherrer data seems a plausible average for U.S. families. On the perhaps unsound grounds that parking charges are imposed on only a small fraction of auto trips, this cost was ignored.

Bus Operating Costs (B)

For planning purposes in 1975, the Metropolitan Transit Commission of the Twin Cities Metropolitan Area used 40 cents per vehicle mile *plus* $11.39 per vehicle hour for off-peak service and for peak service, 40 cents per mile *plus* $13.07 per vehicle hour *plus* $13.69 per vehicle. Average speeds of 10 and 12 miles per hour during peak and off-peak periods and four hours of use during peak periods imply hourly operating costs of $16.19 for off-peak and $20.49 for peak hours.

To estimate capital costs—not included in the MTC formulas—assume a one-horse shay type of bus capable of producing exactly H hours of service over its lifetime. If a bus system supplies A hours of service a week during peak periods of L-hour duration, the system would require a fleet of FA/L buses where F is one plus the fraction of spare buses maintained. The annual capital costs of such a fleet can be written as $C = PFA/ [L R(H/H^*, r)]$ where P is the purchase price of a bus, H^* is the number of hours a year it is used, and $R(H/H^*, r)$ is the present value of a $1, $H/H^* =$ year annuity at an interest rate of r. The derivatives of C with respect to A and the number of off-peak hours of service respectively give the appropriate peak and off-peak capital charges. Assuming a 4 percent real interest rate and using MTC data on 1976 bus prices and system operating characteristics, these charges work out to $3.96 and $2.78.

Number of Travelers per Mile-Hour

Data from a 1970 origin-destination survey indicated that an average of 985 trips originated per square mile-hour in the central cities of the Twin Cities Metropolitan Area during the average of the six leading weekday travel hours.[23] The corresponding figure for the next twelve hours was 570—the hours between midnight and 6 A.M. were ignored. Adjusting to take into account the directional imbalance of peak hour trips leads to estimates of 246 and 143 for main-direction peak and off-peak one-direction flows in the half-mile corridor that the average bus route draws upon. Traffic conditions in the Twin Cities seem considerably less congested than those of most major metropolitan areas in North America. Therefore, to be more nearly representative of the continent, one-direction traffic flows were rounded off to 400 during peak and 200 during off-peak periods for the base calculations to which section 2 mainly refers.

Trip Length (M)

In 1970, the average trip in the Twin Cities area by all modes was 4.87 miles. Although bus trips (4.25 miles) tended to be somewhat shorter than auto trips (5.09 miles),[24] an assumed average trip length of five miles seems reasonable for base calculations.

Arterial Congestion Level (MN/K)

If 400 travelers per mile-hour make five-mile trips in one direction along an artery during peak periods, 2000 travelers per hour pass each point on the artery. Arterial streets in Minneapolis generally have four ten-to-twelve-foot lanes. The *Highway Capacity Manual* (p. 70) indicates the "basic capacity" of a ten-foot lane to be 625 vehicles per hour, if signals are green 50 percent of the time. With two lanes per direction, a peak period volume/capacity ratio of $2000/(2 \times 625) = 1.6$ would be implied if all trips were taken in one passenger automobiles. The corresponding calculations for off-peak periods yield an MN/K value of 0.8. Basic capacities are realized only under ideal conditions. These respective MN/K values were therefore rounded off to two and one for the base calculations in peak and off-peak periods respectively.

Auto Occupancy (a)

Vehicle occupancy rates vary substantially with trip purpose, the lowest being for work trips. In 1970, the average auto engaged in a work trip in the

Twin Cities area carried 1.19 passengers, while the average for all trip types was 1.50 passengers. Since work trips predominate in peak periods, 1.25 and 1.50 passengers per auto were assumed during the peak and off-peak periods respectively.

Time Walking to Bus Stops

Assumption of a rectangular street grid and a uniform distribution of bus travelers in a half-mile wide market centered on a traffic artery leads to the conclusion that the average bus passenger must walk an eighth of a mile perpendicular to the artery and a fourth of the distance between stops if stops are spaced less frequently than every block. A somewhat shorter perpendicular distance results with spacing every block. Ignoring the complication of every-block spacing, the average walks to a bus stop at origin and from a stop at destination aggregate to a fourth of a mile (five minutes) plus half the distance between stops.

Bus Stop Spacing (Y)

In those portions of Minneapolis with a rectangular street network, the average block is an eighth of a mile long by a sixteenth of a mile wide. But stops are generally placed at every corner. Although quarter-mile stop spacing appears to yield the lowest total cost for a bus trip (except for short trips or on lightly traveled routes), eight stops per mile were adopted for base calculations as a reasonable approximation to present practice.

Costs of Arterial Street Expansion

No recent arterial street widening projects have been undertaken in Minneapolis, but the city has been engaged in major residential street paving projects. Taking into account paving, curbs and gutters, catch basins, such miscellaneous work as laying sod, relocating sidewalks, occasional sub-base excavation and fill, and engineering yielded $135,940 as the average cost of a ten-foot wide, one-mile long strip of pavement in 1975. This cost derives from projects in which equipment is brought in to handle five miles or so of contiguous, lightly traveled streets. Widening a heavily traveled artery would involve less efficient use of equipment and additional expense to maintain traffic flow. Doubling residential paving costs to take these additional problems into account seems about the right order of magnitude. The annual costs of summer maintenance and cleaning and winter salting, sanding, and snow and ice removal averaged $1,705 per lane-mile on the

Minneapolis arterial streets classified as County-State Aid Highways between 1970 and 1975. In 1975, a year with above average snowfall, these costs averaged $1,759 per lane-mile.

NOTES

1. Subject, in models 4 and 5, to constraints on auto tolls and the deficits the bus operation may incur in providing service.

2. More precisely, origins and destinations are uniformly distributed either along the artery or on a continuum of streets that intersect it perpendicularly.

3. Apart from the introduction of time spent walking to the bus route, the development of this expression is identical to that in Mohring (1972), pp. 594–95.

4. The traffic engineering literature suggests that any road has a "capacity" in the sense of a maximum rate at which trips can be taken on it. Equation (7) seems to violate this general finding in that it permits the travel rate on a road to exceed its capacity. Nevertheless, employing a relationship like equation (7) seems defensible in analyses of the sort described in this paper. Even though demand may exceed capacity during some time periods, these periods are finite. Most people eventually reach their destinations. (I am indebted to Donald Dewees for this point.)

5. See Mohring (1972), pp. 595–96.

6. Implicit in the third line of equation (14) is the assumption that the bus operator responds to the increased congestion resulting from an additional auto trip by adding a sufficient number of bus hours of service to keep the headway between buses, $1/\chi$, fixed. But it is, after all, bus hours of service—say, $X = \chi M t_b$—that the bus company controls, not χ itself. If the bus company is regarded as holding X rather than χ fixed, the expression for the derivative of costs with respect to N_a would look quite different from equation (14). However, if χ and hence X have been selected so as to minimize total costs, the sum of the second two lines of equation (14) would have the same numerical value as the sum of the corresponding lines in the equation that takes X to be fixed.

7. The assumption implicit in equation (15), that the bus company responds to the additional trip by adding sufficient bus hours to leave bus headways unchanged, implies that the additional trip has no effect on the artery's volume/capacity ratio and hence no effect on auto travel time. Assuming bus hours rather than bus trips fixed leads to a considerably more complicated expression than equation (15) for the effect of an additional bus traveler on total system costs. Just as with auto tolls, if the cost minimizing values of N_b and χ have been selected, either expression would yield the same numerical value for the marginal cost bus fare.

8. In these models, road capacity is held fixed. An increase in total travel therefore leads to an increase in arterial volume/capacity ratios. The resulting reduction in travel speeds tends to offset the increasing returns aspect of the bus system. For some combinations of parameter values studied in section 2, these decreasing returns aspects of the system outweigh its increasing returns features. When this happens, marginal cost fares generate revenues in excess of bus system costs.

9. I have explored the ramifications of this general principle in Mohring (1970) and Mohring (1975).

10. U.S. Bureau of Public Roads (1950), p. 71.

11. Naturally enough, the value of the marginal product of a unit of capacity would diminish with widening of an artery; however, the crudeness of these calculations is such that attempting to adjust table 6.5 to take this bias into account seems pointless.

12. Approximately $290,000 and $300,000 at 6 percent for twenty-five years and infinite lives; $280,000 and $285,000 at 12 percent.

13. In Mohring (1975), pp. 191–95.

14. Kenneth Small has analyzed preferential access to expressway capacity for

buses. His models differ significantly from mine in that they devote much more attention to travel demand, but less attention to bus system optimization. Nevertheless, our results are strikingly similar. In particular, he too found that preferential bus access provides cost reductions that make them a strong second best to marginal cost pricing. See Small (1976).
15. Mohring (1972), pp. 603–4.
16. Solow and Vickrey (1971).
17. Boyd, Asher, and Wetzler (1973), pp. 58–62.
18. Lisco (1967) and Beesley (1965).
19. U.S. Bureau of the Census (1976), p. 11.
20. Winfrey (1969).
21. Liston and Sherrer (1974).
22. Lisco (1967), pp. 50–57.
23. Twin Cities Metropolitan Council (1974).
24. Twin Cities Metropolitan Council (1974), p. 45.

REFERENCES

Beesley, M. 1965. "The Value of Time Spent in Travelling: Some New Evidence." *Economica* 32 (May): 174–85.

Boyd, J. H., Asher, N. J., and Wetzler, E. S. 1973. *Evaluation of Rail Rapid Transit and Express Bus Service in the Urban Commuter Market.* Arlington, Va.: Institute for Defense Analysis.

Lisco, T. 1967. *The Value of Commuters' Travel Time: A Study of Urban Transportation.* Ph.D. diss., University of Chicago.

Liston, L. I., and Sherrer, R. W. 1974. *Cost of Operating an Automobile.* Washington, D.C.: U.S. Federal Highway Administration.

Mohring, H. 1970. "The Peak Load Problem with Increasing Returns and Pricing Constraints." *American Economic Review* 60 (September): 693–705.

———. 1972. "Optimization and Scale Economies in Urban Bus Transportation." *American Economic Review* 62 (September): 591–604.

———. 1975. "Pricing and Transportation Capacity." In *Better Use of Existing Transportation Facilities,* pp. 183–95. Special Report 153 of the Transportation Research Board. Washington, D.C.: National Research Council.

Small, K. A. 1976. *Bus Priority, Differential Pricing, and Investment In Urban Highways.* Ph.D. diss., University of California at Berkeley.

Solow, R., and Vickrey, W. 1971. "Land Use in a Long, Narrow City." *Journal of Economic Theory* 3 (December): 430–47.

Twin Cities Metropolitan Council. 1974. *A Summary Report of Travel in the Twin Cities Metropolitan Area.* St. Paul.

U.S. Bureau of the Census. 1976. *Current Population Reports,* Series P-60, no. 101. Washington, D.C.: U.S. Government Printing Office.

U.S. Bureau of Public Roads. 1950. *Highway Capacity Manual.* Washington, D.C.: U.S. Government Printing Office.

Winfrey, R. 1969. *Economic Analysis for Highways.* Scranton, Pa.: Intext Educational Publications.

7

ASSESSING THE SOCIAL COSTS OF URBAN TRANSPORTATION TECHNOLOGIES

MAHLON R. STRASZHEIM

INTRODUCTION

Whether automobiles constitute the least social-cost urban transportation technology depends on the treatment of external cost in the analysis of comparative cost. Theoretical analysis of externalities, particularly congestion, has been extensive, but satisfactory research into the empirical magnitude of externalities is lacking. Nor has public policy encouraged consideration of external costs. New car emission standards have only recently been established, but under existing law it is not necessary to provide compensation for most types of externality outside the highway right-of-way. Proponents of transit systems argue that the inclusion of auto externalities—particularly pollution and right-of-way damages to nondrivers—in comparative cost analysis would reveal transit as the least social-cost mode. The prospect of higher fuel prices in the future has bolstered the argument of those who claim that auto-dominant systems are not the least social-cost technology.

At the same time, the capital costs of rail transit systems under construction and the operating deficits of existing mass transit systems have risen very sharply. Capital cost of the Metro system being constructed in Washington has tripled in about five years. The BART system in San Francisco is experiencing disappointingly low ridership and high operating costs. Bus systems have also experienced rapid increases in operating costs, and their deficits have risen sharply. If the federal government is unwilling to pay the operating loss, many cities may face very severe tax burdens—particularly the older, Northeastern cities that have large transit systems.

Mahlon Straszheim is a professor of economics at the University of Maryland.

Accurate assessment of all social costs, including externalities, and the imposition of appropriate charges are important if the provision and utilization of transport systems and land-use decisions are to result in an efficient outcome. Since transport and other private and public capital stock in urban areas are typically very durable, misallocation will affect welfare for an extended period.

This chapter takes as its departure point the comparative cost analysis of Meyer, Kain, and Wohl (1965) that showed that auto systems are cost-dominant for all but a few cities with high-density development and high corridor volumes. One of my principal tasks is to determine whether the inclusion of externalities would seriously alter those basic conclusions. Recent evidence on mass transit costs, including imputed charges for capital investments, is reviewed in sections 1 and 2 to determine whether actual operating systems exhibit cost or performance dramatically different than Meyer, Kain, and Wohl projected.

The literature on highway externalities is reviewed in section 3. Although the theory of externalities is well developed, virtually no literature exists on its quantitative application to urban highways. I present estimates of the magnitude of external costs under a range of assumptions.

The fourth section summarizes the theory of pricing and investment in the presence of externalities. Very little analysis has been conducted of the consequences of alternative pricing policies on metropolitan development. The final section reviews several alternative means of imposing user charges or otherwise using the price system to secure an efficient outcome. Administrative and equity considerations are discussed.

1. COMPARATIVE COSTS: THE CONVENTIONAL WISDOM

Meyer, Kain, and Wohl's (1965) analysis of the costs of alternative urban transportation technologies for urban trips of varying length and density has been influential both because of its conceptual insights and because it has proven remarkably accurate for an extended period of time.

Meyer, Kain, and Wohl noted several characteristics. First, travelers consider both the time and money cost of the entire door-to-door trip in making choices; hence valid cost comparisons of modes must be based on systems that provide comparable service in all respects. Second, the density of trip originations and destinations and the line-haul corridor travel volumes are important determinants of the cost of alternative modes. Rail transit systems enjoy substantial scale economies in providing service to a high volume of travelers between two points. Yet the "residential collection" phase of the trip, from place of residence to the rail station, may entail substantial time and money cost and involve schedule delays and uncertainties. In the consideration of total door-to-door cost, lower densities negate the scale economies of rail transit and bus systems in the line-haul portion. Continued decentralization of residences and work places implies much smaller travel volumes between particular points than in pre-World War II periods; the travel markets to be served in urban areas constitute many low-density markets to and from many points.

Meyer, Kain, and Wohl's cost comparisons of auto, bus, and rail transit systems serving peak-hour home-to-work travel markets characteristic of major metropolitan areas reveal that auto travel is cost-dominant in all but the densest corridors of the biggest cities. These comparisons assume 1.4 passengers per car; if car pooling increases auto utilization, auto costs drop sharply. Very few cities have corridor peak-hour volumes in excess of the 5,000 passengers per hour needed for buses to be cost competitive. The auto's overwhelming cost advantage arises from its savings in "driver" costs, which constitute a high proportion of bus operating costs. Smaller buses in lower volume corridors are not cost competitive because of the high driver costs per passenger. Rail transit's scale economies can only be realized at very high volumes. The travel volume at which bus and rail systems are equal in cost depends very substantially on the treatment of rail capital costs. If rail travel is viewed as a sunk cost, and hence a free good, rail may be competitive at the volume of 20,000 passengers per hour; travel volumes twice that level are required to justify constructing a new rail right-of-way.

Keeler and Small (1975) updated this approach with data from the San Francisco Bay Area. Whereas their cost estimates are higher due to the inclusion of time and parking costs, they obtain surprisingly similar results. Keeler and Small compared costs of auto, bus, and BART for several typical commuter trips, employing a variety of assumptions about interest rates, travel volume, and the value of time. Time and parking costs dominate their results. For a twelve mile trip, the total cost for auto is $8.44 or 72¢ per mile. Time costs amount to $2.96, when time is valued at $3.00 per hour. Because of congestion, short-run marginal cost tolls in the peak hour were high, $2.05 of the total trip cost.[1] Parking charges add $2.14 to the price of a trip. Their estimates of externalities, noise cost at .1¢ per mile and pollution at .5¢ per mile, represent less than 1 percent of the total cost. Fuel costs are also a tiny fraction of the total. BART is not "cost competitive" with autos except at very high densities, and buses dominate all modes except at very low densities.

Keeler and Small's estimated bus cost of about 5¢ per passenger mile is less than half that realized by existing urban bus systems. Their results essentially reflect very optimistic assumptions regarding speeds (15 mph during residential collection and downtown distribution and 40 mph in the line haul) and the assumption that all seats are occupied. The latter neglects peaking and stochastic characteristics of demand which preclude full utilization of capacity. If more realistic assumptions regarding utilization of bus

systems are made, Keeler and Small's bus costs would be modified upward
and their study would be another restatement of Meyer, Kain, and Wohl's
result that auto systems dominate.

2. MASS TRANSIT COSTS

The cost of providing current service levels on existing transit systems is
increasing dramatically. Fares cover only a small percentage of total social
costs, and projections indicate that dramatically increased subsidies may be
necessary in the future.

Since a large fraction of transit costs is accounted for by labor, trends in
wage rates and productivity have a major effect on operating costs. Compensation in the transit industry resembles that in manufacturing and other
unionized local public sectors. Average annual wages in mass transit were
$12,489 in 1974, versus $11,000 for all manufacturing. Trends in transit
wage rates are essentially comparable to the rest of the labor force;
whereas money wages have accelerated with inflation in recent years, real
wages have increased about 1.5 percent per year since 1967. In the early
1960s, real wage gains were about 2.5 percent. Transit employment has
declined from 240,000 in 1950 to 156,400 in 1960 and 138,040 in 1970.[2]
(See table 7.1.)

The principal sources of rising mass transit costs are negligible rates of
productivity growth and little or no growth in passenger utilization. Productivity measured in terms of service provided, either employees per
vehicle or vehicle miles per employee, has been remarkably constant over
the long run. Measured in terms of passengers served—for example, revenue
passengers per employee—productivity has declined from 47,687 in 1950

TABLE 7.1. Mass Transit Productivity and Profitability, 1950–74

Year	Number of Employees (thousands)	Vehicle Miles per Employee (thousands)	Revenue Pass per Employee (thousands)	Operating Surplus (millions)
1950	240.0	12.5	57.7	$66.4
1955	198.0	12.4	46.4	55.7
1960	156.4	13.7	48.1	30.7
1965	145.0	13.8	46.9	−10.6
1970	138.0	13.6	43.0	−288.2
1971	139.1	13.3	39.5	−411.4
1972	138.4	13.7	38.0	−513.1
1973	140.7	13.0	37.6	−738.5
1974	153.1	12.6	37.4	−1299.7

SOURCE: U.S. Department of Transportation (1976), *Labor in the Transit Industry*
(Washington, D.C.: U.S. Government Printing Office).

to 42,971 in 1970 and 37,423 in 1974. Much of the increase in unit cost can be traced to declining utilization of the system. Despite the huge investment in capital since 1965, the output/labor ratio has not increased.

Labor productivity has been low for several reasons. Work rules restrict productivity growth in many ways and negate many labor saving advantages of technological innovations in fare collection and vehicle control.[3] As with other local public services, voters have had great difficulty in retaining control over costs. In the publically owned systems strikes have been relatively infrequent, and many states do not extend bargaining rights to public employees. However, since cessation of public services is a very serious disruption, the threat of a strike is quite powerful.

The federal capital grant program has also had an impact. While capital-labor substitution and higher labor productivity were key arguments in support of federal capital grants, the capital grant program provides elaborate job security. Section 13(c) of the 1964 Urban Mass Transportation Act provides that individual worker's compensation and working conditions not be worsened as a result of a federal grant for a period of four years or the length of time the employee has served, whichever is shorter. More recent interpretations of Section 13(c) have resulted in the minimum benefit period being extended to six years. Operating assistance under the 1974 Act, Section 5, has also been conducted under Section 13(c) agreements.[4] Altshuler has argued that Congress could only pass capital assistance legislation with labor's support, and that the latter was conditional on Section 13(c) job security.[5]

The consequences of these provisions are entirely predictable. Management and unions have reached agreement in order to qualify for federal grants, and in virtually all cases management has chosen to retain labor rather than to make severance payments. Barnum (1972) has argued that the transit industry has a long history of "no layoff" policy, and hence Section 13(c)'s impact is minimal.[6] This seems inconsistent with the reductions in the work force throughout the 1950s and 1960s, in the absence of Section 13(c). Faced with increasingly severe operating deficits, management would probably have reduced its labor force if Section 13(c) did not exist.

An accurate determination of the magnitude of the total costs incurred by existing systems is severely hampered by the quality of transit company financial records. A federal requirement for a uniform set of accounts was only recently instituted, and data is as yet unavailable. The biggest source of differences in accounting practices lies in the treatment of capital costs. Depreciation expenses reported in operating accounts typically represent a very small share of capital costs. Since federal and local taxes paid most or all capital investments since 1965, reported operating costs generally omit capital charges for capital investments after that date; hence reported costs approximately correspond to short-run variable costs. A summary of reported operating deficits for all transit companies is presented in table 7.1. By 1974, the operating deficit had risen to $1.3 billion, about 25¢ per ride.

To calculate appropriate capital charges requires an examination of all capital assets, and a determination of which capital assets are sunk costs. Although data on investments prior to 1964 is very incomplete, it is possible to approximate the magnitude of capital costs since the Mass Transit Capital Grant Program began in 1964. Accumulated bus investment was $1,898 billion, and rail transit (equipment and right-of-way) and other investment was $4,639 billion as of 30 September 1976.[7] Assuming that none of the investments since 1964 are treated as sunken costs, at an 8 percent rate of interest, the annual capital charge for investments since 1964 is $658 million—a 25 percent addition to recorded operating cost.[8]

Examination of the costs and ridership of individual systems provides a more accurate view of transit costs, but an elaborate case by case study is beyond the scope of this chapter. An approximation of operating and some portion of capital costs for the twenty-five largest U.S. cities in 1975 is presented below. Capital investment from 1964 to 1976 was converted to an annual capital charge in 1976, using estimated asset lifetimes and an 8 percent rate of interest.[9] Prior capital costs are considered a sunken cost.

Capital charges and financial operating results for mass transit operators in 1975 are summarized in table 7.2. In the case of the five cities with established rail transit systems (New York, Chicago, Philadelphia, Boston, and Cleveland) operating losses of 50¢ to 75¢ per rider were incurred; Fares cover from one-fourth to one-half of operating costs. Annual capital costs equivalent to federally supported capital projects in the period 1964–76 range from 5 to 30 percent of operating costs (and from one-fourth to one-half of fares). These systems were mostly built prior to the federal assistance program, the vehicle comprising most of the investment since 1964. The newest rail transit system, BART is San Francisco, is discussed in greater detail below.[10]

Three cities have rail transit systems under construction—Washington, Baltimore, and Atlanta. It is impossible to interpret reported operating or capital costs since these systems are incomplete. Ridership data reflect bus operations. Continuation of the METRO mass rail transit system under construction in Washington, D.C., is in jeopardy because of rapidly rising construction estimates. Cost estimates for the approximately 100 mile system are about $6 billion. The Secretary of Transportation has become increasingly unwilling to commit more highway funds or Urban Mass Transit Administration (UMTA) grants, and local communities have been reluctant to increase their contribution. Metro's initial operations have resulted in operating deficits. Whether local communities will agree to share operating deficits, or whether the deficits can be financed by area-wide gasoline or other taxes, is highly problematical.

Cities of the third group are those that have bus systems, and where

TABLE 7.2. Transit System Costs in 1975 in the Twenty-five Largest Cities in the United States

City Size (Rank)	City	1975 Riders[a] (millions)	Operating Cost per Rider ($)	Fares/ operating Cost	Total Capital Grants (millions $)	Annual Capital Charge (millions $)	Capital Cost per Rider[b] ($)	Total Costs per Rider
	Existing Rail							
1	New York	2114.0	1.13[d]	0.484	1498	162.7	0.08	1.21
3	Chicago	369.7	...	0.555	576	68.0	0.18	...
4	Philadelphia	255.0	1.46[c]	0.491	352	52.7	0.21	1.67
6	San Francisco/Oakland	202.0	1.25[c]	0.392	519	66.5	0.33	1.58
7	Boston	151.2	...	0.273	641	61.1	0.40	...
9	Cleveland	61.0	0.53[c]	0.493	32	3.5	0.05	0.58
	Rail Under Construction							
8	Washington	218.0	0.78	0.532	503	50.3	0.23	1.01
14	Baltimore	110.0	0.38	0.633	286	33.4	0.30	0.68
20	Atlanta	58.0	0.58	0.245	550	68.9	1.19	1.77
	Bus Systems[a]							
2	Los Angeles	166.0	0.73	0.342	87	16.7	0.10	0.83
5	Detroit	95.9	...	0.480	60	8.6	0.08	...
10	St. Louis	45.0	0.79	0.351	47	8.5	0.18	0.97
11	Pittsburgh	110.0	0.60	0.502	102	14.4	0.13	0.73
12	Minneapolis	50.0	0.69	0.403	60	8.6	0.17	0.86
15	Dallas	26.0	0.42	0.713	31	4.2	0.16	0.58
16	Milwaukee	44.0	0.50	0.742	17	2.6	0.06	0.56
18	Miami	52.0	0.45	0.531	36	3.8	0.07	0.52
19	San Diego	29.0	0.72	0.380	19	2.0	0.07	0.79
21	Cincinnati	38.0	0.59	0.429	30	3.2	0.08	0.67
22	Kansas City	21.0	0.67	0.380	24	2.6	0.12	0.79
23	Buffalo	43.0	0.39	0.738	27	3.0	0.07	0.46
25	San Jose	6.0	1.86	0.088	13	2.1	0.35	2.21

[a] Ridership data for both rail and bus systems when both exist.
[b] Capital costs shared equally by bus and rail transit systems when both exist.
[c] Operating costs refer to rail system only.
[d] Data unavailable for Houston, Seattle, and Denver among the 25 largest SMSAs.

capital grants have principally been used to acquire new buses, bus garages, and maintenance facilities and to acquire the assets of bankrupt private bus operators. The typical fare of about 30¢ per ride covered about one-half the operating costs in 1975. Capital charges for federal capital grants amount to only 10–20 percent of operating costs. Labor costs comprise about 80 percent of the costs of bus systems.

A review of San Francisco's BART system reveals the very high investment costs associated with building new rail transit systems. BART was designed to compete directly with suburban auto commuting. Most of its stations are located outside the central area, far apart, with high speed service between stops. BART was completed before the dramatic increases in construction prices of the early 1970s, at a total capital cost of $1.6 billion. The system was financed through an $800 million bond issue in 1962 and subsequent toll bridge collections, federal grants, and a modest amount of sales taxes. The sales tax is 0.5 percent in the three counties served by BART.

Webber (1976) has summarized ridership levels and financial returns since the system began operations in 1974. Ridership has been dramatically lower than predicted, operating costs more than twice what had been expected initially, and large operating deficits have resulted. In 1976 the fare of 72¢ per ride paid about one-quarter of the total operating cost. When capital costs are added to the operating costs it becomes clear that the system is very expensive indeed. Amortizing BART's capital costs at a 4.1 percent interest rate—the actual rate on its capital borrowing—implies an annual capital cost of $82 million. This together with operating costs results in an average cost per trip of $4.48, on the current ridership basis (about 37¢ per passenger mile). If capital costs are valued at their true opportunity cost—for example, an assumed 8 percent rate of interest and an infinite life—annual capital charges become $127 million and total cost

TABLE 7.3. Section 5 Estimated Mass Transit Operating Deficits (All figures in millions)

	Actual CY 74 Deficit	FY 77 Deficit	FY 77 Section 5[a]	FY 80 Deficit	FY 77–80 Deficit	Allocation as Percentage of Deficit Section 5
New York City	$464	$555	$116	$1123	$3302	17
Five Rail Cities	348	606	107	1001	3185	16
19 Other Large Cities	223	394	195	658	2085	46
Other Urban Areas	215	387	232	649	2052	55
All Urban Areas	1250	1942	650	3431	10624	31

SOURCE: U.S. Department of Transportation, Urban Mass Transportation Administration, "Projected Operating Deficits, FY 77–81" (mimeograph), by Kenneth Orski.
[a] Allocation of Section 5 operating assistance.

approaches $7 per ride at current ridership levels. Even if ridership increases substantially from its current level of thirty-two million trips per year, the full opportunity cost of a trip on BART will be quite expensive. It is also noteworthy that BART is now experiencing wage costs that are only slightly less than those of the local bus system—10.5¢ per passenger mile versus 13.2¢. The large capital investment made by BART has resulted in little substitution of capital for labor.

Based on the experiences of BART and Metro, the social costs of new rail transit systems are very sizeable. The capital costs of such systems dominate even the most optimistic estimates of passenger revenues. In contrast, in existing rail transit systems, bus and rail transit vehicle investments typically are a small fraction of operating costs, with labor costs dominant.

Projections of future operating deficits for mass transit systems are truly sobering. Transit operating costs rose 8 percent annually in real terms from 1965 to 1975. Assuming 4 percent annual increases in ridership, and an 8 percent annual increase in unit costs, operating deficits nationwide will grow to $3.4 billion by fiscal year 1980—$1.1 billion in New York City alone, and another $1 billion in five other rail cities. These projections of deficits will be much understated if several new rail transit systems are completed, and have no better luck than BART. UMTA has made commitments to heavy rail systems in Buffalo, Miami, and Detroit, and to "people movers" (an automated type of fixed guideway system to improve circulation in downtown areas) in Houston, Cleveland, Los Angeles, and St. Paul. These commitments are of various types, most of which as yet fall short of legal commitment of funds.[11] The cost to the public of urban mass transit travel could obviously rise drastically if all these systems are constructed.

3. AUTOMOBILE EXTERNALITIES

The literature on auto externalities often labels all "bad effects," i.e., negative consequences to households, businesses, or local governments, as external costs. This appears to reflect equity considerations; undesirable outcomes traceable to auto use or highway construction must be the responsibility of auto user.

This definition of *externalities* includes many consequences that are essentially income transfers. The circumstance when one agent's actions affect relative prices, and hence the welfare of others, has been called a pecuniary externality. Examination of the types of "externalities" typically ascribed to urban highways reveals that many are pecuniary rather than real. Because of the very long economic lives of much of the private and public capital stock in urban areas, when changes in accessibility or environmental factors are capitalized into property values, changes in prices are often dramatic. For many of the "external costs" so defined, there may be offsetting gains for other parties. Examples include reductions in housing values, business losses resulting from changing shopping patterns, or reductions in a jurisdiction's property tax base. The particular set of income transfers that these price changes represent may or may not constitute a reduction in social welfare, depending on judgments about the distribution of income. Downs' (1970) extensive catalog of "external" costs associated with highway construction and urban renewal contains no attempt to distinguish between real external costs and income transfers.

In order to distinguish between efficiency and equity effects, the standard approach in welfare economics is to include only real externalities. Baumol and Oates (1975) suggested that an externality is present when one individual's utility or production relationships include real variables whose values are chosen by others without attention to the welfare of the former. Another important distinction is between depletable and undepletable externalities. The latter is the public-good case, wherein one person's exposure to an externality does not reduce its availability to others.

Automobile externalities include congestion, as a depletable externality, and undepletable externalities to parties near the right-of-way. For pedogogical purposes the latter is divided into two subclasses in the discussion below—air pollution and right-of-way damages. Right-of-way damages comprise all nonpollution costs borne by those adjacent to the highway right-of-ways, including noise, aesthetic effects, neighborhood disruption, and immobility created by limited access freeway barriers. Only real externalities are included, i.e., effects based on roadway design, usage, or other physical consequences included in recipients' utility or profit functions. Changes in relative prices due to changing location patterns are excluded. *Adjacent* may refer to a substantial distance. This category also embraces all real costs incurred by displaced parties that are *not* presently accounted for in prevailing policies with respect to public acquisition and compensation for real property taken; these are labelled "construction dislocation" costs below.

Estimates of the magnitudes of the major types of real, negative externalities are based on very incomplete information. A best approximation to cost is offered, indicating a sensitivity to key assumptions and areas of uncertainty. It wll be shown that even quite "liberal" assessments of external costs cause only a small percentage increase to perceived auto costs. costs.

A fundamental problem that runs through the discussion is the location-specific nature of automobile externalities. Damage functions associated with the construction and use of a given roadway vary dramatically throughout and between urban areas. Additionally, differences in the cost of reducing the amount of the externality created may exist between areas.

These differences in benefit and cost functions imply that location-specific policies are necessary to achieve an efficient outcome. Public policy has taken very little account of the location-specific nature of the problem; federal policies with respect to new car emissions standards, ambient air quality standards, and compensation for the acquisition of highway rights-of-way are essentially defined on a national basis.

(A) Congestion

The recognition that congestion may be an important externality in highway travel dates back to Pigou's (1920) determination that when an additional driver on a facility reduces the travel speed of others, an externality exists. The time supplied by travelers is itself a scarce resource whose value must be included in the calculation of the total social cost.

Congestion delays are an increasing function of incoming traffic volume for any given highway facility. An extensive highway engineering literature has described relationships between road design, number of lanes, speeds, and traffic volumes (Wohl, 1967). Congestion costs depend also on valuations of time, which will differ among individuals; hence the extent of congestion externalities will depend in part on the composition of road users. Appropriate pricing under such circumstances is discussed in Mohring's chapter in this volume. Where users of a facility have different values of time, as is typical in urban highway facilities, the establishment of any given toll will involve equity judgments since it will overstate the time value for some and understate it for others.

Several studies have estimated congestion costs based on an assumed value of time for the average user. Urban congestion costs are very high during a short period of the day, but very low throughout most other periods. An optimal pricing scheme would entail very high tolls for very limited portions of a given week, normally only a few hours. Walters (1961) estimated congestion costs at 2.2¢ per mile in 1959 in urban areas, with costs as high as 10¢ to 15¢ per vehicle mile during rush hours. Mohring (1964) estimated marginal cost tolls for the Twin Cities in 1958 at about 10¢ per vehicle mile in the morning (thirty minutes) and evening (one hour) peaks, about 6¢ throughout the day, and between 1¢ and 4¢ for the evening. Dewees' (1976) analysis of Toronto streets near the CBD in 1973 revealed peak hour inbound congestion costs that averaged 38¢ per vehicle mile. Keeler's (1975) analysis of San Francisco freeways in 1973 recommended congestion tolls of 16.3¢ per vehicle mile for the six peak hours of the week in the central city, and 1¢ to 3¢ in other periods; for suburban freeways the results were 4.4¢ during the peak and 1¢ to 2¢ at other times.

The sharp nonlinearity in congestion cost functions implies that congestion costs and tolls will be quite sensitive to the amount of capacity and its use. This will vary among cities with different sizes, densities, and road networks. The average congestion cost for all motoring is an aggregation of trips made throughout the day and will be much below peak-hour costs. The typical household makes several trips a day, but only a small fraction occur at the very peak hours. One nationwide survey revealed that 17.9 percent of all vehicle miles, or 16.0 percent of all trips, were made in the two one-hour morning and evening peaks.[12] Another 10 percent of all trips were made immediately before or after the evening peak hour. To summarize, for the largest cities, approximately one-fourth of all auto trips entail substantial congestion costs, whereas very little congestion occurs for the remainder. Five cents a trip or 7.5¢ a vehicle mile, valuing time at $5.00 per hour, would approximate the average congestion toll for all urban trips in the largest metropolitan areas. The implications of these congestion costs for highway pricing and investment are discussed below.

(B) Air Pollution

For the purpose of making cost comparisons among modes, auto pollution externalities are defined to include any costs of reducing emissions, costs of relocation or other averting actions taken by households, and the damage cost to households that remain exposed to pollution emissions.

The cost of pollution externalities will depend on the amount of driving, the fleet mix, and the nature of urban development. Many of pollution's effects are undetermined, and the health effects and their valuation remain subject to debate. EPA (1974) estimated that in 1971 automobiles contributed approximately three-quarters of the carbon monoxide, over one-half of the hydrocarbon, and one-half of the nitrogen oxide emissions in urban areas. Current pollution damages are an inaccurate reflection of costs over the long run, since public policies have been established that will substantially reduce future pollution. Horowitz (1974) estimated that the introduction of newer, cleaner vehicles, will, in 1985, reduce total vehicle emissions by about 75 percent over 1975 levels, less for NOX and more for CO and HC. These are very dramatic improvements over pre-control levels. After about 1985, emission levels will begin to rise slowly as motoring increases offset the emissions savings associated with replacement of older vehicles. Pollution costs after 1985 will increase approximately proportional to the growth in auto driving after that date.

The approach adopted below assumes that public policy is designed to achieve automobile emission levels that correspond to an efficient outcome, where the marginal cost of abatement equals the marginal cost of emissions, conditional on stationary source emissions. The principal expression of congressional judgments on vehicle pollution damage and abatement functions is in the establishment of national ambient air quality and new vehicle emission standards. The 1970 Clean Air Act authorized the Environmental Protection Agency to establish national ambient air quality standards, which include limits on hydrocarbons (HC), carbon monoxide (CO), and nitrous oxide (NOX). Standards for new car emissions limit these pollutants.

Empirical evidence on pollution abatement and damage functions is limited. The discussion below first reviews the literature on the cost of pollution abatement—the cost of reducing pollution to statutory standards from 1968 precontrol levels—and then considers the valuation of residual damages. The implications of these estimates for total automobile externalities costs are noted in subsection D.

Estimation of the cost of emission reductions involves an assessment of the direction of auto technology and a prediction of the future price of fuel. To date, the most complete study of automobile technology is that of the National Academy of Sciences (1974); Dewees' (1976c) summary of the findings of the National Academy of Sciences study is presented below. The evolution in emission standards and estimates of the cost of compliance are shown in table 7.4. The standards prevailing in 1976 represent an 80 percent reduction in emissions from precontrolled levels, using a simple weighted average of hydrocarbons (HC), carbon monoxide (CO), and nitrogen oxide (NOX). Because of extraordinary technological progress, the cost of meeting any given standard is continually declining over time in real terms. The 1973 standards were met by adjusting engine carburetion

TABLE 7.4. Cost over Automobile Life of Meeting Alternative Pollution Standards

Year Standard Achieved	Standard (grams/mile)			Percentage Pollution Controlled	Total Cost over 1970 Vehicle (1974 dollars)
	HC	CO	NOX		
			Dewees		
1973	3.0	28.0	3.1	52	753
1975	1.5	15.0	3.1	63	265
1976	0.4	3.4	2.0	80	473
1977[a]	0.4	3.4	0.4	94	844
1980[a]	0.4	3.4	0.4	94	500
1985[a]	0.4	3.4	0.4	94	0
			Interagency Task Force		
1980[a]	0.4	3.4	0.4	94	1276[b]
1985[a]	0.4	3.4	0.4	94	1135[b]
1980	0.4	3.4	1.0	83	915[b]

[a] Statutory Standard: 90% reduction in all emissions from precontrol levels.
[b] Interagency Task Force cost estimates, defined as cost increment over 1976 model standard, were added to Dewees' cost estimate of reaching 1976 standard. Actual 1976–77 model standard was 1.5 grams/mile HC, 15 grams/mile CO, and 2.0 grams/mile NOX.

and timing to reduce NOX emissions, which reduced fuel efficiency. In 1975 catalytic converters were introduced that burned up pollutants and allowed engine timing to be reset, restoring lost fuel economy.

The least-cost technology and the cost of meeting more stringent standards is subject to greater doubt. If HC and CO emissions were reduced to the statutory limit, but NOX emissions kept at their current level, diesel engines would become the dominant technology. However, diesel engines are incapable of reducing NOX emissions to the statutory standards, and meeting the statutory standards on NOX emissions by using conventional internal combustion engines substantially increases cost. (The least-cost technology is still open to debate.) Dewees estimated that compliance with the statutory standards by 1977 would have cost $844 (in 1974 dollars) over the life of the car, including $302 list price, $75 of maintenance, and $467 in fuel. Deferring the deadline to 1980 reduces the cost to $500.

A recent U.S. Government Interagency Task Force (1977) estimate fuel economy and costs associated with alternative emission standards at about twice Dewees' estimates. Assuming the use of currently available and tested technology, compliance with the statutory standards in 1980 would entail a fuel penalty of about 14 percent and a lifetime cost per vehicle of $803 over the prevailing 1977 new car standards, or $1,276 over 1970 vehicles. Deferring the deadline until 1985 reduces the cost to $1,135 over the life of the car.

To summarize, compliance with the new car emission standards by the early 1980s would entail abatement costs over the life of the car of between $500 and $1,000 over vehicles without emission controls, assuming a gasoline price of 60¢ per gallon. This represents an increase in total operating costs of from 3 to 6 percent. More pessimistic assumptions about the course of future technology might increase abatement costs by 50 percent; a doubling in the price of fuel would also increase abatement costs by about 50 percent.

The second component of social costs, the value of remaining pollution damage, is more difficult to estimate. The use of national air quality and emissions standards presumably reflects the view that administrative costs of unique local standards are too high. In actual fact, local variations in damage functions are dramatic. Federal standards for ambient air quality established by the 1970 Clean Air Act can easily be met in some urban areas but not in others. The value of remaining pollution damage once the statutory standards for new cars are achieved can vary considerably between cities. About three-quarters of all metropolitan areas are currently in compliance with the ambient air quality standards. The sixty-three cities that will require additional transportation control measures for compliance by 1985 include many of the larger cities. The measures include car pooling, reserved bus lanes, gas rationing, limits on on-and-off street parking, and other measures that reduce automobile driving.

One estimate of the value of pollution damage relies on urban property values. Numerous studies have estimated hedonic price equations by relating property values to quality characteristics of the dwelling unit, the neighborhood, and the physical environment.[13] By including air quality variables in the equation, it is possible to determine the market's assessment of pollution damage.

The most carefully conducted study of air pollution to follow this approach is by Harrison and Rubinfeld (1976) and uses 1970 census tract data for Boston. The damage function is nonlinear, with the marginal valuation of a unit of pollution exposure to consumers rising with the level of pollution. The valuation on pollution damage is related to income level. Using the hedonic price equations, property values were calculated for several alternative automobile and transit technologies, including a comparison of the 1971 automobile standards with an auto technology in compliance with the statutory standards. Ingram (1975) estimated pollution levels in each of 500 zones in the Boston Standard Metropolitan Statistical Area using diffusion models that translated emission levels from major expressways into exposure levels in all geographic submarkets. Using Ingram's estimates of exposure, Harrison and Rubinfeld estimated the average change in household property values associated with the two automobile emission levels at $830.

These comparisons provide one measure of pollution damage. If the compliance with the statutory standards that reduces emissions by 90 percent is worth $830 to the typical household, the value of the marginal unit of emission reduction at the statutory standard is very low, and certainly well below $10 for each 1 percent reduction. As presented above, the marginal cost of emission reduction as the statutory standard for new cars is approached is much higher. This suggests that the emissions standards are too strict for Boston. (In addition, Boston has a more serious pollution exposure problem than most metropolitan areas.) Harrison and Rubinfeld's estimates would imply that remaining pollution damages in 1985 would be very small, probably less than $100 per household.

It is difficult to generalize from a single study, and local variations in the severity of pollution damages are significant. Zerbe and Croke's (1975) analysis of Chicago estimated the value of current pollution damage at less than 1¢ per mile.

To summarize, to the extent that public policy reflects society's values, the reluctance to impose additional restrictions on cars suggests that residual pollution damages are relatively small. (Because of problems in organizing the large number of parties damaged, public policy may be biased toward an understatement of pollution damages.) An upper band on the cost of residual damage is given by the product of the amount of emissions and the marginal cost of abatement, each evaluated at the statutory standard. Based on the above estimates of the shape of the marginal cost of abatement function and the amount of emissions reduction, this amount is less than the cost of abatement. One-half cent per mile is used below. In individual cities much higher values may be appropriate.

(C) Right-of-Way

Right-of-way externalities depend on the density and character of urban development and are very location specific. Most right-of-way externalities —noise, smell, and aesthetic effects—are quite pronounced at very nearby properties but diminish with distance. Although a roadway may be visible to residents one-half mile away or may cause residents to alter their local travel due to limited access barriers, these effects are probably judged small by people who are not very near the right-of-way. Very few empirically based reports exists on right-of-way externalities, and measurement is difficult since such factors as "neighborhood disruption" are very subjective concepts.

The approach below uses noise as a proxy for all right-of-way externalities. A limited literature on noise measurement and valuation exists. Noise levels vary with the type of roadway, traffic volumes, speed, mix of cars and trucks, and local topography.

Colony's (1966) analysis of residential property values adjacent to the Detroit-Toledo expressway indicated that values were reduced by 20 to 30 percent, but only for those residences within fifty feet of the right-of-way. Gamble (1974) examined values of properties adjacent to major expressways in four urban areas in the period 1969–71. An index of noise based on a weighted average of traffic noise throughout the day was included in a regression that explained property values. Noise is probably a proxy for all right-of-way effects in his equations. Results varied somewhat with the study area, with the average price reduction $82 per dbA increase in the noise index ("effective perceived noise level in decibels," dbA, is a measure of human reactions to noise-associated air pressure changes). The presence of a freeway would increase the noise index by about 17 dbA over residual noise levels in areas without highways. This implies a decrease in property value of approximately $1500 (in 1970 dollars) associated with the noise. More recent real-estate prices based on realtors' assessments suggests somewhat higher valuations. $7,500 discounts may be appropriate in middle-income suburban areas for immediately adjacent single-family housing, and $2,500 for nonadjacent, noise-impacted properties.

To summarize the consequences of these calculations, consider households with an exposure level above 70 dbA, but neglect the externalities of households that are at lower noise levels. The 70 dbA contour typically varies from 200 to 400 feet along either side of limited access urban freeways.[14] In suburban areas with single-family housing on one-fifth acre lots, approximately 100 houses will border the highway per mile of right-of-way, and another 100 houses will fall within the 70 dbA contour but will usually be separated from the right-of-way by the immediately adjacent property and a local street. Noise costs in this case are one million dollars per mile of right-of-way. The author has no basis for predicting whether nonresidential activities in place of homes would entail larger or smaller costs than these.

In more central residential areas with low- to medium-density apartments, from five to ten households may rent in the space of a single-family lot. Since renters conduct much less of their activity outside of their dwelling unit than do single-family residents, smaller noise discounts are assumed. Adjacent residents' rent is discounted by $25 per month, whereas no noise discount is assumed for nonadjacent renters in the 70 dbA contour. This is equivalent to a perpetuity worth $3,750 at an 8 percent rate of interest. (The assumption of rental noise premiums in perpetuity is based on the premise that noise impacts are capitalized into present land values. Noise compatible activities should be able to obtain land at discount prices in the future, just as they can now.) For the range of rental densities noted above, twenty-five to fifty households per acre, this amounts to costs ranging from $1.8 million to $3.6 million per mile.

In very central locations, noise exposure will be felt largely by business and high-density rental properties. It is very difficult to assess whether total costs would be higher or lower than in medium density residential areas described above. More persons would be exposed but most activity is conducted indoors, in completely enclosed offices and spaces.

These estimated right-of-way externality costs are a significant addition to highway construction costs. For cities of 500,000 to 1 million in population, a four-lane expressway in the CBD would entail a land cost of 2.9 million dollars (in 1973 dollars) and 2.2 million dollars in the suburban fringe of the CBD.[15] Land costs may be less than 35 percent of total capital costs in small cities, but approximately one-half of those in larger cities. Right-of-way damages (based on the real-estate assessments above) could double the cost of land acquisition for roads.

A different type of externality associated with rights-of-way are costs not covered in the land acquisition and construction process. Current laws require compensation to those displaced by a highway right-of-way. In addition to fair market value for real property acquired, certain relocation costs are paid and compensation is made in cases where replacement housing is more expensive.[16] The determination of fair market values has been criticized; in many instances foreknowledge of freeway construction has resulted in curtailment of investment and maintenance, neighborhood deterioration, and a greater number of vacancies. A determination of property value after this process has started will understate the total effect:

for vacant units in the right-of-way, households will have paid their own relocation costs; and congestion and disruption during construction are externalities not covered.

An elaborate analysis of each project would be required to determine the magnitude of costs and whether compensation was appropriate. Both real and pecuniary externalities are involved. The analysis below assumes that prevailing land acquisition costs do not reflect all social costs since they do not provide adequate compensation for those displaced. In the sensitivity analysis two alternative assumptions are illustrated—that prevailing land acquisition costs must be increased 50 and 100 percent to fully account for the externalities associated with displacement. Although allowing dramatically higher compensation, as will be seen, these amounts would add little to total auto costs.

(D) A Retrospective View of Comparative Costs

Different technologies offer different types of service and entail different proportions of money and time costs. Relatively little is known about the particular values consumers place on various time, cost, service, and reliability characteristics.

In making comparisons of auto costs relative to other modes, assumptions regarding the valuation of time and parking costs dominate the results. For any reasonable monetary valuation of time, time costs constitute a sizeable proportion of total costs, especially in middle- and upper-income households. Dewees' (1976) estimates of perceived costs to travelers in Toronto for a variety of modes revealed that time costs may range from one-fourth to three-fourths of total costs. Because public modes typically involve more waiting and greater door to door time in all but the densest travel markets, high valuations of time favor the auto.

No attempt has been made to repeat the accounting procedures used by Meyer et al. (1965) and Keeler et al. (1975). The estimates of transit subsidies and auto externalities presented above are intended to extend earlier cost comparisons that neglected these social costs.

The current operating costs of existing transit systems were about 60¢ per passenger or 12¢ per mile in 1975 for bus travel, and $1.20 per transit rider or 15¢ per mile.[17] An additional 10¢ to 25¢ per passenger in capital costs is being borne by taxpayers. These costs are below that of auto travel —including all externalities and parking costs—as presented below. However, transit systems are not providing service comparable to autos in terms of door to door time or reliability, except in very limited types of markets. (For example, but travel times are often twice those of private automobiles.) The newest rail transit systems achieve higher performance at very

TABLE 7.5. Automobile Costs, Including Externalities

Costs	¢/mile in 1975 prices
Private costs, 1975 vehicle:[a]	
Fuel	2.28¢
Other inputs	10.71
Roadway: land	.57
Roadway: construction	.93
	14.49¢
Undepletable externalities:	
Pollution abatement costs:	
vehicle, maintenance	.37¢
fuel	.47
Residual pollution damage	.50
Right-of-way costs	.57
Construction dislocation	.29
	2.20
Congestion externalities	5.00
Total: private costs plus all externalities	21.69
Additions to total costs under alternative assumptions:	
pollution technology twice as expensive	+ .84
damages to right-of-way twice as expensive	+ .86
price of fuel 90¢/gallon	+2.75

[a] Base case assumes standard size car priced at $4379; fuel price 45¢/gallon net of user charges; and 20 miles per gallon.

great cost. BART rapid rail costs will approximate 35¢ per mile when capital costs are amortized and Washington Metro rail costs will exceed 50¢ per passenger mile.

Auto costs are quite sensitive to assumptions about congestion and parking costs but are otherwise little altered by the inclusion of externalities unless very extreme assumptions are made regarding pollution or right-of-way damages. A summary of both private auto and external costs is presented in table 7.5. Capital costs for roadways, defined on a long-run average cost basis, of 1.8¢ per mile are included in private costs. It is assumed that the legislated fuel economy standard of 28 miles per gallon for new cars by 1985 is met, which implies an average fleet consumption of 20 miles per gallon. Private auto costs (in 1975 prices) for a vehicle meeting 1975 pollution standards are 14.49¢ per mile.

The biggest component of external costs is congestion. As noted, for very limited peak periods, and on certain facilities, congestion costs can be quite substantial; peak-hour charges might be 20¢ per mile, with an average of 5¢ per mile for all trips. External costs of pollution and right-of-way damages are estimated to be 2.2¢ per mile, an 11 percent addition to private costs. Pollution costs are about two-thirds of these externalities costs. The cost consequences of more "liberal" assessments of external costs are also presented. The more pessimistic assumptions regarding pollution technology presented above imply auto costs would be increased by almost 1¢ per mile. If externalities associated with rights-of-way are judged doubly expensive, costs are increased about 1¢ per mile. In short, if the price of gasoline remains at 45¢ per gallon exclusive of taxes, undepletable external costs are a small fraction of total costs. (See table 7.5.)

There are two more extreme assumptions regarding auto externalities that dramatically alter the cost comparisons: reducing pollution emissions significantly below the statutory vehicle emission standards, and placing all highways underground. Based on current technology, the cost of reducing emissions below the statutory standard would probably dramatically increase auto costs and perhaps necessitate a substitute for the internal combustion engine. The cost of underground highway construction is best revealed by examining the cost differentials of at-grade and underground rail transit and bus-way facilities.[18] Underground highway construction would increase highway capital cost on the order of 1,000 percent, and would almost double automobile costs.

Sensitivity analysis reveals fuel prices are more important than externalities, as defined here. It seems quite possible that a doubling of fuel prices in real terms will occur by 1985; this will increase private auto costs by 19 percent and total social costs by 13 percent.

The final cost component nowhere included is parking. Parking fees often differ widely from social costs. Many workers receive free parking from their employer; due to the tax-free nature of this form of compensation, the employer's cost understates the real cost. Much on-street parking in off-peak hours has very low social costs, below parking meter charges. Parking costs may approach $3 per day in downtown areas of the largest cities, but real costs are much below that in the off peak, in suburban areas, and in smaller cities. Parking costs for the work trip in densest areas can be a significant social cost component.

Comparisons of the total social costs of different modes is complicated by the service differentials between auto and transit systems. Auto systems offer a much superior service at a significantly higher social cost. The cost of improving transit service is very high in all but the highest density markets. User charges are clearly well below social costs of all modes. The social costs of urban motoring may be 15 percent or more above privately perceived costs, exclusive of parking, for the non-peak-hour trip. Peak-hour travel costs may be 50 percent or more above privately perceived costs when congestion and parking costs are included.

It is not likely that these cost relationships will change significantly for some time. Although real fuel prices will probably double or triple over a ten-year period, the transit industry will probably be plagued by low productivity growth and low utilization. No dramatic reversion to a denser, more concentrated land-use pattern is evident. An extension of the 8 percent annual rate of increase in real transit costs will double transit costs in ten years and will completely negate the fuel price increases confronting motorists. Technological improvements and auto design changes that increase fuel efficiency are occurring rapidly. It may well be that solar, coal liquification, or other energy technologies will put an upper limit on fossil fuel prices before a means is found to limit the escalation in transit labor costs.

4. PRICING AND INVESTMENT POLICIES AND THEIR IMPACTS

The theory of optimal pricing and investment where congestion and pollution externalities exist has been well developed. Theoretical treatments have elaborated proper pricing and investment criteria under these circumstances, both under first-best assumptions and under a variety of second-best cases in which restrictions are placed on prices or on the level of capacity. There exists a wide variety of institutional or administrative constraints and high transaction costs such that first-best pricing rules cannot be applied, and hence many minor modifications of this theoretical second-best literature could be envisioned.

Definitive conclusions on the consequences of current pricing practices or alternative pricing regimes for travel demand and metropolitan development are absent from the literature. Whereas qualitative results of alternative pricing rules can be deduced, empirical assessment of effects requires that the entire development process be modeled. Only limited success has been achieved in this latter task. (See the chapters by Wheaton and Ingram in this volume.) Monocentric models that examine the relationship between selected transport policies and urban spatial structure have been developed. These could be extended in several directions. Relaxation of the assumption that space can be treated in one dimension—distance to center—requires simulation modeling, which is not far advanced.[19] Quantitative assessment of the effects of transport externalities and pricing policies on city land use are therefore very imprecise.

Theoretical analyses of congestion tolls have been based on a variety of assumptions about demand and cost functions.[20] Perhaps the simplest analysis is that of serving a fixed demand between points by two or more facilities. The least-cost solution requires that the marginal cost associated with an additional user on each road be equal, a solution that will typically require congestion tolls if congestion exists and cost functions for all roads are not identical.

Another application is the case in which travelers may alter, in response to congestion costs, the time of day that they use a given facility. Again, the simplest cases are those in which desired arrival times are fixed, and the problem is to schedule departures so as to minimize travel plus waiting cost. One special case of interest in certain urban contexts is Vickrey's (1969) "pure bottleneck" case, in which a fixed number of travelers must pass through a facility with fixed capacity less than adequate to allow all travelers to complete their use of the facility at the desired times. In the absence of a toll, a queue develops. A toll varying with the magnitude of the demand-capacity imbalance at each point in time internalizes the congestion externality and eliminates the queue.

The more general congestion problem incorporates conventional demand functions, allowing travelers to substitute peak and off-peak trips, trips on different roads, or consumption of other commodities, depending on relative prices. This is attributable to Boiteaux (1956), Strotz (1965), and Mohring (1970).[21] Mohring's paper extended the earlier work by including many of the important second-best cases, including constraints both on prices that could be charged and on permissible deficits. Assume consumer $i(i = 1 \cdots I)$ may allocate his income $r^i - h^i$ (resources less head tax) among these commodities: $x_1{}^i$, trips in period 1; $x_2{}^i$, trips in period 2; and $x_3{}^i$, all other goods. Transport services are provided by a capital facility with annual costs K. Variable costs of producing trips in time period j is $C_j \equiv C(X_j/\alpha_j, K)$ for $j = 1, 2$. α is the fraction of the year when peak demand exists, and $\alpha_1 + \alpha_2 = 1$; is α_1; X_j/α_j is the annual rate of output in period j, when output is produced at a constant rate throughout the year. Resources, r, can be converted into X_3 at a unit price.

The resource allocation problem is to maximize

$$Z \equiv W(U^1 \cdots U^I) + \lambda(\sum_i r_i - \alpha_1 C_1 - \alpha_2 C_2 - K - X_3), \quad (1)$$

choosing prices on the two roads, P_1 and P_2, head taxes, h_i, and the size of the capital facility, K. Differentiating equation (1) with respect to K yields:

$$\frac{\partial K}{\partial K} = -\lambda(\alpha_1 C_{1K} + \alpha_2 C_{2K} + 1) = 0, \quad (2)$$

where C_{1K} and C_{2K} are derivatives of operating costs in the two time periods with respect to capacity, K. Capacity (K) should be chosen such that a dollar spent thereon just offsets the attendant savings in operating costs. Differentiating with respect to prices in the two periods yields:

$$\sum_i W_i \sum_k U_k{}^i X_{kj}{}^i - \lambda[C_{1x}X_{1j} + C_{2x}X_{2j} + X_{3j}] = 0, \quad (3)$$

where C_{1x} and C_{2x} are short-run marginal costs in the two time periods—i.e., $C_{jx} = \partial C_j/\partial(X_j/\alpha_j)$ for $j = 1, 2$. The utility maximization for each household i yields expressions relating $X_{kj}{}^i$, $U_k{}^i$, P_j and $r^i - h^i$; upon substitution into equation (3), two equations result:

$$\begin{bmatrix} S_{11} & S_{21} \\ S_{12} & S_{22} \end{bmatrix} \begin{bmatrix} P_1 - C_{11} \\ P_2 - C_{22} \end{bmatrix} = \begin{bmatrix} 0 \\ 0 \end{bmatrix}. \tag{4}$$

The matrices of S_{jk} are summations across individuals of Hicks-Slutsky pure substitution effects, i.e.,

$$S_{jk} = \sum_i \left(\partial X_j{}^i / \partial P_k - X_k{}^i \cdot \frac{\partial X_j{}^i}{\partial h^i} \right).$$

The matrix of substitution effects is necessarily positive definite, hence equation (4) requires that price equal marginal cost in both time periods. This necessitates a toll equal to the difference between marginal cost and perceived average cost in each period. If the production function for transportation is characterized by constant returns to scale, short-run marginal cost pricing will yield revenues just sufficient to cover capital costs.

The most important second-best case for purposes of analysing urban transport systems in the United States is that in which a single toll is charged for all periods, such as a gasoline tax. Mohring (1970) has extended his model to include this case as well as cases of deficit or surplus financing.[22] In the case requiring no deficit or surplus, the optimal single toll lies between short-run marginal costs of the two time periods. With a single toll constraint, capacity is inefficiently utilized. The capacity chosen in this circumstance is *larger* than would be chosen in the first-best case of equivalent prices and marginal costs in each time period. One consequence of the failure to implement peak/off-peak pricing is the need for more capacity. Mohring's framework is easily extended to include several modes or facilities, times of day, and alternative pricing or financing constraints.

Theoretical analysis incorporating the effects of both congestion and the absence of congestion tolls on metropolitan development has generally been confined to analyses of monocentric models. Two important conclusions emerge from these models. First, the absence of congestion charges in transport prices results in an equilibrium rent gradient that is too flat; hence household residential choices result in a more dispersed urban form than optimal. Second, the appropriate investment rules for transport must be altered in the second-best case in which transport is improperly priced.

Solow (1972) first formulated the problem of nonlinearity in congestion costs in a monocentric model. The principal analytic complication when congestion is included in a monocentric model is the introduction of a differential equation relating land rents and population density. Transport prices for a household living at x depend on travel demand, and hence the number of people living beyond x, which is itself a function of the rent gradient. Two differential equations in land rents, $r(x)$, and transport prices, $t(x)$, must be solved in such models.[23]

The several models of this process differ principally in their assumptions that describe the transport sector or household utility functions. Transport capacity is generally assumed to be proportionate to land devoted to transport. Solow's formulation is outlined below.[24] Households choose a consumption good, c and space, s, and a distance to the CBD, X, so as to maximize $U(s, c) = g \log c + h \log s$, subject to the budget constraint $y = c + r(x) \cdot s + t(x)$, where $r(x)$ is rent at distance X. The equilibrium bid-rent surface is as follows:

$$r(x) = r(l) \cdot \left[\frac{y - t(x)}{y - t(l)} \right] \frac{g + h}{h} , \tag{5}$$

where $r(l)$ is rent at distance l. Land at distance x is devoted to housing in proportion $b(x)$, and transport $1 - b(x)$. $n(x)$ households live at x. For land demanded to equal land supplied at each x implies $s \cdot n(x) dx = 2\pi x b(x) dx$. Since s is a function of land or transport prices, land market clearing can be expressed as a first order differential equation in $t(x)$:

$$n(x) = \frac{2\pi r(1)}{ky} x b(x) \left(\frac{y - t(x)}{y - t(1)} \right) \frac{g + h}{h} - 1 . \tag{6}$$

The cost of transportation is positively related to demand, the sum of the trips by all households living beyond x that commute to the center, and inversely related to capacity as follows:

$$t(x) = \alpha \int_1^x (N(x)/2\pi x(1 - b(x)))^m dx , \tag{7}$$

where $N(x) = \int_x^R n(x) dx = \int_x^R \frac{2\pi x}{s} b(x) \; dx$.

This can be rewritten as

$$\frac{y - t(x)}{y - t(1)} = - \frac{a}{y} (2\pi)^{-m} \left(\frac{N(x)}{x(1 - b(x))} \right)^m . \tag{8}$$

Boundary conditions specify the total population, N, and rents at the center, $r(1)$. Solution of the model requires solution of the two first-order differential equation in $t(x)$ and $n(x)$, equation (6) and (8).

The transport sector in these models is characterized by congestion, but households only perceive the average transport cost, $t(x)$. The consequence is a nonoptimal location pattern. The high congestion costs are incurred near the city center. The optimal toll is a function of x. The imposition of marginal cost tolls would imply a steeper rent gradient near the city center and a flatter gradient at more distant locations. Space per person would also be affected by the imposition of tolls, with higher densities in more close-in locations and the population distribution more skewed toward the city center.

The appropriate investment in transportation is also dependent on the pricing policy pursued. The benefits of adding to transport capacity, as measured by the policy pursued. The benefits of adding to transport capacity, as measured by the savings in travel costs associated with the addition of transport capacity, will be greater in the absence of congestion tolls than if such tolls were employed. Solow (1973) considered the case in which $b(x)$ is a linear function of x. Robson (1976) and Kanemoto (1977) considered the general case in which $b(x)$ could be any continuous function of x, which is a problem in the calculus of variation. The important conclusions of these models are: first, unless congestion tolls are employed, location decisions will be nonoptimal; second, a standard cost-benefit investment criterion in which the benefits of additional capacity in the form of lower transport costs are compared to the investment costs of land leads to nonoptimal results. Land values are an inappropriate measure of social costs in the presence of congestion that is not internalized by congestion tolls. Under most assumptions, these models reveal that in the absence of congestion tolls too many resources are devoted to roads and a more dispersed urban form than optimal results. This is a familiar second-best result, that investment criteria must be altered in the absence of marginal cost pricing.

A useful extension of these models introduces transit as an alternative mode. This permits an analysis of the effects of city size and density, highway congestion, highway and transit pricing and investment policy, and transit technology on mode choice, transit system performance and cost, and rent and density gradients.

The interest in such a class of models derives from the inverse relation of auto performance measures to trip density, whereas just the reverse describes transit performance. As noted, rail transit service is a decreasing cost sector.

The indivisibility associated with bus size and the importance of schedule frequency is such that costs of a given service level exhibit increasing returns over a considerable range of output levels. Higher travel volumes and higher densities of trip originations and destinations near the city center would therefore increase the attractiveness of transit relative to auto systems. Gradients of travel-performance measures of auto and transit systems may intersect, implying a boundary inside which transit is the optimal choice.[25]

In one example of such a model (Duff and Straszheim, 1978), an auto technology as above—characterized by congestion—is combined with a radial transit system with a fixed number of corridors of a given length. Time is included in the utility function. The description of transit technology includes specification of speed, headway, train size, and the number of corridors, which incorporates trade-offs between schedule delays, capacity, and the density of travel. Line-haul time will depend on distance, speed, and the number of stations. Waiting and access time will include the trip to the station and the wait for the train; the former will depend on the number of radial lines and the station spacing, the latter on headway. Costs of providing transit service include a fixed component, related to the number and length of radials, and a variable component, related to use.

Both highway and transit pricing and investment policies must be specified to complete the model. For any given allocation of land to housing, transit, and highways at each distance, marginal and average cost prices can be calculated. The optimal marginal cost toll for each mode will be related to distance because of the congestion externalities for highways and increasing returns for transit. One interesting alternative pricing rule is average cost pricing with tolls insensitive to distance, which approximates current pricing practice. Varying amounts of subsidy to transit or roads, financed by head taxes, could be analyzed, as could policies of cross-subsidy between modes.

Although the specification of transport options is complex, the model reduces to two differential equations in land rents and density. The interdependence arises because density affects travel cost or time and hence bid-rent functions. There are two principal characteristics of the solutions of this type of model. Except under very limited and particular assumptions about utility functions and travel time and cost functions, the equilibrium rent gradient is composed of two intersecting bid-rent functions that correspond to travel on each mode. The least-cost mode choice will depend on distance; a discontinuity will typically occur at the intersection. Since both time and money costs of the two modes are relevant to households, and both time and cost gradients differ by mode, the boundary at which people switch from transit to auto can be inside or outside the distance at which travel time functions intersect.

This class of models has familiar applications in control theory. Derivation of optimal toll gradients given land allocations to the two modes, or derivation of optimal land to the two modes, the boundary, the number of transit radials, and the headway between trains are all control problems.

The characteristic that all households inside a given boundary use transit and all those residing outside use autos arises from the assumption of a common utility function for all households.[26] At any given distance, only one mode can be preferred. Introducing variation in utility functions into the model can produce the result that residents at any distance n differ in their mode choice, a result traceable to differences in their valuation of the marginal rate of substitution of time and money. This added realism substantially increases the complexity of the model but appears to indicate a useful direction for further research.

The qualitative conclusions from these analytic models of congestion pricing and land use are apparent. In the presence of congestion externalities, failure to implement marginal cost tolls results in excessive peak-hour travel and a more dispersed urban form; imposition of such tolls could result in more trips being made in the off-peak hours, shorter trip lengths, and less travel generally. The last can be achieved by multi-purpose trips, and car pooling might be encouraged. Location patterns might also be affected.

Little is known about the empirical magnitude of these adjustments. Available evidence suggests that time elasticities are significantly greater than price elasticities for the majority of drivers. The increased speeds resulting from the imposition of peak-hour tolls would tend to offset the pure price effect of a toll, and hence the demand for peak-hour travel may be quite inelastic with respect to the monetary price. A significant degree of residential relocation seems quite unlikely. The possibilities described above for adjusting trip-making would allow households much flexibility, without mandating alterations in place of work or residence. Peak-hour trips constitute only a fraction of the total number of trips or vehicle miles driven by the typical household. The "gradient" of total household travel costs with respect to residential location would not be significantly altered by the imposition of peak-hour tolls except in a few of the very densest cities with high-volume travel corridors. The significant effects of peak-hour tolls would be improved utilization of highways and reduced need for capacity, rather than a dramatic alteration in land uses.

There has been a similar analytic treatment of pollution externalities. To the extent that pollution damages can be traced to automobile use, a pollution tax related to the volume of traffic and location is appropriate. In the monocentric models, pollution gradients alter land use and rent gradients. An optimal pollution tax gradient can be derived that will remedy the misallocation in the land market (Robson, 1976). Duff and Straszheim (1977) included both pollution and congestion externalities in a monocentric model, with air pollution forming an argument in the utility function. It is possible that the rent gradient will slope upward over some interval if air quality is sufficiently valued and auto emissions are sufficiently great. Alternative engine technologies and pricing rules alter rent and density gradients and city size.

The incorporation of pollution and congestion effects in multi-mode models and optimization through pricing, investment, and pollution regulations considerably extends the complexity of monocentric models. Unfortunately, monocentric models are only the crudest approximation to real-world cities with decentralized employment. The most productive direction for future research of congestion pricing and investment problems would appear to be the devising of more realistic models of urban spatial structure that would include decentralized employment and nonradial travel patterns.

5. PRICING POLICIES:
ADMINISTRATIVE AND EQUITY CONSIDERATIONS

The principal conclusion of this review of urban transportation technology and user charges is that current prices must be substantially increased to reflect full social costs. Although auto externalities will add to auto user charges, transit fares also are much below cost. Highway subsidies are used as an argument in favor of mass transit subsidies. The preferred approach is to rectify pricing deficiencies within the highway program associated with auto pollution, housing dislocation, and other social effects, and to increase transit prices to marginal cost. Continued subsidies of transport are encouraging a more dispersed and a more transport- and energy-intensive pattern of development. Implementation of marginal cost pricing would involve both administrative and equity problems.

An increase in highway user charges to account for externalities would entail congestion tolls and charges for externalities imposed on nonusers. The principal effect of marginal cost tolls would be a reduction in the rate of new construction. Peak-hour congestion tolls could provide major benefits in the form of improved utilization of urban highways and could thus reduce the need for additional capacity. No means has yet been devised to impose tolls that vary by facility and time of day that do not entail excessive administrative costs. Parking charges are a very imperfect proxy for peak-hour congestion tolls. In the case of constant costs in the transit sector, efficiency losses arising from the absence of marginal cost tolls are borne solely by highway users since mode splits do not alter transit prices. If increasing returns exist, underpriced peak-hour highways affect both highway and transit users' welfare.

The principal equity issue involved in the implementation of marginal cost tolls arises because differences in the valuation of time among users implies disagreement about the level of the optimal toll. The marginal cost of another user is the summation of delay costs across all users. If there is no mechanism for beneficiaries of tolls compensating losers, those priced off, each user will be best off if his own valuation of time is used to establish the toll. A voting process by which the median voter's valuation of time is used to define the marginal cost curve will understate the true marginal social cost curve. While the current gasoline tax diverges from a marginal cost toll because it is invariant to time of day and road capacity, differences of opinion will be expressed as to whether current gas taxes are too high or too low.

Difficult administrative problems are also involved in the attempt to devise appropriate user charges that reflect other externalities. Since damages vary by location, as a result of the density and type of surrounding development and other factors, the optimal tax equal to the marginal social damage resulting from each unit of the external effect will vary between locations. The theoretical prescription for undepletable externalities can only be very crudely approximated in practice.

With respect to exhaust pollution, the principal policy must be that of encouraging the purchase of less polluting cars. Altering the design or operation of engines on existing vehicles is not cost effective. Inspection and administrative procedures are costly, and pollution reductions that result from the modification of older engines are not great. Older cars that warrant retrofit constitute an ever declining percentage of the existing fleet. As the fleet mix changes in favor of newer cars, administrative costs of this approach rise relative to the pollution relief benefits.[27]

The current approach of using emissions standards on new cars is administratively simple and in place but has significant disadvantages. Dewees' (1974) arguments for an emissions tax on new cars has much in its favor. Such a tax, based on an estimate of the pollutants emitted over the lifetime of the car, assuming normal driving and maintenance, would be imposed on new cars at the time of purchase. Since abatement cost functions differ between cars, a single emissions standard applied to all cars would be inefficient. Purchasers would be reminded of the pollution cost of a particular vehicle type by the tax imposed at the time of purchase; thus their vehicle choice would be influenced, and manufacturers would have incentives to improve their technology. A pollution tax placed on existing cars would encourage the replacement of polluting vehicles and could be most cheaply administered as part of the annual license tax, with the tax schedule based on the type of car.

Because of the variation in pollution damage functions across cities, nationwide standards or emissions taxes on new cars should be supplemented with local taxes—local license or gasoline taxes could be used as an additional charge in areas where pollution is severe. Such charges could also be used to reflect right-of-way externalities. It is infeasible to design a user charge that reflects locational differences in right-of-way damages, but a unique charge for each metropolitan area could be easily administered through license taxes.

The principal problem with providing compensation to those damaged, assuming that this objective is deemed appropriate, is the difficulty of identifying injured parties; air pollution damages are so diffuse that systematic identification of injured parties would be very difficult. A redistribution of pollution receipts in the form of general tax relief is a very imperfect transfer to those damaged.

Lump-sum compensation for those damaged along the right-of-way must be directed to those people who were located along, or who owned property along, the right-of-way *prior* to the road's construction. Payments could be based on a discounting of future damages, as reflected in market values, assuming no change in activity by the recipients. Households that move into the area after the commitment to construction has been made presumably prefer to suffer externalities in exchange for the opportunity to buy at lower prices, and hence no compensation for damages is appropriate. It would be very difficult to accurately identify the parties who sustained the initial uncompensated capital loss along an existing highway right-of-way. For this practical reason, compensation should be confined to the owners of property that adjoins sites of future construction.

Compensation systems for those who own property alongside prospective facilities might follow two approaches. Changes in property values might be estimated. This method has the advantage that roadway projects may entail both external costs and accessibility benefits, and hence property values will reflect the market valuation of this sum of benefits and costs. Blackburn (1975) has suggested that the government pay 80 percent of any decline in property value; households will be made to share the cost as an incentive to sell their property at the highest price.[28] Appropriate compensation must be determined for parties who choose not to sell. These calculations would involve all the administrative problems in determining fair market value in eminent domain. The alternative and much simpler approach is to base compensation on measured noise levels. Noise might be measured for each project after completion, or payment might be based on an average schedule relating typical noise exposure to the type of facility and its distance from the roadway. In both of these approaches, a trade-off between higher administrative costs and greater equity exists, since the latter is only achieved by making more elaborate measures of noise exposure or estimates of property value assessments at the local level.

Marginal cost pricing would entail substantially higher fares in the transit sector. Marginal cost pricing for mass transit would entail rail transit deficits because of increasing returns to scale. (Bus operations are characterized by constant costs at volumes typical of even very small cities; hence they would be self-financing.) A second-best argument has been made that further transit subsidies are justified because a substitute commodity, highway peak-hour use, is underpriced. The preceding analysis suggests that fares and costs diverge as much for transit as for auto, even when rail transit right-of-way on existing systems is treated as a sunk cost. Even if highways were properly priced to reflect all externalities, user charges would not significantly increase auto costs, except for a few hours each week when peak-hour tolls are high. The cross-elasticities between highway and transit appear to be very low.

Higher transit fares and service curtailment could impose a burden on aged and selected low-income central-city residents. However, an exami-

TABLE 7.6. Percentage of Employed Persons by Mode of Home-to-Work Transportation and Annual Household Income

Annual Household Income	Percentage Distribution of Workers	Private Motor Vehicles	Bus or Streetcar	Train
Less than $3000	5.8	4.0	12.7	1.2
$3000–$3999	5.2	3.8	10.8	2.5
$4000–$4999	5.0	4.1	9.2	3.7
$5000–$5999	7.9	7.6	8.8	15.5
$6000–$7499	12.8	12.9	12.3	11.1
$7500–$9999	18.7	20.2	15.4	14.2
$10,000–$14,999	24.2	26.3	16.3	18.2
$15,000 & over	11.7	12.6	7.9	20.2
Total	100.0	100.0	100.0	100.0

SOURCE: U.S. Department of Transportation (1973), *National Personal Transportation Study: Home-to-Work Trips and Travel,* Report no. 8. August.

nation of the distribution of transit benefits and the characteristics of subsidy financing reveals that prevailing fares and local subsidy schemes are clearly not nearly as progressive as they might appear. Ridership on public transit systems includes both extremes of the income distribution. (See table 7.6.) Bus riders tend to be low income. Rail transit ridership includes a significant proportion of very high-income suburban residents who commute to central-city employment locations; hence the mean income of rail transit riders is well above that of the population in general. Twenty percent of train riders in 1969–70 had incomes in excess of $15,000, the 88th percentile in the distribution of income.

The distribution of benefits among income groups also depends on the structure of transit fares. Because of the use of flat fares, or very limited zone fares, transit prices generally provide the largest subsidies to longer-distance, lower-density trips to the suburbs, benefiting higher-income suburban riders.

Local transit authorities receive support through operating subsidies, reimbursement for reduced school fares, favorable leases, debt guarantees and amortization, and direct provision of such services as police protection. Tax financing of deficits has been obtained through a variety of state and local taxes, principally sales, income, and property taxes.

Examination of transit subsidy financing in particular cities reveals the regressive nature of these arrangements. Straszheim (1969) has described regressive income transfers in Boston that are traceable to the formula for assigning Metropolitan Boston Transit Authority (MBTA) losses to Boston and the surrounding suburbs; Boston taxpayers are subsidizing the losses of MBTA riders who commute from higher-income suburbs. In the case of BART, subsidy benefits are positively related to income, whereas the tax burden is inversely related to income. This occurs because BART's ridership is largely high-income suburban commuters who make very long trips into San Francisco, but the subsidy is financed by area sales taxes and property taxes that tend to be regressive.[29]

The very regressive nature of most local transit subsidy systems is perhaps the best argument for continued federal mass transit subsidies over the short run, assuming that a fiscal transfer to central urban areas is desirable. The existing federal subsidy program is too poorly designed to meet this objective as a tax transfer to the poor or downtown jurisdictions. The grant-in-aid program for capital equipment appears to be financing investments that cannot be financed locally. Subsidizing the price of capital by more than the operating cost subsidy program distorts factor proportions and the choice of technology and encourages transit operators to trade maintenance costs for new equipment.

Federal operating subsidies introduced in 1974[30] constitute about one-tenth of total transit operating costs and one-third of local government tax support. In order to avoid the disincentives associated with basing assistance on the size of the operating deficit, the formula for the distribution of operating subsidies is based largely on population. The formula results in the largest cities receiving the lowest subsidies, measured either as a share of total expenses or on a per rider basis.[31]

The principal alternative to operating cost subsidies is a negative sales tax—a federal contribution for each dollar of local transit receipts. This creates incentives for local authorities to offer services if revenues exceed costs, and at prices that maximize fare revenues. Inelastic demand curves would probably encourage transit companies to increase fares. The efficiency gains of this very close variant of a "free market" outcome must be weighed against certain equity effects. The burden of higher fares would fall both on higher-income suburban riders and on the poor.

NOTES

1. Keeler estimated congestion tolls in San Francisco during the weekly six peak hours at 4¢ to 10¢ per mile in urban-suburban areas, and 16¢ to 40¢ per mile in the central-city area. For all other periods, tolls ranged from 1¢ to 3¢ per mile. The principal difficulty in including these high tolls in the definition of long-run peak-hour auto costs is the implicit but implausible assumption that such tolls would not induce drivers to adjust their travel decisions, particularly with respect to the time of day. If peak-hour tolls were implemented, it seems probable that less congestion would result, and hence the costs that must be borne by peak period users are surely much below Keeler's estimates.

2. U.S. Department of Transportation (1976a), pp. 5–15.

3. Meyer and Gomez-Ibanex (1977).

4. U.S. Department of Transportation (1976a).

5. Altschuler (1975), p. 27.

6. Barnum (1972), p. 321.

7. Based on the author's tabulations of data made available by the Department of Transportation, Urban Mass Transportation Administration.

8. UMTA grants covered 66.6 percent of net project costs until 1973, and 80 percent thereafter, with the nonfederal share, financed by local taxes. It is assumed that federal grants constituted 75 percent of the total project costs in this period. A fifteen-year amortization period is assumed for buses and a twenty-five-year period for rail transit. Alternative assumptions might be made regarding useful lives; though for very long amortization periods, altering the useful-life assumptions has little effect on the results.

9. Assets with different lifetimes were aggregated as follows: buses and related equipment, fifteen years; rail transit vehicles and related equipment, twenty-five years; and right-of-way, rail track, and rail overhead facilities, thirty-five years. (The latter includes some land costs, which should have an infinite life.) Projects for which expenses could not be assigned to individual components were assigned a life of twenty-five years. This procedure neglects difference in costs traceable to the availability of investments at varying dates between 1964 and 1976. This implicitly disregards price inflation and defines capital costs on the basis of initial outlay, a common capital budgeting practice throughout the private sector.

10. Since much of BART's capital costs were financed locally, the capital costs reported in table 7.4 are understated.

11. U.S. Congress (1977), p. 5.

12. U.S. Department of Transportation (1973).

13. Ridker and Henning (1967); Anderson and Croker (1971); Wieand (1973); Rosen (1974); Straszheim (1975); and Kain and Quigley (1975).

14. Gamble (1974). The typical noise emission of a car traveling at 60 m.p.h., passing at a distance of twenty-five feet, is 70 dbA. A quiet residential area will typically exhibit a residual noise level, i.e., a noise level 90 percent of the time, of 43 dbA. A residual noise level of about 60 dbA is typical in more central urban areas.

15. U.S. Department of Transportation (1974), pp. 4-10–4-11.

16. The specific provisions are in Title II of the Uniform Relocation Assistance and Real Property Acquisition Policies Act of 1970 (P.L. 91-646). Compensation for relocation includes actual moving expenses, search costs, and tangible personal property lost, subject to upper limits. Homeowners may receive up to $15,000 for additional interest costs, title searches, and the difference between former and comparable replacement housing. Renters may receive up to $4,000 to cover higher rents on replacement units.

17. U.S. Department of Transportation (1976b). Trip distances were based on Bureau of the Census tabulations of surveys in Philadelphia, Chicago, and San Diego.

18. U.S. Department of Transportation (1974), pp. 3–11, 3–13, 2–15.

19. Surveys that focus on these interactions of several land-use transportation simulation models are Brown et al. (1972) and Ingram (in this volume).

20. For a survey, see Meyer and Straszheim (1970).

21. Earlier analysis was based on the assumption that demand functions in each time period were independent. Steiner (1957) and Williamson (1966).

22. Constraints on pricing can be treated by adding additional constraints to the Lagrangian, equation (1).

23. In the standard models a differential equation in land rents arises because land rents are related to transport prices; the latter depend on land rents under most assumptions.

24. Other authors who have analyzed similar models include Dixit (1973); Oren, Pines and Sheshinski (1973); Mills (1972); Solow and Vickrey (1971); Riley (1974); Mirrlees (1972) and Henderson (1975).

25. Haring, Clobko, and Chapman (1976) constructed a model with public and private modes, but assumed that the bus system was subject to congestion. This specification of similar technology would not appear to capture the essential differences between the modes. Mode choice gradients proved to be highly irregular, affecting the sensitivity of travel costs to assumed capacity and performance parameters of the two modes.

26. The introduction of variation in income would not alter this result except for unusual specifications of utility functions. If a monotonic income gradient existed, only a single boundary indicating a change in mode choice would result.

27. Grad et al. (1975), pp. 231–77.

28. Blackburn (1975), pp. 90–97.

29. Webber (1976), p. 22.

30. Section 5 of the National Mass Transportation Assistance Act of 1964, as amended 26 November 1974.

31. U.S. Department of Transportation (1976b), pp. 8–11.

REFERENCES

Altschuler, Alan. 1975. "The Federal Government and Para-Transit." Presented before the Transportation Research Board, Williamsburg, Va. November 9–12.

Anderson, R. J., and Crocker, T. D. 1971. "Air Pollution and Residential Property Values." *Urban Studies,* vol. 8 (October).

Barnum, David T. 1972. *Collective Bargaining and Manpower in Urban Mass Transit Systems.* Springfield, Va.: National Technical Information Service.

Baumol, Wlliam, and Oates, Wallace. 1975. *The Theory of Environmental Policy.* Englewood Cliffs, N.J.: Prentice Hall.

Blackburn, Anthony. 1975. "A Comprehensive Policy to Ameliorate Adverse Impacts of Transportation Facilities." Cambridge, Mass.: Urban Systems Research and Engineering.

Boiteaux, M. 1956. "Sur la Gestion des Monopoles Publics Astreints a l'Equilibre Budgetaire." *Econometrica,* vol. 24 (January).

Brown, James; Ginn, Royce; James, Franklin; Kain, John; and Straszheim, Mahlon. 1972. *Empirical Modes of Urban Land Use.* New York: National Bureau of Economic Research.

Colony, D. C. 1966. "Study of the Effect, If Any, of an Urban Freeway upon Residential Properties Contiguous to the Right-of-Way." Toledo Research Foundation, University of Toledo.

Dewees, Donald N. 1974. *Automobile Air Pollution: An Economic Analysis.* Cambridge, Mass.: MIT Press.

———. 1976a. "Travel Cost, Transit and Control of Urban Motoring." *Public Policy,* vol. 24.

———. 1976b. "Congestion Costs in Urban Motoring: Some Toronto Estimates." University of Toronto, Research Paper no. 71.

———. 1976c. "The Cost and Technology of Pollution Abatement."

Dixit, A. 1973. "The Optimum Factory Town." *Bell Journal of Economics and Management,* vol. 4.

Downs, Anthony. 1970. *Urban Problems and Prospects.* Chicago: Markham, pp. 192–227.

Duff, Virginia, and Straszheim, Mahlon. 1978. "Congestion and Pollution Externalities in a Multi-Mode Urban Model."

Fisher, Anthony, and Zeckhauser, Richard. 1975. "Averting Behavior and External Diseconomies."

Gamble, H. B. 1974. "The Influence of Highway Environmental Effects on

Residential Prcperty Values." Pennsylvania Institute of Land and Research, Pennsylvania State University, University Park. April.

Grad, Frank; Rosenthal, Albert; Rockett, Laurie; Fay, James; Heywood, John; Kain, John; Ingram, Gregory; Harrison, David, Jr.; and Tietenberg, Thomas. 1975. *The Automobile and the Regulation of Its Impacts on the Environment*. Norman, Okla.: University of Oklahoma Press.

Harrison, David, Jr., and Rubenfeld, Daniel L. 1976. "Housing Values and the Willingness to Pay for Clean Air." Harvard University, Department of City and Regional Plannng, Discussion Paper D76-5. June.

Henderson, J. V. 1975. "Congestion and Optimum City Size." *Journal of Urban Economics* 2 (January): 48–62.

Hicks, J. R. 1936. *Value and Capital*. Oxford: Oxford University Press.

Horowitz, Joel. 1974. "Transportation Controls Are Really Needed in the Air Cleanup Fight." *Environmental Science and Technology*, vol 8 (September).

Ingram, Gregory, and Fauth, Gary R. 1974. *TASSIM: A Transportation and Air Shed Simulation Model*. Springfield, Va.: National Technical Information Service.

Kain, John, and Quigley, John. 1975. *Housing Markets and Racial Discrimination: A Microeconomic Analysis*. New York: Columbia University Press.

Kanemoto, Yoshitsugu. 1977. "Cost-Benefit Analysis and the Second Best Land Use Transportaton." *Journal of Urban Economics*, vol. 4 (October).

Keeler, Theodore E.; Small, Kenneth A.; 1975. "The Full Cost of Urban Transport." Part 3. Institute of Urban and Regional Development, University of California at Berkeley. July.

Meyer, John; Kain, John; and Wohl, Martin. 1965. *The Urban Transportation Problem*. Cambridge, Mass.: Harvard University Press.

Meyer, John, and Gomez-Ibanez, Jose. 1977. *Improving Urban Mass Transportation Productivity*. Department of City and Regional Planning, Harvard University, Research Report R77-1.

Mills, Edwin. 1972. *Studies in the Structure of the Urban Economy*. Baltimore: Johns Hopkins Press.

Mirrlees, James. 1972. "The Optimum Town." *Swedish Journal of Economics*, vol. 74.

Mohring, Herbert. 1964. "Relation between Optimum Congestion Tolls and Present Highway User Charges." In *Traffic Congestion as a Factor in Road-User Taxation*. Washington, D.C.: Highway Research Board of the Division of Engineering and Industrial Research, National Academy of Sciences–National Research Council.

———. 1965. "Urban Highway Benefits." In *Measuring Benefits of Government Investments*. Edited by Robert Dorman. Washington, D.C.: Brookings Institution.

———. 1970. "The Peak Load Problem with Increasing Returns and Pricing Constraints." *American Economic Review*, vol. 60 (September).

Oren, R.; Pines, D.; and Sheshinski, E. 1973. "Optimum versus Equilibrium Land Use Patterns and Congestion Tolls." *Bell Journal of Economics and Management*, vol. 4.

Pigou, A. C. 1920. *The Economics of Welfare*. London: Macmillan.

Ridker, Ronald, and Henning, J. 1970. "The Determinants of Residential Property Values with Special Reference to Air Pollution." *Review of Economics and Statistics,* vol. 59 (May): 246–57.

Riley, John. 1974. "Optimal Residential Density and Road Transportation." *Journal of Urban Economics,* vol. 1.

Robson, A. 1976a. "Cost-benefit Analysis and the Use of Urban Land for Transportation." *Journal of Urban Economics,* vol. 3.

———. 1976b. "Two Models of Urban Air Pollution." *Journal of Urban Economics,* vol. 3 (July).

Rosen, Sherwin. 1974. "Hedonic Prices and Implicit Markets." *Journal of Political Economy,* vol. 32 (January).

Slutsky, E. 1953. "On the Theory of the Budget of the Consumer." In *Readings in Price Theory.* Edited by Kenneth Boulding and George Stigler. London; Allen and Unwin.

Solow, Robert, and Vickrey, William. 1971. "Land Use in a Long Narrow City." *Journal of Economic Theory,* vol. 3.

Solow, Robert. 1972. "Congestion, Density, and the Use of Land in Transportation." *Swedish Journal of Economics,* vol. 24.

———. 1973. "Congestion Cost and the Use of Land for Streets." *Bell Journal of Economics and Management,* vol. 4.

Steiner, Peter. 1957. "Peak Loads and Efficient Pricing." *Quarterly Journal of Economics,* vol. 71 (November).

Straszheim, Mahlon. 1969. "The Federal Mass Transit Capital Grant Program." In *Proceedings of the Transportation Research Forum.* Oxford, Ind.: Richard B. Cross.

———. 1975. *An Econometric Analysis of the Urban Housing Market.* New York: Columbia Universty Press.

Strotz, Robert. 1965. "Urban Transportation Parables." In *The Public Economy of Urban Communities.* Edited by Julius Margolis. Washington, D.C.: Johns Hopkins Press.

U.S. Congress. House. Congressional Budget Office. 1977. *Urban Mass Transportation: Options For Federal Assistance.* Washington, D.C.: U.S. Government Printing Office.

U.S. Department of Transportation. 1973. *National Personal Transportation Study: Home to Work Trips and Travel.* Report no. 8. August.

———. 1974. *Characteristics of Urban Transportation Systems.* Washington, D.C.: U.S. Government Printing Office.

———. Urban Mass Transportation Administration. 1975. "Projected Operating Deficits, FY77-81," by Kenneth Orski.

———. 1976a. *Labor in the Transit Industry.* Washington, D.C.: U.S. Government Printing Office.

———. Urban Mass Transportation Administration. 1976b. *Transportation Operating Performance and the Impact of the Section 5 Program.* Washington, D.C.: U.S. Government Printing Office.

U.S. Environmental Protection Agency. 1974. *Transportation Controls to Reduce Automobile Use and Improve Air Quality in Cities.* Washington, D.C.: U.S. Government Printing Office.

U.S. Government Interagency Task Force. (Administration, Commerce, Energy Research and Development, Environmental Protection, and Transportation). 1977. "Analysis of Effects of Several Specified Alternative Emission Control Schedules Upon Fuel Economy and Costs."

Vickrey, William. 1965. "Pricing as a Tool in Coordination of Local Transportation." In *Transportation Economics.* New York: National Bureau of Economic Research.

Walters, A. A. 1961. "The Theory and Measurement of Private and Social Cost of Highway Congestion." *Econometrica,* vol. 29 (October).

Webber, Melvin. 1976. "The BART-Experience—What Have We Learned?" University of California at Berkeley.

Wieand, K. F. 1973. "Air Pollution and Property Values: A Study of the St. Louis Area." *Journal of Regional Science,* vol. 13 (April).

Williamson, Oliver. 1956. "Peak Load Pricing and Optimal Capacity." *American Economic Review,* vol. 56 (September).

Wohl, Martin, and Martin, Brian. 1967. *Traffic System Analysis for Engineers and Planners.* New York: McGraw Hill.

Zerbe, Richard O., and Croke, Kevin. 1975. *Urban Transportation for the Environment.* Cambridge, Mass.: Ballinger.

THE PROVISION OF LOCAL
PUBLIC SERVICES

8

THEORIES OF GROUP, JURISDICTION, AND CITY SIZE

J. V. HENDERSON

INTRODUCTION

In 1956 Tiebout published a seminal paper that examined community formation and public good choice. Tiebout analyzed the location decisions of the mobile population of an economy, in which people choose among a variety of potential or existing communities with different fiscal features. He argued that, other things being equal, people tend to choose the community that offers them the best fiscal package, given their income and tastes. Accordingly, people with similar demands for public services or similar best fiscal packages will tend to stratify into the same community. Thus in terms of public service demands, the communities that form should be fairly homogeneous internally. Moreover, in the process of choosing between communities, people reveal their preferences for public services by voting with their feet for their desired level of public services.

In the years since Tiebout's article, urban and public finance specialists have taken his ideas and expanded and developed them in two directions: they have developed fully specified and rigorous versions of the original model of local public good consumption and community formation, and they have extended the model to include situations in which people choose among communities on the basis of different earning possibilities, amenities, cost of living, and fiscal features. Utilizing the concepts engendered in the Tiebout model and its extensions, economists have analyzed the allocation of population among regions, cities, and most commonly, the communities and suburbs of a metropolitan area. They have also analyzed the formation of other types of groups, such as social and athletic clubs and community

J. V. Henderson is an assistant professor in the Department of Economics at Brown University.

centers. A common set of questions are analyzed in all these inquiries. What is the optimal number, size, and population composition of the groups (cities, regions, suburbs, and clubs) that form? What is the optimal level of public services provided to each group and what are the optimal methods of financing services? What groups are likely to form in stable market solutions? And under what conditions or set of locally or centrally implemented policies will market solutions correspond to optimal solutions?

For example, concerning suburbanization, I will derive conditions that determine optimal suburb size and public service provision and will show that under certain conditions it is efficient for the population to stratify into different homogeneous suburbs. I will then examine how the use of the property tax to finance public services, the manipulation of zoning instruments, the capitalization of excess fiscal benefits, and suburban growth affect the types of market solutions that actually arise.

This chapter will examine various models of group formation and point out both their common elements and their varying applications.

1.

A Simple Model of Clubs

In this section I outline a simple model of clubs based on McGuire's (1974) work. Consumers in an economy have preference functions $V(x,h,g)$, where h is housing, x is all other goods, and g is public services. x and h are purchased in a market place in which perfect competition prevails and prices equal social opportunity costs. Public services are purchased by joining a club. Within a club, each member consumes the same quantity and quality of public services. Club benefits do not extend or spillover to other clubs.

The total cost of providing a unit of g to each club member is $c(N)$, where N is club size. If g is a pure public good, $dc/dN = 0$. If g is a mixed or congested good, $dc/dN > 0$; with the special case $dc/dN = c/N$, when g is a pure private good produced under constant cost conditions. The usual presumption is that dc/dN is small for low levels of N, reflecting the public nature of the good, but then increases as a club grows. As a club grows it requires greater and greater expenditures to maintain a given quality of services, which reflects (according to the particular type of club or situation) greater spatial dispersion of service benefits, escalating administrative costs, congestion of facilities, or members' preferences for smaller groups. Both the model and the results could be enriched by including g in the $c(N)$ function, but my purpose is served by this (simpler) version.

The problem is to allocate an economy's population amongst clubs in a static situation. I derive optimal solutions and then market solutions under the assumption that the formation of clubs is costless. For simplicity, I assume that all people have identical preference functions (tastes) and that demand for public services and clubs varies only with income. A straightforward extension is to allow tastes to vary also. In deriving solutions, I first assume that all people have identical income and hence identical demand for public services and then I allow incomes to differ.

ALL CONSUMERS IDENTICAL. To find the optimal clubs solution, the optimal characteristics of one club is derived first. Identical people in the economy are treated equally by imposing an equal utility constraint, on equity grounds and to make the optimal solutions comparable to stable market solutions. Therefore, the optimization problem is to maximize

$$V(y\text{-}ph\text{-}c(N)g/N, h, g), \tag{1}$$

where y is consumer income, p is the cost of housing in units of x, $c(N)g/N$ is the average per-member cost of public services; hence x equals $y - ph - c(N)g/N$. Maximizing with respect to h and x yields the usual equality of marginal rate of substitution and ratio of marginal cost condition for housing:

$$\frac{\partial V/\partial h}{\partial V/\partial x} = p. \tag{2}$$

Maximizing with respect to g yields the Samuelson condition for the provision of public services, in which the sum of the marginal rates of substitution in consumption equals the opportunity cost of a unit of g, $c(N)$:

$$\frac{\partial V/\partial g}{\partial V/\partial x} N = c(N). \tag{3}$$

Maximizing with respect to N yields

$$dc/dN = c(N)/N. \tag{4}$$

Assuming marginal cost, dc/dN, starts low and increases with N, as long as it is less than the average cost $(c(N)/N)$, it is efficient to increase club size because the average cost per member of a unit of services is declining. Optimal club size is reached when equation (4) is satisfied and the per-person average cost of providing public services is minimized. This could occur at either a unique value of N or some range of values of N. Note that since $c(N)$ does not contain g, the optimal N is independent of g. If g is included in the $c(N)$ function, optimal club size will vary with g and as McGuire demonstrates, it would be useful to develop a set of diagrams that emphasize the interaction between the demand (equation [3]) and the supply (equation [4]) sides of the model.

Equation (4) specifies a condition for the optimal size of one club. The optimal number of clubs is simply this size divided into the economy's population, with any remainder (or fraction of a club) conveniently ignored. The reason for ignoring any remainder is that if the economy's population is large relative to optimal club size and hence there are many clubs, a remainder can be divided among the clubs with negligible impact upon their size. Dividing the population among identical size clubs ensures that identical citizens are equally well-off and that their utility is maximized.

In the market formation of clubs, entrepreneurs set up clubs—for a nominal (invisible) ex post return—and specify a level of g and a corresponding financial cost for each. Within a club, g is financed on an equal cost-share basis (otherwise members who have been discriminated against will join other clubs). The population chooses amongst potential clubs and market goods. By a costless tâtonnement process, the economy gropes to a stable solution, with equilibria in the housing, all-other-goods, and clubs markets.

With appropriate financing in clubs, the stable market solution will correspond to the optimal solution. The optimality of market solutions may be illustrated as follows: In each club, each person's tax bill is stated to be tg, where t is set so that the total taxes of a club, tgN, are equal to its total expenditures, $gc(N)$; or $t = c(N)/N$. Therefore, $dt/dN = N^{-1}(dc/dN - c/N)$. As long as $dc/dN < c/N$, t will decline as N increases because the marginal financial benefits of an additional member sharing the financing cost (c/N) exceed the congestion cost in the provision of g (dc/dN) of the additional member. When $dc/dN = c/N$—which (from equation [4]) is also the condition that defines optimal club size—t is minimized.

In maximizing $V(x,h,g)$ subject to $y = x + ph + tg$, consumers choose between market goods and a variety of potential clubs. Therefore, at a utility maximum, equation (2) (for housing consumption) will be satisfied; and in choosing g, by choosing among the array of potential clubs with varying g and t combinations, consumers will satisfy $(\partial V/\partial g)/(\partial V/\partial x) = t$. This implies, given that $t = c(N)/N$, that the Samuelson condition (equation [3]) will be satisfied. Under this effective benefit pricing, consumers reveal their preferences for public services in their choice of club. The level of g in each potential club, specified by entrepreneurs, will be affirmed by club members by majority vote. Given homogeneous clubs, there are no political conflicts.

Finally, entrepreneurs will set club sizes to minimize t, the per-member unit tax price of g; and hence club sizes will be optimal. If a potential club does not satisfy the condition for optimal club size, an entrepreneur can set up a different size club that does satisfy this condition and attract the members of the inefficient size club by offering them a higher utility level. (The same comment applies to equation [3].) This also offers the entrepreneur a potential profit equal to a portion of the difference in utility levels of the two clubs; but, of course, the various entrepreneurs who compete for the members of the inefficient club will dissipate any profits by offering higher and higher utility levels. Thus we arrive at an optimal set of clubs.[1]

NONIDENTICAL CONSUMERS.   I will now assume that the population is discretely divided into subgroups that differ in their public-service demand on the basis of differing income. Each subgroup is homogeneous and large enough to support multiple optimal size clubs.[2] An optimal solution requires that the population stratify into different types of club, each of which is homogeneous and satisfies the optimal-size and Samuelson conditions. To illustrate the efficiency of internal homogeneity, suppose that the population is divided into two groups, high- and low-income people, with respectively high and low public service demands.

Assume first that the public service costs are divided equally between members of a club, regardless of income. When homogeneous and mixed clubs are compared, both high- and low-income people are worse off by belonging to mixed clubs. In a mixed club, the Samuelson condition contains a summation of marginal rates of substitution for combined high and low demanders, normally involving a level of public services lying between that provided in high- and low-income clubs. Because there are equal cost shares (which are no longer benefit taxes), there is the same effective unit tax price of g for both high and low demanders, which is also equal to their tax prices in homogeneous communities. Therefore, in general, low [high] demanders consume more [less] public services than they desire and can obtain in a homogeneous community. Both groups would be better off in homogeneous communities.

This reasoning indicates that instituting unequal tax shares (such as benefit taxes in a mixed community) and forcing people into mixed communities for the purpose of redistributing real income or utility is generally an inefficient way to provide public services and redistribute income. This arrangement lowers the potential utility levels of all members in the economy for two reasons. First, any redistribution of income and clubs solution obtained by varying the tax shares within mixed communities can be duplicated by direct income redistribution combined with equal tax shares in mixed communities. But I have shown that for any income distribution (and hence redistribution) with equal tax shares, homogeneity of the communities in which all members consume their desired level of services is most efficient. Second, there is the problem that if public services are affirmed by majority vote, the Samuelson condition will generally no longer be met in mixed communities and only the preferences of the numerically dominant group of people will be reflected.

The free market solution, unconstrained by any institutional restrictions, will provide for optimal stratified solutions. No two groups of people would agree to mix in the same club unless all members pay the same amount. But as we have just shown, with equal cost sharing, both groups are better off with the stratified solution. Therefore, entrepreneurs will design homogeneous communities in which equal cost sharing is ensured.

The model can also be applied to a situation in which there are a variety of different types of public services. For each demand group, each type of service will be provided by a different set of clubs. Then consumers may belong to as many clubs as there are types of public services, with each club perhaps being a different optimal size. This solution will generally arise only if it is possible to costlessly vary club size or jurisdiction for each type of good provided to a consumer.

In the sections that follow, I use this clubs model as a benchmark. In analyzing different situations and models it is necessary, in general, to alter only one or two of the assumptions or features of the basic clubs model.

A Simple Suburbs Model

It is often hypothesized that suburbanization in the United States represents an attempt by fairly homogeneous groups of people to form clubs or jurisdictions for the purpose of consuming certain local public services, particularly education. To adapt the clubs model to analyze the formation of suburbs in a static context requires only a few adjustments in the model. First, membership in a club-suburb is now obtained by buying a house in a certain bounded geographic area, which defines the jurisdiction of the suburb. Second and most critically, the provision of public services is financed by property taxes rather than head or direct benefit taxes. Finally, given institutional restrictions concerning the exclusion of unwanted club members, problems may arise in the market solution when lower-income people join high-income suburbs to turn homogeneous suburbs into mixed communities.

To appreciate the applicability of this version of the clubs model to the suburbanization phenomenon, it is instructive to view a common suburbanization scenario for the United States. Several decades ago, most urban areas were primarily contained in one jurisdictional area and provided public services for a mixture of income groups. Since then, the relative size of the local public sector—especially the public school sector—in the economy has greatly increased. This growth has provided a strong incentive to higher-income people to move beyond the fiscal boundary of the original city and to set up their own fiscal jurisdictions. In the core city, higher-income people are forced by the political process to consume less public services than they desire (as usually suggested by median voter models) and to pay a greater share of the cost of public services than lower-income people, given a tax system based on the value of residential housing. The migration of higher-income has provided the impetus for medium-income people to also leave, since they have become responsible for subsidizing the public service consumption of the lowest income groups. This process of suburbanization has been aided by the development of radial transportation systems that provide quick access to the Central Business Districts (CBD) for suburbanites and by general per-person income growth and city expansion, which have resulted in a demand for relatively cheap, spacious lots and new modern housing that can only be satisfied in the suburbs. Thus a spatial pattern has arisen in which the population has stratified into different, fairly homogeneous suburbs.

Using a clubs model adapted to the suburbanization phenomenon, it can be shown in uncomplicated situations that (a) suburbanization and the resulting jurisdictional fragmentation of a metropolitan area is fiscally efficient; (b) it is efficient for a suburb to be fairly homogeneous; and (c) certain types of zoning may be necessary to attain Pareto-efficient solutions. I also examine more complicated situations in which zoning may prohibit attainment of efficient solutions, heterogeneity in suburbs results, and in which land-use conflicts may arise within a suburb between developers, residents, and potential residents.

The optimal stratification of the population into suburbs in a simple model involves the same consumption of all goods as does the optimal clubs solution of the previous section and the satisfaction of equations (2) through (4). The fundamental nature of the problem is unchanged. The given preference functions are all the same so that demands only vary with income; the optimal solution involves a grouping of people into different spatial jurisdictions by income, where jurisdictions correspond to the clubs of the previous section. This new feature of spatial grouping imposes no extra costs in a simple model, so that optimal consumption bundles and club-suburb sizes are unchanged from the previous section. (Note that to make the solutions directly comparable to clubs solutions, I assume that either the opportunity cost of housing is the same everywhere and that income is exogenous or that all suburbs are equidistant from equal opportunity work places.)

However, market suburbanization solutions will in general no longer be optimal; suburb sizes and public-good choices will still satisfy optimality conditions, but the choice of housing consumption will not. The use of the property tax to finance public services introduces a distortion by raising the price of housing above its social marginal cost, inducing people to reduce their housing consumption to avoid taxes. To demonstrate these points, I utilize Ellickson's (1970, 1971) work to outline the derivation of market solutions.

MARKET SOLUTIONS. The consumer optimization problem is now to maximize

$$V = V(x, h, g) \quad s.t. \quad y - x - p(1 + t)h =$$
$$y - x - \hat{p}h = 0,$$

where p is the producer price of housing, t is the tax rate, and $\hat{p} = p(1 + t)$ is the consumer gross price of housing. Maximizing with respect to x and h yields the housing consumption condition that

$$\frac{\partial V/\partial h}{\partial V/\partial x} = \hat{p}. \tag{5}$$

Examining potential suburbs, only the $\hat{p}$ and g variables facing a consumer vary. Therefore, in choosing among potential suburbs and fiscal packages, consumers want the $\hat{p}$, g combination that maximizes utility. The consumer trade off between $\hat{p}$ and g may be seen by differentiating the utility function and budget constraint for $dy = 0$. In the differentiated utility function, I set $du = 0$, divide through by $\partial u/\partial x$, substitute in equation (5), and then substitute in the differentiated budget constraint (for dx). Rearranging terms, the result is

$$d\hat{p}/dg = h^{-1} \frac{\partial V/\partial g}{\partial V/\partial y}. \tag{6}$$

In figure 8.1 there are sets of indifference curves, I_1 and I_2, whose positive slopes are given by equation (6). As indifference curves shift *down*, utility *increases*. As income increases for a given g, it is possible to show that indifference curves may become steeper (shift right) or less steep (shift left).[3] I assume noncritically that they shift right or the set of indifference curves I_2 in figure 8.1 belongs to a higher-income person than the set I_1.

On the supply side, taxes collected in a suburb equal expenditures: $tphN = gc(N)$, where h is the uniform per-person housing consumption in a homogeneous suburb of size N. Therefore, $t = gc(N)p^{-1} h^{-1} N^{-1}$. Substituting this into $\hat{p} = p(1 + t)$ we get

$$\hat{p} = p + N^{-1} h^{-1} gc(N). \tag{7}$$

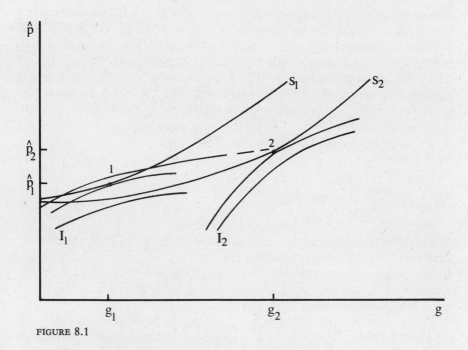

FIGURE 8.1

This is the equation for the supply relationships, S_1 and S_2, in figure 8.1, where the intercept p is the opportunity cost of housing across suburbs and where the positive slope for a given N is

$$\partial \hat{p}/\partial g = N^{-1} h^{-1} c(N) > 0. \tag{8}$$

Also $\partial^2 \hat{p}/\partial g^2 > 0$ or, as we increase g, t and hence $\hat{p}$ must rise at an increasing rate. (Not only must t rise to increase taxes to pay for the increased g but also to maintain taxes used to finance the previous level of g. The per-person tax base, h, is declining as $\hat{p}$ rises due to normal price effects on demand.) The supply curve in figure 8.1 rotates down as per-person income rises in a suburb, because a lower t is needed to finance a given g as the per-person tax base, h, increases.[4] Therefore, S_2 in figure 8.1 belongs to a higher-income suburb than does S_1.

Suburbanization solutions can now be examined. Consider a situation with two income groups. Suburbs are designed by entrepreneurs called land developers. Many developers in a metropolitan area own the land upon which suburbs are formed. This land has the same opportunity cost everywhere, say the cost in farming. Developers may form small coalitions (companies) to avoid the problem of whether one developer's land exactly equals the land area consumed in an optimal size suburb. As before, a stable market solution is generated by a tâtonnement process with consumers choosing the suburb and consumption bundle that maximizes utility. By competing for residents, developers will provide the optimal size suburbs and the desired levels of public services that may be affirmed by a majority vote. In market solutions, optimal perceived suburb size is that which minimizes $\hat{p}$ in equation (7); $\hat{p}$ is minimized when equation (4) is satisfied.[5] In terms of public services, residents will want to reach the lowest indifference curve possible given the supply conditions facing them. With homogeneous suburbs for our two income groups, these are the tangency points 1 and 2 in figure 8.1. From equations (6) and (8) at a tangency point

$$h^{-1} \frac{\partial V/\partial g}{\partial V/\partial y} = h^{-1} N^{-1} c(N) , \qquad (9)$$

or the Samuelson condition—equation (3)—will be satisfied. Therefore, what is violated in the solution is the optimality condition on housing consumption, in which $(\partial V/\partial h)/(\partial V/\partial y)$ should equal p but instead, from equation (5), equals $\hat{p}$. Later I will show that under certain conditions the market will correct this problem also.

I have asserted in the solution that suburbs are homogeneous. Such will definitely be the case in figure 8.1. First, high-income people will never want to admit low-income people because they have a lower tax base, or h, and because they could become numerically, and hence politically, dominant. Second, in figure 8.1, if a low-income person joins the high-income suburb, he will be on an indifference curve going through point 2, the equilibrium in suburb 2. This is a higher indifference curve than for the tangency point 1, and so a lower-income person would be worse off if he left his homogeneous suburb. Stratification is stable.

However, it is possible to specify demand and supply relationships such that lower-income people want to join the higher-income suburb, as is illustrated in figure 8.2. By entering a high-income suburb, low-income people can consume a high level of public services at less than cost, since their pictured tax base is lower than the suburban average. In a market context the question becomes, How do higher-income people exclude lower-income entrants, if as an institutional constraint it is assumed anyone willing to pay the cost of available housing must be admitted to a suburb? That is, there cannot be direct discrimination and exclusion of people on the basis of income.

The most commonly cited method is the zoning of housing. Although zoning is probably the best method of exclusion, given recent U.S. court decisions, exclusionary zoning has an uncertain legal future. Therefore, it is worth considering two other possible exclusionary measures. One is that high-income suburbs can overconsume public services; at point 3 in figure 8.2, low-income people no longer want to enter the high-income suburb.

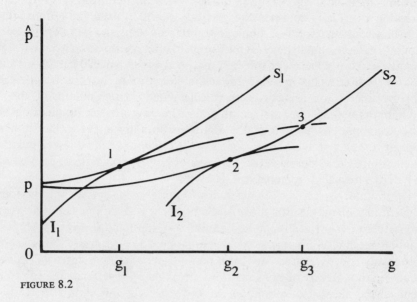

FIGURE 8.2

The other measure is for high-income suburbs to subsidize the provision of public services in low-income suburbs, thereby raising supply curves (taxes) in the high-income suburbs and lowering them in the low-income suburbs until lower-income people no longer have an incentive to join higher-income suburbs. This effective mixing of tax bases while maintaining separate suburbs has the advantage over mixed community solutions of allowing each group to continue to consume its desired level of public services without compromising with or being dominated by another group.

ZONING.   There are a variety of zoning possibilities, several of which are considered here. The first type, which I call implicit zoning, is based on Hamilton's (1975) work. The developer effectively excludes lower-income people by offering housing only at the level demanded by high-income people, from equation (5). This forces potential low-income entrants to overconsume housing and public services as well as to pay the full cost of public services and effectively excludes them. Moreover, using a "perfect" form of this zoning, developers can ensure that residents consume optimal levels of housing rather than the level suggested by equation (5). To accomplish this, developers offer suburbs where the *only* level of housing available is that suggested by equation (2). High-income people will choose to live in this type of suburb since it offers a higher utility level than any other solution. By offering *only* the optimal level of suburban housing, the developer eliminates the "free-rider" problem of individuals reducing their housing consumption to avoid taxes. Fixing housing consumption essentially converts the property tax to a head tax. A problem with this "perfect" form of implicit zoning concerns the developers' perception of the optimal level of housing to offer, since it is not revealed directly in the market place through marginal consumer choices of h (and developers presumably do not know the shape of preference functions). Only by repeated experiments with various g and h combinations in potential suburbs will the optimal combination be revealed as dominating all other combinations. Note that this objection does not apply to the simpler implicit zoning first mentioned, which is used only to exclude lower-income people, since developers can use the level of housing suggested by equation (5) that is revealed by consumer choices.

Unfortunately, implicit exclusionary zoning may not be exceedingly relevant to the analysis of a more realistic world with nonmaleable housing and suburban growth. The implicit zoning solution requires that developers build *all* the housing in the suburb before any sales are made. This is the only totally effective guarantee for initial entrants that later entrants do not consume lower levels of housing. This involves a great financial commitment on the part of the developer, a knowledge of the various preferred architectural designs, and a risk that some housing may never be purchased at a positive profit. Moreover, developers may maximize their profits over time by admitting lower-income residents later. Finally, for life-cycle, income, and family composition reasons, people often prefer to buy housing shells and leave finishing, landscaping, basements, patios, garages, etc., until later.

Thus, communities usually do not rely on implicit zoning but pass explicit zoning ordinances. If suburbs were to zone housing consumption levels, they could achieve with explicit zoning what was achieved with implicit zoning (Hamilton, 1975). Moreover, if suburbs have the "perfect" zoning knowledge to set h equal to that level in equation (2), then in addition to exclusion, they can achieve an optimal clubs solution.

We never see the zoning of housing consumption in practice. Housing is built with a vector of inputs including land, floor space, landscaping, foundations, quality of material, design, etc. To zone housing consumption would require that levels of all these inputs be specified. Communities do not attempt this; there are problems of specification and changing technology and design over time. One way to avoid these technical difficulties is to zone housing *values;* but we do not see this because of problems with the legality of such zoning, problems of consistently evaluating different types of housing, and problems, in the context of inflation, of designing escalator clauses into the zoning laws to ensure that houses have the same real value over time.

Suburbs actually zone minimum levels of only one or two of the housing production inputs, usually lot size or floor space. This eliminates the possibility of perfect zoning. However, this procedure can be effective in excluding lower-income people, but not necessarily because it raises their housing consumption above a no-zoning level. This can be shown as follows.

Suppose that without zoning lower-income people would consume h^* of housing, composed of L^* of land and K^* of capital inputs. A zoning ordinance raises land input to $L^z > L^*$. Unless capital inputs and housing production rise by the same proportion as land (given the same factor prices), the average cost of housing will rise because the ordinance forces inefficient factor proportions and overuse of land relative to capital inputs. Although the average cost of housing, p, rises, the marginal cost, $p + h\partial p/\partial h$, may rise or fall relative to the prezoning level, p^*. We know $\partial p/\partial h < 0$, because as h approaches the level where L^z and K are used in the same proportion as L^* to K^*, the average cost declines towards p^*, the prezoning average and marginal cost: Clearly if marginal cost rises, housing demand will *fall* below h^*. Even if marginal cost falls, housing consumption may not rise because there is an adverse income effect on demand from the rise in average cost.[6] However, zoning L^z at a sufficiently high level raises housing production costs enough to effectively exclude lower-income people. It may be that setting L^z equal to the level used by high-income people will be sufficient to exclude low-income people; thus a distortion of high-income people's land use could be avoided.

SUBURBANIZATION AND CAPITALIZATION.   So far, in this simple characterization of suburbanization, suburbs have been conceived as internally homogeneous in terms of both public service demand and housing consumption. Suppose that preference functions differ such that there are people with identical demands for public services but different demands for housing. What happens if these people group into the same suburbs? Hamilton (1977) examined whether this grouping affects the possibility of attaining Pareto efficient solutions and whether it is necessary for people to stratify on the basis of public service demand alone or in conjunction with housing demand. He also examined the effect of mixed housing communities on the efficient set of housing prices within and between suburbs and the efficient set of zoning regulations in a market context.

Suppose that there are two types of consumers with identical public service demands—high housing consumers (h people) and low housing consumers (l people)—and three suburban communities—homogeneous high housing, homogeneous low housing, and mixed (h, l, m). Total population is fixed. Assume that there is a suburban population range over which average costs of providing services are minimized and that all three suburbs fall within this range.

In the homogeneous suburbs, the price of housing is equal to the opportunity cost, p, given competitive developers. The level of public services satisfies the Samuelson condition and is the same in the h and l suburbs.

Therefore, the tax rate is lower in the h suburb since its per-person tax base is higher. Hamilton assumes there is "perfect" zoning, so that housing consumption in the homogeneous suburbs satisfies equation (2) and Pareto efficient solutions obtain. Per-person consumption bundles in the h and l suburbs are g, h_h, x_h and g, h_l, x_l, respectively; the equilibrium tax rates are t_h and t_l, respectively.

The solution in the mixed community will also be Pareto efficient if the people there have the same consumption bundles as in the homogeneous suburbs. In a market solution this is achieved as follows.

Suppose the developer sets housing consumption in the mixed community at h_h and h_l for h and l people, respectively, and sets public services at g. Since the same level of g is provided in all three communities but the m community has a mixed tax base, t_m should be greater than t_h but lower than t_l. Therefore, if the price of housing in the mixed community remains equal to the opportunity cost, p, h people will not have enough post-tax income to buy x_h and l people will be able to buy more than x_l. To ensure that x_h and x_l are consumed and that people of equal income are equally well-off everywhere, the price of housing in the mixed community must be adjusted so that the sum of housing and tax costs for h and l people in the m community is the same as in their respective homogeneous communities.

For h people this implies $p_h h_h + p_h t_m h_h = p h_h + p h_h t_h$, where p_h is the unit price of housing facing h people in the mixed suburb. Therefore,

$$p_h = p\, \frac{1 + t_h}{1 + t_m}. \tag{10}$$

Similarly for l people

$$p_l = p\, \frac{1 + t_l}{1 + t_m}. \tag{11}$$

Given $t_l > t_m > t_h$, this implies $p_l > p > p_h$.

These housing price differences reflect in rental terms the *full capitalization* of the net fiscal benefits (or costs) of living in mixed relative to homogeneous communities. Moreover, this solution (if attained in the market) is stable; one can conclude that stratification on the basis of housing and public service demand is not a prerequisite for Pareto efficiency. Consumers in the mixed community are satisfied with the solution, since they achieve the same utility as homogeneous suburbanites. The developer is satisfied, since it can be shown that the *average* price of land in the mixed community is the opportunity cost, p. Moreover (given a costless tâtonnement process), for this capitalization to occur in the mixed community homogeneous communities need not actually form; the possibility of their formation is sufficient.

Note that "perfect" implicit or explicit zoning is required for two reasons: zoning housing to be h_h and h_l eliminates the "free-rider" problem of some people reducing their housing consumption to avoid property taxes; in the mixed community, zoning prevents recontracting—h people renting portions of their low-priced high-demand housing to low housing demanders. Such recontracting would, of course, lead to an equalization of all land and housing prices in the mixed community. This would in turn lead to the dissolution of the community, since either the h or the l people would not have equal utility with their counterparts in homogeneous communities.

Of course, a mixed community is not a prerequisite for Pareto efficiency. Moreover, it is improbable that developers have the knowledge to effect "perfect" zoning. However, the analysis is most relevant. The alternative to mixed-housing communities is stratification on the basis of both housing and public service demand, which could result in communities that are too small to adequately exploit scale economies or Samuelson publicness in the provision of services. However, if all communities that have approximately the same public service demands were lumped together, the resulting communities might be of efficient size. Then, if developers or communities effected implicit or explicit zoning that prevented recontracting in mixed housing-demand communities, the above analysis indicates the types of price differences among land uses because of capitalization within the mixed communities.[7] In addition, if the utilized zoning approximates "perfect" zoning, we approximate a Pareto efficient solution.

POSSIBLE INEFFICIENCIES FROM JURISDICTIONAL FRAGMENTATION IN A METROPOLITAN AREA.   Under certain conditions the competitive suburbs model (with decentralized fiscal jurisdictions) will not yield Pareto efficient solutions without some type of centralized intervention. I will consider three problems, all of which envision a metropolitan area setting—suburbs ringed around a core city, where most of the area's commercial activity occurs.

The first problem is that suburbanites may use the public facilities of the core city—by commuting there to work or recreation—without paying. This represents the traditional spillover or externality situation in which the public service benefits of one jurisdiction extend beyond its boundary. If Coase (1960) type agreements do not arise, everyone is made better off by a central metropolitan authority taxing the spillover recipients according to their marginal benefits and using the money to subsidize the provision of the spillover goods. Connally (1970) and Pauly (1970) presented analytical examples of tax subsidy solutions. Whether the suburbanites actually benefit from this program depends in part on whether they have to pay taxes on intramarginal units of public services already provided (which they have been consuming for free) or only on the increases in services following the internalization of the externality. Bradford and Oates (1974) questioned the relevance of the suburban spillover problem by pointing out that suburbanites may contribute more fiscally to the core city in user fees and wage and sales taxes than they receive in benefits. Since core cities have a high proportion of the metropolitan area's industrial and commercial base, they benefit from property taxes on productive capital (not found in the suburbs). Alternatively stated, suburbanites, by commuting to work in the core city and thus contributing to the labor force needed to maintain and attract the core city capital base, confer a fiscal benefit on the core city in terms of a greater tax base (assuming that commercial activity gives more than it takes fiscally). Of course, these suburbanites avoid environmental disamenities that would result from industries locating in their suburbs.

The second problem deals with the issue of industrial location in suburbs. So far all suburbs have been entirely residential and personal income has been given exogenously; now I will account for the fact that incomes are not exogenous but people earn money by working in the core city. Although suburbs may remain entirely residential, as analyzed by Fischel (1975), the location of commercial activity in suburbs has potential benefits as well as costs. The benefits are an increased tax base and convenient work access for residents. The cost is potential environmental disamenities. For a suburb that is deciding whether to admit commercial activity (and to what extent), there is a potential spillover problem among suburbs. If one suburb allows for industrial activity, all the neighboring suburbs benefit from the increased work access without suffering much of the disamenities. This raises the possibility that suburbs will not allow sufficient industrialization, since they are not paid for the benefits that spillover into other suburbs. Central intervention may be needed to encourage efficient levels of suburban industrialization.

The third problem concerning decentralization deals with the issue of income redistribution. If it is desirable to redistribute income from high- to low-income people in a metropolitan area, this redistribution cannot be accomplished by decentralized jurisdictions since low-income suburbs and core cities cannot increase their income by taxation. Central authority is needed to transfer money from high- to low-income communities.

HETEROGENEITY IN SUBURBS.   In practice, one informally classifies suburbs as belonging to categories such as high-income, upper-middle income, middle-income, etc. Although this carries the suggestion and indication that suburbs are relatively homogeneous, a middle-income suburb, for example, may still contain people with considerable differences in income and housing consumption. The possibility of suburbs being nonhomogeneous in housing demands and income, although still homogeneous in public service demands, has already been considered. There are a variety of additional reasons, apart from institutional or historical constraints, why suburbs tend to be only relatively homogeneous.

For example, in the preceding analyses consumers were divided into homogeneous groups, each sufficient in size to support a suburb. Suppose instead no group of identical income people is large enough to support a suburb. Therefore, mixed suburbs will form to foster exploitation of the Samuelson publicness of public services. If majority voting is used to determine the level of services, in a median voter model (Inman, in this volume) the median voter will be the only resident who consumes at a tangency point in figures 8.1 and 8.2. However, we should expect suburbs to contain people of similar income, since they have similar tax bases and demands for public services. This will minimize political conflicts and fiscal disparities and allow residents to consume at *almost* a tangency point. If suburbs can effectively regulate their own sizes, they will choose the lowest income level at which to admit people. In deciding whether to admit the next person down the income scale, suburbs will want to know if his tax payments (which, being the lowest in the community, will be less than c/N) will equal or exceed the marginal cost of providing him with public services (for it to be possibly beneficial to admit him, $\partial c/\partial N < c/N$). The community will also be concerned with his impact upon political decision-making.

Another basis for heterogeneity has been suggested by Berglas (1976) in the context of regional models; Berglas's model can be adapted to a suburban context. Suppose, that suburbs have industrialized—given production, transportation, and commuting conditions in the metropolitan area. People in the metropolitan area vary in skill and hence in income and public service demands. Berglas assumes critically that all types of skilled people are needed in production. Finally in adapting Berglas model to a suburban context it is necessary to assume that there is little cross-commuting between suburbs or that, due to high commuting costs, people tend to work only in the suburb in which they reside. Although this last assumption is at odds with the concept of a metropolitan area as a ring of bedroom communities surrounding a core-city working area, it may not be implausible as regards very large metropolitan areas.

If metropolitan suburbs all produce the same goods, then they will all require the same mix of production skills. If residents only work in their own suburb, suburbs will all contain the same uniform mix of people and there will be no tendency toward homogeneity. Some nonuniformity of mixture, but not complete homogeneity, follows if suburbs produce different types of good. In that case, a suburb's population will contain relatively more people from the skill group used most intensively in the production of that suburb's good.

The application of Berglas's work to a suburban setting begs the questions, Why is there not cross-commuting between suburbs to weaken the

link for a consumer between suburbs of residence and of work? Why do
these industrial suburbs not have adjacent, fiscally independent bedroom
suburbs that house people with different skills and public service demands.
An answer lies in historical and institutional factors. Suburbs may have
started out as relatively homogeneous, fairly high-income bedroom communities. However, once they industrialized (for such reasons as changing
transportation technology, general city growth, core city and suburban
financial problems), there was no space for adjacent bedroom suburbs to
form. Moreover, since low-skill and low-income people were not welcome
in other suburbs, an industrialized suburb had to admit people of different
skills and public service demands to meet its industry's labor demands.

A final basis for heterogeneity arises in a dynamic context. Although
suburbs may initially be homogeneous, it may benefit both developers and
initial residents to later admit people of different income and public service
demands.

Adapting Suburbs Models to a Dynamic Context

Following Henderson (1977b), I add a second time period to the earlier
analysis. Most of the population stratifies into suburbs in the first period;
in the second there is some population growth in each income group, but
not enough to push the initial suburbs beyond their optimal population
range nor enough to form a second suburb for any income group. To
maximize later profits, developers in the first period set aside vacant land
rented out at opportunity cost (agriculture) for future residents. The opportunity cost is the same in both periods. For simplicity I assume land rather
than housing is consumed in this section. Lot size provided in the first
period is not malleable and cannot be changed in the second period. Initial
residents rent the land for both periods at a price fixed in period 1. Hence,
suburbs cannot readily be redesigned and people are generally "locked-in"
to their land consumption. (In general, it will not be profitable to sublet
and move in the second period.)

In the first period the formation of suburbs is competitive; developers
compete for initial residents. In the second period developers have some
degree of monopoly power, assuming (from period 1 suburb formation)
that suburbs are strongly ordered by public good levels and per-person
income. A new resident will choose between existing suburbs. His first
feasible choice, given appropriate land prices, will be the suburb with people
with income similar to his. Higher-income suburbs will generally not want
to admit him, because of his relatively low land consumption. He will not
want to enter a lower-income suburb, because of his higher probable land
consumption and their relatively low levels of public services. Thus, he will
be willing to pay a rental premium to live in the similar income suburb.

The question is, How do developers or residents exploit this monopolistic situation? The answer may be found by examining the people who are entering one suburb and by deriving optimal strategies for developers and suburbs. (Edelson, 1975; White, 1975.) To limit the possibilities considered, I assume that all residents in the second period must be assessed at the same unit price of land, without discrimination between new and old residents. The assessed price is denoted by a. It is assumed that there are no lump-sum or head taxes and that the developer controls the rental of all vacant land.

Suppose that in the second period the developer has more similar-income customers than he can accommodate on his vacant land. He will then try to get the highest price per unit of land that he can, by selling as little land as possible to each customer without driving them to a lower-income suburb. Given that $t\bar{a}$ is fixed in $\hat{p} = p + t\bar{a}$, the developer charges the highest $\hat{p}$ and p that he can, such that indirect utility is $V(y, g, \hat{p}) \geq \bar{u}$, where $\bar{u}$ is the utility level available in the next-best suburb. This rental exceeds the implicit per-period rental paid by initial residents. If the developer does not have enough customers to follow this policy, he will increase the lot size offered and lower his unit price (as long as his total profits increase) and he will try to sell to lower- (or higher-) income people who are willing to pay a premium above opportunity rent to live in this suburb. That is, if a developer has a lot of vacant land, it is to his benefit to allow the community to become heterogeneous (and in a multiperiod model, to accelerate development).

Under this policy, since all residents are assessed at the same price but new entrants choose a lower land consumption, given they face higher per-period market prices, new similar- or lower-income entrants have a lower tax base than older residents and are a fiscal burden to the community. (If land is assessed at the per-period rental price *initially* paid by any resident, new entrants, who pay higher prices than first period residents, have a lower [higher] tax base if the price elasticity of demand for land is greater [less] than 1.)

In contrast, given a fixed assessment price, the optimal policy for initial residents is to force each subsequent entrant to consume as much land as possible through zoning regulations. This maximizes the revenue from each resident, given a fixed cost of providing him with public services. Given an alternative utility level, $\bar{V}$, available to new entrants in another suburb, $\hat{p}$ and hence p must fall to induce new residents to remain in the suburb and consume more and more land as the zoned lot size increases. The amount that the community can raise lot size is limited by the fact that p cannot fall below the opportunity cost of land in agriculture or developers will not rent land to new residents.

Given these conflicting objectives, what are possible equilibrium solutions and patterns of land prices across suburbs and time? There are a variety of possibilities that depend on the assumptions chosen; to give a flavor of the types of results, I present one situation. Assume that any zoning restrictions must be imposed in period 1 and apply equally to earlier and later residents. (Without this, residents in period 2 could simply impose the zoning solution presented above.) Second, assume that in the textual discussion initial residents have naive expectations and expect prices and consumption patterns of first period residents to persist into the second period. Therefore, they have no rationale for imposing zoning restrictions, and developers can then impose their best second period solution, presented above.[8] This has interesting implications for prices across time and suburbs.

In the second period in the lowest-income suburb, n, the price of land will be what lowest-income residents are willing to pay to live in that suburb as opposed to their next-best alternative, which may be the core city. The lower limit on this price is the opportunity rent in agriculture. In the next-income suburb, $n - 1$, the price of land equals the price $n - 1$ people are willing to pay there as opposed to the n suburb. Hence, $p_{n-1} > p_n$. Similarly, in the $n - 2$ suburb, the price is what $n - 2$ people are willing to pay to live there as opposed to their best alternative, $n - 1$. Hence, $p_{n-2} > p_{n-1} > p$.[9] This argument implies a scaffolding effect in which prices in period 2 rise continuously as we move up the income scale in suburbs. What does this imply for prices across time?

Suppose that the profits from vacant land sold in the second period are fully anticipated by developers. What does this imply for first period prices? In deciding at what price to sell to initial residents, developers have the choice of selling to suburbanites now and forming a suburb or renting to farmers at opportunity cost for both periods. The opportunity to form a suburb means that the developer can sell to second period residents at a greater than opportunity cost price. Accordingly developers will compete for these initial residents so as to be able to form a suburb and get these higher second period prices. To compete for initial residents developers lower their prices below opportunity cost and at the limit initial residents will effectively capture the profits from the high second period prices. One can, of course, take the argument a step further back and argue that competitive developers will shift the profits to the initial land owners (farmers) by attempting to outbid each other when buying up the land.

2.

In this section I turn to models of a system of cities or regions. While the same notions of group or community formation and of determination of market equilibrium pertain, the underlying basis for population grouping and the formal structure of the model are somewhat different from the original Tiebout and clubs models. As explained in Wheaton's chapter in this volume, in partial equilibrium models of a single city (Mills, 1967), people group or agglomerate in a city to exploit economies of scale in the production of the city's export goods. The spatial character of cities is represented by the monocentric model of a city, in which all people work in the Central Business District (CBD) and live in the surrounding doughnut shaped residential area. Internal commuting and transport costs usually limit the city's spatial area and population. As city size increases, the average commuting distance to the CBD increases, the average housing rental price increases, and the average industrial transport cost may increase.

From the partial equilibrium model of a single city, economists have proceeded to analyze a general equilibrium model of a system of cities (Beckmann, 1968; Mirrlees, 1972; and Henderson, 1974b). These models are concerned with the pattern of trade, the allocation of population and investment among cities, and the determination of the equilibrium and optimum number and size of cities in an economy. I will examine these problems, with a view to answering the following questions: (1) What is the basis and nature of a system of cities? (2) What conditions define the optimal characteristics of a system of cities? (3) Why do cities tend to specialize in the production of different types of goods? (4) What sort of investment and labor location problems arise in a system of cities? (5) How does a model of a system of cities fit in with the usual aggregate international trade and growth models of an economy? (6) What types of externalities arise in a system of cities and do local governments need national government help to solve these externality problems?

One Type of City

First, I will solve for the characteristics of an optimal set of cities and then see under what conditions market solutions are optimal. In designing an efficient set of cities, the welfare of two groups of people must be considered: laborers who work in cities and whose welfare is a function of income, city cost of living, and such urban (dis)amenities as leisure consumption, which is a function of commuting time; and the owners of the capital invested in cities. The latter need not live in the city where their capital is employed, or in any city at all. I assume that they live either on the edges of cities or in the countryside and that their amenity consumption and cost of living are exogenous to the problem. Therefore, their welfare is reflected solely by the return earned on their capital.

The criteria for efficient resource allocation in an economy are usually obtained by maximizing the utility of a representative individual while holding the utility of all others constant and subject to production, spatial, and resource constraints. To make these planning solutions consistent with possible stable market solutions with nondiscriminatory government policies, as in the clubs solutions, two additional constraints are imposed on the problem: people with the same skills and tastes must achieve equal utility levels; and cities that face identical production and consumption conditions must be identical in size and characteristics. If cities are to be identical, they must have the same capital-to-labor (K/N) ratio. To solve for optimal city size, the maximization problem is carried out for one representative city; then that city's size is divided into the economy's population to solve for the optimal number of cities (any population remainder leftover, is ignored).

In the representative, monocentric city, all of the city's export good is produced in the CBD and shipped to the marketing-transport node at the very center of the city and either sold to city residents or exported. In the residential sector, a resident at distance u from the city center consumes the export good $x(u)$, import good $z(u)$, housing $h(u)$, and leisure $e(u) = T - tu$, where T is fixed nonworking time and t is the time it takes to commute a unit distance (round trip) to the city center to work. Therefore, the optimization problem is to maximize utility, $V = V(x(u), z(u), h(u), e(u))$, for a representative individual subject to the constraint that all city residents have the same utility level and subject to the following resource, spatial, and production constraints.

Where N is city population, u_0 is CBD radius, u_1 is city radius, $N(u)$ is residential population at location u (the ring distance u from the city center), and $n(u)$ is business employment at location u, the city's population equals total residential population equals total employment or

$$N = \int_{u_0}^{u_1} N(u)\,du = \int_0^{u_0} n(u)\,du \,.$$

Where $k(u)$ is per-person capital used in housing at location u or total business capital employed at location u, city capital stock, K, is fully employed, or

$$K = \int_0^{u_0} k(u)\,du + \int_{u_0}^{u_1} k(u)N(u)\,du \,.$$

There are also constraints that state that total residential—$l(u)N(u)$—or business—$l(u)$—land demanded at each location equals land supplied $(2\pi u)$ and constraints defining per-person housing production—$h(u) = h(l(u), k(u))$—and leisure consumption at each location. The identical city constraint is represented by the city facing a capital-to-labor (K/N) ratio equal to the national endowment ratio.

The final constraint is a balance of trade or consumption-production constraint, stating that the value of city consumption plus rental payments on capital is equal to the value of city production (assuming the opportunity—agricultural—rent of urban land is zero). Where $x(u)$ and $z(u)$ are per-person consumption of exports and imports at location u and p_z is the (say, international) price of z in units of x, the value of city consumption is

$$\int_{u_0}^{u_1} (x(u) + p_z z(u)) N(u) du .$$

City rental payments are $p_k K$, where p_k is fixed. This means that the utility of city residents is maximized by holding the utility of capital owners fixed. The value of city production available at the marketing transport node is

$$\int_0^{u_0} G(N) x(k(u), n(u), l(u)) (1 - t_x u) du .$$

The x function represents firms' own constant returns to scale technology; and t_x is the cost in x of shipping a unit x a unit distance. $G(N)$ is a Hicks' neutral shift factor where $dG/dN > 0$, representing industry economies of scale *external* to the firm.

These scale economies are the basis for urban agglomeration. They also present a possible externality problem in market solutions, because when a person migrates he affects the efficiency of firms and the productivity of all factors in the cities he enters and leaves. In making location decisions, he does not account for these external effects; hence, under certain conditions, he may make socially inefficient location decisions.

The optimization problem just outlined yields the following optimal city size condition (Henderson, 1977b; see also Mirrlees, 1972, for a similar condition; and Dixit, 1973, for related analyses).

$$\frac{\partial V/\partial h}{\partial V/\partial x} h(u) + p_z z(u) + x(u) = G(N) \frac{\partial x}{\partial n} (1 - t_x u) \qquad (12)$$

$$+ \epsilon X/N + K/N(G(N) \frac{\partial x}{\partial k} (1 - t_x u) - p_k),$$

where ϵ is defined as $(dG/dN)(N/G)$, the elasticity of scale effects with respect to city population; and X is the total net city output of x.

The left-hand side of equation (12) is the social cost to the economy of adding one resident to the city. This is the value of a new resident's consumption of x, z, and h (taken from the total available to the city), such that all residents have equal utility. Note that commuting times borne by this resident are not a direct social cost to the city, although any differential leisure loss borne by the new resident relative to other residents must be compensated with market goods to maintain equal utilities.

The right-hand side of equation (12) is the social benefit of an additional resident. The first term is the private marginal product of the resident and the second is his positive externality effect on total city output. Therefore, the first two terms are his social marginal product (SMP). The third term is the net benefit/loss to the city from employing the resulting additional capital to maintain the national K/N ratio in the city.

In summary, equation (12) states that at optimal city size the marginal social benefits of increasing city size just equal the marginal social costs. This size divided into the economy's population yields the optimal number of cities. To determine if equation (12) will be satisfied in a market economy, I first interpret equation (12) in a market context.

The Pareto-efficient solution relevant in a free market economy is one in which factors are paid the value of their private marginal product. In that case the capital effect—the last term of equation (12)—equals zero. The wage rate, p_n, equals $G(N) \, \partial x/\partial n \, (1 - t_x u)$; and $(\partial V/\partial h)/(\partial V/\partial x) = p(u)$, the price of housing. We assume that land rental income in the city is divided equally between residents by a city land bank company or by the city government. (This avoids introducing a third class of people, or rentiers.) The left-hand side of equation (12) will be a resident's expenditures, which must equal his income, or the wage rate plus his land rent share. Accordingly, equation (12) reduces to

$$\text{land rent share} = \epsilon X/N. \tag{13}$$

This defines a general relationship that must hold in a market economy when any individual city is of efficient size. It has a simple intuitive explanation.

The benefit of an additional resident to other city residents is the increase in production available to them, $\epsilon X/N;$ their cost is the additional land rent share that must be allocated to the new resident. Since per-person land rent in a city starts at a miniscule level and then rises with city size and marginal scale effects are positive (but perhaps declining), the net benefit of additional residents starts off positive and then declines to zero at optimal city size, as land rent shares increase and scale effects wane.

WILL THE MARKET GENERATE PARETO EFFICIENT SOLUTIONS? Under the assumption of only one type of city, equations (12) and (13) are generally satisfied in stable market solutions. Henderson (1977*b*, chs. 3, 4) demonstrated this in a general equilibrium model of a system of monocentric cities. The reasoning is much the same as for the market attainment of optimal club size in section 1. If there are entrepreneurs (land developers) who set up cities, competition will force them to set up cities of efficient size and capital and labor will be attracted to cities of efficient size.

That developers are concerned with the interests of two groups of people, capital owners and laborers, presents interesting problems but does not preclude Pareto-efficient solutions. Henderson (1974b and 1977b) showed that in the neighborhood of efficient city size, laborers generally suffer and capital owners generally gain from increases in city size. The reason is that although both gain on the income side through increased factor productivity, laborers also experience consumption loss in the form of reduced leisure time caused by increased commuting distances. Capital owners who are not city residents do not experience these losses. Developers implicitly trade off the marginal gain to capital owners against the marginal loss to laborers; at equilibrium city size the marginal gain equals the marginal loss. Alternatively stated, at equilibrium city size the monetized sum of laborers' utilities and capital owners' rental is maximized. Such a maximum can only occur if while one element is held constant the other is maximized. This, of course, corresponds to the welfare maximization problem stated above, in which laborers' utility is maximized for a given return to capital. Thus in this situation, the condition that defines equilibrium city size can be shown to be equivalent to equation (13).

Satisfying this condition is necessary for stable market solutions. For example, if cities are larger than those specified by equation (13) a developer could set up a city of efficient size, pay competitive capital rentals and utility levels, and have a profit left over (this must be, since the monetized sum of possible utility levels plus capital rentals is higher at the efficient city size than otherwise). Other entrepreneurs would adjust their existing or potential city sizes in an effort to duplicate these profits. The competition between developers for laborers and the investment necessary to set up the cities that will earn these profits will lead to labor and capital market adjustments and the dissipation of profits to the point where all cities are of efficient size, profits are zero, and capital rentals and utility levels are consistent with the optimal solution.

The Pareto-efficiency of market solutions in this context also makes sense from an externality perspective. Laborers move to equalize private marginal location benefits between cities, whereas, from a social perspective, they should incorporate into their calculus any external effects of migration and equalize social marginal location benefits. However, because in this simple situation all cities are identical, the magnitude of external effects will be equal between cities; and when laborers move to equalize private location benefits they will also incidentally equalize social benefits.

There are three objections to modeling market equilibrium as suggested above. First, land developers may not have the resources, knowledge of the nature and parameters of optimal city size, or the freedom from institutional constraints to ensure market attainment of efficient solutions. However, even in a world of ignorant developers the efficient solution is the only one that is stable with respect to any disturbance. Second, it is conceivable that in the interests of increasing their own welfare, laborers (through unions) or capital owners might lobby politically for national policies that would decrease or increase city sizes. Third, it is difficult to envision cities springing up or dissolving instantaneously in response to changing market conditions. As with the club and suburbs models, the system-of-city models are meant to indicate tendencies and the nature of long-run solutions in an economy.

PUBLIC GOODS.   So far I have assumed that external economies of scale are the basis for agglomeration in cities. Suppose instead or in addition that people agglomerate in monocentric cities to exploit the Samuelson publicness of public goods. In the optimization problem outlined at the beginning of this section, pure public goods would enter utility functions and public service costs would enter the balance-of-trade constraint. Optimizing yields the same optimal population condition as does equation (12), given that an additional resident may consume the existing level of *pure* public goods at zero cost (Henderson, 1977*b*). The market interpretation of equation (12) is the same, except that residents are taxed to finance public services. Assuming that public services are provided on an equal cost-share for equal-income residents and that marginal (but not necessarily intramarginal) scale effects, or ϵ, are zero, the market interpretation of equation (12) becomes

per-person land rent share = per-person tax share.   (14)

To city residents, the marginal cost of an additional resident is the land rent share that he gets and the marginal benefit is the tax share he incurs.

This result was originally derived by Flatters, Henderson, and Mieszkowski (1974) in a regional Ricardian increasing cost model, in which a system of regions is generated much like a system of cities. Another implication of equation (14) is that total taxes equal total public expenditures, which equal total land rents in a city. Public services may be financed best by taxing away all land rental income and using only that revenue to finance public services. (This implication does *not* depend on the way in which land rent income is distributed [Flatters, Henderson, and Mieszkowski, 1974].) This is equivalent in a local context to Henry George's 1879 proposal that public expenditures be financed solely by a tax that taxes away all land rental income (above frontier rents, which are zero agricultural rents here) (George, 1938). This analysis is thus a modern vindication of George's proposal.

Nonidentical Cities

So far I have discussed city size when there is only one type of city. Suppose that there are two or more types of city and each city specializes in the production of a different traded good or bundle of goods. Specialization occurs when no production benefits or positive externalities follow from the location of two different industries in the same city. If the industries are located together, because workers in both industries are living and commuting in the same city, the spatial area of the city and the average commuting cost for a given level of scale economy exploitation in any one industry are raised. Separating the industries in different cities allows for greater scale economy exploitation in each industry relative to a given level of commuting costs and city spatial area. The extent of specialization is limited by the cost of trade between different types of city and production interrelations between industries. Industries that use each other's inputs, a common labor force, or a common public good or such intermediate non-traded inputs as a specialized transport system will tend to locate together.

I now examine a situation in which there are only two types of city, one specializing in x production and the other in z production. I initially assume that there is adequate economy population for just *one* city of each type, so that the optimization problem is simply to allocate the population between the two cities. Thus cities will probably not be of individually efficient size and the optimal number of cities is assumed at the outset to be two.

The optimization problem outlined in section 1 can easily incorporate a second type of city by the addition of employment, spatial, and equal utility constraints for the second type of city and by the use of full-employment and production-consumption constraints for the economy as a whole. Given the new optimization problem, the optimal population allocation condition becomes (Henderson, 1977b, chap. 4)

$$(G(N)\partial x/\partial n(1 - t_x u) + \epsilon X/N)$$

$$-\left(\frac{\partial V/\partial h}{\partial V/\partial x} h(u) + x(u) + \frac{\partial V/\partial z}{\partial V/\partial x} z(u)\right)$$

$$= \left(\frac{\partial V/\partial z}{\partial V/\partial x} (F(N)\partial z/\partial n(1 - t_z u) + \epsilon_z Z/N)\right) \tag{15}$$

$$-\left(\frac{\partial V/\partial h}{\partial V/\partial x} h^z(u) + x^z(u) + \frac{\partial V/\partial z}{\partial V/\partial x} z^z(u)\right),$$

where ϵ and ϵ_z are scale effect elasticities. In the first [second] line of equation (15), following the discussion of section 1, the first expression in large parentheses is the social marginal product (SMP) of labor in city x [3]. The second expression is the consumption cost, or social marginal cost (SMC), of labor in city x [3]. Therefore, equation (15) may be written informally as

$$\text{SMP}_x - \text{SMC}_x = \text{SMP}_z - \text{SMC}_z. \tag{15a}$$

This states that the gap between SMP and SMC should be equalized in all cities. For example, if $\text{SMP}_x - \text{SMC}_x > \text{SMP}_z - \text{SMC}_z$, city x is underpopulated. Since the gap between per-person productivity and consumption is greater in city x, a person may be moved from city x to city z without affecting utility levels and there would be a residual of goods leftover.

The basic concern is whether equation (15) will be satisfied in a market economy. The basic problem in attaining efficient city sizes, given more than one type of city, is due to the existence of different degrees of external scale economies in different types of city. If marginal scale economies differ between cities, laborers will not equalize social location benefits when they move to equalize private location benefits between cities. To determine under what conditions a city may be over- or underpopulated in a market economy, I will interpret equation (15) in a market context in which land rents are distributed equally among residents of a city. Following the derivation of equation (13), equation (15) becomes

$$\epsilon(X/N) - \text{city } x \text{ land rent share} = \epsilon_z(Z/N) \tag{16}$$
$$- \text{city } z \text{ land rent share}.$$

Suppose the x city is larger than the z city (due to differences in intramarginal scale economies or relative export demands), so that land rent shares are probably greater in x cities. If marginal scale effects are lower [higher] in x cities, then x cities must be overpopulated [may be underpopulated]. In either case, to encourage optimal population movement, federal intervention will be necessary to tax people in overpopulated cities or subsidize people in underpopulated cities.

Note that this analysis rejects a partial equilibrium approach to the determination of optimal city size. Under an approach in which each city is viewed on its own, if SMP > SMC for a city, immigration should be subsidized. This is incorrect since such a policy would draw population from other cities where SMP > SMC. Immigration should only be subsidized if the *gap* between SMP and SMC is greater in some cities than in others.

This externality analysis is concerned with population allocation at the margin. In the present context there is another problem. Cities are individually best off by satisfying equations (12) and (13), where SMP

$=$ SMC; whereas with a limited number of cities, Pareto-efficient solutions for the economy as a whole usually involve a gap between SMP and SMC. This provides a basis for individual cities to nonoptimally try to restrict (or enhance) their size and force some of the population into additional very small, inefficient size cities.

If there are many cities of each type, however, both this global problem and the externality population allocation problem disappear. As the number of cities of each type increases, the gap between SMP and SMC in each type of city declines until at the limit it is zero; or all cities can approach their individually efficient size (the remainder problem referred to above disappears). Then equations (12), (13), (15), and (16) will all be satisfied.

AGGREGATE CONSTANT RETURNS TO SCALE. When the number of cities of each type becomes very large, so that all cities approach their individually efficient size, we have at the national or aggregative level a constant returns to scale situation. Then, for example, a doubling of factor endowments in the economy simply doubles the number of each type of city, with utility levels, capital rentals, and city sizes unchanged (assuming the same relative traded good demands). Henderson (1974b, 1977b) uses this fact to argue that the basic international trade theorems (Rybczynski and Stolper-Samuelson) and growth theorems (balanced and golden-rule growth) can be applied directly and hold for large economies with many cities. This provides a direct and auspicious link between urban and mainstream economic theory.

PURE PUBLIC GOODS. If we reintroduce pure public goods as the basis for urban agglomeration, in an economy with a population adequate for only one x and one z type city, the optimal population allocation condition is the same as equation (15). Interpreting this in a market context, assuming public services are financed by equal tax shares for similar people and assuming marginal scale economies, ϵ, are zero, yields:

land rent share in city x — tax share in city x = land rent in city z — tax share in city z. (17)

To simplify (17) further and isolate the public good problem, assume that land rents go out of the system to a separate group (rentiers). Then (17) becomes

tax share in city x = tax share in city z. (17a)

When will this condition be satisfied in a market economy? Suppose that x cities are larger (due, say, to greater intramarginal scale economies).

The unit tax price of public goods is $1/N$, where N is city population and the unit cost of public services is set at 1 unit of x. Since N is larger in the city x, the per-person unit tax price is lower. The relative levels of per-person public expenditures and tax shares between cities is determined by the compensated price elasticity of demand for public services. If this elasticity equals $|-1|$, per-person expenditures and taxes will always be equal between cities, regardless of tax prices, given equal utility levels between cities. However, if the elasticity is greater [less] than $|-1|$, expenditures are greater in the low [high] tax price x [z] city; and the x [z] city is underpopulated. Thus optimality generally requires federal intervention.

This problem in public service provision has been termed a *fiscal externality,* in the sense that when a person migrates he affects the tax prices of all residents in the cities he enters or leaves, but he does not account for these effects in making his migration decisions. It is also useful to view the problem from another perspective. From equation (17a), this problem of potential misallocation of population can be solved by the allocation of tax shares on a national basis (so that similar people pay the same taxes regardless of location)—the same comments apply to the distribution of land rent shares when evaluating equation (17). Tax *shares* do not in themselves affect or directly represent production or consumption capabilities in the economy; therefore, we want to ensure that they do not influence location decisions. Equalizing shares nationally, will remove any incentive to move based on tax shares; location decisions will be based solely on local marginal productivity and public good consumption conditions. However, with national financing, the national government would have to pay for local public services, which presents the problem of the correct assessment of local preferences and the satisfaction of the local Samuelson condition in the provision of local services.

The results contained in equations (17) and (17a) were originally derived (by Flatters, Henderson, and Mieszkowski, 1974) in a model where population is to be allocated between two regions with different natural resources. As a general rule, the introduction of other externality considerations (such as land rent shares, scale economies, congestion in public good consumption or transportation) simply adds additional terms to each side of equations (15) and (17) that state the magnitude of the particular externality. To evaluate the over- or underpopulation of a city or region, simply add the different externality effects for a city and compare the totals for different cities.

Pollution Externalities

It is instructive to examine externalities that affect the internal allocation of resources within cities. The externalities that are most commonly

modelled in a spatial context are road congestion and air pollution externalities. Since Wheaton covers road congestion externalities in this volume,
I will briefly review the main results of air pollution models.

In a monocentric model of a city, air pollution results from firms in the
CBD employing raw materials that lead to the emission of airborne wastes.
These emissions cause air pollution or a decline in the air quality amenity
that enters residents' utility functions; they may also affect production
efficiency (ignored here). Pollution may be abated by devoting resources
to antipollution activity. For a given level of business emissions, the further away a CBD firm is from the residential area, the less its emissions
influence residential air quality; they have a proportionately greater opportunity to disperse vertically and fall out in the CBD before reaching residences. Similarly, the further away residents are from industrial areas, the
less pollution they experience.

A comprehensive environmental policy consists of the following components:

(a) *Pollution taxes.* As Baumol and Oates (1976) demonstrated in a
nonspatial context, to induce firms to use optimal levels of raw materials,
optimal production techniques, and to engage in optimal levels of antipollution activity, firms must be charged for their pollution damages. The
unit tax price for pollution facing firms should equal the marginal value of
damages (to air quality) experienced by residents from increments to
pollutants. In a spatial context (Tietenberg, 1974, and Henderson, 1977a),
the level of pollutants assessed to firms (and evaluated at the spatially
invariant tax price) is an increasing function of their emissions and a
decreasing function of their distance from residential areas.

(b) *Land-use zoning or discriminatory land-use taxes.* The free market
determination of the border between residential and commercial areas will
in general be nonoptimal (Stull, 1974). The free market will tend to
equalize land rents that reflect the private marginal product of land at the
border of competing uses—in this case, residential and commercial. However, there are two externalities present. Increasing the size of commercial
areas allows for greater emission dispersion within the commercial area
before emissions reach residents; thus for commercial emissions, an increase in the commercial area may increase residential air quality (Henderson, 1977a). On the other hand, increasing the relative size of commercial areas in many spatial models results in residents living closer to
commercial areas and polluting sources (Stull, 1974). Given these opposing externality affects it may be desirable to either increase or decrease the
size of the commercial area by means of zoning or discriminatory land-use
taxes, relative to the free market level.

(c) *Distributing pollution tax proceeds.* The extensive literature on this
subject, reviewed in Baumol and Oates (1976), is inconclusive on how to
best distribute pollution tax proceeds. Whether a local government directly

or indirectly distributes its pollution tax proceeds to local residents or the national government intervenes and distributes some or all local tax proceeds nationally, the tax-proceed income of local residents and the benefits from locating in that area are affected. Thus the distribution of local tax proceeds will affect population movements to and from the locality and the number of pollution victims and laborers in different localities. Henderson (1977a) points out that this question falls naturally into the framework of the theory of optimal population allocation discussed above. Consider an economy composed of two polluting monocentric cities. The condition for optimal population allocation is the same as equation (15) (given that the use of raw materials, not population per se, is the cause of pollution). If marginal scale economies, ϵ, are zero, if land rents go to a separate group (rentiers), and if there are no public services, the market interpretation of (15) is simply

$$\text{pollution rebate share in city } x = \text{pollution rebate share in city } z. \tag{18}$$

Optimality would be guaranteed in equation (18) if the national government collected all pollution tax proceeds and distributed them nationally on an equal basis (for similar people). Then following the same reasoning used in the discussion of public good financing, migration decisions would be neutrally affected by the distribution of tax proceeds and there would be no incentive to move nonoptimally between cities for the purpose of increasing pollution tax proceeds income. In a model in which there is no equal utility constraint on similar people, the same neutrality effect could be achieved by the distribution of a city's local tax proceeds to initial residents (regardless of whether they stayed or migrated) but not to new residents. Once the various other possible externalities underlying equation (15) are reintroduced back in the model, pollution tax proceeds could also be distributed nonneutrally to encourage optimal population reallocation, necessitated by the existence of other externalities.

One question of interest in the literature is whether the implementation of optimal pollution policies in a locality is likely to increase or decrease city size (Henderson, 1974a, and Tolley, 1974). Suppose that in a two-city economy, prior to the enactment of optimal environmental policies, production in the x city results in heavy pollution, whereas production in the z city results in little or no pollution. Moreover suppose that, with the enactment of optimal environmental policies, a very small amount of employment in antipollution activity is needed to reduce pollution in city x from its high levels to almost zero. The cost of employing labor in the x city should decline, since the wages needed to attract laborers and compensate them for living in the polluted x city relative to the z city will decline. The effect of this decline in wages on x's production costs could exceed the opposing effects of pollution taxes and costs of antipollution employment. In that case, the decline in x's production costs would lead to an increase in x demand and city x production and population relative to city z.[i] The basic idea is that firms, by imposing disamenities on residents, inadvertently raise the costs of employing laborers in polluted localities. If they can be induced to collectively reduce pollution, their production costs could fall. Moreover, even if x production costs rise, laborers in the city will still be made better off (providing some pollution tax proceeds are retained in the city) by the enactment of optimal pollution policies and they could be made initially relatively better off than city z residents (who may benefit from a relative increase in z demand plus some portion of city x tax proceeds). There could still be an increase in x city population despite the relative increase in x production costs.[10]

NOTES

1. A basic question pointed out to me by Tom Woodward is why we need membership clubs at all. Public services could be provided on a pay-as-you-use basis, open to anyone, and people would choose to consume at clubs that provide the level of services they desire. Therefore, clubs need only arise in more complicated situations in which membership ensures exclusivity or period-by-period financial solvency and guaranteed use.

2. Alternatively, we can assume that the optimal club size condition is satisfied over a range of N, and subgroup sizes always fall within this range. Therefore, there will be one club corresponding to each type of consumer.

3. $\partial (dp/dg)/\partial y = h^{-1} \dfrac{\partial V/\partial g}{\partial V/\partial y} y^{-1} \left[y \left(\dfrac{\partial V/\partial g}{\partial V/\partial y} \right)^{-1} \partial \left(\dfrac{\partial V/\partial g}{\partial V/\partial y} \right) / \partial y - h^{-1} y \partial h/\partial y \right].$

If the first term in the square brackets, the income elasticity of the marginal evaluation of public services, is positive and greater than the income elasticity of housing demand, then *indifference curve slopes increase* with income. Otherwise, they decrease.

4. The effect of income changes on the supply relationship (holding g constant) is

$$\partial p/\partial y = -gc(N)N^{-1}h^{-2}\partial h/\partial y < 0.$$

5. From equation (7), p is minimized when

$$\partial p/\partial N = h^{-1}gc(N)N^{-2}(-1 + (dc/dN)N/c) = 0$$

or when $dc/dN = c/N$, as in equation (4).

6. The greater the number of inputs that are zoned, the greater the magnitude of $\partial p/\partial h$ is and the more likely h is to increase and approach that at which where $p = p^*$.

7. Note that capitalization will occur only relative to possible alternative homogeneous communities. Since such alternative communities may be inefficient in size, actual capitalization will be less than that indicated in equations (10) or (11), with the actual magnitude dependent on the difference in public service costs between the mixed and potential homogeneous suburbs.

8. Because any zoning restrictions apply equally to all residents and because all land is assessed at the same price, (with effective zoning) new and old residents contribute equally to taxes and initial residents cannot fiscally exploit new residents. Therefore, if initial residents do not have naive expectations, all land may simply be

zoned at the level most desired by them, given price. In this way, they consume
optimally and cannot be exploited by new residents. Developers will thus capture the
monopolistic profits in period 2; the discussion of prices in the next two paragraphs
also applies to this situation.

9. This assumes developers do not price discriminate or set lot sizes to extract
consumer's surplus, as in Edelson, 1975. This latter assumption imposes no constraints
here, where developers have more potential similar income entrants than they can sell
land to.

10. If this is the case, there must be a substitution away from x consumption into
nontraded goods consumption, such as housing, to support employment in the x city.
Henderson, 1974a, and Tolley, 1974.

REFERENCES

Baumol, W. J., and Oates, W. E. 1975. *The Theory of Environmental Policy.*
Englewood Cliffs, N.J.: Prentice-Hall.

Beckmann, M. 1968. *Location Theory.* New York: Random House.

Berglas, E. 1976. "Distribution of Tastes and Skills and the Provision of Local
Public Goods." *Journal of Public Economics* 6: 409–23.

Bradford, D. F., and Oates, W. E. 1974. "Suburban Exploitation of Central
Cities." In *Redistribution Through Public Choice.* Edited by H. M. Hochman and G. Peterson. New York: Random House.

Buchanan, J. 1965. "An Economic Theory of Clubs." *Economica* 32: 1–14.

Buchanan, J., and Goetz, C. 1972. "Efficiency Limits of Fiscal Mobility."
Journal of Public Economics 1: 25–45.

Coase, R. 1960. "The Problem of Social Cost." *Journal of Law and Economics*
3: 1–64.

Connally, M. 1970. "Public Goods, Externalities, and International Relations."
Journal of Political Economy 78: 279–90.

Dixit, A. K. 1973. "The Optimum Factory Town." *Bell Journal* 4: 637–51.

Edelson, N. 1975. "The Developer's Problem or How to Divide a Piece of Land
Most Profitably." *Journal of Urban Economics* 2: 349–65.

Ellickson, B. 1970. *Metropolitan Residential Location and the Local Public
Sector.* Ph.D. diss. Massachusetts Institute of Technology.

———. 1971. "Jurisdictional Fragmentation and Residential Choice." *American Economic Review* 61: 334–39.

Fischel, W. 1975. "Fiscal and Environmental Considerations in the Location
of Firms in Suburban Communities." In *Fiscal Zoning and Land Use.* Edited
by E. S. Mills and W. E. Oates. Lexington, Mass.: D.C. Heath.

Flatters, F.; Henderson, V.; and Mieszkowski, P. 1974. "Public Good Efficiency
and Regional Fiscal Equalization." *Journal of Public Economics* 3: 99–112.

George, Henry. 1938. *Progress and Poverty.* New York: Modern Library.

Hamilton, B. W. 1975. "Zoning and Property Taxation in a System of Local
Governments." *Urban Studies* 12: 205–11.

———. 1977. "Capitalization of Intrajurisdictional Differences in Local Tax
Prices." *American Economic Review* 66: 743–53.

Henderson, J. V. (1974a). "Optimal City Size: The External Diseconomy Question." *Journal of Political Economy* 82: 373–88.

————. 1974b. "The Sizes and Types of Cities." *American Economic Review* 64: 640–56.

————. 1977a. "Externalities in a Spatial Context." *Journal of Public Economics* 7: 89–110.

————. 1977b. *Economic Theory and the Cities*. New York: Academic Press.

Inman, R. 1979. "Demand for Urban Public Services." In *Current Issues in Urban Economics*. Edited by P. Mieszkowski and M. Straszheim. Baltimore: Johns Hopkins University Press.

McGuire, M. 1974. "Group Segregation and Optimal Jurisdictions." *Journal of Political Economy* 82: 112–32.

Mills, E. S. 1967. "An Aggregative Model of Resource Allocation in a Metropolitan Area." *American Economic Review* 57: 197–210.

Mirrlees, J. A. 1972. "The Optimum Town." *Swedish Journal of Economics* 74: 114–36.

Pauly, M. V. 1970. "Optimality, Public Goods, and Local Government." *Journal of Political Economy* 78: 572–85.

Stull, W. 1974. "Land Use and Zoning in an Urban Economy." *American Economic Review* 64: 337–47.

Tiebout, C. 1956. "A Pure Theory of Local Expenditures." *Journal of Political Economy* 64: 416–24.

Tietenberg, J. H. 1974. "Comment." *American Economic Review* 64: 462–66.

Tolley, G. S. 1974. "The Welfare Economics of City Bigness." *Journal of Urban Economics* 1: 324–45.

White, M. J. 1975. "Firm Location in a Zoned Metropolitan Area." In *Fiscal Zoning and Land Use*. Edited by E. S. Mills and W. E. Oates. Lexington, Mass.: D. C. Heath.

9

THE FISCAL PERFORMANCE OF LOCAL GOVERNMENTS: AN INTERPRETATIVE REVIEW

ROBERT P. INMAN

> Budgets are not merely affairs of arithmetic. In a
> thousand ways they go to the root of prosperity of
> individuals, the relation of classes, and the strength
> of kingdoms.
>
> *William Gladstone*

INTRODUCTION

If there has been a dominant theme to urban domestic policy in the last ten years it has been that of urban problems, new legislation, and observed failures. It has been a frustrating and discouraging experience, one born of high expectations and poor information. We simply did not appreciate the full complexities of the urban economy when the "solutions" of the 1960s were developed.

One of the principle actors that we did not understand was local government. Yet local governments have been and continue to be among the major providers of all goods and services within the urban sector. As simple

Robert P. Inman is associate professor, Department of Finance and Department of Economics, University of Pennsylvania.

This work was supported in part by grants from the Ford Foundation and the National Science Foundation. A preliminary version of this paper was presented to the Harvard University Faculty Seminar on Urban Public Economics, to the Organizations Workshop of the University of Pennsylvania, and to the Committee on Urban Economics, Columbus, Ohio Conference (May, 1977). The comments of the many participants are gratefully acknowledged. Philip Cook, Malcolm Getz, Richard Nelson, Bernard Saffran, Thomas Romer, and Howard Rosenthal also provided very useful comments on an earlier version of this paper. The editorial assistance and substantive comments of Peter Mieszkowski and Mahlon Straszheim were particularly helpful. Special thanks go to my tutor in fiscal politics Julius Margolis.

"creatures of the state," local governments were perceived as public-serving bodies that played according to the legal rules; give them money, and they will spend it by the guidelines. But experience has taught us that the rules were their own. If federal and state legislators were to use local governments as policy vehicles—as was the intention with urban renewal, compensatory education, and model cities programs—it soon became apparent that we had better understand how the local budgetary process allocates public resources. Our purpose here is to see how far we have come toward such an understanding.

This chapter builds from a central premise: local governments produce something of social value but, for immutable structural reasons, often do it poorly. What local governments provide are public service outputs and after tax-or-transfer income for residents of the urban economy. But scale economies in production or consumption, diversity of tastes for local public outputs, and informational asymmetries between consumer-voters and supplier-politicians render extremely improbable the provision by local governments of outputs to achieve a socially optimal allocation. Since structural imperfections in the urban public economy preclude our ever building perfect local governments, we must manipulate the ones that we have.

Yet to rationally influence local fiscal choices we must be able to predict the effects of policy on the behavior of local governments. The efficacy of any remedy depends crucially on how local governments and their residents respond to its incentives. There is no guarantee that policies directed toward local fiscal reform will work. In fact, federal or state efforts at reform, undone by local fiscal adjustment, may actually make matters worse.

Section 1 summarizes much of what we now know empirically about the determinant of local expenditure and tax decisions.[1] The two commonly used behavioral models of local budgeting—the median voter model and the dominant party model—are presented, and the econometric results developed within these frameworks are reviewed. Not surprisingly, these models often prove too restrictive to portray the complicated processes they are meant to describe. Extensions in two general directions seem particularly important.

First, the production process for local public services assumed within these models treats public goods as technologically equivalent to private goods. Varying degrees of congestability from pure Samuelsonian public goods ("more services for you means no less for me") to service breakdown under heavy use (e.g., "stop and go" highway travel) are not allowed. In addition, production is assumed to be technologically efficient at all levels of output, that is, management techniques and management preferences are ignored. Section 2 corrects these omissions by explicitly incorporating public service technologies and administering bureaucracies into the budget model.

Second, although changes in the environments of cities stimulate a reflex budgetary reaction, the cities themselves are presumed to have no impact on, or control over, this environment. Factor prices, grants-in-aid, tax base, and population are all assumed to be exogenous to the local budgetary process. Section 3 drops this fiction and summarizes and extends recent attempts to place local budgeting within a general equilibrium specification of the metropolitan political economy.

Section 4 concludes the survey. Our progress toward building a policy-relevant predictive model of local fiscal performance is assessed and the priorities for future research are presented.

1. RECENT WORK AND NEW DIRECTIONS

The Determinants Studies and Fiscal Policy

The 1960s saw a major increase in research by economists and political scientists into the determinants of local fiscal behavior. The results pointed to a fairly consistent set of conclusions: states or cities with higher per-capita income, larger fiscal bases, greater unemployment, a greater percentage nonwhite, more extensive urbanization, and higher state plus federal aid, generally spent more on public services. Gramlich (1969a) has provided a useful overview of this early literature. Typically, local expenditures (EXP) were hypothesized to be simple linear functions of per-capita income (I), per-capita grants-in-aid (A), various socioeconomic characteristics (SES), and a normally distributed error term (u):

$$\text{EXP} = \beta_0 + \beta_1 I + \beta_2 A + \beta_3 SES + u. \tag{1}$$

The estimated income coefficient (β_1) ranged from .01 to .09, implying that a dollar's increase in per-capita income stimulated a one to nine cent rise in local spending. Of central concern was the effect of grants-in-aid on local spending. Grants were considered "stimulative" if $\beta_2 > 1$—that is, if one dollar of aid induced more than a one dollar increase in local outlay. If $\beta_2 < 1$, then grants replaced local spending, and aid resulted in a "substitution" of federal for local money. When $\beta_2 = 0$, this substitution was complete. Most of the early studies obtained estimated of β_2 that were significantly greater than 1, a result that might have been expected if the federal and state requirements to "spend and match" were at all binding in this period.

Two suggestive conclusions emerged from this early work. First, a systematic relationship between local spending, as determined by a political process, and the economic and demographic characteristics of the community was observed; the proportion of the expenditure variation "explained" by income, aid, and SES generally exceeded 0.5 in cross-section studies and was well over 0.9 in time-series work. Second, grants-in-aid were consistently significant and positive in these equations. At a time when U.S. cities were facing severe fiscal pressure and local service quality was declining, it appeared that there was at least one policy instrument that could make a difference. For both political economists and urban policy analysts, the topic of local fiscal performance appeared promising for future work.

The new research soon appeared. For whereas the early determinants studies were suggestive, the usefulness of the results themselves was seriously marred by econometric problems. First, the model specifications as typified by equation (1) were rarely more than an ad hoc collection of variables that seemed to work. Hypothesis testing was not an issue. The central danger with such strict empiricism is that key variables may be omitted. If the omitted variable (e.g., fiscal base) is correlated with the included variables (e.g., income and aid), then the estimated effects of exogenous changes in the included variables will be biased. The income coefficient, β_1, will, for example, measure both the marginal effect of income on expenditures and a portion of the effect of fiscal base on spending. Such biased parameter estimates may lead us to push some policies that will not work or to reject other policies that will. The problem can only be avoided by formally modeling the budgetary process, generating hypotheses about model specification and variable effects, and *then* testing for the effects econometrically.

But there were other difficulties with the early studies. The bulk of the determinants work was based on aggregated data of state plus local government expenditures. Yet the primary concern in micro-urban policy analysis is with the effect of policy on *a* local government. Aggregated data will yield accurate estimates of micro-behavior only if all the micro-units that comprise the aggregate react identically to changes in the variables. The estimated effects of policy on local spending will be an average of the true effects for all local units in the aggregate. The question is, of course, how serious this aggregation bias is likely to be. A comparison of the results of Brazer (1959), for central cities, Henderson (1968), for counties, and Sharkansky (1967), for state governments, suggests that the prediction error due to aggregation may be large. Limiting the analysis to politically and geographically similar local units (e.g., center cities, suburban school districts, rural towns) seems a wise first step toward avoiding this bias.

The final serious error of these early studies was their inappropriate specification of the major policy variable—grants-in-aid. The federal and state aid structure to local governments includes both exogenous, or lump-sum, aid (e.g., state school foundation aid grants, federal revenue sharing) and matching grants-in-aid (e.g., percentage equalization school aid, federal welfare aid). Previous analyses did not distinguish between these two forms of transfer but combined them in a single grants variable that measured the dollar value of total aid received. There are two problems with this specification of the aid variable. First, unless correct simultaneous equation procedures are employed, consistent estimates of this total aid effect cannot be obtained. Oates (1968) and others have rightly criticized past work on this account.[2] Second, even if correct estimation procedures are employed, the estimated effect of total aid on local spending may be of only marginal usefulness in policy planning. A priori, lump-sum aid as a pure budget transfer might be expected to have a very different impact on fiscal decisions than matching aid, which operates as a price reduction for the aided service. The coefficient on the total aid variable, however, is an estimate of a weighted average (weights unknown) of these "budget" and "price" effects. If policy consists of small proportional changes in all aid programs, then the weights will be unaffected and the (correctly estimated) total aid coefficient will give reasonable predictions of the expenditure response to aid. But such uniform mark-ups in all existing aid are rarely the tools of policy. For most matters of local fiscal policy, the separate price and income impacts of matching and exogenous aid on local fiscal performance must be known.

Although hinting that something systematic was going on, this early empirical work on local fiscal choice was therefore more suggestive of problems to be avoided than of answers to be used. The central difficulties stemmed from a lack of a firm conceptual framework upon which to build and interpret the empirical analyses. The recent work of Gramlich (1968, 1969b), Henderson (1968), and Barr and Davis (1966) has filled this void and has become the basis for the major empirical studies of recent years.[3]

Fiscal Choice in the Demand Framework

The fundamental innovation of Gramlich, Henderson, and Barr and Davis was to view the process of local fiscal choice as an "as if" preference maximization subject to a budget constraint. Preferences are specified over local public services and after tax-or-transfer incomes while the budget constraint requires local revenues from taxes and subventions to equal local expenditures on public output. The optimization process used to describe local fiscal choice yields a set of demand equations for output and local revenue (or, equivalently, private income) as functions of the net cost of outputs, before tax income, and fiscal base.

The optimizing, demand function specification has two clear advantages over the ad hoc approach of past determinants studies. First, the potential role of Federal and state fiscal policy variables can be clearly stipulated and specific hypotheses as to their effects on local choices can be tested. Second, because of legal requirements for a balanced budget, the between service effects of service-specific policies (e.g., matching aid) can be explicitly incorporated into the analysis through the model's imposed budget constraint. To understand these strengths and to correctly interpret the derived empirical results, the preference maximizing model of local fiscal choice must be specified in somewhat greater detail.

The analysis assumes a continuous, quasi-concave preference function representing *individual* preferences for current period local service outputs (denoted by the vector $\tilde{G}$) and after tax, private income $(Y)—P(\tilde{G}, Y)$. For the moment, I shall assume that individuals are myopic and neglect investment (i.e., future public services) and new debt financing (i.e., a future lien on private income). Unless individual (or family) tastes and incomes are identical across all residents of a local political unit, a central issue for the demand approach must be *whose* preferences are to define $P(\cdot)$. This question is discussed in detail below. Here I derive the demand specification from the maximizing framework, given that someone's— whether resident, elected official, or party boss—preferences define $P(\cdot)$.

Within the demand framework, the chosen preference function must be maximized subject to the individual's corresponding budget constraint. All local governments face a legal requirement to balance the revenues raised (taxes and grants-in-aid) against the dollars spent.

For each public service, dollars are allocated to labor (L_i) and materials (M_i) to produce the public *facilities*—denoted $X_i = \psi_i(L_i, M_i)$—that are then used by the town's N residents to yield an equal flow of public *services* per resident—denoted $G_i = g_i(X_i, N)$.[4] There is a service cost schedule that corresponds to the service production technology. Within the demand approach, this cost structure generally assumes the form:

$$C_i = c_i(w_i, s_i) \cdot X(L_i, M_i), \tag{2}$$

where w_i and s_i are the assumed exogenous factor prices of labor and materials, respectively. As the specification of the current service cost index $c_i(\cdot)$ is independent of X_i, the facilities production relationship $\psi_i(L_i, M_i)$ is implicitly assumed to be linear homogenous—i.e., Cobb Douglas with constant returns to scale.[5] The average cost of public facilities for service i is the constant $c_i(w_i, s_i) = (C_i/X_i)$. Finally, within this cost and production structure, the city's budget constraint must balance taxes (T), lump-sum aid (Z), and matching aid (at rates m_i for current expenditures) against current expenditures $(\sum c_i X_i)$. The constraint is specified as:

$$T + Z = \sum_i c_i(1 - m_i)X_i. \tag{3}$$

There is a counterpart to the city fiscal constraint in equation (3) for those individual residents within the city whose preferences are presumed to be the basis of $P(\tilde{G}, Y)$. To draw the connection, the demand approach assumes that each service's facilities, X_i, translate into per-resident service outputs, G_i, on a per-capita basis. Formally, $G_i = g_i(X_i, N)$ becomes $G_i = X_i/N$. In a like manner, city taxes can be transformed into individual tax burdens and incomes. For each resident, current period after-local-tax income is defined by $Y = I - tb\pi$, where I is current before-tax income, t is the current effective tax rate against the individual's current tax base b, and π is the individual's net burden per dollar of local taxes after the deduction of local taxes and the awarding of local tax credits when paying federal or state income tax. In all states, $0 < \pi < 1$ with values falling between 0.60 to 0.85 for most local taxes.[6] If B is the city's tax base per resident (including commercial-industrial property), then $t = T/BN$. Substituting t into Y and solving for T and then substituting this expression into equation (3) along with $X_i = G_iN$, gives the following *individual* budget constraint with local services and financing:

$$I + \tau z = \sum_i \tau c_i(1 - m_i)G_i + Y, \tag{3'}$$

where,

τ = The resident's net share of per capita taxes, $= (b/B)\pi$, and

z = lump-sum aid per capita $= Z/N$.

Having specified an individual preference function, $P(\cdot)$, and *that individual's* corresponding budget constraint in equation (3'), the process of fiscal choice in the demand framework is described by an "as if" maximization of $P(\cdot)$ subject to (3'). The result: a series of current period public service demand equations,

$$G_i = f_i(p_1 \cdots p_n; 1; \tau z + I)(i = 1 \cdots n); \tag{4}$$

and a current period private income equation,

$$Y = y(p_1 \cdots p_n; 1; \tau z + I), \tag{5}$$

where $p_i(= \tau c_i(1 - m_i))$ is the net "tax price" of service i, 1 is the price of current private income, and τ, z, and I are defined as above. Y is related to total taxes by the identity $T \equiv N(I - Y)/\tau$. Equations (4) and (5) constitute a complete system of fiscal choice demand equations, except for our neglect of local public investment and net long-term borrowing.

The inclusion of borrowing and public investment in the demand framework is problematic at best. Presumably, the individual's preference function specified as $P(\cdot)$ includes future public services and private income as well as current services and income. In the simplest case of intertemporal choice, borrowed funds can be invested in public capital formation for increased future services but at a cost in reduced future income, when debt plus interest is repaid. Strictly speaking, public investment should continue until the extra benefits from increased investment just compensates for lost future income. A lower interest rate lowers the cost of public investment and should stimulate such expenditures. The individual's budget constraint is no longer defined just by current before tax income (I) but by current plus (discounted) future before-tax income; that is, by wealth. Within this framework investment and future income equations analogous to equations (4) and (5) can be hypothesized, where wealth now replaces I and the exogenously determined interest rate is included as a price in all equations.

A *realistic* extension of equations (4) and (5) to the intertemporal setting is more demanding. The primary difficulty stems from the crucial fact that the residents and politicians who make today's budgetary choices may not be tomorrow's residents and politicians. In a world of perfect information—in which future city residents know the size of the debt burden and the capital stock they will inherit—current residents have an incentive to anticipate the preferences of new residents and to invest accordingly. This strategy will maximize the resale value of homes and businesses now within the city. But such a strategy creates problems for the demand model, grounded as it is in a specified *individual's* preference function. With perfect information, current expenditures will be allocated to satisfy today's preferences, but debt and borrowing decisions will depend on current residents' assessments of future residents' preferences and income. Thus both today's and tomorrow's preferences and income must be specified.

If information on the part of future residents is at all imperfect, there will still be problems for empirical analysis of local investment and borrowing behavior: it is possible for debt financing to be used as a transfer device. Future residents may be forced to pay for current residents' services or tax relief, as borrowing finances the current budget. Although only the current residents' preferences and income are needed to model intertemporal choice in this case, the demand model must specify the potential for such debt-financed exploitation of future residents. Such a measure should define the myriad of institutional restrictions now imposed by state governments on local borrowing—notably debt limits and interest rate ceilings.

Although it is difficult to satisfactorily extend the demand model of local choice into the intertemporal framework, controlling for variations in borrowing cost and anticipated future income by including municipal bond interest rates (or bond ratings) and the past rate of income growth in equations (4) and (5) may be sufficient to obtain good estimates of the effects of *current* prices, income, and aid on *current* expenditures and taxes. On this basis, the estimation of equations (4) and (5) can proceed.

Within the structure of equations (4) and (5), how federal and state fiscal policies *might* influence local services and financing can now be seen. In this model, matching aid (m), deductions and credits for local taxes (defining π), and fiscal base guarantees (setting B) operate as price changes that influence service spending by own price and cross-price effects. Inflation, interest rate assurance, and federal and state tax deduction policies for income from municipal bond interest influence the net real cost of local borrowing and impact upon the local fiscal process as a de facto change in local prices. Lump-sum aid and any macropolicy effects on residential real income operate as exogenous shifts in the income-plus-aid constraint, $\tau z + I$.

Therefore, the demand approach provides a helpful organizing framework for analyzing local fiscal choice and debating policy reform. The real issue is, of course, whether the resulting specification, once estimated, proves to be an accurate predictor of local fiscal performance. Predictive power is the real test of any model's structure. To face this test, the demand framework must first select a governing preference function, $P(\cdot)$.

The Demand Framework Applied: Whose Preferences?

The choice of a specifying preference function is fundamentally a prediction about who governs local fiscal choices. Many candidates have been offered —Banfield and Wilson (1963) give a long list—and numerous case studies on local politics (e.g., Banfield, 1965) have described the "winners" in various U.S. communities. In much of this case-study literature, the choice of who will govern is seen as a subtle bargaining game in which the rules are defined by local history and the outcome depends on local personalities. The extremely localized character of the choice process makes the prediction of the individual winners a hazardous exercise, at best. Indeed, local "noise" may dominate any common structure and render the identification of $P(\cdot)$, and hence accurate fiscal predictions, statistically impossible. But this is a testable proposition, and the final verdict will come only from empirical analyses with specified preference functions. To date, the literature has offered two alternatives: the median voter model and the dominant party model. Both are grounded in democratic politics, but each arises from very different assumptions about the workings of that process.

THE MEDIAN VOTER MODEL. The median voter model of local fiscal choice, derived from the Hotelling theory of spatial competition,[7] places the resident voter and the election process on center stage. Voters determine budgetary outcome. Financial or institutional barriers to running for political office are low, and an elastic supply of candidates seeking office emerges. Voters are well-informed on budgetary issues, voting costs are insignificant, and because of social pressure or a moral commitment to the process of democracy, all voters vote. Candidates must please the voters if they hope to be elected. Rule is by majority decision and through a process of campaign adjustment—the candidate or, equivalently, the budgetary package favored by the median (50th percentile) voter stands to win.[8] Deviation from the median voter's preferred outcome will insure a candidate's defeat, as an opponent will arise to satisfy those preferences. $P(\cdot)$ therefore represents the preferences of the voter in the median position of the town's demands for local services.

As applied in empirical analyses, the median voter specification for $P(\cdot)$ employs two further restrictions. First, each local government is assumed to supply only one service financed by a fixed tax structure. This guarantees that local budgets are one dimension issues—is there more or less spending? Extension of the median voter logic to multidimensional issues demands improbable restrictions on voter preferences.[9] Second, the median voter in each locality is identified as the one with the town's median family income. Local fiscal choice therefore reduces to an "as if" maximization of the $P(\cdot)$ that corresponds to the family with the median income, subject to that family's fiscally defined budget constraint (equation [3']).

Bergstrom and Goodman (1973) have derived five conditions sufficient for $P(\cdot)$ to correspond to the preferences of the median-income family:

1. All sample cities have income distributions that are simple proportional shifts of each others' distributions;
2. Each family's share of local tax cost (τ) is a constant elasticity function of family income $(\tau = aI^\epsilon)$;
3. All families have identical log-linear demand for public services as a function only of income and tax shares $(G = AI^\alpha \tau^\beta)$;
4. The relevant elasticities do not violate the condition $\alpha + \beta\epsilon \neq 0$;
5. All families vote their true preferences (i.e., "sincere," not strategic, voting).

Conditions 1 and 2 allow us to define voter tax shares (τ) as a simple function of family income. More generally, $\tau = \pi b/B$, but if conditions 1 and 2 are valid, then this general specification can be reduced to $\tau = aI^\epsilon$.[10] Condition 3 is the commonly used log-log demand curve specification, under the assumption that the prices of nonpublic goods and services are constant (and therefore represented within the term A).[11] Condition 4 insures that family demand for public services will be a monotone function of family income.[12] Voters can therefore be ranked along the spending continuum from low to high, with low-income families demanding low spending when $\alpha + \beta\epsilon > 0$ (G as a monotonically increasing function of I) and high-income families demanding low spending when $\alpha + \beta\epsilon < 0$ (G as a decreasing function of I). If all voters vote sincerely (condition 5), the

median position in this spending distribution will correspond to the level
of G preferred by the family with the median income.

In addition to clarifying the conditions sufficient for the median voter to
median income correspondence, Bergstrom and Goodman importantly
extended the usual model. Specifically, condition 3 is relaxed to allow
expressed demands for G to depend on family characteristics other than
income—for example, religion, ethnic group, age, and most importantly,
whether or not people vote. Under the Bergstrom-Goodman extension,
a new condition is defined:

> 3′. All families in a population subgroup j $(j = 1 \cdots n)$ in city i
> have a log-linear demand for public services as a function of
> family income, tax shares, city-wide characteristics $f(S^i)$, and
> a group specific constant term, $G = A_j f(S^i) \tau^\beta I^\alpha$.

For a sample of cities satisfying conditions 1, 2, 3′, 4, and a requirement
of sincere voting (3′ obviates full voter participation), the median quantity
of public services demanded in town i, denoted $G_m{}^i$, will be given by:

$$G_m{}^i = \Phi(\rho_1{}^i \cdots \rho_n{}^i) A_j f(S^i) \tau_{jm}^{i\beta} I_m^{i\alpha}, \tag{6}$$

where $\rho_1{}^i \ldots \rho_n{}^i$ is the portion of city i's population in each family subgroup
$(\sum \rho_j{}^i = 1)$, I_m^i is the median-family income in city i, τ_{jm}^i is the tax share
of a family with the median income in a chosen reference group j $(\tau_{jm}^i = a_j{}^i I_m{}^\epsilon)$, and A_j is the constant term of the demand curve common to all
families in reference group j. For single service, majority rule budgetary
processes that satisfy the extended Bergstrom-Goodman axioms,
equation (6) is the correct (nonstochastic) specification of the community's
demand for local services.

This is an important result. For the first time, the logical connection
between a community demand function and individual demand functions
has been drawn in a way that is useful for empirical analysis. In addition,
and directly related to the present task, the specification in equation (6)
allows a direct test of the validity of the conventional *assumption* that the
median quantity demanded is in fact that quantity preferred by a voter with
the city's median income.

Inman (1978c) has developed a test of this hypothesis using the Bergstrom-Goodman framework. In the special case in which the value of the
city subgroup function $\Phi(\rho_1{}^i \cdots \rho_n{}^i)$ is equal to 1, it is evident from equation (6) and condition 3′ that $G_m{}^i$, the median quantity demanded, is in
fact equal to the quantity of services preferred by the individual median-
income voter: $G_m{}^i = A_j f(S^i) \tau_{jm}^{i\beta} I_m^{i\alpha}$. Thus when $\Phi = 1$, subgroup effects
"wash out" and the voter with the median town income is decisive. His
preference function and budget constraint alone defines town i's spending
level. When $\Phi^i < 1 (>1)$, a voter who demands less (more) than the

median-income voter is decisive in local politics. To see if $\Phi \gtrless 1$, subgroups must be defined and $\Phi(\cdot)$ specified.

Inman estimated equation (6) for a sample of fifty-eight Long Island school districts, whose budgets are annually approved in a majority-rule referendum. Ten community subgroups that completely cover each city's population are identified. The population is first separated into poor (income < \$6000/year) and rich (income > \$6000/year) nonvoters and then into eight mutually exclusive voter groups on the basis of family characteristics: home ownership (owner or renter), Catholic school (user or not), and age of the head of household (older or younger than 64).[13] Of the ten groups, the nonvoters were in the majority; on average, 80 percent of the families in the sample districts did not vote. Of the voters, the majority (on average, 65 percent of the voters) were homeowners who used or had used local public schools and whose heads of household were younger than 64. The next largest voter bloc (19 percent) were renters and public school users whose family heads were younger than 64. Members of the third largest voting group (7 percent) were young homeowners who used Catholic schools; the forth largest voter group (6 percent) were old, non-Catholic homeowners.

The typical application of the median voter model to school budgeting has assumed that all families vote and are members of the young, home-owning, public-school-using subgroup. Hence all families belong to a single community subgroup in which income is the only distinguishing characteristic; axiom 3 rather than 3' applies. Thus the median quantity demanded is that preferred by the median-income voter (i.e., $\Phi \equiv 1$). What happens when other subgroups appear? Imagine that initially some young, homeowning, public-school users do not vote. If the nonvoters are drawn randomly from the voter distribution, the median position will be unaffected and the above result ($\Phi \equiv 1$) applies. If—as survey evidence suggests (see Verba and Nye, 1972)—more of the nonvoters are drawn from the lower end of the income (and spending) distribution, then the median budget position ($G_m{}^i$) should increase above that originally preferred by the median-income family—that is, Φ should be greater than 1.

If some of the homeowner-voters positioned just below the new median quantity are replaced by renter-voters and if renters do not bear (or perceive themselves to not bear) the full burden of local school taxes, then the renters will vote for expanded school spending and the median quantity should rise still further. Replacing public school users with nonusers, by allowing Catholic homeowners and elderly homeowners to become voting subgroups, should have the opposite effect on $G_m{}^i$; the preferred median quantity should fall as these "no votes" enter the referendum. To capture all of these subgroup effects, Inman specified the political subgroup shift term in equation (6), $\Phi(\cdot)$, as:

$$\Phi = \{P^{\phi_0 + \phi_1 PCL6}\} \exp (\phi_2 PCOLD + \phi_3 PCRENT \qquad (7)$$
$$+ \phi_4 PCCATH + v),$$

where P is the rate of voter participation, PCL6 is the percentage of families with income less than \$6000 per year, PCOLD is the percentage of families whose heads are older than 64 years, PCRENT is the percentage of dwelling units occupied by renters, PCCATH is the percentage of families with children in Catholic schools, and v is a normally distributed error term with a common mean ($= 0$) and variance ($= \sigma_v^2$) across all districts. The error term captures all unmeasured determinants of the voting outcome— e.g., rainy weather on voting days or school board errors in "reading" voter preferences.[14]

The specification in equation (7) adopts the largest community sub-group—homeowner, public school user, young—as the reference group j for the full specification of G_m^i in equation (6). When all families vote ($P = 1$), all families belong to reference group j (PCOLD = PCRENT = PCCATH = 0), and there are no political errors in recording voter preferences ($v = 0$), then from equation (7) $\Phi \equiv 1$ and G_m^i is that quantity preferred by the median-income family in reference group j. This is exactly what the median voter model requires. Shifts in the median quantity away from that preferred by a median-income family occur as nonvoters, the elderly, renters, and Catholics are introduced into the analysis. From the discussion above, we anticipate $\phi_1 > 0$, $\phi_2 < 0$, $\phi_3 > 0$, and $\phi_4 < 0$.

Inman's empirical results largely confirm these hypotheses. Substituting equation (7) into equation (6) and estimating for the sample of Long Island school districts showed that all coefficients were of the expected sign. Particularly significant, statistically and quantitatively, was the effect of the elderly on G_m^i; the elasticity of the chosen spending level with respect to PCOLD centered near -0.3. The implied values of Φ are of primary interest here. Is the median-income, public-school-using homeowner decisive? Generally, yes.

All the parameters, their variances and covariances, and the variance of v for equation (7) are estimated. Assuming that each district's population characteristics are nonstochastic, a mean value and a variance for each town's Φ^i ($i = 1 \cdots 58$) can be calculated. The expected values of Φ^i range from a low of 0.8 to a high of 1.03 with a mean value for the sample of 0.9. The elderly bloc has a dampening effect, so that on average school spending conforms most closely to those levels preferred by families within the young homeowner reference group with *lower* than median income. The standard errors of the Φ^i's are large, however, averaging nearly 0.45. Thus, when Inman tested the null hypothesis that the Φ^i's equaled 1, it could not be rejected at any reasonable level of significance.

These results offer only one test of the hypothesis that the median-income voter is decisive in local politics and that it is his preferences that underlie $P(\cdot)$. For this sample of school districts, it appears to be a reasonable working assumption. At most, the prediction bias is 20 percent ($\phi = .8$) and more often it is 10 percent or less. Whether these results generalize to other samples, other services, or to big city governments remains to be seen. If not, the dominant party model offers one alternative specification to be tested.

THE DOMINANT PARTY MODEL.   The dominant party model is the implicit basis for the early empirical work of Gramlich (1969b), Henderson (1968), and Inman (1971a, b) and the more recent work of Gramlich and Galper (1973) on big cities, Ehrenberg (1973) on public employees, Sloan (1977) on welfare, and Olsen (1972), Brown and Saks (1975), and McGuire (1977) on education.

In contrast to the median voter model's annual struggle among many candidates, the dominant party specification views local politics as an occasional two-party fight for office from which a clear and controlling winner emerges. Elections are held every two or four years, and the majority party after each election is given full control over the local fisc. The parties are seen as well-disciplined organizations whose candidates adhere to the party line. (*Party* is here used for any organization that, through candidates, seeks to control the local budget.) Entry barriers to the formation of new parties or to the generation of independent candidates are high. Voters in the strong party model are pushed into the background; they have only minimal control over party performance. Issues are complex; voting is costly. Voters rarely vote, and when they do, the individual's vote is often easily controlled through small favors or friendships offered by one party or the other. Party resources—patronage jobs and dollars—largely control election results, and past winners, because of their control over the local budget, generally have easier access to such resources. Favors granted are favors rewarded. The result is long runs of one-party rule. Only major scandals, legal limitations on reelection, or long-term demographic shifts can undo control.

For what kinds of communities and for what types of governments might this dominant party model be an accurate description of local politics? Multiservice governments in medium to large cities seem a good guess. Dollars that flow across several services to a variety of locations will be exceedingly difficult to monitor. Even when dissatisfaction is observed among one group within the city, finding other disgruntled voters may be quite costly. Information on budget performance is necessarily fragmented in a large city with multiservice governments. As long as political persuasion involves some fixed cost per voter, election costs and entry barriers will rise with city size.

Who sets $P(\cdot)$ in the dominant party model? Barro (1973), Wittman

(1973), and Margolis (1974) have hypothesized that the local political party bosses, bent on maximizing their own long-run welfare, will define $P(\cdot)$. Through the decisions to spend and to tax, income generating favors can be granted. Budgetary outcome will be defined by the bosses' preference for income. Political income from budgetary activity is maximized subject to the budget constraint in equation (3'), specified for mean after- and before-tax income.[15] This is the framework that, for example, implicitly underlies the budgetary models of Gramlich (1968, 1969b) Gramlich and Galper (1973), Henderson (1968), and Inman (1971a, b).

Romer and Rosenthal (1978) have offered another variant of dominant party budgeting. In contrast to the specification that totally ignores voters, the Romer-Rosenthal budget model allows a limited referendum "check" on the chosen budget. The bosses must submit the budget for annual referendum approval, but there are a limited number of times the vote can be taken and the bosses pick the budget for the "yes-no" votes. The politicians are assumed to be budget maximizers. The strategy is to select as large a budget as can possibly win. If the selected budget fails, the politicians are forced to live with the existing, lower budget. In a majority rule referendum, any status quo budget equal to or greater than the median budget will remain; the bosses will never propose less and nothing larger can pass. An interesting case is the one in which the status quo is below the median voter-preferred budget; a budget larger than the median can be approved by a majority in a one-time, "yes-no" vote. Some voters, located slightly below the median budget, will vote for an expansion above the median rather than a return to the lower, much less desirable status quo. The lower the status quo is, the larger the number of voters who find it unattractive and, therefore, the larger the majority approved, politician proposed budget is. Thus in the Romer-Rosenthal model, referendum approved budgets will be greater than or equal to median preferred budgets. In such a political environment, the decisive voter preferences that define $P(\cdot)$ and equation (3') will belong to a family in the upper tail of the preferred spending distribution.

The evidence for or against the dominant party framework is largely anecdotal. Case studies of local school politics reveal budget maximizing superintendents backed by pro-education blocs of upper-income parents. There are numerous studies that attest to voter ignorance, the disincentives to become informed, and the high cost in time and money of running for local office. In many cities the prerequisites for monopoly power in local politics are present.[16]

Jackson's (1972) time series study of Cleveland has provided one of the few systematic budget studies of a probable dominant party city. Over the twenty-five year sample period, Cleveland had only three administrations: Thomas Burke from 1945 to 1953; Anthony Celebrezze and his hand-picked successor Ralph Locher from 1953 to 1967; and Carl Stokes from 1967 to the end of the sample, 1970. (Stokes served, however, until 1971). Jackson found stable budget rules over each administration and, of main interest here, no major break in the spending pattern for the sample period. A more direct test of the dominant party framework versus the median voter model was provided by the tax equations. In the property tax and "other-tax" equations, Jackson estimated the effect of the mayor's plurality on the annual tax increase. With only one exception, all challengers over the period 1945–70 ran on a "control spending" platform. If the incumbent mayor or his party won, then a median voter explanation should predict expanded budgets and increased taxes. Though the incumbent always won, Jackson found the plurality variable to be insignificant in the property-tax equation and significantly positive, but with only a small quantitative effect, in the "other-tax" equation.

Jackson's results are, of course, only suggestive of the dominant party model and in no way provide a direct test of the model's structure. Further research, with more refined data on voting patterns and politicians' income, is clearly needed if we are to identify the dominant party, the median voter, or a hybrid model as the preferred specification of local budgeting.

But discerning political structure may be a bonus for the task of fiscal planning. The reduced-form demand equations specified in (4) and (5), if good predictors, may be adequate.

The Demand Framework Applied: Results Summarized

Tables 9.1 and 9.2 summarize much of the recent empirical literature, and the results are largely self-explanatory. The elasticities of G $(=X/N)$ with respect to each independent variable are listed by services. For the income and lump-sum aid variables, the tables also give the marginal dollar increase in own expenditure or revenue following a one dollar increase in I and z.[17]

Some general conclusions emerge from the results in table 9.1. With only few exceptions, all local public services are price inelastic against the four alternative price variables. The estimated personal income elasticities of demand for local services are also generally less than one, with the exception of housing and urban renewal (~ 1.1), parks and recreation (~ 1.0), welfare (~ 1.2), and investments in future public service (~ 1.1). Most local services qualify as necessities. Exogenous aid elasticities are all low, with all but one estimate (Inman, 1971*a, b,* education) falling between 0 and 0.40. What is encouraging for the demand framework in which politics are reduced to an individual choice process, is that most of the price and income elasticities for local services, estimated from city data, are within the range of estimates obtained for their corresponding commodi-

TABLE 9.1. Demand for Local Services

Service	Price Elasticities with Price Measured As:				Income Elasticity ϵ_I $(dExp/dI)$	Exogenous Aid Elasticity ϵ_z $(dExp/dz)$
	$b/B = (\tau)$	B	$(1-m)$	c		
Education						
Bradford-Oates (1974)[d]	−.36				.65	
Ehrenberg (1973)[a]		.1 to .36	−1 to −1.6	−.57 to −.09	.54	
Feldstein (1971)					.47	.21, federal aid .06, state aid
Gramlich-Galper (1973)			0		(.02)	(.1, revenue sharing aid) (.6, for exogenous education aid)
Inman (1971a, b)	−.37 to −.51				.56 (.005)	.71 (.69)
Inman (1978)	−.31		−.20		.6 to .75	.23 to .40
Ladd (1975)[b]	−.14 to −.16		−.48		.46	.03
Lovell (1977)					.24 to .39	
Olsen (1972)						(.27)
Pack-Pack (1975)	−.07				.34 (.041)	
Peterson (1975)	−.25 to −.70				.85 to 1.35	
Weicher (1972)					(.001)	(.41 to .58)
Health and Hospitals						
Ehrenberg (1973)[a]				−.51 to −.26	.43 to .51	.12 to .15
Gramlich-Galper (1973)			−.74		~0	(.1, for revenue sharing) (.6, for exogenous health aid)
Inman (1971a, b)			−.34		.52 to 1.31 (.004)	(0)
Jackson (1972)					0	(0 to .02)
Housing and Urban Renewal						
Gramlich-Galper (1973)			−.74		~0	(.1, for revenue sharing) (.6, for exogenous housing aid)

TABLE 9.1. (*Continued*)

Service	Price Elasticities with Price Measured As:				Income Elasticity	Exogenous Aid Elasticity
	$b/B = (\tau)$	B	$(1-m)$	c	ϵ_I (dExp/dI)	ϵ_z (dExp/dz)
Inman (1971a, b)			− .10		1.1 (.001)	0 (0)
Jackson (1972)						(0 to .01)
Parks and Recreation						
Bergstrom-Goodman (1973)	−.19				1.32	
Ehrenberg (1973)[a]				− .60 to − .39	.21	.06 (∼0)
Gramlich-Galper (1973)			− .92		.99 (.01)	.34 (.10)
Inman (1971a, b)			− .50		(.003)	(.02)
Jackson (1972)						
Pack-Pack (1975)	−.23				1.01	
Protection (Police and Fire)						
Bergstrom-Goodman (1973)	−.25				.71	
Ehrenberg (1973)[a]				− .35 to − .01	.60	.16
Gramlich-Galper (1973)			− .71		.61 (.01)	(−.06)
Inman (1971a, b)			− 1.00		(.01)	0 (0)
Jackson (1972)						
Pack-Pack (1975)	−.19					(.04 to .10)
Weicher (1972)					.52 (.001)	(.05 to .07)
Public Works						
Ehrenberg (1973)[a]				− .64 to − .40	.33 to .45	.10 to .13 (∼0)
Gramlich-Galper (1973)			− .92		.79 (.01)	.13 to .28 (.14)
Inman (1971a, b)			− 1.00		(.01)	(.0 to .02)
Jackson (1972)						
Weicher (1972)					(.001)	(.03 to .10)

TABLE 9.1. (Continued)

Service	Price Elasticities with Price Measured As:			Income Elasticity ϵ_I $(dExp/dI)$	Exogenous Aid Elasticity ϵ_z $(dExp/dz)$
	$b/B = (\tau)$	B $(1-m)$	c		
Welfare					
Ehrenberg (1973)[a]			−1.13 to −1.33	1.2	.34
Inman (1971a, b)		−.04		0 (0)	.30 (.04)
Investment					
Gramlich-Galper (1973)				1.12 (.07)	(~0)
Inman (1971a, b)		−.04		0 (.01)	0 (~0)
Total Expenditures					
Bergstrom-Goodman (1973)	−.23			.64	
Ehrenberg (1973)[c]			−.68	.75	
Gramlich-Galper (1973)				(.05 to .095)	.22 (.25 to .43)
Inman (1971a, b)				(.04)	(1.0)
Jackson (1972)					(.2)
Ladd (1976)	−.31 to −.56			.34 to .89	

NOTES: Income and exogenous aid elasticities are reported without parentheses. The marginal effects of income and aid are reported within parentheses.
[a] Ehrenberg's results give the elasticity of labor employed with respect to the corresponding wage (under column "c"), income, and exogenous aid variables.
[b] Based on Ladd's results in table 1, equation 1.
[c] Real total expenditures in the Ehrenberg study is total employment.
[d] Strictly speaking, Bradford and Oates use the ratio "school children to population" as a measure of the relative tax price for education.

ties, using individual household data. For example, the health and hospital elasticities are only slightly larger than those obtained by Newhouse and Phelps (1974), Feldstein (1974), and Davis and Russell (1972); the education elasticities correspond to those obtained in the micro-voting studies of Peterson (1975) and Rubinfeld (1977); the housing elasticities fit the bounds set by Polinsky (1977); the welfare elasticities correspond to Feldstein's (1975*b*) recent work on individual charity giving; and the investment price and income elasticities are consistent with the low price elasticity and the constant marginal propensity to save out of income of most savings studies.

Inman (1971*a*), and Ehrenberg (1973) have estimated cross-price expenditure effects as part of a general budgeting model and found the effects to be small. Ehrenberg reports that in his study of local employment budgets, only changes in the education wage produced significant employment response in other services with the cross-wage elasticity near 0.1. Inman's expenditure model showed a similar pattern. Only the price of education proved statistically significant on a consistent basis in the "other-service" expenditure equations and the cross-price elasticities were never larger than 0.05. Given that own price elasticities are less than one and that cross-price effects are trivial, an increase in matching aid will generally lead to a net decline in own city expenditures, implying tax or debt relief. Inman found that most of the released dollars were channeled into debt relief.

Table 9.2 summarizes the effects of tax credits and deductions (summarized in the net burden "price" π), the net interest cost of local borrowing (i), income, and exogenous aid on taxation and long-term borrowing. An increase in credits or allowed deductions for a local tax reduces the net direct burden of that tax (π falls), which should encourage its use relative to other finance instruments and, perhaps, stimulate local spending. In Inman's (1971*a*) study of local taxation in forty-one large U.S. cities, the elasticity of property taxes with respect to that tax's π is negative (-1.49). Because property taxes dominate total local taxation, there is also a negative elasticity of total taxes with respect to the weighted average of the individual tax's π's (-1.22). The use of local income taxes appears insensitive to own credits and deductions in Inman's sample (forty-one large U.S. cities). But only eleven of his cities had legal access to the tax; thus, the estimate of tax use with respect to π, although negative, was imprecise. The net burden price π did not vary sufficiently for sales tax for a price elasticity to be estimated.

An increase in the net interest cost of local borrowing reduces borrowing marginally but has no quantitatively significant effect on the use of taxes. This is to be expected, since bond market and legal restrictions limit long-term debt financing to capital expenditures.

What is particularly interesting in table 9.2 is the large (-1.49) esti-

TABLE 9.2. Financing Local Services

	Price Elasticities with Price Measured As:		Income Elasticity	Exogenous Aid Elasticity
	π^a	i	ϵ_I $(d\mathrm{Rev}/dI)$	ϵ_z $(d\mathrm{Rev}/dz)$
Total Taxes				
Gramlich-Galper (1973)			(.05 to .095)	(−.57 to −.75)
Inman (1971a)	−1.22	∼0	1.0 (.02 to .04)	∼0 (∼0)
Jackson (1972)				(−.80)
Property Taxation				
Inman (1971a)	−1.49	∼0	1.2 (.03)	∼0 (∼0)
Income Taxation				
Inman (1971a)	∼0	∼0	1.2 (.01)	∼0 (∼0)
Sales Taxation				
Inman (1971a)		∼0	.5 (∼0)	∼0 (∼0)
Debt				
Inman (1971a)		−.02	∼0 (∼0)	∼0 (∼0)

NOTES: Income and exogenous aid elasticities are reported without parentheses. The marginal effects of income and aid are reported within parentheses.

ᵃ Each city observation's net burden per dollar of local taxes in Inman's (1971a) study is defined for total taxes as the weighted average of each individual local tax's value of π, as the local property tax value of π for the property tax equation, and as the local income tax value of π for the income tax equation. The net burden of local sales taxes was ∼1 for all observations in Inman's sample so the deduction-credit effect could not be estimated for sales taxes. In Inman's study the federal plus state income tax rate used to calculate the effect of deductions on π was the nominal rate for the city's mean income.

mated elasticity of local property taxation with respect to changes in tax credits or deductions (measured in π). A 10 percent fall in π from its current average value of 0.65, say through the introduction of a 6.5 percent property tax credit, will lead to 15 percent rise in large cities' use of property taxation. Since the net direct burden of a local tax on residential income after federal and state credits and deductions equals πT, this large elasticity of T with respect to π gives the paradoxical result that the new tax credit in fact increases the direct burden of the tax! The 10 percent fall in π is more than offset by the 15 percent rise in T, leading to a net 5 percent increase in the tax's direct burden (πT). The local government's fiscal response to credits appears to have undone the credit's intended property-tax relief. For Inman's sample of large U.S. cities, this increase in property taxation goes first into reducing local sales taxation (the estimated cross-price elasticity of local sales taxation with respect to property tax credits is −.64) and then into increased local spending (total taxes rise by 12 percent for the 10 percent fall in property tax π). There is relief, but not where expected.

The effects of increased mean family income are also summarized in tables 9.1 and 9.2. Current and capital expenditures increase with income (table 9.1), with the rise financed almost entirely from increased taxes (table 9.2). The share of extra revenue raised from property and income taxes rises as city mean income rises—the elasticity of property and income taxes with respect to income exceeds 1—whereas the relative use of sales taxation falls (ϵ_I for sales taxes < 1). Overall, Inman's tax results in table 9.2 suggest a unitary elasticity of total taxes with respect to income, near the upper end of table 9.1's estimated income elasticities of expenditures.

Particularly interesting and important is the wide range of estimates in tables 9.1 and 9.2 of the effect of revenue-sharing aid on local tax relief. Inman's study predicts no tax relief. The Gramlich-Galper study predicts from $0.50 to $0.75 in tax relief per dollar of aid received. Jackson's work estimates that $0.80 per dollar of aid goes into tax reductions. Who is right? Possibly all three, since the three studies estimate different segments of a nonlinear relationship between expenditure and exogenous aid. From table 9.1, all the elasticities of local expenditures with respect to z center near 0.3 for varying samples and expenditures, suggesting a constant elasticity of *total* expenditures with respect to z. Figure 9.1 shows the "true" curve. Inman, Gramlich-Galper, and Jackson all estimated *linear* models

Figure

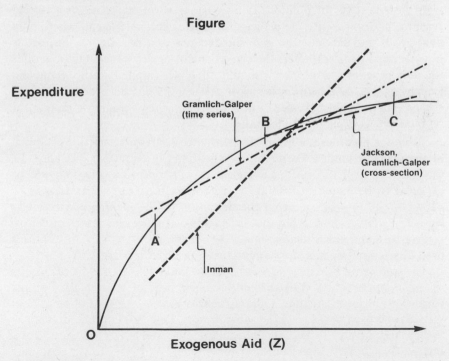

FIGURE 9.1

for different segments of the curve. Jackson, using only high aid observations (Cleveland), estimated the segment marked BC, where dExp/dz~.2 and tax relief is $0.80 per dollar of aid. Gramlich-Galper obtained their dExp/dz~.25 estimate (=$0.75 tax relief) from a sample of ten very large U.S. cities, also in the BC range. Their lower estimate of tax relief with dExp/dz~.43 ($0.57 tax relief) is from aggregate time series data for all U.S. cities for the period 1954/72. These aggregate expenditure and aid data are likely to be dominated by medium to large cities with z aid in the range AC. Inman's forty-one city sample includes not only Cleveland, New York, and a few other high aid cities but also many Southern and Western cities that received little exogenous aid in his sample year. Using an unweighted linear regression to estimate the full range (OC) of the true line, Inman obtained much higher expenditure effects, dExp/dz~1, and no tax relief. His estimates of the marginal tax effects of aid are approximately accurate for low aid cities but are likely to be poor predicators for cities that already receive large z aid. For these cities, the Gramlich-Galper and the Jackson estimates are probably more accurate.[18]

Beyond the Demand Model: New Directions for Research

Although the fiscal demand model described above can be easily embellished with the adjectives of politics, its main story is an economic one. Local resource allocations are the choice of *a single* economic agent, where only final goods and services can give satisfactions and one dollar, no matter how received or spent, offers the same benefits as any other. Outputs offer the only benefits and all money is fully fungible. Implicit in this economic framework are rather strong a priori restrictions on the process of fiscal choice. They should be tested, and if rejected, a new research strategy will be required to explain the violations.

Table 9.1 provides the estimates needed to test two restrictions implicit in the demand model. From the specifications in equations (4) and (5), the elasticities for the various components of service tax prices should be expected to be equal in absolute value for each service—that is, $\epsilon_{G,\tau} = \epsilon_{G,c} = -\epsilon_{G,B} = \epsilon_{G,(1-m)}$. From the definition of the income constraint as $\tau z + I$, it should be observed that for each service, the elasticities of G with respect to z and I are related as $\epsilon_{G,z} = (\tau z/I)\epsilon_{G,I}$.[19] Are these restrictions even approximately met by the results summarized in table 9.1?

The studies by Feldstein (1975a) and by Ladd (1975) of Massachusetts school districts in FY 1970 provide a direct test of the equality of the various tax price elasticities. Ladd estimated $\epsilon_{G,\tau}$ at -0.31 and $\epsilon_{G,(1-m)}$ at -0.48, whereas for basically the same sample, Feldstein estimated $-\epsilon_{GB} = -0.28$ and $\epsilon_{G,(1-m)} = -1$. The elasticities, $\epsilon_{G\tau}$ and $-\epsilon_{GB}$ are quite close, but $\epsilon_{G,(1-m)}$ differs significantly from both. Why the low (absolute) elasticity with respect to base or tax shares and the high (absolute) elasticity with respect to matching aid? Ladd's subsequent work suggests an answer.

The major source of variation in the net tax share (τ), defined as b/B, probably comes from variations in the commercial-industrial tax base across communities. Yet if the commercial tax base is thought to be highly sensitive to increases in local school tax rates, towns may feel constrained in increasing education for fear of losing their base. This sensitivity to the loss of the commercial base would not be observed for truly exogenous changes in matching rates. Thus, we would expect the estimate of the price elasticity using (b/B) to be less in absolute value than estimates of the price elasticity derived from exogenous variations in matching rates. A local choice process in tune with the wider realities of the public economy of which it is a part might reasonably react differently to changes in commercial base and matching aid. Ladd tested this hypothesis and found it true. Cities behaved "as if" a 10 percent rise in the commercial base reduced the residential share in local taxes by only 8 percent, whereas a 10 percent rise in the industrial base reduced the residential share by only 4.5 percent. A rise in the matching rate of 10 percent reduced the residents' share by the full 10 percent. When these behavioral reactions were admitted into the specification of local tax shares, Ladd found that the $\epsilon_{G,\ (1-m)}$ was *not* significantly different from the *adjusted* $\epsilon_{G,\tau}$. The message seems clear. Cities exist as part of a wider network of local governments, not in isolation, and that reality can have a significant effect on how they choose to spend their money. With the exception of Ladd's work, no demand studies have made a serious effort to accommodate this fact.

The result of comparing exogenous aid and personal income elasticities is equally clear against the strict structure of the demand model. Of the work reviewed here, only Feldstein's (1975a) study of Massachusetts school districts comes close to meeting the proposed test, $\epsilon_{G,z} = (\tau z/I)\epsilon_{G,I}$. As $0 \simeq \tau z/I \leq 0.1$ generally, Feldstein's estimates for state aid imply $\epsilon_{G,z} = 0.06 \simeq (0.1)(0.47) = 0.1\epsilon_{G,I}$. The expenditure effect of exogenous aid and income can also be formulated as a comparison of marginal expenditure effects. In the demand model, $d\text{Exp}_i/dI = \tau(d\text{Exp}_i/dz)$ should result. In fact, the full budget expenditure effects of a $1.00 increase in exogenous aid range from a low of $0.30 ($0.70 to tax relief) to a high of $1.00 (no tax relief), whereas a $1.00 increase in personal income rarely increases local public expenditures by more than $0.10 with at least $0.90 staying in the private sector. As $\tau \geq 0.6$ for most observations in these studies, the aid to income correspondence required by the individual preference maximizing model is clearly not observed. Gramlich and Galper have called this observed reluctance of the public and private sectors to trade dollars at the going terms-of-trade $(dI/dz = -\tau)$ the "flypaper effect"—money is not fungible but rather sticks where it hits. Again, it is apparent that there may be something more to local fiscal choice than static individual utility maximization.[20] Of course, the question is what?

In additional to the two budget "fungibility" requirements, the strict demand model, as generally estimated, uses three additional restrictions that also require examination. First, public services are assumed to be provided through a "private goods" technology, with public output (G) directly proportional to input (X) and inversely proportional to users (N)—$G = X/N$. But public services by nature may involve significant economies in sharing (doubling N need not halve G) and one suspects that the quality of the local environment (income level, job opportunity, pollution) must also matter as determinants of G. To omit these facts from the model of fiscal choice and its final demand equations may lead to a serious misinterpretation of the parameter estimates of the included variables. Second, factor prices, notably wages and the rate of matching aid, are assumed to be exogenous. The presence of labor scarcities, public employee unions, and federal "grantsmanship" make this assumption suspect. Again, biased parameter estimates may result. Third, the hypothesized process of political choice, reduced as it is to an "as if" maximization of an *individual* preference function, must strike most political scientists and politicans as a major departure from reality. Politics is compromise not dominance. But to describe compromise empirically, bargaining models that detail the players, their resources, and the rules of the game are needed. Not one but many demand systems must be specified and aggregated through a description of local compromise.

Although it offers a significant contribution to our understanding of local budget-setting through its emphasis on choice under a revenue constraint, the demand model is far from the final word. Technology, unions, "grantsmanship," and bureau bargaining have all been neglected. Yet these forgotten elements may each have a significant impact on local fiscal choice. Research to accommodate these facts has recently begun.

2. BUDGETS, OUTPUTS, AND BUREAUS

With two implicit assumptions about the technology of local service provision, the demand studies reviewed in section 1 have been able to side-step the difficult problems of specifying and estimating the production process of local service output. By first assuming that labor, materials, and capital can be combined through a constant return to scale technology into a package denoted X and called "facilities" (e.g., roadmiles, police patrols, fire stations, park acreage, classrooms, and hospital beds), a constant factor cost index ($c(\cdot)$) can be specified that when divided into total (or current) expenditures will define $X(= \text{Exp}/c(\cdot))$. By next assuming that local public output (G) flows to residents from a per-capita (or per-user) sharing of the facility, $G = X/N$, the demand studies are able to define the dependent variable G as deflated expenditure per capita—$G = \text{Exp}/c(\cdot)N$. The estimated elasticities summarized in table 9.1 give the percentage change in G, measured as $\text{Exp}/c(\cdot)N$, for the percentage change in prices, income, or exogenous grants-in-aid. Although these restrictions on local service technology are plausible, it is premature to assume that they hold without formal testing. If they are not valid, the results in table 9.1 may be biased estimates of price, aid, and income effects or, worse still, may be altogether without meaning. Permitting the unrestricted technology, $G = g\{X(L, M, K), N\}$, it is no longer certain that factor-cost deflated per-capita expenditures will define G. If not, the dependent variable of the usual demand models has no clear interpretation. Expenditures are not outputs—to ignore this may lead to biased conclusions as to the efficacy of fiscal policy. It is important the demand model's strict assumptions about technology be relaxed. Budget models must estimate a technological specification along with spending if the true effects of fiscal policy on local public outputs are to be measured.

Technology Within the Budget Model: The Reduced Form Approach

In three recent papers, Bergstrom and Goodman (1973), Borcherding and Deacon (1972), and Pack and Pack (1975) have attempted to estimate the technology of local service provision within the framework of the demand model of local choice. Their work is a first attempt to deal with the difficulties of technology's inclusion in the budget model.

Their model is simple but broad enough to retain the real dilemma: How do we estimate demand behavior and service technology within a consistent framework? The demand model is the median voter model that identifies the decisive voter as a resident with median-family income. The demand equation is a log-linear relationship between output (G), the median voter's income (I), and tax price (p)—$G = AI^\alpha p^\beta$, where the median voter's tax price (p) is defined as his share (τ) of the cost per-person per-unit of service $(C(G)/GN)$.

The cost schedule of providing G follows from the specification of the service technology. Facilities (X) are produced by a Cobb-Douglas technology with labor (L) and capital (K)—$X = L^\theta K^\delta$—whereas public services per resident are provided through a constant elasticity congestion technology—$G = X/N^\epsilon$. The parameter ϵ is the congestion elasticity and measures the percentage increase in X needed to hold G constant for a percentage rise in N. For pure public goods, $\epsilon = 0$, and for private goods, $\epsilon = 1$. Values of ϵ in the range $0 < \epsilon < 1$ indicate quasi publicness whereas $\epsilon > 1$ indicates congested public services. With fixed factor prices, the minimal costs for producing X are given by $C(X) = cX\eta$, where c is a function of factor prices and the parameters θ and δ and where $\eta = 1/(\theta + \delta)$. Substituting $X = GN^\epsilon$ into $C(X)$ defines $C(G)$. The tax price p can now be defined, which when substituted into the demand equation along with the relationship $G = X/N^\epsilon$, gives a demand equation for facilities. The final step is to note that the cost of facilities defines $X = (C(X)/c)^{1/\eta}$, which can be equated to the demand for facilities equation to give a reduced form expenditure equation of the form:

$$C = \hat{A}I^{\hat{\alpha}}(\tau c)^{\hat{\beta}}N^{\hat{\epsilon}},$$

which can be estimated from available data using ordinary least squares regression procedures. The estimated parameters, $\hat{\alpha}$, $\hat{\beta}$ and $\hat{\epsilon}$, depend on the underlying demand (α and β) and technological (ϵ and η) parameters of the structural model.[21]

The identification of the four structural parameters from the three estimated reduced form parameters requires one identifying restriction. Bergstrom-Goodman and Borcherding-Deacon both assume $\eta = 1$—that is, the facility production technology is constant returns to scale. With this assumption and the fact that their reduced form parameter estimates imply $\eta\epsilon \simeq 1$, we conclude that $\epsilon \simeq 1$. Local public services are therefore assigned a private goods sharing technology: a 10 percent rise in users requires a 10 percent rise in facilities to maintain service output.

Such a conclusion is premature. All that is really known from the reduced form results themselves is that the product $\eta\epsilon$ is close to 1. The "identification" of the two technological parameters separately requires the prior knowledge that $\eta = 1$. Yet the available evidence is not convincing on this point. Walzer (1972), for example, found $\eta \neq 1$ for police services, and Hirsch (1965) and Kemper and Quigley (1976) found $\eta = 1$ for refuse collection. For other services, we just do not know;[22] and even in this simple form, the reduced form approach will not provide the answer.

Is the reduced form approach a mistake? Not at all. First, the reduced form framework of Bergstrom-Goodman explicitly introduces technology into the budget model and thereby controls for possible omitted variable bias. This is a significant gain.[23] Second, the estimated elasticity $\hat{\epsilon}$ on the new variable N does provide new information *if interpreted correctly*. (I should add that Bergstrom-Goodman, Borcherding-Deacon, and Pack-Pack are all wisely cautious in their use of the new parameter.) The studies show that generally $\epsilon\eta \simeq 1$. Within the utility maximizing demand model framework, that $\epsilon\eta = 1$ has an important implication. When true, it can be concluded that the median-income voter whose demand curve is being estimated behaves "as if" an increase in the user population imposes no utility loss upon him. Over the city-size range considered here (10,000 to 150,000 in Bergstrom-Goodman), the median-income voter will be indifferent between large or small cities that provide equal levels of public output. The facility cost increase needed to accommodate more users is just offset by the tax saving of having more residents to share the cost.[24] That utility loss on the public sector side are negligible with rising population can be an important fact when designing optimal city size. (See Henderson in this volume.)

Although these gains with this reduced form model are important, for the design of local fiscal policy it is generally necessary to know how dollars spent translate into output received. The reduced form approach will not give us independent estimates of this technology. A structural methodology that relates service output to facility or factor input is therefore needed.

Technology Within the Budget Model: A Structural Approach

The literature on public service technologies is rich and growing, particularly for such important local services as education, health, crime control, and transportation.[25] My objective is to determine how this technology should be specified and estimated once it is realized that public outputs and factor inputs are simultaneously determined as part of a budgetary process.

A simple model of a one-service government illustrates the approach. Assume that the fiscal choice process can be represented by a representative preference function $P(\cdot)$ over public output (G) and private income (Y) and (for the moment) that factor prices, grants-in-aid, and the number of users (N) are all exogenous. Taxes must cover expenditures on labor (L) and capital (K) inputs purchased at wage w and rental price r, respectively. Inputs employed provide facilities to be shared by the N users, where facility effectiveness depends not only on the number of users but also upon the exogenous environment (Q) in which the user-facility interactions take place. (Students learn more from a given teacher with more able classmates present; police are more effective in neighborhoods that practice self-surveillance.) The budget and production process can therefore be characterized by the "as if" maximization of $P(G, Y)$, subject to the production constraint, $G = g\{(X(K, L), N, Q\}$, and the budget constraint, $Y = I - \tau(1 - m)\{wL + rK\}(1/N) + \tau z$. For empirical analysis, a stochastic, three-equation model of the budget-cum-production process can be now specified:

$$l = l(p_w, p_r, 1; I + \tau z; N, Q; \mu), \tag{8}$$

$$k = h(p_w, p_r, 1; I + \tau z; N, Q; v), \tag{9}$$

$$G = g(l, k, N, Q; \omega), \tag{10}$$

where l and k are labor and capital per user, $p_w = (1 - m)\tau w$, $p_r = (1 - m)\tau r$, and μ, v, and ω are the unobserved determinants of l, k, and G, respectively.

Several recent studies have specified and estimated budget-production systems, such as the one specified in equations (8) through (10). The results are instructive, both for their content and for the methodological insights they provide.

Two studies of the education budget process, one by Hambor, Phillips, and Votey (1973) and the other by Brown (1972), most closely approximate the full model in equals (8), (9), and (10). For these studies, as for all work on public services output, a crucial problem is how to measure output. The vast literature on educational outputs will not be reviewed here (Boardman et al., 1977), but one methodological point should be stressed. When specifying an output measure, the metric must be cardinal—that is, unique up to a linear transformation—before there can be meaningful talk of marginal products, returns to scale, or public service congestion. As their measure of the performance of a state school system, Hambor et al., have adopted the probability of a student in the state passing the national selective service test. This is an acceptable, cardinal measure of output; and they find that education so measured is a private good. A 10 percent rise in input (our X, measured by the teacher wage bill as a proxy for quality-adjusted teaching units), holding pupils (our N) fixed, leads to a 10 percent rise in the pass-to-failure ratio (our G), whereas a 10 percent rise in pupils, holding the wage bill fixed, leads to a 10 percent decline in the pass-to-failure ratio. These results follow from a direct estimation of a production function.

In his study, Brown chose to measure school system performance directly by pupil test scores. However, individual test scores are not unique, cardinal measures of achievement gains. For example, the logarithm of the score contains the same information as the score itself and is therefore an equally valid output measure. Yet the marginal effects of inputs on outputs measured by the score or the logarithm of the score are clearly different. There is no a priori reason to prefer one measure over the other. Nonetheless, Brown's work is valuable. Policy relevant budget elasticities can still be calculated. Unfortunately, the results are not very encouraging for those who wish to influence test performance through local fiscal policy. Although the number of teachers per pupil can be increased through aid—the elasticity of teachers per pupil with respect to net wages (p_w) is −0.425, with respect to fiscal base is 0.12 to 0.61, and with respect to lump-sum aid is 0.08 to 36—the teacher-pupil ratio has no statistically significant effect on test scores. Increased teacher quality measured by experience and training does improve test performance. But, alas, the fiscal variables have no significant effect on these variables. For Brown's sample at least, a fiscal policy towards education is limited to being a tax relief policy.

Getz (1978) has estimated a production-cum-budget model for fire services. Outputs are measured by the number of fires per dwelling and the average property loss per fire, with each measure disaggregated by single-family dwelling, multi-family dwelling, commercial property, and industrial property. Fires are prevented and losses reduced through the allocation of labor (firefighters and fire inspectors) and capital (stations, hydrants per square mile, and equipment per station), given population and the threat of fire (defined by the socioeconomic characteristics of the city).

In contrast to Brown's results for education, Getz's analysis of fire services does show a potentially significant effect of fiscal policy on service output. The key service input that explains fire protection is the number of stations per square mile. Increasing the density of stations has a dramatic effect on losses per fire; the elasticity of losses with respect to stations per square mile is -0.7 for residential property and -0.8 for commercial property. Further, stations per square mile is negatively related to the net wage of firefighters with an elasticity of -0.40. Thus a 10 percent decline in net wages from, for example, a new matching aid program will lead to roughly a 3 percent ($= 0.4 \times 0.8$) decline in residential and commercial fire losses. A fall in labor cost will also increase the likelihood that a city will adopt fire safety and inspection programs, the other main deterrents of fires and fire loss.

The results of Phillips and Votey (1975) on the control of crime also suggest that fiscal policy may have a significant impact of public output. In a study of felony offenses per capita for California counties, Phillips and Votey specified a simultaneous three-equation model in the spirit of equations (8) and (10) (capital and equipment expenditures were not included). The rate of criminal offenses per capita (the measure of G) depends on the socioeconomic environment (our Q), the probability of conviction, and the severity of punishment. The probability of conviction in turn depends on the number of law enforcement personnel per capita (our l) and on the number of offenses as a measure of the load upon the system. The employment of law enforcement officers is finally a function of police wages (tested and found exogenous), median county income, the rate of offense, and the ratio of violent and nonviolent crime. Again, a decline in the net wages of the key labor input appears to impact favorably on output. The elasticity of the crime rate with respect to net wages was equal to 0.68. Thus for California counties, a 50 percent matching grant for police salaries is estimated to reduce the crime rate by about one-third.

The studies by Carr-Hill and Stern (1973, 1977) are more notable for their approach to the problems involved in estimating public service production functions than for their actual results. This research stands as an important qualifier to the work described above, for it illustrates just how tenuous production function results can be when output is not measured carefully. Although increased population increased the crime rate for given inputs as would be expected—a 10 percent rise in N increased the crime rate per capita by 1 percent—police and dollar inputs had perverse effects on the control of reported crime. For their 1961 and 1966 samples, in-

creasing both police and expenditures per capita increased reported crime!
On the surface the results imply more police will cause more crime, but
read correctly they reveal that more police cause more *reported* crime. The
measured output variable is not *true* but reported per-capita crime. It is
perfectly plausible that more police will lead to more reported crime even
while the number of crimes committed is declining. This is an econometric
problem of measurement error and unobservables. It was dealt with carefully by Carr-Hill and Stern, who proposed one procedure, an application
of the recent econometric work on multiple indicators (see Joreskog and
Goldberger, 1975) to escape this difficulty. The problem of output measurement will remain a major barrier to the full estimation of the budget-cum-
production models, but the work of Carr-Hill and Stern suggests, at least
in principle, that it need not be an insurmountable one.

Bureaus and Production of Public Output

The budgeting-cum-production model described by equations (8) through
(10) would surely strike city budget officers and political scientists as a
peculiar characterization of a political budgetary process. By reducing the
process to an "as if" maximization of an unspecified preference function,
subject to production and budget constraints, politics has been, in effect,
assumed away.

   A central political institution in local budgeting, and the one that controls the public sector production process, is the local service bureau. The
role of the service bureau in the production of local public outputs, like the
role of management in the production of private goods, has been largely
neglected in previous empirical work.[26]

   To formally introduce bureaucracy into the budget-production model,
a great deal of analytic simplicity can be gained by recognizing two common institutional facts about the structure of local budgeting: (1) the
main point of conflict over dollars is between the executive branch (mayor
or city manager) and the service bureaus (the elected city council is generally a weak vetoing agent); and (2) the service bureaus determine output subject to the negotiated spending level. Informational asymmetries
between the executive and the council on the budget and between the
executive and the bureaus on production largely dictate this division of
control. Local budgeting therefore becomes a two-stage process in which
stage one—the budget stage—determines service spending and stage two—
the production stage—determines resource allocations across inputs to set
output. Compromise between opponents defines the outcome at each stage.

   Of primary interest here is the potential role of the bureaucracy in the
production of local services. Through selection of the production technology, the labor skill mix, and for many services, even the clientele, the

bureaus dictate who gets what from a given local budget. The purely "economic" budgetary model in equations (8) through (10) must be extended to include bureau preferences and this potential for control. Labor and capital intensity now become functions of the relative bargaining position of the relevant bureau. And perhaps most important, the number of service users (N) or the percentage of the eligible population who are favored with special treatment may now become endogenous to the budget-production process. Resources can be spent intensively on a small percentage or extensively on a large percentage of eligible clients. The bureau's allocation problem is to then choose a mix of service quality (G) and the eligible population (N) subject to its budget constraint and its production technology.

How should the budget model be generalized and the recipient equation specified to include autonomous bureaus? Each bureau is an agent speaking for itself and on behalf of its service clientele. The executive branch of government (mayor, city manager) is the agent for all parties and as such must arbitrate the conflicts, between the various bureau-client groups and between bureaus generally and the taxpayers. The executive's success as arbitrator is measured by the expected utility from playing the arbitrator's role, in turn defined by the probability of reelection or reappointment, earnings (legal and illegal) if reelected, and out-of-office income. The probability of re-election and the level of in-office earning will depend on the arbitrated budget allocations. Participants in the budget game derive their power from their control over the arbitrator's well-being. Bureaus that are monopoly providers of high-demand services among the probable voters—middle- and upper-income, generally—will be favored through their implicit control over reelection. Bureaus that can provide patronage, authorize construction, or regulate commercial activity have control over the sources of political income and will also probably be favored. In budget negotiations therefore, public health care, libraries, and welfare services should do poorly, whereas police, education, public works, and urban renewal should do well.

The specification of the recipient equation should also attempt to detail determinants of bureau and executive preference and each party's relative strength in the bargaining game. In most instances, the executive branch is ill-equipped to monitor bureau decisions on G and N; thus bureau preferences are likely to be controlling. One might expect that, given budget and technology, the portion of the eligible population serviced (N) should be negatively related to bureau preferences for service quality (in turn a positive function of employee professionalism), negatively related to available competition from other towns and private providers, and positively related to legislatively or judicially imposed standards for service equity.

Although a few empirical studies have recently attempted to integrate the bureau-executive bargaining process explicitly into the budget-cum-production model, the results, though suggestive, are at best tentative.[27] The design of a rational urban fiscal policy may not be possible, however, without a firm understanding of local bureaus. As the level and distribution of public services are largely the perogatives of city bureaucracies, it is imperative that we discover *their* rules for public resource allocations.

3. TOWARD A POLITICAL ECONOMY OF THE BUDGETARY PROCESS

Previous budget and production studies of local governments, concentrating as they have on the specification and estimation of the within-city budget and production process, have generally assumed that the local unit is a passive member of the broader metropolitan political economy. For any individual community, factor prices, grants-in-aid, tax base, and town residents are assumed given, dictated by area-wide markets or central policy. Yet the history of public employee unions, the rise of the "grantsmen," and the emerging fiscal crisis tell a decidedly different story, particularly for larger U.S. cities within regional economies. Changes in today's service level, the number of recipients, or local taxes may lead to future alterations in the local tax base and even in the socioeconomic composition of the community. The assumption in past work that prices, aid, tax base, and residents are given confines us to a partial equilibrium vision of what is assuredly a general equilibrium reality. Only recently have we begun to look beyond these blinders; the first results, which are reviewed here, strongly indicate the need to understand this wider, more complex environment of local budgeting.

Local Fiscal Choice with Endogenous Wages

The major dollar component of any local budget is the wage bill, in which changes in aggregate labor expenditure can come either from a change in wages (w) or a change in employment (l). Both are, of course, important, as such expenditure changes translate into tax changes that in turn affect local private income. Yet changes in labor have an added interest. An increase in employees per resident-user (l) leads, via the local production function, to increased local services (G). For reasons of policy, it is important that we understand the determinants of public employment and wage changes. When wages are endogenous to the budgetary process, a wage equation must be appended to our basic specification in equation (8) through (10).

What evidence do we now have that local public wages might be endogenous? In a study of 259 small New Jersey school districts, Frey (1975) found that union bargaining had no significant effect on teachers' wages; districts in which bargaining took place had 1.3 percent higher base teacher pay than districts without bargaining. In their study of California county crime control and police expenditures, Phillips and Votey (1975) formally tested an endogenous wage model and concluded that salary per criminal justice employee was independent of the number of employees. For these two studies of predominantly rural, small local governments, wages were exogenous to the budget process.

Studies with large-city samples give a decidedly different picture, however. Schmenner (1973) in a pooled time-series, cross-section study for eleven large U.S. cities (Providence was the smallest city included) for 1962–70 found that unionization had a significant effect on local wages. The estimated elasticity of teacher and police-fire wages with respect to the percentage of employees unionized was 0.05 and 0.15 respectively. In cities with formal collective bargaining agreements, teachers wages were 8 percent higher than in cities without such agreements. In a more detailed study of public unions' effects on wages, Ehrenberg and Goldstein (1975) found even stronger aggregate effects. In their work, unionization within a service is allowed to impact both on the service's own wage and, through a spillover effect, on the wages of other services. The cross-service effects are most significant among services that use interchangeable, semi-skilled labor —public works, parks and recreation, and sanitation and sewage. For example, moving from 0 to 100 percent unionized in parks and recreation increases own wages by 7 percent but the wages in sanitation-sewage by 11 percent and streets and highways by 15 percent. Full unionization of all public employees within a service drives wages up through own plus cross-effects by an estimated minimum of 7 percent for general control to a maximum of 28 percent for sanitation-sewage. Ashenfelter (1971) has pointed to a possible upward bias in these estimated unionization effects when the sample's percent unionized falls within the middle ranges, say 20 to 80 percent. Yet Ashenfelter, working with a "clean" sample for firefighters (percent unionized is either 0 or 100), still found a 10 percent wage effect with full unionization.

Ehrenberg-Goldstein also found evidence of monopsony wage power for their large city samples. (Schmenner also found monopsony power in his teacher wage equation, but not in his police and firemen wage equations.) Cities that are large in population relative to the rest of their Standard Metropolitan Statistical Area (SMSA) pay significantly lower wages than cities that are relatively small. Union power or no, a monopsonistic employer faces an endogenous wage schedule. For large cities with monopsony power in small regions or for cities that must face unions with the power to influence wages, the presumption that wage and labor inputs are jointly

determined is a hypothesis that must be tested. Ignoring the wage determination process may lead to biased coefficient estimates and a false
understanding of the efficacy of fiscal policies.

What are the implications of observing a local fiscal influence on public
wages? A central question here is what effect if any fiscal policy will have
on the wage level. When local wages are endogenous, increases in grants-in-
aid, community fiscal base, or income may lead to increases in both l and w.
Since a wage increase will consume new fiscal resources just as a labor
increase does, yet the higher w offers no compensating rise in services,
fiscal planners who aim at improving local public outputs through such
measures as revenue sharing will surely want to know the effect of those
policies on w. The effect may be substantial.

Schmenner (1973) has provided estimates of the impact of local fiscal
base (say through the relocation of commercial property or base-equalizing
aid) on public employer wages. His estimates give an elasticity of wages
with respect to fiscal base of 0.05 for teachers, 0.16 for police officers and
firemen, and 0.2 for workers in other common services (parks, highways,
public works, libraries). Tentative but still reasonable order-of-magnitude
estimates of the effect of revenue-sharing aid on wages can be derived from
the results in table 9.1. The elasticity of the local wage bill with respect to an
exogenous change in aid $(\epsilon_{wl, z})$ equals the sum of the elasticity of wages
with respect to aid $(\epsilon_{w, z})$ plus the elasticity of labor with respect to aid
$(\epsilon_{l, z})$. If the wage bill is a constant share of expenditures (as the evidence
suggests), then $\epsilon_{wl, z}$ can be measured by the expenditure elasticities
reported in table 9.1. The Ehrenberg estimates reported in table 9.1 provide
estimates of $\epsilon_{l, z}$. The elasticity $\epsilon_{w, z}$ can now be estimated as the difference,
$\epsilon_{wl, z} - \epsilon_{l, z}$. Ehrenberg's estimates are based on samples of large and small
cities, but fortunately the aid elasticities (reported as ϵ_z in table 9.1) are
reasonably consistent within expenditure categories across the various
studies. Thus our estimated $\epsilon_{w, z}$ from the many samples in table 9.1 is
probably still a reasonable estimate of the average effect of aid on wages.
For large cities (using Ehrenberg and Inman's, 1971a, b, estimates of
$\epsilon_{wl, z}$), $\epsilon_{w, z} = 0.55$ ($= 0.71 - 0.16$) for education, $\epsilon_{w, z} = 0.28$ for parks,
$\epsilon_{wz} = 0.15$ for public works, and $\epsilon_{w, z} \sim 0$ for all other services. For education in smaller cities and school districts, $\epsilon_{w, z} \sim 0$ (using Feldstein, 1975a,
Inman, 1978c, and Ladd, 1975.) The aid to wage elasticities for other
services for small cities could not be estimated using table 9.1.

Although these estimates of the elasticity of wages with respect to tax
base and grants-in-aid are only first approximations, they seem well within
the bounds of reason. Yet if these orders of magnitude are even approximately correct they raise the possibility of a strong wage dilution to the
effectiveness of urban fiscal policy. In reasonable cases, as much as 80
percent of any aid increase may find its way into higher public wages![28]
That is worthy of concern, particularly if the policy intention of grants-in-

aid is to increase services or reduce taxes. More precise estimates of the role of aid in the wage-setting process are of course needed before policy is redesigned. The potential importance of the wage effects involved, however, elevate it to a research topic of first priority.

"Grantsmanship" and Local Budgeting

One of the major problems with the very early econometric efforts to predict local fiscal behavior was their inappropriate specification of the grants-in-aid structure. By aggregating all aid, whether matching or lump-sum, into a single dollar-aid variable, simultaneity was introduced into the analysis and the ability to predict the separate fiscal effects of the two aid instruments was lost. Fortunately, the recent fiscal demand models have correctly specified the aid structure as consisting of its two components: dollar levels of exogenous lump-sum aid that influence fiscal choice as an income change and matching rates that impact as changes in service price. Presumably, this solved our problems. Yet the recent experience of local governments in the aids process suggests we should be less sanguine. The culprit now is "grantsmanship," the process of "winning" federal and state assistance.

The central source of difficulty is what are known as project grants. As of 1970, of the 370 federal grants-in-aid authorizations, 280 were designated as project assistance—matching aid distributed to selected local governments on a project by project basis following approval of a locally submitted proposal. Grants money must be specifically applied for, and an administered federal agency determines the winners. It is highly unlikely that the submitted proposals will just exhaust the budget of the granting agency. If not, allocations across competing local governments must be made. This process of "grantsmanship" introduces new players—the federal and state bureaucracy—and new statistical problems—the possibility of endogenous matching *rates*—into our analysis.

If local governments are "matching-rate-takers" and all local governments apply and receive some aid, then there will be no formal difficulty. There will be a "clearing" matching rate, as the administrative agency simply spreads its appropriation at an equal matching rate over all projects. The uniform rate will be defined by $m = \{$Aid Appropriation$/\Sigma$ Project Requests$\}$; so defined, m is clearly exogenous to any individual city's decision to tax or to spend. Such an aid allocation rule need not be an unreasonable characterization of federal agency behavior; it is easy to administer and everyone gets something. But if the federal or state administering agency pursues a more sophisticated strategy, the local's own allocation decisions may significantly affect its chances of receiving an award and the level of its matching rate. In effect, the local matching rate may become a negotiated price reduction, where the rate m becomes a function of the local's own spending level, its "grantsmanship" ability, the number of other applicants, the administering agency's preferences for favoring a few or many localities (perhaps tempered by Congressional preferences as well—see Plott, 1968), and the level of agency's appropriation. A matching rate equation may therefore be a necessary complement to our basic budget model in equation (8), (9), and (10), not only to avoid simultaneous equation bias as spending determines m but also to expose the federal bureaucratic determinants of local aid. A matching rate equation provides the needed look at how aid is actually disbursed.

For what services will a matching rate equation be necessary? As most project aid applies to the investment budget, it is here that greatest care is necessary. In an interesting analysis of the administration of one project grant—Department of Housing and Urban Development's Basic Water and Sewer Facilities program—Chernick (1976) has specified and estimated a matching rate equation. His results are suggestive. There is strong evidence that the "clearing rate" specification does not apply to this program. Although in the first years of the grant local matching rates showed little variation across communities receiving aid (the mean matching rate was 0.6 with a standard deviation of 0.06), as the administering agency gained experience, final rates began to spread (mean m rose to 0.62, with the standard deviation rising to 0.12). In addition, not all applicants received aid—HUD was discriminating. The towns that received aid were the large, income-poor towns with city managers (the trained "grantsmen"!). Further, submitting several applications rather than just one significantly improved the city's chance of receiving an award.

Two of the budget studies summarized earlier have actually included matching aid equations as endogenous components of their fiscal models. The first, by McGuire (1977), is an econometric sequel to his earlier (1975), theoretical discussion of endogenous aid. The analysis estimates a school spending equation in which both the matching rate and lump-sum aid are endogenous. To identify all parameters, McGuire assumed that city budgets can be described by an "as if" maximization of a linear homogeneous preference function. Thus, to gain added information about the aid structure, McGuire found it necessary to constrain his demand model a priori. The main conclusion is that educational aid, although nominally constrained to be spent only on public education, is in fact fully fungible into other services and the "matching" or price effect often required in such grants can be avoided. Federal or state rules for aid use can apparently be circumvented by the locals, a discouraging fact for those who wish to manipulate local school allocations through such matching aid schemes as Title I of the Elementary and Secondary Education Act or "District Power Equalizing."

While McGuire constrains his demand model to identify the full aid structure, the second study, by Inman (1971a), imposes the prior restrictions on the aid structure to permit a more general demand model. Inman assumed that for all *current* expenditure categories, matching aid is provided via the "clearing rate" model. These rates were therefore estimated as $\hat{m} = \{$Aid Appropriations$/\sum$ Project Expenditures$\}$. Using these estimated current budget matching rates and data on total aid and current expenditures, a "residual aid" equation composed of investment matching aid plus lump-sum aid was estimated as part of the full budget model. For the largest forty-one U.S. cities for the decade 1960–70, Inman found that lump-sum aid and capital matching aid were mildly redistributive—more aid and higher matching rates for poor towns—and favored older cities.

Public Budgets and the Private Sector

Like positive economic research generally, the recent empirical work on local fiscal choice has respected the understood separability of public, governmental activities and the private market. The assumption that these two sectors do not interact, except through exogenously set public policies, has been a maintained hypothesis for much of the research reviewed here. It is a limiting and potentially misleading premise. Dropping this assumption and admitting local governments as active (and reactive) members of the general urban economy is an important topic for future research. Two directions seem particularly promising. The first is to explore the interaction of fiscal choice and tax base. The second is to examine the effect of private market substitutes on the provision of local public services.

FISCAL BASE.   In the U.S. urban public economy, in which property taxation is the dominant form of local revenue, changes in local tax *rates* and local spending may have significant feedback into local tax *bases*. The change in the base may in turn induce further change in local spending. The private sector capital, housing, and land markets are the source of the feedback.

The central danger in neglecting this interrelationship between tax bases and local budgeting is the biased policy view that may result. First, when the feedback is neglected but the tax base is included as an explanatory variable in a fiscal model, such as equations (8) through (10), biased estimates of the behavioral coefficients may result. But further, even if appropriate two-stage least squares procedures are employed to estimate the budget model, the resulting parameter estimates will yield only the *impact* effect of policy changes on service and income. The regression procedure gives estimates of the marginal effect of policy *while holding the tax base constant.* To predict the *equilibrium* effect of policy, where aid influences spending and tax base, and tax base in turn influences spending and aid, a tax base equation is needed as a structural part of our fiscal model.[29]

Three recent studies have attempted to embed a tax base equation within the budget model. Inman (1977), in a study of Long Island suburban school districts, has specified a school spending model with endogenous land values, housing stocks, and firm investments. Although households are allowed to move, firms are assumed to remain in their original locations. The adjustments following fiscal change therefore approximate an intermediate time horizon rather than a true long run. Inman found that the impact (no feedback) effects of fiscal changes on local spending and taxes were 2 to 20 percent larger in absolute value than the general equilibrium effects. Thus the error in neglecting these effects is not trivial.

Oates, Howrey, and Baumol (1971) and Bradford and Kelejian (1973) have specified and estimated residential income equations as part of a fiscal model of center-city and suburban spending. The two studies provide conflicting answers to the important question of whether the center city can attract tax base (in this case measured as residential income) by increasing its levels of own-financed local services. Using data from the decade 1950 to 1960, Oates et al., found a very strong positive effect. A $1 per capita tax-financed increase in center city spending increases next year's median city income by $6 and the equilibrium median city income by $120! After formally incorporating the generally pro-poor bias in center-city finances (the rich pay more in taxes than they receive in services), Bradford and Kelejian found the opposite result. The rich leave as spending rises. A 10 percent rise in tax-financed expenditures ($\sim$ $30 per person) by a center city will lead to a 10 percent fall in the percentage of the region's middle and upper class residents who live within the city's borders.[30]

These studies are only initial efforts on this important topic, but they clearly point to one fact: local taxable capacities and budgetary choice are intimately intertwined. The private economy has wrapped the strands together. Sound urban fiscal policy requires that we understand the ties and make our policy decisions within the bounds that they impose.

THE PRIVATE PROVISION OF LOCAL SERVICES.   Local governments are no longer monopoly providers of many local public services. Private schools, voluntary and profit-making hospitals, swim clubs, sanitation companies, and private protection agencies now offer significant competition to the public provision of local services. What are the implications of this new competition for local fiscal performance and the design of policy? Two points are at issue: Under what conditions will residents prefer private to public providers, and what will be the impact (short run) and the equilibrium (long run) effects on local service provision of resident "exit" to the private sector?

Three recent studies—Barzel (1973), Barzel and Deacon (1975), Inman (1978b)—have examined the exit decision and its consequences. Each treats the decision to exit to a private provider as a purely economic choice. The question is simply which mode of service provision—uniform public output paid for through taxes or discretionary output paid for through prices—offers the resident the preferred consumption bundle. If service levels are too low within the public sector, the individual may prefer to pay both his local taxes and the extra cost of private services to replace or to supplement the inadequate public output. If public goods are normal goods with respect to income, the rich are the most probable exiters.

The exit of the rich will have two offsetting effects on public service provision. First, the once high demanders of public output are now low demanders; the rich exiters become tax bill minimizers. This creates political pressure for reduced public output. On the other hand, fewer residents are now using the public service, which means (when public services are "congestable" goods) that the remaining residents enjoy an output increase for their original tax payment. The tax-price of public services to the remaining users therefore declines. This creates pressure for increased public output. Brown and Saks (1977) have estimated the exit effect on school spending directly for a large sample of Michigan districts, and their results imply an exit elasticity of −0.4. An increase of 10 percent in the fraction of students in private school implies a 4 percent decline in spending for the average district.

As with all else within the urban public economy, there is a dynamics to this exit process too. As the very rich families exit and public spending falls, new families may find the private sector alternative attractive. They leave, and spending falls again. The end result may be a two class system of local service provision. The high- and middle-income families are within the high-spending private sector while the poor remain in the (now) low-spending public sector. The current public-private division in hospital services is an example of the exit process taken to an extreme.

Knowledge of these public-private interactions is fundamental for urban fiscal planning. Fiscal policies that initially look redistributive and promise to equalize the distribution of local public services may eventually have just the opposite effect. Since the rich are increasingly taxed to support improved services for the poor, they may prefer to exit and reduce redistribution by voting "no" for local public services. The poor who the initial redistribution was designed to help may now lose on two accounts. As the rich stop supporting the public system, real input may decline; but perhaps more importantly, as the rich exit, peer group production spillovers from rich to poor may be lost.[31]

Without arguing the normative value of a two-class system (remember that the upper-income groups are now able to buy their individually pre-ferred service level, a clear efficiency gain), that it can arise and that its social welfare implications are potentially significant are two strong reasons to learn more about the subtle feedback between the public and private sectors of the metropolitan economy.

CONCLUSION: FISCAL CHOICE AND FISCAL POLICY

A central concern of U.S. domestic policy in the last fifteen years has been the fiscal performance of local governments. Declining major cities have left the immobile poor and elderly holding the I.O.U.'s of past excesses. Bonds due and pensions promised will leave a large burden in increased taxes or reduced services for those who, for reasons of age, poverty, or race, cannot escape the center cities.

As troublesome as the big city crisis seems to be, the fiscal performance of suburban governments creates problems too. In a world of mobile families "shopping" for their own best fiscal package, significant external effects with such mobility may be ignored. If for reasons of high com-muting costs individuals work and live in the same community, a fiscal system of tax and service sharing may induce an inefficient allocation of labor within the private sector (see Henderson in this volume). Perhaps more importantly, if there are significant peer group effects in the provision of local services such that the mixing of rich and poor or the able and less able increases the output for the disadvantaged while only marginally reducing the output of the advantaged, then heterogenous communities may be preferred. The present fiscal system of property-based taxation with mobile households ignores these favorable externalities and discourages beneficial integration. Yet even without high commuting costs or peer group effects in service provision, the suburban fiscal economy as now financed may be inefficient. If all households are not fully mobile, the local property tax may impose a relatively high excess burden on consumers in the housing market. This criticism also applies, of course, to the center city's use of the property tax.

To meet these problems—to ease the pain of secular adjustment and to improve resource allocation generally—compensatory relief for the victims of big city decline may be desired in the short run, but structural reform of the urban fiscal economy will be needed in the long run.

The primary instruments of local fiscal reform within a federalist system are grants-in-aid: revenue-sharing or lump-sum aid, matching aid, fiscal base equalizing aid ("district power equalization"), tax credits (the "circuit-breaker"), deduction of local taxes, tax-exempt municipal bonds, or direct subsidy for local borrowing. These policies can be designed as compensatory devices targeted to residents of the center city, as structural remedies to stem big-city decline, or to improve resource allocation and encourage residential integration.

But understanding the causes of local fiscal problems and suggesting remedies is only part of the task of designing urban fiscal policy. The effectiveness of any remedy crucially depends upon how local governments and their residents respond to the policy's incentives. Will revenue-sharing aid designed to compensate city residents in fact lead to the residents' preferred level of tax relief and increased spending, or will aid find its way into further wage increases or a nonoptimal mix of tax and spending changes? Will fiscal base equalization aid aimed at reducing the disincentives for rich and poor to live together have that effect, or will it prove too redistributive for the rich, thereby encouraging their exit into a competitive private system? Will tax credits or tax deductions designed to relieve the burden of local property taxation reduce that burden, or will local governments' expansionary response to the lower burden per dollar of tax so stimulate the use of property taxation that total burdens *after credits* in fact increase?

As the above questions imply, there is absolutely no guarantee that local fiscal policies will work. Reform undone by local fiscal adjustment may actually make matters worse. The research surveyed here seeks to prevent well-meaning policies from having unwanted outcomes. But as the results in sections 1 through 3, make clear, knowledge of local fiscal choice is uneven. Against some fiscal problems we can proceed with confidence, against others we must operate more from faith than fact.

Our understanding seems most secure when predicting the short-run effects of reform on income. The impact of policy on expenditure is reasonably well detailed in table 9.1, and table 9.2 describes the impact of policy on taxes and on borrowing for multi-service, large city governments. The effects on current and future residential income follow from the budget identity. The estimated aid parameters (e.g., $d\text{Exp}/dz < 1$) imply that grants-in-aid can be used for local tax relief, particularly for already high-taxation cities. But from table 9.2 it can be seen that tax credits and interest rate subsidies will have only small and perhaps negative (tax burden increasing, p. 290) effects on current and future incomes.

The next steps toward a complete fiscal model of residential after-tax income are the further analysis of the determinants of local service costs, notably local wages, and the development of a long-run model of spending-taxes-borrowing through the specification and estimation of a local tax base equation. An econometric fiscal model with endogenous wage and tax base disaggregated to the level of a center city plus its suburban fringe would be most useful. We are close; both the methods and the data are available.

We are not very close, however, to understanding the effect of fiscal policy on the production of local service output. As the review of the budget-cum-production model has made clear, we have only begun to understand the process of turning public dollars into public outputs. Sound empirical analyses will require four ingredients: (1) measures of public output; (2) specifications of the production technology; (3) a behavioral model of bureau decision-making on input allocation, technology selection, and output mix; and (4), for those services in which peer group effects are important determinants of output (e.g., education, crime control, housing quality), behavioral models of racial or income integration and private sector service provision. Each is necessary. The analysis in sections 2 and 3 has outlined a strategy for such research.

We are still further from understanding the important role of the political choice process in determining budget outcome. Though the research on median voter models and bureaucracy behavior have been useful first attempts in this direction, much remains to be done. The public sector demand machinery is complex. Voters seldom decide on budgets directly, and when they vote they are often uninformed about not only the possible outcome but also their "tastes." Who knows how much we are willing to pay for programs that provide new services? Elected and appointed officials may have a good deal of latitude in setting budgets. But then, what are their objectives? And what formal and informal rules constrain their choices? Past empirical work based on the individual demand model has focused on the budget constraint as primary. Now the constraints of the *process* of collective choice must be formally introduced into our empirical analysis. The conceptual work of Margolis (1974), Breton (1974), and Barro (1973) are good bases from which to build.

Finally, there is one area of research, not been discussed in this review, that deserves attention—the normative theory of grants-in-aid. Grants will probably continue to be the primary instruments of fiscal reform in the urban public economy. As we have seen, how aid alters the income and service levels of individuals is an exceedingly complex matter; predicting outcome is far from trivial.

But there is another side to policy. As the Cheshire Cat said to Alice, before you choose you must know "where you want to get to." A normative theory of grants-in-aid, building on the methods of the new theory of optimal taxation and commodity pricing can help map the way from first principle and desired outcome through the behavioral complexities of budgetary choice to the preferred urban fiscal policy.[32] Only against the standard of normative analysis can we judge the effectiveness of policy.

Local governments now spend $120 billion per year, requiring 10 percent of personal income and constituting approximately 30 percent of all nondefense public spending.[33] Local government is a major U.S. "industry" whose performance, perhaps as much as any other, defines the quality of our urban life. To monitor and improve their performance, accurate empirical descriptions of local fiscal choice—descriptions that are true to both the economic and the political forces within the urban sector—are needed. Useful research will demand a judicious blend of behavioral and normative economic and political analysis with the institutional facts of local budgeting. Improved urban resource allocation is the reward for the added effort.

NOTES

1. There is an equally large and suggestive case study literature on the local budgetary process, which I will not review systematically, although I will draw occasionally upon it to stress a point. The reader is referred to Banfield (1965) for more details. See also the recent surveys in Hawley and Lipsky (1976).

2. Some recent authors, although recognizing the problem, have tried to argue that for their samples matching aid is trivial and simultaneous equation bias is not an issue. See Ohls and Wales (1972) and Gramlich (1969b). Generally, the argument runs: although the nominal provisions of the aid program indicate a matching formula, the total level of appropriated aid is fixed by legislation and therefore the program is not truly an open-ended price subsidy with received local aid dependent on local expenditures. This argument must be used carefully. If local governments compete for the fixed pool of aid resources by increasing local expenditures, and if the limited aid is not spread equally but is awarded to larger projects or high-spending cities, then simultaneous equations bias will still be present. A presumption of simultaneity and the use of a consistent estimation procedure seem prudent. The bias may be small (see Marsh, 1975), but we ought to test for it.

3. I have singled out these three studies because of their direct attempts to test empirically the implications of their new models. Scott (1952) had previously proposed a form of the Gramlich-Henderson specifications, and Bowen (1943) anticipated the Barr-Davis model by more than twenty years.

4. Capital inputs that are being ignored for the moment can be assumed to be "inherited" from prior budgetary periods. Generally, $X_i = \psi(L_i, M_i, K_i)$, where K_i is fixed in the current period by past investment.

5. As $\psi(\cdot)$ is linear homogeneous $c_i(\cdot)$ can be defined as:

$$c = \left\{\frac{w}{\alpha}\right\}^\alpha \left\{\frac{s}{1-\alpha}\right\}^{1-\alpha},$$

where α is labor shares in total *current* expenditures on service i (subscript i is understood). From the theory of consistent aggregation (Green, 1964) we can define $X = C/c$.

6. The family's net burden of one dollar of local taxes under the assumption of no tax shifting is defined as $\pi = (1-r-\lambda)$, where r is the family's marginal federal plus state income tax rate if local taxes are deductible and λ is the rate of tax credit for local taxes. Estimation of π for various income classes for the forty-one major U.S. cities appear in Inman (1971a).

7. The basic specification of spatial politics finds its intellectual start in Hotelling (1929). Bowen (1943) developed and extended the framework to problems of budgetary choice, and Downs (1957) overlayed the needed institutional analysis. For a good review of more recent developments, see Riker and Ordeshook (1973, chap. 11 and 12).

8. The process of adjustment always moves to the median position in the distribution of preferred budgets. Starting at a position below the median will produce a vote with more than 50 percent of voters preferring an expansion of expenditures. Starting with a budget above the median will produce a vote with more than 50 percent preferring contraction. No matter what the initial budget, convergence is to

the single equilibrium at the median position. This single equilibrium position, independent of the starting budget, occurs only with 50 percent majority rule. Political choice systems requiring a two-thirds or three-quarter vote for victory will give outcomes contingent on the starting budget. For empirical analysis, the single equilibrium result is an obvious advantage. Fortunately, most local political choice processes operate with a majority rule constitution. The discussion will be limited to this case.

9. See Riker and Ordeshook (1973, pp. 106–9) and Kramer (1973).

10. Edelson (1974) and Lovell (1977) show that for one case of the Bergstrom-Goodman model the tax price term for the median income voter is a function not only of median income but also of the spread in the town's income distribution, measured by the coefficient of variation in the income distribution. But if condition (1) holds, the coefficients of variation of all towns' income distributions are equal to each other. Thus the "income spread effect" on tax prices falls within the constant term when defining τ. This is the key role of condition (1).

Condition 2 hypothesizes a particular specification for the tax share specified generally as $\pi b/B$. For most local governments, each resident's tax base (b) is the assessed value of his or her home. If the assessment rate is a constant elasticity function of home value (Edelstein, 1977, and Berry and Bednarz, 1975) and home value is a constant elasticity function of income (Polinsky, 1977, and most housing demand studies), then tax base will be a constant elasticity function of income, say $b = \theta I^\epsilon$. Substituting b into the general form of τ, gives $\tau = (\theta \pi / B) I^\epsilon = a.I^\epsilon$, as hypothesized in condition 2.

11. Sato (1972) discussed the functional form of $P(\cdot)$ implicit in the use of a log-log demand system.

12. Substituting the definition of τ from condition 2 into the demand curve in condition 3 gives $G = (Aa^\beta)I^{\alpha+\beta\epsilon}$, with $\partial G/\partial I \gtrless 0$ as $\alpha + \beta\epsilon \gtrless 0$.

Brown and Saks (1977) have challenged assumptions 3 and 4, noting that for most private market commodities it is not observed that the desired share of income allocated to the good is monotonic with respect to income. If the share relationship for local public services (G/I) is not monotonic with respect to income, then identifying the median voter with the median-income position will be an error. What we may then observe are coalitions of the rich and the poor, both of whom prefer that a high (or low) share of income (i.e., tax rate) be allocated to public services, ganging up against the middle class. Brown and Saks tested this proposition for a sample of Michigan school districts and found it to be true, at least for very income heterogenous cities. For more income homogenous suburbs, assumptions 3 and 4 are probably still acceptable.

13. The eight voter groups are defined by the eight combinations of the three characteristics—e.g., homeowner, non-Catholic school user, young; homeowner, non-Catholic school user, old; etc.

14. The specification in equation (7) is obviously a simplification of a more exact representation of $\phi(\rho_1 \ldots \rho_{10})$ for Inman's ten subgroups. It is, however, the best that can be done with published data. For a discussion of possible bias, see Inman (1978c).

15. If W is legal and illegal income from political office, $P(W)$ defines the politician's preference for income and $W(G, N\cdot\bar{Y})$ defines the "income production function" of political wealth from budgetary activities, then $P(W(G,N\cdot\bar{Y}))$ is to be maximized subject to the city budget constraint. Diminishing marginal utility to wealth and diminishing "marginal income productivity" in budget activities are assumed. The *city* budget constraint reduces to equation (3′), if b and π are proportional to I (a reasonable assumption). Then summing over all residents and dividing by total population gives $\bar{Y} = \bar{I} - t\bar{b}\bar{\pi}$, where $\bar{b}$ and $\bar{\pi}$ are the values of b and π for the individual (or family) with the mean before-tax income $(\bar{I})$.

16. See Banfield and Wilson (1963), the case studies in Banfield (1965), and Crecine (1969), and Wildavsky (1975, chap. 6).

17. Some studies did not report all the data needed to calculate both elasticity and the marginal dollar effect. What could be calculated is reported in table 9.1.

18. The experience of the first year following revenue sharing for a sample of sixty-three counties, towns, and larger cities saw approximately $0.92 of every revenue sharing dollar allocated to expenditures ($0.31 to new spending, $0.61 to

programs maintenance against inflation), $0.07 to direct tax reductions, and $0.01 to long-term debt reductions. See Nathan et al. (1975, table 8.3).

19. Letting $\tau z + I = I'$, we know $\epsilon_{GI}\epsilon_{II'} = \epsilon_{GI}' = \epsilon_{Gz}\epsilon_{zI'}$ or $\epsilon_{Gz} = \epsilon_{GI}(\epsilon_{II'}/\epsilon_{zI'})$, from which the above restriction follows.

20. One might try to rationalize the "flypaper effect" as a statistical rather than a behavioral anomaly. If measured exogenous aid is less transitory than measured private income, then the estimated slope of the expenditure-aid line will be closer to its true (permanent aid) slope than will be the estimated slope of the expenditure-income line to its true (permanent income) slope. If exogenous aid is not transitory, so dExp$/dz$ is "true", then even its lower estimate of 0.3, with $\tau = 0.6$, will require a "true" dExp$/dI$ of 0.18 for the demand model's restriction to be valid. As most estimates of dEpx$/dI = 0.05$ to 0.10, a 100 percent bias in an estimate of expenditure-income slope due to transitory income must be argued for.

21. The reduced form parameters are related to the structural parameters as $\hat{\alpha} = \eta\alpha/q$, $\hat{\beta} = \eta\beta/q$, $\eta\epsilon = (\hat{\epsilon}/\hat{\beta} + 1)$, where $q = 1 - \beta(\eta - 1)$. Note that we can only identify the product $\eta\epsilon$ and the ratio α/β directly from the reduced form parameter estimates.

22. One point of clarification should be emphasized here. To identify η estimates of a *facility* cost schedule, where (C/X) is a function of X, are needed. Much of the work on service costs have in fact estimated the relationship between (C/N) and N. Hirsch (1965) reviewed that literature. Borcherding-Deacon (1972, p. 894) seem to have confused these two relationships when they appealed to Hirsch's review for support of their assumption that $\eta = 1$.

23. Strictly speaking, all that is identified in the reduced form approach is the ratio of the income to price elasticities, $\alpha/\beta = \hat{\alpha}/\hat{\beta}$. Without the prior restriction on η or ϵ we cannot identify the absolute values of α or β. This conclusion holds for *all* the studies in table 9.1. The omitted variable bias is thus for the true ratio (α/β). We find that in those studies that omit N, the ratio $(\hat{\alpha}/\hat{\beta})$ is significantly smaller in absolute value than the estimated ratio obtained from the Bergstrom-Goodman and Pack-Pack studies that include N.

24. The median voter's utility is defined by $P(G, Y)$, where $G = g(X, N)$ and $Y = I - \tau C(X)/N = Y(X, N)$. The derivative of $P(.)$ with respect to N, holding service output (G) fixed at some level G_0 is:

$$\partial P/\partial N = \partial P/\partial Y \{\partial Y/\partial N + \partial Y/\partial X(dX/dN)_{G=G_0}\}.$$

As $\partial Y/\partial N = \tau C/N^2$ and $\partial Y/\partial X = -(\tau/N)(\partial C/\partial X)$, $\partial P/\partial N$ can be rewritten as:

$$\partial P/\partial N = (\partial P/\partial Y)(\tau)(X/N^2)(\partial C/\partial X)\{1/\eta - \epsilon\},$$

which equals 0 when $\eta\epsilon = 1$.

25. The most recent works contain good bibliographies of the literature. See Murnane (1975) or Boardman et al. (1977) on education, Grossman (1976) on health, Cook (1977) on crime, and Keeler and Small (1977) and Inman (1978a) on transportation.

26. Though there have been useful conceptual treatises on the topic. See Downs (1967), Tullock (1965), Niskanen (1975), and Breton (1974).

27. Two recent studies—one by Sloan (1977) of the U.S. welfare system and one by Brown and Saks (1975) of local education—have estimated budget models with equations analogous to $N=n(.)$ included. The results are suggestive. Sloan, for example, found that an increased welfare budget has only a small effect on the number of eligible recipients who receive benefits. Most of the budget increases are allocated to improved benefits (i.e., higher service quality) for those already receiving assistance. This bias toward quality is what one might expect from such a professionally dominated bureaucracy as welfare.

Using a slightly different specification of the model, Brown and Saks estimated the effect of budget and bureau preference on the variance of school test scores. In a two group school system—honors (denoted as N) and nonhonors students—it is possible to show that for reasonable values of N and service quality (G) as the number of favored students falls and as G increases to those who remain, the variance of school test scores rise. Brown and Saks found that after holding total input levels fixed, more professionally oriented school systems (measured as the percentage of teachers with master's) and school systems with greater private or other public school competition (measured as parental socioeconomic status) had lower N's and larger G's (i.e., variance of test scores increased). These results are consistent with the bureau model outlined above.

In a different context, Feldstein (1977) has estimated a hospital behavior model in which he observed a similar and significant bias toward high quality (G) and restricted case load (N) as budgets are increased through increased insurance coverage.

28. If labor costs (wl) are a constant share (ϕ) of expenditures, then $wl = \phi\mathrm{Exp}$ and the total effect of aid on expenditures can be approximated by:

$$\phi d \, \mathrm{Exp} = ldw + wdl,$$

where $dw = \epsilon_{w,z}.w(dz/z)$ and $dl = \epsilon_{l,z}.l(dz/z)$. Substituting and rearranging the terms gives:

$$d\mathrm{Exp} = \left(\frac{\mathrm{Exp}}{z}\right)\epsilon_{l,z}\Delta z + \left(\frac{\mathrm{Exp}}{z}\right)\epsilon_{w,z}\Delta z.$$

For a typical large city school system $(\mathrm{Exp}/z) \cong 1.4$ and using $\epsilon_{l,z} = 0.16$ and $\epsilon_{w,z} = 0.55$, $\Delta z = \$1$ is allocated $\$0.22$ to buy more labor and $\$0.77$ to higher wages.

29. A reduced form spending equation from the full model could also be estimated to give the equilibrium effect on spending of changes in the model's exogenous variables. A fiscal-base equation will still be needed, however, to specify the reduced form spending equation.

30. The elasticities were calculated assuming 40 percent of the center-city residents had income in the lower fifth of a region's distribution and that the center city occupied about 40 percent of the region's land area. Bradford and Kelejian's table 1 provided the needed parameter estimates.

31. The loss of such spillovers may be particularly crucial for public education. See Henderson, Miezkowski, and Sauvageau (1976) and Summers and Wolfe (1977).

32. The reader unfamiliar with the optimal tax literature could profitably begin with Sandmo (1976) and Stern (1976). Federal grants are, of course, subsidies to local public services. Atkinson (1977) provided a nice analysis of the optimal design of one subsidy, housing allowance, and his methodology should generalize. As externalities are a prominent source of market failure in the urban public sector (see Henderson in this volume), the work by Diamond (1973) on optimal pricing and externalities should also be a useful guide.

33. Figures calculated for the 1972 budget and income figures published in the *Statistical Abstract of the United States,* 1974, tables 402, 405, and 409.

REFERENCES

Ashenfelter, O. 1971. "The Effects of Unionization on Wages in the Public Sector: The Case of Fire Fighters." *Industrial and Labor Relations Review* 24 (January): 191–202.

Atkinson, A. B. 1977. "Housing Allowances, Income Maintenance and Income Taxation." In *The Economics of Public Services.* Edited by M. S. Feldstein and R. P. Inman. London: The MacMillan Press.

Barro, R. 1973. "The Control of Politicians: An Economic Model." *Public Choice* 14 (Spring): 19–42.

Banfield, E., and Wilson, J. Q. 1963. *City Politics.* Cambridge, Mass.: Harvard University Press.

Banfield, E. 1965. *Big City Politics*. Cambridge, Mass.: Harvard University Press.

Barr, J., and Davis, O. 1966. "An Elementary Political and Economic Theory of Local Governments." *Southern Economic Journal* 33 (October): 149–65.

Barzel, Y. 1973. "Private Schools and Public School Finance." *Journal of Political Economy* 81 (January/February): 174–86.

Barzel, Y., and Deacon, R. 1975. "Voting Behavior, Efficiency, and Equity." *Public Choice*, Spring, pp. 1–11.

Bergstrom, T., and Goodman, R. 1973. "Private Demand for Public Goods." *American Economic Review* 63 (June): 286–96.

Berry, B., and Bednarz, R. 1975. "A Hedonic Model of Prices and Assessments for Single-Family Homes: Does the Assessor Follow the Market or the Market Follow the Assessor?" *Land Economics* 51 (February): 21–40.

Boardman, A. E.; Davis, O. A.; and Sanday, P. R. 1977. "A Simultaneous Equations Model of the Educational Process." *Journal of Public Economics* 7 (February): 23–50.

Borcherding, T., and Deacon, R. 1972. "The Demand for Services of Non-Federal Governments." *American Economic Review* 62 (December): 891–901.

Bowen, H. 1969. "The Interpretation of Voting in the Allocation of Economic Resources." Reprinted in *Readings in Welfare Economics*. Edited by K. Arrow and T. Scitovsky. Homewood, Ill.: Richard D. Irwin.

Bradford, D., and Oates, W. 1974. "Suburban Exploitation of Central Cities and Government Structure." In *Redistribution Through Public Choice*. Edited by H. M. Hochman and G. E. Peterson. New York: Columbia University Press.

Bradford, D., and Kelejian, H. 1973. "An Econometric Model of the Flight to the Suburbs." *Journal of Political Economy* 81 (May/June): 566–89.

Brazer, H. 1959. "City Expenditures in the United States." National Bureau of Economic Research Occasional Paper No. 66. New York.

Breton, A. 1974. *The Economic Theory of Representative Government*. Chicago: Aldine.

Brown, B. 1972. "Achievement, Costs, and the Demand for Public Education." *Western Economic Journal* 10 (June): 198–219.

Brown, B., and Saks, D. 1975. "The Production and Distribution of Cognitive Skills Within Schools." *Journal of Political Economy* 83 (June): 571–94.

———. 1977. "Income Distribution and the Aggregation of Private Demands for Local Public Education." East Lansing: Michigan State University.

Carr-Hill, R., and Stern, N. 1973. "An Econometric Model of the Supply and Control of Recorded Offences in England and Wales." *Journal of Public Economics* 2 (November): 289–318.

———. 1977. "Theory and Estimation in Models of Crime and Its Social Control and their Relations to the Concepts of Social Output." In *The Economics of Public Services*. Edited by M. Feldstein and R. Inman. London: MacMillan.

Chernick, H. 1976. "The Economics of Bureaucratic Behavior: An Application to the Allocation of Federal Project Grants." Ph.D. diss. University of Pennsylvania.

Cook, P. J. 1977. "Punishment and Crime: A Critique of Current Findings Concerning the Preventive Effects of Punishment." *Law and Contemporary Problems* 41 ((Winter): 164–203.

Crecine, P. 1969. *Governmental Problem-Solving: A Computer Simulation of Municipal Budgeting*. Chicago: Rand McNally.

Davis, K., and Russell, L. 1972. "The Substitution of Hospital Outpatient Care for Inpatient Care." *Review of Economics and Statistics* 54 (May): 109–20.

Diamond, P. 1973. "Consumption Externalities and Imperfect Corrective Pricing." *Bell Journal of Economics and Management Science* 4 (Autumn): 526–38.

Downs, A. 1957. *An Economic Theory of Democracy*. New York: Harper and Row.

———. 1967. *Inside Bureaucracy*. Boston: Little, Brown.

Edelson, N. 1974. "Budgetary Outcomes in a Referendum Setting." In *Property Taxation and the Finance of Education*. Edited by R. Lindholm. Madison: The University of Wisconsin Press.

Edelstein, R. 1976. "The Equity of Real Estate Property Tax: An Empirical Examination of the City of Philadelphia." University of Pennsylvania.

Ehrenberg, R. 1973. "The Demand for State and Local Government Employees." *American Economic Review* 58 (June): 366–79.

Ehrenberg, R., and Goldstein, G. 1975. "A Model of Public Sector Wage Determination." *Journal of Urban Economics* 2 (July): 222–45.

Feldstein, M. S. 1794. "Econometric Studies of Health Economics." In *Frontiers of Quantitative Economics*, vol. 2. Edited by M. D. Intrilligator and D. A. Kendrick. Amsterdam: North-Holland Publishing.

———. 1975a. "Wealth Neutrality and Local Choice in Public Education." *American Economic Review* 65 (March): 75–89.

———. 1975b. "The Income Tax and Charitable Contributions: Part I—Aggregate and Distributional Effects." *National Tax Journal* 28 (March): 81–100.

———. 1977. "Quality Change and the Demand for Hospital Care." *Econometrica* 45 (October): 1681–702.

Frey, D. E. 1975. "Wage Determination in Public Schools and the Effects of Unionization." in *Labor in the Public and Nonprofit Sectors*. Edited by D. Hamermesh. Princeton, N.J.: Princeton Univeristy Press.

Getz, M. 1979. *The Economics of the Urban Fire Department*. Baltimore: The Johns Hopkins University Press.

Gramlich, E. 1968. "Alternative Federal Policies for Stimulating State and Local Expenditures: A Comparison of Their Effects." *National Tax Journal* 21 (June): 119–29.

———. 1969a. "The Effects of Federal Grants on State-Local Expenditures: An Review of the Econometric Literature." *Proceedings of the 62nd Annual Conference on Taxation*, pp. 569–93. Lexington, Ky.: National Tax Association.

———. 1969b. "State and Local Governments and Their Budget Constraints." *International Economic Review* 10 (June): 163–81.

Gramlich, E., and Galper, H. 1973. "State and Local Fiscal Behavior and Federal Grant Policy." *Brookings Papers on Economic Activity* 1: 15–58.

Green, H. A. J. 1964. *Aggregation in Economic Analysis.* Princeton, N.J.: Princeton University Press.

Grossman, M. 1976. "A Survey of Recent Research in Health Economics." National Bureau of Economic Research Working Paper No. 129. March.

Hambor, J.; Phillips, L.; and Votey, H. 1973. "Optimal Community Educational Attainment: A Simultaneous Equations Approach." *Review of Economics and Statistics* 55 (February): 98–103.

Hawley, W. D., and Lipsky, M. 1976. *Theoretical Perspectives on Urban Politics.* Englewood Cliffs, N.J.: Prentice-Hall.

Henderson, J. 1968. "Local Government Expenditures: A Social Welfare Analysis." *Review of Economics and Statistics* 50 (May): 156–63.

Henderson, V.; Mieszkowski, P.; and Sauvageau, Y. 1976. *Peer Group Effects and Educational Production Functions.* Ottawa: Economic Council of Canada.

Hirsch, W. 1968. "The Supply of Urban Public Services." In *Issues on Urban Economics.* Edited by H. Perloff and L. Wingo. Baltimore: The Johns Hopkins Press.

Hotelling, Harold. 1929. "Stability in Competition." *Economic Journal* 39 (January): 41–57.

Inman, R. P. 1971*a. Four Essays on Fiscal Federalism.* Ph.D. diss. Harvard University.

————. 1971*b.* "Towards An Econometric Model of Local Budgeting." *Proceedings of the 64th Annual Conference on Taxation,* pp. 699–719. Lexington, Ky.: National Tax Association.

————. 1975. "Grants in a Metropolitan Economy—A Framework for Policy." In *Financing the New Federalism.* Edited by W. Oates. Baltimore: The Johns Hopkins University Press.

————. 1977. "Micro-fiscal Planning in the Regional Economy: A General Equilibrium Approach." *Journal of Public Economics* 7 (April): 237–60.

————. 1978*a.* "A Generalized Congestion Function for Highway Travel." *Journal of Urban Economics* 5 (January): 21–34.

————. 1978*b.* "Optimal Fiscal Reform of Metropolitan Schools: Some Simulation Results." *American Economic Review* 68 (March): 107–22.

————. 1978*c.* "Testing Political Economy's 'As If' Proposition: Is the Median Income Voter Really Decisive?" *Public Choice* (Winter).

Jackson, J. 1972. "Politics and the Budgetary Process." *Social Science Research* 1 (April): 35–60.

Joreskog, K., and Goldberger, A. 1975. "Estimation of a Model with Multiple Causes of a Single Latent Variable." *Journal of the American Statistical Association* 70 (September): 631–39.

Keeler, T., and Small, K. 1977. "Optimal Peak-Load Pricing, Investment and Service Levels on Urban Expressways." *Journal of Political Economy* 85 (February): 1–25.

Kemper, P., and Quigley, J. 1976. *The Economics of Refuse Collection.* Cambridge, Mass.: Ballinger.

Kramer, J. 1973. "On a Class of Equilibrium Conditions for Majority Rule." *Econometrica* 41 (March): 285–97.

Ladd, H. F. 1975. "Local Education Expenditures, Fiscal Capacity, and the

Composition of Property Tax Base." *National Tax Journal* 28 (June): 145–58.

———. 1976. "Municipal Expenditures and the Composition of the Local Property Tax Base." In *Property Taxation, Land Use and Public Policy*. Edited by A. Lynn Jr. Madison: University of Wisconsin Press.

Lovell, M. 1977. "Spending for Education: An Exercise in Public Choice." Middletown, Ct.: Wesleyan University.

McGuire, M. 1975. "An Econometric Model of Federal Grants and Local Fiscal Response." In *Financing the New Federalism*. Edited by W. Oates. Baltimore: The Johns Hopkins University Press.

———. 1977. "A Method for Estimating the Effect of a Subsidy on the Receiver's Resource Constraint: With An Application to U.S. Local Governments." College Park, Md.: University of Maryland.

Margolis, J. 1974. "Public Policies for Private Profit: Urban Governments." In *Redistribution Through Public Choice*. Edited by H. M. Hochman and G. E. Peterson. New York: Columbia University Press.

Marsh, L. 1975. "Weicher's State Aid and Local Expenditures Model and the Simultaneous Equations Controversy." *Natural Tax Journal* 28 (December): 459–61.

Murnane, Richard. 1975. *The Impact of School Resources on the Learning of Inner City Children*. Cambridge, Mass.: Ballinger.

Nathan R.; Manvel, A.; and Calkins, S. 1975. *Monitoring Revenue Sharing*. Washington, D.C.: Brookings Institution.

Newhouse, J., and Phelps, C. 1974. "Coinsurance, the Price of Time, and the Demand for Medical Services." *Review of Economics and Statistics* 56 (August): 334–42.

Niskanen, W. 1975. "Bureaucrats and Politicians." *Journal of Law and Economics* 18 (December): 617–43.

Oates, W. 1968. "The Dual Impact of Federal Aid on State and Local Government Expenditures: A Comment." *National Tax Journal* 21 (June): 220–23.

Oates, W. E.; Howrey, P.; and Baumol, W. 1971. "The Analysis of Public Policy in Dynamic Urban Models." *Journal of Political Economy* 78 (January/February): 142–53.

Ohls, J., and Wales, T. 1972. "Supply and Demand for State and Local Services." *Review of Economics and Statistics* 54 (November): 424–30.

Olsen, E. O. 1972. "A Method for Predicting the Effects of Different Forms of Outside Aid on Local Educational Expenditure." Santa Monica: RAND Corporation Working Note, December.

Pack, H., and Pack, J. 1975. "Local Public Goods and the Tiebout Hypothesis: An Alternative Approach." Fels Discussion Paper No. 71. University of Pennsylvania.

Peterson, G. 1975. "Voter Demand for Public School Expenditures." In *Public Needs and Private Behavior in Metropolitan Areas*. Edited by J. Jackson. Cambridge, Mass.: Ballinger.

Phillips, L., and Votey, H. 1975. "Crime Control in California." *Journal of Legal Studies*. 4 (June): 327–50.

Plott, C. 1968. "Some Organizational Influences on Urban Renewal Decisions." *American Economic Review* 58 (May): 306–21.

Polinsky, M. 1977. "The Demand for Housing: A Study in Specification and Grouping." *Econometrica* 45 (March): 447–61.

Riker, W., and Ordeshook, P. 1973. *An Introduction to Positive Political Theory.* Englewood Cliffs, N.J.: Prentice-Hall.

Romer, T., and Rosenthal, H. 1978. "Bureaucrats vs. Voters: On the Political Economy of Resource Allocation by Direct Democracy." *Public Choice*, (Winter).

Rubinfeld, D. 1977. "Voting in a Local School Election: A Micro Analysis." *Review of Economics and Statistics* 59 (February): 30–42.

Sandmo, A. 1976. "Optimal Taxation—An Introduction to the Literature." *Journal of Public Economics* 6 (July/August): 37–54.

Sato, K. 1972. "Additive Utility Functions with Double-Log Consumer Demand Functions." *Journal of Political Economy* 80 (January/February): 102–24.

Schmenner, R. 1973. "The Determination of Municipal Employee Wages." *Review of Economics and Statistics* 55 (February): 83–90.

Scott, A. D. 1952. "The Evaluation of Federal Grants." *Economica* 19 (November): 377–94.

Sharkansky, I. 1967. "Some More Thoughts About the Determinants of Government Expenditures." *National Tax Journal* 20 (June): 171–79.

Sloan, F. 1977. "A Model of Income Maintenance Decisions." *Public Finance Quarterly* 5 (April): 139–74.

Stern, N. 1976. "On the Specification of Models of Optimum Income Taxation." *Journal of Public Economics* 6 (July/August): 123–62.

Summers, A., and Wolfe, B. 1977. "Do Schools Make a Difference?" *American Economic Review* 67 (September): 639–52.

Tullock, G. 1965. *The Politics of Bureaucracy.* Washington, D.C.: Public Affairs Press.

Verba, S., and Nye, N. H. 1972. *Participation in America: Political Democracy and Social Equality.* New York: Harper and Row.

Walzer, N. 1972. "Economies of Scale and Municipal Police Services: The Illinois Experience." *Review of Economics and Statistics* 54 (November): 431–38.

Weicher, J. 1972. "Aid, Expenditures, and Local Government Structure." *National Tax Journal* 25 (December): 573–83.

Wildavsky, A. 1975. *Budgeting: A Comparative Theory of Budgetary Processes.* Boston: Little, Brown.

Wittman, D. 1973. "Parties as Utility Maximizers." *American Political Science Review* 67 (June): 490–98.

10

CENTRAL CITIES: FISCAL PLIGHT AND PROSPECTS FOR REFORM

WILLIAM H. OAKLAND

1. INTRODUCTION: CENTRAL-CITY FISCAL STRESS

The past twenty years have been characterized by a dramatic reversal in the economic and social fortunes of many large central cities in the United States. There has been a loss of employment and population, income has fallen relative to the suburbs, and the fiscal condition of many central cities has become extremely weak. The difficulties of New York City, although unique in some respects, stem in part from a set of underlying factors that are present in many of our older large central cities.

There is no need to document the demographic consequences of central-city decline, since they are discussed elsewhere in this volume.[1] However, it is useful to highlight those factors that relate to fiscal distress. Of particular significance are various measures of central-city-suburban disparities, because they lie at the root of the central-city fiscal problem. Relative conditions in the suburbs serve as a powerful check on the central city's fiscal behavior, since city residents or business firms have the option of relocating to the suburbs in response to a relatively unfavorable fiscal climate in the city.

That the decline of the central city has been accompanied by a corresponding weakening of its relative fiscal strength is persuasively demonstrated by table 10.1, which shows per capita income for the eighty-five largest Standard Metropolitan Statistical Areas (SMSA). With only a few exceptions, per-capita income grew more slowly between 1960 and 1973 in the central cities than in their suburbs. Moreover, the *level* of per-capita

William H. Oakland is a professor of economics, Ohio State University, and senior fellow in public finance, Academy for Contemporary Problems.

The author expresses his gratitude to Peter Mieszkowski and Dick Netzer for many helpful suggestions.

TABLE 10.1. Per Capita Income, Central City and Outside Central City Areas, 1960 and 1973

	1960			1973		
Region and SMSA	cc	occ	Ratio of cc to occ	cc	occ	Ratio of cc to occ
East						
Bridgeport	$1967	$2613	.75	$3643	$4648	.78
Hartford	2104	2521	.83	3428	4761	.72
Washington, D.C.	2406	2432	.98	4901	5809	.84
Baltimore	1866	2063	.90	3595	4517	.79
Boston	1919	2363	.81	3678	4617	.79
Springfield	1888	2078	.90	3451	4037	.85
Worcester	1935	1901	1.01	3763	3926	.95
Jersey City	1963	2107	.93	3691	4032	.91
Newark	1792	2747	.65	2964	5232	.56
Paterson	2053	2646	.77	3902	5363	.72
Albany	1985	1989	.99	3888	4165	.93
Buffalo	1913	2113	.90	3409	4004	.85
New York	2306	2734	.84	4309	5088	.84
Rochester	2072	2259	.91	3716	4619	.80
Syracuse	2152	1922	1.11	3717	3847	.96
Philadelphia	1875	2272	.82	3678	4394	.83
Pittsburgh	1943	1945	.99	3618	3962	.91
Providence	1843	1823	1.01	3749	3864	.97
Mean	1999	2251	.90	3727	4488	.83
Standard Deviation	160	303	.11	396	587	.10
Midwest						
Chicago	2293	2662	.86	3984	4975	.80
Fort Wayne	2105	1957	1.07	3850	4406	.87
Gary	1936	2022	.95	3563	4091	.87
Indianapolis	2031	2179	.93	4104	3931	1.04
Des Moines	22.6	2035	1.08	4051	4251	.95
Wichita	2082	1896	1.09	3906	3502	1.11
Detroit	2005	2261	.88	3817	4736	.80
Flint	2045	1721	1.18	3858	4075	.94
Grand Rapids	1937	1943	.99	3603	3894	.92
Minneapolis	2218	2178	1.01	4141	4467	.92
Kansas City	2176	2105	1.03	4012	4333	.92
St. Louis	1801	2192	.82	3292	4179	.78
Omaha	2139	1846	1.15	3979	3610	1.10
Akron	2124	2012	1.05	3887	4071	.95
Cincinnati	2043	2031	1.00	3657	3920	.93
Cleveland	1856	2693	.68	3160	4773	.66
Columbus	1885	2310	.81	3547	4376	.81
Dayton	1973	2127	.92	3308	4292	.77
Toledo	2012	2009	1.00	3745	4340	.86
Youngstown	1876	1936	.96	3421	3920	.87
Madison	2214	1873	1.18	3938	4304	.91
Milwaukee	2105	2305	.91	3809	4628	.82
Mean	2049	2104	.98	3756	4231	.89
Standard Deviation	132	239	.12	277	364	.10

TABLE 10.1 (*Continued*)

Region and SMSA	1960			1973		
	cc	occ	Ratio of cc to occ	cc	occ	Ratio of cc to occ
South						
Birmingham	1570	1347	1.16	3177	3738	.84
Mobile	1747	1101	1.58	3428	2668	1.28
Jacksonville	1611	1814	.88	3686	*	*
Miami	1838	2101	.87	3592	4635	.77
Tampa	1798	1724	1.04	3757	4016	.93
Atlanta	1934	1918	1.00	3903	4631	.84
Columbus	1534	1287	1.19	3446	2672	1.28
Louisville	1764	1946	.90	3687	4016	.91
Baton Rouge	1855	1493	1.24	3480	3320	1.04
New Orleans	1740	1673	1.03	3319	3544	.93
Shreveport	1859	1307	1.42	3436	2648	1.29
Jackson	1756	921	1.90	3641	2640	1.37
Charlotte	1975	1443	1.36	4314	3521	1.22
Oklahoma City	1981	1850	1.07	3967	3793	1.04
Tulsa	2298	1560	1.47	4217	3114	1.35
Knoxville	1486	1570	.94	3457	3334	1.03
Memphis	1651	1220	1.35	3562	2982	1.19
Nashville	1288	1934	.66	3731	3895	.95
Austin	1688	1520	1.11	3634	3679	.98
Corpus Christi	1616	1122	1.44	3188	2372	1.34
Dallas	2219	1906	1.16	4432	4055	1.09
El Paso	1579	1405	1.12	2947	2173	1.35
Fort Worth	1946	1782	1.09	3747	3862	.97
Houston	2062	1735	1.18	4128	3896	1.05
San Antonio	1427	1937	.73	2892	4430	.65
Norfolk	1658	1613	1.02	3550	3821	.92
Richmond	1940	2055	.94	4074	4494	.90
Mean	1771	1603	1.14	3644	3537	1.06
Standard Deviation	232	315	.25	383	701	.20
West						
Phoenix	2013	1741	1.15	4118	4092	1.00
Tucson	1886	1942	.97	3714	4176	.88
Anaheim	2138	2361	.90	4032	4059	.99
Fresno	1984	1702	1.16	3494	3274	1.06
Los Angeles	2603	2453	1.06	4569	4419	1.03
Sacramento	2476	2069	1.19	4076	3947	1.03
San Bernardino	2103	1812	1.16	3708	3643	1.01
San Diego	2301	2054	1.12	4215	3876	1.08
San Francisco	2596	2516	1.03	4762	4964	.95
San Jose	2205	2390	.92	4026	4978	.80
Denver	2275	2050	1.10	4560	4428	1.02
Honolulu	2176	1689	1.28	4306**	**	**
Albuquerque	2109	1393	1.51	3835	2656	1.44
Portland	2284	2026	1.12	4029	4323	.93
Salt Lake City	2105	1693	1.24	4109	3404	1.20

TABLE 10.1 (*Continued*)

Region and SMSA	1960			1973		
	cc	occ	Ratio of cc to occ	cc	occ	Ratio of cc to occ
Seattle	2664	1989	1.33	4545	4228	1.07
Spokane	2077	1770	1.17	3781	3286	1.15
Tacoma	1986	1815	1.09	3709	3757	.98
Mean	2221	1970	1.14	4088	3990	1.04
Standard Deviation	229	305	.14	354	591	.13
Total Mean	1987	1948	1.05	3784	4019	.96
Standard Deviation	254	383	.21	385	675	.17

SOURCE: ACIR, *Trends in Metropolitan America,* Washington, 1977, pp. 38–40.
  * City and county consolidated with only four small municipalities excluded and therefore relationships are not applicable.
  ** City and county consolidated and therefore relationships are not applicable.

income was lower in the central city, in 1973, in all Eastern cities and all but two Midwestern cities. In the South and the West, on the other hand, no clear picture of the level of income emerges.

Table 10.2 shows additional evidence of the weakened central-city fiscal condition. The table indicates that employment *growth* was substantially more rapid in the suburbs than in the central city, with the largest disparities existing in the East and Midwest. Such shifts of employment are of considerable fiscal consequence because of the tax revenues they generate.[2] The latter consideration also applies to retail sales, particularly if the central city levies a sales tax.

The combined effect of the shift in relative income and in shares of employment and retail sales was a seriously impairment of the central city's property tax base. Table 10.3 shows the market value of taxable property for a sample of twenty older large cities for the years 1961 and 1971. Column (4) of the table indicates that in only one case did the growth of per-capita taxable property in the central city exceed that of the suburbs. Moreover, by 1971, only four of the twenty central cities had a greater property tax base than their suburbs. In ten of the cases, the central city base stood 10 percent or more below the SMSA average, and in three cases, the differential stood at 40 percent or more. This primacy of the suburbs is a relatively new phenomenon, as the data for 1961 indicate.

A direct consequence of a smaller property-tax base is the need for a higher property tax rate to produce a given revenue stream per capita. A tax base differential between the city and the metropolitan area of 10 percent implies a city-suburban tax *rate* differential in excess of 20 percent for the *same level* of per-capita revenue.[3] The *true* tax rate disparity, how-

TABLE 10.2. Growth of Total Employment, Manufacturing Employment, and Retail Sales for Central Cities (CC) and Outside Central Cities (OCC), by Region, 1960–73[a]

Region	Percent Change in Total Employment, 1960–70	Percent Change in Manufacturing Employment, 1963–72	Percent Change in Retail Sales, 1963–72
Northeast			
CC	− 2.4	−18.9	27.2
OCC	3.5	15.4	120.6
Midwest			
CC	7.0	3.0	54.4
OCC	65.0	27.2	138.5
South			
CC	23.1	38.3	107.4
OCC	43.2	64.2	179.8
West			
CC	28.0	24.0	82.9
OCC	38.4	82.9	158.0
United States			
CC	15.8	14.2	71.5
OCC	45.8	36.4	152.0

SOURCE: U.S. Advisory Commission on Intergovernmental Relations, *Trends in Metropolitan America* (Washington, D.C., February, 1977).
[a] Unweighted average of individual cities.

ever, must reflect the *actual* patterns of revenue requirement. However, as the last four columns of table 10.3 show, the central city must raise considerably more revenue than the metropolitan average—often as much as 20 percent more. Such a differential, *by itself,* would generate a tax rate discrepancy of approximately 50 percent.[4]

If such a discrepancy simply reflected differences in city-suburban consumption of public services, the tax surcharge would correspond to a benefit fee. However, few observers of the urban scene would venture such a hypothesis. Instead, the higher city expenditures are usually attributed to one or more of the following: services rendered to suburban commuters; public goods enjoyed by the entire metropolitan community but provided and paid for by the central city; redistributive services provided to the urban poor who are concentrated in the central city; cost of ameliorating some of the social diseconomies caused by the clustering of the urban poor; and most recently, waste. Whatever the source of the higher expenditures, however, from the standpoint of the middle- and upper-income family, the added expenditures are nonproductive. Hence, for such groups the tax sur-

TABLE 10.3. Property Tax Base and Own Source Revenues for Central Cities and Suburbs in Select Metropolitan Areas

City	Market Value of Taxable Property per Capita* 1971				1961				Local Revenues per Capita** 1970			
	CC (1)	OCC (2)	SMSA (3)	(3)÷(1) (4)	CC (5)	OCC (6)	SMSA (7)	(7)÷(5) (8)	CC (9)	OCC (10)	SMSA (11)	(11)÷(9) (12)
New York	10,459	16,157	12,271	1.17	6,801	7,128	6,891	1.01	493	402	464	.94
Chicago	11,150	13,189	12,205	1.09	8,046	8,247	8,133	1.01	281	303	292	1.04
Philadelphia	5,363	9,019	7,540	1.40	3,255	3,666	3,477	1.07	321	232	268	.83
Baltimore	5,889	11,701	9,160	1.55	4,022	5,683	4,801	1.19	286	240	260	.91
Cleveland	11,893	14,389	13,482	1.13	9,226	9,867	9,573	1.04	376	299	327	.87
St. Louis	9,173	10,548	10,186	1.11	5,920	6,701	6,422	1.08	375	210	253	.67
Pittsburgh	6,182	6,674	6,572	1.06	5,021	4,534	4,656	.92	315	205	229	.73
Buffalo	7,856	7,247	7,456	.95	7,024	5,338	6,025	.86	289	293	292	1.01
Cincinnati	10,732	11,043	10,941	1.02	7,700	6,783	7,153	.92	475	177	274	.58
Newark	4,634	12,378	10,787	2.32	3,953	5,773	5,336	1.35	421	331	350	.83
Washington, D.C.	12,371	13,666	13,323	1.08	7,048	7,361	7,246	1.03	594	296	375	.63
Milwaukee	9,527	13,168	11,308	1.19	5,304	6,556	5,699	1.07	371	239	306	.82
Boston	8,058	8,928	8,763	1.09	5,483	5,274	5,321	.97	443	299	333	.77
Kansas City	11,555	12,682	12,226	1.06	7,949	6,674	7,229	.91	347	213	285	.82
Atlanta	14,547	12,259	13,078	.90	8,117	3,849	5,978	.74	318	196	240	.75
Rochester	9,955	9,002	9,322	.93	....	....	....		359	283	309	.86
Providence	8,665	9,218	9,089	1.05	....	....	....		236	181	192	.81
Akron	11,838	13,898	13,063	1.10	....	....	....		298	200	240	.81
Louisville	9,695	9,064	9,341	.96	5,752	6,414	6,058	1.05	302	186	237	.78
New Orleans	8,842	11,391	9,945	1.12	5,176	3,406	4,630	.89	228	162	199	.87

* SOURCE: Compiled from information in U.S. Bureau of Census, *Taxable Property Values,* 1972 and 1962.

** SOURCE: U.S. Advisory Commission on Intergovernmental Relations, *City Financial Emergencies.* (Washington, D.C., 1973)

charge for higher city public expenditures must be added to that arising
from tax base considerations. Not uncommonly, a city-suburban tax rate
disparity of 70 percent emerges.[5] This growing disparity is the essence of
the central-city fiscal crisis.

Although the evidence provided above makes it clear that, relative to
their suburbs, the economic fortunes of most central cities have been
declining, it is not the case that the problem is equally severe in all areas.
This is shown by table 10.4, which presents an index of "Central-City
Hardship" for fifty-five large SMSAs. The index, developed by Nathan and
Adams (1976), attempts to measure the comparative economic disadvantage of central cities vis-a-vis their suburbs. Specifically, it is a composite
of various measures of city-suburban economic disparities.[6]

Because it is sensitive to the choice of underlying economic indicators,
the specific ranking shown in table 10.4 should be viewed only as suggestive. Nevertheless, two features of the table are quite robust: (1) the wide
variation in conditions between metropolitan areas; (2) the concentration
of economically weak central cities in the old industrial North. The former
property indicates that the solution to central-city fiscal problems should
not take the form of help per se to cities but should be selectively targeted.
The second characteristic suggests that much of the problem may be due
to the inflexible geographic boundaries that characterize older Northern
cities. The importance of each of these considerations will become apparent
in the discussion to follow.

TABLE 10.4. Central City Hardship Index, 1970

City		City		City	
Newark	422	Columbus, Ohio	173	Toledo	116
Cleveland	331	Miami	172	Tampa	107
Hartford	317	New Orleans	168	Los Angeles	105
Baltimore	256	Louisville	165	San Francisco	105
Chicago	245	Akron	152	Syracuse	103
St. Louis	231	Kansas City, Mo.	152	Allentown	100
Atlanta	226	Springfield, Mass.	152	Portland, Ore.	100
Rochester	215	Ft. Worth	149	Omaha	98
Gary	213	Cincinnati	148	Dallas	97
Dayton	211	Pittsburgh	146	Houston	93
New York	211	Denver	143	Phoenix	85
Detroit	210	Sacramento	135	Norfolk	82
Richmond	209	Minneapolis	131	Salt Lake City	80
Philadelphia	205	Birmingham	131	San Diego	77
Boston	198	Jersey City	129	Seattle	67
Milwaukee	195	Oklahoma City	128	Ft. Lauderdale	64
Buffalo	189	Indianapolis	124	Greensboro, N.C.	43
San Jose	181	Providence	121		
Youngstown	180	Grand Rapids	119		

SOURCE: Adams and Nathan (1976).

2. SOURCES OF CENTRAL-CITY FISCAL DIFFICULTIES

A survey of the literature in urban public finance would reveal a plethora of "explanations" for the central-city fiscal crisis.[7] At the risk of over-simplification, however, most arguments can be classified under one or both of two broad hypotheses:

1. It is a by-product of and perhaps a contributor to the process of urban decentralization.

2. It is the consequence of excessive expenditures by central-city governments.

Apart from differences in underlying mechanism, what clearly distinguishes the two hypotheses is the locus of responsibility for the condition itself. In one case, the city government is the unfortunate victim of circumstance; in the other, the city is directly responsible for its own plight. Such a distinction has obvious implications for remedial action.

The Decentralization Hypothesis

According to the first hypothesis, the fiscal difficulties of central cities can be traced to the interaction of relatively fixed political boundaries with the powerful forces of population growth, urbanization, and urban decentralization. Together with natural population increase, the process of rural to urban migration led to the "filling up" of the central core of urban areas, requiring subsequent growth to spill outside the central-city jurisdiction. At the same time, powerful forces were at work decentralizing economic activity within urban areas.[8] Given fixed central-city boundaries, decentralization resulted in a declining city *share* of urban population and private sector employment and in many instances caused an absolute *decline* in these magnitudes.

Such a reduction in numbers would be of little *fiscal* consequence if city government revenues and expenditures were affected equally. Although definitive evidence has yet to be produced, it is widely believed that most business enterprises contribute more to the local government treasury than they withdraw in public service costs.[9] This is to be expected because business firms often impose costs upon a community that are not reflected in budgetary outlay. In effect, the fiscal "profits" serve as compensation for environmental and related costs associated with business activity. Without such compensation the community has incentives to "zone out" business firms.[10] The suburbanization of population also has adverse fiscal consequences for the central city principally because it has been largely confined to middle- and upper-income groups.[11] Because local government taxes are assessed on bases that are positively correlated with income, city government revenues decreased faster than did population.

On the expenditure side, the best available evidence suggests that most local public service costs are proportional to the user population.[12] However, this does not necessarily imply that expenditures will fall as fast as central-city population will. Some public services are designed to serve the entire metropolitan area (e.g., museums, zoos, central libraries, etc.). Moreover, the immigration of the rural poor actually increases the need for redistributive city public services.[13] Hence, the cost of central-city public services will fall at a rate slower than that of population.

The process of decentralization increases fiscal disparities between city and suburbs, making the tax-price of public services higher in the central city than in the suburbs. Hence, businesses and households have a fiscal incentive to relocate to the suburbs. Because taxes rise with income, the incentive is greatest for households in upper-income brackets. By similar reasoning, it is in the interest of suburban communities to see to it that relocation is confined to higher-income groups. Fiscal considerations are therefore seen to be operative on both the supply and the demand sides of the urban housing market.[14]

Whether this process will continue depends critically on the sensitivity of locational decisions to fiscal cost differentials. Although the empirical evidence on this point is quite incomplete, the weight of what there is appears to be on the side of those who would deemphasize fiscal considerations.[15] Nevertheless, even though fiscal factors may not have played a major role in past relocations to the suburbs, they may prove to be a force to be reckoned with in the future. If decentralization continues unabated in the immediate future, as most experts would predict, fiscal incentives for relocation will increase accordingly.

The Over-Expenditure Hypothesis

A number of factors may have combined to produce excessive expenditures by central-city governments. One, which may have had particular applicability to New York City, was the existence of substantial site rents for central-city locations. As an alternative to outright confiscation, which raises serious political and legal questions, property tax financed public services constitute a more acceptable means of making central-city site rents more widely available to city residents. In recent years, improvements in transportation and communication technology have seriously eroded central-city locational advantages. High levels of city public services can now be sustained only by onerous tax burdens on business and upper-income residents. The alternative, expenditure reduction, is vigorously opposed by those who benefit from public services but contribute little toward their cost—e.g., low-income households and households with particular characteristics, such as having children of school age. Hence the fiscal crisis of city governments emerged with the disappearance of central-city locational rents.[16]

An alternative but not necessarily inconsistent version of the over-expenditure thesis places the major share of the blame upon excessive compensation of public employees. Exponents of this view point to the rapid growth of public employee compensation during the past two decades along with recent evidence that government wage levels stand above those for comparable positions in the private sector.[17, 18] To a large extent, this favorable performance of government wages has been attributable to the unionization of public employees that occurred at a rapid pace during the period.

The ability of unions to extract higher wages may be substantially greater in the public than in the private sector, because many public services are demanded inelastically, owing to the "essential" nature of the service.[19] Moreover, public employees, because they are also constituents, can invoke a "political" demand for their services.[20] In a recent study, Hamermesh (1974) estimated that public employee unions may have rased municipal expenditure by approximately 12 percent in 1966.

Not only do central cities appear to be more susceptible to unionization, but their unions appear to be more effective than their suburban counterparts. Suburban communities tend to be more closely substitutable for each other than for the central city. In other words, competition among suburbs curbs union power in such jurisdictions. This is evidenced by central-city wages standing 11 percent above the average for their metropolitan area in large SMSAs during 1975.[21] Furthermore, evidence from the Bureau of Labor Statistics shows that public employee wages in large central cities exceed those of the private sector as well as of the federal government.[22] However, the most fiscally damaging effect of unions may not be to raise wage levels; it may be to raise employment levels above the optimum. In a declining environment, public employee unions may be a powerful check on reductions in force warranted by the declining clientele for central-city services. For a sample of declining cities examined by Peterson (1975), public employment per capita rose by 41 percent during 1964–73, despite a 10 percent decline in population in the same cities.

Other versions of the overexpenditure argument have been advanced. Some economists, such as Netzer (1977), suggest that a large part of the problem is poor management and its accompanying low worker productivity. Peterson (1976), on the other hand, is among those who argue that the blame rests with the "Great Society" programs of the sixties. Such programs raised the public service expectations of the city poor, but federal financial support of the programs was short-lived, placing responsibility for their continuation on already financially strapped central cities.

To recapitulate, two major sources of central city fiscal problems have been identified: (1) decentralization of urban areas; (2) excess expenditure. Although each has its distinctive flavor and have obviously different implications for policy, they share a number of characteristics. The forces that promoted decentralization in the first model reduce central-city land rent in the second. More importantly, the result of excessive city wages or public services will give rise to a city-suburban fiscal disparity similar to that discussed in the first model. Hence, fiscal incentives to relocate to the suburbs will exist in both models. From a locational standpoint, it matters little to business firms and upper-income groups whether their city taxes are used to support the services of poor city households (model 1) or the higher wages of city government workers (model 2). What matters is that such redistributive burdens can be avoided by locating in suburban communities. In a meaningful sense, therefore, the *consequences* of central-city fiscal problems are independent of their source.

3. CONSEQUENCES OF CENTRAL-CITY FINANCIAL PROBLEMS

Simply because some central cities are confronted with severe financial difficulty is not sufficient ground for intervention by higher governmental authorities.

Fiscal Collapse

One potential problem is the complete financial collapse of certain central cities. To the extent that such a collapse is accompanied by a prolonged breakdown of public service delivery in the central core of the urban area, the social cost will be staggering. Intervention by higher levels of government is clearly indicated and would undoubtedly be forthcoming. Happily, however, total collapse is not a serious prospect for even the most seriously pressed central cities. At worst, such cities might default on some of their outstanding debt. Here the immediate problem is one of deciding which creditors to pay and not one of sustaining vital city services. Therefore, the appropriateness of external assistance should be largely independent of the technical act of default and should hinge instead upon factors that underlie the fiscal problem.

There is one exception to this dictum. If the default by one city threatens the financial integrity of other cities, one could justify federal intervention on "externality" and "free-rider" grounds. However, only a very few large cities have made extensive use of short-term debt and thus are highly vulnerable to serious risk of default. It seems highly improbable, therefore, that the financial community will be stampeded into a liquidity drain on other cities should one city default.

Misallocation of Regional Public Goods

Poor central-city fiscal health may aggravate problems of resource misallocation that arise from central-city provision of metropolitan-wide public goods. Such goods can be simultaneously enjoyed by all residents of the urban community. As a first approximation, therefore, the optimal level of such goods is independent of the distribution of population between city and suburbs. However, the willingness and ability of the central city to provide such services is reduced by migration from city to suburbs. Willingness is reduced because only those benefits that accrue to city residents are relevant to the decision process. Ability is reduced to the extent that the *per-capita* city resource base is adversely affected by outmigration from the city. Moreover, willingness and ability are reduced if the cost of public goods is artificially inflated by union power or mismanagement. Thus, whether poor central-city fiscal health is due to decentralization or to excessive spending, it will lead to the underprovision of metropolitan-wide public goods.[23]

Inefficient Locational Decisions

A second source of resource misallocation arises from the interaction of locational choice and fiscal disparity. To the extent that upper-income groups and business firms relocate to the suburbs in order to avoid high central-city taxes or inferior city public services, resources become spatially misallocated. The migrant taxpayer enjoys a reduction in taxes and an increase in transportation costs, with the former clearly outweighing the latter. However, the fiscal savings to the migrant unit is exactly offset by a loss to remaining city taxpayers. The net result, then, is an increase in total transportation costs—which is a social waste.[24]

Fiscally induced migration may also give rise to another source of inefficiency. It is often alleged that perverse peer-group effects result from an increased concentration of poor households within the central city. Examples of such effects include increased crime rate, proliferation of slum housing, and decreased scholastic achievement. Since fiscally induced migration can be expected to be selectively concentrated among above-average-income households, peer-group diseconomies must be considered to be one of its costs.[25] Unfortunately, little is known about the magnitude of peer-group costs, even though persuasive evidence of their presence exists in the literature.[26]

Inequitable Fiscal Relations

The principal source of dissatisfaction with present central-city fiscal conditions may not be related to economic efficiency but rather to considerations of equity. As a first approximation, the cost of the local public services consumed by poor households can be assumed to be borne by the middle- and upper-income residents of the jurisdiction in which the poor reside. Obviously, such redistributive costs are greatest in those communities in which the concentration of poor is highest—namely, the central city in most urban areas. Since all urban residents benefit from the reception of public services by the poor, equity would require a household's redistributive burden to be independent of the community in which it resides.

A similar argument is often made with respect to central-city public services rendered to suburban commuters and shoppers. However, the magnitude of the net cost of such services may be substantially exaggerated. Neenan (1972) found in his study of Detroit that commuters adequately compensated the city for the public services they received.

In summary, the fiscal difficulties that currently confront our central cities involve both real economic costs and inequities. Inefficiencies arise with respect to the provision of urban-area public goods and household location choices. On the equity side, there is an unfair redistributive burden on central-city residents. Policies for the alleviation or elimination of current city fiscal ills should be judged in terms of their ability to deal with these undesirable consequences of current arrangements as well as their success in avoiding new inefficiencies or inequities.

Capitalization of Fiscal Cost Differentials

Before turning to a discussion of policy alternatives it is necessary to digress briefly and consider a potential flaw in the argument. So far, we have tacitly assumed that city-suburban fiscal disparities are reflected in actual cost differences as perceived by a household. In the Ricardian tradition, however, one could argue that all fiscal differentials will be offset by rent differentials.[27] Hence, high city taxes would be capitalized into land values. In this case, inequities cannot be said to exist because the inferior fiscal climate of the central city is completely offset by lower site value rents. Whatever burden was created by high city taxes fell completely upon the landowner at the time that the tax increase was anticipated.

Although this may itself constitute an inequity, it is of limited policy significance because it would be extremely difficult if not impossible to ameliorate; i.e., the current set of landowners will generally not coincide with the historical set. More important for our own purposes, existing fiscal disparities do not create an equity concern if complete capitalization occurs.

Moreover, there would be no basis for concern about nonneutralities in locational choice. Since they are completely offset by land value adjustments, fiscal disparities can have no effect on locational choice.[28]

Although the capitalization hypothesis has considerable appeal and may explain depressed central-city property values, its underlying assumptions are at variance with the situation under discussion. It is well known, for example, that if land is not of uniform quality but varies, say with distance to the Central Business District (CBD), tax differentials are not fully reflected in land value and will thus have real allocation effects.[29] More important for our purposes, even if land in the central city were of uniform quality, complete capitalization would not occur. For fiscal cost differentials are a positive function of household income. Thus, land value cannot reflect fiscal cost differentials for *all* income classes. Instead, land value will adjust to the fiscal differential of a marginal buyer of land.[30] Those with income above that level will still suffer some redistributive burden of city taxation. Moreover, the income level of a "marginal" buyer is apt to be quite low. As Hamilton (1976) has pointed out, those with low income can outbid those with higher income for sites in communities that are heterogeneous with respect to income. Such bids are of no consequence in suburban communities, because of exclusionary zoning. However, they may serve as a floor on central-city property value, thereby negating capitalization for anyone with above-average income.

Thus, the case for capitalization cannot be made on a priori grounds. The question must be resolved empirically. Unfortunately, definitive evidence is lacking for this important issue.[31] Until such evidence is forthcoming, the burden of proof would appear to be upon those who advocate the capitalization hypothesis.

4. POLICIES TO COPE WITH OVEREXPENDITURE

If central-city fiscal problems are primarily the result of mismanagement, waste, or union power, the appropriate course of action is obvious—eliminate the excess expenditure. Unfortunately, this is easier said than done. The difficulty of measuring the output of government services precludes the construction of valid productivity measures on which the expenditure cutbacks must be based. Furthermore, even if the particular source of inefficiency could be identified, resolution of the problem is by no means assured. For example, if excess employee compensation is found to be the culprit, powerful unions or binding prior arrangements (e.g., pensions) may preclude the lowering of wages or fringe benefits. The situation is made even worse if unions believe that external relief is forthcoming. To provide fiscally pressed cities with external financial assistance may be tantamount to an invitation for further waste. Elsewhere in this volume,

Inman has estimated that as much as 80 percent of an increase in grants-in-aid to large cities may find its way into public employee wages. If this result is valid, external aid would only increase wasteful expenditure and have little effect upon the underlying problem.

The preceding considerations suggest that, should the problem be one of overexpenditure, the best course of action is to confront city and union officials with the consequences of their actions—persistent and severe budget crises. By withholding external relief or making relief conditional on the adoption of austerity measures, powerful pressure is applied. New York's experience is proof that a tough approach can successfully produce sharp budget cuts. Such a policy carries considerable risk of serious disruption in the delivery of local public services in some cities.

Evidence that the fiscal ills of central cities may be due to overspending usually takes the form of per-capita expenditure comparisons. At the simplest level of sophistication, expenditures of fiscally weak cities can be compared with those of an average local government. Netzer (1977) found that municipal outlay in eleven "mature" cities exceeded the national average for local governments by roughly two-thirds. As Netzer himself recognized, however, this may have little to do with the overspending hypothesis. Table 10.5 shows that per-capita municipal expenditures rise relentlessly with city size. Since all of Netzer's cities fell into the two highest size classes, higher expenditure could be due simply to population size. This can be taken as evidence of spending excess only if one is willing to hypothesize that *per-capita* overexpenditure is primarily a function of population size. Another possibility, at least as plausible, are scale diseconomies that arise from the need for increased remedial public services (e.g., those due to congestion) as city size increases. Alternatively, since the central-city share of population declines over a broad range of city sizes, the higher expenditure could be due to Margolis' (1961) well-known "municipal overburden" hypothesis—i.e., the tendency of central-city expenditure to rise as its share of the SMSA population falls. In short, to

TABLE 10.5. Municipal Expenditures by City Size, 1975

Population Size	General Expenditure per Capita
<50,000	209.78
50,000– 99,999	313.56
100,000–199,999	404.01
200,000–299,999	451.05
300,000–499,999	485.83
500,000–999,999	605.65
>1,000,000	995.03

SOURCE: Bureau of the Census, *City Government Finances in 1975–76* (Washington, D.C.: Government Printing Office, September, 1977).

demonstrate that expenditure levels of fiscally distressed cities exceed those for the average municipality is unpersuasive evidence of overspending.

Perhaps the most convincing evidence to date for the overspending hypothesis has been produced by Peterson and Mueller. Peterson (1976) found that large declining cities spend roughly 65 percent more per citizen on common functions than large growing cities. Mueller (1975), examining a similar set of cities, arrived at a similar conclusion with respect to public employees per capita. He also found that the wages of public employees were higher in declining than in growing cities.

Because the comparison is restricted to large cities, size cannot explain the spending differential. Furthermore, since the declining city category is composed almost exclusively of fiscally distressed cities and the growing category consists of financially healthy cities, one is tempted to place the blame for poor fiscal health upon the sharply higher expenditures of declining cities.[32]

If there were no other differences between declining and growing cities, this conclusion would be difficult to reject. Closer inspection of the data, however, reveals that they differ in another important respect. The proportion of the metropolitan population residing within city boundaries in declining cities is double that in growing cities. As indicated above, city per-capita expenditure rises as its share of the urban population falls. Such a relationship is often explained in terms of greater *relative* costs of servicing commuters and providing area-wide public goods. Perhaps as important, however, is that the city's share of low-density suburbs declines with its population. Now suburbs spend considerably less per capita for public services than do central cities.[33] This partly reflects factors already mentioned—commuter costs and metropolitan-wide public goods—but it also reflects the reduced need for services related to high density and concentrations of poverty.

For these reasons, then, the expenditure differential between growing and declining cities should be normalized for the effect of varying city population share. This can be done by aggregating public expenditures by all local governments in an SMSA. Such a measure is not only invariant to the city share of population but is also independent of the structure of local government. Hence, it is possible to widen the range of comparison from common functions to all functions. In table 10.6, per-capita total expenditure and employment are shown for metropolitan areas with declining and growing central cities. For comparative purposes, Peterson's findings for cities alone are also shown.

The table reveals that differentials are sharply reduced if the comparison is made between all local governments instead of central-city governments alone. For per-capita expenditure, the differential is reduced from 67 percent to 19 percent; for per-capita employment, it disappears altogether. If Honolulu, where the state pays the full cost of primary and secondary

TABLE 10.6. Fiscal Characteristics of Local Governments in Large U.S. Cities and SMSAs

Characteristics	(1) Large Growing Cities	(2) Large Cities Growing in Population 1960–70, Now Declining	(3) Large Declining Cities	(4) $(3) \div (1)$
Municipal Expenditures per capita, Common Functions, 1973[a]	$152	$195	$264	1.67
Direct General Expenditures per capita (all local governments), 1975[b]	$607 ($634)	$773	$726	1.19
Municipal Workers per 1,000 Residents, Common Functions, 1973[a]	8.7	10.5	13.0	1.49
Government Workers per 1,000 Residents (all local governments), 1975[c]	34.9	38.1	34.8	1.00
Central City Share of SMSA[d] Population, 1974	67.3%	40.9%	33.8%	...

[a] Figures taken from George E. Peterson, "Finance," in *The Urban Predicament,* ed. Gorham and Glazer (Urban Institute: Washington, D.C., 1976), p. 48.

[b] SOURCE: U.S. Bureau of Census, *Local Government Finances in Selected Metropolitan Areas and Large Counties: 1974–75.*

[c] SOURCE: U.S. Bureau of Census, *Local Government Employment in Selected Metropolitan Areas and Large Counties: 1974–75.*

[d] SOURCE: U.S. Bureau of Census, *City Government Finances in 1974–75,* and [b] above.

education, is excluded from the group of growing cities, the expenditure differential falls to 15 percent. Moreover, if differences in private sector wage levels are considered, two-thirds of the remainder of the differential is accounted for.[34] Thus, we are able to account for all but 5 percent of Peterson's expenditure differential. It appears that if excess expenditure is indeed the source of central-city fiscal difficulty it will have to be shown in some other way.

As was argued above, one possibility is that excessive expenditure is characteristic of all large cities, whatever their fiscal condition. Differences in fiscal health among cities would primarily reflect differences on the revenue side of the budget. Although the hypothesis that all large cities overspend is difficult to establish by comparison of aggregate expenditure, it receives some support from an examination of public sector wages. Ehrenberg and Goldstein (1975) found evidence that wages tend to be higher in large cities even if differences in private sector wages are taken into account. Similarly, studies by Field and Keller (1976) and Perloff (1971) show that, in large cities, public employee wages exceed those in the private sector. In addition, Inman found that 80 percent of increases in grants may be absorbed by higher wages in large cities.[35] All of these results suggest that there may be some validity to the overspending hypothesis in large cities.

Nevertheless, the evidence is far too weak at this point to warrant as harsh and potentially disruptive a policy as would be warranted by the overspending hypothesis. For example, in the Field and Keller (1976) study, wages were shown to be higher in only fourteen of the twenty-four cities studied. Moreover, Inman's results are extremely sensitive to the elasticity of city government expenditures with respect to exogenous grants-in-aid. If other empirically derived values of this parameter were substituted, the estimate of the wage effects of grants would fall to zero. Finally and most importantly, wage differentials of the size that have been estimated would appear to be too small to cause a *major* fiscal problem. Even if wage differentials are as high as 10 percent—a higher figure than those typical in Field and Keller (1976)—*total expenditure* would be increased by only 5 percent—a figure that would hardly seem to warrant a crisis.[36]

The latter consideration prompts speculation that overspending by large cities, to the extent that it exists, is more likely to be found in *employment* levels as opposed to *wage* levels. Excessive employment could arise from low worker productivity or public services that have dubious social value. In either event, the excess would probably show up in terms of abnormally high employment levels for particular categories of public expenditure. Research into this issue would involve the development of expenditure or employment norms for particular public services. This task may prove difficult because of the problem in measuring public-service output. Nevertheless, it would be extremely useful to identify expenditure categories for which a particular jurisdiction deviates significantly from the norm. Such information would enable efforts for measuring output to be focused as well as raising the question as to whether the abnormal expenditure (whether due to waste or higher service levels) is justified.

5. POLICIES TO COPE WITH DECENTRALIZATION-INDUCED FISCAL ILLS

If the city fiscal problem is not primarily due to overexpenditure, some form of external relief may be warranted to ameliorate or mitigate the adverse efficiency and equity consequences of poor central-city financial health. As a matter of general strategy, policies should be directed toward the reduction of the fiscal disparity that currently exists between central city and suburbs. It is precisely that disparity that gives rise to the locational distortion and intrametropolitan difference in redistributive burden. Because the spectrum of policy options is so wide, a convention is needed to keep the discussion to manageable length. Ours will be to focus upon those alternatives that have received the greatest attention in the policy literature. Only at the very end of the discussion will new departures be considered.

Replace the Property Tax with an Income Tax

One way of reducing fiscal disparity between city and suburbs is to reform the central-city revenue system in such a way as to place a larger share of the city tax burden upon suburban residents. This amounts to finding a substitute for the property tax, since central cities rely most heavily on this instrument for locally raised revenue. The most obvious alternative is a city income tax.

An income tax will be most effective in reaching suburban residents if it applies to all income earned within the city as well as upon income of residents wherever earned. Essentially, this enables the central city to tax the income of suburban commuters. Such an approach also has dynamic advantages in situations of out-migration. A city would lose the tax proceeds from a migratory household only if the unit also changed its location of work. Similarly, if a firm relocated to the suburbs, the city would continue to enjoy tax receipts as long as workers continued to reside within the city.

It is not enough, however, to demonstrate that the income tax can be "exported" to suburban residents. It is also necessary to show that it is exported to a greater degree than the property tax. This may be difficult because the property tax is widely believed to be substantially exported.[37] One mechanism for tax exporting is the federal income tax. Because of its deductibility, the property tax can be viewed as being shared with all other residents of the nation.[38] However, deductibility is not restricted to the property tax—it extends to local income taxes as well. Hence, it is not relevant to the choice of tax instruments.[39]

If property taxes upon nonresidential property are shifted forward in the form of higher sales prices, there results another mechanism for exporting property taxes. This is because a large fraction of business sales are to non-city residents. Even if shifted backwards, however, business property taxes will be heavily borne by non-city residents, either as commuters or as absentee shareholders and landlords. Since nonresidential property accounts for approximately one-half the total property tax base, it is clear that exportation of property taxes can be substantial. Thus, the advantage of income taxes in reaching nonresidents may be more apparent than real.

From the standpoint of the state government, which must ultimately approve a city income tax, the relevant magnitude is the fraction that can be exported to out-of-state residents. Unless the city is located near the state border, exportation of the income tax is likely to be minimal. Moreover, when the city is near a border, adoption of a city income tax may invite retaliation.

Thus, tax exporting considerations may actually provide grounds for preferring the property tax to the income tax. The city may have little to gain by switching to the income tax, whereas the state may have a considerable amount to lose. Of course, all of this depends upon the validity of the shifting assumptions for the nonresidential property tax. Such assumptions might appear to be inconsistent with the "new view" of the property tax, which argues that only tax *differentials* can be shifted.[40] However, they are perfectly consistent. From the standpoint of the city and state, the full amount of property tax will have excise effects—the appropriate base is those prices that would prevail in the absence of the tax.

Before leaving this topic, one caveat is in order. Central-city property tax rates may now be so high as to obviate exportation of further increases in tax rate. In other words, the elasticity of the central-city tax base may be sufficiently high to preclude further exportation. It may be that, at the margin, other revenue sources may be more effectively exported.

Increased Application of User Charges

User charges are generally discussed in terms of improving the efficiency to which public services or the environment are utilized. They are seldom analyzed from the point of view of reducing city-suburban fiscal disparity. This lack of emphasis may reflect the belief that the revenue potential of user charges is modest and much too insignificant relative to the fiscal difficulties of central cities. Yet user charges, in 1975, comprised 20 percent of own source general revenue for cities with more than 50,000 inhabitants.[41] If we include receipts of city-owned utilities, the figure goes much higher. Thus what may be true of user charge revenue from only one activity is definitely not true for all activities taken together.

To be successful in reducing fiscal disparity, a user charge must be collected from nonresidents, preferably from those who reside in the suburbs. Thus our attention should focus upon those public services whose clientele is composed of a significant number of nonresidents. This would seem to characterize three major categories: (1) cultural and recreational facilities; (2) transportation services; (3) water and sewer services.

Under the first category are city libraries, museums, zoos, civic centers, etc. Each of these services is amenable to user charges. However, each of these services is like a pure public good in the relevant range; hence, user charges will introduce deadweight efficiency losses. Furthermore, use by poor households is apt to be quite sensitive to price. The effect of the user fee, then, may be to remove the services from those who can least afford them and who can perhaps most productively utilize them. In principle, the latter effect can be avoided by the issuance of identity cards or vouchers to poor families. However, given the limited revenue potential of such charges, this may raise collection costs to prohibitive levels.

The second area—transportation—has long been thought to need user charges to promote economic efficiency. To date, however, virtually no action has been taken to rationalize the city transportation system through user charges. This is unfortunate; the revenue yield of an efficient system of highway tolls would be substantial and a good deal of the revenue would be derived from commuters. Hence, it would be an excellent vehicle for reducing city-suburban fiscal disparity. However, the transportation toll increases the cost of travel in the city to at least a subset of travelers. Only if the proceeds of such a toll are employed to reduce transportation cost can these travelers be said to gain from the toll. If not, they have an incentive to conduct business elsewhere. If so, such revenues are not available for reducing fiscal disparity. To the extent that this group is significant, therefore, the effectiveness of highway user charges to directly reduce fiscal disparities is reduced.

In most metropolitan areas water and sewer services are provided by a single authority. If the city has control over this authority, it may have an excellent tool with which to reduce fiscal disparity. Because of scale economies, provision of water and sewer services is a natural monopoly.[42] This monopoly power could be used to extract additional revenue from suburban residents. Even if discriminatory rates are prohibited the city could price the system to produce a profit that could be used for general expenditures. Such action is not without precedent. In the aggregate, city water revenue exceeded current costs and debt services by $229 million in 1975.[43]

One might object to the use of water charges to generate general revenue because of the efficiency loss from setting price above marginal cost. However, this objection is based on the premise that current prices actually reflect marginal cost. More likely, current prices reflect the original cost of water and sewer systems that is, for most mature cities, far below replacement value. A substantial price increase may be in order simply to achieve marginal cost pricing. Since the demand for water and sewer services is relatively low, the excess burden resulting from greater-than-marginal cost prices is apt to be quite modest, particularly compared to the efficiency cost of poor city fiscal health.

Restructuring of Local Government

Metropolitan government is often advocated as the appropriate response to the fiscal ills of mature cities. The tax base of surrounding suburban jurisdictions is larger in per-capita terms and outlays for public services are lower than in the central city. Since the typical mature city (see table 10.3) has a per-capita resource base that is 15 to 20 percent lower and per capita own-financed outlays that are 20 percent higher than the metropolitan average, the central-city resident could enjoy a tax-burden reduction of roughly one-third from consolidation.[44]

Metropolitan government, almost by definition, would eliminate most of the fiscal difficulty that confronts mature central cities. With only one jurisdiction, fiscal disparity cannot exist, nor can inequities arising from differential redistributive burdens. Furthermore, since all of those who benefit from area-wide public goods are included in the decision-making jurisdiction, there is no longer a prima facie expectation that such goods would be underprovided.

Why then has metropolitan government been adopted in so few cases, particularly in the industrial north? For one thing, there is considerable suburban opposition to such a charge. Just as the city taxpayer could expect some relief, the typical suburban resident could expect a tax increase to accompany consolidation. In many situations this increase could amount to at least 25 percent.

Somewhat surprisingly, there is often considerable central-city opposition to consolidation. Such opposition usually reflects concern that a metropolitan government would not be as responsive to the needs of city residents. These fears may not be without foundation. If the budgets of areas with metropolitan government (usually located in the "sunbelt") are examined, one finds that public services are at substantially lower levels than in urban areas with mature central cities.[45] This occurs despite the often higher percentage of poor residents in the former areas. Thus, the poor in "healthy" sunbelt cities may be worse off than those in declining northern cities.

Centralization of public services can be expected to be accompanied by uniformity of provision.[46] However, the appropriate level of public services may be markedly different in the inner city than in the suburban ring. For example, trash pickup should probably be more frequent in the inner city because of its greater density and relative lack of storage facilities. Similarly, the need for fire protection is apt to be considerably greater in older, central-city neighborhoods than in the suburbs. Therefore, it is probable that a uniform provision of services throughout the metropolitan area would be extremely wasteful.[47] Although there is no legal requirement that services be provided in such a fashion, casual empiricism suggests that uniformity accompanies centralization.

One might object to the preceding argument on the grounds that there is absolutely no basis for believing that *existing* governmental structure is optimal. Indeed, in most mature cities, existing boundaries are more likely to reflect historical accident than an attempt at optimization. A strong case can be made that existing cities are too large for the efficient provision of the services they now provide. The needs of affluent city suburban neighborhoods are apt to be quite different from those of poor slum neighborhoods. Whether there would be a net loss in efficiency from further consolidation cannot be established on a priori grounds. The resultant pattern of government services will probably fit more closely the needs of some city residents and less closely those of some suburban residents. Furthermore, a metropolitan government could be expected to outperform the present system with regard to the provision of area-wide public goods. Therefore, only by careful empirical work can the relative efficiency of metropolitan government be settled. In the political arena, however, most observers would agree that the issue has been settled.

Metropolitan Base Sharing

Some of the difficulties of metropolitan government can be avoided if consolidation is restricted to the revenue side of the budget. Existing local jurisdictions would retain their identity, thus maintaining existing responsiveness to citizen needs and also avoiding the bureaucratic cost that is alleged to accompany increased governmental size. An example of such an approach is "base sharing." Under this arrangement, a portion (or all) of each jurisdiction's property tax base is assigned to a pool that is then shared by every jurisdiction in the metropolitan area.[48] The bases for sharing can vary, but one popular version is to guarantee each jurisdiction equal per-capita receipts for any particular tax rate. In effect, such a program would eliminate disparities in per-capita tax base. In terms of table 10.3, the central-city tax base would shift from column (1) to column (3), assuming total sharing.

Each community would be free to set its own tax rate and hence its own level of expenditure. For the typical city shown in table 10.3, the city resident would be afforded tax relief of approximately 20 percent if current expenditures were sustained. This not only narrows incentives for relocation but also induces the central city to spend more on area-wide public goods. With a larger tax base, the tax price of such services is reduced. Thus, base sharing would favorably impact on each of the three problems now associated with poor central-city fiscal health.

Nevertheless, tax-base sharing is not without its limitations. The tax price for *all* government services is reduced, not simply those that are pure public goods. Hence, we may observe an unwarranted expansion of other city services.[49] Much more serious, however, are the perverse signals provided by tax-base sharing. Under the arrangement, few communities will find it profitable to permit the location of commerce and industry within their borders. This reflects the fact that a community's costs, governmental and environmental, rise with the addition of industry, whereas its tax receipts are imperceptibly changed. In other words, base sharing eliminates the benefits to a community from the entry of new business activities without eliminating the associated costs. Such communities would no doubt respond by zoning out new business activity in an attempt to pass on the costs to its neighbors. The consequences for regional development are potentially disastrous. Thus, complete base sharing, particularly for the property tax, is not practical if land-use controls rest at the community level. At best, urban jurisdictions can share some portion of their tax base. The appropriate portion cannot be ascertained without further research. However, it is unlikely to be more than half. Unfortunately, as the shared portion is diminished, so are benefits to city residents.

Metropolitanizing Select City Functions

If one of the adverse consequences of current fiscal arrangements is the underprovision of area-wide public goods, an obvious solution is to change the locus of responsibility from the city government to a metropolitan authority, or in some cases to a regional authority. Indeed, recent years have witnessed a proliferation of metropolitan districts.[50] To date, however, emphasis has been upon those activities with a high "bricks and mortar" content—e.g., water and sewers, bridges and tunnels, airports, etc. Relatively little has been done with respect to less capital-intensive services, such as public health, environmental control, crime laboratories, libraries, museums, etc.

Although it is true that area-wide provision of public goods will probably be more efficient, it may not always spell tax relief for central-city residents. Such would be true for water and sewer services, in which case the city might surrender a potentially powerful tool for exporting taxes to suburban residents. It would also be true if centralization of the function led to business or household relocation. For example, if the location of an airport is important to business location decisions, the choice of site under the two different institutional arrangements can be expected to vary. Thus, it would not be uncommon for the central city to vigorously oppose the regionalization of some of its activities.

State Assumption of Responsibility for Local Functions

Centralization of service responsibility need not stop at the metropolitan level; there are many who would propose shifting functions to the state level. Such action has been particularly urged for elementary and secondary education; the courts have increasingly challenged disparities in service level or tax effort that result from local provision.[51] Furthermore, some observers believe that a state takeover of education is an essential ingredient in a successful strategy for resolving the central-city fiscal problem. However, interest in state assumption of service responsibility has not been restricted to education but has included public welfare, public employee pensions, airports, and transit systems, among others.[52]

Few would quarrel with the proposition that the nonfederal share of welfare and related service costs should be borne by state government. Although such a position can be defended on equity grounds, it is most persuasively presented in terms of the categorical imperative that local government should not try to redistribute income. The ease of relocation makes such action self defeating as well as a source of deadweight efficiency loss. Although similar arguments can be made against a state redistribution policy, mobility may be considerably less among states than among localities within a state. Hence, state action can be justified in second-best terms.

In practice, the preceding logic appears to have been accepted by policymakers. With a few noticeable exceptions, the nonfederal share of welfare cost is borne almost entirely at the state level. This has had particularly favorable consequences for central cities, since they house a disproportionate share of urban poor. Whatever the method used to finance the state program, central-city residents are almost certain to gain fiscal relief. But in some states, such as California, Wisconsin, and New York, a substantial fraction of welfare cost remains at the county level. Because the countries in which central cities are located are nearly as fiscally disadvantaged, state assumption of responsibility is clearly indicated.

Agreement about state assumption of education is much less widespread. Although education outlays absorb by far the largest share of aggregate local government revenue within the central-city jurisdiction, it is by no means clear that state assumption will reduce central-city-suburban fiscal disparity. Furthermore, considerable efficiency loss can be expected to accompany a state takeover of the schools.

Reduction of fiscal disparity is in doubt because of the interplay of several key facts: (1) expenditure per pupil in the central city generally lies significantly above the state average, often exceeding the outlay in the city's own suburbs; (2) under present state and federal aid programs, the city receives above-average aid per pupil and considerably more than its suburbs; (3) the number of public school children per capita is lower in the central city than in its suburbs.

The significance of (1) is that city residents will have to contribute toward the cost of increased expenditures in other jurisdictions, particularly rural school districts. The effect of (2) is to provide greater incremental relief to noncity jurisdictions, particularly the suburbs. Finally, (3) implies that the central city would receive less *per capita* than its suburbs even if it received as much per-pupil relief (which it would not).

Each of these factors means that the central city's share of additional state outlay will fall short of its population share. On the other hand, its share of additional state taxes will be less than its population share. Since the situation is exactly reversed in the suburbs, it is not possible to determine a priori whether the city-suburban fiscal disparity would be reduced. In the author's study of the Baltimore, Maryland, metropolitan area, it appeared that these disparities would be slightly *increased*.[53]

At the same time that fiscal relief may be modest, state takeover of education may entail considerable efficiency loss. Such loss arises from the uniformity that would probably accompany centralization. The loss would be considerable because of the diversity that currently characterizes local provision. Bradford and Oates (1974) estimated the loss from state provision to be 50 percent of aggregate education outlay for New Jersey.

With the exception of welfare, identification of services that may be suitable for transfer to the state level is quite difficult. Clearly, such programs should have the property that the central city devotes a substantially greater fraction of its resources to the activity than do the suburbs. On the other hand, they should also have the property that efficiency loss from centralization should be small. The latter translates into little diversity of provision among jurisdictions. But this would appear to be contradictory to the first requirement.

The nature of the contradiction is clearly illustrated by local police protection. Per capita outlays by large central cities for police protection are considerably larger than those of their suburbs. Thus, state provision would afford considerably differential fiscal relief to the central city. However, if one considers the other consequences of centralization of police services, the case becomes less persuasive. First, local control of police services has long been thought essential to personal freedom. It is not inconceivable that certain minorities would be subject to discrimination under state-wide provision. Furthermore, charges of police brutality or complaints of insufficient security are much less likely to produce a response in the state capitol than in the local city hall. Along the same line of reasoning, the composition of police activity between, say, traffic control and crime prevention, would not tend to be as sensitive to jurisdictional differences under a centralized regime.

Although it might be argued that these difficulties could be avoided by limiting centralization to the financing of police services (maintaining local administration), substantial problems would remain. Aggregate resources for police service would still be determined centrally. More importantly, the same would be true of the allocation of local shares. Such distribution would presumably be based upon need, but there is no good single index of need. If the crime rate were to be the basis for allocation, each local jurisdiction would have a strong incentive to overstate its index. In addition, the crime rate would not reflect other needs for police services, such as traffic control.

Similar arguments could be made about the state assumption of other functions. For example, if corrections were to be solely a *state function,* the location of facilities would be plagued by the same problems faced by the old postal service. In essence, the problems that would arise from central provision are the basic reason that such activities were delegated to local government in the first place. And the local level is probably where responsibility for most currently provided local services should remain.

Financial Assistance from Higher Levels of Government

The last alternative to be considered is financial assistance from higher governmental levels to fiscally troubled cities. Such assistance could come from either the state or federal government and it could be categorical or completely unrestricted. However, it is unlikely that such assistance could be restricted only to fiscally distressed cities. For one thing, fiscal distress is a matter of degree rather than a discrete characteristic, and for another, it would be politically impractical to target aid so selectively. Hence, the assistance would probably take the form of a general program for which many local governments qualify but by which fiscally ill central cities are particularly benefited. If this latter requirement is not satisfied, the program may provide little in the form of relief to central cities since residents of central cities will be required to contribute to the finance of the program.[54]

It is clear that problems of underprovision of urban area-wide public goods can be handled by the grants mechanism. What is required is a categorical assistance program that provides for state or federal sharing of program costs. This effectively reduces the tax price to the central city, thereby inducing it to increase provision of the public good. Since the degree of underprovision will increase as the central-city population and business tax base decreases, the federal or state share should be adjusted upward over time. Furthermore, since the degree of underprovision will vary among central cities, state action would appear preferable to federal action because of the political difficulty of varying federal shares spatially.

Even if the categorical aid programs are successful in promoting efficient levels of urban public goods, the disparity problem will remain. The "income" effect of the categoricals will singly be too small to make serious inroads into city-suburban fiscal disparity. A separate program that provides unrestricted aid is necessary to satisfy this objective. In other words, a program of general assistance to "needy" governments is needed.

Before considering alternative assistance programs, it should be pointed out that economists have long been critical of programs directed to the needs of poor governments or poor regions. The objection is that if the ultimate target of the programs are the poor constituents of a government or the poor residents of a region, the objective can be best served by programs directed at poor people per se. The indirect approach will not only provide unintended benefits to nonpoor individuals but it will also distort locational choice or the mix of private versus public services. Such an argument was directed against General Revenue Sharing and, to my knowledge, has never been successfully refuted.[55]

The argument does not apply in the present case, however. Although the concentration of poor households within a central-city jurisdiction brings about the problem, the objective of general governmental assistance is not to raise the income of the poor. Instead, the aim is to neutralize the locational distortions and the redistributional inequities that the spatial concentration of poor people brings about. A program of general government aid is ideally suited for this purpose. Although the elimination of poverty would also accomplish the same objective, justification for such action must be made primarily on other grounds.

Let us turn to a discussion of the alternatives. First, consider existing programs of general purpose assistance. At the state level, such aid constitutes only 10.5 percent of all state assistance to local government. Furthermore, such aid often takes the form of sharing a tax source on the basis of origin—a formula that could hardly be considered beneficial to central cities. Hence, current state general assistance programs are much more likely to exacerbate the difficulties of central cities than to relieve them.[56]

The situation at the federal level is considerably different. The emergence of the "New Federalism" in the late sixties gave rise to a number of programs that could be considered as general assistance to local governments, including central cities. The most famous of these programs is General Revenue Sharing (GRS), enacted in 1972. Also well known is the Community Development Block Grant (CDBG), which, although restricted to community development activities, is generally considered as general aid because the scope of its potential services is so wide. Most recently, Congress has enacted a number of "countercyclical" aid programs, including: (1) an expansion of public service employment under the Comprehensive Employment and Training Act (CETA); (2) a program of accelerated public works; (3) countercyclical revenue sharing. Although (1) was purportedly restricted to new public service positions, it is widely believed that beleaguered governments are using these funds as substitutes for their own revenue.[57] Similarly, (2) has had the effect of substituting for local government capital outlay and hence serves as a form of general budgeting relief.

The aggregate impact of these programs has been startling. Table 10.7 shows that for a sample of fifteen cities, federal grants grew from only 5.2 percent of own source general revenue in 1967 to nearly 46 percent in 1978. Although not all of this increase was due to the programs outlined above, much of it was. For example, the changes between 1976 and 1978 of more than 17 percentage points was entirely due to countercyclical aid programs. This massive increase in federal aid has led one observer to label

TABLE 10.7. Direct Federal Aid as a Percentage of Own Source General Revenue, Selected Cities and Fiscal Years 1957–78

City	"Nathan's Urban Conditions Index"	Fiscal Years				Exhibit: Per Capita Federal Aid[b]	
		1957	1967	1976	1978 Est.	1976	1978 Est.
St. Louis	351	0.6	1.0	23.6	54.7	$ 86	$233
Newark	321	0.2	1.7	11.4	55.2	47	251
Buffalo	292	1.3	2.1	55.6	69.2	163	218
Cleveland	291	2.0	8.3	22.8	68.8	65	217
Boston	257	*	10.0	31.5	28.0	204	203
Unweighted averages	302	0.8	4.6	29.0	55.2	113	222
Baltimore	226	1.7	3.8	38.9	53.3	167	258
Philadelphia	216	0.4	8.8	37.7	51.8	129	196
Detroit	201	1.3	13.1	50.2	69.6	161	248
Chicago	201	1.4	10.9	19.2[a]	38.7	47	107
Atlanta	118	4.3	2.0	15.1	36.0	52	150
Unweighted averages	192	1.8	7.7	32.2	49.9	111	192
Denver	106	0.6	1.2	21.2	24.2	98	140
Los Angeles	74	0.7	0.7	19.3	35.7	54	120
Dallas	39	0	*	20.0	17.8	51	54
Houston	37	0.2	3.1	19.4	22.7	44	68
Phoenix	20	1.1	10.6	35.0	58.3	57	116
Unweighted averages Bottom 5 Cities	-55	0.5	3.1	23.0	31.7	61	100
All 15 Cities	183	1.1	5.2	28.1	45.6	95	171

* Less than 0.05 percent.

[a] Percentage based on federal aid excluding general revenue sharing. Funds withheld pending judicial determination.

[b] Based on 1975 population.

SOURCE: John Shannon "Our Central Cities: Creatures of the State and Wards of the Federal Government." Paper given before the Committee on Taxation, Resources and Economic Development, Cambridge, Mass., October 22, 1977.

central cities "creatures of the state but wards of the federal government."[58]

Table 10.7 also indicates that much of the recent increase in aid has been targeted toward the more mature cities of the United States. The "urban conditions" index of the table essentially serves as a proxy for the central cities of the Northeast and Midwest.[59] In 1978 such cities received nearly twice as much per capita as the newer cities of the Southwest and West.

Thus, it is apparent that the federal government has responded to the fiscal crisis of central cities. Undoubtedly the rapid expansion of fungible aid to older cities helped insure that they did not share the same fate as New York City during the recent economic downturn. It is unlikely, however, that the fiscal difficulties of cities are behind us. The forces of decentralization will continue to operate, giving rise to a need for further assistance. More importantly, however, is the temporary and ad hoc nature of many existing programs of federal assistance. In principle, all countercyclical assistance will disappear with economic recovery. Since the financial difficulties of cities will not significantly diminish with recovery, termination of countercyclical assistance will produce serious difficulties for many cities. Thus a more permanent basis for aid is necessary. Even if countercyclical assistance did not terminate, however, it would be desirable to identify more appropriate bases for allocating federal assistance. Unemployment, the principal factor in existing programs, may be a relatively poor indicator of relative fiscal stress. It is important, therefore, to identify more appropriate allocation formulas.

The appropriate basis for distributing federal aid should be determined directly from the problems it is intended to address. In the present case these problems consist of the locational distortions and inequities that arise from central-city-suburban fiscal disparity. The latter, in turn, reflect the fact that the poor do not fully pay for the public services they consume. The deficit is covered through taxes on middle- and upper-income residents and business. The source of fiscal disparity, then, is the differential redistributive burden carried by central-city residents and businesses. In effect, such groups bear the costs of the local public service consumption of the urban poor. Fiscal disparity would be eliminated if the state or federal government absorbed these service costs. Responsibility for providing the public needs of the poor would then be put on a footing similar to what is currently the case for the private needs of the poor.

In effect, I am suggesting that the state or federal government must bear the fiscal loss suffered by local governments on their poor population. Although the measurement of such loss is conceptually difficult, per-capita own-financial expenditure might be a useful approximation. Thus a community's allotment could be set equal to the product of per-capita own revenue and poverty population. Elsewhere I have estimated the cost of such a program to be approximately $6 billion for 1973, about the same level as General Revenue Sharing.[60]

Despite the similarities in total cost, the two programs are considerably different. While the grant formula under the General Revenue Sharing is quite complicated, it can be approximated by a per-capita allocation adjusted by relative income and relative tax effort. No attempt is made to specifically allow for the extent of poverty within the jurisdiction.[61] Thus, it is likely that General Revenue Sharing falls far short of eliminating city-suburban fiscal disparities.

CONCLUSION

The principal tenet of this chapter is that the financial difficulty of many large cities is the consequence of a structural flaw in our method of providing local services. The defect arises because local governments, consciously or not, engage in the redistribution of income. Because most local government services are rendered without regard to the tax contribution of the recipient, those who pay little in taxes (i.e., the poor) are subsidized by those who pay a lot (i.e., the rich). For a number of reasons, the nation's older central cities house a disproportionate share of their area's poor. Hence, income redistribution is greater in the central cities than in the suburbs, creating incentives for the well-to-do and business firms to relocate to the suburbs. Equally important, it is in the interest of suburban localities to attract and retain individuals who yield "fiscal surpluses" and repel those who create "fiscal losses." The process, then, may be self-reinforcing and cumulative in its effect. "Rich" governments grow richer and "poor" localities grow poorer.

That local (or even state) governments are not suitable agents for income redistribution is generally recognized by analysts and policy-makers alike. This recognition has been manifested in a massive upsurge of federal activity in social services, as well as a heavy involvement of states in the funding of such services at the local level. Although difficulties have been encountered in the formulation of an acceptable program, it is generally agreed that the federal government should assume the total financial burden of welfare. Although efforts to remove the burden of social welfare programs from local government should be applauded, there is a powerful argument that such steps are grossly inadequate to eliminate income redistribution at the local level of government. This argument is based upon the observation that social welfare services constitute but a small fraction of locally financed expenditure, the vast majority of which consists of services rendered to the public at large (e.g., education, fire and police protection, parks, etc.). Because the poor contribute little, if anything, toward the financial support of such services, they receive significant redistributive benefits. Hence, the locational distortions described in the previous paragraph remain. Furthermore, such distortions are apt to be most pronounced in our older urban areas, because the existing proliferation of local governments allows individuals and business firms considerable flexibility in the choice of community of residence, and because in such areas the poor are heavily concentrated in the central city, making redistributive burdens there much heavier than in adjacent localities. In rural areas, on the other hand, redistributive considerations play a secondary role to employment opportunities in the locational choice. Similarly, the considerable metropolitanization of local government in "sunbelt" states allows much less opportunity for individuals to avoid redistribution through migration. However, in the latter instance, redistribution can be avoided by providing many services through the private sector or restrictive private "clubs"—which may also produce an inefficient allocation of resources.

This conception of the problem, though in no way a comprehensive view, nevertheless suggests an approach by which the federal or state government might neutralize adverse fiscal incentives and at the same time ease the plight of hard-pressed localities. It points toward a program of intergovernmental grants designed to compensate local governments for the money they lose on the high-cost, low-revenue components of their population. Such a program, if properly designed, could neutralize the incentive for localities to exclude taxpayers who do not pay their way and to bid competitively for those who do. It could remove the fiscal element in locational choice. And it could compensate local governments for the burdens they assume in servicing the high-cost citizens who reside within their boundaries.

NOTES

1. See Mieszkowski's chapter in this volume. See also Berry and Dahmann (1977).
2. Greytak and Cupoli (1977) have estimated that the average private sector job yielded $626 in tax receipts to the District of Columbia government. For similar results for New York City see Bahl and Greytak (1976).
3. This is based upon the assumption that the central-city population is equal to that of the suburbs. For large cities, the figure actually stood at 79 percent in 1973. See ACIR (February 1977).
4. I do not mean to imply that the *property tax* differential will actually be 50 percent, since the city may use other revenue sources. Nevertheless, the 50 percent figure is representative of tax burden differentials.
5. See note 4.
6. The index is a simple average of city-suburban disparity with respect to: (1) unemployment rate; (2) dependency rate; (3) educational level; (4) income level; (5) poverty rate; (6) crowded housing. For more details, see Adams and Nathan (1976).
7. A small sample of this burgeoning literature would include: Peterson (1976), Berry (1975), Oates et al. (1971), Gramlich (1976), Hirsch (1971), Reischauer et al. (1975), Bradford and Kelejian (1973), Shefter (1977), Rothenberg (1977), and Neenan (1972).
8. For a discussion of these forces see Muth (1969), Mills (1972), and Meyer, Kain, and Wohl (1965).
9. For a dissenting view, however, see Hirsch (1970), chapter 12.
10. For an elaboration of this argument see Fischel (1975) and Fox (1978). To the extent that the community is large relative to its labor market, business firms may also confer an employment benefit. In such cases a community may be willing to suffer fiscal "loss" on its business enterprise.
11. See Mieszkowski, this volume.
12. See Hirsch (1970), chapter 8.
13. For a quantification of the net budget impact of low-income migrants to the central city see Crowley (1970).
14. For formal models of fiscally induced decentralization, see Rothenberg (1977), Oates et al. (1971), and Neenan (1972).

15. See Oakland (1978). The major evidence that fiscal differentials have played a role in suburbanization is found in Bradford and Kelejian (1973).

16. For an elaboration of this argument see Shefter (1977).

17. For the most comprehensive statement of this view see Bahl and Campbell (1976). For a more popular view see Peirce (1975).

18. Solid data on comparative wages in the public and private sector are scarce. However, Melvin Reder (1975) found that average hourly earnings of state and local employees grew more rapidly than those of private sector workers between 1959 and 1969. Other empirical studies of wages in the public sector have been done by Ashenfelter (1971), Ehrenberg (1973), and Schmenner (1973).

19. This argument is most clearly spelled out by Wellington and Winter (1969). For an opposing view see Burton and Krider (1970).

20. For a formal model of this effect see Courant et al. (1977).

21. U.S. Department of Commerce (1976).

22. Field and Keller (1976). For earlier estimates see Perloff (1971).

23. One might argue that the fundamental problem is city provision of area-wide public goods and not poor fiscal health per se. However, as long as central cities *do* provide for such services it would seem legitimate to view the problem as exacerbated by poor city fiscal health.

24. Not all fiscally induced migration will cause inefficiency. If movement occurs in order to obtain a better match between tastes and the availability of public services efficiency can be promoted. See Tiebout (1956).

25. "Peer-group" effects may themselves constitute an important stimulus to out-migration. Such subsequent round effects must be included in our computation of the inefficiencies associated with fiscally induced migration.

26. See, for example, Henderson, Mieszkowski, and Sauvageau (1976).

27. For a rigorous statement of this principle, see Hamilton (1976).

28. Note that in this case the threat of relocation is sufficient to lead to complete capitalization.

29. In particular, the capital intensity of fiscally disadvantaged sites will be reduced. See Mieszkowski (1972).

30. Those familiar with the municipal bond literature will recognize this argument.

31. Oates (1972) has shown that, at the margin, increases in property taxes decrease property values; the converse is true for increases in expenditure. Although this suggests that capitalization of fiscal differentials occur, *on average,* it says nothing about property values to specific income groups.

32. Alternatively, one could place the blame for poor fiscal health upon slow growth. A moment's reflection, however, suggests that the two hypotheses need not be inconsistent. Negative growth could be responsible for high *per capita* expenditures.

33. See Columns (9)–(12) of table 10.3.

34. According to the U.S. Bureau of Labor Statistics, manufacturing wages were 18 percent lower in "growing" cities than in "declining" cities.

35. See Inman's chapter in this volume.

36. The calculation assumes a ratio of total wages to total expenditures of 50 percent.

37. For a discussion of tax exporting see McLure (1967).

38. It is true that for all local governments taken together, nothing is gained by the deductibility. However, from the standpoint of a *single* locality or state, it is appropriate to view the tax as exported.

39. However, it is extremely relevant for user charges that are not deductible under the federal income tax.

40. See Mieszkowski (1972). Along this line, Peter Mieszkowski has argued that if *all* cities switch from a property tax to an income tax, export effects cancel each other out. This assumes, however, that all consumers of exported commodities reside in cities. If they do not, central cities will lose from the switch since their exportable base per capita exceeds the national average, but their imports of taxes fall below the national average. Furthermore, the argument under consideration is restricted to such a policy change by fiscally pressed central cities.

41. U.S. Bureau of the Census (1977).

42. The creation of the Environmental Protection Agency has enhanced this monopoly power, because the agency has made it much more expensive for small communities to operate their own sewer systems.

43. U.S. Bureau of the Census (1977).

44. This probably overstates the benefit to the city resident because some "leveling up" of service levels between city and suburbs is likely to accompany consolidation.

45. For example, per capita noneducation, noncapital expenditures were $195 in Houston in 1975. Comparable figures for all cities with populations in excess of 1 million were $730 and for cities between one-half million and 1 million, $415. See U.S. Bureau of the Census (1977).

46. This aspect is given a nice treatment in Oates (1972).

47. See Bradford and Oates (1974).

48. For a good description of base sharing see Lyall (1975).

49. Such an argument tacitly assumes the present tax price to be optimal for nonpublic goods. If this is not the case, the argument could conceivably go the other way.

50. See Advisory Commission on Intergovernmental Relations (September, 1976).

51. See Berke and Callahan (1972).

52. See Bahl and Vogt (1975).

53. See Oakland (1974).

54. This seems to be occasionally overlooked. For example, the mayor of New York City supported general revenue sharing even though it was clear his constituents would pay more in federal taxes than they would obtain in revenue sharing assistance.

55. Musgrave and Polinsky (1971).

56. Although such a remark strictly applies only to state general purpose and programs, there is evidence that it also applies to all state aid. See Mushkin and Biederman (1975).

57. Peterson (1976), p. 90.

58. Shannon (1977).

59. The urban conditions index was developed by Richard Nathan and set forth in testimony before the Joint Economic Committee on July 28, 1977. It is a composite of three indexes: (1) growth of population 1970–73; (2) percentage pre–1939 housing; (3) the percentage of the population below the poverty level.

60. Oakland (1976).

61. Such a factor was considered in the debate surrounding renewal of revenue sharing, but it was beaten back. See Nathan and Adams (1977).

REFERENCES

Advisory Commission on Intergovernmental Relations. 1976. *Improving Urban America*. Washington, D.C.: U.S. Government Printing Office. September.
———. 1977. *Trends in Metropolitan America*. Washington, D.C.: U.S. Government Printing Office. February.

Ashenfelter, Orley. 1971. "The Effect of Unionization on Wages in The Public Sector: The Case of Fire Fighters." *Industrial and Labor Relations Review* 24 (January): 191–202.

Bahl, Roy, and Campbell, Alan. 1976. "The Fiscal Dilemma of Central Cities: An Evaluation of Causes and Policy Reforms." Metropolitan Studies Program, Syracuse University. April.

Bahl, Roy, and Greytak, David. 1976. "The Response of City Government Revenues to Changes in Employment Structure." *Land Economics* 52 (November): 415–34.

Bahl, Roy W., and Vogt, Walter. 1975. *Fiscal Centralization and Tax Burdens.* Cambridge, Mass.: Ballinger.

Berke, J. S., and Callahan, J. J. 1972. "Serrano v. Priest: Milestone or Millstone for School Finance." *Journal of Public Law* 21 (1972): 64–65.

Berry, Brian J. L. 1975. "The Decline of the Aging Metropolis: Cultural Bases and Social Process." In *Post Industrial America: Metropolitan Decline and Inter-Regional Job Shifts.* Edited by Sternlieb and Hughes. New Brunswick, N.J.: Rutgers University Press.

Berry, Brian J. L., and Dahmann, Donald C. 1977. *Population Redistribution in the United States in the 1970s.* Washington, D.C.: National Academy of Sciences.

Bradford, D., and Kelejian, H. 1973. "An Econometric Model of the Flight to the Suburbs." *Journal of Political Economy* 81 (May–June): 566–89.

Bradford, D., and Oates, W. 1974. "Suburban Exploitation of Central Cities and Government Structure." In *Redistribution through Public Choice,* pp. 43–90. Edited by H. Hochman and G. Peterson. New York: Columbia University Press.

Burton, John F., and Krider, Charles. 1970. "The Role and Consequences of Strikes by Public Employees." *Yale Law Journal* 79 (January): 418–40.

Courant, P.; Gramlich, E.; and Rubinfeld, D. 1977. "Public Employee Market Power and the Level of Government Spending." Discussion Paper No. 110, Institute of Public Policy Studies, University of Michigan. July.

Crowley, Ronald W. 1970. "An Empirical Investigation of Some Local Costs of Migration to Cities, 1955–60." *Journal of Human Resources* 5: 11–23.

Ehrenberg, Ronald G. 1973. "The Demand for State and Local Government Employees." *American Economic Review* 63 (June): 366–79.

Ehrenberg, Ronald G., and Goldstein, G. 1975. "A Model of Public Sector Wage Determination." *Journal of Urban Economics* 2 (July): 222–46.

Field, C., and Keller, R. 1976. "How Salaries of Large Cities Compare with Industry and Federal Pay." *Monthly Labor Review* 99 (November): 23–8.

Fischel, William A. 1975. "Fiscal and Environmental Considerations in the Location of Firms in Suburban Communities." In *Fiscal Zoning and Land Use Control.* Edited by E. Mills and W. Oates. Lexington, Mass.: Lexington Books.

Fox, William F. 1978. "Local Taxes and Industrial Location." *Public Finance Quarterly* 66 (January): 93–114.

Gramlich, Edward M. 1976. "The New York City Fiscal Crisis: What Happened and What is to be Done?" *American Economic Review* 66 (May): 415–29.

Greene, Kenneth; Neenan, William; and Scott, Claudia. 1976. "Fiscal Incidence in the Washington Metropolitan Area." *Land Economics* 52 (February): 13–31.

Greytak, David, and Cupoli, Edward. 1977. "Revenue Implications of Alternative Tax Systems in the Context of a Changing Central City Employment Structure: The Case of Washington, D.C." Occasional Paper No. 33, Metropolitan Studies Program, Syracuse University. June.

Hamermesh, Daniel S. 1975. "The Effect of Government Ownership on Union

Wages." In *Labor in the Public and Nonprofit Sectors,* pp. 227–55. Edited by Daniel Hamermesh. Princeton, N.J.: Princeton University Press.

Hamilton, Bruce W. 1976. "Capitalization of Intrajurisdictional Differences in Local Tax Prices." *American Economic Review* 66 (December): 743–53.

Henderson, V.; Mieszkowski, P.; and Sauvageau, Y. 1976. *Peer Group Effects and Educational Production Functions.* Ottawa: Economic Council of Canada.

Hirsch, Werner Z. 1970. *The Economics of State and Local Government.* New York: McGraw Hill.

———. 1971. "Fiscal Plight: Causes and Remedies." In *Fiscal Pressure on the Central City,* pp. 3–40. Edited by Hirsch et al. New York: Praeger.

Lyall, Katherine. 1975. "Tax-Base Sharing: A Fiscal Aid Towards More Rational Land Use Planning." *AIP Journal* 41 (March): 90–100.

Margolis, Julius. 1961. "Metropolitan Finance Problems: Territories, Functions and Growth." In *Public Finances, Needs, Sources and Utilization.* Edited by J. Buchanan. Princeton: Princeton University Press.

McLure, Charles. 1967. "Tax Exporting in the United States: Estimates for 1962." *National Tax Journal* 20 (March): 49–77.

Meyer, J.; Kain, J.; and Wohl, M. 1965. *The Urban Transportation Problem.* Cambridge, Mass.: Harvard University Press.

Mieszkowski, Peter. 1972. "The Property Tax: An Excise Tax or A Profits Tax." *Journal of Public Economics* 1 (April): 73–96.

Mills, Edwin. 1972. *Urban Economics.* Glenview, Ill.: Scott, Foresman.

Muller, Thomas. 1975. *Growing and Declining Areas: A Fiscal Comparison.* Washington, D.C.: The Urban Institute.

Musgrave, R. A., and Polinsky, M. 1971. "Revenue Sharing: A Critical View." *Harvard Journal of Legislation* 8 (January): 197–208.

Mushkin, Selma J., and Biederman, Kenneth R. 1975. "Defining Tax and Revenue Relations." In "States' Responsibilities to Local Governments: An Action Agenda," p. 168. Center for Policy Research and Analysis of the National Governors' Conference. October.

Muth, Richard. 1969. *Cities and Housing.* Chicago: University of Chicago Press.

Nathan, Richard. 1977. "Testimony before the Joint Economic Committee." 95th Cong., 1st Sess., 28 July *Congressional Record* 123: 450–76.

Nathan, Richard, and Adams, Charles. 1977. *Revenue Sharing: The Second Round.* Washington, D.C.: Brookings Institution.

———. 1976. "Understanding Central City Hardship." *Political Science Quarterly* 91 (Spring): 47–62.

Neenan, William. 1972. *Political Economy of Urban Areas.* Chicago: Markham.

Netzer, Dick. 1977. "Public Sector Investment Strategies in the Mature Metropolis." Presented at the Symposium on Strategies for the Maturing Metropolis, St. Louis, Missouri. June 6–8.

Oakland, William. 1974. "Incidence and Other Fiscal Impacts of the Reform of Educational Finance: A Case Study of Baltimore." Baltimore Urban Observatory, City Planning Department, Baltimore.

———. 1976. "A Rationale for Federal Government Intervention in Housing:

Distortions Arising From Present Fiscal Arrangements at the Local Government Level." In *Housing in the Seventies Working Papers,* pp. 459–73. Washington, D.C.: Government Printing Office.

—————. 1978. "Local Taxes and Intraurban Industrial Location: A Survey." In *Metropolitan Financing and Growth Management Policies: Principles and Practice,* pp. 13–30. Edited by G. Break. Madison: University of Wisconsin Press.

Oates, Wallace E. 1972. *Fiscal Federalism.* New York: Harcourt Brace Jovanovich.

Oates, W. E.; Howrey, G.; and Baumol, W. 1971. "The Analysis of Public Policy in Urban Models." *Journal of Political Economy* 79 (January/February): 142–53.

Peirce, Neal. 1975. "Public Worker Pay Emerges as a Growing Issue." *National Journal* 7 (August 23): 1198–1206.

Perloff, Stephen. 1971. "Comparing Municipal Salaries with Industry and Federal Pay." *Monthly Labor Review* 94 (October): 46–49.

Peterson, George. 1976. "Finance." In *The Urban Predicament,* pp. 35–118. Edited by Gorham and Glazer. Washington, D.C.: The Urban Institute.

Reder, Melvin. 1975. "The Theory of Employment and Wages in the Public Sector." In *Labor in the Public and Nonprofit Sectors.* Edited by Daniel Hamermesh. Princeton, N.J.: Princeton University Press.

Reischauer, Robert D.; Clark, Peter K.; and Cuciti, Peggy L. 1975. *New York City's Fiscal Problem,* Background Paper no. 1, Congressional Budget Office. Washington, D.C.: U.S. Government Printing Office.

Rothenberg, Jerome. 1977. "Endogenous City-Suburb Governmental Rivalry Through Household Location." In *The Political Economy of Fiscal Federalism.* Edited by W. Oates. Lexington, Mass.: Lexington Books.

Schmenner, Roger. 1973. "The Determination of Municipal Employee Wages." *Review of Economics and Statistics* 55 (February): 83–90.

Shannon, John. 1977. "Our Central Cities: Creatures of the State and Wards of the Federal Government." Presented to the Committee on Taxation, Resources and Economic Development (TRED), Cambridge, Mass. October 22.

Shefter, Martin. 1977. "New York City's Fiscal Crisis: The Politics of Inflation and Retrenchment." *Public Interest,* no. 48 (Summer), pp. 98–127.

Stocker, Frederick D. 1976. "Diversification of the Local Revenue System: Income and Sales Taxes, User Charges, Federal Grants." *National Tax Journal* 29 (September): 313–22.

Tiebout, Charles. 1956. "The Pure Theory of Local Expenditures." *Journal of Political Economy* 64: 416–24.

U.S. Department of Commerce, Bureau of the Census. 1976. *Local Government Employment in Selected Metropolitan Areas and Large Counties: 1975.* Washington, D.C.: U.S. Government Printing Office. August.

—————. 1977. *City Government Finances, 1975–76.* Washington, D.C.: U.S. Government Printing Office. September.

Wellington, Harry H., and Winter, Ralph K., Jr. 1969. "The Limits of Collective Bargaining in Public Employment." *Yale Law Journal* 78 (June): 1107–27.

11

SCHOOL DESEGREGATION
AS URBAN PUBLIC POLICY

CHARLES T. CLOTFELTER

INTRODUCTION

Public schools are the single most important component of local public expenditures, accounting for some 45 percent of local direct expenditures (U.S. Bureau of the Census 1976, p. 20). Roughly one-half of all couples either have a child in public school or have a child who will attend public school;[1] about 90 percent of all children attend public school. This ubiquity is combined with a widely acknowledged role in the personal development of children that lends education an unparalleled importance among public services. Given this importance, it should not be surprising that a fundamental change in educational policy would have important effects among households as well as among students.

School desegregation is one such fundamental policy change that has been widely applied in recent years. The indications of deep feeling over this policy abound. Citizens have, on one hand, sought to affect the direction of this policy through demonstrations, boycotts, and school board elections. An alternative response has been for families to take their children out of the school system. Indeed, one of the most urgent questions surrounding urban school desegregation is whether or not the policy is itself causing whites to leave city schools for suburban and private schools. Such "white flight" would not only frustrate the aim of school desegregation but also, to the extent that there is additional white suburbanization, actually increase the degree of residential segregation. Determining the relationships between school desegregation and "white flight" is therefore one of the

Charles T. Clotfelter is an assistant professor of economics, Bureau of Business and Economic Research, University of Maryland.

The author would like to thank Anthony Pascal and the editors for helpful comments.

most significant questions regarding the evaluation of desegregation as a
social policy in urban areas.

The purpose of this chapter is to contribute to the evaluation of school
desegregation as an urban policy, abstracting as much as possible from the
surrounding constitutional and philosophical issues. The first section describes the evolution of the present school desegregation policy as it affects
urban areas and discusses the measurement of desegregation. The second
section summarizes the broader urban context of the "white flight" debate
and discusses the educational implications of desegregation. The third section describes a number of empirical studies of the relationship between
school desegregation and "white flight." The final section presents an
evaluation of school desegregation in terms of simple normative concepts
commonly used by economists.

1. DEFINING AND MEASURING DESEGREGATION POLICY

What is the government policy on school desegregation? If one were to
proceed by examining patterns of urban school attendance, it would be
exceedingly difficult to identify a single policy; at least two sources of
variation in desegregation policy would be observed. The first concerns the
breadth of coverage of desegregation within metropolitan areas. Desegregation in most metropolitan areas is carried on in central cities separately from
suburbs. Because of the relative concentration of blacks within central
cities, such central-city desegregation results in disparate racial contact between city and suburban schools. In a few urban areas, however, a policy
of metropolitan desegregation is followed, in which desegregation is carried
out with some uniformity throughout the urban area. A second manner in
which desegregation policies differ is in the extent of desegregation within
individual districts. The degree of racial homogeneity among schools in a
single district varies widely, ranging from large differences resulting from
residential patterns to near uniformity under desegregation plans that call
for a degree of "racial balance." To understand the reasons for both of
these differences, it is necessary to review the judicial history that shapes
present urban desegregation policy.

Legally segregated schools were declared unconstitutional in the 1954
Brown v. *Board of Education* decision.[2] This ended the segregated school
systems in such border cities as Baltimore, Washington, and St. Louis but
had only the most limited effect in the Southern cities. A few cities, such as
Little Rock and Atlanta, began desegregation slowly; but by 1964 only 1.2
percent of black students in the South went to school with whites.[3] White
schools were often technically open to blacks, but in effect a dual system
persisted. The Supreme Court decision that apparently signaled the beginning of an aggressive judicial attack on the remaining segregated systems

in the South was *Greene* v. *County School Board of New Kent County* in 1968, which stated that freedom of choice plans were in general not effective and therefore not acceptable.[4] In 1971 the Court ruled in *Swann* v. *Charlotte-Mecklenberg Board of Education* that proper desegregation plans could require the busing of pupils.[5] That case concerned the metropolitan school district that includes Charlotte, N.C.; that area was thus the first to be put under a policy of metropolitan desegregation. It is worth noting, however, that this desegregation plan required no crossing of jurisdictional boundaries. Since most central-city school districts are politically separate from their neighboring suburban districts, this decision generally implied only that busing could be used for central-city desegregation, a potentially quite different policy from the metropolitan plan followed in Charlotte.

Until 1972 the Supreme Court required desegregation only where de jure segregation had existed, which left Northern and Western cities free of the stringent conditions set down in previous cases. But in the Denver *Keyes* v. *School District No. 1* case, the Supreme Court enunciated a rule by which to judge Northern school segregation. If "intentional state action" had been used to foster segregated plans—by such tactics as gerrymandering attendance areas, segregating "feeder" systems, or building and using schools in such a way as to maintain segregation—Northern districts could be treated like Southern districts and be required to desegregate.[6] This case opened the door to desegregation in the major cities of the Northeast, Midwest, and West. Major central-city desegregation orders have been enforced in Boston, San Francisco, and Detroit. The Detroit case, *Milliken* v. *Bradley,* was particularly important in that the question of metropolitan desegregation across boundary lines was also an issue. The advocates of the metropolitan plan argued that a city-only plan would lead to "white flight" and eventually to an all-black city school system. In a 5 to 4 decision, the Court ruled against metropolitan desegregation in Detroit but left open the possibility under other circumstances.[7] Those circumstances were apparently present in the Wilmington case of *Evans* v. *Buchanan,* in which a circuit court declared unconstitutional a Delaware law prohibiting busing between Wilmington and its suburbs.[8]

Although the Supreme Court continued to expand the application of desegregation remedies over the period from *Brown* until *Milliken,* one limitation remained firm: innocently-conceived de facto segregation— segregation that has resulted from individual behavior rather than state action—has not been a target of desegregation policy.[9] In several recent cases, the Supreme Court has elaborated upon this limitation. In a case involving the Pasadena schools, the Court lifted a requirement that the system adjust attendance boundaries yearly in order to avoid having "a majority of any minority" in any school. In doing so, it reiterated that constitutional desegregation does not require any particular degree of racial balance among schools.[10] Another decision limited the extent of busing used to desegregate the Austin city schools. The Court argued that busing could be used to remedy the segregation caused by past official actions, but could not be used to push desegregation further. "Thus, large-scale busing is permissible only when the evidence supports a finding that the extent of integration sought to be achieved by busing would have existed had the school authorities fulfilled their constitutional obligations in the past."[11] Whether this means that school desegregation efforts will eventually be abandoned, when the effects of official segregation are ruled to have been remedied, is as yet unclear; but it is conceivable that school-desegregation policy is headed in the direction of the Northern-style de facto system, minus any official actions designed to encourage that segregation. For those who have relied on achieving desegregation by "opening up the suburbs" and dispersing low-income housing throughout the metropolitan area, another recent Supreme Court decision appears to establish a similar barrier. In judging suburban zoning laws that often result in residential segregation, the Court ruled that such zoning is constitutional as long as it does not have a "racially discriminating intent."[12]

Measures of School Desegregation

In this chapter, school desegregation will be measured in terms of contact between white and black children in public schools, no matter how it comes about. It will be measured in general by examining the racial composition of individual schools. There has been considerable debate over how desegregation should be defined, some maintaining that it should refer only to court-ordered racial mixing, not to mixing that results from changing residential patterns.[13] If complete information were available for all school districts, it would clearly be desirable to distinguish different desegregation experiences according to such characteristics as the degree to which neighborhood integration influenced school composition, the degree of intervention by the courts, the extent of community involvement in the decision process, the extent of busing, and the climate of racial relations within schools.[14] Since comparable data on such aspects of desegregation are quite difficult to obtain, it seems reasonable simply to use the extent of racial mixing in schools as the best reflection of desegregation policy. Some social scientists have gone as far as to argue that racial mixing that results from neighborhood integration should be distinguished from "true" desegregation, but this dichotomous approach is less useful and, moreover, is mistaken. Even residentially-induced mixing is the result of an explicit desegregation policy, that is, a policy that *allows* white and blacks to attend schools together. The reverse of this policy, de jure segregation, was the rule in many states until 1954 and in some Southern states well into the 1960s.[15] The abandonment of de jure segregation itself, even though gradual at times, was therefore a tremendous change in desegregation policy, one which has likely had important effects on the development of Southern urban areas. While racial mixing due to neighborhood transition is appropriately viewed as desegregation, it remains essential to separate the effects of such school desegregation from those of neighborhood integration on white household movement.

A number of different measures of segregation and desegregation have been used in studying public school enrollment, including the measure of dissimilarity associated with Taeuber and Taeuber.[16] I have chosen to discuss two indices developed by Coleman et al. (1975). Their presentation is useful here, because they illustrate two basic but differing ways to measure desegregation and because the authors have calculated indices using recent data for schools in a number of urban areas. One measure of racial composition as proposed by Coleman et al. is a measure of white pupils' exposure to blacks:

$$X_w = \frac{1}{W} \sum W_i \, (\% \, B_i) , \qquad (1)$$

where $\% B_i$ is the proportion of blacks in school i, W_i is the number of whites in that school, and W is the total number of white students in the district. This exposure index is the average racial composition faced by white children. If the racial composition of schools is a determinant of decisions by whites to move or enroll their children in private schools, it would appear that changes in such an exposure rate would be the proper measure of desegregation. However, the exposure rate has one major flaw as a useful measure of school desegregation: it is affected by the proportions of whites and blacks in the public schools. Therefore, the rate confounds the effects of desegregation policy with the effects of the district's demographic characteristics.

To counterbalance this weakness, Coleman et al. define an index of segregation (R) that relates the actual degree of racial contact to the maximum degree dictated by the proportion of blacks in the district (p_b):

$$R = \frac{p_b - X_w}{p_b} . \qquad (2)$$

Like the Taeuber index, it has a range of 0 to 1 (or 0 to 100), with 0 indicating complete racial balance in all schools ($p_b = X_w$) and 1 indicating complete segregation.[17] This segregation index is superior to the exposure index in measuring the degree to which desegregation has approached its limit within a district. But it is not at all clear that white parents confronted with desegregation are concerned about R rather than the extent of white exposure (X_w).

TABLE 11.1. Measures of Racial Composition, Desegregation, and Change in White Enrollment for Twenty-three Central-City School Districts, 1968 and 1973

District	Proportion Black		White Exposure (X_w)		Segregation (R)		Percent Change in Whites,
	1968	1973	1968	1973	1968	1973	1968–73
New York	.31	.37	.17	.18	.47	.50	−18.6
Los Angeles	.23	.25	.03	.05	.86	.79	−22.6
Chicago	.53	.58	.08	.07	.86	.88	−28.1
Philadelphia	.59	.61	.21	.17	.64	.72	−16.3
Detroit	.59	.70	.20	.27	.66	.62	−36.6
Houston	.33	.41	.04	.11	.89	.72	−33.0
Baltimore	.65	.70	.19	.21	.71	.69	−18.6
Dallas	.31	.41	.03	.13	.91	.69	−25.7
Cleveland	.56	.57	.09	.08	.85	.87	−17.4
Memphis	.56	.68	.04	.47	.92	.31	−35.1
Milwaukee	.24	.31	.06	.09	.75	.73	−17.2
San Diego	.12	.14	.04	.06	.66	.53	− 8.4
Columbus	.26	.30	.10	.13	.60	.56	−13.4
Tampa	.19	.19	.04	.18	.78	.04	−13.6
St. Louis	.64	.69	.12	.11	.82	.85	−28.7
New Orleans	.67	.77	.19	.34	.72	.57	−39.8
Indianapolis	.34	.41	.11	.25	.67	.39	−26.0
Boston	.27	.34	.11	.12	.60	.63	−16.9
Atlanta	.62	.81	.09	.42	.85	.48	−62.4
Denver	.14	.18	.04	.12	.69	.31	−21.3
Albuquerque	.02	.03	.01	.02	.43	.25	+ 1.1
San Francisco	.28	.31	.17	.28	.38	.07	−40.5
Charlotte-Mecklenberg	.29	.33	.10	.32	.66	.03	−11.4

SOURCE: Coleman et al. (1975, Appendix 1, revised).

Table 11.1 presents indices calculated by Coleman et al. for the twenty-three largest central-city school districts in 1968 and 1973, ranked in order of 1972 enrollment.[18] The segregation indices are generally lower in the smaller districts. In addition, the levels of white exposure tend to be highest in Southern cities and a few, predominantly black, Northern cities. The effect of increasingly stringent desegregation requirements over the period 1968–73 is readily apparent in the indices shown in the table. Whereas Southern cities had segregation indices as high or higher than non-Southern cities in 1968, by 1973 indices for these Southern cities were generally among the lowest in the country. The least segregated districts in 1973, by this measure, were Tampa and Charlotte, both of which are county-wide systems that have desegregated in response to court orders.

A final point regarding the measurement of desegregation made by Coleman et al. is that a significant amount of racial separation is due to segregation between districts rather than within them. That is, even if segregation were eliminated within districts, schools in central cities would still differ widely in racial composition from suburban schools. To capture this metropolitan segregation, they calculated segregation indices for twenty-two metropolitan areas by treating districts as units instead of schools. Two conclusions can be drawn on the basis of these calculations. First, the degree of between-district segregation varies greatly. In large cities with predominantly black central cities and white suburbs—such as Chicago, Detroit, St. Louis, and Washington—indices are high; in cities with large or metropolitan districts—Tampa, Memphis, San Diego—indices are low. Second, between-district segregation is increasing in almost all large cities, evidence of the racial polarization that has been characteristic of large U.S. cities. Only in Washington, where the public school system is virtually all-black and the ghetto is expanding into suburban counties, did the index fall between 1968 and 1972.

2. THE "WHITE FLIGHT" DEBATE AND URBAN SCHOOLS

Jencks et al. (1972, p. 156) have suggested that "the most important effects of school desegregation may be on adults, not on students." Probably the most important such effect has been the white exodus from many central-city school systems. Whether it is concern for educational quality, fear of disruptions, or simple-minded prejudice, it seems clear that many whites are opposed to desegregation on a large scale, particularly when children are assigned to schools outside their neighborhoods. A 1974 survey found that busing was opposed by 82 percent of whites who were interviewed (Farley, 1975, p. 14). This opposition has been pointed to as a factor in the loss of thousands of white students from desegregating districts. Atlanta is often cited as an example: that city's system lost over 60 percent of its white enrollment between 1968 and 1973. In Memphis, white enrollment fell 44 percent between 1971 and 1973 after a desegregation order. Such white exodus is not confined to cities in the Deep South. In Prince George's County, Maryland, the white student population has fallen by 25 percent since a 1972 desegregation order that called for busing. Whereas forty-six schools had a majority of black enrollments before the order, sixty-seven have black majorities today.[19] An even more precipitous loss of whites has occurred in Boston, where a 1973 court order was followed by a 37 percent drop in white enrollment over the next three years.[20] Losses such as these are usually referred to as "white flight," but it is useful to point out that what is being measured is the *net loss* of whites. No matter what the combination of gain and loss, it is clear that such loss tends to make central-city schools even more predominantly black and thus increases the typical racial disparity between city and suburban school systems. What is not obvious, however, is the extent to which this white exodus and subsequent "resegregation" is caused by the policy of school desegregation itself. Specifically, if school desegregation has an independent effect on

white residential choices, then the policy of central-city desegregation would
be expected to increase metropolitan segregation of schools and housing
compared to a policy of metropolitan desegregation. The choice between
the two policies would therefore be of crucial importance, as Justice
Douglas evidently believed. In his dissenting opinion in *Milliken* v. *Bradley,*
Douglas stated: "When we rule against the metropolitan area remedy we
take a step that will likely put the problems of the Blacks and our society
back to the period that antedated the 'separate but equal' regime of
Plessy v. *Ferguson.* . . ."[21] This policy distinction underscores the importance of the empirical question of desegregation and "white flight."

Factors in "White Flight"

Clearly, the principal empirical problem is to distinguish that portion of
white loss, if any, due to desegregation from that portion due to other
causes. Urban economists have been among the first to document and provide a rationale for the movement of households to the suburbs as well as
for the predominance of whites among those new suburban residents. At
least three sets of factors explain this mostly white and middle-class suburbanization: relatively innocent market forces, including rising incomes
and changes in production and transportation technology; public policies
providing subsidies to transportation and middle-income housing; and outright discrimination against blacks, causing them to be concentrated in central cities and underrepresented in suburbs relative to their economic
status.[22] Central-city crime and city-suburban fiscal disparities have also
been suggested as possible stimulants of this white-middle-class flight.[23] It
is therefore clear that "white flight"—perhaps by some other name—would
exist in the absence of school desegregation. This indicates the need to
study the effect of desegregation policy withn a larger model of urban
residential location, including the necessity of separating the effects of
neighborhood integration, or ghetto expansion, from those of school desegregation. Since school racial composition often follows the neighborhood pattern, this separation may be quite difficult to achieve in practice.

There is one more factor in white enrollment loss that must be distinguished. Demographic changes have produced a shift over time in the age
distribution of the population, and these changes have affected whites
differently from blacks. The result has been a decline in overall white school
enrollment: over the period 1968 to 1974, the total number of whites enrolled in elementary and secondary schools in the United States fell an
average of 0.75 percent per year. Since 1971 the yearly decrease has
exceeded 1.25 percent. These declines, combined with a gradually increasing black school population, have raised the percentage of blacks among

all elementary and secondary students from 13.4 percent in 1968 to 14.4 percent in 1974.[24]

The Educational Importance of Desegregation

In the evaluation of school desegregation as a policy, some of the effects most worthy of consideration are those that occur in the public school classrooms. It is important to know how school desegregation may affect both the level and distribution of educational services provided to students. Specifically, three effects of school desegregation can be distinguished. The first is obviously that school racial compositions change. Second, the amount and quality of school services provided to students are inevitably redistributed; students who are transferred exchange one set of teachers and school resources for another. Third, it is probable that these two effects cause a change in the level of educational services provided. To see why this may occur, it is useful to refer to the theoretical and empirical work on educational production functions.

A general production function for the education of a single child may be written:

$$e = f(\bar{b}, \bar{r}, \bar{p}) , \qquad (3)$$

where e is educational output and $\bar{b}$, $\bar{r}$, and $\bar{p}$ are vectors of inputs related to the child's family background, the resources available at his school, and the student's peer group at school. Although there are important conceptual difficulties in measuring educational output (e), most studies have measured this output in terms of achievement test scores or changes in achievement levels.[25] Among the inputs to the production process, school authorities have considerable control over two sets: school resources (including teachers) and the composition of the student body, that is, vectors $\bar{r}$ and $\bar{p}$. Desegregation policies involve changes in both of these groups of inputs, the peer group change probably being more dramatic in most cases. Accordingly, desegregation will in general affect the level and distribution of educational outputs received by individuals—even when the system's aggregate student composition and resources are held constant. For example, if the achievement of disadvantaged children is enhanced by the presence of middle-class children but there is no offsetting peer group effect for the latter, the integration of both groups will lead to an increase in aggregate achievement. However, if the achievement of middle-class children suffers as a result of mixing, then it is important to compare the size of these losses with the gains in achievement by disadvantaged students.

Probably the best known attempt to estimate the effects of various inputs in the production of this educational output is the so-called Coleman

Report (Coleman et al., 1966). That study concludes that, in predicting achievement, any effect of school inputs, including teachers, is greatly outweighed by the family background of students and the characteristics of fellow students in school. The report seems to allow for the possibility that racial integration would raise the achievement of blacks as long as schools do not become predominantly black. Because factors such as class are not adequately controlled for, the existence of this effect is highly uncertain.[26] Since the publication of the Coleman Report, there have been dozens of studies estimating educational production functions. In a review of many of these studies, Averch et al. (1972, p. 48) arrived at a conclusion not very different from that of the Coleman Report: "Research into educational effectiveness by means of the input-output approach has not, as yet, yielded consistent results regarding the importance of school resources. Background factors tend to dominate the results."

Other empirical studies of the educational process using individual pupil data are particularly interesting because they do not require aggregation across schools. Hanushek (1971) used data for third graders from a large California school system and separately estimated functions for Mexican-Americans and two groups of whites. He was able to reject the weak hypothesis that individual teachers make no difference in achievement, but teachers' experience and their amount of graduate education are not significant. Other teacher characteristics do turn out to be significant in some equations—for example, teachers' verbal ability and their recentness of educational training, for white students whose fathers work at manual occupations—but there is little consistency in the results. Summers and Wolfe (1974) worked with a sample of students in the Philadelphia school system and in general found considerable variation in the effect of school resources and peers on individual achievement. For example, high-achieving students are helped by having experienced teachers, but this is not true for low-achievers. School characteristics that have a generally positive effect on student achievement are small class size and the quality of the colleges attended by teachers. In addition, students seem to be helped by being in schools with a large proportion of high-achievers, a high degree of racial heterogeneity, and a low incidence of disruption. Henderson et al. (1976, 1977) looked at individual data from a quite different school system: the French-speaking Catholic schools in Montreal. They found that school resources, including teachers, "have no apparent, consistent, or large impact on achievement" (1976, p. 62). The only policy variable that appears to be important is the intelligence of fellow classmates. Moreover, this effect is positive but concave, implying that mixing weak and strong students will tend to help the former more than it hurts the latter.

Dozens of studies have looked specifically at the effects of school desegregation on achievement and a number have investigated effects on racial attitudes and other important personal characteristics. Regarding achievement, Coleman et al. (1966) and Summers and Wolfe suggest that desegregation may result in achievement gains. Jencks et al. (1972, p. 106) summarized much of the evidence on the effect of desegregation by calculating that placing all black children in desegregated classrooms would raise black achievement by 20 percent of the difference between white and black average scores. However, Armor's study (1972) supports the conclusion that integration has no impact on the achievement of blacks. In a recent exhaustive survey of all the studies on this question, St. John (1975) concluded that the data used have not been adequate to provide a definitive test of the effect of school desegregation on student achievement. She did not find support for either a positive effect for blacks or a negative effect for whites.[27] According to St. John, two major problems with experimental design that stand in the way of clearer findings are the short time period covered by most studies and the general inability to hold constant the atmosphere facing black students in the desegregated schools.[28] One recent study that attempted to solve the first of these problems is Gerard and Miller's (1975) longitudinal study of desegregation in Riverside, California. They were able to follow some students for up to six years in a desegregation process involving several minority groups. They found little evidence that desegregation has any effect on achievement: minority children did not gain and majority children did not suffer. Taken together, the research on the effect of desegregation on student achievement has failed to turn up evidence of any strong effect.

Aside from the effect of desegregation on the production of education—and therefore the question of allocation—it is quite clear that school desegregation is an important redistributive policy in that it redistributes (in-kind) the school resources and teachers to which students are exposed. The Coleman report concluded that, prior to the active desegregation efforts in the late 1960s and early 1970s, inequities in expenditures between schools within regions were minimal compared to differences between regions. However, disparities between white and black schools were significant when the mean verbal achievement scores for teachers were compared (Armor 1972, pp. 192, 194). Studies of disparities within single school systems showed that both per-pupil expenditures and average years of teacher experience in public schools were negatively correlated with the proportion of blacks enrolled.[29] Even if it does nothing else, school desegregation should tend to equalize the distribution of resources in providing public education. Of course, this kind of redistribution would also be possible with other redistributive policies, such as compensatory grants to poor districts or vouchers to poor families. However, if desegregation of the student body has a real effect on achievement or attitudes, such grant schemes would not be fully redistributive. Such a view is implicit in the 1954 ruling that separate schools are inherently/unequal. Therefore, apart from any aggregate effects it may have on achievement, school desegregation must certainly be considered an important policy in the redistribution of school resources.

3. EMPIRICAL ANALYSIS OF THE "WHITE FLIGHT" QUESTION

In empirical studies of the effect of desegregation policy on "white flight," one source of statistical information has been used more than any other— the school enrollment data for individual schools, broken down by race, published by the Office of Civil Rights (OCR) of the Department of Health, Education, and Welfare. But some studies have used other data sources, at least in part, and it is useful to separate the "white-flight" studies according to the data source used.

Studies Based on OCR Data

Since 1967 the OCR has compiled annual enrollment data by race for the school systems that contain most of the elementary and secondary students in this country. Because these data are available on the level of the individual school, it is possible to determine the degree of racial segregation that exists between schools (though not segregation by classroom that may exist within schools). It is important to note several limitations of these data, however. First, only public schools are included in the survey. Private school enrollment in response to desegregation is therefore not directly observable. Second, the boundaries of school districts do not necessarily correspond to jurisdictions for which other social and economic data are available. Third, the only measure of "white flight" obtainable from these data—loss of white students—is far from definitive. It is impossible to separate losses due to residential relocation from those due to private school enrollment. These are conceptually quite different phenomena, which certainly have different implications for patterns of residential segregation. On the other hand, it is the total loss in white enrollment that seems to be of the greatest public interest.

Probably the most extensive analysis of the "white flight" question using these data is contained in Coleman et al. (1975). Using pooled time series and cross section data for central-city school systems between 1968 and 1972, they estimated equations with the basic form

$$\%\Delta W = a + b_1\Delta R + b_2 p_b + b_3 \ln N + \sum_{i=4}^{I} b_i Z_i + u, \qquad (4)$$

where $\%\Delta W$ is the proportional change in white students over one year using the white enrollment in the previous year as base, ΔR—see equation

TABLE 11.2. Coleman et al. Basic Regression Results

Equation	2.1	2.2	2.3	2.4
ΔR	.279 (.062)	.056 (.026)	−.459 (.184)	−.349 (.151)
Proportion black	−.133 (.028)	−.090 (.014)	.051 (.037)	−.026 (.019)
ln N	.000 (.008)	−.042 (.010)	.003 (.006)	−.039 (.009)
R-SMSA			−.210 (.044)	−.102 (.025)
$\Delta R \times$ South			.148 (.198)	.244 (.145)
$\Delta R \times$ Prop. black			1.770 (.307)	.511 (.215)
$\Delta R \times R$-SMSA			.561 (.494)	.894 (.314)
South			−.006 (.010)	−.002 (.006)
Constant	.013	.452	−.039	.414
R^2	.29	.26	.60	.40
Number of observations	105	226	105	226

SOURCE: Coleman et al. (1975), p. 59, revised.

NOTE: Dependent variable is $\% \Delta W$, according to equation (4). Standard errors are in parentheses.

(2) above—is the change in the measure of school segregation p_b is the proportion black in the district in the previous year, N is the number of students in the district in the previous year, and the Z_i's are the other variables, including interaction terms. School desegregation policy is taken to be reflected in ΔR. Thus the central empirical question of the effect of desegregation on "white flight" turns on the estimated effect of ΔR. The regressions are estimated for two samples of central districts, the largest twenty-one and the next forty-six.[30] Coefficients and standard errors are shown in table 11.2. In equations (2.1) and (2.2), decreases in the index of segregation (indicating desegregation) are associated with decreases in numbers of white students, holding constant the size and racial composition of the school district. The equation thus implies that school desegregation itself stimulates white loss. The related coefficients are statistically significant, but the magnitude of this "desegregation" effect is larger in the sample of large districts. The proportion of blacks apparently has the expected effect of stimulating white loss, and district size is associated with more rapid white losses in the sample of smaller districts.

In order to hold constant other possible factors in white flight, Coleman et al. estimated two principal variations on equations (2.1) and (2.2). First, they estimated each equation substituting individual constant terms for each district for the single intercept and found that the coefficients of ΔR changed very little. This specification is quite a bit more appealing in that it allows for different rates of growth and decline in various cities independent of desegregation. In a second variation of the basic equation, a Southern dummy variable, a measure of between-district segregation in the metropolitan area (R-SMSA), and several interaction terms were added to equation (4). The resulting regressions are shown in equations (2.3) and

(2.4) in table 11.2. The effect of increased metropolitan segregation—that is, between central cities and suburbs—is generally to accelerate white loss. The effect of the Coleman et al. desegregation variable ΔR, in contrast to equations (2.1) and (2.2), varies greatly between cities, generally reaching its greatest magnitude in cities with large proportions of black students.

The study by Coleman et al. raises a number of methodological concerns, including the question of the proper measure of desegregation. The problem with this measure is simply that the Coleman et al. measure—the change in an index of segregation—may have almost no importance in white parents' enrollment decisions; it is white exposure to blacks that seems to matter most to white parents. For example, between 1968 and 1973 the segregation indices in Denver and Atlanta fell by approximately the same amount (.38 and .37, respectively), indicating similar desegregation experiences. For Denver, the proportion of blacks to which the average white student was exposed rose from .044 to .123. In the predominantly black Atlanta system, however, that exposure rate rose from .093 to .420, certainly a dramatically greater degree than in Denver. The notion that whites would respond similarly to these changes is unconvincing. The difference between these cases is partly captured by the interaction variables in equations (2.3) and (2.4), but the desirability of a desegregation variable that would measure the change in the average white exposure to blacks is not thereby diminished. The econometric problem with this approach is, of course, that a simple measure of change in white exposure would be a function of "white flight" and therefore would be inadmissible as a predetermined variable. The question of proper specification is discussed below.[31]

A second problem with the analysis is the absence of explicit consideration of other determinants of white exit from the schools, an omission that could bias the estimated effect of desegregation. Although the data do not allow an explicit identification of white exit due to residential relocation, it is nevertheless desirable to control for factors that might in any case be associated with rapid suburbanization; white family income levels, the rate of job decentralization, the size and growth of the black population in the central city, and the land area of the central city compared to that of the urbanized area would all be expected to affect the rate at which whites relocate in the suburbs. The level of white income would also be expected to influence the ability of whites to enroll in private schools.[32]

There are several other criticisms of the Coleman et al. study. One is that its sample includes cities that annexed land over the period of study; another is that the study depends upon the extensive desegregation of a few Southern cities with both large changes in R and high rates of white loss, notably Atlanta and Memphis. It is suggested that Southern cities are somehow fundamentally different from Northern cities and that desegregation experiences cannot be extrapolated to the Northern case. Given the small amount of evidence comparing responses to desegregation between regions, there seems to be little support for this notion.[33] A final criticism is that measures of desegregation must take into account more than simple changes in racial composition of schools. As noted above, it remains a possibility that racial mixing via busing may produce different effects than mixing achieved in other ways. A reexamination of the Coleman et al. data (Clotfelter, forthcoming) attempts to take account of some of these criticisms by using a modified sample and including several new explanatory variables. In addition, desegregation is measured by the change in white exposure to blacks, correcting for the effects of white loss. The resulting estimates generally support the conclusions of Coleman et al. that desegregation has a significant effect on white enrollment loss and that the effect is most pronounced in the larger districts. The estimates also indicate that desegregation has a nonlinear effect on white loss, becoming a significant factor only above a certain threshold.

Two other studies that used the same OCR data are noteworthy because they present the opposite conclusion from Coleman et al.—that desegregation does *not* cause any additional "white flight." Farley (1975) measured school segregation by a Taeuber index of dissimilarity, and desegregation by changes in that index. Using OCR data from a sample of districts, both central city and metropolitan, he regressed percentage change in white pupils between 1968 and 1972 on the change in the segregation index. No other variables were included. He found no statistically significant relationship. Because this segregation variable, like ΔR in Coleman et al., does not measure white exposure to blacks, and furthermore because there is no racial composition variable included, this result should not be surprising. A second study, by Rossell (1975–76), incorporated OCR data in conjunction with supplementary data on the extent of explicit reassignment for desegregation. Like Farley, she found no relationship between desegregation and "white flight."[34] Rossell's measure of desegregation was the percentage of blacks reassigned for desegregation plus the percentage of whites reassigned (a measure with a theoretical maximum of 200). This measure has the virtue of being exogenous but the weakness that it may be only weakly related to the extent of white exposure to blacks. The analysis centers on a comparison of the average rate of white loss before desegregation with the rate afterward. The date of segregation is defined as the date of the order(s) explicitly reassigning students. This definition of course rejects the notion of desegregation as simply a change in school racial composition. An example will indicate that this definition can be quite misleading. Using her methodology, Rossell set 1974 as the year of desegregation for Atlanta (Rossell 1976, table 4). Yet it is clear that the Atlanta system experienced increasing levels of desegregation after the end of the de jure system in 1961. The average white exposure to blacks in that system increased from .000 in 1960 to .420 in 1973.[35] Moreover, the difficulty in defining any one date as *the* date of desegregation is increased by the probable tendency of white families to anticipate court orders and leave public schools before they are actually ordered to desegregate.

Studies Using Other Data

Empirical analysis based solely on the net movement of students is not sufficient to yield conclusions concerning the separate effects of desegregation on white residential location and on private school enrollment. Thus, it has been necessary to turn to other data sources. Dealing first with the question of residential location, the theory of how desegregation ought to affect location is analogous to the well-known Tiebout hypothesis (Tiebout 1956). If white families prefer predominantly white schools, just as they might prefer parks or large public libraries, the desegregation of some (for example, central-city) schools would be expected to have two simultaneous effects in the short run. First, demand for housing in the predominantly white (suburban) districts would rise, driving up rents and house prices in those districts. How much prices in predominantly white districts would rise would depend on the intensity of white demand and the relative housing supply in predominantly white districts. At the same time, whites with the greatest willingness to pay for segregation—primarily those with children—would tend to purchase this relatively higher priced housing and leave those who are indifferent to school desegregation to enjoy reduced central-city housing prices. Both a price effect and a rearrangement effect, by family composition, would therefore be expected in the short run, that is, over the period in which the housing stock is relatively inelastic. In the longer run, any sustained shift in white housing demand toward the suburbs would be expected to result in an increased proportion of all whites living in suburbs over what would have existed in the absence of a policy of central-city desegregation.

I have conducted empirical tests of two of these three rather distinct hypotheses. In order to examine the effects of school desegregation on housing prices in the white submarket, I studied a sample of stable and predominantly white census tracts in the Atlanta metropolitan area whose public high schools nevertheless underwent varying degrees of racial change during the 1960s (Clotfelter 1975a). This relatively independent movement of neighborhood and school composition was made possible by a unique historical event: the end of de jure segregation in Atlanta schools during this period. Unlike Northern cities, where school racial compositions have historically reflected neighborhood compositions, the case of a Southern city allowed the statistical separation of the two effects on housing prices. Percentage changes in single-family house prices are explained by the average change in the percentage of blacks in local high schools attended by whites, the percentage change in a weighted average of distances from employment centers, changes in percentage of new housing units, median number of rooms per unit, and blacks in the tract, and a dummy variable for tracts bordering on tracts with significant racial change. The estimated equation indicates that the coefficient for changes in racial composition of schools has a negative and statistically significant effect, implying a decrease in house prices of about 4.7 percent in response to an increase of 10 percent in the proportion of blacks in school. Since this result is estimated for stable and predominantly white tracts and since, in addition, two other variables were included to reflect the effects of any remaining racial change, it seems reasonable to take this as an estimate of the independent price effect of school racial composition in this metropolitan area.

The possibility of rearranging white households on the basis of family composition was tested using a crude measure of the proportion of blacks in public schools attended by whites: zero in years of de jure segregation, and the proportion of blacks among the tract's children in other years (Clotfelter 1975b). For both Baltimore and Atlanta, the proportion of the white population aged fourteen or younger was negatively associated with this measure of desegregation, holding constant the racial composition of the tract and allowing the age structure of whites to vary over time.[36] Similar results were obtained for a different sample that used a direct measure of school racial composition. That study supports the hypothesis that whites with children are the first to make residential moves in response to school desegregation. When schools were segregated, the typical Southern "marble-cake" residential patterns had no effect on the racial composition of schools. But with the advent of desegregation, white parents tended to move away from integrated tracts.[37]

In contrast to the difficulty of measuring white residential responses to school desegregation, it is relatively straightforward to measure the alternative response of private school enrollment. It is likely that the supply of private schooling is quite elastic, even when school quality is considered. Therefore, any shifts in white demand for private schooling induced by school desegregation are easily observed and long-run equilibrium levels of private enrollment are achieved with little delay. If private schooling is assumed to be supplied everywhere at constant cost, the demand for private schooling by whites can be expressed in general as

$$E = g(Y, D, Z), \tag{5}$$

where E is the proportion of whites that attend private school, Y is a measure of white income, D is a measure of desegregation, and Z represents other relevant determinants of demand. Ascertaining the effect of desegregation on white flight involves measuring the derivative of E with respect to D. There are three questions of special interest related to this derivative. First, is there a "tipping point," or threshold, beyond which white response to desegregation increases significantly? Second, are high-income whites more sensitive to changes in school racial composition than lower-income whites? Third, are factors other than racial contact most important in explaining the effect of desegregation on white behavior?

At least three empirical studies of private school enrollment are relevant to these questions. All three use data from Southern states in which desegregation has been applied on a metropolitan or county-wide basis. In my 1976 study, I characterized desegregation policy in Mississippi as a school district's choice concerning what proportion of its black students to assign to schools with whites. Where W is total white enrollment and B is black enrollment in public schools, this proportion (c) defines the potential racial composition of district schools attended by whites in the event that no whites left:

$$D = cB/(cB + W). \tag{6}$$

As noted above, this potential racial composition is more appropriate than the actual racial composition because it is independent of the extent of white private school enrollment. In estimating equation (6), the data were found to be better explained by nonlinear functions of the desegregation variable D than by a simple linear function. One nonlinear function used involves a maximum likelihood search for a threshold, or "tipping point," in white responses to desegregation in the form of a change in slope at a particular racial composition in the eligible school population (θ). The estimated equation is

$$E = -.109 - .084\,FS + .059\,MY + 6.51\,PC25$$
$$\quad\ (.222)\ \ (.214)\qquad (.241)\qquad\quad (2.50)$$
$$+.406\,D + 2.445\,(D - \theta)^*\quad R^2 = .679,$$
$$\ (.162)\qquad (.480)$$

$$\tag{7}$$

where E is the proportion of whites in private schools, FS is the average white family size, MY is the mean white family income in 1969, $PC25$ is the proportion of white families with incomes over \$25,000, $(D-\theta)^*$ equals $D-\theta$ when $D>\theta$ and zero when $D\leq\theta$, and θ is .572. This equation indicates that potential racial composition (D) has a positive and significant effect on white private school enrollment. Furthermore, the sensitivity of whites increases markedly beyond potential compositions of about 50 percent black, as indicated by an increase in slope from 0.4 to 2.8. A similar nonlinear effect is implied by other functional forms, as shown by the cubic

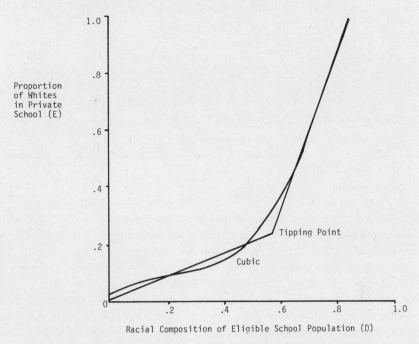

FIGURE 11.1 Demand for Private School Enrollment as a Function of Desegregation: Two Alternative Functional Forms

form—in which D^2 and D^3 are substituted for $(D-\theta)^*$—in figure 11.1. To the extent that these findings are applicable to other desegregating districts, they imply that white private school enrollment will tend to be modest in districts where white children outnumber black.

Giles et al. (1975, 1976) employed data from a sample of whites in seven Florida school systems. Using the actual proportion of blacks in school as a measure of desegregation, they show that the proportion of whites who leave the public system and enroll in private schools remains fairly constant up to a racial composition of 30 percent black and then increases above that level. They viewed this as evidence of a racial threshold at this point, confirming other studies of schools and neighborhoods that indicate tipping points in that vicinity. This 30 percent level is quite reasonable for the case of Florida school desegregation, but there is no reason to expect tipping points in different circumstances to be the same. Indeed, it is reasonable to believe that a tipping point is a function of demand for an alternative (in this case, private schools) and the supply of that alternative. Given higher levels of income in Florida than in Mississippi, it is conceivable that any tipping point would be lower in Florida. As for the effect of income on responses to desegregation, table 11.3 presents findings by Giles et al. indicating that for every level of racial

TABLE 11.3. Proportion of White Parents Who Transferred Their Children to Private Schools, 1972–73

Income	Percentage Black in Former Public School 1972–73			
	0–29	30–39	40–49	50 +
Less than $12,000	1.1	2.7	3.0	4.3
$12,000 to $17,999	2.2	6.5	6.5	8.3
$18,000 and over	4.1	13.5	14.4	14.0
Total	2.3	6.8	5.6	7.2

SOURCE: Giles et al. (1975, p. 87).

composition, the proportion of whites leaving public school increases with income. This finding supports the notion that "white flight" tends to increase economic, as well as racial, segregation.

A third study, by Farrell et al. (1977), emphasizes fiscal variables in explaining private school enrollment. In their analysis of North Carolina counties, the authors found, reasoning that the added expense of such transportation would tend to cause substitution from public to private education, that the amount of court-ordered busing (indirectly measured) had an independent effect on private school enrollment. However, how such a comparatively minor element of educational expenditures alone could have such an effect on the public-private choice remains unexplained. More compelling is the authors' explanation for the observed positive correlation between the percentage of blacks in a district and rate of private school enrollment. If fiscal discrimination against black schools is greatest in counties with large black populations, they argue, the redistribution that accompanied desegregation may have caused the largest decreases in educational resources for whites in those counties, and thus the largest increase in demand for the private alternative.[38] As the authors implied, it is impossible, using these models, to distinguish this hypothesis from the hypothesis that whites avoid desegregated schools because they prefer segregated schools.

Directions for Research

The empirical work on this question leaves many unanswered questions, most of which will be difficult to answer before new data (including the 1980 census) become available. Among the most important are: What is the full extent of residential relocation resulting from the white response to central-city desegregation? To what extent does private school enrollment result in similar rates of white loss where metropolitan desegregation is implemented? To what extent do relocation and private school enrollment act as substitutes where both are options? Is private enrollment in the South and in desegregated systems elsewhere likely to be a long-run form of white avoidance, or can we expect to see a return of whites from the private schools to the public systems? What will be the resulting economic composition of the whites who remain in the public schools? Can we expect decreases in local spending for public schools where whites have enrolled in private schools? How do the desegregation experiences of whites and blacks vary by family income? Are the responses of black families to desegregation similar to those of white families? More generally, what proportion of private avoidance of desegregation can be attributed to class rather than to racial mixing? What proportion is due to the fiscal redistribution implicit in desegregation? Given the variety of desegregation experiences across cities, it may be impossible to answer all of these questions precisely. But given the broad coverage of desegregation in urban schools and the apparent size of the short-run responses, these issues will probably continue to have important implications for the development of urban areas and the distribution of educational services.

4. EVALUATING DESEGREGATION POLICY

Because it is a policy that has been indirectly mandated by the Constitution, through the Supreme Court, school desegregation has been subjected to little of the systematic normative analysis applied to many other important social policies. This section suggests the outlines for such an analysis. None of this is to imply that desegregation policy should be made according to any but constitutional standards. On the other hand, for the purposes of policy consideration, the Constitution as currently interpreted should not always be taken as an unalterable constraint; for example, a constitutional amendment could conceivably be adopted to allow metropolitan desegregation to cross over boundaries even where no state action had been deemed responsible for segregation.

If normative analysis is relevant to the evaluation—that is, if logically or legally prior principles do not dominate economic criteria—the commonly used normative criteria of efficiency and equity may be applied to the evaluation of this policy. The fundamental efficiency-related question follows from the role of desegregation in redistributing educational resources and changing the composition of schools, discussed in section 2. For simplicity, consider a school system with just two kinds of student, each with a given educational production function. For students of each group, achievement (E) is a function of school resources and exposure to students in the other group. Given these production relationships, the school system's budget constraint, the cost of inputs, and the size of both student groups, the school system faces a production possibilities frontier of the form $G(E_1, E_2) = 0$. The production of education for these groups may be rival, in which achievement gains by one group can be achieved only at the expense of the other group. Whether or not strict rivalry is normally the case in education is uncertain, one case in which it almost certainly must be is where students of group 1 are segregated from those of group 2. Alternatively, there may be jointness over some ranges in educating both groups. This would be the case where students of both groups share the same classrooms and where each group benefits from achievement by the other.

Community preferences concerning educational achievement of the two student groups may be summarized as the set of community indifference curves formed by $V = V(E_1, E_2)$. This function implies that the community has preferences regarding only the achievement levels of each group and not, for example, the degree of contact between the two student groups or the level of resources given to each. These community indifference curves embody distributional preferences as well as evaluations of the marginal social value of increased educational achievement. The optimal community allocation of resources will be characterized by the usual condition,

$$\frac{\partial V/\partial E_2}{\partial V/\partial E_1} = \frac{\partial G/\partial E_2}{\partial G/\partial E_1}. \tag{8}$$

Two cases are of particular interest. Where all gains in achievement are equally valuable and no group is given extra weight due to redistributional aims, the community indifference curves are straight lines with a slope of -1 ($V = k[E_1 + E_2]$), and school resources are allocated so as to maximize total achievement. In contrast, where the community insists on strict equality of achievement, indifference curves are of the form $V =$ (min $[E_1, E_2]$) and the optimum will normally be located on the 45° angle line. More generally, if the community does not discriminate between the two groups, the community indifference curves will be symmetrical; the marginal rate of substitution of the nth unit of E_1 is the inverse of that for the nth unit of E_2.

School desegregation may be adapted to this model by viewing that policy as a reallocation of school resources. For example, assume the national community or government has preferences described by curves V_1 and V_2 in figure 11.2. If desegregation involves a redistribution of resources from student group 2 to student group 1, and as a result achievement levels shift from combination d to c, then desegregation can be said to be an improvement in allocation.[39] To see how a school system might have arrived at d in the first place, it is sufficient to suppose that some local communities have allocated school resources on the basis of preferences that

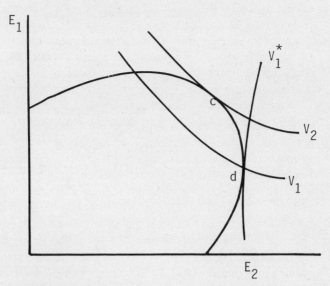

FIGURE 11.2   Community Preferences and Educational Production Possibilities

are quite distinct from those of the nation as a whole. For example, a set of preferences that placed primary importance on achievement in group 2 might be described by an indifference curve such as $V_1{}^*$. An even more extreme case would result if achievement by group 1 was a "bad"; indifference curves would then slope up to the right.[40] In summary, school desegregation may be an instrument for improving the "grand" efficiency of public education, where efficiency is defined by national, rather than local, preferences.

More generally, desegregation is likely to have costs and benefits of various kinds, in addition to changes in achievement, for families of different races and income levels. If opinion polls are taken at face value, white households with children in school often bear a net cost due to desegregation.[41] The greater the weight given to such costs as compared to the benefits others receive from desegregation, the less likely it is that desegregation plans will be desirable in terms of overall welfare criteria. One may go a step further and look at the distribution of these costs among whites alone. Where schools are desegregated, these costs are borne by whites with children either directly, by going to a desegregated school, or indirectly, by paying private school tuition or by accepting a property value decrease and moving to relatively higher-cost suburban housing.[42] Since it is in central cities that desegregation is typically most intense, it is probable that, among whites, those who bear this tax tend to have the lowest incomes.[43] Among whites, the policy of central-city desegregation is therefore regressive.[44] When the possible benefits received by blacks are considered, this regressivity may be mitigated or entirely eliminated. Finally, the criterion of horizontal equity, or equal treatment of equals, may be applied as well as distributional equity. It seems clear that the specific policy of central-city desegregation violates this principle. Whites living in central cities and suburbs, who are otherwise similar, are treated quite differently. In contrast, metropolitan desegregation does not appear to have this defect.

In summary, a full evaluation of school desegregation policy must consider the social costs as well as the social benefits of the alternative policies. Perhaps the most important social cost is the additional "white flight," which appears to be strong despite the methodological problems present in studying it. However, to what extent these trends will result in long-term residential and economic resegregation remains to be seen. One trend that suggests the possibility of longer term segregation is the dramatic decline in the number of school-age children. This decline should provide white and middle-class black families with children increased opportunities for two means of avoiding central-city schools: rearrangement, because such families will be able to relocate in suburbs at less premium; and private school enrollment, because there will be more resources per child. Evidence of other costs of desegregation, such as those due to increased prejudice or decreased self-confidence, seems quite tenuous and subject to reversals with the passage of time. On the benefit side, there is as yet little empirical basis for the notion that racial desegregation produces measurable achievement gains, though the evidence of such an effect for the French Canadian group indicates that the problem needs more complete analysis. It is quite possible, however, that desegregation may yet be found to have beneficial effects on the success of black graduates in the job market, presumably as the result of changes in characteristics unmeasured by achievement tests. Finally, the social benefits of integration per se must be included in a full evaluation of this policy, as difficult as they may be to measure. As stated before, the framework here described ignores such potentially overriding issues as the constitutionality of any given policy instrument. When such a consideration is brought up, it is possible that all the costs mentioned here may be outweighed, but this does not seem to be necessarily so.

NOTES

1. Estimate based on proportion of couples with at least one child under eighteen in 1974 (53.9 percent) and the proportion of children who attended public school (90.7 percent). U.S. Bureau of the Census (1975), p. 43; U.S. Bureau of the Census (1976a), p. 7.

2. *Brown* v. *Board of Education,* 347 U.S. 483 (1954).

3. U.S. Commission on Civil Rights (1976), p. 4.

4. 391 U.S. 430 (1968).

5. *Swann* v. *Charlotte-Mecklenberg Board of Education,* 402 U.S. 1 (1971).

6. *Keyes* v. *School District No. 1, Denver, Colorado,* 413 U.S. 189 (1972), 198, U.S. Commission on Civil Rights (1976), p. 5.

7. 418 U.S. 717 (1974).

8. John MacKenzie, "Court Backs City-County Busing Plan," *Washington Post,* 18 November 1975, p. A-1.

9. For an elaboration of these points see Taylor et al. (1975) and Amaker (1974).

10. *Pasadena City Board of Education* v. *Spangler,* slip opinion no. 75-164 (1976).

11. *Austin Independent School District* v. *United States,* slip opinion no. 76-200 (1976). In *Dayton Board of Education* v. *Brinkman* (1977), the Court further refined this principle by ruling that desegregation remedies could be used to redress only the "incremental segregation effect" of past official segregation. Slip opinion no. 76-539 (1977), 13.

12. *Village of Arlington Heights* v. *Metropolitan Housing Development Corp.,* slip opinion no. 75-616 (1977), 12. For a detailed analysis of the development of recent desegregation policy see Kirp (1977).

13. See Jackson (1975) and Rossell (1975–76, p. 677).

14. In his comment on the current paper, Anthony Pascal states the need for obtaining data and performing analysis in order to distinguish the effects of desegregation resulting from freedom of choice and neighborhood integration from that resulting from court-ordered reassignment: "The distinction is important because we have no evidence which leads us to believe that families residing in a given place will respond similarly to 'natural' incursions into their local schools and to mandatory reassignment plans which may entail long distance bussing of their children into unfamiliar and, many feel, possibly hostile environments. Theory would suggest that the latter will appear much more costly and evoke more extreme responses. Employing the details of reassignment plans as independent variables in a multivariate analysis appears to me the only way to clarify the situation."

15. This reasoning may be taken further, to argue that even de facto segregation is the result of two sets of official actions—assignment of pupils to specific schools and compulsory attendance. See Kirp (1977, p. 124).

16. See Taeuber and Taeuber (1972), Appendix A. For an application of this index to school desegregation see Farley (1975). This and other measures are discussed in Zoloth (1976).

17. A comparable segregation index could be calculated on the basis of the black exposure rate and the proportion of whites in the district.

18. Washington, D.C., is not included by Coleman et al.

19. Lawrence Feinberg and Elizabeth Becker, "White Pupil Enrollment Dips Dramatically in Prince George's," *Washington Post,* 1 December 1976, p. C-1.

20. "Whites Flee Boston Schools," *Washington Post,* 10 November 1976, p. A-23.

21. 418 U.S. 759 (1974).

22. Straszheim (1974) documents this underrepresentation in home ownership.

23. Bradford and Kelejian (1973) show that middle-class suburbanization is stimulated by unfavorable tax-expenditure packages in central cities.

24. U.S. Bureau of the Census (1976a), p. 7.

25. For a discussion of these conceptual difficulties see Bowles (1970).

26. See also Cohen et al. (1972).

27. In possible support of the relevance of Henderson et al. for the United States' case, St. John found some evidence for a curvilinear relationship between black achievement and percentage white.

28. These problems of experimental design also lead to difficulties in determining other effects of desegregation. Nevertheless, St. John has said there is evidence that the self-confidence of blacks is often reduced by desegregation and that prejudice may be either intensified or reduced.

29. The correlations of the percentage of blacks with per-pupil expenditures and average years of teacher experience are respectively: —.29 and —.50 for Washington, D.C., elementary schools in 1970; and —.48 and —.16 for Atlanta high schools in the 1960s. Sources: Charles Clotfelter, "The Effect of School Inputs on Achievement Among Elementary School Children," unpublished paper, May 1971; and Jesse Burk-

head, photocopy of "Atlanta Data: Matrix of Correlations among Dependent and Independent Variables," data used in Jesse Burkhead, Thomas G. Fox, and John W. Holland, *Input and Output in Large-City High Schools,* Education in Large Cities Series (Syracuse: Syracuse University Press, 1967).

30. For a detailed description of the samples, see Coleman et al. (p. 56).

31. Simultaneity bias is also possible in regressions based on equation (4). If whites tend to leave disproportionately from schools with high proportions of blacks, the measure of segregation will rise when there is white flight and ΔR will be less than it would have been without flight. Coleman et al. appear to have recognized the desirability of using a measure of change in exposure and proposed a measure that could be used as an exogenous variable (p. 57n and Appendix 2).

32. One study critical of Coleman et al. on this point is Jackson (1975). He reestimated earlier Coleman equations, explaining changes in white enrollment between 1970 and 1972 by ΔR and ΔX_w for the period 1968 to 1970. Although he did not present the estimated equations, he reported that the two-year version of ΔX_w is significant when demographic variables are included.

33. See Clotfelter (1976b and forthcoming).

34. According to Armor (1977, p. 43) both Farley and Rossell have modified their conclusions and agree that white flight from desegregation occurs "under certain circumstances."

35. Coleman et al. (1975, Appendix 3, revised).

36. For Baltimore, the coefficient of this proxy for school racial composition was —.296 (with a standard error of .041) and for Atlanta it was —.192 (.041). A 10 percent increase in the percentage of blacks in this measure would be associated with decreases in the proportion of whites under fourteen years of age of about 3 percent in Baltimore and 2 percent in Atlanta.

37. Another attempt to measure the effect of school desegregation on white relocation is Lord and Catau's (1977) study of intradistrict white transfers in the Charlotte-Mecklenberg area following the imposition of a metropolitan desegregation order. They found that the proportion of blacks during the postdesegregation period and the presence of busing have negative effects on the net gain in white enrollment from these intradistrict moves, a finding that would appear to support the importance of rearrangement of white households noted above. However, the measure of the postdesegregation racial composition of schools appears to be contemporaneous with the measures of white movement and is thus an endogenous variable whose coefficient is subject to a negative bias.

38. For evidence that discrimination against blacks in public education was greatest where the proportion of blacks was highest, see Freeman (1972).

39. For a similar analysis of the distribution of police services see Shoup (1964).

40. Similar models of white discrimination against blacks in public education are discussed in Freeman (1972). For a theoretical analysis of the fiscal implications of such discrimination, as well as the subsequent redistribution implicit in desegregation, see Borcherding (1977).

41. Farley (1975, p. 14) reports that 82 percent of whites (and 35 percent of blacks) opposed busing in 1974.

42. In a city of identical tastes and incomes among whites, the city-suburban price differential would equal the minimum of (a) the present value of direct desegregation costs or (b) the present value of private school tuition. To the extent that tastes vary and rearrangement of whites occurs, these housing price differentials are lessened.

43. Conventional desegregation is also experienced disproportionately by lower-income whites. Using the Coleman data, Cohen et al. (1972, p. 351) calculated the correlation between the percent of blacks in schools and the social class of whites to be —.462 in grade 1 and —.668 in grade 6.

44. Similar analyses of the incidence of the military draft have been made; see Tobin (1970).

REFERENCES

Amaker, Norman C. 1974. *"Milliken v. Bradley:* The Meaning of the Constitution in School Desegregation Cases." In *"Milliken v. Bradley": The Implications for Metropolitan Desegregation.* Edited by U.S. Civil Rights Commission. Washington, D.C.: U.S. Government Printing Office.

Armor, David J. 1972*a.* "The Evidence on Busing." *Public Interest* 29 (Summer): 90–126.

————. 1972*b.* "School and Family Effects on Black and White Achievement: A Reexamination of the USOE Data." In *On Equality of Educational Opportunity,* pp. 168–229. Edited by Frederick Mosteller and Daniel P. Moynihan. New York: Vintage Books.

————. 1977. "The Dangers of Forced Integration." *Society* 14 (May/June): 41–44.

Averch, Harvey A.; Carroll, Stephen J.; Donaldson, Theodore S.; Kiesling, Herbert J.; and Pincus, John. 1972. "How Effective Is Schooling?" RAND Report R-056-PCSF/RC. March.

Borcherding, Thomas E. 1977. "An Economic Approach to School Integration: Public Choice with Tie-ins." *Public Choice* 31 (Fall): 53–77.

Bowles, Samuel. 1970. "Towards an Educational Production Function." In *Education, Income, and Human Capital.* Edited by W. Lee Hansen. New York: National Bureau of Economic Research.

Bradford, David F., and Kelejian, Harry H. 1973. "An Econometric Model of the Flight to the Suburbs." *Journal of Political Economy* 81 (May/June): 566–89.

Clotfelter, Charles T. 1975*a.* "The Effect of School Desegregation on Housing Prices." *Review of Economics and Statistics* 57 (November): 446–51.

————. 1975*b.* "Spatial Rearrangement and the Tiebout Hypothesis: The Case of School Desegregation." *Southern Economic Journal* 42 (October): 263–271.

————. 1976. "School Desegregation, 'Tipping,' and Private School Enrollment." *Journal of Human Resources* 11 (Winter): 28–50.

————. 1979. "Urban School Desegregation and Declines in White Enrollment: A Reexamination." *Journal of Urban Economics,* vol. 6 (April).

Cohen, David K.; Pettigrew, Thomas F.; and Riley, Robert T. 1972. "Race and the Outcomes of Schooling. In *On Equality of Educational Opportunity,* pp. 114–37. Edited by Frederick Mosteller and Daniel P. Moynihan. New York: Vintage Books.

Coleman, James S.; Campbell, Ernest Q.; Hobson, Carol J.; McPartland, James; Mood, Alexander M.; Weinfeld, Frederic D.; and York, Robert L. 1966. *Equality of Educational Opportunity.* 2 Vols. Washington, D.C.: U.S. Government Printing Office.

Coleman, James S.; Kelley, Sara D.; and Moore, John A. 1975. "Trends in School Segregation, 1968–73." Urban Institute Paper 722-03-01.

Farley, Reynolds. 1975. "School Desegregation and White Flight." Presented at the Symposium on School Desegregation and White Flight, Center for National Policy Review and Center for Civil Rights. August.

Farrell, Claude H.; Hyman, David N.; and Ihnen, Loren A. 1977. "Forced Busing and the Demand for Private Schooling." *Journal of Legal Studies* 6 (June): 363–72.

Freeman, Richard B. 1972. "Black/White Economic Differences: Why Did They Last So long?"

Gerard, Harold B., and Miller, Norman. 1975. *School Desegregation: A Long-Term Study.* New York: Plenum.

Giles, Michael W.; Gatlin, Douglas S.; and Cataldo, Everett F. 1975. "White Flight and Percent Black: The Tipping Point Re-examined." *Social Science Quarterly* 56 (June): 85–92.

———. 1976. *Determinants of Resegregation: Compliance/Rejection Behavior and Policy Alternatives.* National Science Foundation.

Hanushek, Eric. "Teacher Characteristics and Gains in Student Achievement: Estimation Using Micro Data." *American Economic Review* 61 (May): 280–88.

Henderson, Vernon; Mieszkowski, Peter; and Sauvageau, Yvon. 1976. *Peer Group Effects and Educational Production Functions.* Ottawa: Economic Council of Canada.

Henderson, Vernon; Mieszkowski, Peter; and Sauvageau, Yvon. 1977. "Peer Group Effects and Educational Production Functions." Paper presented to the Committee on Urban Public Economics. Philadelphia.

Jackson, Gregg. 1975. "Reanalysis of Coleman's 'Recent Trends in School Integration.'" *Educational Researcher* 4 (November): 21–25.

Jencks, Christopher; Smith, Marshall; Acland, Henry; Bane, Mary Jo; Cohen, David; Gintis, Herbert; Heyns, Barbara; and Michaelson, Stephen. 1972. *Inequality.* New York: Basic Books.

Kirp, David L. 1977. "School Desegregation and the Limits of Legalism." *Public Interest* 47 (Spring): 101–28.

Lord, Dennis, and Catau, John. 1977. "School Desegregation Policy and Intra-School District Migration." *Social Science Quarterly* 57 (March): 784–96.

Murnane, Richard J. 1975. *The Impact of School Resources on the Learning of Inner City Children.* Cambridge, Mass.: Ballinger.

Pettigrew, Thomas F., and Green, Robert L. 1976. "School Desegregation in Large Cities: A Critique of the Coleman 'White Flight' Thesis." *Harvard Educational Review* 46 (February): 1–53.

Pincus, John, and Pascal, Anthony H. 1977. "Education and Human Resources Research at Rand." RAND Paper P-5748. January.

Rossell, Christine H. 1976a. "A Reply to Professor Coleman's Response."

———. 1976b. "School Desegregation and White Flight." *Political Science Quarterly* 90 (Winter): 675–95.

St. John, Nancy H. 1975. *School Desegregation Outcomes for Children.* New York: Wiley.

Straszheim, Mahlon R. 1974. "Housing Market Discrimination and Black Housing Consumption." *Quarterly Journal of Economics* 88 (February): 19–43.

Summers, Anita, and Wolfe, Barbara L. 1975. "Equality of Education Opportunity Quantified: A Production Function Approach." Philadelphia Federal Reserve Research Paper.

Taeuber, Karl E., and Taeuber, Alma F. 1972. *Negroes in Cities*. New York: Atheneum.

Tax Foundation. 1974. *Facts and Figures on Government Finance 1973*. New York: Tax Foundation.

Taylor, William L.; Benjes, John E.; and Wright, Eric E. 1975. "School Desegregation and White Flight: The Role of the Courts." Presented at the Symposium on School Desegregation, Center for National Policy Review and Center for Civil Rights. August.

Tiebout, Charles M. 1956. "A Pure Theory of Local Expenditures." *Journal of Political Economy* 64 (October): 416–24.

Tobin, James. 1970. "On Limiting the Domain of Inequality." *Journal of Law and Economics* 13: 263–78.

U.S. Bureau of the Census. 1975a. *Statistical Abstract of the United States 1975*. Washington, D.C. U.S. Government Printing Office.

———. 1975b. *Current Population Reports*. Series P-20, no. 294. "School Enrollment—Social and Economic Characteristics of Students, October 1975." Advance Report, June 7.

———. 1976c. *Governmental Finances 1974–75*. GF75 no. 5. September.

Zoloth, Barbara S. 1976. "Alternative Measures of School Segregation." *Land Economics* 52 (August): 278–98.

IV

HOUSING MARKETS
AND HOUSING POLICIES

12

WHAT HAVE WE LEARNED
ABOUT URBAN HOUSING MARKETS?

JOHN M. QUIGLEY

INTRODUCTION

Most economic analyses of urban phenomena, both positive and normative, rest upon current conceptions of behavior and resource allocation in the urban housing market. The operation of this market determines the configuration of a substantial fraction of the capital stock found in urban areas. At the same time, however, this market determines the spatial distribution of these stocks and the geographical locations of different kinds of residential households. Attention to this central feature of the housing market—determining levels of investment and capital stocks and spatial distributions of suppliers and demanders—distinguishes research on housing by urban economists from that undertaken by other specialists. The theory of resource allocation in the housing market underlies the analysis of such diverse questions as transportation investment policies, the fiscal position of central cities, and the extent and location of slums.

This chapter reviews the research underlying our current conceptions of the housing market, emphasizing the distinctly urban or intrametropolitan aspects of the market.[1] The perspective on housing that receives attention by urban economists analyzes the characteristics of the housing commodity and investigates the microeconomic determinants of demand by consumers, of supply by landlords and builders, and of factors influencing the form of metropolitan areas.

In large part, our increased understanding of the urban housing market has arisen from a more careful and realistic consideration of several special

John M. Quigley is associate professor of economics at Yale University.

This chapter has benefited from the comments and suggestions of Susan Ackerman, Eric Hanushek, Peter Mieszkowski, Richard Muth, Richard Nelson, Dick Netzer, Mahlon Straszheim, Mitchell Polinsky, Raymond Struyk, and James Sweeney.

features of residential housing that distinguish this market from others. The chapter begins by isolating these distinguishing characteristics. Following this, section 2 introduces the single characteristic of housing—accessibility—that had been the focus of attention, until quite recently, for urban economists studying the housing market. We then review recent research on the demand for housing services, including analyses that recognize the dimensionality of the bundle of housing services. The review of recent work on the supply side of the market discusses models of the production of new housing and the filtering and transformation of existing dwelling units by landlords in response to market conditions. This chapter indicates that during the past decade substantial progress has been made in understanding the complex market for housing services, particularly the behavior of housing demanders. Conversely, our understanding of the microeconomics of housing supply is still quite rudimentary, and empirical evidence on supplier behavior is notably weak.

1. THE PECULIAR NATURE OF HOUSING MARKETS

The principal features of the housing commodity that distinguish it from most goods traded in the economy are its relatively high cost of supply, its durability, its heterogeneity, and its locational fixity. Many commodities exhibit one of these features; it is the interaction of these distinguishing characteristics that complicates theoretical and empirical analysis of the housing market.

The high cost of housing construction implies that houses are expensive, that a large rental market exists, and that mortgage repayment makes owner-occupied housing an attractive instrument of wealth accumulation. In addition, financing costs make the level of new construction of dwelling units and the occupancy cost for prospective purchasers quite sensitive to macroeconomic policy.

The durability of housing implies that there are fairly narrow bounds to the rate of disinvestment in existing structures. Housing lasts a long time; older structures may become "obsolete," but they do not necessarily lose substantial market value because of their vintage. Housing services (the flows of consumption) are "emitted" by a configuration of residential housing (the stock) over an extended period of time.

Together, durability and supply cost indicate that it is typically quite expensive to convert a unit in the existing stock from one configuration to another, which suggests that the supply curve for housing services is inelastic, even over relatively extended periods, and even if the supply of newly constructed units is rather elastic. Substantial quasi rents may accrue to particular units in any market run, and the long-run is very long indeed.

The heterogeneity of housing indicates that housing units differ in a number of important dimensions, quantitatively and qualitatively, and thus that units that command the same market price may be viewed as substantially different by both suppliers and demanders.

Locational fixity implies that the spatial characteristics of housing units— their location with respect to other dwelling units, employment, shopping centers, and neighborhood amenities—are purchased jointly with structural characteristics. The close proximity of housing units in urban areas indicates that there may be important physical or social externalities inherent in the location chosen for housing consumption. Locational fixity also suggests that dwelling units may differ greatly in their accessibility to production or consumption activities, a factor that has been greatly emphasized in the urban economics literature. Finally, at least in the United States, the spatial location chosen for housing consumption is the admission ticket to those goods and services provided by local government—the choice of a dwelling unit is the choice of a school district and a "mill rate." Thus, given the fragmented structure of local governments in U.S. metropolitan areas and the American tradition of local autonomy, the housing market is intimately connected with the means of financing the local public sector.

Durability, heterogeneity, and fixity together indicate that "the" housing market is really a collection of closely related, but segmented, markets for particular packages of underlying commodities differentiated by size, physical arrangements, quality, and location. These submarkets are, however, connected in a predictable way. At neighboring locations, differences in prices between submarkets cannot exceed the short-run cost of converting a housing unit from one submarket to another. If there were no location-specific component of the housing commodity, then at different sites, variations in prices within any submarket could not exceed transport cost differentials for the marginal consumer. However, a price inelastic demand for some of the attributes jointly purchased, combined with inelastic supply in the short run, may make the pattern of housing prices much more complex, even in a market in temporary equilibrium. In the extreme, if the demands for some locational aspects of housing services are relatively price inelastic and if the supply of dwellings is fixed, then the equilibrating forces of substitution in demand will not equate prices over space to marginal transport differentials. The equilibrating competition of demanders may permit significant segmentation of the market over locations (that is, large quasi rents will accrue to particular locations); similarly, the competition of suppliers may permit significant segmentation of the market over types of housing accommodations (that is, large quasi rents, up to the cost of conversion, will accrue to different types of dwelling units at the same location). The "equilibrium" set of housing prices in an urban area may be quite complicated indeed.

Clearly, any economic analysis of the housing market must abstract from this complex reality. Without *some* simplification, theoretical and empirical research can hardly be expected to yield any insight. It is true, of course, that "everything depends upon everything else," but without imposing some simplifying (and hence unrealistic) structure on the nature of the housing market, this observation hardly aids the understanding of human behavior. To evaluate the contributions of disparate strands of recent housing market research, it is important to note how various strategies have "cut through" this complexity by making simplifying assumptions. We can then ask how well suited the simplifications are, in principle, for understanding a particular aspect of market behavior and, given the simplifications, whether the results are relevant or useful in understanding the behavior of real actors in the market.

2. WHERE WE HAVE BEEN: LOCATIONAL FIXITY AND ACCESSIBILITY

A point of departure for the review of housing market research presented a decade ago by Muth is his observation that "[U]ntil quite recently, most writings on urban residential land and housing markets tended to neglect accessibility. They emphasized instead the dynamic effects of a city's past development upon current conditions, and preferences of different households for housing in different locations. . . ."[2]

Many of the seminal insights about the operation of housing markets were derived in the mid sixties from the observation that housing and employment accessibility are jointly purchased. This insight, plus the assumptions that there exists a single urban workplace and that housing is produced competitively from land and "nonland" by a constant returns technology, led to a number of important propositions—about the form of urban areas in long-run equilibrium, the intra-metropolitan distribution of housing, and the location patterns of urban households. The principal conclusions of the monocentric model are: (1) residential densities decline with distance from the central place; (2) densities decline at a decreasing rate; (3) housing prices decline with distance, also at a decreasing rate; (4) the land price gradient is steeper than the housing price gradient; (5) households with higher incomes locate further from the central place.[3]

These results are based upon the ingenious model developed initially by Alonso and Wingo in 1961, generalized by Mills in 1967, and synthesized by Muth in 1969. These conceptual results, derived from what is, in the late 70's the "standard model" (to use Solow's [1973] terminology) of the urban area, were not well-known within the economics profession at large a decade ago, but they were available to many students of urban economics through pre-prints and through intermediate papers published by Richard Muth (1964) among others.

Elaborations of the monocentric model are reviewed and criticized in

Wheaton's chapter. For the analysis of housing markets per se, it is sufficient to note that at present the applicability of these mathematically sophisticated "new urban economics" models to the study of housing markets is tenuous at best;[4] and that there exists considerable skepticism among some, and controversy among others within the discipline, regarding the potential research benefits of further extensions, which may be mathematically ingenious but economically uninteresting.[5]

These judgments partly reflect an evaluation of the research strategy implicit in these analyses. In concentrating upon the long-run features of the housing market, these extensions assume that "housing" can be represented as a scalar instead of a vector of attributes and that consumer choice can be described in two dimensions—"how much" and "where." In addition, the important features of fixity and durability in housing are completely ignored, since this long-run perspective implies that the distribution of housing over space conforms to the distribution that would be observed if the urban area were built anew.

At the same time that these theoretical extensions were undertaken, a number of scholars, expanding upon the empirical findings of Colin Clark, tested the qualitative implications of the "standard model" of the spatial distribution of housing services within metropolitan areas. An extensive empirical literature has investigated the relationship between the distance from the city center and the intensity of economic activity, for example, residential density. These studies—typically, the estimation of density gradients (regressions relating distance to log-density) for various urban areas in the United States and in other developed countries (Mills, 1970; Mills, 1971; Niedercorn, 1971)—generally fail to reject the hypothesis of a convex density relationship. With Mills' ingenious method it has also been possible to estimate population density gradients historically, beginning in 1880,[6] for some U.S. cities. These historical analyses suggest a systematic decline in central densities and in gradients across time periods. At a descriptive level, these results indicate strikingly that the postwar decentralization of workplaces, the suburbanization of households, and the resulting spatial changes in housing demands in urban areas have been no more pronounced than the decentralization that occurred a generation earlier—central densities of population and employment have regularly declined, as have their gradients, for as far back in time as we have data.

It has been argued that the convexity (or even the log-linearity) of population density functions provides a direct test of the "standard model," at least as it applies to housing markets (White, 1977). At best, this is a quite weak test of these class of models. Empirical evidence shows that estimates of density-distance relationships are highly sensitive to the partitioning of geographical units (Kemper and Schmenner, 1974). More important, as noted by Harrison and Kain (1974), plausible density gradients can be derived from assumptions about the nature of the housing stock (for example, by assuming an infinite durability of housing) that are diametrically opposed to those of the standard theory.

3. THE DEMAND FOR THE COMPOSITE COMMODITY "HOUSING SERVICES"

It would appear that a simple strategy for gaining a general understanding of the behavior of housing consumers would be to abstract completely from intrametropolitan choices and to assume a single valued measure of housing services. It should then be a simple matter to estimate the price and income elasticities of demand from market data on housing in the same way as demand curves have been estimated for countless other goods. However, measuring the importance of price and income in housing demand has not proved to be a simple matter at all. In part, the dispersion of price and income elasticity estimates results from traditional measurement problems—sample selectivity, econometric specification, and the like (see de Leeuw, 1971, for a review of these measurement problems and a presentation of the empirical evidence as of 1971). In part, however, the interpretation of empirical evidence depends upon the peculiar characteristics of the housing commodity.

First, consider the costliness and durability of housing: housing expenditures represent a large fraction of income, and it is costly for any household to change the configuration of housing services received (by modifying its current dwelling unit or by searching and moving to another unit). Thus, the appropriate concept of income is less clear-cut than in the study of most commodities. Housing durability and high transaction costs imply that the relevant notion of income for analyzing consumer choice is a "normal" or long-run income as opposed to annual income. This by itself suggests that the estimates of income elasticity obtained from observations based on consumers randomly grouped by income will be larger than those obtained when individual households are the units of observation,[7] a finding consistent with the empirical evidence assembled over the past few years (Aaron, 1975; Hanushek and Quigley, 1979; King, 1973; Maisel, Burnham, and Austin, 1971).[8] Since de Leeuw's review of the cross-sectional evidence on income elasticities in 1971, several studies that use individual households as units of observation and employ some measure of permanent income have been reported (Carliner, 1973; Kain and Quigley, 1975). These studies typically report statistically significant elasticities with respect to *both* annual and permanent income, with a higher elasticity estimate computed for permanent income.

In addition, the permanent income elasticities reported in these microeconomic studies are generally smaller than those derived from grouped data.[9] The review of this evidence presented by Kain and Quigley (1975) provides several possible rationalizations of these findings—for example, the existence of a peer-group, or relative-income, effect influencing housing consumption—as does the analysis by Vaughn (1976), which emphasizes simultaneous equations bias, but the general conclusion remains: "none [of these explanations] completely reconciles the differences in income elasticity estimates."[10]

The conceptual and empirical problems in estimating the price elasticity of housing demand arise from quite different considerations. In the market for housing, "prices" are never directly observed. Market transactions produce monthly rents for flows of housing service or market values for stocks of housing capital. Neither of these is a price. They are expressed in units of price-times-quantity.

Thus, in aggregate analyses that relate housing consumption to income and price, price is usually approximated by inter-urban (or inter-temporal) variations in construction cost indices (Muth, 1960), or in more recent work, by the average cost for an arbitrarily specified dwelling unit, gathered by the Bureau of Labor Statistics for different U.S. cities (de Leeuw, 1971). (The BLS indices are described and criticized by Gillingham, 1975). Estimates of the price elasticity of housing demand based upon these indices have ranged from about −0.3 to −0.9 (Carliner, 1973; de Leeuw, 1971; Maisel, Burnham, and Austin, 1971).

The recent paper by Polinsky (1977) attempts to reconcile these differences in price elasticities (as well as the differences in long-run income elasticities) estimated from grouped and ungrouped data. Part of the reconciliation reflects "standard" econometric problems—the particular specification and measurement of housing prices relative to the prices of other goods employed in various studies. In part, however, the proposed synthesis emphasizes theoretical issues in housing markets and builds upon the results discussed in section 2. The reconciliation of empirical findings is based upon the inherent jointness in the housing consumption and location decision and the meaning of housing "prices," between as well as within markets. Polinsky's analysis considers the effect of specification errors upon price and income elasticity estimates arising in three kinds of samples: sample *a,* individual households within a single housing market; sample *b,* individual households drawn from several housing markets; and sample *c,* averaged data drawn from several housing markets. The theory reviewed in section 2 suggests that higher-income households will consume more housing and will locate where housing prices are lower within a housing market (see note 3). On the other hand, higher-income households are more likely to live in cities with higher average incomes and housing prices. Thus, if housing demand is price inelastic:

1. Estimates of income elasticities obtained from the bivariate regression

of housing expenditure on income in sample *a* will be biased downwards, since housing expenditures will fall as price decreases with distance and higher-income households will choose more distant locations.

2. Estimates of income elasticities obtained from the bivariate regression on sample *c* will be biased upwards, since the increase in prices in cities with higher incomes causes expenditures on housing to rise, and in the bivariate regression, this is attributed to income.

3. Estimates of income elasticities obtained from the bivariate regression on sample *b* will also be biased (the intra-city residential location pattern imparting a downward bias) but moderated by the magnitude of the inter-market effect—i.e., the positive bias imparted, assuming price inelasticity, by neglecting the positive relationship, on average, between household income and housing prices across cities.

4. Similarly, if a regression is estimated for sample *b* between housing expenditures, income, and some average metropolitan price index (e.g., from BLS budget data), the downward bias in the estimated income elasticity is larger (since the average price term holds the inter-market effect constant to the extent that incomes and prices are positively correlated across cities). Of course, if prices and incomes are perfectly correlated, then the bias is equivalent to that in case 1; if prices and incomes are completely uncorrelated, the bias is equivalent to that in case 3.

5. Finally, in regression 4 the estimated price elasticity based upon the average price is, in general, biased upwards (towards zero).[11]

This taxonomy proves very useful in narrowing the range of empirical estimates of "the" income elasticity of demand, at least if demand is price inelastic;[12] overall this reconciliation of prior evidence suggests a slightly inelastic demand for housing of about 0.7 to 0.9 with respect to long-run income.

With regard to estimates of the price elasticity of demand, there is less empirical evidence available, since housing prices are not directly observed. However, a few studies have "measured" housing prices, other than as a market-wide average in samples gathered across cities. (i.e., case 5 above which leads to an upward bias.) These analyses (Muth, 1971; Polinsky and Ellwood, 1979) have used samples of Federal Housing Administration (FHA) appraisal and sale data to derive estimates, that vary by observation, of unit prices for housing and have used these price estimates in subsequent investigations of the price and income elasticities of housing demand. Analytically, this involves estimating the parameters of the production function (assumed of the constant elasticity of substitution [CES] form) that relates housing output to land and nonland inputs and then substituting the parameters into the cost function to estimate the competitive price (that varies for each unit in the sample) per unit of housing.[13] Each price is interpreted as the competitive equilibrium price of the homogeneous good "housing services" at a particular location—an output price that varies only with the substitution of capital for land inputs in response to land price premiums. Expenditures on housing are then regressed on income and these unit prices; in logarithmic form, the coefficient of the price term is one plus the price elasticity of demand. The results of these studies (which used FHA data on newly constructed homes and their occupants across different cities and time periods), suggest a price elasticity of about —0.7 for owner occupants.

These qualitative results are supported in a more recent study in which Hanushek and Quigley (1978a) used the results of one part of the housing allowance experiment to estimate the price elasticity of housing demand for renters. For some households participating in the experiment, the unobserved housing prices have been reduced experimentally by various percentages (i.e., some households receive percentage rebates on rental contracts). By observing the behavior of these households over time, it is possible, in principle, to estimate the sensitivity of housing consumption to price variation. Price elasticity estimates are derived within a stock adjustment framework (see Hanushek and Quigley, 1979; Muth, 1960) that distinguishes between the long-run and short-run effects of price variation upon observed demand. Panel data on experimental and control households in two metropolitan areas permit the replication of the empirical results for several time periods. For these two samples, the long-run price elasticity estimates (statistically identical for all replications) are about —0.5 and —0.7. These results are in rather close agreement with those estimated indirectly from the parameters of the production function for new housing.

There seems to be some professional consensus that, in the aggregate and over the long run, housing demand is slightly inelastic with respect to income and with respect to price. In the short run, we may well expect significant lags in household response to variations in income and price, since there are large transaction costs associated with the search for alternate accommodation. Evidence from panel data on individual households confirms the importance of these lags in adjustment—to variations in income for a national sample of households (Roistacher, 1977) and to variations in income and price for longitudinal samples of individual households in particular metropolitan areas (Hanushek and Quigley, 1978a, 1979).

4. THE COMPLEXITY OF "HOUSING SERVICES": HETEROGENEITY AND HEDONIC MEASUREMENT

The definition of housing services employed above—the assumption that housing services is a homogeneous good available at a single price—is quite useful in certain instances, since it permits a unique mapping from rents or housing values to a single quantity. This conceptual apparatus is clearly central to the research themes discussed so far. Nevertheless, for many analytic and descriptive purposes, especially at the microeconomic level, the assumption is patently unreasonable. During the past decade, considerable intellectual resources have been devoted to understanding the relationship between the market prices of rental and owner-occupied dwelling units and the components of housing services imbedded in them. This strand of analysis, the development of so-called hedonic indices, was seldom applied to housing a decade ago (Griliches' 1961 paper that applied the same methodology to automobiles seems to have stimulated only one application to housing markets [Nourse, 1963]). Today, there is considerable literature on the dimensionality of housing services.

The recent interest in applying these methods to housing markets owes much to the new theories of consumer behavior, developed in the mid sixties by Lancaster (1966) and others, which postulate that households have demands for the underlying characteristics inherent in all traded commodities and that households combine purchased characteristics with time inputs to "produce" satisfactions. When these theories are applied to housing markets, the natural question is: in what way is the complex and heterogeneous bundle of physical and spatial characteristics provided by the choice of a dwelling unit reflected in its price in trade? From observations on the market prices of dwelling units and on these underlying characteristics, it is possible to estimate the relationships empirically. The regression of market value or monthly rent upon the set of characteristics yields their implicit prices.

If the market is in equilibrium and if the statistical model is properly specified, then the hedonic regression indicates the market's valuation of each of the components of housing services jointly purchased by a household and jointly supplied by a landlord. Within the discipline of urban economics, this research strategy has been applied to housing markets by using the average characteristics of census tracts and later by using rich samples of data on the prices paid for individual dwelling units and descriptions of the quantitative and qualitative aspects of these units, their structures, parcels, and microenvironments. (Ball, 1973; Grether and Mieszkowski, 1974; Kain and Quigley, 1970a; King and Mieszkowski, 1973; Lapham, 1971).

Such a strategy requires the definition and measurement of the set of characteristics and the choice of the functional form for analysis; both issues are largely empirical. With regard to functional form, it has been argued that the semi-log function is more plausible (Griliches, 1971) since it is consistent with a rising supply price for individual characteristics.[14] Most authors have chosen the linear, semi-log, or logarithmic form for analysis, presumably on the grounds of convenience and without rigorous statistical experimentation.[15] (This is hardly surprising, since rigorous analysis of functional form is conditional upon an agreed specification of the independent variables.) So far, this strand of empirical research has been employed: to provide empirical tests of the importance of workplace accessibility, so emphasized in the early theoretical literature, in determining housing prices; to investigate the type and importance of local externalities in affecting the market valuation of housing services; to analyze the relationship between local taxes, public services, and property values; and to provide a rich description of the components of the heterogenous commodity "housing services."[16]

Workplace Accessibility

With regard to the importance of workplace accessibility, the empirical evidence is somewhat mixed. Various authors have measured accessibility in different ways—for example, as travel time (or distance, or cost) to the central business district, or as a generalized workplace accessibility index derived from gravity models. By and large, the estimated coefficients of such measures in hedonic regressions are significant; observed market prices vary with accessibility. Holding other factors constant, however, the independent effect upon housing prices of distance or generalized accessibility to workplaces is not large (see Ball, 1973, for a review of thirteen recent studies); relative to the important structural and qualitative characteristics, the effect of distance is, in fact, rather small. In part, these general findings may simply reflect the negative covariance between accessibility and measures of housing quality or vintage arising from the historical growth pattern of U.S. cities—the tendency for older, more obsolete, and lower-quality dwelling units to be located closer to traditional central employment centers. In part, however these empirical results may reflect the limitations of a long-run equilibrium interpretation applied to durable configurations of residential capital. As noted above, in a temporary equilibrium positive and negative quasi rents may be associated with particular sites and housing configurations. In many housing markets, these location premiums may be large relative to accessibility premiums.

The Importance of Externalities

With regard to the question of externalities, analyses of hedonic prices have provided direct evidence of the effect of air pollution (Anderson and Croker, 1971), residential blight (Kain and Quigley, 1970b), and neighborhood characteristics (Kain and Quigley, 1970a) on property valuation. In addition, and perhaps of much more importance, these analyses have indicated the effect of social externalities and racial composition on housing prices. These implications of recent studies are reviewed in the chapter by Yinger in this volume.

In the regression that relates property values to characteristics of housing services external to the dwelling unit—for example, measures of ambient air quality (with the other relevant characteristics of the properties held constant)—the regression coefficient provides an estimate of the capitalized value of air quality. How should these estimates be interpreted?

Despite a number of theoretical and empirical analyses of hedonic prices, there still seems to be some confusion about the precise meaning of these empirical findings. Some authors appear to interpret hedonic regressions as representing supply curves, others as representing demand curves (see note 14). In general, hedonic representations of implicit prices are neither. The hedonic regression represents an estimate of the (upper) envelope of bid-rent functions of *different* households for particular housing components. For any housing attribute, each bid-rent function is defined as locus of unit payments and amounts of that attribute yielding equal utility, with the consumption of other housing attributes held constant. However, the same regression also represents the (lower) envelope of the offer functions of *different* suppliers for distinct housing characteristics. For any housing attribute, each offer function is defined as the locus of unit prices and amounts of that attribute supplied that yield the same profit, with the supply of other attributes held constant. Demanders' bids vary by a set of characteristics (i.e., by income and taste); suppliers' offers presumably vary as well (i.e., by short-run cost conditions). Thus the joint envelope traced out by the hedonic regression need not reveal anything about the underlying structure of supply or demand.[17]

When first presented, estimates of the capitalized value of air quality (Freeman, 1971; Anderson and Crocker, 1971; Ridker and Henning, 1967), were often interpreted as if they revealed demanders' willingness to pay for air quality, and thereby indicated the market return to pollution abatement policies.

The previous argument indicates, however, that only if consumers were identical in their demands for all housing characteristics would the hedonic function reveal consumers' willingness to pay for air quality or for any other externality. In this special case, of course, the hedonic regression would not be the envelope of the bid-rent functions of groups of consumers with differing demands; it would be the single bid-rent function of any consumer. Thus it would directly reveal the income-compensated demand, or willingness to pay, by all consumers.

Even under these stringent conditions, however, it does not follow in general that estimates of changes in aggregate property values accurately reflect the market return to public policies that affect amenity levels. Again, there still seems to be some confusion regarding the underlying logic. Consider a public policy that changes the schedule of amenities (e.g., ambient air quality) in a single urban area. Without the assumption that the urban area is small and that there is perfect equilibration (e.g., residential mobility) among urban areas, the utility levels of residents within any one urban area will be affected by any change in the schedule of amenity levels provided.[18] Thus the increase in capitalized values at one location from an increase in the amenity level at that location depends upon changes in the amenity level at all *other* locations. In the isolated urban area, aggregate increases in amenity levels result in increases in aggregate values, but these changes in values are underestimates of the aggregate willingness to pay (since in an isolated urban area these consumers enjoy higher levels of utility following the general improvement in amenities). With perfect mobility among urban areas, however, the level of utility of identical consumers is equal across cities and is exogeneous to a change in the amenity level in one city (again, if it is small enough). Thus, subject to these restrictions, changes in property values reflect the aggregate willingness to pay for changes in amenity levels.[19]

This divergence in implications has led to a distinction in the literature between models of equilibrium in a "closed" (i.e., isolated) urban area and models of equilibrium in an "open" urban area (i.e., a small city whose residents can move costlessly to any other city in an equilibrium system of urban areas). Such models have recently been applied to the theoretical analysis of public finance and tax incidence (Arnott and MacKinnon, 1977; Polinsky and Rubinfeld, 1978).

Taxes and Public Services

The most widely quoted paper on local public finance is unquestionably "A Pure Theory of Local Expenditures' (Tiebout, 1950) which introduced the adjective *Tiebout* into professional jargon. As is well known, the positive model of Tiebout argues that the system of local government provision of public services at fixed tax prices *may* provide a conceptual solution to the problem of preference revelation for those public goods provided by the non-federal sector. Normatively, the Tiebout view suggests that this system *may* allocate these public goods as efficiently as the private sector allocates private output. The leap from the informal model of Tiebout to the reality of metropolitan finance involves several specific features of public goods, tax instruments, and consumer behavior. It is clear, however, that if there is any diversity in demand among consumers for the local public goods that can be produced by tax revenues, then the existence of many jurisdictions that provide alternative levels of public goods and taxes at the same commuting radius does permit consumers to increase their well-being by allowing them a choice among jurisdictions.

Many of the key questions in applying this perspective to local government—how diverse are demands? What determines the level of public good expenditure chosen? How are these expenditures used to produce outputs?—are considered in the chapters by Inman and Mills in this volume.

The existence of location-specific packages of public outputs and taxes does have particular implications for the analysis of urban housing markets, since housing, public services, and taxes are chosen jointly by consumers. These implications are, in fact, more-or-less independent of the positive and normative prescriptions of the original Tiebout model. (Recall that Tiebout nowhere considered the link between housing or land demands and consumption of local public goods and, thus, the specifics of capitalization). If consumers have preferences over the goods produced by local government, and if mobility is sufficiently high, we should expect property values to be higher in communities with more attractive packages of public goods. For the same reason, with other things held constant, we should expect lower housing values in jurisdictions with higher tax rates on real property.

A number of recent analyses have investigated the effect of these public-sector attributes on metropolitan housing prices by including measures of effective tax rates and public services in hedonic regressions on property values. However, the measurement of the relevant public-service concept is itself a difficult matter. Consider schools, which account for more than one-half of local expenditures. Does the bid for a property by a household in the housing market vary with the level of local spending or physical resources per child (inputs), with the average level of achievement of students (gross outputs), or with an estimate of the increased performance of particular children (value added)? Most studies have considered only the effect of the capitalization of inputs on housing prices. Oates's 1969 analysis considered the effects of variations in school spending and effective tax rates on housing values for a sample of suburban New Jersey jurisdictions. Oates found clear evidence that per-student school expenditures are capitalized into higher values and that differences in tax rates are reflected in market prices. Holding other things constant, Oates estimated that about two-thirds of the variation in annual tax rate is capitalized (and in a subsequent analysis of the same data [1973], virtually all the variation is capitalized) into differences in values. These results are roughly consistent with subsequent analyses of communities in the Boston area by Orr (1968) and by Heinberg and Oates (1970), and are also similar to results reported by Pollakowski (1973) based upon a small sample of San Francisco communities. In contrast, an analysis of individual housing units in the New Haven area by King (1973) revealed no evidence of the capitalization of tax differentials. Of course, this latter result (based upon a sample of individual properties) could be attributed to the wide variation in effective property taxes within jurisdictions that has been reported in the literature on assessment practices (Black, 1972). An analysis of the housing market in a single jurisdiction, St. Louis (Kain and Quigley, 1970a), where tax rates and school spending are presumably more uniform, suggested further that gross output measures (average test scores of students) are capitalized into the prices for both rental and owner-occupied housing. This finding is confirmed in a more recent study that measured student performance across suburban school districts (Peterson, 1973).

A recent paper by Edel and Sclar (1974) argues that if the supply of local public goods is in long-run equilibrium across communities, there will be no capitalization of local public service benefits or taxes into housing values. The authors presented a series of cross-sectional analyses of Boston communities that suggest a declining average capitalization of school spending over a forty-year period. They attribute this to movements towards long-run equilibrium in the provision of schools across communities. However, in the Edel and Sclar analysis long-run equilibrium is defined simply as equal provision of public services across jurisdictions. Without differences in service provision, capitalization is of course impossible.

The implications of these results about the capitalization of taxes and public services in housing prices are often discussed as if they verified Tiebout's positive (or normative) model. They do provide evidence that the tax and public service packages provided by different communities influence consumers in their choice of the heterogeneous bundle of residential services. However, the implications of the "invisible foot" for efficiency in the provision of public goods and services at the local level depend upon many other considerations—for example, whether (or how) the characteristics of residents themselves affect the production of public service outputs (Bradford, Malt, and Oates, 1969) and how citizens react to output choices (Hirschman, 1975). Recent analyses, by Rose-Ackerman (1979) and Rothenberg (1977) among others, that combine models of political behavior with the housing market models discussed in section 2 and with assumptions of costless mobility, yield *highly ambiguous results* in terms of economic efficiency. For example, Rose-Ackerman demonstrated that an equilibrium pattern of location and service provision need not exist, even in a simple model, and that fragmented service provision may be inferior on efficiency grounds to uniform public goods provision in an urban area.

5. THE DEMAND FOR THE COMPONENTS OF THE HOUSING COMMODITY

A number of studies have attempted to integrate the three strands of research reviewed so far. These studies investigate the determinants of consumer demand (discussed in section 3), while recognizing the heterogeneity of housing—that is, by incorporating, in some form, information about the unit prices of the underlying components of the housing bundle (section 4). Superficially, these studies appear to be based upon far more realistic assumptions than were their predecessors; they are certainly intended to address far more realistic questions about consumer choice in the housing market than simply "How much?" and "Where?" (the implicit scope of the research reviewed in section 2). In fact, these studies are somewhat less general than they appear.

There have been three closely related approaches to the larger questions of consumer choice.

The Demand for Bundles of Characteristics

Two research efforts have partitioned, a priori, the housing-services expenditures of a sample of consumers into implicit payments for a limited number of "composite commodities" or aggregates of underlying characteristics by utilizing hedonic price indices for a metropolitan housing market. The earlier of these researches (Kain and Quigley, 1975) assumed a linear additive form of the metropolitan wide hedonic price index, which implies that the unit price of each underlying component of the housing commodity is constant throughout the housing market. Estimates of the unit prices are used to partition household expenditures on housing (a hedonic price vector times a vector of housing services) into several components (dwelling unit quality, interior space, neighborhood quality, and exterior space). Then household demands for these components of housing services are estimated jointly as a function of household income and sociodemographic characteristics. The econometric results suggest a systematic pattern of substitution; not only the pattern of substitution between housing services consumed and other goods revealed in the aggregate studies of housing demand, but also substitution in demand among components of the bundle of housing services. They reveal, for example, higher income elasticities of demand for housing quality than for space and systematic reallocations in response to variations in family size and composition. In this analysis, the implicit assumptions about the price structure of the market are strong; since it is assumed that the unit price of each component of the housing bundle is constant throughout the market, the model ignores the importance of variations in quasi-rents across locations.

Two recent papers by King (1975, 1976) extended this analysis of the demand for bundles of housing characteristics. King recognized that the unit price of particular housing characteristics may vary within the metropolitan housing market due to excess supplies of particular types of residential housing at specific locations or to some interaction between accessibility and other housing characteristics. He used hedonic regressions to estimate the implicit prices of the underlying housing characteristics separately for several geographical regions within a single housing market; then he used these price weights to partition housing expenditures into components (the same four) for a metropolitan sample of households. His subsequent analysis related consumption of these commodities to the income of each household and the prices prevailing in its chosen region of the market. The results revealed not only significant differences in income elasticities across the components of housing services, but also systematic substitution in consumption in response to intramarket price variation.

The assumptions about household behavior implicit in this analysis are equally strong. One must assume not only that these a priori categories exhaust the relevant characteristics valued in housing, but also that there is no substitution among spatial areas by consumers in registering their demands for these components of housing services. Within any housing market, households certainly do make substitutions among spatial locations. However, in this econometric specification, households choose the structure of prices as well as the levels of consumption of each composite commodity. If households choose among price sets by choosing a spatial location, then their consumption opportunities are defined by the envelope of the hedonic price surfaces. Of course, within this model all households would then face the same relative prices. Thus, without strong restrictions upon the substitution possibilities among locations (that is, an assumption that for some reason households first choose a neighborhood and only later choose housing characteristics in response to relative prices), the results are difficult to interpret.

In addition to these attempts to model the household consumption decision simultaneously for an exhaustive set of housing components, there have been a number of studies that have concentrated on the choice of a single attribute of the housing bundle: the tenure choice decision. As previously noted, for institutional and historical reasons, mortgage repayment makes home ownership an attractive vehicle for wealth accumulation, especially by middle-income households. Moreover, in the United States a significant fraction of all direct public subsidies to housing consumers has been in the form of tax advantages to home ownership. A number of studies (Birnbaum and Weston, 1974; Kain and Quigley, 1972) have analyzed the relationship between the demand for owner-occupancy (or for new purchase), income, and household demographics (and sometimes wealth). Earlier studies that analyzed tenure choice within a single housing market implicitly assumed that all households faced the same relative prices for rental and owner-occupied dwellings. In similar studies across housing markets, little serious effort was made to evaluate the price sensitivity of choice. More recently, however, Struyk (1976) has attempted to measure the variations in the price of owner-occupied, relative to rental, housing that individual households face. He accomplished this end by calculating the average implicit subsidy to owner occupancy and by measuring differential occupancy costs for the two types of accommodation. The results suggest that households are responsive to relative price variation in their demand for owner occupancy.

Better evidence is presented in an unpublished paper by Harvey Rosen (1977). Based upon income, family size and financial information, his study computed the potential tax subsidy to home ownership for each observation in a sample of individual households. Rosen then related the probability of home ownership to household income, demographic characteristics, and to the ratio of net homeowner and renter costs. The empirical results suggest that in their choice of the amount of housing and its form of tenure, households are sensitive to the tax-induced variations in relative prices.[20]

The Influence of Workplace-Related Prices

Two studies have utilized the variations in the worksites of households to allow the envelope of housing prices to vary by household, permitting subsequent investigation of the relationship between demand for components of housing services, income, and the intramarket relative price of housing attributes.

Straszheim (1973, 1975) estimated the price surface for several components of housing services (e.g., structure type, lot size) by the hedonic methods described earlier. The entire structure of prices is allowed to vary for a large number of geographic areas within a metropolitan housing market. Essentially, this analysis produces a contour map of the prices of specific housing attributes throughout the market. Now, assuming that the location of work is predetermined for each household, Straszheim estimated the envelope for prices for each component of housing by summarizing the price level from each workplace at an average distance (commute time).[21] Thus, depending upon the location of the worksite, the envelope of housing prices varies in a complex way for different households in the same housing market. The subsequent demand analysis relates observed household choices of housing characteristics to income and these relative prices. This strategy generalizes the demand analyses, since it provides estimates of both direct and cross price elasticities of demand for several components of housing services.

Quigley (1976) also relied upon household-specific workplaces to derive an envelope of housing prices that varies for consumers within the same metropolitan housing market. A workplace-specific travel cost[22] was added to the market price for each of several types of housing (i.e., specified combinations of housing components) available at each residential site.[23] The minimum price for each housing type constitutes the envelope faced by consumers with different incomes and workplaces.[24]

The housing demand problem was described as a discrete choice among housing types—a function of the underlying characteristics of the alternative types of housing, the incomes and demographic attributes of households, and the relative prices they face. The discrete choice model, estimated empirically by maximum likelihood techniques, suggests a strong pattern of substitution among components of housing services, particularly residential density and housing quality, in response to intra–housing-market price variations.

A comparison of these two related approaches to the analysis of housing demand shows that each makes strong but somewhat different assumptions about the nature of housing markets and household behavior. Straszheim assumes that each component of housing services can be purchased separately at any site in the metropolitan area (at varying prices, to be sure), but allows each household to vary in its valuation of travel time.[25] The latter analysis recognizes that households typically do not have the opportunity to purchase any combination of housing components—they must make a tied purchase of discrete bundles of components. However, Quigley's analysis makes the assumption that commuting time prices are constant for all households with the same income. This assumption is widely used in urban transportation research, but it is nevertheless somewhat restrictive.[26] Both models provide strong evidence that the observed demands of households for the components of housing services are highly responsive, not only to income differences, but also to intrametropolitan price variations that arise from worksite location. The spatial pattern of housing stock and the geographical pattern of housing prices are reflected in consumer demand in a complex but predictable manner.

The Direct Estimation of Utility Functions for Housing Components

Three recent analyses (Wheaton, 1977a, 1977b; Galster, 1977) have approached the modelling of household demand for the characteristics of dwelling units in a manner complementary to those just discussed. As noted before, the optimizing choices of housing consumers can be described as points on the lower envelopes of the price surfaces they face. Equivalently, in equilibrium the housing price surface of the urban area itself reflects the upper envelope of the bids different kinds of households are willing to make for alternative locations. This implies that identical households employed at the same worksite should achieve identical utility levels even though they have chosen different locations and housing components. Their choices should be along a common bid-rent function for housing components.

The models developed by Wheaton and Galster directly estimate the common utility function underlying the equilibrium bid-rent function. Galster assumes an arbitrary monetary valuation of commuting time;

Wheaton assumes that commuting time per se is valued by consumers. In either case, from information about income, housing payments, and out-of-pocket transportation costs, they estimate the parameters of a common utility function defined over housing components and other goods (i.e., income net of housing and transport costs). Conditional upon the form of the utility function (assuming Cobb-Douglas, CES, and—in Galster's work—a power transformation) and the assumption about travel time valuation, these analyses provide direct estimates of the marginal rates of substitution between particular components of the housing bundle (e.g., between a measure of the quality and the interior size of dwelling units) for households stratified by income and sociodemographic characteristics.[27] As might be expected, the empirical results of these studies indicate an increasing marginal valuation of most housing components with income (i.e., a decreasing marginal utility of income); however, Wheaton's results in particular also suggest pronounced differences in marginal rates of substitution with income (e.g., holding other things constant, an increasing valuation of exterior space relative to interior space with income) and with family size and composition.

These models assume, as does Straszheim's, that households have the opportunity to purchase any combination of housing components and that the price structure of the urban area is fully adjusted to its temporary equilibrium position. Finally, it should be noted that the application of such models to households in urban areas with decentralized workplaces, requires a knowledge of the equilibrium wage gradient for identical labor.[28]

6. HOUSING DEMAND: SOME SUMMARY OBSERVATIONS

In selecting a particular dwelling unit, households simultaneously choose a large array of particular characteristics—a structure type, a configuration of rooms, a neighborhood, and a journey to work. Thanks to the original contributors to the urban economics literature, a part of this choice process has been rather carefully analyzed—the trade-off between the journey-to-work component and a stylized representation of the remaining components of the housing bundle. The resulting theory is internally consistent and yields an equilibrium pattern of housing and location within urban areas that bears a rough resemblance to casual observation and to statistical summary data on urban areas.

Recent work on the demands for residential housing has proceeded in two directions. First, improved econometric techniques and the central insight of this original work have reduced the uncertainty regarding the parameters of the aggregate demand curve for housing services. Second, a more detailed consideration of the housing commodity has led to analyses of the substitution of components within the bundle of housing services in response to variations in household income and demographic composition. This more general conception of housing markets has also resulted in analyses that have investigated the role of intrametropolitan variations in housing price and worksite locations in motivating consumer choice. The empirical results of these studies are also consistent with our general knowledge of household location and housing choice in urban areas.

Compared to the earlier literature on housing market choice, however, these recent departures are less general, since the supply side of the market is only considered in a superficial way. The outcomes on the demand side of the market should, of course, provide a set of incentives to landlords and builders to modify the stock of housing in response to demand pressure.

The following sections review recent developments in modelling the behavior of housing suppliers.

7. THE SUPPLY OF HOUSING

As noted in the introduction, more than 90 percent of the housing services consumed in urban areas in any year are emitted by dwelling units from the pre-existing stock of housing. More generally, year to year variations in the housing services supplied in a metropolitan area arise from three sources: new construction of dwelling units by builders; the conversion of existing housing capital from one type of accommodation to another, presumably in response to perceived profitability; and the operation and maintenance decisions by owners of existing dwelling units, which affect the quantity of services provided by a given configuration of capital. These operation and maintenance decisions are made by landlords as well as owner-occupants, who rent housing services to themselves. Of course, decisions about operation and maintenance policy may result in the withdrawal of a given dwelling unit from the stock, either through demolition or abandonment. Presumably, individual landlords make operation and maintenance decisions to maximize profit, and owner-occupants are motivated to maximize utility.

During the past decade, much less theoretical and empirical work has been undertaken to unravel these complex supply phenomena. For example, in contrast to the considerable research efforts to investigate the aggregate demand curve for housing services, there have been only a few attempts (de Leeuw and Ekanem, 1971, Smith, 1976) to estimate the aggregate supply relationship for urban housing. (This does not include the large-scale simulation efforts—de Leeuw and Struyk, 1975; Ingram et al., 1972; and Bradbury et al., 1977—discussed elsewhere in this volume. Each of these models does estimate a housing supply curve, or something that closely resembles one. However, it is remarkable that, excluding these three complex and large-scale efforts, the preponderance of work on housing markets is so oriented to the demand side).

In part, this relative lack of progress can be traced to the real analytical difficulties encountered by the unobservability of a single housing quantity (market data provide evidence in the units of price times quantity). Our lack of understanding of supply phenomena is partly attributable to the difficulty in observing the behavior of decision makers at the micro level; that is, individual landlords, the physical components they offer on the market, and their gross rentals and investment strategies. Finally, this lack of progress may be attributed, in part, to the difficulty in conceptualizing the ways in which the various segments of the housing market interact to produce price incentives and to affect suppliers' expectations.

We begin our investigation of housing supply with a review of analyses of the aggregate supply of housing. Then we investigate several studies of housing production decisions—for new construction and for the services provided by the existing stock. Finally, we review several efforts to integrate the behavior of the various actors in supplying housing services; this involves a reconsideration of the familiar issue of the filtering of housing units—analyses of the life cycle, as it were, of dwellings.

Estimates of the Aggregate Supply Curve

The analysis of the supply elasticity of rental housing by de Leeuw and Ekanem (1971) illustrates the difficulties inherent in making inferences about supplier behavior in the aggregate. The aggregate evidence these authors relied on was obtained from a cross-section of Standard Metropolitan Statistical Areas (SMSAs). Because differences among SMSAs in rents, incomes, input costs, etc., tend to persist for long periods, the de Leeuw-Ekanem results may be interpreted as long-run estimates of the price-supply relationship. "Long run" in this sense may be on the order of ten or twenty years. It is the period in which producers have time to build additional units, to alter their operation and maintenance policies, or to make conversion decisions with respect to housing types or capital configurations, but it is obviously not a sufficiently long run for producers to depreciate completely the existing stock.

In their paper, de Leeuw and Ekanem estimated reduced form supply and demand relationships for rental housing and, conditional upon exogeneous estimates of the price and income elasticities of demand, deduced the overall supply elasticities in the rental housing market. On the demand side, the authors postulate that the quantity of rental housing services per household is a function of real income and the level of rents relative to other prices. On the supply side, average rents for a standardized unit are assumed to be a function of the prices of capital and operating inputs, of vacancy rates, of the number of households, and of the quantity of housing services per household.[29] For a sample of thirty-nine metropolitan areas, the authors have average values for these variables (they rely on the BLS estimates of the average rental price for a standardized unit; capital and operating prices also come from BLS tabulations). However, they do not have direct information on the (unobserved) quantity of housing services consumed per household. Thus they estimate the reduced form relationship across cities between average rents, on the one hand; and the prices of capital and operating inputs, the number of households, real income, the general price level, and vacancy rates, on the other hand. The conceptual model implies that rents will vary positively with input prices and negatively with vacancy rates, and that positive coefficients on the other variables will be significant only if supply is less than perfectly elastic (i.e., only if upward shifts in demand affect rents, after controlling for the effects of input prices and vacancies). The econometric results indicate that these other variables are significant and positive, implying an inelastic supply of housing in the long run. Further, when the model is solved algebraically for the supply elasticities (conditional upon exogeneous estimates of the price and income elasticities of demand, assumed to be -1 and $+1$ respectively), the elasticity of the supply of housing services with respect to output price (rent) is about 0.5 in this "long run." The estimated supply elasticity with respect to capital prices is between -0.5 and -0.2; with respect to the prices of operating inputs the supply elasticity is between -0.3 and 0. This evidence seems to be in sharp contrast to previous analyses that concentrated on the responsiveness of new construction to prices (Muth, 1960).

However, severe problems are encountered in interpreting this evidence. First, to believe that a positive coefficient on income in the reduced form relation results from upward shifts in housing demand (which increase rents in the long run) it must be assumed that there are no systematic measurement errors associated with income in the estimate of rent for a standardized dwelling unit across cities. This is very hard to swallow.[30] Second, a subsequent investigation by Grieson (1973) that used the same body of data indicated that plausible alternative formulations of the structural model, which yield identical reduced form relationships, imply much higher estimates of the supply elasticity of housing services.[31]

On balance, it is certainly possible to regard the evidence of de Leeuw and Ekanem on the aggregate supply elasticity of rental housing as highly ambiguous and as an underestimate of the true relationship between prices and the supply of housing services.

The Production Conditions for New Housing

Several recent studies have investigated the way in which inputs of residential capital can be substituted for land inputs to produce new units of housing services, again a single-valued commodity that is presumed in this framework to be the ultimate object of consumer demand. Muth's (1972) extension of the research reported in his 1967 paper is representative of these recent production analyses. From tabulated data on newly constructed dwelling units, Muth obtained the average sale price, (an appraisal of) the average market value of the land inputs, and the average amount of land used for new single-family housing in a sample of U.S. cities. From this information, the average value of capital inputs and the average land price can be computed; price indices for residential capital are available from other sources.

In a competitive market the ratios of marginal products will equal the ratios of factor prices. If it is assumed that the production relationship is of the CES form with constant returns to scale, then the elasticity of substitution of land for nonland in production can be estimated from the (logarithmic) regression of factor shares (i.e., land value divided by capital value) upon factor prices (land prices divided by capital prices). Muth's estimate of the elasticity of substitution, based upon several specifications of this model, is about 0.5.[32] If these results are interpreted literally, they suggest that in response to declining land prices with distance from downtown, the elasticity of housing services output per unit of land increases with distance. In equilibrium (in the long-run sense discussed in section 2), this implies that *relative* population densities increase at more distant locations as the urban population increases. These results may thus be interpreted as an explanation of the decrease in density gradients over time observed in most cities (see section 2)—a long-run equilibrium explanation that ignores rising income or employment decentralization but that assumes full adjustment of the stock of residential capital.

The Production and Supply of Used Housing

Several studies have expanded upon the production function approach to consider the output of housing services from used dwelling units. Rydell (1976) estimated the production relationship between land, fixed capital, and operating services for used multi-family dwelling units. This analysis assumes a constant elasticity of substitution between any pair of inputs (i.e., a three parameter CES production function with constant returns to scale). Empirical results from a single city, obtained from heroic assumptions in the light of data availability, also support the conclusion that the ratio of percentage change in input proportions to the percentage change in their relative prices is about 0.5.

It is, of course, more difficult to interpret this type of finding literally for used housing than it is for newly constructed dwellings. The intensity of residential development on parcels is affected by the prices existing at the time of investment (more specifically, by discounted expected future prices). However, once an investment has been made, it becomes quite costly to modify capital intensity other than by undermaintenance or minor structural transformations. Thus we may expect that a positive or negative "development gap" will be associated with the vintage of construction; input proportions are only weakly related to current prices and are more strongly related to the relative prices associated with the construction vintage. Unfortunately, in Rydell's analysis, it is difficult to interpret any vintage effect upon the production relationships.[33]

Ingram and Oron (1977) postulated a slightly more complex textbook model of the production of housing services and used it to perform "numerical experiments" (as distinct from statistical estimation) of supplier behavior. According to their analysis (simplified slightly in this presentation), housing services are subscripted by structure type and are defined in terms of two characteristics: "structure quality" and "neighborhood quality." Structure quality is produced by three factors: land (infinitely durable), operating inputs (a given flow), and capital (with some depreciation rate).

The capital specific to each structure type is, in turn, assumed to have two components: "structure capital" (the minimum stock of capital required to produce structure quality), which does not depreciate; and "quality capital" (required to produce structure quality in excess of the minimum), which depreciates at a rate affected by maintenance policy. Thus, in this formulation, structure capital does not enter into the production decisions that relate to existing dwelling units and is only a factor in calculations about new construction or conversion among structure types. One implication of this formulation is that dwelling units that produce larger amounts of structure quality will have higher depreciation rates (for a given maintenance policy) than those producing small quantities. In maximizing their profits, landlords choose a level of operating inputs and a maintenance policy; they also calculate whether it would be profitable to alter a given structure type.

In choosing current period levels of operating inputs and maintenance expenditures, the landlord maximizes the present value of net revenues subject to the production relationship and an accounting relationship between capital, maintenance, and depreciation. If the demand relationship between gross rents and structure quality is known, then the optimal maintenance path and the level of operating inputs are straightforward calculations.[34]

Conditional upon this optimal maintenance strategy, conversion among structure types is a simple extension. With exogenous conversion and new construction costs, the landlord will choose the best of the best—that structure type which, for the optimum maintenance and operating input decision over the planning period, maximizes the present value of the parcel.

In much of the analysis of operations and maintenance, Ingram and Oron investigated the implications of borrowing constraints that (they assume) operate whenever optimal current expenditures exceed cash flow (gross rents). (It is curious that the authors emphasize imperfect capital markets in their analysis of current period decisions but ignore its more important effect on the profitability of conversion.) The authors perform several numerical experiments, using this textbook model in combination with assumed and estimated parameter values. These results quite properly emphasize the general importance of operating inputs and maintenance in the analysis of housing markets but provide few testable propositions about behavior.

If the determinants of maintenance and operating expenditures are considered more generally, owner-occupants and landlords would be expected to behave somewhat differently. In general, given identical input prices and market demand conditions, we should expect higher levels of activity among owner-occupants than among landlords, since the former will derive utility as well as profit from renting particular housing commodities to themselves. A recent paper by Sweeney (1974c) has formally investigated this difference in incentives. The analysis suggests that owner-occupants will invest more resources in maintenance, will time investments earlier, and in general, will produce more specialized housing commodities than landlords, who face uncertainty in demand and who derive no satisfaction from investment. Alternatively, the theoretical analysis may be interpreted in terms of higher moving costs for owner-occupants who are thus less likely to move as their given dwelling unit ages—and consequently are more likely to invest in maintenance. With lower moving costs, there is a higher mobility rate among potential occupants of rental properties. These units will therefore be allowed to depreciate faster and households with lower housing demands will come to occupy them.

Quantitatively, the level of investment in housing supply by owner-occupants is surprisingly large; for example, it appears that the value of home improvements by owner-occupants is about one-half as large as the value of new single-family construction in any year. There has been one empirical analysis (Mendelsohn, 1977) of home improvements by owner-occupants, which investigated the probability of a household's engaging in investment activity and the conditional level of that investment. The results imply an income elasticity of home improvement expenditures by owner-occupants on the order of 0.6. Since much of the labor used in such activities is not purchased, the income relationship in terms of market values may be considerably larger.

Struyk and Ozanne (1977) have investigated the investment behavior of landlords and owner-occupants as revealed by changes in the housing services emitted by their dwelling units. They proceeded by matching individual dwelling units in the housing inventory at two points in time in a single metropolitan housing market. The data consist of a matched sample of Boston dwelling units in 1960 and 1970.

The maximization of profits (over an assumed ten-year time horizon) subject to a particular production function that relates housing services to the initial stock of housing and to capital and labor inputs yields a functional relationship between housing services, the initial level of service, the price of housing output, and the unit price of inputs.[35] Again, this relationship cannot be estimated directly, so the authors present estimates of the relationship between the quantity of housing services provided by a dwelling unit in 1970, the initial quantity observed in 1960, and output price variations. Based upon these regressions (and a supplemental analysis that estimates decennial changes in quantities) the authors made inferences about the elasticities of supply from the existing stock of rental and owner-occupied housing, conditional upon exogeneous information about the changes in input prices during the period.

The unobserved quantities of housing services are estimated from a Laspayres index. A hedonic regression that relates housing characteristics to rents and housing values in 1960 yields implicit prices or weights for each characteristic; these weights are applied to the characteristics of dwelling units in 1970 to arrive at a quantity index. In principle, this technique produces a consistent measure of housing quantities; in fact, its application produces an important bias in empirical work. Since only a limited number of dwelling unit characteristics are available for the estimation of the hedonic index, errors of measurement in the quantity of housing services are reflected in errors of measurement of the *opposite* sign in the price of housing services (since price times quantity equals rent). Thus, statistical estimation of the supply relationship between quantity and price is biased in a predictable way. The spurious relation between quantity and price is negative; therefore the estimated supply response will be biased towards zero. The estimated supply elasticities (about 0.2 for rental units and 0.2 to 0.4 for owner-occupied units, after adjustment for factor price changes) are probably lower bound estimates of the "true" elasticity of supply from the existing stock of structures.

The Integration of Supplier Behavior

It is commonly observed that newly constructed residential housing tends to be concentrated in the upper tail of the quality distribution. Once built and inhabited by upper-income households, who demand higher quality, housing generally deteriorates. In addition, as incomes and demands rise and as technical change advances, used dwellings tend to become obsolete. These two factors suggest that over their life cycle, dwelling units filter down to lower-income levels. Alternatively, as households at the upper end of the income distribution move to occupy new dwelling units, the units they vacate are available for occupancy by lower-income households. During the late fifties and early sixties, several "theories" of the filtering process emerged—detailed descriptions of the reallocation of households by income class among the existing stock as new construction enabled households at the highest-income level to leave vacancies available to those remaining. These assignment models of filtering shared one crucial deficiency, namely, that depreciation and deterioration of dwelling units was assumed to be exogeneous to the bids of households for occupancy. The limitations of such strong assumptions were pointed out by Lowry (1960); many of the papers reviewed in this section (e.g., Rydell, 1976; Ingram and Oron, 1977; Struyk and Ozanne, 1977) were attempts to understand the extent to which the depreciation and quality decline of dwelling units is endogeneous. Previous work had generally assumed a Leontief relation between operating inputs and capital and a Cobb-Douglas (or CES) relation between land and capital inputs.

In contrast to these efforts to include operating and maintenance inputs directly in housing supply models, a recent analysis by Muth (1973) takes the traditional filtering model to its logical conclusion. Muth's formulation analyzed the assignment problem of matching households to a stock of dwelling units whose characteristics depend only upon vintage. In this formulation, the initial level of housing services provided by a dwelling unit and its depreciation path are functions of vintage (i.e., year of construction) only. If income, and hence housing demand, grows at a constant rate and if the path of production prices is known, then for a given depreciation and discount rate, the initial level of housing services and the retirement age for a new dwelling (chosen by producers to maximize profits) will be determinate. Once chosen, housing units of a given vintage will be invaded over time by relatively lower-income households as a result of both depreciation of units and increases in absolute income. Relatively lower-income households will continually displace higher-income households from dwellings of a given vintage unless the price of that vintage (i.e., of that age-specific quantity of housing services) exceeds new construction costs for that quantity. From this rigid model, Muth calculated relative occupancy rates by vintage, rental expenditure, retirement age, and paths of residential succession based upon assumed market parameters.

In contrast to this deterministic world of filtering, two papers by Sweeney (1974a, 1974b) have integrated the depreciation of dwellings, new construction, and the process of succession in occupancy within a single model. Sweeney's basic model is applied to a restricted class of segmented markets, one in which all related commodities are ranked in discrete quality levels from "best" to "worst." Note that this assumes that all consumers make identical quality distinctions within the commodity class.

Consider the rental housing market; abstract from locational considerations and assume it is composed of a finite number of discrete quality levels, each characterized by a market price, a number of dwelling units, and a number of occupying households. Housing units are constructed at various levels in the hierarchy and they can only filter down the hierarchy of markets. The rate at which dwelling units filter down, however, depends directly upon the maintenance strategies adopted by landlords.[36]

The rate at which units deteriorate from a given level is directly proportional to the number of dwelling units at that level and inversely proportional to the average length of tenure of dwelling units at that level. Profit-maximizing landlords will choose a maintenance policy during the unit's tenure at any level that maximizes the discounted stream of net revenue— i.e., the discounted revenue minus the maintenance expenditure during its tenure at any level, plus its discounted value at the next lowest level. This implies that the value of a unit in any position in the hierarchy can be calculated by recursion once its final scrap value is known. Thus, the value of a unit at a given level in the hierarchy is an increasing function of all prices at and below that level and is independent of prices at higher levels. Similarly, profit from new construction at a given level is an increasing function of all prices at and below that level.

Under these general conditions, Sweeney demonstrated that the average tenure time of housing units at a given quality level is an increasing function of the price of housing at that level, is a decreasing function of the price of housing at all lower levels, and is independent of prices at higher levels.

Sweeney placed more or less standard restrictions on consumer demand, sufficient to imply that in response to small price changes households will change their chosen quality by, at most, one level and that, as prices rise, some families will no longer rent units in the hierarchy (i.e., they will "double up" or move away). Under these fairly general behavioral assumptions, Sweeney demonstrated that a competitive solution exists, that is, there is a set of prices declining throughout the hierarchy that insures a matching of suppliers to demanders within each level. The level in the hierarchy at which prices are zero corresponds to the level at which demand is also zero. The dynamic equilibrium implies a steady rate of new construction within the hierarchy and a steady filtering of dwelling units throughout the hierarchy, with the profits of suppliers at competitive levels and with consumers as well-off as possible.

Subsequently, the author demonstrated that this equilibrium is unique, thereby permitting a highly stylized analysis of several classes of housing-market programs. For example, Sweeney proved that there exists a construction subsidy program that reduces the equilibrium rental prices at all levels in the hierarchy below some arbitrary level. He further demonstrated that this result does not hold for an arbitrarily chosen construction subsidy program but only for a restricted class of possibilities. This provides something of an answer to the filtering debate of the early sixties—whether and under what conditions construction subsidies raise the welfare of low-income households by reducing their housing prices. Sweeney's analysis also provides some insight into the implications of demand subsidies and their potential effect on the welfare of nonsubsidized households.

Several problems are raised in interpreting the results of this important strand of research. These do not arise merely because the assumptions noted here are quite strong (although they are, of course). Rather, the uniqueness of the competitive equilibrium and the subsequent comparison of dynamic equilibrium depend on an additional assumption, namely, that the total lifetime of a dwelling unit is an increasing function of each rental price. Clearly this is very restrictive indeed, for it implies that the increased tenure time at a particular level in response to a price increase at that level must exceed the decreased tenure time at all other levels in the hierarchy. This assumption may be correct in some situations, but it surely is not generally valid. Naturally, once this assumption is abandoned it is possible, at least in principle, to rank multiple equilibria preferentially—for example, to make comparisons between equilibrium solutions with varying rents for low-quality dwellings.

However, despite these limitations the commodity hierarchy model provides real insight into the segmented market for housing services and provides a rigorous and plausible analysis of the filtering of dwelling units among submarkets. Although this analysis is still a long way from practical application, the basic approach has been used by Ohls (1975) in a subsequent simulation study of housing policies and has been incorporated—somewhat crudely—in econometric analysis.

CONCLUSIONS

This chapter has surveyed some of the progress made during the past decade in understanding the behavior of suppliers and demanders of residential housing in urban areas. The point of departure is a featureless plain containing a number of undifferentiated consumers with a common worksite. In such a world, the system of housing prices performs a truly heroic function; it causes different amounts of housing to be produced by landlords at different locations and, simultaneously, it causes households to be utterly indifferent to the amount and location of their housing. If consumers were differentiated by income alone, the price system would again compute everything required to characterize the behavior of housing suppliers, housing demanders, household locations and urban form. Unfortunately, this world gets complicated if consumers are differentiated by other characteristics or if they have differing transport demands. If housing is differentiated as well, and more to the point, if it lasts a long time, then the aesthetic appeal of that heroic price set is diminished. Given a convenient structure of assumptions on all these complications, a single price structure could be deduced with the assistance of a large-scale computer, but its properties would be heavily dependent upon many specifics. However, the "solution" provided would be to the market for urban housing!

Much of the progress noted in this paper has resulted from attention to these many specifics—to those features that distinguish the search for a fixed point in the urban housing market from other searches in other markets. Some real progress has been made in characterizing the kinds of households that choose to consume specific attributes of the bundle of housing services and in describing and analyzing the character of the housing bundle itself. Progress has been made in relating the location of the existing stock of dwelling units and the decentralized nature of worksites to a more complete characterization of consumer demands. In addition, there exists a greater understanding of the interrelation of housing submarkets from the viewpoint of suppliers and demanders, and of their responses to changes in an existing set of relative prices.

However, by any standard, relatively less progress has been made in characterizing the decisions of individual landlords in this market, and systematic econometric evidence is notably weak. For example, despite their critical importance, there has been little analytical work on the formation of price and profitability expectations by landlords or on the relationship between the character of particular neighborhoods and expectations about future market conditions. Descriptive information gathered by George Sternlieb and his associates (1962, 1973) at several points in time and across several housing markets strongly suggests that landlords' notions about the return on equivalent investment vary among neighborhoods and, not surprisingly, that this affects their behavior as housing suppliers. Yet uncertainty and externalities have not been prominent in economists' formal models of supplier behavior. Ironically, implicit judgments about the effect of externalities and expectations upon supplier decisions have provided the principal economic motivation for many categorical and formula grant programs.

NOTES

1. As an industrial sector, the housing industry is also distinctive. For example, housebuilding in the United States is characterized by small scale production, large financial capital requirements, labor intensive production techniques, and a relatively low rate of technical progress. A review of recent research focusing on these aspects of housing would be quite different from the perspective adopted here. Unfortunately, such a review would also be very short.

There is, of course, some overlap between the price theoretic and industrial organization perspective. For example, intraurban housing markets are affected by the pattern of local regulation. The pattern of regulation may, in turn affect the structure of the industry. The chapter by Mills in this volume considers the former in some detail. See Muth and Wetzler (1976) and Oster and Quigley (1977) for recent evidence on the latter.

2. Muth (1968), p. 300.

3. This last proposition depends also on the plausible assumption that the income elasticity of housing demand exceeds the elasticity of marginal transport costs with respect to income.

4. This is hardly surprising, since mathematical tractability virtually requires that the assumption of long-run (as opposed to temporary) equilibrium be maintained. For more on this, see below.

5. Mills and MacKinnon's review (1973) of this genre questions the cost-benefit ratio of this allocation of research expertise and indicates that the most tempting mathematical extensions of the monocentric model may not further an understanding of urban economics. A more extreme statement of conflicting judgments may be found in the published views of Mirlees, Richardson, and Solow (1973).

6. More precisely, to compute the intercept and the gradient from two pieces of information—the level of activity in the central city and the level of activity in the entire urban area—leaving no degree of freedom.

7. This is a straightforward errors-in-variables argument: random deviations of observed income about permanent income will tend to cancel in computing averages.

8. Equivalently, high transaction costs indicate that the observed consumption of housing by any household may deviate considerably from its equilibrium or desired level of housing based upon current income and demographics (Hanushek and Quigley, 1978b; 1979).

9. Several papers (Maisel, Burnham, and Austin, 1971; Smith and Campbell, 1979) attribute this discrepancy to some form of "aggregation bias." In general, conditional upon the specification of the model, aggregation merely affects the efficiency of parameter estimates, unless units of observation are aggregated by values of the dependent variable.

10. Kain and Quigley (1975), p. 171.

11. The reasoning here is a bit more subtle. To the extent that average incomes and average housing prices are correlated across cities, an increase in income increases the probability that a household will be located in a city of higher average income. Since the relative income of the household will be lower after a move to a higher-income city, it will locate closer to the city center, where prices are yet higher. Again, with price inelastic demand, this understates the change in expenditures with respect to price.

12. Since the bivariate estimates of income elasticity from sample b and sample c bracket the "true" values.

13. This strategy relies upon an exogenous estimate of the value of land for each observation on housing units, which is available in FHA appraisals. See also section 7, below.

14. This specification is, however, not consistent with equilibrium on the demand side, and the diminishing marginal utility of additional units of each characteristic. See "The Importance of Externalities," below.

15. Indeed, there appears to be only one paper (Goodman, 1978) that investigates the functional form of the hedonic relationship. That study concludes, on the basis of Box-Cox tests that the appropriate functional form is (roughly) the square root relationship between price (P) and housing attributes (x): $\sqrt{P} = \beta x$.

16. In addition, these research techniques have broad practical applications in improving the assessment of real property and in increasing the reliability of price indices. (See, for example, Schafter, 1977).

17. See Sherwin Rosen (1974) for a lucid discussion of these issues.

18. See Courant and Rubinfeld (1978) and Pines and Weiss (1976) for reviews of these issues emphasizing different aspects.

19. It should be emphasized that these stylized results say very little about the distribution of benefits between landlords and tenants of a real public policy in an urban area. Polinsky and Shavell (1976) have analyzed a more general case (in which migration is not costless and in which consumers' price and income elasticities of demand matter) that indicates the divergence of benefit measures and willingness to pay. A more realistic setting is analyzed by Rose-Ackerman (1977). Within a "not fully open" urban area, Rose-Ackerman demonstrated that the relationship between

aggregate rents and benefits depends not only upon the price and income elasticities of demand for housing (or in this special case, land) but also upon the specifics of the public program—for example, a program that provides uniform, equalizing, or selective benefits to communities.

20. Rosen's empirical results suggest that the elimination of the subsidy to home-ownership would reduce homeownership rates modestly, by about 4 to 5 percent. There is reason for caution in the interpretation of these numerical results, since the model is estimated for a (national) sample of households in different local markets, and it is assumed that each household faces a horizontal supply curve for owner-occupied and rental housing.

21. Each "contour map" is summarized by its "elevation" and "gradient" from each workplace. The details of this estimation are quite laborious and are summarized by Straszheim (1973).

22. This assumes that travel time is valued at a constant price (as a proportion of hourly wages) for each household.

23. See the chapter by Ingram in this volume for an elaboration on these house-hold-specific price surfaces, termed gross prices.

24. A contour map is produced for each housing type. From a given workplace, the elevation of each point is raised by the transport costs (given the income of a household). The envelope of prices for any household is the minimum point on each contour map.

25. This is, in fact, somewhat inconsistent with the procedure for defining the envelope of prices. See note 21.

26. In addition, the estimation technique used in the latter analysis assumes a specialized property of discrete choice (the so-called independence of irrelevant alter-natives). Not too much should be made of this limitation, however, since McFadden (1978) has shown in a recent unpublished paper on residence choice that Quigley's empirical model is similar (but not identical) to a more general model that is free of this restricted property.

27. The actual estimation technique is slightly more complex and the assumptions are slightly stronger, since income classes (and not identical incomes) are the basis for stratification. See Wheaton, 1974b, for details.

28. This is because the equilibrium bid-rent surface must equalize utility levels for ex ante identical households with different workplaces, and hence transport costs, to the same residential locations.

29. The form of the last two variables was chosen to investigate potential sources of diseconomies of scale in housing supply by factoring housing services into proxies for housing services per unit of capital stock and levels of (new and existing) capital stock. As the authors admit, these proxy variables do "not correspond very closely to the concepts."

30. In collecting price data, the BLS do not control in a systematic way for the quality of neighborhoods. As noted in section 3, there is ample evidence that neigh-borhood characteristics are capitalized into rental prices and that the consumption of these attributes of housing varies positively with income. Thus, it appears, at least to me, that the positive relationship between rents and incomes says little about the supply elasticity of housing services.

31. Other published evidence of very large supply elasticities provided by Smith is far less reliable, since it is based upon the interpretation of an apparently unidenti-fied regression equation (Smith, 1976, p. 401, n. 26).

32. More recent work (Polinsky and Ellwood, 1979) that applies an identical strategy to a national sample of about 10,000 single, detached dwelling units con-cludes that the best estimate of the elasticity of substitution is about 0.45. However, it should be noted that Koenker's replication (1972) for new multi-family housing within a single city results in estimates substantially higher.

33. This is because, as the model is specified, the age of the building mechanically affects the quantity of services actually provided by a multi-family complex. More-over, in this model the price of services declines with the quantity provided. The estimated equations also "control for" the number of dwelling units and buildings per

property. The net effect of these assumptions is to strain (perhaps beyond credibility) the assumption of constant returns needed to interpret the production parameters.

34. To avoid using an optimal control framework, Ingram and Oron made very simple assumptions about expectations: they assumed a fixed time horizon and a static demand relationship. A more extended treatment of dynamics, but not of expectations, is provided by Dildine and Massy (1974).

35. The production relationship is somewhat specialized. Specifically, it is assumed that the production function for housing services at the end of the period is the initial level of services (depreciated) plus a constant elasticity relationship between capital and labor supplied during the period. The elasticity of substitution between capital and labor is constant, but with diminishing returns assumed. However, the elasticity of substitution between the initial stock of services and the capital-labor composite is infinite.

36. Investment policy, by assumption, cannot move a dwelling unit up the hierarchy.

REFERENCES

Aaron, Henry J. 1975. *Who Pays the Property Tax?* Washington, D.C.: Brookings Institution.

Alonso, William. 1964. *Location and Land Use.* Cambridge, Mass.: Harvard University Press.

Anderson, Robert J., and Croker, Thomas D. 1971. "Air Pollution and Residential Property Values." *Urban Studies* 8 (October): 171–80.

Arnott, Richard J., and MacKinnon, James G. 1977. "The Effects of the Property Tax: A General Equilibrium Simulation." *Journal of Urban Economics* 4 (October): 389–407.

Ball, Michael J. 1973. "Recent Empirical Work on the Determinants of Relative House Prices." *Urban Studies* 10: 213–31.

Birnbaum, Howard, and Weston, Rafael. 1974. "Homeownership and the Wealth Position of Black and White Households." *Review of Income and Wealth* 20: 103–19.

Black, David E. 1972. "The Nature and Extent of Effective Property Tax Rate Variations within the City of Boston." *National Tax Journal* 25 (June): 203–10.

Bradbury, K.; Engle, R.; Owen, I.; and Rothenberg, J. 1977. "Simultaneous Estimation of the Supply and Demand for Household Location in a Multizonal Metropolitan Area." In *Residential Location and Urban Housing Markets.* Edited by Gregory K. Ingram. New York: National Bureau of Economic Research.

Bradford, D.; Malt, R.; and Oates, W. 1969. "The Rising Cost of Local Public Services: Some Evidence and Reflections." *National Tax Journal* 22 (June): 185–202.

Carliner, Geoffrey. 1973. "Income Elasticity of Housing Demand." *Review of Economics and Statistics* 55 (November): 528–32.

Courant, P., and Rubinfeld, D. 1978. "On the Measurement of Benefits in an Urban Context: Some General Equilibrium Issues." *Journal of Urban Economics* 5 (July): 346–56.

de Leeuw, Frank. 1976. "The Demand for Housing: A Review of the Cross Sectional Evidence." *Review of Economics and Statistics* 53 (February): 1–10.

deLeeuw, Frank, and Ekanem, Nkanta F. 1971. "The Supply of Rental Housing." *American Economic Review* 61 (December): 806–17.

deLeeuw, Frank, and Struyk, Raymond J. 1975. *The Web of Urban Housing.* Washington, D.C.: Urban Institute.

Dildine, Larry L., and Massy, Fred A. 1974. "Dynamic Model of Private Incentives to Housing Maintenance." *Southern Economics Journal* 40 (April): 631–39.

Dixit, Avinash. 1973. "The Optimum Factory Town." *Bell Journal of Economics and Management Science* 4 (Autumn): 637–51.

Edel, Matthew, and Sclar, Elliott. 1974. "Taxes, Spending, and Property Values: Supply Adjustment in a Tiebout-Oates Model." *Journal of Political Economy* 83 (September/October): 941–54.

Freeman, A. Myrick. 1976. "Air Pollution and Property Values: A Methodological Comment." *Review of Economics and Statistics* 53 (November): 415–16.

Galster, George C. 1977. "A Bid-Rent Analysis of Housing Market Discrimination." *American Economic Review* 67 (March): 144–55.

Gillingham, Robert. 1975. "Place to Place Rent Comparisons." *Annals of Economic and Social Measurement* 4 (Winter): 153–73.

Goodman, Allen C. "Hedonic Prices, Price Indices, and Housing Markets." *Journal of Urban Economics,* forthcoming.

Grether, D. M., and Mieszkowski, Peter. 1974. "The Determinants of Real Estate Values." *Journal of Urban Economics* 1 (April): 127–46.

Grieson, Ronald E. 1973. "The Supply of Rental Housing: Comment." *American Economic Review* 63 (June): 433–36.

Griliches, Zvi. 1961. "Hedonic Price Indices for Automobiles: An Econometric Analysis of Quality Change." In *The Price Statistics of the Federal Government.* New York: National Bureau of Economic Research.

———. 1971. *Price Indices and Quality Change.* Cambridge, Mass.: Harvard University Press.

Hanushek, Eric A., and Quigley, John M. 1978a. "What Is 'the' Price Elasticity of Housing Demand." Public Policy Analysis Discussion Paper no. 7803. Rochester, N.Y.: University of Rochester.

———. 1978b. "An Explicit Model of Residential Mobility." *Land Economics* 54 (November): 411–29.

———. 1979. "The Dynamics of the Housing Market: A Stock Adjustment Model of Housing Consumption." *Journal of Urban Economics* 6 (January).

Harrison, David, and Kain, John F. 1974. "Cumulative Urban Growth and Urban Density Functions." *Journal of Urban Economics* 1 (January): 61–98.

Heinberg, J. D., and Oates, W. E. 1970. "The Incidence of Differential Property Taxes on Urban Housing: A Comment and Some Further Evidence." *National Tax Journal* 23 (March): 92–98.

Hirschman, Albert O. 1975. *Exit, Voice, and Loyalty.* Cambridge, Mass.: Harvard University Press.

Ingram, Gregory K.; Kain, John F.; and Ginn, J. Royce. 1972. *The Detroit Prototype of the NBER Urban Simulation Model.* New York: National Bureau of Economic Research.

Ingram, Gregory K., and Oron, Yitzhak. 1977. "The Behavior of Housing Producers." In *Residential Location and Urban Housing Markets*. Edited by Gregory K. Ingram. New York: National Bureau of Economic Research.

Kain, John F., and Quigley, John M. 1970a. "Measuring the Value of Housing Quality." *Journal of the American Statistical Association*. 65 (June): 532–48.

————. 1970b. "Evaluating the Quality of the Residential Environment." *Environment and Planning* 2: 23–32.

————. 1972. "Housing Market Discrimination, Home Ownership, and Savings Behavior." *American Economic Review* 62 (June): 263–77.

————. 1975. *Housing Markets and Racial Discrimination*. New York: National Bureau of Economic Research.

Kemper, Peter, and Schmenner, Roger. 1974. "The Density Gradient for Manufacturing Industry." *Journal of Urban Economics* 1 (October): 410–27.

King, A. Thomas. 1973. *Property Taxes, Amenities, and Residential Land Values*. Cambridge, Mass.: Ballinger Publishing.

————. 1976. "The Demand for Housing: A Lancastrian Approach." *Southern Economics Journal* 43 (October): 1077–87.

————. 1975. "The Demand for Housing: Integrating the Roles of Journey to Work, Neighborhood Quality, and Prices." In *Household Production and Consumption*. Edited by Nester E. Terleckyj. New York: National Bureau of Economic Research.

King, A. Thomas, and Mieszkowski, Peter. 1973. "Racial Discrimination, Segregation, and the Relative Price of Housing." *Journal of Political Economy* 81 (May/June): 590–606.

Koenker, Roger. 1972. "An Empirical Note on the Elasticity of Substitution Between Land and Capital in a Monocentric Housing Market." *Journal of Regional Science* 12 (August): 299–305.

Lancaster, Kelvin J. 1966. "A New Approach to Consumer Theory." *Journal of Political Economy* 74 (April): 132–57.

Lapham, Victoria. 1971. "Do Blacks Pay More for Housing?" *Journal of Political Economy* 79 (November/December): 1244–57.

Lowry, Ira S. 1960. "Filtering and Housing Standards: A Conceptual Analysis." *Land Economics* 36 (November): 362–70.

Maisel, Sherman J.; Burnham, James B.; and Austin, John S. 1971. "The Demand for Housing: A Comment." *Review of Economics and Statistics* 53 (November): 410–12.

McFadden, Daniel. 1978. "Modelling the Choice of Residential Location." *Transportation Research Record*, forthcoming.

Mendelsohn, Robert S. 1977. "Empirical Evidence on Home Improvements." *Journal of Urban Economics* 4 (October): 459–68.

Mills, Edwin S. 1967. "An Aggregative Model of Resource Allocation in a Metropolitan Area." *American Economic Review* 57 (May): 197–210.

————. 1970. "Urban Density Functions." *Urban Studies* 7 (February): 5–20.

————. 1972. *Studies in the Structure of the Urban Economy*. Baltimore: Johns Hopkins Press.

Mills, Edwin S., and MacKinnon, James. 1973. "Notes on the New Urban Economics." *Bell Journal of Economics and Management Science* 4 (Autumn): 593–601.

Muth, Richard F. 1960. "The Demand for Non-Farm Housing." In *The De-*

mand for Durable Goods. Edited by Arnold C. Harberger. Chicago: University of Chicago Press.

―――. 1961. "The Spatial Structure of the Housing Market." *Papers of the Regional Science Association* 7: 207–20.

―――. 1964. "The Variation of Population Density and its Components in South Chicago." *Papers of the Regional Science Association* 15: 173–83.

―――. 1968. "Urban Residential Land and Housing Markets." In *Issues in Urban Economics.* Edited by Harvey S. Perloff and Lowdon Wingo. Baltimore: Johns Hopkins Press.

―――. 1969. *Cities and Housing.* Chicago: University of Chicago Press.

―――. 1971. "The Derived Demand for Urban Residential Land. *Urban Studies* 8 (October): 243–54.

―――. 1973. "A Vintage Model of the Housing Stock." *Papers of the Regional Science Association* 30 (November): 141–56.

Muth, Richard F., and Wetzler, Elliot. 1976. "The Effect of Constraints on House Costs." *Journal of Urban Economics* 3 (January): 57–67.

Niedercorn, John H. 1971. "A Negative Exponential Model of Urban Land Use Densities and Its Implications for Metropolitan Development." *Journal of Regional Science* 11 (December): 317–26.

Nourse, Hugh O. 1963. "The Effects of Public Housing on Property Values in St. Louis." *Land Economics* 39 (November): 434–41.

Oates, Wallace E. 1969. "The Effects of Property Taxes and Local Spending on Property Values: An Empirical Study of Tax Capitalization and the Tiebout Hypothesis." *Journal of Political Economy* 77 (November): 957–71.

―――. 1973. "The Effects of Property Taxes and Local Spending on Property Values: Reply." *Journal of Political Economy* 81 (July): 1004–8.

Ohls, James C. 1975. "Public Policy toward Low Income Housing and Filtering in Housing Markets." *Journal of Urban Economics* 2 (April): 144–71.

Orr, L. 1968. "The Incidence of Differential Property Taxes on Urban Housing." *National Tax Journal* 21 (September): 253–62.

Oster, Sharon M., and Quigley, John M. 1977. "Regulatory Barriers to the Diffusion of Innovation: Some Evidence from Building Codes." *Bell Journal of Economics* 8 (October): 361–77.

Perloff, Harvey S., and Wingo, Lowdon, eds. 1968. *Issues in Urban Economics.* Baltimore: Johns Hopkins Press.

Peterson, George E. 1973. "The Effect of Zoning Regulations on Suburban Property Values." Washington, D.C.: Urban Institute Working Paper 1207-24. March.

Pines, David, and Weiss, Yoram. 1976. "Land Improvement Projects and Land Values." *Journal of Urban Economics* 3 (January): 447–61.

Polinsky, A. Mitchell. 1977. "The Demand for Housing: A Study in Specification and Grouping." *Econometrica* 42 (March): 447–61.

Polinsky, A. Mitchell, and Ellwood, David T. "An Empirical Reconciliation of Micro and Grouped Estimates of the Demand for Housing." *Review of Economics and Statistics,* forthcoming.

Polinsky, A. Mitchell, and Rubinfeld, Daniel. 1978. "The Long Run Effects of a Residential Property Tax and Local Public Services." *Journal of Urban Economics* 5 (April): 241–62.

Polinsky, A. Mitchell, and Shavell, Steven. 1976. "Amenities and Property Values in a Model of an Urban Area." *Journal of Public Economics* 5 (January/February): 119–30.

Pollakowski, Henry O. 1973. "The Effects of Property Taxes and Local Public Spending on Property Values: Comment." *Journal of Political Economy* 81 (July): 994–1003.

Quigley, John M. 1976. "Housing Demand in the Short Run: An Analysis of Polytomous Choice." *Explorations in Economic Research* 3 (Winter): 76–102.

Quigley, John M., and Weinberg, Daniel H. 1977. "Intra-Metropolitan Residential Mobility: A Review and Synthesis." *International Regional Science Review* 2 (Fall): 41–66.

Richardson, Harry W.; Solow, Robert S.; and Mirrlees, J. A. 1973. "Comments on Some Uses of Mathematical Models in Urban Economics." *Urban Studies* 10: 259–70.

Ridker, Ronald G., and Henning, John A. 1967. "The Determinants of Residential Property Values with Special Reference to Air Pollution." *Review of Economics and Statistics* 49 (May): 246–56.

Roistacher, Elizabeth A. 1977. "Short-Run Responses to Changes in Income." *American Economic Review* 67 (February): 381–86.

Rose-Ackerman, Susan. 1977. "On the Distribution of Public Program Benefits Between Landlords and Tenants." *Journal of Environmental Economics and Management* 4 (June): 167–84.

————. 1979. "Market Models of Local Government: Exit, Voting, and the Land Market." *Journal of Urban Economics* 6.

Rosen, Harvey. 1977. "Housing Decisions and the U. S. Income Tax: An Econometric Analysis." Econometric Research Program Memorandum no. 218. Princeton, N.J.: Princeton University.

Rosen, Sherwin. 1974. "Hedonic Prices and Implicit Markets: Product Differentiation in Pure Competition." *Journal of Political Economy* 82 (January): 34–55.

Rothenberg, Jerome. 1977. "Endogeneous City-Suburb Rivalry through Household Location." In *The Political Economy of Multi-level Government*. Edited by Wallace E. Oates. Lexington, Mass.: D. C. Heath.

Rydell, C. Peter. 1976. "Measuring the Supply Response to Housing Allowances." *Papers of the Regional Science Association* 37: 31–54.

Schafer, Robert. 1977. "A Comparison of Alternative Approaches to Assessing Real Property." *Assessors' Journal* 12 (June): 81–94.

Schnare, Ann B., and Struyk, Raymond J. 1976. "Segmentation and Urban Housing Market." *Journal of Urban Economics* 3 (April): 146–66.

Smith, Barton A., and Campbell, J. M. 1979. "Aggregation Bias and the Demand for Housing." *International Economic Review,* forthcoming.

Smith, Barton A. 1976. "The Supply of Urban Housing." *Quarterly Journal of Economics* 90 (August): 389–405.

Solow, Robert S. 1972. "Congestion, Density and the Use of Land in Transportation." *Swedish Journal of Economics* 74 (March): 161–73.

Sternlieb, George. 1969. *The Tenement Landlord.* New Brunswick, N.J.: Rutgers University Press.

Sternlieb, George, and Burchess, Robert W. 1973. *Residential Abandonment: The Tenement Landlord Revisited*. New Brunswick, N.J.: Rutgers University Press.

Straszheim, Mahlon. 1973. "Estimation of the Demand for Urban Housing Services from Household Interview Data." *Review of Economics and Statistics* 55 (February): 1–8.

———. 1975. *An Econometric Analysis of the Urban Housing Market*. New York: National Bureau of Economic Research.

Struyk, Raymond. 1976. *Urban Homeownership*. Lexington, Mass.: D. C. Heath.

Struyk, Raymond J., and Ozanne, Larry. 1977. "The Price Elasticity of Supply of Housing Services." Washington, D.C.: Urban Institute. (Mimeograph.)

Sweeney, James L. 1974a. "A Commodity Hierarchy Model of the Rental Housing Market." *Journal of Urban Economics* 1 (July): 288–323.

———. 1974b. "Quality, Commodity Hierarchies, and Housing Markets." *Econometrica* 42 (January): 147–60.

———. 1974c. "Housing Unit Maintenance and the Mode of Tenure." *Journal of Economic Theory* 8: 111–38.

Tiebout, Charles M. 1956. "A Pure Theory of Local Expenditures." *Journal of Political Economy* 64 (October): 416–24.

Vaughn, Garrett A. 1976. "Sources of Downward Bias in Estimating the Demand Income Elasticity for Urban Housing." *Journal of Urban Economics* 3 (January): 45–56.

Wheaton, William C. 1977a. "Residential Decentralization, Land Rents, and the Benefits of Urban Transportation Investment." *American Economic Review* 67 (March): 136–43.

———. 1977b. "A Bid Rent Approach to Housing Demand." *Journal of Urban Economics* 4 (April): 200–17.

White, Michelle J. 1977. "On Cumulative Urban Growth and Urban Density Functions." *Journal of Urban Economics* 4 (January): 104–12.

Wingo, Lowdon. 1961. *Transportation and Urban Land*. Baltimore: Johns Hopkins Press.

13

PREJUDICE AND DISCRIMINATION IN THE URBAN HOUSING MARKET

JOHN YINGER

INTRODUCTION

Racial prejudice and racial discrimination are important influences on the structure of American cities. Families of all races choose where to live partly on the basis of their racial prejudices, and racial discrimination constrains the housing choices of many minority families. In order to determine implications for public policy, this chapter reviews what is known about the effects of racial prejudice and racial discrimination on the urban housing market. The racial groups considered are blacks and whites.

Precise definition of several terms is crucial for the discussion that follows. *Racial prejudice* is an inflexible, deeply felt *attitude* about members of a particular racial group. In the context of this chapter, prejudice is an aversion to living near an individual of another race, regardless of the attributes of that individual. *Racial discrimination* is *behavior* that denies members of a racial group the rights or opportunities given to other groups, regardless of the formal qualifications of that group for those rights or opportunities. Two types of discrimination are of particular concern here: *price discrimination* occurs when a seller charges members of one group higher prices than members of another group for equivalent products; *exclusion* occurs when a seller refuses to sell or rent housing at a particular location to members of one racial group.[1]

A *racial price differential* exists when members of different racial groups pay different amounts for equivalent products. This term is purely descriptive. A common confusion is to equate the terms *price discrimination* and

John Yinger is an assistant professor, Department of City and Regional Planning, Harvard University.

I am grateful to Paul N. Courant, Peter Mieszkowski, and Mahlon Straszheim for their comments.

price differential; price discrimination is sufficient to cause a price differential, but it is not necessary. It is also convenient to distinguish between price differentials *within* neighborhoods and price differentials *between* types of neighborhoods. For example, blacks and whites who live in the same neighborhood may pay the same amount for housing even if the price for comparable housing is much higher in mostly black neighborhoods than in mostly white neighborhoods.

Racial residential segregation is a measure of the physical separation of the residential locations of different races. *Complete* racial segregation exists when no location contains members of more than one race. *Segregation* is another purely descriptive term. This paper determines the implications for segregation of various types of behavior, such as discrimination. Racial *integration,* the inverse of racial segregation, is a measure of the extent to which blacks and whites live together. The term *complete integration* is used in two ways: it refers to either a uniform distribution or a random distribution of blacks and whites in an urban area. Segregation (or integration) has two dimensions: degree and pattern. The *degree* of segregation indicates to what extent the races live in separate places, and the *pattern* of segregation describes the distribution of the races in an urban area. One often-mentioned pattern of segregation is a black *ghetto,* the clustering of the black population in a central location.

1. THEORIES OF RACE AND URBAN STRUCTURE

Theories about race and urban structure introduce the racial prejudice of households or racial discrimination by the sellers of housing (or both) into an equilibrium model of the urban housing market. These theories therefore determine the impact of prejudice and/or discrimination on the pattern of residential location (including racial segregation) and on the relative price and quantity of housing consumed by blacks and whites. Since racial discrimination in housing is illegal, its existence is sufficient to justify government intervention in the housing market.[2] The link between racial prejudice and government intervention is less direct, and people with different values are likely to disagree about the extent of government intervention that is called for by the existence of prejudice without discrimination. Thus, for policy purposes, it is important (1) to carefully distinguish the logical implications of models based on prejudice alone from those of models that include discrimination and (2) to determine which of these types of model is supported by the evidence. The remainder of this section is devoted to the first task; section 2 is devoted to the second.

Household Prejudice and Urban Structure

In a model of an urban area, racial prejudice is defined as a disutility of whites or blacks from living with or near members of the other race. The degree to which a household at any particular location lives with or near members of the other case is measured by racial composition, $r(u)$, which is defined to be the proportion of the population at and around location u that is black. Prejudice is measured by the effect of $r(u)$ on a household's utility function. This subsection examines models that include household prejudice, but not discrimination by the sellers of housing.

The effect of $r(u)$ on utility has been characterized in two ways. The first alternative views prejudice as disutility from living *near* members of the other race. This approach assumes that complete racial segregation exists, with blacks in the city center, and measures prejudice as a function of distance from the black-white border—we call models based on this approach *border models*. The second alternative views prejudice as disutility from living *with* members of the other race. Under this approach, the pattern of segregation is derived, not assumed. Because this formulation of prejudice is analogous to the more general formulation of a neighborhood amenity, we call these models *amenity models*.

A model of prejudice and urban structure requires assumptions about prejudice; surveys of racial attitudes, many of which are reviewed by Pettigrew (1973), are an important source of information about these assumptions. In surveys conducted in the late 1960s, 35 percent of whites said they would or might move, and 51 percent said they would object, if a black family moved in next door; 71 percent said they would or might move if many blacks moved into their neighborhood. Similarly, 43 percent of whites said that whites have the right to exclude blacks from white neighborhoods, and 63 percent opposed laws forbidding discrimination in housing. According to these surveys, white prejudice has subsided somewhat over time, but substantial white prejudice against blacks still exists.

Black attitudes exhibit greater variation. In one survey in the late 1960s, 74 percent of blacks preferred neighborhoods with both black and white residents and 16 percent of blacks preferred black neighborhoods. In another survey, 48 percent of blacks preferred neighborhoods that were half white and half black and 13 percent preferred neighborhoods that were all or mostly black. These stated preferences for integration are somewhat stronger than those given in surveys in the early 1960s. These results appear to contradict the reasonable assumption that most blacks, like most whites, prefer living with members of their own race. However, these surveys do not distinguish between racial attitudes and attitudes about housing. Since integrated neighborhoods often have higher quality houses and better services than all-black neighborhoods, these survey results may simply reflect blacks' preference for better housing. Racial attitudes need not be separated from attitudes toward housing in order to build an urban model, but it should be remembered that the assumption that the behavior of many black households is motivated by a preference for integrated neighborhoods is not simply an assumption about blacks' racial attitudes.

BORDER MODELS.   The literature on border models of racial prejudice and urban structure has grown out of an article by Bailey (1959). The Bailey model is discussed by Muth (1969) and incorporated into a more general model of an urban area by Courant (1974) and Rose-Ackerman (1974). These models are reviewed and extended by Courant and Yinger (1977).

Bailey's original model assumes that blacks and whites are completely segregated, that whites prefer to live away from blacks, and that blacks prefer to live near whites. Under these conditions, whites will be willing to pay more for housing in the white interior than near the black-white border and blacks will be willing to pay more near the border than in the black interior. In a competitive housing market, sellers will convert housing from white to black occupancy (or vice versa) until the price of housing is equal on both sides of the border. It follows that, in equilibrium, the price of housing will be highest in the white interior and lowest in the black interior.

Both Courant and Rose-Ackerman incorporate Bailey-like assumptions about prejudice into an equilibrium model of an urban area. Their main assumption is that the utility of prejudiced white households increases with distance from the black-white border, u^*. Let $r(u)$ be a measure of distance from u^* for a white household living u miles from the central business district (CBD)—that is, a measure of racial composition. Then the formal statement of this assumption is that $r'(u)$ is positive near u^* but drops to zero for locations far from u^*.

A white household's utility function is $U_w(Z, H, r[u])$, where Z is a composite consumption good and H is housing services; and its budget constraint is $Y = P_zZ + P(u)H + T(Y, u)$, where Y is income, P_z is the price of Z, $P(u)$ is the price of housing at location u, and $T(Y, u)$ is commuting costs from the CBD to u.[3] Maximizing U_w subject to the budget constraint yields

$$P_w'(u) = -(\partial T/\partial u)/H + [\partial U_w/\partial r(u)] \, r'(u)/\lambda H \tag{1}$$

where λ is a Lagrangian multiplier. In an urban model, equation (1) is interpreted as a market condition indicating the housing price function, $P_w(u)$, that results in locational equilibrium for whites. It reveals that the slope of this equilibrium function, which is called the white price-distance function, is of indeterminate sign. If $\partial U_w/\partial r(u)$, which is positive, is large enough, $P_w'(u)$ will be positive; but at distances far from u^*, where $r'(u)$ is zero, $P_w'(u)$ is negative. Thus, white prejudice flattens the white price-distance function and may cause it to be upward sloping near u^*.

The assumptions about racial prejudice in border models have two serious problems. First, Bailey's model assumes that there is complete segregation and that blacks prefer to live near whites. These assumptions are contradictory; blacks who prefer to live near whites will simply move into white neighborhoods. Muth argues that *all* whites have a stronger preference for white neighborhoods than do *any* blacks. This assumption removes the contradiction, but it is not realistic. If even a few blacks strongly prefer white neighborhoods, and a few whites are indifferent about the race of their neighbors, then those blacks will outbid those whites in largely white neighborhoods and the simple dichotomy between black and white areas will be invalid.

Second, the amount that a household is willing to pay to live in a particular neighborhood depends on that household's income as well as on its tastes. Therefore, even if Muth's assumption about tastes is true, a high-income black may outbid a low-income white for a house in a white neighborhood. As Courant puts it, blacks have an incentive to "hop" over whites with lower incomes. This hopping leads to more than one border, thereby contradicting a basic assumption of the models. According to some simple simulations carried out by Courant and Yinger, high-income blacks have an incentive to hop unless white prejudice is extremely strong, that is, unless whites are willing to pay at least 40 percent more for their housing in order to live as far from blacks as possible. If some high-income blacks are willing to pay 5 percent more for their housing to be in integrated neighborhoods, then hopping occurs unless whites are willing to pay at least 50 percent more to be far from blacks.

Thus there is a fundamental problem with the logic of border models: their implications for the pattern of racial segregation contradict their basic assumptions about that pattern. This contradiction provides two insights into the relationship between prejudice and urban structure. First, in a competitive housing market, whites' racial prejudice may lead to complete racial segregation but will not lead to a pattern of segregation with all blacks in a central ghetto. Instead, it will lead to a pattern that involves rings of high-income blacks outside of low-income whites. Consider, for example, complete segregation by income class and, within income class, complete segregation by race. The border-model logic suggests that this is an equilibrium configuration as long as the black taste for integration is less than the white taste for segregation.

The second insight can be illuminated by considering the case of high- and low-income classes of both blacks and whites, with all blacks concentrated in the city center. In this case, high-income blacks have an incentive to hop over low-income whites. But if they do, both classes of whites will be worse off. High-income whites will be worse off because their social distance from blacks will be decreased; low-income whites will lose because they will live inside a second black-white border and therefore be near essentially twice as many blacks as before. In short, all prejudiced whites have an incentive to prevent high-income blacks from hopping over low-income whites; the pattern of segregation with all blacks in a central ghetto is a public good for the white community, which can be purchased by excluding blacks from white areas.

AMENITY MODELS.   Amenity models of racial prejudice, which have been developed by Schnare (1976) and Yinger (1976), assume that households care about the racial composition of their own location, but not about that of other locations. Amenity models are in the tradition of Schelling's (1972) "tipping" model, which shows how white prejudice leads a neighborhood to change from largely white to all black once a few blacks have moved in. Schelling does not consider the role of housing prices in racial transition, but prices have been introduced into his model by Schnare and MacRae (in press). Amenity models differ from Schelling's model in that they examine housing prices and racial segregation in an entire urban area instead of in a single neighborhood.

Like border models, amenity models include $r(u)$—some measure of racial composition—in the utility function of prejudiced households. Furthermore, the household locational equilibrium condition is derived in the same way: in an amenity model, equation (1) still defines the appropriate price-distance function for whites.[4] However, amenity models include no assumptions about the pattern of segregation, so that a black-white border does not necessarily exist and $r(u)$ cannot be defined by reference to a border. Instead, $r(u)$ is defined as the percentage of the population at location u that is black, and the utility of a prejudiced white household decreases as $r(u)$ increases. Furthermore, $r(u)$ is determined endogenously. To find the locational equilibrium for whites, an amenity model must derive an equilibrium $r(u)$—that is, an equilibrium pattern of segregation—and insert that it into equation (1).

Note that any $r(u)$ function is consistent with equilibrium for whites if the market price-distance function is defined by equation (1). The trick is to find an $r(u)$ function that is consistent with equilibrium for both blacks and whites. Furthermore, competition in the housing market makes price discrimination impossible; blacks and whites must be charged the same $P(u')$ at any u' where both races live. Thus, to find an equilibrium, we must first derive the locational equilibrium condition for blacks, $P_b(u)$, that is analogous to equation (1) for whites, and then find an $r(u)$ that equates $P_w(u)$ and $P_b(u)$ at all locations where both races live.

It is now apparent that complete integration is an equilibrium. If there is complete integration, then $r(u)$ is constant, $r'(u)$ is equal to zero, and the second term drops out of equation (1) and the analogous equation for blacks. Thus, $P_w(u)$ and $P_b(u)$ are both found by integrating

$$P_w'(u) = -(\partial T/\partial u)H = P_b'(u) .$$
(2)

This same differential equation is found in an urban model without prejudice (see Mills, 1972b). Thus, with complete integration, the price-distance function reflects the trade-off between housing and transportation costs that exists in a world without prejudice, and since racial composition is the same everywhere, no household can move away from the race against which it is prejudiced. Complete integration is, however, an unstable equilibrium. A slight decrease in $r(u')$ will make u' the preferred location for prejudiced whites. These whites will move to u', thereby changing the racial compositions of other locations and causing more moves. The end result of all these moves cannot be determined from the model.

Amenity models also reveal that if some blacks prefer to live in integrated areas, complete segregation is not an equilibrium.[5] We can establish this result in three steps. First, complete segregation implies that racial composition is constant throughout the white area, so that $r'(u)$ equals zero in the white area and the slope of the price-distance function in the white area is the same as it would be without prejudice. The same is true for the price-distance function in the black area. Second, competition in the housing market causes the price of housing to be the same on either side of the black-white border. Thus, the black and white price-distance functions, both unaffected by prejudice, meet at the black-white border, and the combined price-distance function is the same as it would be without prejudice. Third, to complete the proof, note that whites are in equilibrium (the price-distance function reflects transportation costs and whites prefer the white area to the black area), but blacks are not. Although the price-distance function reflects transportation costs, blacks prefer integrated areas, so they would gain utility by moving into locations in the white area, and thereby integrating them. In making such moves, blacks are exactly compensated for their increased transportation costs by lower housing prices, but they gain utility by being in an integrated neighborhood. Hence, complete segregation is not an equilibrium.[6]

The two main insights about prejudice and urban structure provided by amenity models are similar to those from border models. The first is that with realistic assumptions about black preferences, no pattern of complete segregation—let alone a central ghetto—is an equilibrium. The second insight is derived from the assumption that whites value neighborhood stability; because of the lack of a stable equilibrium in a competitive market, the white community has an incentive to purchase the public good "stability" through discrimination against blacks.[7]

Discrimination and Urban Structure

The models in this subsection consider the impact of discrimination on urban structure, but do not consider the impact of prejudice on household location.

Racial discrimination in housing is carried out by the sellers of housing themselves or by landlords or real-estate brokers who are their agents. Surveys by the National Committee Against Discrimination in Housing (NCDH, 1970), Denton (cited in Foley, 1973) and Sheppard (1976) have uncovered widespread discriminatory practices by landlords. For example, Denton's 1970 study of rental housing in the San Francisco area concludes that "the vast majority [of apartment owners] discriminate. . . . Their usual tactics for avoiding integration are delay and red tape, i.e., the minority prospect gets delay and the white prospect gets the apartment. Where housing is as tight as it is in the Bay Area, discrimination becomes difficult to prove and easy to practice. If a minority prospect can be held off for as little as four hours, it is usually time to get a bona fide white tenant signed up." [Cited in Foley, 1973, p. 98.] Real-estate brokers discriminate by using their control over information about houses that are for sale. The NCDH study found that brokers used the following tactics with black customers: telling the buyer no houses meeting his specifications are currently available when such houses actually are available; showing houses only in black, fringe, or changing neighborhoods; saying that a house is sold when it is not; misrepresenting the price or other terms of the transaction; delaying until a white buyer is found; and refusing to help the buyer find a mortgage. Similar tactics were reported by Denton (cited in Foley, 1973) and by Mandelbaum (1972). "Steering" blacks into certain neighborhoods appears to be the most common discriminatory tactic used by brokers.[8]

WHY SELLERS DISCRIMINATE.   Monopoly power, seller prejudice, and buyer prejudice have been suggested as explanations for discrimination by the sellers of housing or their agents.

Monopoly Power. The well-known model of classical price discrimination can be applied to housing. Classical price discrimination occurs if the market for a product can be divided into submarkets and if the following conditions are met: (1) buyers cannot switch submarkets; (2) the product cannot be bought in one submarket and resold in another; and (3) the seller faces a different price elasticity of demand from the group of buyers in each submarket. The last condition implies that the seller has some market power in at least one submarket; otherwise, all the price elasticities facing a single seller would be infinite. Given these conditions, a profit-maximizing seller will charge a higher price to a group with a lower price elasticity. To be precise, the seller will set the price for group i equal to $MC[1 + (1/u_i)]$, where MC is marginal cost and u_i is the price elasticity for group i. (See Robinson, 1969.)

In the case of housing, sellers can identify blacks, and prohibitions against subletting can be included in leases. On the other hand, little is known about the black and white price elasticities, and a single seller of housing may not have such market power. Even if a single seller has market power, price discrimination can exist only when the same sellers operate in both the black and white submarket. If these two submarkets are in different locations and involve different sellers, then, by definition, price discrimination is impossible; a price differential between the two submarkets may exist, but it cannot be caused by price discrimination. Thus, the plausible assumption that sellers operate in small neighborhoods implies that price discrimination can only occur in integrated neighborhoods. (See Stengel, 1976.)

Seller Prejudice. The approach to discrimination developed by Becker (1957) has been applied to housing by King and Mieszkowski (1973) and to durable goods by Masson (1973). According to this approach, the sellers of housing (and/or their agents) have an aversion to dealing with blacks and will sell to blacks only if they receive a premium for doing so. Thus, their own prejudice leads sellers to practice price discrimination against blacks or—if they cannot obtain a price high enough to compensate them for dealing with blacks—to refuse to sell to blacks.

Lee and Warren (1976) combine the notions of seller prejudice and seller search. In their model, prejudiced white landlords "search" by waiting for white tenants to appear; if blacks arrive during the waiting period, the landlords refuse to rent to them. Lee and Warren devise a formula for the optimal waiting time for a prejudiced landlord under the assumption that blacks and whites pay the same rent. If the discount rate is high enough, landlords will rent to the first customer, black or white, but, in general, prejudiced landlords will exclude blacks for a certain time period and then rent to them if no white tenants have appeared. Lee and Warren also examine the case in which blacks and whites pay different rents. They derive a formula for the minimum "bribe" a black tenant must pay in order to override a prejudiced landlord's decision to wait. This bribe is greater the less time the landlord expects to have to wait for a white tenant.

Household Prejudice. The third explanation for discrimination by sellers or their agents is the prejudice of white buyers. Even in a competitive housing market, sellers may respond to the prejudice of their white customers by discriminating against blacks.

One example of this type of explanation for discrimination is found in the work of Muth (1969). He argues that since whites have a strong preference for living with other whites, the "landlord's refusal [to rent to Negroes] may be interpreted as based on a desire to avoid the loss of white tenants" (p. 108). Note that Muth's argument has two steps. First, whites will move out of an apartment building when blacks move in, thereby insuring complete segregation. Second, the prejudice of white renters gives landlords an incentive to refuse to rent to blacks, that is, to discriminate. But if whites are willing to pay more than blacks to live in an all-white apartment building, the landlord simply has to set the rental at the level whites are willing to pay. Since no blacks will want to live in the building at that price, a profit-maximizing landlord will not have to discriminate.[9] If, on the other hand, the landlord sets the price too low, not only will he have to exclude blacks in order to keep his white tenants, he also will not be maximizing his profits.

Expanding on Muth's brief discussion, let us build a simple competitive model in which a landlord rents Q identical apartments so as to maximize his rental income. In this model, both blacks and whites are prejudiced, so that the amount they are willing to pay for apartments in a given building is a decreasing function of the number of people of the other race who live in that building. Furthermore, landlords are able to exclude blacks from their building if they choose to do so. Now if Q_b is the number of apartments rented to blacks, then R_w, the rent a single landlord can charge whites, is a decreasing function of Q_b, and R_b, the rent he can charge blacks, is an increasing function of Q_b. A landlord chooses Q_b so as to maximize his income, which is equal to $R_b(Q_b)Q_b + R_w(Q_b)(Q - Q_b)$.

In this model, the landlord's decision-making rule is very simple. If $R_b(Q)$, the rent blacks will pay when $Q_b = Q$, is greater than $R_w(O)$, the rent whites will pay when $Q_b = O$, he will set the rent of an apartment at $R_b(Q)$ and have an all-black building. If $R_w(O)$ is greater than $R_b(Q)$, he will set the rent of an apartment at $R_w(O)$ and have an all-white building. This rule does not involve any discrimination. Simply by setting the rent at the greater of $R_b(Q)$ and $R_w(O)$, the landlord is certain that members of the group he does not want will be unwilling to pay for his apartments.

Discrimination appears when this model is placed in the context of a city in which black demand is increasing. The above rule indicates that a landlord will keep the rent at $R_w(O)$ until black demand increases to the point where $R_b(Q)$ is greater than $R_w(O)$; then the landlord will switch to an all-black building. However, racial transition involves two types of cost. First, if rents are not protected by leases, average rents will decline during racial transition, since neither blacks nor whites are willing to pay as much for an apartment in an integrated building. If rents are protected, then all whites will move out when the first black moves in and more than normal vacancies will result.[10] Second, in order to find a new tenant, a landlord must advertise the apartment, interview applicants, check the applicants' credit references, and execute needed maintenance on the apartment. Thus, unless $R_b(Q)$ exceeds $R_w(O)$ by more than the per-tenant transition cost (t), the landlord will want to retain his white tenants; however, it may not be possible to do so without discriminating. Suppose black demand shifts upward, so that $R_b(O)$ is greater than $R_w(O)$, and suppose the black demand curve is fairly flat, so that $R_b(Q)$ is less than $[R_w(O) + t]$. In this case, if the landlord sets the price at $R_w(O)$, blacks will move in, transition will occur, and the landlord will lose income; it is therefore in the landlord's economic interest to exclude blacks until $R_b(Q)$ is greater than $[R_w(O) + t]$.

This analysis reveals the importance of the slope of $R_b(Q_b)$ and the size of t. Very little is known about these two quantities. As noted earlier, surveys indicate that many blacks prefer integrated neighborhoods, and several studies (reviewed below) have measured the differences between what blacks pay in all-black and in integrated neighborhoods. However, none of these studies examines price differentials among blacks across apartment buildings; even if blacks prefer integrated neighborhoods, they may prefer to live in all-black apartment buildings.[11]

The prejudice of white households and the structure of the real-estate industry give real estate brokers an incentive to discriminate against blacks. Brokers act as agents for owners who want to sell their houses and provide information and expertise for prospective house buyers. Brokers' income is in the form of commissions from owner-sellers. To earn a commission, a broker must attract a customer to his (or her) office, match that customer with a house in his files (called a *listing*), and find financing for the "matched" customer. Now consider a broker who works in a community of prejudiced whites. If this broker sells to blacks in that community, he or she will lose prestige in the community. This loss will result in fewer prospects coming to the office and hence in fewer commissions. This loss may be made up by more advertising, but only by raising costs. A broker's prestige in a particular community may also have been acquired over a long period of time and may therefore be very difficult to replace. The second step of the broker's job, finding listings and matching them with customers, also depends on a broker's prestige. Many brokers seem to fear a loss of listings if they sell to a black in a white neighborhood. For example, in a survey of brokers in the New York area in 1972, Mandelbaum (1972) found that "the white community is the source of almost all their business, and brokers fear that many whites would not give listings to agencies that show homes to blacks."

The attitudes of other brokers reinforce these incentives to discriminate. Until the early 1960s, the punishment for a broker who sold to a black in a white neighborhood was often expulsion from the local real-estate board and loss of the many services provided by the board (Helper, 1969). Furthermore, exclusionary policies were actively supported by the organization that sponsors local boards, the National Association of Realtors (NAR). Recent civil-rights legislation makes it illegal to expel a broker from a real-estate board for selling to a black, and NAR now officially supports freedom of choice in housing, but brokers can still refuse to cooperate with a broker who sells to a black in a white neighborhood. For example, the NCDH (1970) reports that a broker brought suit against several other brokers on the grounds that they conspired "to drive her out of business by advising customers and clients not to deal with her because she would sell homes to people of a minority race" (p. 69).

In addition, black brokers have been systematically excluded from NAR-affiliated local real-estate boards and associated multiple listing services. As recently as 1962, a national survey found only 18 local real-estate boards with one or more black members (Helper, 1969). Many boards now have black members, but blacks are still seriously underrepresented on these boards, even relative to their proportion in the real-estate profession. Elaborate entrance requirements and high membership fees still effectively limit black participation (NCDH, 1970).

The multiple listing service (MLS) is a dramatic recent development in the real-estate industry. To some degree, the MLS breaks the broker's ties to a particular community and opens up the flow of information about houses. Since few black brokers have access to an MLS and since an MLS does not eliminate white brokers' incentives to discriminate, the impact of these services on discrimination is undetermined.

A broker must also find financing for the potential buyer. In the past, discrimination by lending institutions has reinforced discrimination by brokers (Helper, 1969). More research is needed on the current relationship between lending institutions and the racial practices of brokers.

THE IMPACT OF DISCRIMINATION ON URBAN STRUCTURE. Theories about the impact of discrimination on urban structure combine a view of why sellers or their agents discriminate with assumptions about the urban housing market.

Classical Price Discrimination. As noted earlier, the model of classical price discrimination can be applied to housing within integrated neighborhoods. If blacks are less responsive than whites to price changes by a single seller, this model implies that there will be a positive black-white price differential within such neighborhoods. It has no implications, however, for the degree or pattern of racial residential segregation.

Seller Prejudice. To examine the impact of seller prejudice on urban structure, let us assume that after entry, in long-run equilibrium, sellers in the housing market range from unprejudiced to strongly prejudiced.[12] In this case we can construct a market supply curve of housing for blacks by adding horizontally the supply curves of groups of sellers, starting with the least prejudiced. With constant costs, group i has a horizontal supply curve set at P_w, the white equilibrium price, plus d_i, the premium group i requires in order to deal with blacks. Thus, the market supply curve for blacks is an increasing step function, with the unprejudiced group on the bottom step and the most prejudiced group on the top step. The black demand curve for housing intersects this supply curve on a step representing some group of sellers, say G_j, with an intermediate level of prejudice, and the equilibrium price for blacks is $(P_w + d_j)$. Groups with less prejudice than G_j sell to blacks at the equilibrium price and make a profit. Group G_j sells either to blacks at $(P_w + d_j)$ or to whites at P_w; that is, this group practices price discrimination. Groups with more prejudice than G_j sell to whites at price P_w and exclude blacks.

Except for its spatial implications, this model is similar to the models of labor-market discrimination developed by Arrow (1973). In Arrow's model, segregation applies to each firm; in our model it is determined by the distribution of firms throughout a city. If very prejudiced sellers operate next to unprejudiced sellers, our model predicts that a city will be highly integrated. But sellers who are very prejudiced and who practice exclusion may cluster because there are external economies to exclusion; it is much easier for a seller to exclude blacks if he is backed up by neighboring sellers. In this case, our model predicts that a city will be highly segregated, with a few integrated areas where members of a group G_j are located. Note that this model is incomplete; it does not explain what prevents unprejudiced sellers from selling to blacks in white areas.

Search Models with Discrimination.   Masson (1973) and Courant (1978) introduce seller prejudice into models of buyer search. Masson begins with a model in which buyers search for the lowest price for a single unit of some durable good. Buyers continue to search as long as their expected utility after one more unit of search is greater than the utility associated with the lowest price they have already found $(=P)$. This expected utility is the sum of (1) the (negative) cost of search in the form of lost leisure, (2) the probability of finding a price higher than P in the next search multiplied by the utility associated with P, and (3) the sum, over all possible prices below P, of utility at each price multiplied by the probability of getting that price.

From the seller's point of view, the demand curve in this model is probabilistic. A seller does not know if any individual buyer will accept a particular price, so the seller must set prices according to an expected price elasticity of demand. As in most search models (Rothchild, 1973), the seller has some market power, because further searches are costly to the buyer. The seller quotes a price equal to $MC[1 + (1/u)]$, where MC is marginal cost and u is the (noninfinite) expected price elasticity. Thus prices are set in the same way as in classical price discrimination, except that u is an expected elasticity.

Masson then assumes that *some* sellers are prejudiced against blacks and charge a premium for dealing with them. In this case, the distribution of prices facing blacks is higher than the distribution facing whites. More formally, when blacks undertake another search, they are more likely than whites to find a price higher than P, and they face a higher distribution of prices below P. From what we have said about expected utility, it follows that "blacks will be less likely to search given any past number of searches and lowest observed price" (Masson, p. 182) and therefore that sellers do not expect them to be as responsive as whites to an increase in price; that is, the expected price elasticity is lower for blacks than for whites. It follows that all sellers—including the unprejudiced—will charge blacks more than they charge whites.

Masson's model links classical price discrimination and seller prejudice. Sellers have some market power because it is costly for buyers to search, and blacks have a lower price elasticity than whites because—thanks to a few prejudiced sellers—they are less likely than whites to gain from further searches. Thus, if individual sellers sell to both blacks and whites, the existence of search costs and of a few prejudiced sellers is enough to satisfy the conditions for classical price discrimination. Furthermore, if sellers have small market areas, and if sellers with similar preferences cluster, the Masson model, as that of seller prejudice, implies that there will be a price differential between the black and white submarket.

Courant's model examines an owner-occupied housing market that is divided into n different neighborhoods. Buyers must choose where to search as well as whether to search. Courant assumes that black buyers perceive that in neighborhood j there is a nonzero probability, g_j, that a white seller will be prejudiced and refuse to deal with blacks. A black searching in neighborhood j therefore anticipates a probability, a_j, that he will be confronted with discrimination. This probability is equal to g_j times the fraction of sellers in neighborhood j who are white. If F_j, the cumulative distribution of utilities associated with the distribution of houses and of prices in neighborhood j, is the same in all neighborhoods, then for blacks, search is clearly most promising in the neighborhood with the lowest value of a_j. Blacks will identify the neighborhood with the lowest a_j and search there if they have an expected utility gain from doing so; they will prefer to search in an all-black neighborhood, where $a_j = 0$. Beginning with any distribution of blacks and whites in neighborhoods, this type of search behavior by blacks will eventually lead to complete segregation, but not to any particular pattern of segregation.[13]

Courant also shows that a higher price in black areas than in white areas is consistent with equilibrium for buyers. For black buyers, the expected utility from searching in a white neighborhood is lower than the expected utility from searching in a black neighborhood, even if the distribution of prices is higher in the black neighborhood, as long as less utility is lost from the higher prices than is gained from the lower search costs. The size of the price gap that is consistent with equilibrium clearly increases with the lowest value of a_j in a white neighborhood. If the housing or public services are better in white neighborhoods than in black neighborhoods, blacks must trade off the higher utility from the better services and the possible lower prices in white neighborhoods against the higher search costs there.

Exclusion Models. Models of the effect of exclusion on urban structure can be found in the work of Downs (1960), Kain (1969), and Stengel (1976). These authors assume that the housing market is split into black and white submarkets, which are physically separate because sellers in the white submarket refuse to deal with blacks. Furthermore, these models assume that exclusion is so pervasive that sellers in border neighborhoods do not sell to blacks unless the price differential between the submarkets is very high. Consequently, a large black-white price differential exists in equilibrium. These models are incomplete, however, since they do not explain why exclusion is so pervasive. For example, they do not explain why blockbusters do not open border neighborhoods, or even neighborhoods at the outer edge of the city, to blacks until the price differential is eliminated.

A disequilibrium explanation for price differentials in an exclusion model was suggested by Becker (1957) and has been expanded by Haugen and Heins (1969). King and Mieszkowski (1973) label this explanation the "Rate-of-growth hypothesis." This hypothesis assumes that blacks live in a central ghetto and that the primary source of new housing for blacks is racial transition at the border. The exclusion of blacks from white areas is implicitly assumed. Given this pattern of racial segregation and racial transition, increases in the black demand for housing due to migration or natural population growth or higher incomes lead to a higher price for housing in the black ghetto than in the white parts of the city. Since there are long lags in the housing market, this price differential may persist for a long time. Thus the rate-of-growth hypothesis explains how exclusion may lead to a higher price for housing in the black ghetto than elsewhere, but it does not explain why exclusion is so pervasive.

Prejudice and Discrimination in an Urban Model

This subsection shows how the effect of prejudice on household location decisions and the effect of seller and broker discrimination on urban structure can be combined in a single model.

To begin with, Courant and Yinger (1977) suggest that exclusion can be added to a border model. This addition makes the multi-income-class border model logically consistent; hopping by blacks does not occur because blacks are excluded from white areas. Blacks are completely segregated in the city center and the white price-distance function is defined by equation (1)—adjusted for the range in white incomes. However, these results are now due to the interaction of discrimination and prejudice, not just to the prejudice of white households. Any empirical support for the model—such as support for its predictions about the pattern of housing prices—is evidence that there is discrimination as well as prejudice.

A second possibility, suggested by Yinger (1976), is to add exclusion to an amenity model. In this case $r(u)$, which describes the distribution of blacks and whites in an urban area, is determined by the partial or complete exclusion of blacks from some locations. Thus, discrimination prevents moves by blacks and housing prices adjust to reflect white prejudice, as in equation (1), so that whites are in equilibrium. This model can be tested by determining whether housing prices actually take the form specified by equation (1). Evidence that prices take this form indicates that blacks cannot be in equilibrium and supports the hypothesis that blacks are prevented from moving by discrimination.

Finally, it is possible to introduce the following assumptions about household prejudice into Courant's (1978) search model: (1) although there is a range in white prejudice, whites prefer not to live with or near blacks; (2) some blacks prefer to live in integrated areas and some to live in all-black areas. Now if, except for racial factors, the distribution of utilities is the same in all white neighborhoods, white buyers choose where to search according to the racial characteristics of each neighborhood. The most prejudiced whites bid the most for housing that is the farthest from the ghetto; hence, the level of white prejudice increases with distance from the ghetto. Since all white owner-sellers were once buyers, this result implies that a_j increases with distance from the ghetto. Black buyers who prefer integration will search for housing in white areas if the utility they gain from better services and possibly lower prices in those neighborhoods is large enough to offset their higher search costs there. Note, however, that they will search in the neighborhoods at the black-white border, since the value of a_j is lowest there.

Real-estate brokers in stable white neighborhoods are interested in their long-run profits in those neighborhoods. They invest heavily in developing contacts in those neighborhoods so that buyers and sellers will know about them and arrange sales through them. In neighborhoods far from the border, the high value of a_j prevents search by black buyers who might trigger racial transition and thereby undermine the brokers' investments: consequently, it is in the brokers' interest to keep the value of a_j high, and even to increase it, by dramatizing exclusionary behavior by owner-sellers, by convincing owners not to sell to blacks, and by practicing exclusion themselves. The white community reinforces such broker behavior; whiteness is a public good that is preserved by bringing social pressure to bear on less prejudiced members of the community. If effective, social pressure increases a_j.

Blockbusters are intermediaries who are not attached to a particular neighborhood. They make their profits on individual transactions, not on long-run investments in prestige in a single neighborhood. To arrange a sale to a black, a blockbuster must find a seller in the white submarket who is willing to deal with a broker without an established reputation and who, despite his own prejudice and the social pressure from his neighbors and local brokers, is willing to sell to a black. Such sellers are undoubtedly hard to find, so that a blockbuster will have high search costs. These costs will increase with distance from the black-white border. In short, the incentives of buyers of both races, of established brokers, and of blockbusters interact to prevent sales to blacks outside of black or border neighborhoods.

2. EVIDENCE ABOUT RACE AND URBAN STRUCTURE

The theories we have considered make many predictions about urban structure. In this section we will examine the empirical work on race and urban structure to discover which predictions are supported by the evidence.

Residential Segregation

The most visible racial characteristic of the urban housing market is racial residential segregation. We therefore begin our discussion of evidence about race in the housing market by reviewing what is known about both the *degree* and the *pattern* of racial segregation.

THE DEGREE OF RACIAL SEGREGATION.   The degree of racial residential segregation is usually measured by an index. For extensive discussions of the various indexes, see Taeuber and Taeuber (1965, Appendix A) or Zoloth (1976). These indexes divide a city or an urban area into subareas, usually census tracts or blocks, and calculate the extent to which blacks and whites (or any other two groups) live in separate subareas.

Dissimilarity Index (D). The dissimilarity index measures the dispersion of the racial compositions of subareas around the racial composition of the entire city. It is defined to be

$$D = (100) \sum_i | N_i(b_i - b) | /2Nb(1 - b),$$

where N is population (for the entire city or subscripted by subarea) and b is the proportion of the population that is black (in the city or subarea i). The numerator of the expression sums the absolute deviations in racial composition from the city mean. The denominator expresses the maximum value of the numerator, so that the index goes from zero (complete integration) to one hundred (complete segregation). Algebraic manipulation leads to the more easily calculated form

$$D = (100)(\tfrac{1}{2}) \sum_i | (B_i/B) - (W_i/W) | ,$$

where B is a number of blacks (for the city or subarea i) and W is a number of whites (in the city or subarea i). The dissimilarity index can also be interpreted as the minimum percentage of the black population (or of the white population) that would have to move in order to achieve complete integration.

The dissimilarity index is easy to compute and to interpret, but it has an important disadvantage: Zoloth shows that D depends on the division of the black population between the group of subareas with above-average proportions of blacks and the group of subareas with below-average proportions of blacks, but not on the distribution of blacks within each of these two groups. In other words, bringing an all-black subarea one percentage point closer to the average racial composition of the city, b, has the same effect on the index as bringing a subarea only slightly less integrated than average one percentage point closer to b. The "payoff" to desegregation is linear.

Exposure Index (E). A second index measures the exposure of blacks to whites (or vice versa). An individual black's exposure to whites is defined as the proportion of the population in that person's subarea that is white. The average exposure of blacks is

$$\sum_i B_i(1 - b_i)/\sum_i B_i = \sum_i B_i(1 - b_i)/B.$$

Dividing this expression by its maximum value $(1 - b)$ and subtracting the result from one yields the exposure index

$$E = (100)\{1 - \sum_i B_i(1 - b_i)/[B(1 - b)]\}.$$

As Zoloth points out, this index is like a dissimilarity index with a quadratic payoff function instead of a linear one. In symbols, it can be derived by dividing the expression $\Sigma N_i(b_i - b)^2$ by its maximum value. The value of E clearly is affected by transfers of blacks within the group of subareas that have below-average proportions black.

Calculations. Sørenson et al. (1976) calculate *D* using block data from 1940 to 1970 for 109 large cities. The indexes for the segregation of whites and nonwhites in 1970 range from 61.4 to 97.8, with a mean value of 81.6. Indexes for the segregation of blacks and whites in 1970 are several percentage points higher than these nonwhite-white indexes. According to these indexes, the degree of racial segregation is very high; on average, 82 percent of nonwhites or whites would have to move in order to have a completely integrated city. The 1970 average for the nonwhite-white indexes is significantly lower than the 1960 average of 86.1 (or the 1950 average of 87.3 or the 1940 average of 85.2). Since the standard deviation of the 1960 indexes is 7.7, the drop between 1960 and 1970 is fairly large. Indeed, about 90 percent of the cities experienced some decline in the index between 1960 and 1970.

Schnare (1977) calculates *E* for nonwhite-white segregation using tract data for 130 metropolitan areas in 1960 and 1970. The mean value of *E* (weighted by population) is 52.6 in 1960 and 55.8 in 1970, and the value of *E* increases in all but 31 areas. A comparison of these calculations of *D* and *E* suggests that in 1970, as compared to 1960, fewer nonwhites lived in tracts with below-average percentages nonwhite, but nonwhites were much more heavily concentrated in tracts that were almost entirely non-white.

Most of the theories discussed in section 2 either assume or predict complete segregation, perhaps with some integration in border areas; the evidence just presented, therefore, is not much help in choosing among the theories. Trends in the degree of segregation also do not help us choose; even if the evidence about these trends were consistent, it could be explained by trends in either prejudice or discrimination. Several studies, including Taeuber and Taeuber (1965), Pascal (1967), and Schnare (1977), have discovered that most of the degree of racial residential segregation cannot be explained by the relatively low socioeconomic status of blacks. This finding also does not help us to choose among the theories in section 1; it is consistent both with a model based on discrimination and with a border model that has segregation by income class as well as by race.

THE PATTERN OF RACIAL SEGREGATION.   The question most frequently asked about the pattern of segregation has been how centralized blacks are relative to whites.[14] To begin to answer this question, let us look at some aggregate numbers presented by Hermalin and Farley (1973): although 14.4 percent of the population in the twenty-nine largest urbanized areas is black, only 4.6 percent of the suburban population in those areas is black, whereas 25.9 percent of the central-city population is black. Reid (1977) provides a more complete measure of the relative centralization of blacks by comparing population density functions for blacks and for whites in a sample of thirty-three central cities. Using census tract data for 1960 and 1970 to estimate the well-known exponential form for the density function, he finds that in every city except one, black population density falls off much more steeply than white population density with distance from the CBD; that is, blacks are much more centralized than whites. Reid also calculates that in 1970 the average distance from the CBD was 2.2 miles for blacks and 4.8 miles for whites.

Only a small part of the relative centralization of blacks can be explained by their relatively low socioeconomic status. Kain and Quigley (1975) report that in all of the eleven largest SMSAs, a higher percentage of whites with incomes below $3,000 than of blacks with incomes above $10,000 live in the suburban ring. On average, 53.1 percent of low-income whites and only 25.9 percent of high-income blacks live in the suburban ring. Kain and Quigley also regress residential location, measured in miles from the CBD, on a large number of income and family characteristics, using a large sample of blacks and whites in St. Louis in 1967. They find that the number of miles expected on the basis of the average black characteristics and the coefficients of the white regression (4.39 miles) is much larger than the average actual black location (3.19 miles). Another possible test of the relationship between socioeconomic status and centralization would be to regress density gradients, such as those estimated by Reid, on the socioeconomic characteristics of blacks and whites and to compare actual and expected gradients for blacks. Mills (1972a) has estimated this type of regression for all races together, but no one has estimated separate regressions for blacks and whites. A related issue is addressed by Reid, who finds that changes in black density gradients between 1960 and 1970 cannot be explained by changes in black socioeconomic characteristics.

Although incomplete, the evidence indicates that blacks are much more centralized than expected on the basis of their socioeconomic characteristics. This evidence is not consistent with a model based on prejudice alone. As argued earlier, a border model could lead to rings of blacks alternating with rings of whites, with blacks of a given income just inside whites of that income. This residential pattern is characterized by complete segregation but predicts that blacks will be only slightly more centralized than whites. Furthermore, it predicts that high-income blacks will live outside low-income whites, and it is therefore contradicted by the finding that low-income whites are more suburbanized than high-income blacks. This evidence is consistent with models based on discrimination. Exclusion prevents blacks from moving out of the city center or makes search more costly for them outside the city center. Consequently, exclusion leads to a clustering of blacks in the city center, with high-income blacks living in more central locations than low-income whites.

Black-White Price Differentials

The literature on black-white price differentials in housing asks whether blacks pay more than whites for comparable housing. In other words, the question is whether blacks pay more for housing than whites, after accounting for differences in the characteristics of the housing consumed by blacks and whites. The relevant characteristics include the physical attributes of houses, the types of lots, and the quality of neighborhoods. The most direct method of controlling for housing characteristics is multiple regression analysis; this review is therefore restricted to studies that estimate hedonic regressions for housing.[15]

Specification is a key issue in regression analysis; if important explanatory variables are left out of a regression, the coefficients will be biased.[16] The types of racial explanatory variables in an estimate of the black-white price differential are: race of the household, racial composition of the neighborhood, and submarket. Since the studies that consider all three types find them all to be important, studies that do not consider all three are likely to yield seriously biased results; therefore, this review will only discuss studies that consider at least two racial variables.

Another issue in regression analysis is whether to use grouped data, such as census tract data, or data for individual households. In estimating racial price differentials in housing, grouped data automatically introduce bias into regression coefficients because they prevent the consideration of one type of racial variable—race of the household. Furthermore, the grouping of data leads to imprecise coefficient estimates and biases the estimates of standard errors (Johnston, 1972). Studies based on grouped data will therefore not be considered. Finally only studies based on post-1965 data will be reviewed.[17]

REVIEW OF INDIVIDUAL STUDIES. *King and Mieszkowski (1973).* King and Mieszkowski analyze the effect of racial variables on apartment rents in New Haven, Connecticut, in 1968–69. Their sample, obtained from an extensive survey of 220 rental units, contains information on utilities included in the rent, physical and quality characteristics of the apartment, and characteristics of the neighborhood. Their data also allow them to control for three household characteristics—lack of information about housing, family size, and welfare status—that have been suggested as explanations for black-white price differentials.

King and Mieszkowski define their racial variables on the basis of three zones: the white interior, the black-white boundary zone, and the ghetto. By their criteria, a block is in the ghetto if it is 60 to 100 percent black and the blocks around it are 60 to 100 percent black; a block is in the white interior if it is less than 3 percent black; everything else is in the boundary zone. They define the following dummy variables: BOUND-*B* equals one for black households in the boundary zone; BOUND-*W* equals one for white households in the boundary zone; GHET-*B* equals one for black households in the black ghetto; and GHET-*W* equals one for white households in the ghetto. They also include a variable for families headed by black females. The coefficients of GHET-*B* and GHET-*W* are of about the same magnitude and are significant at the 10 percent level or above. The coefficient of BOUND-*W* is significantly negative, and the coefficient of BOUND-*B* is very small and insignificant. Since the dependent variable is rent per square foot, the average rent and floor area for each race in each zone must be used to translate these coefficients into percentages. After performing the necessary translations, one finds that compared to a white in the white interior, a black in the ghetto pays 9.3 percent more, a black at the boundary pays no more, and a white at the boundary pays 7.5 percent less. Within the boundary zone, a black pays 8.0 percent more than a white. These price differentials are substantially larger for female-headed black families.

Yinger (1978). The study by Yinger is based on data collected by Kain and Quigley (1975) for 266 owner-occupants in St. Louis in 1967. These data, which were obtained from a survey, contain a large set of neighborhood characteristics as well as information on dwelling unit size and quality. Yinger tests two different specifications of racial variables in a regression of house values on housing characteristics. The first specification employs the four variables defined by King and Mieszkowski: GHET-*B*, GHET-*W*, BOUND-*B,* and BOUND-*W*. Two different definitions of the ghetto and the boundary zones are used. The first defines the zones by racial composition. Tracts below 5 percent black are defined to be in the white interior, and those above 85 percent black are defined to be in the ghetto. The second definition explicitly locates the zones in space, with the boundary zone located between the ghetto and the white interior. The classifications of tracts into zones using these two definitions are similar, but not identical. A hedonic regression is then performed using each definition of zones to calculate the four racial variables. The only significant coefficient in both regressions is that of GHET-*B,* which has a value of about 10 percent and is significant at the 5 percent level. In addition, BOUND-*B* is positive (with a value of 17 percent) and significant at the 5 percent level using the second definition of the zones.

The second specification includes three types of racial variables: (1) race of the household (RACE); (2) dummy variables for each zone, defined by racial composition (INT for the boundary, BLK for the ghetto); and (3) racial composition interacted with the zone dummies (PBL-WHI for the white interior, PBL-INT for the boundary, and PBL-BLK for the ghetto).[18] The boundary zone is defined as any tract from 40 to 80 percent black, and the ghetto is any tract over 80 percent black. This specification estimates a separate slope and intercept for the racial composition term in each zone. All of the variables in this specification are significant at the 5 percent level, except for those that refer to the boundary zone (where there are few observations), which are significant at the 10 percent level. The coefficients, which are in percentage form, are as follows:

	Coefficient	t-Statistic
RACE	.15	1.94
INT	.26	1.53
BLK	.27	2.17
PBL-WHI	−.0062	−2.68
PBL-INT	−.0088	−1.50
PBLE-BLK	−.0184	−2.47

These coefficients indicate that blacks pay 15 percent more than whites within any given neighborhood, that prices are 26 percent higher in the boundary zone and 27 percent higher in the ghetto than in the white interior, and that the price of housing declines within each zone as the racial composition of the zone increases. For a 10 percentage point increase in racial composition, these declines vary from 6 percent in the white interior to 18 percent in the ghetto.[19]

Little (1976). Little uses a large sample (3,400 observations) of single-family houses that sold in 1970 in the St. Louis metropolitan area. His dependent variable is the sale price of the house, and the independent variables are 5 linear combinations (derived using factor analysis) of 20 physical and neighborhood characteristics of housing. Two of the neighborhood variables are the percentage of the population in a tract that is nonwhite (NONWHITE) and the percentage of the population in adjacent tracts that is nonwhite (NONWHITEADJ). On the basis of the regression coefficients and factor weights, Little calculates that a 10 percentage point increase in NONWHITE leads to a $1644 drop in the price of a house (9.7 percent of the mean sale price) and that a 10 percentage point increase in NONWHITEADJ leads to a $1378 drop in price (8.1 percent of the mean).

Little's specification, which is similar to the one used by Bailey (1966), is difficult to interpret. Its two racial variables cannot determine if the effect of racial composition is the same for blacks and whites or the same in the white submarket and the black submarket. Consequently, it reveals nothing about black-white price differentials within a tract or between the black and white submarkets. And since the race of the household is not included in the specification, the coefficients are likely to be biased.

Schnare (1976). Schnare was able to combine census tract data with the public-use sample of individual housing units for owner and renter housing in Boston in 1970. The resulting data set, which consists of 3364 owner-occupied units and 3985 rental units, allowed her to carry out hedonic regressions with detailed data for the structural characteristics of units, the characteristics of households, and the socioeconomic characteristics of neighborhoods. Schnare's specification of the racial variables, which is the same as the one employed by Gillingham (1973), consists of a binary variable for the race of the household and the proportion of the population in the tract that is black. The binary variable is not significant in either the owner or the renter regression. The coefficient of the proportion black variable is —.04 in the owner regression and .08 in the renter regression, and significant in both regressions at the 5 percent level. These coefficients are difficult to interpret, however, because they do not allow us to distinguish the effect of racial composition within a submarket from a price differential between the black and white submarkets.

Schafer (in press). Schafer further analyzes the 1970 sample of rental houses used by Schnare. He divides the sample into four submarkets (central city ghetto, central city transition area, central city white area, and suburban white area), estimates a separate hedonic regression for each submarket, and determines how much the average housing bundle in each submarket would cost if valued at the implicit prices for the other submarkets. (The average housing bundle is defined to have the average quantity of each housing characteristic.) He finds that, except for the lowest-quality bundle, all bundles would rent for more in the ghetto than in the suburban area. The differentials range from —1.9 to +36.4 percent. Similar calculations reveal that bundles generally rent for less in the transition area and in the central-city white area than in the suburban area.

Schafer then estimates separate regressions for blacks and whites in each submarket and calculates three more sets of indexes using the results.[20] The first set of indexes determines whether blacks and whites pay the same amount within any given submarket. He discovers that in the ghetto, blacks pay from 13.5 to 515.6 percent more than whites for equivalent housing, depending on the quality of the bundle. Blacks also pay more than whites in the white suburban area; the differential goes from 8.0 to 51.0 percent depending on the bundle. In transition and central-city white areas, blacks pay more than whites for six of the eight bundles considered; the highest differential is 353.9 percent in the transition area and 13.9 percent in the central-city white area.

Schafer's third set of indexes measures price differentials among whites; compared to what they pay in suburban areas, whites pay from 5.4 to 67.5 percent less for bundles in the ghetto and pay less for almost all bundles in the transition area and the central-city white area. The final indexes provide the same information for blacks—compared to what they pay in suburban areas, blacks get discounts of about 10 to 20 percent on low-quality bundles (except in the central white area) and pay premiums of 5 to 150 percent on high-quality bundles in the three other submarkets.

Galster (1977). Galster shows how the functional form for a hedonic regression for housing can be derived from an urban model. He tests his results using about 1100 owner and renter observations gathered by Kain and Quigley (1975). Galster begins with a household maximization problem similar to the one discussed in section 1. By assuming specific functional forms for utility, he derives bid-rent functions of the form $Y - k(t) - B = f(t,q_i)$, where Y is annual income, $k(t)$ is (estimated) yearly commuting costs to location t, B is annual housing expenditures (rent plus utilities for renters; taxes, maintenance, interest, and utilities for owners), and q_i is a vector of housing characteristics. Galster stratifies his sample by age of head, number of children, and income and estimates separate regressions for four black and six white strata.

The q_i in Galster's regressions for black households include two racial variables: percentage white in the tract and a binary variable for the ghetto (tracts greater than 95 percent black). The coefficient of percentage white is significant at the 10 percent level for only one of the four strata, where it indicates an increase in rents of $6 per year for every 10 percentage point increase in percentage white. The coefficient of the ghetto variable is large and negative and is significant at the 10 percent level or above for two strata. This variable indicates that rents are as much as $700 lower in the ghetto than elsewhere.

Galster argues that if blacks outbid whites for units currently occupied by whites, then discrimination must be restricting the housing choices of blacks. He also discovers, however, that the amount a white stratum bids for its own average bundle is frequently $200 to $300 less than the amount bid for that bundle by other white strata, and concludes that this disparity represents housing market frictions. Thus he argues that there will be evidence of discrimination if blacks outbid whites by more than these market frictions. Galster then calculates what each black stratum would bid for the average housing bundle of each white stratum in border neighborhoods. Such neighborhoods are defined as being between 35 and 80 percent black and located next to the ghetto. These calculations reveal that middle-class blacks outbid all but the richest white stratum by an average of $700 per year. This bid differential exceeds Galster's estimates of market frictions by 20 to 50 percent of the white rent in border neighborhoods. Note that Galster's test is essentially the same as Schafer's. Schafer calculates what would happen to the price of the average housing bundle consumed by whites in each type of neighborhood if that bundle were switched to a black family. Galster does the same type of calculation for border neighborhoods. His results—at least for middle-class blacks—are similar to Schafer's. However, Galster does not perform the other half of Schafer's test; he does not ask what whites would bid for the average black bundle.

SUMMARY OF EVIDENCE ABOUT PRICE DIFFERENTIALS.   These six studies can be summarized by focusing on three key aspects of the pattern of housing prices: the relationship between racial composition and the price of housing; the black-white price differential within housing submarkets; and the black-white price differential between submarkets.

Racial Composition. Five studies provide information about the relationship between racial composition and the price of housing. Schnare and Little include racial composition variables in their regressions, but their specifications are seriously flawed because they do not enable us to separate the relationship between racial composition and price within a submarket from a price differential between submarkets. Three studies allow us to isolate the relationship between racial composition and price within the white submarket. King and Mieszkowski discover that whites pay 7.5 percent less in the boundary zone than in the white interior. Yinger finds that price declines as percentage black increases in both largely white areas and boundary areas. This decline is equal to 6 percent for every 10 percentage point increase in black population in largely white areas and to 9 percent for every 10 percentage point increase in black population in boundary areas. Schafer ascertains that whites pay less in ghetto, transition, and central-city white areas than in the white suburbs. These discounts are largest in the black ghetto, where, depending on the bundle, they range from —5 percent to —68 percent.[21]

Thus, three studies find that the prices whites pay drop substantially as percentage black increases. Since the percentage of the population that is black decreases with distance from the ghetto, these results support the view of white prejudice that appears in both border models and amenity models. However, it is important to remember that white prejudice alone cannot account for these results, since they are all based on a specification that involves a central ghetto—a pattern of segregation that is not consistent with models that include prejudice but not discrimination. Thus these results indicate that white prejudice should be included in models based on discrimination. For example, Yinger shows that his results about racial composition are predicted by an amenity model when the white function is Cobb-Douglas and the distribution of blacks throughout the urban area is determined by discrimination against blacks.

Results about racial composition and prices in the black submarket are inconclusive. King and Mieszkowski find that blacks pay 2 percent more in the ghetto than in the boundary zone. Galster's results imply that middle-class black households pay about $6 less rent per year for every 10 percentage point increase in the white population, and that blacks pay from $200 to $700 less per year in the ghetto than elsewhere. Yinger discovers that prices decline 18 percent for every 10 percentage point increase in black population in a ghetto tract. And Schafer finds that blacks pay from 10 to 35 percent less for low-quality bundles, and from 6 to 48 percent more for high-quality bundles, in the ghetto than in the suburbs. The co-efficient of Galster's ghetto variable and Yinger's and Schafer's results are consistent with the view that many blacks would prefer to live in an integrated area because of the higher-quality housing there.

Price differentials within submarkets. A second aspect of urban residential structure is the black-white price differential within submarkets. King and Mieszkowski detect an 8 percent differential in the boundary zone and no differential in the ghetto. Yinger discovers a 15 percent price differential in both the ghetto and the boundary zone. Schnare finds no significant differential for either owners or renters. However, using the same rental data as Schnare, Schafer uncovers very large black-white price differentials within all submarkets. These differentials, which depend on the bundle being examined, range from 14 to 516 percent in the ghetto, from —9 to 354 percent in transition areas, from —41 to 14 percent in central-city white areas, and from 8 to 51 percent in suburban areas. In all submarkets, these differentials tend to increase with the quality of the bundle. Finally, Galster finds that in border neighborhoods, middle-class blacks pay from 20 to 50 percent more than whites.

These large black-white price differentials within submarkets are not consistent with models based only on racial prejudice. They are predicted by classical price discrimination, seller prejudice, and Masson's search model applied to housing. They are also consistent with other models that include discrimination.

Price differentials between submarkets. Five studies provide information on the black-white price differential between submarkets. As noted earlier, however, two of the studies (Little and Schnare) cannot separate a price differential between submarkets from the effects of racial attitudes. The other three studies are easier to interpret. King and Mieszkowski ascertain that a black at the boundary pays the same rent that a white pays in the white interior, but that both blacks and whites in the ghetto pay 9 percent more than whites in the white interior. Yinger finds that prices are 26 percent higher in the boundary zone and 27 percent higher in the ghetto than in the white interior. Finally, Schafer discovers that, compared to the price of units in the white suburban area, the prices of units in the ghetto range from 2 percent less to 36 percent more; the prices of units in transition areas are about 1 percent less; and units in central-city white areas range from 8 percent less to 2 percent more. Hence, all three studies find that housing units, especially high-quality units, are more expensive in the ghetto than in the white interior. The only exception is Schafer's estimate that the lowest-quality units are 2 percent cheaper in the ghetto than in white suburban areas.

These results are not consistent with models that include household prejudice but not discrimination. They are predicted by exclusion models, seller prejudice, and Courant's search model. Models with a range in the strength of seller prejudice and the combination of Masson's and Courant's search models predict both a black-white price differential within integrated neighborhoods and a black-white price differential between the ghetto and the white interior. Finally, note that only theories with both household prejudice and seller discrimination predict that price will vary with racial composition and that there will be both within-submarket and between-submarket price differentials. The evidence presented in this section—especially the findings of the studies that examine racial composition and both types of price differential (King and Mieszkowski; Yinger; Schafer)—strongly supports these theories.

Racial Differences in Housing Consumption

A black-white price differential between neighborhoods can be caused by a restriction on the quantity of housing supplied to blacks. Furthermore, black-white price differentials within or between neighborhoods will cause blacks to substitute other goods for housing. One can therefore test for discrimination by measuring black-white quantity differentials in housing as well as by measuring black-white price differentials. In order to measure quantity differentials between blacks and whites (or between ghetto residents and nonghetto residents), one must start with a model of the demand for housing, which depends on income, family size, a family's position in its life cycle, and the price of housing; a quantity differential exists if blacks and whites with the same demand characteristics consume different quantities of housing.

Two studies examine black-white quantity differentials in housing. Straszheim (1975) analyzes a sample of 28,000 households in San Francisco in 1970, and Kain and Quigley (1975) analyze the St. Louis data described earlier. Both studies indicate that blacks consume smaller amounts of housing attributes than do whites with similar income and life-cycle characteristics. In the Kain and Quigley study, these quantity differentials are particularly large for the quality characteristics of housing (such as ratings of the condition of a house or its neighborhood) and small or nonexistent for the size characteristics of housing (such as square feet of floor area). These results support the hypothesis that discrimination restricts the quantity of housing consumed by blacks.

Although both studies are done thoughtfully, there is room for more work on this topic. Straszheim shows how to include prices—he first estimates implicit prices for housing attributes using hedonic regressions and then includes these prices as independent variables in demand equations for individual housing attributes—but his study is based on data with only three control variables for life-cycle characteristics. The Kain and Quigley study has much more satisfactory life-cycle data, but it leaves out prices. In short, neither study adequately controls for demand variables.

Race and Home Ownership

Without discrimination, one would expect a black family to be as likely to own a house as a white family with the same income and in the same position in its life-cycle; hence, another test for discrimination in housing is to look for racial differentials in the probability of home ownership, carefully controlling for household characteristics. Note that home ownership can be treated in the same manner as the housing attributes in the previous section. The demand for home ownership is a function of income and family characteristics, the price of owner-occupied houses, and the price of rental housing.

Four recent studies provide detailed information about race and home ownership. Kain and Quigley (1972; 1975) use their St. Louis data, Birnbaum and Weston (1974) use a 1967 national sample of 900 households, Straszheim (1975) uses the San Francisco sample described earlier, and Roistacher and Goodman (1976) use 1971 data for a sample of about 5000 households in the twenty-four largest metropolitan areas. All four studies indicate that blacks are much less likely to own houses than are whites with similar life-cycle and socioeconomic characteristics. For example, the probability of owning a house, $P(\text{own})$, is found by Kain and Quigley to be 9 percentage points lower, and by Roistacher and Goodman to be 26 percentage points lower, for blacks than for whites with similar characteristics. These results are further evidence of discrimination against blacks.

Several issues about race and home ownership remain unresolved.[22] First, the estimation of demand functions for home ownership requires price variables, but only Straszheim uses them. As noted before, however, Straszheim's data has inadequate controls for life-cycle characteristics. Second, the effect of wealth on home ownership has not been determined. Birnbaum and Weston find that when household wealth is included as an independent variable in a demand equation for home ownership, $P(\text{own})$ is never much lower for blacks than for whites and may be slightly higher. Roistacher and Goodman, on the other hand, ascertain that the black-white gap in $P(\text{own})$ is not affected by including household savings as an independent variable. As Kain and Quigley point out, the right way to solve this dilemma is to estimate wealth and $P(\text{own})$ simultaneously; after all, home ownership allows a household to accumulate wealth. However, no simultaneous estimation has yet been attempted.

Finally, the evidence for recent movers is not fully analyzed. Kain and

Quigley discover that for recent movers the probability of purchasing a house, $P(\text{pur})$, is 9 percentage points lower for blacks than for whites. But Roistacher and Goodman find no black-white differential in $P(\text{pur})$ and conclude that there has been a "substantial reduction in discrimination against blacks currently making the buy-or-rent decision." This conclusion is premature. $P(\text{pur})$ depends on the probability of purchase given previous owner status, $P(\text{pur}|\text{own})$, and on the probability of purchase given previous renter status, $P(\text{pur}|\text{rent})$. If black owners expect to face discrimination, they may be unwilling to move unless they are sure of finding a house, so that $P(\text{pur}|\text{own})$ may be much higher for blacks than for whites; this higher value may offset the lower value of $P(\text{pur}|\text{rent})$ for blacks that is due to discrimination. Consequently, $P(\text{pur})$ may be the same for blacks and whites despite discrimination.[23]

CONCLUSION: LESSONS FOR PUBLIC POLICY

The evidence reviewed in this chapter overwhelmingly supports the proposition that racial discrimination is a powerful force in urban housing markets. Only a theory that involves discrimination can explain why blacks are concentrated in a central ghetto, why blacks pay more for comparable housing than whites in the same submarkets, why prices of equivalent housing are higher in the ghetto than in the white interior, and why blacks consume less housing and are much less likely to be home owners than whites with the same characteristics. This evidence of discrimination, based on recent data, makes a convincing case for government intervention in the housing market.

The evidence also points to the importance of white prejudice in the urban housing market. According to the studies presented here, white prejudice has a strong and consistent influence on the amount whites are willing to pay for housing in different neighborhoods. This strong white prejudice is the fundamental source of the interconnected incentives that support discriminatory behavior in the housing market. It feeds and is fed by the economic incentives for discrimination by landlords and real-estate brokers. Furthermore, discrimination by whites conditions the search behavior of black buyers. These interconnections are by no means the end of the story; lending institutions, developers, and local zoning boards are all affected by white prejudice, and there is evidence that they have all helped to support discrimination in housing (McEntire, 1960; Foley, 1973). More research is required on the role these institutions play in discrimination.

The existence of strong white prejudice also implies that policies to prevent discrimination may not bring about integration. This point has been emphasized by Muth (1969), who argues that open-housing policies will have little effect on racial residential segregation because whites simply are

not willing to live with blacks. It is important, however, to separate the
goal of eliminating discrimination from the goal of promoting integration.
There may be good reasons for the government to promote integration, but
the case for government intervention to eliminate discrimination stands on
its own. Antidiscrimination legislation should not be judged by its ability
to foster integration. Furthermore, eliminating discrimination is a policy
goal about which people with very different views about integration should
be able to agree. Belief in the right of blacks to buy housing on equal terms
with whites is compatible with belief in the development of the ghetto and
of black self-reliance, as well as with belief in the dispersal of blacks
throughout an urban area: discrimination both drains resources from blacks
in the ghetto and prevents blacks who want to leave the ghetto from doing
so.[24]

Many types of policy have been proposed to deal with discrimination in
housing. One type is prohibitive legislation, often called open-housing
legislation. The Civil Rights Act of 1968 outlaws discrimination in the sale,
rental, or financing of housing. Some transactions (such as the sale of a
house by its owner) are exempt from this legislation, but discrimination in
these transactions is also illegal according to the 1968 Supreme Court
decision in *Jones* v. *Mayer*. The evidence reviewed in this chapter suggests
that this legislation has by no means eliminated discrimination in urban
housing markets. This limited impact is caused partly by the lack of enforcement powers in the 1968 legislation and partly by the inherent difficulty of proving that discrimination, which often takes the form of restrictions or distortions of information, has taken place. To be effective,
prohibitive legislation would have to allow the government to gather
evidence about discrimination and to bring this evidence to court.[25]

Lowry (1968), Downs (1968), and Pascal (1970) have proposed a
different type of policy, namely, the awarding of desegregation bonuses to
communities or individuals. "One version of the scheme calls for the establishment of a metropolitan agency that would subsidize, at some predetermined percentage of the value of the transaction, any sales or rental
transaction that would cause a convergence between the fraction of, say,
blacks in a neighborhood and the fraction of blacks in the metropolitan
area as a whole" (Pascal, 1970, pp. 428–29). To evaluate these bonus
schemes on the basis of their ability to lower discrimination (not their
ability to foster integration), it is appropriate to examine their impact on
each of the actors in the housing market. First, they do not compensate
whites in a neighborhood into which a black moves; therefore they do not
change those white's incentives to discriminate. Second, bonuses may
appear to compensate blacks for the high search costs in white neighborhoods, but they probably end up in the sellers' pockets. Remember that
search costs give a seller some market power, particularly when the buyer
has few options. Finally, these bonus schemes, like the price differential

between the ghetto and largely white neighborhoods, only alter the terms
for selected housing transactions; they do not change the fundamental
economic incentives that lead landlords and brokers to discriminate. In
short, our analysis indicates that bonus schemes would have little impact
on discrimination in housing.

A third approach to policy is to try to improve the flow of information
in the housing market. To begin with, the government could encourage the
flow of information through existing institutions. The most important
example of this type of policy involves multiple listing services. Although
the Civil Rights Act of 1968 forbids discrimination in access to multiple
listing services, large membership fees and strict eligibility requirements
have limited the access of minority brokers to these services. Federal programs to subsidize the training of minority brokers and to increase their
access to multiple listing services would greatly increase the flow of housing
information to minorities; indeed, such policies are probably the single type
of government action that would have the most dramatic impact on discrimination in owner-occupied housing—and at relatively low cost. Another
policy alternative is for the federal government to subsidize private organizations that help blacks find housing outside the ghetto and other organizations that counsel black house hunters.

The federal government could also improve the flow of information by
creating new housing market institutions. For example, the NCDH (1970)
has proposed the establishment of a central agency for real-estate listings
and apartment advertisements. A voluntary central listing agency would
increase the flow of information to some degree, but the requirement that
all listings or advertisements in an urban area be posted for a certain number of days before an offer could be accepted would be necessary to break
the hold of brokers and landlords over the flow of information. A mandatory listing agency would allow the government to make sure that accurate
information was passed on to minority buyers or renters and that any
minority families who wanted to bid on a particular house would have a
chance to do so.

Opening up the flow of information with one of these policies would
begin to change the incentives facing brokers. Open access to multiple listings or a central listing agency would make it difficult for brokers to discriminate, so that white buyers and sellers could no longer avoid brokers
who sold to blacks in white neighborhoods. Thus a broker's long-run profits
might not decline if he sold to a black. Indeed, it might be possible to get
some broker backing for these policies; brokers who are worried about
losing business if they do not discriminate, but who are not otherwise
averse to dealing with blacks, should be glad of a program that will get
them off the hook. And to the extent that increased information lowers
landlords' transition costs, it will also lower their incentive to discriminate.

These optimistic comments about the elimination of discrimination are purely hypothetical. Optimism is unjustified without effective and enforced policies to break down the incentives and the ability of brokers and landlords and the white community to discriminate. Instead of hoping for that long run when discrimination will disappear, economists should join in the search for such policies.

NOTES

1. It has been argued that exclusion is a type of price discrimination, because no seller would refuse to sell to a minority if the price were high enough. This broad definition of price discrimination is confusing, because it does not refer to observable behavior. An incorrect inference based on this definition is that the absence of price discrimination implies the absence of discrimination. According to the definitions in the text, exclusion can exist without price discrimination. For more discussion of prejudice and discrimination see Simpson and Yinger (1974, ch. 2).

2. The text states the legal case for government intervention when there is discrimination. An economic case for government intervention can also be made: according to widely accepted values, discrimination in housing is inequitable; it is also inefficient in that it distorts the trade-offs facing blacks in the housing market. To be specific, it limits the employment opportunities of many black workers and lengthens the distance others must commute; it forces blacks to live in central cities where the public services, particularly education, tend to be poor; and it perpetuates a system that restricts the opportunities of black Americans. The legislation that forms the legal case grew, in part, out of this economic case.

3. Border models and amenity models assume, for analytical convenience, that all workers commute to the central business district (CBD). Although this assumption is unrealistic, this author believes that it does not lead to misleading results about prejudice and urban structure. For example, we will show that these models cannot explain the well-documented fact (see section 2) that blacks are clustered around the CBD. And if these models cannot explain this fact with a monocentric assumption, they certainly could not explain it when there are suburban employment centers pulling blacks away from the CBD.

4. An example of a solution to the differential equation (1) is given by Yinger (1976), who shows that if whites have Cobb-Douglas utility functions and per-mile transportation costs (t) are constant, then $P_w(u) = K (Y-tu)^{1/k}D_w [r(u)]$, where K is a constant of integration, k is the proportion of income (net of commuting costs) spent on housing, and D_w is a function that describes how $r(u)$, the amenity "racial composition," affects the utility of prejudiced whites. This result is identical to price-distance functions derived for locational amenities such as air pollution (see, for example, Polinsky and Rubinfeld [1977]). Racial composition differs from other amenities in that it is determined by the decisions of many households—even though it is given for a single household.

5. Schelling (1972) and Schnare and MacRae (in press) show that complete segregation is usually the only equilibrium for a *single* neighborhood. Schnare (1976) argues that this result applies to an entire urban area; the text argues that it does not. Also remember that complete segregation can be an equilibrium in a border model.

6. For a detailed proof see Yinger (1976). Note that blacks who prefer some integration to complete segregation may not want to be the only black in an otherwise all-white neighborhood. If so, a single black does not have an incentive to move into the white area, but it is in the interest of blacks to act together to achieve their most preferred level of integration. With a range of black tastes, cooperation may not be necessary. Blacks who prefer any level of integration to complete segregation will be the first to move. They will be followed by blacks who prefer integration to complete segregation as long as they have at least one black neighbor, and so on.

7. A similar argument has been made by Straszheim (1975): since whites know

that the tipping process (described by Schelling, 1972) will take place as soon as a few blacks move in, whites act to keep blacks out even if they would not mind a few black neighbors in equilibrium.

8. For a thorough legal analysis that shows why racial steering is illegal see Aleinikoff (1976).

9. In a search model there is a nonzero probability that a black will be willing to pay the white price. Thus the landlord may have to discriminate against a few blacks in order to keep an all-white building. This possibility deserves more rigorous treatment, but is not explicitly mentioned by Muth.

10. The argument that increased vacancies during racial transition give landlords an incentive to discriminate has also been made by Pascal (1970, pp. 412–13).

11. A variety of assumptions about black preferences can be considered in the model in the text. A black preference for integrated apartment buildings means that blacks will pay the highest rent when Q_b is equal to some $Q_b{}^*$. This preference does not affect the landlord, who still discriminates as long as $R_b(0) > R_w(0)$ and $R_b(Q) < [R_w(0) + t]$. A black preference for largely white apartment buildings means that $R_b{}'(Q_b)$ is negative. This preference gives landlords an incentive to exclude blacks even with no transition costs; if it is very strong, apartment buildings may be integrated in equilibrium, with landlords practicing price discrimination against blacks.

12. The usual approach in the literature (Masson, 1973, Muth, 1969) is to assume that because unprejudiced sellers make a profit, they will enter the housing market and drive P_b down to P_w. At these prices, prejudiced sellers refuse to deal with blacks, have less business, and (unless costs are constant) go bankrupt. This approach leads to the unrealistic conclusion that all sellers of housing are unprejudiced. Furthermore, it does not explain where the prejudiced sellers go. Is there some other market that has only prejudiced sellers?

13. This argument has been made on a less formal basis by Pascal (1967, p. 127n).

14. Another question is: how concentrated are blacks relative to whites? In all of the forty-seven cities with black populations over 50,000, the majority of blacks live in tracts over 50 percent black. This concentration has been increasing over time (see U.S. Commission on Civil Rights [1975]). Furthermore, largely black tracts are almost always clustered near the CBD. This author looked at ghetto tracts (over 80 percent black) in a 1970 sample of twenty-seven cities with 2 or more ghetto tracts. In sixteen of the cities, all of the ghetto tracts were contiguous and very near the CBD. In four other cities, 90 percent or more of the ghetto tracts were in two clusters near each other and near the CBD. In one other city, 3 of the 4 ghetto tracts bordered on the CBD. Only two cities (Pittsburgh and Houston) had more than 1 significant ghetto area.

15. One study (Straszheim [1975]) estimates hedonic regressions but is not reviewed here because it is based on data with only 4 housing characteristics. For reviews of several studies that do not use regression analysis, see Boston et al. (1972) and Kain and Quigley (1975).

16. The bias caused by excluding a variable is equal to the partial correlation between the included variable and the excluded variable times the true coefficient of the excluded variable (Johnston, 1972, p. 169). Since most variables in a hedonic regression for housing are correlated with race of household, the exclusion of this variable is liable to lead to severe biases. Straszheim (1975) points out that if implicit prices for housing characteristics vary across submarkets, then pooling submarkets in a single regression leads to bias by, in effect, excluding submarket-characteristic interaction variables. The importance of this type of bias is not clear. Using an F-test, Straszheim and Lapham (1971) detect a significant difference in implicit prices across submarkets, but neither study has adequate data on neighborhood characteristics; Yinger (1978) discovers no significant difference (see n. 19).

17. Studies by Kain and Quigley (1970 and 1975), Lapham (1971), Olsen (1974), and Berry (1976) are not reviewed because they have a single racial variable; studies by Muth (1969) and Daniels (1975) are not reviewed because they use grouped data; and studies by Bailey (1966) and Gillingham (1975) are not reviewed because they use pre-1965 data.

18. To be precise, PBL-INT is defined to be (PBL−40)×(INT) and PBL-BLK

is defined to be (PBL—80)×(BLK), where PBL is the percentage of the population that is black. These variables are defined in this way so that INT and BLK will measure percentage deviations in price at 40 and 80 percent black, respectively, from the price in an all-white neighborhood. RACE equals one for blacks and zero for whites.

19. Yinger also splits his sample between the black submarket and the white submarket, runs separate regressions for each submarket, and calculates, like Kain and Quigley (1975), what various housing bundles would cost in each submarket. The appropriate F-test does not reveal a significant difference in implicit prices between the two submarkets, and the price differentials calculated by indexes are very similar to the ones reported above.

20. Schafer calculates the price of the average bundle consumed by each race in each submarket using the implicit prices from the regression for each race in each submarket. The price differentials discussed in the text are made as indicated from the price calculations for 8 bundles (4 submarkets times 2 races) and 8 sets of implicit prices (again, 4 submarkets times 2 races).

21. According to one of Courant and Yinger's (1977) simulations, whites must be willing to pay at least 40 percent more for housing in the white interior than on the white side of the black-white border in order to prevent hopping by high-income blacks. Other simulations place this required premium as high as 110 percent. None of these estimates indicates that white prejudice is that high. King and Mieszkowski find that whites pay 7.5 percent more, Yinger that they pay 24 percent, and Schafer that they pay at most 35 percent more to live in the white interior instead of at the border.

22. Another issue should be mentioned: logit analysis has more desirable statistical properties in a regression with a dichotomous dependent variable (such as home ownership) than either ordinary or generalized least squares (see Pindyck and Rubinfeld [1976, ch. 8]). Of the studies mentioned above, only Roistacher and Goodman use logit analysis.

23. A numerical example: according to evidence in Roistacher and Goodman and in Kain and Quigley, it is reasonable to assume that for whites $P(\text{pur}|\text{rent}) = .2$; $P(\text{pur}|\text{own}) = .32$; m_R (the proportion of movers who were renters) $= .60$; and m_O (the proportion of movers who were owners) $= .40$. For blacks, it is reasonable to assume that $P(\text{pur}|\text{rent}) = .15$, $P(\text{pur}|\text{own}) = .80$ $m_R = .85$ and $m_O = .15$. Thus $P(\text{pur}) = m_R P(\text{pur}|\text{rent}) + m_O P(\text{pur}|\text{own}) = .248$ for both blacks and whites despite discrimination. Roistacher and Goodman estimate that $P(\text{pur}) = .253$ for both blacks and whites.

24. There is a large body of literature on the development versus dispersal debate; see Kain (1968) and Harrison (1974).

25. For a review of the legislation outlawing discrimination in housing, see U.S. Commission on Civil Rights (1975); a brief review is in Straszheim (1974); a review of the enforcement efforts can be found in Quigley (1974). One way for the government to gather information about discrimination would be by using pairs of "testers." Each pair consists of a black person and a white person with similar socioeconomic characteristics. The members of a pair go separately to a landlord or real estate broker to inquire about housing. Discrimination exists if the black person is quoted a higher price or less favorable terms for the same housing or if the black person is only shown housing in black and transition neighborhoods.

REFERENCES

Aleinikoff, T. A. 1976. "Racial Steering: The Real Estate Broker and Title VIII." *Yale Law Journal* 85: 808–25.

Arrow, Kenneth J. 1973. "The Theory of Discrimination." In *Discrimination in Labor Markets*, pp. 3–33. Edited by Orley Ashenfelter and Albert Rees. Princeton, N.J.: Princeton University Press.

Bailey, Martin J. 1959. "A Note on the Economics of Residential Zoning and Urban Renewal." *Land Economics* 35: 288–92.

———. 1966. "Effects of Race and Other Demographic Factors on the Value of Single-Family Homes." *Land Economics* 42: 215–20.

Becker, Gary S. 1957. *The Economics of Discrimination.* Chicago: University of Chicago Press.

Berry, Brian J. L. 1976. "Ghetto Expansion and Single-Family Housing Prices: Chicago, 1968–1972." *Journal of Urban Economics* 3: 397–423.

Birnbaum, Howard, and Weston, Rafael. 1974. "Home Ownership and the Wealth Position of Black and White Americans." *Review of Income and Wealth* 20: 103–18.

Boston, John; Rigsby, Leo C.; and Zald, Mayer N. 1972. "The Impact of Race on Housing Markets: A Critical Review." *Social Problems* 19: 382–93.

Courant, Paul N. 1974. "Urban Residential Structure and Racial Prejudice." Institute of Public Policy Studies, discussion paper no. 62. Ann Arbor: University of Michigan.

———. 1978. "Racial Prejudice in a Search Model of the Urban Housing Market." *Journal of Urban Economics* 5: 329–45.

Courant, Paul N., and Yinger, John. 1977. "On Models of Racial Prejudice and Urban Residential Structure." *Journal of Urban Economics* 4: 272–91.

Daniels, C. 1975. "The Influence of Racial Segregation on Housing Prices." *Journal of Urban Economics* 2: 105–22.

Downs, Anthony. 1960. "An Economic Analysis of *Property Values and Race* (Laurenti)." *Land Economics* 36: 182–88.

———. 1968. "Alternative Futures for the American Ghetto." *Daedalus* 97: 1331–78.

Foley, Donald L. 1973. "Institutional and Contextual Factors Affecting the Housing Choices of Minority Residents." In Hawley and Rock (1973).

Galster, George C. 1977. "A Bid-Rent Analysis of Housing Market Discrimination." *American Economic Review* 67: 144–55.

Gillingham, Robert F. 1975. "Place to Place Rent Comparisons." *Annals of Economic and Social Measurement* 4: 153–73.

Harrison, Bennett. 1974. *Urban Economic Development.* Washington, D.C.: Urban Institute.

Haugen, Robert A., and Heins, A. James. 1969. "A Market Separation Theory of Rent Differentials in Metropolitan Areas." *Quarterly Journal of Economics* 83: 660–72.

Hawley, Amos H., and Rock, Vincent P., ed. 1973. *Segregation in Residential Areas.* Washington, D.C.: National Academy of Sciences.

Helper, Rose. 1969. *Racial Politics and Practices of Real Estate Brokers.* Minneapolis: University of Minnesota Press.

Hermalin, Albert I., and Farley, Reynolds. 1973. "The Potential for Residential Integration in Cities and Suburbs: Implications for the Busing Controversy." *American Sociological Review* 38: 595–610.

Johnston, J. 1972. *Econometric Methods,* 2d ed. New York: McGraw Hill.

Kain, John F. 1968. "Housing Segregation, Negro Employment, and Metropolitan Decentralization." *Quarterly Journal of Economics* 82: 175–97.

———. 1969. "Effect of Housing Market Segregation on Urban Development."

In *Savings and Residential Financing: 1969 Conference Proceedings,* pp. 89–108. Edited by Donald P. Jacobs and Richard T. Pratt. Chicago: U.S. Savings and Loan League.

Kain, John F., and Quigley, John M. 1970. "Measuring the Value of Housing Quality." *Journal of the American Statistical Association* 5: 532–48.

————. 1972. "Housing Market Discrimination, Home Ownership, and Savings Behavior." *American Economic Review* 62: 263–77.

————. 1975. *Housing Markets and Racial Discrimination.* New York: National Bureau of Economic Research.

King, A. Thomas, and Mieszkowski, Peter. 1973. "Racial Discrimination, Segregation, and the Price of Housing." *Journal of Political Economy* 81: 590–606.

Lapham, Victoria. 1971. "Do Blacks Pay More for Housing?" *Journal of Political Economy* 79: 1244–57.

Lee, Chung H., and Warren, E. H., Jr. 1976. "Rationing by Seller's Preference and Racial Price Discrimination." *Economic Inquiry* 14: 36–44.

Little, James T. 1976. "Residential Preferences, Neighborhood Filtering and Neighborhood Change." *Journal of Urban Economics* 3: 68–81.

Lowry, I. S. 1968. "Housing." In *Cities in Trouble: An Agenda for Urban Research,* pp. 4–26. Edited by Anthony H. Pascal. Santa Monica: RAND Corporation.

Mandelbaum, Joel. 1972. "Race Discrimination in Home Buying Resists Tough Laws." *New York Times,* 3 December 1972, sec. 8, pp. 1, 10.

Masson, Robert T. 1973. "Costs of Search and Racial Price Discrimination." *Western Economic Journal* 11: 167–86.

McEntire, Davis. 1960. *Residence and Race.* Berkeley: University of California Press.

Mills, Edwin S. 1972a. *Studies in the Structure of the Urban Economy.* Baltimore: Johns Hopkins University Press.

————. 1972b. *Urban Economics.* Glenview, Ill.: Scott, Foresman.

Muth, Richard F. 1969. *Cities and Housing.* Chicago: University of Chicago Press.

National Committee Against Discrimination in Housing. 1970. "Jobs and Housing: A Study of Employment and Housing Opportunities for Racial Minorities in Suburban Areas of the New York Metropilitan Area." Interim Report. New York: NCDH.

Olsen, Edgar O. 1974. "Do the Poor or the Black Pay More For Housing?" In von Furstenberg et al. (1974).

Pascal Anthony H. 1967. *The Economics of Housing Segregation.* Santa Monica: RAND Corporation.

————. 1970. "The Analysis of Residential Segregation." In *Financing the Metropolis.* Edited by John P. Crecine. Beverly Hills: Sage.

Pettigrew, Thomas F. 1973. "Attitudes on Race and Housing: A Social-Psychological View." In Hawley and Rock (1973).

Pindyck, Robert S., and Rubinfeld, Daniel L. 1976. *Econometric Models and Econometric Forecasts.* New York: McGraw-Hill.

Polinsky, A. Mitchell, and Rubinfeld, Daniel L. 1977. "Property Values and the Benefits of Environmental Improvements: Theory and Measurement."

In *Public Economics and the Quality of Life,* pp. 154–80. Edited by Lowdon Wingo and Alan Evans. Baltimore: Johns Hopkins University Press.

Quigley, John M. 1974. "Indirect Policies to Reduce Residential Segregation." In von Furstenberg et al. (1974).

Reid, Clifford E. 1977. "Measuring Residential Decentralisation of Blacks and Whites." *Urban Studies* 14: 353–57.

Robinson, Joan. 1969. *The Economics of Imperfect Competition.* 2d ed. London: St. Martin's Press.

Roistacher, Elizabeth A., and Goodman, John L. 1976. "Race and Home Ownership: Is Discrimination Disappearing?" *Economic Inquiry* 14: 59–70.

Rose-Ackerman, Susan. 1975. "Racism and Urban Structure." *Journal of Urban Economics* 2: 85–103.

Rothchild, Michael. 1973. "Models of Market Organization with Imperfect Information: A Survey." *Journal of Political Economy* 81: 1283–1308.

Schafer, Robert. (In press.) "Racial Discrimination in the Boston Housing Market." *Journal of Urban Economics.*

Schelling, Thomas. 1972. "A Process of Residential Segregation: Neighborhood Tipping." In *Racial Discrimination in Economic Life.* Edited by Anthony Pascal. Lexington, Mass.: Lexington Books. pp. 157–84.

Schnare, Ann B. 1976. "Racial and Ethnic Price Differentials in an Urban Housing Market." *Urban Studies* 13: 107–20.

———. 1977. "Residential Segregation by Race in U.S. Metropolitan Areas: An Analysis Across Cities and Over Time." Contract report no. 246-2. Washington, D.C.: Urban Institute.

Schnare, Ann B., and MacRae, C. Duncan. In press. "The Dynamics of Neighborhood Change." *Urban Studies.*

Sheppard, Nathaniel, Jr. 1976. "Race Discrimination Found Pervasive in Rental of Manhattan Apartments." *New York Times,* 28 June 1976, pp. 1, 44.

Simpson, George Eaton, and Yinger, J. Milton. 1972. *Racial and Cultural Minorities: An Analysis of Prejudice and Discrimination.* 4th ed. New York: Harper and Row.

Sørenson, Annemette; Taeuber, Karl E.; and Hollingsworth, Leslie J., Jr. 1975. "Indexes of Racial Residential Segregation for 109 Cities in the United States, 1940 to 1970." *Sociological Focus* 8: 125–42.

Stengel, Michell. 1976. *Racial Rent Differentials: Market Separation and the Ghetto Housing Market.* East Lansing: Michigan State University.

Straszheim, Mahlon R. 1974. "Housing Policy." In von Furstenberg et al. (1974).

———. 1975. *An Econometric Model of the Urban Housing Market.* New York: National Bureau of Economic Research.

Taeuber, Karl E., and Taeuber, Alma F. 1965. *Negroes in Cities: Residential Segregation and Neighborhood Change.* Chicago: Aldine.

U.S. Commission on Civil Rights. 1975. *Twenty Years After Brown: Equal Opportunity in Housing.* Washington, D.C.: U.S. Government Printing Office.

Von Furstenberg, George; Harrison, Bennett; and Horowitz, Ann R. 1974. *Patterns of Racial Discrimination.* Vol. 1: *Housing.* Lexington, Mass.: Lexington Books.

Yinger, John. 1976. "Racial Prejudice and Racial Residential Segregation in an Urban Model." *Journal of Urban Economics* 3: 383–406.

————. 1978. "The Black-White Price Differential in Housing: Some Further Evidence." *Land Economics* 54: 187–206.

Zoloth, Barbara S. 1976. "Alternative Measures of School Segregation." *Land Economics* 52: 278–98.

14

URBAN HOUSING POLICY

JOHN C. WEICHER

INTRODUCTION

This chapter discusses the economics of housing policies and the role of economics in policy-making. It does not address broader issues of urban policy; economic development, transportation, fiscal problems, and the provision of public services, are all excluded, even though policies in these areas can significantly affect housing markets. This narrow focus results from the increasing policy roles of economic analysis and economists. There was no similar chapter in *Issues in Urban Economics*. Instead, there was one chapter on housing markets by Muth (1968) and another on urban policy by Campbell and Burkhead (1968). Neither devoted much attention to housing policy. In this they reflected current professional interests; urban economists then tended to concentrate on models of urban spatial structure, which were not easily adapted to policy analysis. In the ensuing decade, however, there has been much more research directly relevant to housing policy, and economists have played a larger part in policy formulation.

This chapter first briefly describes trends in housing conditions and then surveys major policies and programs, concentrating on those designed to improve the housing of low-income households. The remainder of the chapter discusses the contribution of economics to housing policy, divided roughly into positive and normative categories. The third section adopts the policy-maker's viewpoint and describes how research can be—and has been—useful, given the goal of improving housing. The final section considers housing programs from the economist's perspective, summarizing

John C. Weicher is a senior research associate at The Urban Institute.

I would like to thank Edgar O. Olsen for a useful discussion of the National Housing Policy Review, and John L. Goodman, Jr., and the editors for helpful comments on an earlier draft of this chapter.

both the general literature on the framework for evaluation and the detailed analysis of specific programs. The impact of this literature on policy is also reviewed.

1. TRENDS IN HOUSING QUALITY

The national housing goal of the United States, as established by Congress in 1949, is "a decent home and a suitable living environment for every American family."[1] While an explicit definition of "decent" (or for that matter, either "suitable" or "living environment") has never been formally adopted, the reports and hearings that led up to that goal indicated particular concern over the number of units "in need of major repairs," or lacking complete plumbing. Physical inadequacy is still commonly measured by these categories. Housing space also attracted Congressional attention. Inadequate space was defined in terms of the relationship between the size of the unit and the number of people living in it. The two most frequently cited types of inadequacy were "overcrowding" (more than 1.5 persons per room in the unit) and "doubling up" (two or more families in the same unit).[2] The latter problem was especially acute for returning servicemen.

Data on the incidence of these phenomena show marked, steady improvement from 1940 to 1976, to the point that very few households are now living in conditions that would have been considered unacceptable in 1949 (table 14.1). By all these measures, the United States is close to achieving the goal of a "decent home," as originally conceived. (Some minimum of inadequate housing will probably remain, unaffected by any policy; for example, the 1976 data show some 22,000 households with incomes above $25,000 who do not have complete plumbing in their dwellings.)

TABLE 14.1. Measures of Housing Inadequacy, 1940–76
(Percent of Occupied Housing)

Inadequacy	1940	1950	1960	1970	1976
Lacking some or all plumbing	55.4	34.0	14.7	5.5	2.6
Dilapidated or needing major repairs	18.1	9.1	4.6	3.7	...
Overcrowded (more than 1.5 persons per room)	9.0	6.2	3.8	2.0	1.0
"Doubling up" (married couples without own household)	6.8	5.6	2.4	1.4	1.2

SOURCES: Sixteenth Census of the United States: 1940, Housing, vol. 2, part 1; Census of Housing: 1950, vol. 1, part 1; 1970 Census of Housing, Components of Inventory Change, HC(4)-1; Annual Housing Survey: 1976, United States and Regions, Part B; Current Population Survey, Series P-20 (various years).

The data in table 14.1 are aggregate figures. However, data for various groups in the population show the same trend, albeit with numerous gaps and changes in coverage. For example, 80 percent of nonwhite households lacked complete plumbing in 1940, compared to 8 percent of black households in 1976. The decline in overcrowding was similarly pronounced, from 23 to 3 percent. Parallel improvements occurred in rural areas, where units without plumbing dropped from 75 to 8 percent, and overcrowding dropped from 14 to 1 percent. Data on housing by income, available since 1950, show comparable improvement among the poor, whether measured by real income or as a fraction of the income distribution. Little information was compiled for the Hispanic population prior to 1970, but figures since then show that the incidence of both deficiencies had been halved by 1976. All these groups have worse housing than the population as a whole, but the elimination of deficiencies is rapid. The limitations of these data are often frustrating but do not appear to invalidate the reported trends.

The quality improvement has been partly obscured by the problem of defining and measuring the overall condition of the unit. From 1940 through 1960, Census enumerators made such ratings, but after reevaluation of the 1960 data showed a high frequency of misclassification, the Bureau decided to terminate them (U.S. Bureau of the Census, 1967). Estimates were provided for 1970, based on smaller samples than in prior Censuses, with less geographic detail (U.S. Bureau of the Census, 1973), but there have been no later figures, and none are planned.

As the old quality measures become obsolete or are discontinued, new ones are desirable. To some extent, they are already being used. The earlier definition of overcrowding has already been superseded by a ratio of "more than 1.0" persons per room. By this definition, also, overcrowding is declining sharply, from 15.8 percent in 1950 to 4.6 percent in 1976; in a few years a still lower ratio may become the norm.

New standards can be readily designed for overcrowding, since the concept can be measured on a continuum. But quality gradations for other characteristics are not continuous, so different criteria are needed. Partly for this reason, the Department of Housing and Urban Development and the Bureau of the Census have conducted an Annual Housing Survey (AHS) since 1973, which contains data on some thirty deficiencies.[3] Although the data now available (through 1976) cover too short a period to establish trends for the deficiencies not previously enumerated, the AHS reports small but significant declines in most of them. It also includes a new question on overall housing condition, in which residents (not Census enumerators) are asked to rate the structural condition of their dwellings. In 1976, 2.8 percent considered their housing "poor."

Some studies have begun to explore ways of using the AHS to measure housing quality. Two papers by Wieand and Clemmer (1977) and Goedert and Goodman (1977) have examined the pattern of deficiencies across units. Neither finds that any single deficiency is a good proxy for quality, based on its correlation with other deficiencies or with characteristics of households. Goedert and Goodman conclude that "the prospects for developing a single, simple measure of housing quality are dim."[4]

These results suggest that economists may well have a major role in the development of future standards. In the past, the profession has not; the plumbing and crowding criteria were devised by housing specialists from other disciplines. Economists are typically uncomfortable with norms that allow for no trade-offs and have stressed the multidimensionality of the bundle of services provided by a dwelling. This approach could usefully be applied to the development of new standards of quality, more refined than those used for the past thirty years and reflecting the greater well-being and better housing of the population.

2. THE DEVELOPMENT OF HOUSING POLICY

Housing policy in the United States has had two primary purposes: to encourage home ownership and to improve the housing of the poor. The programs to promote these objectives have typically been distinct; indeed, prior to the formation of the Department of Housing and Urban Development (HUD) in 1966, separate agencies were responsible for each goal. But there has been some overlap, and many of the policies designed to help low-income families have borrowed important elements from the home-ownership programs; a discussion of the latter is therefore useful in explaining the development of programs for the poor.

FHA Insurance

Federal policies to increase home ownership began during the Great Depression. The main vehicle was the Federal Housing Administration (FHA), created in 1934.[5] Like most subsequent housing programs, FHA operated in the mortgage market rather than directly in the housing market. Prior to the Depression, the typical home mortgage ran for less than ten years, had a loan-to-value ratio of about 50 percent, and provided for repayment of interest only over the life of the mortgage, with a single "balloon payment" of the entire principal at expiration. FHA encouraged the use of a new type: long-term, high loan-to-value ratio (and therefore low down payment), and self-amortizing, with repayment of both principal and interest at a fixed amount each month over the life of the loan. FHA insured such mortgages, assuming the risk of any loss due to default. Funds to pay the losses came from an insurance premium levied on individual mortgagors. The system was intended to be self-supporting, with the insurance premiums equal to outlays for defaults plus administrative expenses.

Even with the premium (which has usually been 0.5 percent of the out-standing principal balance of the mortgage each year), the longer term and lower interest rate brought the monthly mortgage payment down to a level at which many more families could afford it. The program is known as "Section 203," the section of the 1934 National Housing Act that established it.

FHA mortgage insurance has been widely viewed as a success on several grounds. The proportion of homeowners has risen from 44 percent of all households in 1940 to 65 percent in 1976, though the precise contribution of FHA has never been studied. The program proved to be actuarially sound: the premiums have more than covered the losses and administrative costs and the mutual mortgage insurance fund has steadily accumulated reserves that by 1976 totalled just under $2 billion.[6]

This showed lenders that long-term, self-amortizing mortgages could be profitable, and lending institutions were increasingly willing to make such loans without FHA insurance, at terms that borrowers found more attrac-tive. It also showed that mortgage insurance could be profitable. The first private mortgage insurance company began operations in 1957, and by 1970, there were about a dozen such firms.

With this increased competition, FHA's market share has declined markedly, from a pre–World War II high of over 30 percent of new home mortgages to around 7 percent in the mid-1970s.[7] While there has been little serious analysis of its decline, a recent study has concluded that private mortgage insurance is probably the most important contributing factor (Kaserman, 1977). These firms typically insure only the "top quarter," or a similar fraction of each loan, at less cost than FHA charges for insuring the full amount; lending institutions are willing to accept the risk that they will be unable to sell the home for 75 percent of the out-standing loan balance. Private firms have been especially able to attract the "better" borrowers because of FHA's single-premium structure, under which all borrowers pay the same insurance rate, regardless of risk differ-entials. Thus the decline of FHA has been manifested both in a lower volume of insurance and in a lower quality of loans for its remaining business. Since 1971, Section 203 has experienced significant increases in the average loss per claim, and is actuarially sound chiefly because of its past reserve accumulations.

Because FHA was designed to increase home ownership, particularly among middle-income households, loans have always been subject to legislated dollar mortgage limits. With inflation, the limits have steadily restricted FHA's market potential, and Congress has raised them regularly. Many housing analysts blame the decline of FHA on the limits, but Kaser-man finds that they have had a minor impact.

FHA's decline has generated an evaluation process to see if it should attempt to reattain its original role, seek new goals, or simply wither away

(U.S. Department of Housing and Urban Development, 1977). Since much of its remaining activity is among relatively low-income homebuyers, a common suggestion is to expand this function, perhaps with an explicit geographic or racial focus on central cities or minorities. To the extent that such mortgages are riskier than FHA's traditional business, either insurance premiums would need to be raised or subsidies would be required. The latter approach would blur, if not effectively eliminate, the distinction between the two original policy purposes.

Public Housing

Subsidies for low-income families began slightly later, when public housing was established in 1937. Under this program, local housing authorities buy and raze slum property and build new rental housing in its stead. The federal subsidy originally covered the capital cost of the projects, with operating costs paid by the tenants. The subsidy mechanism is somewhat complicated: the authority sells its own tax-exempt and federally guaranteed bonds; the federal government then pays principal and interest to the authority, which in turn pays the bondholder. This device reduces federal budget outlays by reducing the interest rate required to induce investors to buy the bonds but at the same time creates an indirect cost, because the interest rate is determined by the income tax bracket of the marginal investor, while those in higher brackets receive a greater deduction. The foregone taxes generated by the exemption appear to be much greater than the increase in interest costs needed to float a taxable, federally guaranteed bond issue.[8] A recent study estimated that the exemption cost almost as much as the total direct federal and local expenditures for public housing (U.S. Department of Housing and Urban Development, 1974). However, the increase in interest costs for taxable bonds would produce a visible federal budget outlay and would reduce the number of units that could be subsidized out of any given amount, whereas the indirect effect of tax exemption on federal revenue is much more obscure, and to the extent that it generates pressure to hold down the level of expenditures, is likely to be spread among all programs. The tax exemption of public housing bonds was the first of many techniques designed to minimize budget outlays for housing.

Over time, the federal payment has been extended to include part of the operating cost of the projects. This change grew out of a concern that very-low-income households were so poor that they could not afford to pay even the maintenance and utilities of their apartments without spending "too much" of their income on housing. In 1969 Congress limited the rent of a tenant to 25 percent of his or her income, if this was less than the operating costs. In so doing, Congress substantially changed the nature of the subsidy

—from one conditioned on part of the cost of the unit to one conditioned on income. By 1976 operating subsidies amounted to about 40 percent of operating costs and 25 percent of the total federal outlay on public housing.

Originally, all projects were built under contract to the local authority, but this procedure was modified during the 1960s to permit the purchase of new, privately built projects under the "turnkey" programs. These numbered over 200,000 units, out of a total of 1.3 million, by 1972. A more radical departure was the Section 23 leased housing program, enacted in 1965, under which local authorities could sign leases with private landlords for existing apartments, and the federal government would make the same subsidy payments as for new units. This program was not large—it encompassed about 65,000 units by 1972—but it was a major conceptual change.

Public housing has been through several cycles in popularity. About one-half the units were built during either World War II, the early 1950s, or the late 1960s; production was sharply cut immediately after each period. Public housing was suspended in 1973, and reactivated in 1976. It primarily serves very-low-income households. The median tenant income was around $3500 in 1976, compared to a national median of $12,000. Minorities, especially blacks, and young households are disproportionately represented. Two-thirds of the households contain no workers; less than one-third are married couples. In view of the popular stereotype of tenants as "welfare mothers," it is perhaps surprising that almost one-half had no children, but about one-fourth had three or more. However, the incidence of large families is higher in public housing than among all eligible households.

Urban Renewal

In 1949 a new form of subsidy was created in the urban renewal program. Urban renewal had many purposes, most of them beyond the scope of this chapter (Rothenberg, 1967; Weicher, 1973), but it was in part a means of bringing down the cost of building. Localities employed their power of eminent domain to acquire urban land; the buildings were then razed and the land resold at auction to private developers. The subsidy thus took the form of a partial write-down of land costs. Since land typically represents only about 20 to 25 percent of the cost of a new dwelling, this partial subsidy was not an effective device to lower housing costs, and in fact the program came under intense criticism, particularly after 1960, for its perverse income redistribution effects: it demolished housing for the poor and replaced it with housing for the upper half of the income distribution. It was also attacked for razing a significant volume of standard housing along with the substandard units. Increasingly, Congress sought to redirect the program toward assisting the poor. Finally, it was replaced in 1974 with

the Community Development Block Grant program (CDBG), which provides funds that local governments can use for renewal projects of their
choice or for a variety of such other purposes as construction of water and
sewer facilities and development of public parks. The block grant reduces
the local government's incentive to engage in urban renewal (Weicher,
1976) and there has been some concern among housing officials that not
enough of the funds are spent on renewal (Nenno, 1976). In 1977 a program of Urban Development Action Grants (UDAG) was created as a
supplement to CDBG. These grants are awarded by HUD for specific
redevelopment projects, which is essentially the system used for urban
renewal, so it may be reappearing under another name.

Interest Subsidies

Up to 1961 the FHA programs and subsidies for low-income households
proceeded on separate tracks. Since the former were widely perceived as
successful, and the latter as much less so, a new program was created in
that year that combined FHA insurance with subsidies. It was designed for
those who were too well-off to be eligible for public housing but too poor
to take advantage of the FHA home ownership program. FHA insured
mortgages on apartment projects owned by nonprofit or limited-dividend
corporations, if the mortgages were issued at below-market interest rates.[9]
The lower interest rate and the limits on profit were to be reflected in
lower rents. In order to induce private lenders to write mortgages at below-
market rates, the Federal National Mortgage Association (FNMA) was
empowered to buy the loans from the originators at face value. (FNMA
was established by Congress in 1938 as a secondary market facility for
FHA mortgages. It could borrow in the capital market to buy mortgages
from their originators, on the theory that it would draw funds from areas
where savings were high relative to mortgage demand and buy mortgages
in areas where they were low.) The net effect of this complicated arrangement was that FNMA lent money at below-market interest rates to private
sponsors to build moderate-income housing. This was known as the Section
221 (d)(3) BMIR (below market interest rate) program.

The program had a relatively short life. The interest rate subsidy proved
to be insufficient to make the apartments attractive to most moderate-
income families, and the budget impact was very large, since each mortgage
purchased by FNMA showed up, dollar for dollar, as a federal budget
outlay. Subsequently, FNMA would receive payment of principal and
interest from the mortgagor over the life of the mortgage, so that the outlay
in the first year would be partially offset later. The subsidy was essentially
the difference between a forty-year stream of payments capitalized at perhaps 5 to 6 percent and at the 3 percent subsidized interest rate. But in

the accounting of the federal budget, the face value of the mortgage was recorded as an outlay in the initial year, with a very small offsetting receipt. The resulting large one-year deficit made the program politically vulnerable.

The 1961 legislation also created a "Section 221 (d) (3) 'market rate'" program, which extended FHA insurance to apartment project mortgages with longer terms and lower down payments than had been customary. These apartments were not originally subsidized, but in 1965 Congress enacted the "rent supplement" program, under which the federal government could make rental payments on behalf of tenants to the sponsors of Section 221 (d) (3) projects. This permitted very-low-income families, similar to those in public housing, to live in the "market rate" projects. Rent supplements were something new, and very controversial at the time. The subsidy was based on the income of the tenant; the federal government paid the difference between 25 percent of his or her income and the rental value of the apartment. Previous subsidies under public housing, urban renewal, and Section 221 (d) (3) had been tied to the cost of the unit; a family had to pay the subsidized rent from its own resources, without extra assistance. (The 25-percent-of-income limit for public housing tenants was enacted later, in 1969.)

Rent supplements effectively served the same income group as did public housing, while the BMIR apartments were not affordable by most moderate-income families. Section 221 (d) (3) had thus missed its target, despite enormous budget outlays, and in 1967 the National Commission on Urban Problems, chaired by former senator Paul Douglas, recommended its termination (National Commission on Urban Problems, 1969). It was superseded in 1968 by another program that combined interest rate subsidies with FHA insurance, known as Section 236. This provided a large subsidy at lower budget impact, by paying the subsidy annually to the project owner (which could be a profit-making firm, unlike the Section 221 programs) rather than by buying the mortgage outright. In this respect, the subsidy mechanism was similar to that used for public housing. It differed, however, in that the mortgage was issued by a private lender, at the market interest rate. The federal government would then pay the difference between the monthly payment needed to amortize the mortgage and the amount needed to amortize it at a lower interest rate, which could be as low as 1 percent. The subsidy was partly conditioned on income; tenants were required to pay 25 percent of their income for rent, or more if this was inadequate to meet payments on a 1 percent mortgage. Rent supplements were also available for those families that still could not afford the apartments, making both moderate- and low-income families eligible. The income limit was set at 135 percent of that for public housing in each locality. In order to hold down costs, dollar mortgage limits per apartment were enacted.

Section 236 got off to a fast start. By 1971 more apartments had been built under it than during the entire Section 221 (d) (3) BMIR program. (Although existing projects were eligible for both programs, over 90 percent of the subsidized units in each were newly constructed.) It also reached the target income groups. In 1976 about one-half the tenants had incomes between $5,000 and $8,000, with a median of $5,700. Tenants are somewhat younger and households are smaller than in public housing, and more occupants are employed.

Subsidized Home Ownership

A parallel series of programs to encourage home ownership for lower-income families was also created during the 1960s. These began in 1961 with Section 221 (d) (2), which authorized FHA insurance, without subsidy, for longer-term, lower down payment loans, on riskier borrowers, than had heretofore been the case. As with the original Section 203, this was used extensively to buy existing homes; about 60,000 new and 300,000 existing homes were insured during the 1960s. In 1968, Section 235 introduced subsidies for home purchase, on the same formula as Section 236. No down payment was required. In fact, the mortgages were typically for larger amounts than the sale price, to cover part of the closing costs. The buyer spent about $100 and was then entitled to move in. Mortgage limits were set well below the prices of most homes then being built. They ranged from $15,000 to $20,000, compared to a median new home price of over $25,000 in 1969. The houses were also much smaller, with fewer amenities, than the typical new home.

Like its counterpart, Section 235 grew quickly, with over 300,000 new and 80,000 existing homes subsidized during its first four years. Buyers had markedly lower incomes than traditional homeowners. The median income of families in the program was $6500 in 1972, compared to $12,300 for all buyers in 1973. Most were young, and the program had a strong geographical concentration in the South and West, where construction costs and home prices were generally lower, so the comparison of current nominal income overstates the extent to which assisted families would not have bought homes without the program, but it seems clear that they were on balance significantly worse-off financially than the usual buyer.[10]

Programs and Problems

By the end of 1972 all the major programs had run into serious problems of one sort or another. Sections 235 and 236, as well as Section 221 (d) (2) and (d) (3) before them, were proving to be actuarially unsound:

actual defaults were high and projected defaults exceeded the value of the mortgage insurance premiums. There were several reasons for this. Most visibly, there were scandals, particularly in the Section 235 existing home program (Aaron, 1972; U.S. Congress, 1970, 1971). Inexpensive houses, of low quality, were bought by real-estate "speculators" who made cosmetic improvements and bribed FHA inspectors to certify that the houses met program standards. They were then sold to eligible families. Often the homes needed major repairs shortly after the new owners moved in, which they could not afford. Default and abandonment was a frequent response. Even in the absence of fraud, the same economic incentives existed for families who wanted to move within a year or two of buying the house. In both instances, the owner found it profitable to act as a renter, treating the closing costs as a security deposit and ignoring the miniscule equity built up in the home (typically less than the cost of selling it) during the first few months of the thirty-year mortgage.

The subsidy formula inadvertently compounded the problem. Buyers were required to pay 20 percent of their income or the amount needed to amortize the mortgage at 1 percent, whichever was higher. Thus, the formula was perverse when maintenance or other operating costs increased. The families that received the maximum subsidy had to meet these cost increases from their own resources, whereas higher-income families that paid 20 percent of their income would have the subsidy raised to cover all cost increases until the 1 percent limit was reached. A 1973 HUD evaluation argued that the major problems were inherent in the program design;[11] other analysts (e.g., Downs, 1973) have stressed the possible gains from improved administration.

When the homes were abandoned, for any reason, the lenders foreclosed. Under the terms of the mortgage insurance, HUD paid the face value of the mortgage and acquired title to the house, which would then be offered for sale. This process worked reasonably well for Section 203; the default rate was low, and the homes acquired by HUD could be resold without great difficulty. But defaults on subsidized homes and apartments were much higher, and the rate of resale did not keep pace. The HUD-held unsold inventory of homes rose from 27,000 in 1960 to 62,000 in 1969, then to 149,000 by 1972; the inventory of apartments went from 4,000 in 1960 to 54,000 in 1972.

Mortgage insurance provided a market test of housing programs, which is relatively rare among government activities. Section 203 had passed that test; the subsidized programs failed it. It was increasingly probable that the insurance funds for these programs would be unable to meet the claims upon them, and that Congress would have to make appropriations for them. This raised the cost substantially. Nor could HUD sell many of the defaulted properties at prices near the original mortgage amount. Sale at a lower price was an admission of mistake, and also appeared in the budget as an expenditure of the difference between mortgage amount and sale price in the year of sale. But withholding the house from the market in the hope that the full mortgage amount could be recouped generated continuing, though smaller, outlays for protection and management. Moreover, a vacant house was often a target for vandals, creating problems for the neighborhood in which it was located.[12]

Section 235 in particular was attacked as inequitable, enabling beneficiaries to live in better housing than people whose incomes were too high to qualify for the program. The resentment is exemplified by one letter to a senator:

> One other thing struck my eye today. An ad for new houses in the $17,000 class being offered to low-income families for $200 down and $100 a month. This made possible by Government subsidy. In the meantime, my wife and I both work to make the payments on our 30-year-home of $136 a month and support our family without the aid of the government. Can you explain to me why I should be taxed to help someone else buy a home that I myself could not afford to live in?[13]

At the same time, urban renewal and public housing were continuing to come under criticism. Some public housing projects were beset by crime and other problems and were so undesirable that they had high vacancy rates, despite the large subsidies received by tenants. The most spectacular "problem project" was Pruitt-Igoe in St. Louis. This was widely praised when it opened in the mid-1950s, but by 1971 it was largely vacant and vandalized, and the City of St. Louis and HUD concluded that much of it should be razed. Demolition of three buildings in 1972 attracted national attention and became a symbol of "what's wrong with public housing."

Section 8

During the early 1970s there was increasing political recognition that the housing programs were not working as desired, and a search for alternatives, culminating in President Nixon's unexpected suspension of all the programs on 8 January 1973. The task force that he then established, the National Housing Policy Review, proposed a major policy shift to a "demand-side" subsidy to be given directly to the family, which could be used for new or existing housing, rather than the customary "supply-side" subsidies tied to specific, usually new, housing units. To achieve this policy, the Section 23 leased public housing program was revised to become Section 8 of the 1974 Housing and Community Development Act. Section 8 differs from Section 23 in several ways. Families with income up to 80 percent of the local median—well above most public housing limits—are eligible. A household receives a commitment from the federal government to pay part of its rent, and then uses this entitlement to seek its own housing. The housing must meet certain quality standards, defined in detail by the local housing authority that administers the program. The federal government pays the subsidy to the local authority, which in turn pays the landlord.

The subsidy formula is also an innovation. It pays the difference between the rent on a standard quality unit (called the Fair Market Rent, or FMR) and 25 percent of the recipient's income. Tenants have some financial incentive to seek housing that rents for less than the FMR in that they also receive part of the difference; a 1976 survey indicated that almost half were receiving this payment, although for most it was minimal.[14] Recipients are limited in choice; they cannot spend more than 25 percent of their income for rent, and they cannot rent a unit for more than the FMR. A novel feature is that low-income tenants who live in standard quality housing (that rents for no more than the FMR) but also pay more than 25 percent of their income for rent, can receive a subsidy while remaining in their current residence. This provision recognizes that most existing housing meets the traditional definition of "decent."

The Section 8 subsidy mechanism for new projects is more like the "supply-side" programs. Private developers and state housing agencies submit project plans to HUD, which promises to subsidize tenants in those it approves. The sponsor is thus guaranteed the FMR on all occupied units, for a period of twenty years. Higher FMRs are set for new projects, to reflect construction costs rather than market rents for standard housing. FHA insurance is also available, but projects need not be insured.

Section 8 is thus a pure income transfer for tenants subsidized in place, and a housing subsidy of the traditional type for new projects. For those who move from one existing dwelling to another, the quality standards impose limits on the extent to which the program is simply a transfer; some may be induced to live in better housing than they would have chosen with an unrestricted cash payment.

Like Section 236 before it, Section 8 started quickly. The program began subsidizing tenants in existing housing during 1975, and by the end of 1976 over 140,000 were being assisted—more than double the number in the first two years of the Section 235 and 236 existing programs combined.

New construction proceeded more slowly, but by the end of September 1977 about 135,000 apartments had been started, two-thirds as many as in the first three years of Section 236. The program served the same income groups as public housing and rent supplements. In mid-1976 tenant median income was estimated as $3800 (U.S. Department of Housing and Urban Development, 1976). About 40 percent of the households received some wage income; 70 percent had a female head. Minorities were participating roughly in proportion to their share of the eligible population. Most households contained only one or two persons; large families were under-represented.

Policy Since 1974

When Section 8 was enacted there was substantial interest in a still less restricted demand-side subsidy, and HUD had in fact begun an experiment with such a "housing allowance." This experiment includes low-income owners as well as renters; it imposes no FMR or percent-of-income ceiling on expenditures or quality, and it subsidizes the individual directly. A renter need not tell the landlord that he or she is being assisted, unlike Section 8, in which landlords must agree to participate. (The experiment is described more fully in RAND, 1977.) This approach has attracted wide attention among economists, and is sometimes viewed as the logical next step after Section 8 (Kain and Schafer, 1977; Nourse, 1976a). It was not adopted in 1974, partly because the experiment was just beginning. Since then, policy has shifted back toward new production. Even as Section 8 was being adopted, housing starts were dropping; 1975 recorded the lowest level since 1946. Also, the program suspensions of 1973 were being challenged in Congress and in the courts as a violation of the Constitutional power of the Congress to appropriate money. At the beginning of 1976, therefore, Section 235 was revived in a modified form, using funds appropriated but not spent prior to January 1973. The program is limited to newly constructed homes, and the maximum subsidy was set at the difference between the mortgage payment at the market interest rate and at a 5 percent rate (instead of 1 percent). The revised program was thus aimed at a higher-income group than the original. Later in 1976 Congress reactivated the traditional public housing construction program, shifting funds requested for Section 8.

Since President Carter has taken office, the trend has continued. In his final budget, President Ford proposed a "modified block grant" approach for Section 8. Localities would be promised a specific dollar amount of subsidy and could choose to subsidize new or existing units, instead of being assigned a given number of each. This plan is somewhat similar to the Community Development Block Grant that replaced urban renewal. It was not adopted by the incoming administration. Also, early in 1977, advocates of welfare reform proposed to fold housing subsidies into welfare, creating an unrestricted income transfer in lieu of all current programs. HUD vigorously opposed this, and it was not part of the final proposal. Instead, President Carter's first budget proposed an expansion of the Section 8 new construction program. The revised Section 235 program has been liberalized and may be extended to existing housing once again. In early 1978, also, the General Accounting Office recommended that Section

236 be revived (U.S. Comptroller General, 1978). Thus, at this writing, the panoply of programs is much like that of 1972, and may become still more similar.

3. THE ECONOMICS OF HOUSING MARKETS: POLICY IMPLICATIONS

Although economists have not until recently played a major direct role in the formulation of housing policy, the noneconomists who have been policy-makers have utilized—usually implicitly—some sort of economic "model" of housing markets and some notions about the empirical magnitudes of key parameters. This section describes the "models" underlying the major types of policy and assesses the professional research insofar as it provides evidence on their validity.

Prior to 1974, housing policy generally sought to increase the supply of standard housing available to lower-income households. In contrast, the Section 8 existing program has sought to increase housing demand. The relative effectiveness of these two approaches in increased housing consumption depends on supply and demand elasticities, most critically on the supply response in the private market. Production-oriented programs have greatest impact in a market in which supply is very inelastic, and demand is inelastic with respect to income and elastic with respect to price. These programs have built new units for lower-income households, to rent at below-market prices. They increase supply to the extent that landlords and builders do not react by reducing the number of units they offer. If private supply is very elastic, the net effect of the program is that publicly supported housing displaces private standard housing, and there is little increase in consumption or decrease in price. In these circumstances, a demand-side subsidy is the only kind of policy that can be very effective at all in improving the quality of housing occupied by low-income households. If, on the other hand, private supply is quite inelastic, a demand subsidy will result in large price rises and little consumption change.

Housing Supply

Elsewhere in this volume, Quigley reviews the scanty empirical work on housing supply. Most studies have concluded that supply is highly elastic in the "long run" (e.g., Muth, 1960; Smith, 1976), and this has been the predominant professional view. There is conflicting evidence, notably the work of de Leeuw and Ekanem (1971), although subsequent reanalyses using their model and data by Grieson (1973) and by Vaughn (1976) suggest a much higher elasticity, particularly for lower-quality housing.

Preliminary evidence from the housing allowance experiments also suggests that supply is highly elastic, though no attempt has yet been made to estimate an elasticity (RAND, 1977).

The choice of policy depends not only on the comparative statics of the two strategies but also on the dynamic process of adjustment. Policymakers have higher rates of time preference than economists and may favor a policy whose ultimate effect is less desirable, if its short-term results are clearly preferable. There are few studies of the adjustment of the housing stock to a change in demand. Muth (1960) estimated that about one-third of the difference between the current and desired stock will occur each year; at this rate, adjustment is over two-thirds complete in three years, and over 90 percent complete in six. His model also implies that prices rise above their initial level in response to increased demand, then gradually decline back to it. De Leeuw and Ekanem (1973) conclude that both the stock and the rent gradually rise to their new, higher equilibrium levels, with about 60 percent of the response occurring within three years. More recently, Mayo (1977) has analyzed the long-run adjustment by participants in the housing allowance experiment in Pittsburgh and Phoenix, finding that they increase consumption by 20 to 25 percent of the difference between actual and desired levels each year.

Taking any of the empirical results at face value, the policy-maker confronts a somewhat unpleasant choice. With elastic supply, as estimated by Muth, demand stimulus will increase housing consumption in the long run, while new construction subsidies will not; but the initial response will be an increase, perhaps sharp, in rents. With the inelastic supply and sluggish adjustment of de Leeuw and Ekanem, rent increases are less of a short-run problem, but more than one-half the demand-induced increase in housing expenditure will eventually be dissipated in higher rents.

Demand

The relative efficacy of the two basic strategies also depends on demand parameters, at least to the extent that supply is less than perfectly elastic. The income elasticity of demand is especially relevant, both because it helps to determine the extent of housing improvement generated by a demand-based subsidy and because income changes are surely one of the most important exogenous (to the housing policy-maker) factors affecting consumption.

Modern empirical research on the income elasticity of demand utilizes permanent income as the relevant concept, rather than current income, given the high transaction costs associated with altering housing consumption patterns. In the two decades since permanent income elasticity estimates first appeared, the preponderance of opinion has varied. Writing in

1971, de Leeuw concluded that the bulk of the evidence indicated an elasticity of 1.1 to 1.5 for owner-occupants and 0.8 to 1.0 for renters. Most of the studies he examined used aggregate cross-section data. Since then, a number of analyses of microdata sets have reported much lower elasticities, so that a 1977 paper by Polinsky reconciling the various estimates argues that the elasticity is probably around 0.75,[15] and Quigley (in this volume) reports a professional consensus that demand is slightly inelastic with respect to income.

The difference between the estimates of de Leeuw and Polinsky is less important to the policy-maker than to the professional economist. It is clear that the elasticity is not zero, and equally clear that not all of a demand-based subsidy will be spent on housing—both positions that have been forcefully argued in political debates. More important is the conclusion in most studies that renters have lower elasticities than owners. This reduces the attractiveness of demand subsidies, since low-income renters are the principal target group for housing programs. Most studies also find lower elasticities with respect to current than to permanent income, and the former concept is still given substantial weight in policy formulation. It is common to find comparisons of rent-income ratios across income classes used to show that low-income households have high housing cost "burdens," without considerations of negative transitory income (Birch et al., 1973).

The price-elasticity of demand is relevant for housing policy in two senses. Most programs have lowered the price of housing to the subsidy recipients, and production programs are justified in part on the basis that they will lower the market price of standard housing, and thus increase consumption by increasing supply. The quality improvement will, of course, be greater, the more elastic the demand. If it is very inelastic, price reduction programs become very expensive. (Ironically, program effectiveness in this sense conflicts with economic efficiency; the more elastic the demand, the greater the deadweight loss compared to an income transfer, from the standpoint of the subsidy recipients.)

The empirical evidence reviewed by Quigley suggests a price elasticity slightly below unity, although economists have often concluded that it is "close enough" to unity for many analytical purposes. As with income, the difference is not significant for policy. Whether price elasticity is slightly below, at, or somewhat above unity, the consumption increase generated by production programs will be similar, and a large part of any subsidy will be spent to "buy out the base," i.e., pay people to do what they would do anyway, rather than to improve quality or increase production.

Price and income elasticities are also relevant to the issue of financial burden, which has been suggested as a new "quality" standard, supplementing the physical measures described in section 1 (Frieden and Solomon, 1977). A common rule of thumb is that the housing expense/income ratio should be constant, usually at 0.25. In fact, the proportion of renters paying more than 25 percent of their income for rent has risen steadily since World War II—from 31 percent in 1950 to 44 percent in 1976. (Far fewer owners—about 22 percent—had such ratios in 1976, up from 19 percent in 1974, the earliest data available.) This is usually regarded as evidence of a decrease in supply, and therefore a "problem," without reference to demand. Economists, of course, look at both sides of the market, and seldom take this rule of thumb seriously. But its widespread appeal demonstrates that basic economic concepts are still not well understood by housing analysts who are not economists.

Housing Submarkets and Policy

Many policies are directed at submarkets for housing with specific attributes rather than at the housing market as a whole. One of the most important is the market for "low-income" housing, which means, approximately, dwellings meeting, but not greatly exceeding, some minimum quality standards. Policies to increase the supply of such housing have included both the direct subsidy programs described in section 2 and the construction of much higher-quality housing, on the theory that the increased supply will depress the price of existing housing to the point where lower-income households can afford "decent" housing.

This latter process is widely known as "filtering." There is a substantial literature concerning it, which Quigley reviews in this volume. For policy purposes, the important parameter is the extent to which the price per unit of housing service declines as the number of units of service in a dwelling (i.e., its quality level) also declines. If the price does not fall, then filtering does not help low-income households; they can improve their housing only by increasing expenditures, which they are likely to do only if their income increases. The filtering literature has rarely focused on price change, although there are important exceptions. Lowry (1960) argued that price declines could not occur because landlords would earn a below-market return on their investment. They would then disinvest, by reducing maintenance expenditures, and quality would deteriorate until the original price per unit of service and rate of return were reestablished. Recently, Sweeney (1974) and Ohls (1975) have constructed more rigorous models that permit prices to vary with quality and have simulated housing policies. Both found that a production program can lower the price per unit of service for dwellings of lower quality than those produced. In Sweeney's model, this occurs only if more new housing is created than was originally demanded at the equilibrium price; the program must replace all units provided privately at that quality level. Unless quality is very narrowly defined, this has almost certainly not happened. Indeed, one of the major criticisms of subsidy programs is that they help a small fraction of the eligible population. Ohls simulates both a very large public housing program (approximately fifteen times the actual construction in the past four decades) and a demand subsidy that achieves the same quality improvement; the latter costs about 25 percent less. Under both simulations, prices rise slightly for middle-income families.

None of these analyses include empirical work.[16] Some estimates of the actual patterns of prices per unit of housing service have been derived by de Leeuw and Struyk (1975). Four out of six Standard Metropolitan Statistical Areas (SMSAs) showed sharp price declines for housing below the minimum quality established by local building codes for new units, suggesting that a filtering process could be occurring.

There are also some studies of the submarket for substandard housing. Farb (1971) concluded that supply is highly elastic and demand inelastic, which indicates that income transfers are more likely to improve quality than slum clearance and new construction. Davis, Eastman, and Hua (1974) studied changes in substandard housing during the 1960s, but owing to the data limitations described in section 1, they were unable to make precise quality comparisons and found conflicting results on the relative importance of income increases and subsidized production in raising quality.

The tenure choice decision is another major topic of interest to policymakers. The professional literature tends to focus on income and demographic factors (Straszheim, 1975), but most programs have sought to lower the price of owning housing relative to renting it. Thus the literature has not been directly relevant to policy, although recently Struyk (1976) has attempted to analyze price sensitivity indirectly, by translating price changes into equivalent income changes. His results suggest that tenure choice is quite responsive to price. More attention has been given to the estimates of the cost of various policies, notably Aaron's (1972) work on the income tax treatment of home ownership, but as yet this has not affected policy.

There are many other relevant submarket classifications. Proposals are common, and are sometimes adopted, to stimulate the market for housing of a certain age (new; or old, such as pre-1940), by location (central city; or rural), or by price (under $40,000). Research has rarely been used, or been useful, for the analysis of such proposals; but the hedonic approach might be used here, as well as in measuring housing quality, to contribute effectively to policy formulation.

4. ECONOMIC EVALUATION OF HOUSING PROGRAMS

The economic evaluation of housing subsidies starts from the well-known theoretical proposition that, from the recipient's point of view, an income transfer is preferable to a subsidy in kind of equal dollar value. Economists then ask: Why subsidize housing? If an income transfer increases the well-being of a low-income family to a greater extent than a housing subsidy, at the same cost to the taxpayer, what is the reason for providing the subsidy that gives less satisfaction?

Macroeconomic Considerations

A common argument for subsidized production programs is that they increase output and provide economic stimulus. This macroeconomic effect is given great weight by noneconomists; it is sometimes regarded as a third major goal of housing policy, and has been used by advocates of each subsidy program in turn.

Economists tend to find the argument less compelling, since the resources used in housing programs have alternative uses, including other countercyclical programs. In addition, it is important to distinguish between the macroeconomic effect of housing production in general and subsidized housing for low-income families in particular.

The complex relationship between housing and the business cycle lies beyond the scope of this chapter; much recent research is reported in Gramlich and Jaffee (1972) and Ricks (1973). But the basic data indicate that subsidy programs have almost certainly not been effective countercyclical policy tools. The housing industry recovered from the 1960 trough without significant assistance from Section 221: subsidized multifamily starts did not reach 10,000 a year under the program until 1964, whereas overall production rose from 1.25 million in 1960 to 1.60 million in 1963, which was the third highest yearly figure recorded to that date. Similarly, Section 8 new construction did not occur in significant volume until 1977, when total starts were already running at an annual rate of 1.90 million, up from a trough of about 1 million at the end of 1974. Section 236 and the Section 211 (d) (2) and 235 home ownership programs also did not have a marked countercyclical effect. Although these were new programs, requiring administrative development before any construction, long lead times occur even under established programs. Public housing projects have historically required about a year of federal processing before site acquisition, let alone new construction, can begin (National Commission on Urban Problems, 1969).

More fundamentally, there is some evidence that subsidized housing production substantially substitutes for unsubsidized production. Swan (1973) has estimated that about 85 percent of the starts under Section 235 and 236 during 1969–72 would have occurred without the programs; mortgage interest rates were driven up in the process of reaching equilibrium in the mortgage market. The period studied was perhaps not ideal, since the programs were most important during the minor recession of 1970 and the housing boom of 1971–72. There has been no similar analysis of more severe recessions. Even if Swan's findings were reversed for other periods, however, the long lags would greatly reduce the countercyclical effectiveness of subsidized production.

Externalities: Property Values

In evaluating housing programs, economists have usually ignored macro-economic considerations and assumed full employment. Under that assumption, the economic justification for housing subsidies, whether tied to production or not, must be based on market failure. The most detailed framework for analyzing urban programs has been developed by Rothenberg (1967) in his study of urban renewal. Much of it is not germane to housing subsidies, which typically have the relatively simple purpose of raising the quality of housing occupied by low-income households, since urban renewal is a broader program with nonhousing objectives and its central feature— the utilization of eminent domain to overcome a "prisoner's dilemma" in urban land markets in order to improve the efficiency of land use—is not relevant. Housing subsidies thus can be justified to the extent that good housing is underproduced in the market, which will occur if housing generates externalities.

Externalities of two kinds have been identified: the effect of housing quality on the value of nearby property, and the "social costs of slums."[17]

The argument that good housing increases the value of adjacent property is widely accepted by real-estate professionals. It applies not only to substandard housing but to all quality levels: the better a given house is, the greater is the value of housing in the neighborhood. However, it has often been used as a rationale for subsidized low-income housing, in particular.[18]

The empirical evidence on this externality is limited. The hedonic literature has shown the difficulty of isolating the effect on value of any one attribute, such as the quality of adjacent housing, and the theoretical problems are compounded by a lack of data.

Given the difficulties, it is not surprising that there have been few studies of subsidized housing. Nourse (1963) analyzed the effect of three public housing projects in St. Louis over twenty-two years, comparing the price changes for individual properties near the projects to changes in three control neighborhoods. By confining the sample to parcels that were sold at least twice during the period, he avoided the problems inherent in comparing different properties. Schafer (1972) subsequently used the same methodology to study a Section 221 (d) (3) project in Los Angeles. Neither found any evidence that the projects raised property values.

A somewhat different technique was employed by Ferrera (1969) in a study of urban renewal and public housing in Chicago. Using block data from the 1940, 1950, and 1960 Censuses, he found that prices rose differentially within a one-block ring around one public housing project during the 1950s. Subsequent investigation showed that this ring was being converted to commercial use; the project did not include any stores, although it increased the number of residents in the area. It is likely that this effect would be offset by declining commercial property values in nearby neighborhoods.

More recently, DeSalvo (1974) studied the neighborhood effect of the Mitchell-Lama middle-income housing subsidy program in New York City. This state and local government program is somewhat similar to Section 221 (d) (3) BMIR in that it subsidizes the interest rate on apartment project mortgages, through the municipal bond tax exemption, to achieve lower rents. DeSalvo compared the changes in assessed property values within three blocks of each of fifty projects to borough-wide changes, from the beginning of each project to fiscal year 1968–69. He found a 5 percent greater annual average change in assessed value around the projects than in the borough as a whole. Although this is the largest study yet undertaken, it suffers from the use of assessed rather than market values. Weicher and Zerbst (1973) have presented evidence that assessors systematically err in their estimates of the market value of externalities. Since the projects are expected to raise land values, the assessor may conclude that they do so, without reference to market transactions.

None of these studies provides strong evidence that social benefits exist. Nourse (1976*b*) has hypothesized that building codes may have effectively internalized the externalities, and raised housing quality. Mills (1976) expressed an alternative view: that the externality is real, but that its empirical magnitude, and therefore its policy significance, may be small—on the order of 5 to 15 percent of the amount invested in a house. This brackets DeSalvo's results.

Mills further argued that the subsidy justified by the externality is probably already provided to owner-occupants by the income tax provisions that allow them to deduct mortgage interest and property taxes and suggested extending the same deduction to renters, in preference to housing subsidy programs.

Externalities: "Social Costs"

The "social costs of slums" has received much more attention than their effect on the value of adjacent property. Rothenberg (1967), for example, argued that they probably provide the most important argument for urban renewal. These costs include crime and delinquency, fires, disease and death, and mental illness and psychological problems. These are only partly externalities. A fire in a substandard house will first affect the residents. Until its spreads to other property, no externality is created. The same distinction is relevant for disease, although communicability varies widely. Crime and mental illness would appear to be the extreme cases: the former is a pure externality, the latter probably close to a purely private cost, at least within the family.

The argument that slum housing increases the incidence of these unpleasant phenomena antedates housing programs by many years. In most early studies, however, characteristics of housing were not separated from characteristics of people, so that the marginal effect of housing was not measured (Dean, 1949; Fisher, 1959). Gradually this deficiency has been ameliorated, and the standards of research have risen. There is now a large literature on the relationship of housing to these "social costs," much of it in disciplines other than economics.

Perhaps the most recent exhaustive evaluation of the research on housing and health is by Kasl (1976), who reviewed 178 studies in the fields of public health, medicine, and social psychology. He concluded that, ". . . the link between parameters of housing and indices of physical health has not been well supported by the reviewed evidence, at least not in any direct sense . . . the association between housing and mental health . . . is supported only by the weakest, most ambiguous studies. . . . The best designed studies do not demonstrate any mental health benefits, and it now appears that some of our most cherished hopes—such as raising educational and occupational aspirations by moving people out of slums—never will be realized."[19] Kasl cited evidence that people are more satisfied in better housing, which may be regarded as one aspect of mental health. He also qualified his conclusions by noting that current research techniques probably understate the effect of housing on health, because that effect is likely to be mediated through other processes. In the language of economics, what we have now are largely reduced-form relationships derived from unspecified structural models, rather than the models themselves.

Kasl is an epidemiologist. Few if any economists have reviewed this literature as extensively. Within the profession, interpretations differ. The range of opinion can be illustrated in reference to what is probably the best-known evaluation, a longitudinal study by Wilner and his associates (1962) of public housing residents in Baltimore. Kasl termed it the "classical" study. It compared tenants in public housing to a similar control group over a three-year period that spanned the move from substandard housing to the project. Reviewing the results, Muth concluded: "In matters relating to health and personal adjustment . . . differences were small and did not systematically favor public housing tenants."[20] (This is essentially also Kasl's conclusion.) Nourse is somewhat more positive: "Better housing improved the health and school performance of children because they had fewer accidents and days of illness. The differences were not found among persons over 35 years of age."[21] Rothenberg is still more positive, citing five specific findings that better housing was associated with improved health, including lower incidence of infectious childhood disease.[22] He did not discuss those instances where no association was found.

Research into the relationship between housing and crime has also been primarily the province of noneconomists and suffers from the same problem of isolating the effect of housing. A study by Lander (1954) is particularly noteworthy: a strong simple correlation between housing and delinquency disappeared in a multivariate analysis controlled for race and education. Summarizing the field, Rothenberg (1976) concludes that "Once again, there is not a body of decisively persuasive evidence linking bad housing per se with crime."[23]

In the case of fire, there is more evidence of a link with housing. Syron (1972) found fire losses in Boston to be highly correlated with housing conditions, which is consistent with Weicher's (1972) result that local expenditures on fire protection are affected by housing conditions; the latter study did not show any relationship between housing and expenditures for police or public health. Syron's findings are plausible, but they do not demonstrate the presence of an externality; and the expenditure comparisons, even if interpreted to show that fewer resources are required to achieve a given level of protection, indicated that savings were minor compared to other benefits and costs of urban renewal.

Although there are differences of opinion and interpretation, the disagreement among economists is less than among housing analysts generally, because standards of research methodology are more clearly established. Thus, Rothenberg stressed the difficulty of empirical work, arguing that research so far does not show that externalities do *not* exist,[24] Aaron concluded that it has not been shown that they *do* exist,[25] and Mills stated that, "Undoubtedly, the important causes of these problems [social costs] are poverty, racial conflict, etc. none of which represent housing market failures."[26]

Finally, it should be noted that much of the literature is concerned with the effect on the individual; there is still less evidence for externalities than for direct effects. From the standpoint of housing policy, the more important question is not whether housing affects health but whether it affects the neighbors' health.

Income Distribution and Equity

Most economists who have analyzed specific housing programs have ignored externalities and treated the programs simply as income redistribution mechanisms. This approach has been taken in part because different techniques and data are needed to study redistribution; several analysts (Aaron and von Furstenberg, 1971; Bish, 1969) have explicitly stated that externalities are being ignored "without prejudice" to their importance. But the literature also reflects the view that externalities are probably minor; the nearly unanimous conclusion is that the production programs are inefficient forms of redistribution, a criticism that is more appropriate, the less serious is market failure.

One reason for this conclusion is that all of the programs are inequitable—they provide a large benefit to the small number of households participating, but nothing to a very large number who are equally eligible. For example, some 850,000 households with income under $5000, out of 17.7 million in that income range, were living in public housing in 1972, thirty-five years after the start of the program. Fewer than 10 percent of those in any income bracket were helped by all programs combined (U.S. Department of Housing and Urban Development, 1974).

There is also a problem of vertical equity. Both public housing and rent supplements are concentrated among the lowest income households, but each subsidizes many who are better-off than others who receive no benefit. Among those who do participate, benefits are inversely related to income, as is desirable (Aaron, 1972; Barton and Olsen, 1976; Bish, 1969; U.S. Department of Housing and Urban Development, 1974). But the opposite occurs in Section 235 and, to a lesser extent, in Section 236; higher-income families have higher subsidies, apparently because they are living in more expensive houses and apartments and because the subsidy is conditioned on family size as well as income (U.S. Department of Housing and Urban Development, 1974).

Inefficiency in Production

The programs have also been consistently criticized for inefficiently providing assistance to their direct beneficiaries. One source of inefficiency is that housing is produced more expensively by government than by private enterprise. Resource misallocation is most germane for public housing, where construction is undertaken under contract to local authorities and where the subsidy formula, until 1969, was based only on some components of cost.

Muth concluded that payment of capital costs by the federal government creates an incentive for local housing authorities to build better quality units, needing less maintenance, than they would if required to purchase both capital and current operating inputs at market prices. Based on his estimate (1971) of the elasticity of substitution between these inputs, he calculated (1973) that costs are 21 percent higher as a result of the subsidy formula.

Another approach was taken by de Leeuw and Leaman (1972), who compared actual costs under the Section 23 leased housing program, where units are privately built, to those under conventional and turnkey public housing. They found the latter programs to be 42 and 37 percent more expensive, respectively, in large part because of the foregone federal income tax revenues resulting from the tax exemption of local authority bonds. An additional factor, not mentioned by de Leeuw and Leaman but implicit in their data, is that Section 23 units were not subject to the Davis-Bacon Act. This law requires that the locally prevailing wage must be paid on federal construction projects, including public housing and Section 236. Administratively, prevailing wages are typically determined to be the union scale, even in areas where little housing is built by union workers (Gould, 1971).

Smolensky (1968) also analyzed project cost data, concluding that units cost 25 percent more than equivalent private existing dwellings. When the tenant's payment is subtracted from cost and rent, the additional housing provided through the program cost 55 percent more than if it had been provided privately. More recently, Barton and Olsen (1976) found that the costs of New York City units were about 10 percent above their market values, and the additional housing cost about 20 percent more. Their study contains the most sophisticated estimates of market rents for public housing units to date.

These cost increases differ from the usual economic concept of inefficiency, though they implicitly include the effects of resource misallocation. The higher cost of public housing units is analogous to the higher price charged by a monopoly. Both represent income transfers, which in the public housing case are paid to labor, and perhaps to the program administrators who perform some of the functions of private landlords and mortgage lenders.[27] Economic inefficiency arises to the extent that fewer units are subsidized because of these costs, which depends on the elasticity of "demand," or the willingness of the government or the taxpayers to subsidize more units if costs are lower. On the other hand, the inefficiency occurs because of cost-raising constraints imposed by the government, which demands the housing in the first place, a situation quite different from private monopoly. The government agencies may act in ignorance of the true cost of their practices; but some cost increases may be transfers that gain political support for the program, and without them, fewer units would be built.

In-kind Transfers and Welfare Loss

A second source of inefficiency, which has received more study, arises from the in-kind nature of the subsidy. A dollar in cash will make its recipient better-off than a dollar's worth of any good, unless the demand for that good is completely inelastic. Beneficiaries of housing subsidies can buy or rent a particular unit at a price below its market value. The welfare loss from this in-kind transfer can be measured as $\frac{1}{2}\Delta P\Delta Q$, where ΔP is the price subsidy and ΔQ is the difference between the quantity of service provided by the subsidized unit and by the unit the household would otherwise occupy. Clearly, the more elastic the demand for housing, the larger the difference between the quality of the unit originally occupied and that which the household would like to occupy, and thus the greater the welfare loss.[28]

Empirical studies of the welfare loss in public housing began to appear during the mid-1960s, shortly before publication of Perloff and Wingo's *Issues in Urban Economics*. Estimates of the market rent of the apartments, the price elasticity of demand, and the amount that would be spent for housing in the absence of the program, are required to calculate the loss. Prescott's (1964) estimate of market value in 1965 was based on the assumption that local authorities set rents at the legal maximum (80 percent of the rent for equivalent private units). Since rents averaged $60 a month, he calculated the market rent at $75. His figure was subsequently used by Smolensky and by Olsen and Prescott (1969). Based on his own analysis of the subsidy formula, Muth (1973) concluded that local authorities could provide housing at 27 percent of the cost to a private builder; if they did so, the equivalent 1965 private rent would have been $177. These figures place bounds on the market rent and, given the tenant's payment, the market value of the subsidy.

Fortunately, the previous expenditures of households admitted to public housing are collected as program data. They have been used by Olsen and Prescott (1969) and Kraft and Olsen (1977) to measure consumption without the program. The former study assumed a unitary price elasticity and estimated a welfare loss of about 22 percent of the market value of the subsidy. The latter employed a Cobb-Douglas utility function to estimate indifference maps for tenants, estimating the welfare loss at 27 percent. More recently, Barton and Olsen (1976) used a displaced Cobb-Douglas function and found the loss to be 25 percent.

Aaron and von Furstenberg (1971) have developed a more sophisticated analytical framework. Using a constant elasticity of substitution (CES) utility function to estimate a welfare loss of 10 percent or less for public housing and 18 percent for Section 235 and 236, they concluded that, "If there are large inefficiencies in federally-assisted housing, they will have to be found empirically on the cost side."[29] Data limitations may be responsible for the relatively small public housing figure. Aaron and von Furstenberg used aggregate data for all low-income households to estimate housing expenditures in the absence of the program, rather than individual observations. Olsen and Prescott had earlier estimated the welfare loss at 2 to 10 percent with data for all low-income households, compared to the

22 percent figure for their tenant sample. Also, aggregation can substantially affect the results. Kraft and Olsen calculated the welfare loss for each individual separately and then substituted the sample means for the variables into their formula. They found the average benefit to be 25 percent higher in the latter case and the welfare loss only 3 percent, instead of 27. The choice of utility function is also relevant. Aaron and von Furstenberg derived a price elasticity of around 0.5, well below the unitary elasticity implied by the Cobb-Douglas function and the figures typically found in the literature (Quigley, in this volume).

More recently, Murray (1975) has calculated welfare loss in public housing by using both utility functions to construct indifference maps. For a sample of newly admitted tenants, he estimated mean welfare loss at 20 percent for the Cobb-Douglas specification, compared to 16 percent for the CES. These figures are of course quite similar. But Murray also tested the hypothesis that either is the true specification, with discouraging results: he rejected the CES specification for over one-half the family size and composition groups in his sample, and the Cobb-Douglas form for all of them.

Perhaps the largest welfare loss has been estimated by Muth, in a different manner from most studies. He used his own previous empirical work, suggesting a price elasticity of 1.25, and his estimate of the market value of a public housing unit to calculate a loss of 45 percent, far larger than the inefficiency from the production subsidy.

There have been few analyses of other programs. DeSalvo (1971, 1975) has independently developed a framework similar to that of Aaron and von Furstenberg and used a Cobb-Douglas function to estimate the inefficiency in the New York City Mitchell-Lama program. He found a large welfare loss of 45 percent.

The National Housing Policy Review

Through 1972 economic evaluation of housing programs was primarily an academic exercise, with little effect on policy. This pattern changed with the National Housing Policy Review (NHPR). It was headed by an economist, Michael Moskow, and as part of the basis for its recommendations, a research group composed largely of economists evaluated the major programs.

The analysts concentrated on equity and efficiency. They rejected the macroeconomic rationale for production subsidies and evaluated the programs from an economic rather than a budgetary perspective. This approach was completely new to housing policy-makers. In the words of one veteran civil servant, "Why should we have economists looking at these programs now? We never had them here before!"[30]

TABLE 14.2. Estimated Efficiency of Subsidized Housing Programs

Program	Annual Cost per Household	Percentage Improvement in Housing	Production Efficiency	Transfer Efficiency	Program Efficiency
Section 236	$1051	51%	.70	.71	.50
Section 236 with rent supplement	1901	....	.84	.64	.54
Section 221 (d) (3) with rent supplement	1310	....	.75	.64ᵃ	.48
Section 235	1051	35	.87	.90	.79
Section 502 (Farmers Home Administration)	813	92	.85	.82	.70
Public Housing	1750	71	.74	.75	.55
conventional	....	....	.71	....	....
turnkey	....	....	.81	....	....
Section 23 leased	....	....	.97	....	....

SOURCE: National Housing Review, *Housing in the Seventies* (Washington, D.C.: U.S. Government Printing Office, 1974), table 4, p. 92; table 5, p. 94; and calculations from p. 127.

ᵃ Assumed to be the same as the estimate for Section 236 with rent supplement.

The NHPR concluded, as had previous independent studies, that the programs were seriously inequitable. It also found them all to be inefficient, for diverse reasons. Table 14.2 summarizes the quantitative estimates of efficiency. The first column contains estimates of the total per-unit cost, including administrative costs, foregone property or income taxes, and defaults in excess of premiums for the insured programs, as well as the actual subsidies. Although interesting, the relative magnitudes should not be over-emphasized, since the programs serve different population groups and generate different degrees of improvement in housing and general well-being. Estimates of the housing improvement are shown in the next column; the degree of improvement is roughly inversely related to the income level of the subsidy recipients.

The remaining columns contain measures of efficiency. Production efficiency is the ratio of the market value of the extra housing provided by a program to its total direct and indirect costs; this measure had earlier been used by Smolensky.

The most detailed calculations of production efficiency were developed for public housing. Yearly development, administrative, and operating costs for each of a sample of projects in eleven cities were discounted to 1971, using a market interest rate. This procedure had been used by de Leeuw and Leaman and by Smolensky to adjust for the tax-exempt status of the bonds. The costs were then compared to hedonic estimates of market rents, based on previous studies by Olsen (1972) for New York City and Gillingham (1973) for five other cities, also adjusted to 1971. Separate valuations for conventional, turnkey, and leased units were computed and compared to the production cost figures of de Leeuw and Leaman. These comparisons indicated that leased housing was markedly more efficient, and contributed to the decision to expand and revise Section 23.

For the newer rental subsidy programs, it was more difficult to calculate the extent to which subsidized units cost more than private housing. A 1973 HUD construction cost subsidy found a 20 percent differential, based on a multivariate analysis (including more than 20 characteristics of the units) of a sample that comprised both Section 236 and 221 (d) (3) projects. Beyond this, HUD rent surveys showed a difference of zero to 10 percent, but the degree of comparability was more questionable. With this range of estimates, the analyst settled on 10 percent as a measure of central tendency in each program. The differential becomes a much larger figure when the tenant's rent is subtracted from both terms to measure the subsidy inefficiency, which varies inversely with the depth of the subsidy. The cost difference was the most important source of production efficiency for each program.

The second most important was foregone income taxes. For Section 236 (both with and without rent supplement), it was more than double the administrative costs and the expected loss from foreclosure combined; for the earlier rent supplement program, it was slightly larger than the latter two. Estimates of foregone taxes were based on the questionable assumption that investors in subsidized projects would not find other tax shelters. However, even under the opposite assumption—that the federal government received no additional revenue—production efficiency would have increased only from 0.70 to 0.74 for Section 236, from 0.84 to 0.86 for Section 236 with rent supplement, and from 0.75 to 0.80 for Section 221 (d) (3) rent supplement units.[31]

Estimating the production efficiency of the home ownership programs was more difficult, since the typical new Section 235 home was not comparable in size or amenities to most unsubsidized homes built at the time. A cost survey in nine cities found that the price per square foot of house was about 10 percent lower for the subsidized homes; however, land costs were included in the price, without adjustment for lot size or location. In the absence of better data, the analysts assumed that construction costs would be the same for equivalent new homes and applied that assumption to existing homes. This generated the higher production efficiency in the home ownership programs. Administrative costs became the major source of inefficiency, particularly for Section 235, which was marginally actuarially sound in 1973; shortly thereafter it ceased to be so.

The production inefficiency calculated for public housing is close to the estimates of Muth and of Barton and Olsen. Independent evaluations of the other programs have not been undertaken. They would be particularly desirable, since the NHPR estimates clearly rest heavily on the construction cost differentials. The most detailed critique of the study (U.S. Library of Congress, 1974) concentrated on these differentials and argued that lower numbers were equally plausible, but there has been no further work.

Estimates of transfer efficiency came from Murray's study, then in progress, and from two samples of public housing tenants, using the formula earlier developed by Olsen and Prescott. One of these samples was subsequently reanalyzed by Kraft and Olsen (both of whom worked on the NHPR), with the more sophisticated techniques described earlier. Benefit calculations were very close to those of the NHPR.

Murray's indifference maps for public housing tenants were also used to estimate transfer efficiency for the other programs, based on the family's expenditure on other goods and the market value of the housing unit. The expenditure data came from samples of Section 236 tenants and Section 235 owners, stratified by family composition. The validity of this procedure depends on the extent to which the tastes of public housing tenants are similar to those aided by other programs. The correspondence is probably closest for the rent supplement programs, whose beneficiaries have about the same income and racial composition as public housing tenants. Other program beneficiaries are less obviously comparable, differing by income, race, or location. The racial difference is probably least important, given the evidence of similar demand functions by race (Reid, 1962; Straszheim, 1975). The application of indifference maps for low-income families to estimate benefits for those better-off is valid if the indifference curves of each family are homothetic. There are few independent studies of the newer programs to serve as a check on this methodology. The NHPR calculated a lower welfare loss than Aaron and von Furstenberg for Section 235 but a higher one for Section 236. No estimate is as high as DeSalvo's 45 percent figure for the Mitchell-Lama program. Section 235 has the highest transfer efficiency because the buyers have higher income and smaller housing improvements; their preferences are thus less distorted by the program.

The final column of table 14.2 is the product of the preceding two. Program efficiency is the fraction of program cost, direct and indirect, that increases the recipient's welfare. It is not a measure of economic efficiency, since production efficiency includes transfers to others besides subsidy recipients.

The NHPR study, and the academic research on which it is based, clearly have limitations. The evidence indicates that the simpler utility functions used so far are, at best, rather imprecise approximations. Also, the conclusions depend heavily on the estimates of the higher cost of building subsidized units. But despite its limitations, this body of research has, within a surprisingly short time after economists began to study the programs seriously, improved the ability of policy-makers to make informed decisions.

Arguments for Subsidized Production

While most of the literature is explicitly or implicitly critical of the subsidized production programs, some economists do support them. Their leading advocate within the profession has probably been Anthony Downs (1973). His advocacy, however, is not based on efficiency or equity grounds. He acknowledged that Section 236, and probably Section 235, are inherently inefficient; but he argued that the degree of inefficiency and program abuse and fraud could be reduced through better administration. He attributed the inequities to an inappropriate policy focus on the housing quality of low-income households, instead of their general economic welfare, and recommended some form of direct financial assistance—such as a subsidy to use the existing inventory—for those who live in adequate units, but at high cost.

Downs favored production subsidies on three grounds: (1) to stimulate the economy; (2) to expand the total housing stock and reduce the upward pressure on prices; (3) to achieve some economic integration, enabling low-income households to live in suburbs from which they would otherwise be excluded.

The first two arguments have been considered earlier; the research so far suggests that neither is particularly strong, although there is certainly room for further study. Even if subsidized production expands supply, however, it can mitigate price increases only to the extent that supply is inelastic. Several other economists, including Musgrave (1976) and Chinitz (1976), have argued for production subsidies on this ground, combined with income transfers. The elasticity of supply is fundamentally an empirical question; the evidence discussed in section 3 suggests that it is fairly high and that subsidized production would therefore not be effective.

Downs' third justification depends on the existence of externalities for low-income households from living in high-income areas. An obvious source of externalities is the local public-service sector, which typically provides such important services as education and police protection, more or less uniformly over a political jurisdiction or neighborhood. Public policy on service provision is the subject of another paper in this volume (Inman), and will not be considered here.

A related rationale has been advanced by Kain (1976), who argued that the programs are, or can be, an effective means of alleviating racial discrimination in housing. Discrimination, like public service provision, is addressed elsewhere in this volume (Yinger). There has been no systematic analysis of its relationship to subsidized production, although Kain's contention is plausible. Section 236 may have contributed to racial integration of suburban areas, at least on a small scale.[32] The most important consideration, however, is whether there are more efficient means of reducing discrimination.

CONCLUSION

When Tobin reviewed Friedman and Schwartz's *Monetary History of the United States* in 1965, he devoted most of his space to a critical discussion of technical issues. But in the last section he turned to monetary policy, and his tone changed:

> Enough of the parochial disputes of monetary theorists . . . I think that economists today—though they differ sharply in theoretical approach and political color—would agree very widely on the major practical and operational issues of these nine decades. I prefer to end with this note of operational agreement rather than theoretical discord. . . . Economists are likely to show a united front when the occasion arises to second-guess the decisions of men of affairs.[33]

Tobin's words surely apply to urban economists when they address housing policy. Regardless of their conclusions on the magnitude of the income elasticity of demand, or even the elasticity of supply, most economists have argued against the subsidized production programs of the past forty years. As part of the NHPR, over twenty economists—representing a broad spectrum of the profession—were asked to evaluate them from various standpoints (U.S. Department of Housing and Urban Development, 1974). Although a few favored the current programs for the reasons discussed at the end of section 4, the large majority preferred either unrestricted income transfers or some form of rent certificate, along the lines of the Section 8 program that was enacted the next year, or the housing allowance.

The distinction between a housing allowance and an income transfer is important, because the latter can be used to constrain the recipient's choice to "decent" housing, however narrowly defined (Mills, 1976). But in the policy context, the difference between them is small, compared to the difference between either one and conventional public housing or Section 236. These latter programs "create" housing.

Thus, from the policy-maker's perspective, there is a distinctly "economic" point of view. The appearance of a professional consensus exists basically because economists approach housing policy with the prior conviction that it is better to give people money than housing, unless there is evidence to the contrary. As policy tends to move toward renewed emphasis on subsidized production, this consensus among economists is likely to appear still broader.

NOTES

1. P.L. 87–181, sec. 2.
2. U.S. Congress, Joint Committee on Housing, 1948, pp. 8–9; and Part 2, p. 9.
3. U.S. Bureau of the Census, 1973–76, Part B.
4. Goedert and Goodman, 1977, p. 29.
5. The history of mortgage credit policy, particularly with respect to home owner-ship, is described in Semer et al. (1976a). Recently, both Aaron (1972, ch. 5–6) and the National Housing Policy Review (1974, ch. 3) have reviewed these programs from an economic perspective.
6. Unless otherwise noted, data on HUD programs and on housing generally is taken from the HUD Statistical Yearbook for various years from 1967 to 1976. The later yearbooks typically repeat program information for earlier years, so that nearly all data appears in the 1976 edition (the latest in print at this writing), with the exception of characteristics of residents of subsidized housing, which are usually pub-lished only for the current year.
7. U.S. Department of Housing and Urban Development, 1977, p. 10. Figures for mortgages on existing homes are less readily available, but the data suggest a similar pattern (U.S. Department of Housing and Urban Development, 1967–76, 1967 edition, p. 75, and 1975 edition, pp. 48, 274). The (later) Veterans Administration mortgage guarantee program has followed a parallel course. Its market share peaked in the early 1950s at about 16 percent of new homes and has since fallen by more than one-half. VA requires no down payment or mortgage premium, and guarantees up to 60 percent of the loan amount, rather than the full value insured by FHA.
8. Surveys of the development of public housing are provided by Semer et al. (1976b) and the National Commission on Urban Problems (1969). The latter also contains a defense of the tax exemption and an explanation of its utilization as a means of financing the program. For comparisons of alternative methods of financing state and local government capital expenditures see Galper and Petersen (1971).
9. FHA has long had relatively smaller programs for insuring apartment buildings. Section 207, the basic program, was most important in the decade after World War II, when FHA-insured buildings may have constituted over one-half of all new projects. Since then, FHA's share has declined markedly to 10 to 15 percent of unsubsidized units. Kaserman argued that the reasons for the decline include attractive terms offered by conventional lenders and the costs imposed by the Davis-Bacon Act, which requires union wages for construction workers. (This Act does not apply to FHA-insured new homes.)
10. This survey perforce omits numerous smaller programs for special groups, such as the elderly or American Indians, and special types of housing. Most have rung minor changes on the mechanisms described in the text. The largest is the "Section 502" program of the Farmers Home Administration within the Department of Agriculture, which provides 235-like subsidies for new homes in rural areas. Section 502 lies outside the geographic scope of this paper, but Aaron (1972) and the NHPR (1974) have evaluated it.
11. U.S. Department of Housing and Urban Development, 1974, p. 106.
12. There have been a number of programs to sell these units. The best known is probably "urban homesteading," in which abandoned homes are given "as is" to families, often chosen by lottery, who agree to move in, make repairs, and live in them for a fixed period. The program has attracted wide attention since it was begun locally in Philadelphia and Wilmington in the early 1970s. From the standpoint of HUD's property disposition, it is a politically acceptable way to recognize that the houses have a zero market value in their current condition.
13. Aaron, 1972, p. 139.
14. U.S. Department of Housing and Urban Development, 1976, p. 1.
15. Polinsky relies heavily on studies of FHA homebuyers in reaching this con-clusion, because these studies coincidentally satisfy the constraints derived from his theoretical analysis of econometric issues. They tend also to report lower income elasticities than studies that use non-FHA data; the difference is shown most clearly

in a study of both types of buyers by Smith and Campbell (1975). It is possible that FHA encourages home purchase by households with relatively weak preferences for housing; but the estimates may be lowered by the FHA mortgage limits, which truncate the upper end of the sales distribution. Only those high-income households that wish to spend a small fraction of their income on housing will be eligible for FHA insurance.

16. Several studies have traced the actual "chains of moves" of individual households. Occupants of newly constructed units are surveyed to ascertain their former residences, the new occupants of these units are then surveyed in turn to ascertain their prior locations and so on until the chain ends, typically with a new household. These studies generally focus on changes in housing quality, rather than price, and thus contribute little to knowledge about filtering. Brueggeman (1976) has reviewed them from the standpoint of policy relevance.

17. This phrase has been used by Rothenberg (1967, pp. 54–56 and ch. 10) and in the literature of other disciplines to encompass a variety of undesirable social phenomena. Despite the potential for confusion with the technical economic concept of social cost, the terminology is retained here in the absence of any other commonly used short phrase for conveying the same meaning.

18. Fisher (1959, pp. 8–12) has reviewed the use of externalities as a justification for public housing.

19. Kasl, 1976, p. 296.

20. Muth, 1976, p. 194.

21. Nourse, 1976b, p. 248.

22. Rothenberg, 1976, p. 277–78.

23. Rothenberg, 1976, p. 279.

24. Rothenberg, 1976, pp. 279–80.

25. Aaron, 1972, p. 12.

26. Mills, 1976, p. 209.

27. The income tax exemption for housing authority bonds also represents in part an income transfer to high-income bond buyers, although the process is more indirect and the motivation of the exemption is apparently to lower direct program costs, rather than to assist bondholders.

28. The welfare loss formula in the text applies if the household can choose a unit having the quantity of housing service that it desires at the subsidized price. However, typically the household is offered a particular unit, having a specified quantity of service that may not be the same as the desired quantity. If it is not, then the welfare loss can be greater or less than $\frac{1}{2} \Delta P \Delta Q$.

29. Aaron and von Furstenberg, 1971, p. 190.

30. Private conversation with the author during the summer of 1973.

31. Foreclosure losses were estimated to be twice as large in the earlier program, perhaps because of its limitation to nonprofit sponsors; a recent analysis of Section 236 by the General Accounting Office concludes that profit-making sponsors have had lower default rates (U.S. Comptroller General, 1978).

32. U.S. Department of Housing and Urban Development, 1974, pp. 103–4.

33. Tobin, 1965, p. 482.

REFERENCES

Aaron, Henry J. 1972. *Shelter and Subsidies*. Washington, D.C.: The Brookings Institution.

Aaron, Henry J., and von Furstenberg, George M. 1971. "The Inefficiency of Transfers in Kind: The Case of Housing Assistance." *Western Economic Journal* 9 (June): 184–91.

Barton, David M., and Olsen, Edgar O. 1976. "The Benefits and Costs of Public Housing in New York City." Madison: University of Wisconsin, Institute for Research on Poverty Discussion Paper 373–76.

Birch, David; Atkinson, Reilly III; Clay, Philip L.; Coleman, Richard P.; Frieden, Bernard J.; Friedlaender, Ann F.; Parsons, William L.; Rainwater, Lee; and Teplitz, Paul V. 1973. "America's Housing Needs, 1970 to 1980." Cambridge, Mass.: Joint Center for Urban Studies of M.I.T. and Harvard University.

Bish, Robert L. 1969. "Public Housing: The Magnitude and Distribution of Direct Benefits and Effects on Housing Consumption." *Journal of Regional Science* 9: 425–38.

Brueggeman, William B. 1976. "An Analysis of the Filtering Process with Special Reference to Housing Subsidies." In *Housing in the Seventies: Working Papers*, 2: 842–56. Washington, D.C.: U.S. Government Printing Office.

Campbell, Alan K., and Burkhead, Jesse. 1968. "Public Policy in Urban America." In *Issues in Urban Economics*, pp. 577–649. Edited by Harvey S. Perloff and Lowdon Wingo, Jr. Baltimore: The Johns Hopkins Press.

Chinitz, Benjamin. 1976. "The Role of New Construction Subsidies in National Housing Policy." In *Housing in the Seventies: Working Papers*, 1: 483–90.

Davis, Otto A.; Eastman, Charles M.; and Hua, Chan-I. 1974. "The Shrinkage in the Stock of Low-Quality Housing in the Central City: An Empirical Study of the U.S. Experience over the Last Ten Years." *Urban Studies* 11 (February): 13–26.

Dean, John P. 1949. "The Myths of Housing Reform." *American Sociological Review* 14 (April): 281–88.

deLeeuw, Frank. 1971. "The Demand for Housing: A Review of Cross-Section Evidence." *Review of Economics and Statistics* 53 (February): 1–10.

deLeeuw, Frank, and Ekanem, Nkanta F. 1971. "The Supply of Rental Housing." *American Economic Review* 61 (December): 806–17.

———. 1973. "Time Lags in the Rental Housing Market." *Urban Studies* 10 (February): 39–68.

deLeeuw, Frank, and Leaman, Sam H. 1972. "The Section 23 Leasing Program." In *The Economics of Federal Subsidy Programs*. Part 5: *Housing Subsidies*, pp. 642–59. U.S. Congress, Joint Economic Committee. Washington, D.C.: U.S. Government Printing Office.

deLeeuw, Frank, and Struyk, Raymond J. 1975. *The Web of Urban Housing*. Washington, D.C.: The Urban Institute.

DeSalvo, Joseph S. 1971. "A Methodology for Evaluating Housing Programs." *Journal of Regional Science* 11: 173–85.

———. 1974. "Neighborhood Upgrading Effects of Middle-Income Housing Projects in New York City." *Journal of Urban Economics* 1 (July): 269–77.

———. 1975. "Benefits and Costs of New York City's Middle-Income Housing Program." *Journal of Political Economy* 83 (August): 791–805.

Downs, Anthony. 1973. *Federal Housing Subsidies: How Are They Working?* Lexington, Mass.: Lexington Books.

Farb, Warren E. 1971. "An Estimate of the Relative Supply and Demand for Substandard Rental Housing in Major U.S. Cities." Ph.D. diss. Washington University, St. Louis.

Ferrera, Salvatore V. 1969. "The Effect of Urban Renewal and Public Housing on Neighboring Property Values and Rents in Chicago." Ph.D. diss. University of Chicago.

Fisher, Robert Moore. 1959. *Twenty Years of Public Housing*. New York: Harper.

Frieden, Bernard J., and Solomon, Arthur P. 1977. "The Nation's Housing: 1975 to 1985." Cambridge, Mass.: Joint Center for Urban Studies of M.I.T. and Harvard University.

Galper, Harvey, and Petersen, John. 1971. "An Analysis of Subsidy Plans to Support State and Local Borrowing." *National Tax Journal* 24 (June): 205–35.

Gillingham, Robert F. 1973. "Place to Place Rent Comparisons Using Hedonic Quality Adjustment Techniques." Washington, D.C.: U.S. Bureau of Labor Statistics Research Discussion Paper no. 7.

Goedert, Jeanne E., and Goodman, John L., Jr. 1977. *Indicators of the Quality of U.S. Housing*. Washington, D.C.: The Urban Institute.

Gould, John P. 1971. *Davis-Bacon Act: The Economics of Prevailing Wage Laws*. Washington, D.C.: American Enterprise Institute for Public Policy Research.

Gramlich, Edward M., and Jaffee, Dwight M., eds. 1972. *Savings Deposits, Mortgages and Housing*. Lexington, Mass.: Lexington Books.

Grieson, Ronald E. 1973. "The Supply of Rental Housing: Comment." *American Economic Review* 63 (June): 433–36.

Inman, Robert. "The Fiscal Performance of Local Government: An Interpretative Review." In this volume.

Kain, John F. 1976. "Background Paper on Housing Market Discrimination and Its Implications for Government Housing Policy." In *Housing in the Seventies: Working Papers,* 1: 394–405. Washington, D.C.: U.S. Government Printing Office.

Kain, John F., and Schafer, Robert. 1977. "Urban Housing Policies." Columbus, Ohio: Conference of the Committee on Urban Economics, May.

Kaserman, David L. 1977. "An Econometric Analysis of the Decline in Federal Mortgage Default Insurance." In *Capital Markets and the Housing Sector,* chapter 15. Edited by Robert M. Buckley, John A. Tuccillo, and Kevin E. Villani. Cambridge, Mass.: Ballinger.

Kasl, Stanislav V. 1976. "Effects of Housing on Mental and Physical Health." In *Housing in the Seventies: Working Papers,* 1: 286–304. Washington, D.C.: U.S. Government Printing Office.

Kraft, John, and Olsen, Edgar O. 1977. "The Distribution of Benefits from Public Housing." In *The Distribution of Economic Well-Being*. Studies in Income and Wealth, vol. 41. Edited by F. Thomas Juster. New York: National Bureau of Economic Research.

Lander, Bernard. 1954. *Towards an Understanding of Juvenile Delinquency*. New York: Columbia University Press.

Lowry, Ira S. 1960. "Filtering and Housing Standards: A Conceptual Analysis." *Land Economics* 36 (November): 362–70.

Mayo, Stephen K. 1977. *Housing Expenditures and Quality*. Part 1: *Report on Housing Expenditures Under a Percent of Rent Housing Allowance*. Cambridge, Mass.: Abt Associates.

Mills, Edwin S. 1976. "Housing Policy as a Means to Achieve National Growth

Policy." In *Housing in the Seventies: Working Papers,* 1: 202–14. Washington, D.C.: U.S. Government Printing Office.

Murray, Michael P. 1975. "The Distribution of Tenant Benefits in Public Housing." *Econometrica* 43 (July): 771–88.

Musgrave, Richard A. 1976. "Policies of Housing Support: Rationales and Instruments." In *Housing in the Seventies: Working Papers,* 1: 215–33. Washington, D.C.: U.S. Government Printing Office.

Muth, Richard F. 1960. "The Demand for Non-Farm Housing." In *The Demand for Durable Goods,* pp. 29–96. Edited by Arnold C. Harberger. Chicago: University of Chicago Press.

————. 1968. "Urban Residential Land and Housing Markets." In *Issues in Urban Economics,* pp. 285–333. Edited by Harvey S. Perloff and Lowdon Wingo, Jr. Baltimore: The Johns Hopkins Press.

————. 1971. "Capital and Current Expenditures in the Production of Housing." Stanford: Stanford University Center for Research in Economic Growth memo 123.

————. 1973. *Public Housing: An Economic Evaluation.* Washington, D.C.: American Enterprise Institute for Public Policy Research.

————. 1976. "The Rationale for Government Intervention in Housing." In *Housing in the Seventies: Working Papers,* 1: 192–201. Washington, D.C.: U.S. Government Printing Office.

National Commission on Urban Problems. 1969. *Building the American City.* New York: Praeger.

Nenno, Mary K. 1976. "First Year Community Development Grant Experience: What Does It Mean?" *Journal of Housing* 33 (April): 171–75.

Nourse, Hugh O. 1963. "The Effect of Public Housing on Property Values in St. Louis." *Land Economics* 39 (November): 433–41.

————. 1976a. "Can We Design the Housing Allowance for Learning?" *American Real Estate and Urban Economics Association Journal* 4 (Spring): 97–104.

————. 1976b. "A Rationale for Government Intervention in Housing." In *Housing in the Seventies: Working Papers,* 1: 243–50. Washington, D.C.: U.S. Government Printing Office.

Ohls, James C. 1975. "Public Policy Toward Low Income Housing and Filtering in Housing Markets." *Journal of Urban Economics* 2 (April): 144–71.

Olsen, Edgar O. 1972. "An Econometric Analysis of Rent Control in New York City." *Journal of Political Economy* 80 (November/December): 1081–110.

Olsen, Edgar O., and Prescott, James R. 1969. "An Analysis of Alternative Measures of Tenant Benefits of Government Housing Programs with Illustrative Calculations from Public Housing." Santa Monica: RAND Corporation.

Polinsky, A. Mitchell. 1977. "The Demand for Housing: A Study in Specification and Grouping." *Econometrica* 45 (March): 447–61.

Prescott, James R. 1964. "The Economics of Public Housing: A Normative Analysis." Ph.D. diss. Harvard University.

Quigley, John M. "What Have We Learned About Housing Markets?" In this volume.

RAND Corporation. 1977. *Third Annual Report of the Housing Assistance Supply Experiment*. Santa Monica: RAND Corporation.

Reid, Margaret G. 1962. *Housing and Income*. Chicago: University of Chicago Press.

Ricks, R. Bruce, ed. 1973. *National Housing Models*. Lexington, Mass.: Lexington Books.

Rothenberg, Jerome. 1967. *Economic Evaluation of Urban Renewal*. Washington, D.C.: Brookings Institution.

―――. 1976. "A Rationale for Government Intervention in Housing: The Externalities Generated by Good Housing." In *Housing in the Seventies: Working Papers*, 1: 267–85. Washington, D.C.: U.S. Government Printing Office.

Schafer, Robert. 1972. "The Effect of BMIR Housing on Property Values." *Land Economics* 90 (August): 282–86.

Semer, Milton P.; Zimmerman, Julian H.; Frantz, John M.; and Foard, Ashley. 1976*a*. "Evolution of Federal Legislative Policy in Housing: Housing Credits." In *Housing in the Seventies: Working Papers*, 1: 3–81. Washington, D.C.: U.S. Government Printing Office.

―――. 1976*b*. "A Review of Federal Subsidized Housing Programs." In *Housing in the Seventies: Working Papers*, 1: 82–144. Washington, D.C.: U.S. Government Printing Office.

Smith, Barton A. 1976. "The Supply of Urban Housing." *Quarterly Journal of Economics* 90 (August): 389–406.

Smith, Barton, and Campbell, John. 1975. "The Demand for Housing: A New Look at Urban Empiricism." San Diego: Meeting of the Western Economic Association, June.

Smolensky, Eugene. 1968. "Public Housing or Income Supplements—The Economics of Housing for the Poor." *Journal of the American Institute of Planners* 34 (March): 94–101.

Straszheim, Mahlon R. 1975. *An Econometric Analysis of the Urban Housing Market*. New York National Bureau of Economic Research.

Struyk, Raymond J. 1976. *Urban Homeownership*. Lexington, Mass.: Lexington Books.

Swan, Craig. 1973. "Housing Subsidies and Housing Starts." *American Real Estate and Urban Economics Association Journal* 1 (Fall): 119–40.

Sweeney, James L. 1974. "A Commodity Hierarchy Model of the Rental Housing Market." *Journal of Urban Economics* 1 (July): 288–323.

Syron, Richard F. 1972. "An Analysis of the Collapse of the Normal Market for Fire Insurance in Substandard Core Areas." Federal Reserve Bank of Boston Research Report no. 49.

Tobin, James M. 1965. "The Monetary Interpretation of History." *American Economic Review* 55 (June): 464–85.

U.S. Bureau of the Census. 1967. "Measuring the Quality of Housing." Washington, D.C.: Working Paper no. 25.

―――. 1973. *1970 Census of Housing, HC(6), Plumbing Facilities and Estimates of Dilapidated Housing*. Washington, D.C.: U.S. Government Printing Office.

————. 1973–76. *Annual Housing Survey*. Washington, D.C.: U.S. Government Printing Office.

U.S. Comptroller General. General Accounting Office. 1978. "Section 236 Rental Housing—An Evaluation with Lessons for the Future."

U.S. Congress. House. Committee on Banking and Currency. 1970. *Investigation and Hearing of Abuses in Federal Low- and Moderate-Income Housing Programs*. 91st Cong., 2d sess. Washington, D.C.: U.S. Government Printing Office.

————. 1971. *Interim Report on HUD Investigation of Low- and Moderate-Income Housing Programs*. 92d Cong., 1st sess. Washington, D.C.: U.S. Government Printing Office.

U.S. Congress. Joint Committee on Housing. 1948. *Housing Study and Investigation*. Final Majority Report, 80th Cong., 2d sess. March 15. Washington, D.C.: U.S. Government Printing Office.

U.S. Department of Housing and Urban Development. 1967–76. *HUD Statistical Yearbooks*. Washington, D.C.: U.S. Government Printing Office.

U.S. Department of Housing and Urban Development. National Housing Policy Review. 1974. *Housing in the Seventies*. Washington, D.C.: U.S. Government Printing Office.

U.S. Department of Housing and Urban Development. Office of Policy Development and Research. 1976. "A Report to the Secretary on the Section 8 Existing Housing Program." June 30.

————. 1977. *Future Role of FHA*. Washington, D.C.

U.S. Library of Congress. Congressional Research Service. 1974. *Critique of "Housing in the Seventies."* Washington, D.C.: U.S. Government Printing Office.

Vaughn, Garret A. 1976. "Sources of Downward Bias in Estimating the Demand Income Elasticity for Urban Housing." *Journal of Urban Economics* 3 (January): 45–56.

Weicher, John C. 1972. "The Effect of Urban Renewal on Municipal Service Expenditures." *Journal of Political Economy* 80 (January/February): 86–101.

————. 1973. *Urban Renewal: National Program for Local Problems*. Washington, D.C.: American Enterprise Institute for Public Policy Research.

————. 1976. "The Fiscal Profitability of Urban Renewal Under Matching Grants and Revenue-Sharing." *Journal of Urban Economics* 3 (July): 193–208.

Weicher, John C., and Zerbst, Robert H. 1973. "The Externalities of Neighborhood Parks: An Empirical Investigation." *Land Economics* 49 (February): 99–105.

Wieand, Kenneth, and Clemmer, Richard L. 1977. "The Annual Housing Survey and Models of Housing Services Output." Washington, D.C.: Meeting of the American Real Estate and Urban Economics Association, May.

Wilner, Daniel M.; Walkley, Rosabelle Price; Pinkerton, Thomas C.; and Tayback, Matthew. 1962. *The Housing Environment and Family Life*. Baltimore: The Johns Hopkins Press.

Yinger, John. "Prejudice and Discrimination in the Urban Housing Market." In this volume.

V

URBAN LAND-USE CONTROLS

15

ECONOMIC ANALYSIS
OF URBAN LAND-USE CONTROLS

EDWIN S. MILLS

INTRODUCTION

Serious scholarly analysis of land-use controls, especially by economists, is of remarkably recent origin. City planning literature has the longest history of publication on land-use controls, but until recently it rarely met the scholarly standards of other social sciences. Legal scholars have a better record than economists of writing on land-use controls, but few analytical papers on the subject appeared in law journals more than a decade or two before the mid-1970s.

Economists had almost nothing to say about land-use controls before the 1960s. Tiebout's 1956 classic, which hardly mentioned land-use controls but which forms the basis for the theory of exclusionary zoning, is almost the only pre-1960 piece on the subject by an economist that is still worth reading.

There does not appear to be a good reason why economists have ignored land-use controls for so long. The basic characteristics of land as an input whose main peculiarity is inelastic overall supply were well understood by classical and neoclassical economists. Zoning and other land-use controls are forms of market regulation similar to those that have been studied by economists for decades in their application to transportation, utilities, agriculture, and other industries. Furthermore, the subject is indisputably important in that there is a potential for misallocation of valuable resources in land markets. The share of land rents exceeds that of agricultural value added and that of value added in many other regulated industries in U.S.

Financial support provided by grants from the Ford and the Sloan Foundations and by a Department of Housing and Urban Development Contract.

I am indebted to Jeffrey Wolcowitz and Jeffrey Smisek for research assistance and to Carl Christ, Bruce Hamilton, and Peter Mieszkowski for comments.

national income. Most important, misallocation of urban land inevitably entails misallocation of other valuable resources, such as transportation inputs and outputs and the time of commuters and shoppers. The probable reason for neglect of land-use controls by economists is that these controls are administered by local governments, and economists have only recently undertaken serious analysis of local government activities.

The important economic issues of urban land-use controls are, of course, in the area of applied welfare economics. Both efficiency of resource allocation and equity in income distribution are involved. The most basic legal justification for land-use controls is the prevention of resource misallocation by unregulated private markets because of external economies or diseconomies, monopoly power, or some other factor. An economist's job is to inquire into the nature and magnitude of the market failure and the controls that will best avoid misallocation. The equity issue arises mainly because of the belief that certain patterns of local government finance, in conjunction with land-use controls, affect the distribution of income or at least the ability of local governments to redistribute income. Regarding equity, the applied welfare economist's job is to ask what structure of local government leads to land-use controls and other actions that satisfy an appropriate criterion of equity. Obviously, there is no guarantee that the same organization of local government will satisfy both the efficiency and the equity criteria.

Government actions can be analyzed either normatively or positively. In normative analyses economists try to ascertain the government activities that will satisfy particular welfare criteria, such as socially efficient resource allocation. In positive analyses economists seek to explain government actions as functions of the environments in which they operate, just as the positive theory of the firm seeks to explain a firm's actions as functions of its market environment. Governments respond to incentives just as people do as household members or as employees of a profit-making firm. Fragmented suburban governments are likely to respond quite differently to wishes of constituents than would a single metropolitan area government. There has been no more fruitful application of the positive theory of government than in the analysis of the interaction between local government finance and land-use controls.

What Are Land-Use Controls?

Modern governments have a panoply of regulatory, tax, and expenditure programs. Every such program affects resource allocation, and since virtually all resource allocation takes place on land, virtually all government programs affect land uses. But there is agreement among writers on the subject that land-use controls refer to a narrower range of programs whose explicit purpose is to regulate land uses. The relevant set of programs is nevertheless broad and diverse.

The central land-use control is zoning, meaning designation of a set of zones within which certain activities are permitted. A recent tendency is to designate many zoning categories, which inevitably gives power to zoning boards to decide into which category a particular activity fits. Other important land-use controls are: a mapped-street ordinance, a legal map showing existing and proposed streets; subdivision controls, which impose controls on developers who want to subdivide and develop a tract of undeveloped land; building and housing codes, which regulate construction, maintenance, and use of structures; and architectural controls, which regulate structure design, mainly for aesthetic purposes. For a complete set of definitions and uses made of these controls see Yearwood (1971).

A Historical Sketch of the Development of Urban Land-Use Controls

Good presentations of the historical development of urban land-use controls in the Anglo-Saxon world have appeared, apparently for the first time, in recent years. Two comprehensive works, at about the level of detail of interest to most economists, are *The Taking Issue* (Bosselman et al.) and *Land Use Controls in the United States* (Delafons). Whereas earlier works on the history of urban land-use controls in the United States concentrated on the twentieth century, recent works trace the subject back much further. There is no better example than land-use controls of the continuity of social institutions in the Anglo-Saxon world.

Private property consists of a set of related rights to use and dispose of property in the interest of its owner, a "bundle of sticks" to use the infelicitous legal term. Every society places restrictions on these rights—removes, breaks or bends some sticks in the bundle. There is no broad category of property on whose use more, or more complex, restrictions have been placed than on land. Inevitably, the concern of legislatures and courts has focused on defining the kinds of restrictions that can be imposed consistently with constitutional and legislative requirements. Courts have been especially concerned to define circumstances under which imposition of restrictions so impairs property rights that the owner must be compensated, the "taking issue." Until very recently, legislatures, courts, and relevant administrative agencies have shown remarkably little concern with analyzing the content of land-use controls: what controls in combination with what kinds of other government action will achieve what social goals equitably and efficiently? The fundamental theme of this chapter is that the result is a web of complex, redundant, inconsistent, and ineffectual controls that furthers no coherent set of social goals. Although this conclusion will be developed in subsequent sections, it is stated here because it prejudices each step of the argument.

Monarchs have apparently restricted the use of their subjects' land as long as they have had the power to do so. Roman emperors restricted business locations (Yearwood, 1971). The right of the sovereign to seize or control use of nobles' land was a perennial source of conflict in medieval England and was a major issue in Magna Carta. What would now be called low density zoning, ana complete construction bans, were used in Elizabethan London (Bosselman et al., 1973).

English colonists brought to North America a moderately strong tradition of government land-use controls, which was applied intermittently during the colonial and later periods despite strong opposition to government interference with property rights. Starting at least as early as the seventeenth century and continuing without interruption after the revolution, local governments segregated noxious activities and controlled building materials and the details of construction for both safety and aesthetic reasons.

Although the trend of land-use controls was consistent before and after the revolution, their constitutional basis changed. The basis for land-use controls in the U.S. Constitution is the obligation of governments to pass laws that protect the health and welfare of the population. Until after the Civil War the constitutional preeminence of state governments and their created, local governments in regulating land use was unchallenged. There was no federal legislation and almost no federal court cases bearing on the subject. There was no local government legislation relating to land-use controls that would now be called comprehensive, but the trend of ad hoc controls continued. State courts did not hesitate to give local governments broad powers to regulate land use for valid public benefits under the police power provision of the Constitution.

Until the Civil War, most state court cases on land-use controls related not to the right of governments to control use, but to the "taking" issue. The Fifth Amendment contains the clause, ". . . nor shall private property be taken for public use without just compensation." Courts have consistently enforced this provision when private land has been seized for government use. But most regulations consist of the removal of a few sticks from the bundle of property rights, and courts have grappled at length with the issue of compensation. The taking issue has been the subject of a recent thorough, though partisan, essay (Bosselman et al., 1973).

Although the judicial history of the "taking" issue is complex and convoluted, courts have been willing to give local governments remarkably broad prerogatives to regulate land use in the public interest under the police powers without requiring compensation. The courts' attitude has been that the right to property does not entail the right to use the property to the detriment of others. The right to own a car or a weapon does not entail the right to use those properties in a manner dangerous to others. Thus, laws and administrative actions to prevent owners from using land in ways that are detrimental to public health and welfare do not require compensation. Such laws are assumed by the courts to impose only peripheral restrictions on property rights—to remove only a few sticks from the bundle. Only if controls remove sticks thought to constitute the essence of ownership have courts construed regulation as effectively taking the property.

Whatever the merits of the courts' attitude toward the "taking" issue, one cannot but be amazed at the naïvete of the courts' failure to recognize the blatantly special interest nature of many land-use controls. A good example is provided by what some authorities refer to as the first zoning law in the United States. After several discriminatory laws against orientals had been struck down as unconstitutional during the 1880s, San Francisco and other California communities zoned laundries out of many of their neighborhoods as a way of confining orientals to special districts (Delafons, 1969). This case is typical. The courts could not say that avoiding nuisances from laundries by excluding them from certain areas was not a valid exercise of police power, yet the real purpose of the laws was to discriminate against a particular group of people.

Following this success, cities in California and elsewhere gradually adopted "districting" as a means of confining to certain city districts activities that were nuisances or were otherwise unwanted. At the same time, building height controls were introduced in some cities. By the beginning of the First World War more than two dozen cities had adopted districting or height controls (Delafons, 1969). But it was in New York City during World War I that the two ideas were combined and instituted on a large enough scale to justify the term *comprehensive zoning*. Once again, the ostensible motives seem quite different from the real motives.

In the early years of the twentieth century there was rapid multiplication of the number of tall buildings and expansion of garment manufacturing—usually carried on in lofts in the upper stories of buildings—in and below midtown Manhattan. Both trends, but especially garment manufacturing, attracted large numbers of poorly paid female workers. The Fifth Avenue Association, a merchants' organization, was concerned that the comings and goings of lower-class workers would be bad for business in the exclusive shops of the area; they became convinced that limitations on building height would help limit the number of female clerical workers, but would especially slow the spread of garment manufacturing. A commission established on their behalf recommended height controls, setback requirements, and bulk controls. In 1916, a successor commission recommended comprehensive zoning, height controls, setback requirements, and bulk controls throughout the city.

It is clear that land-use controls were becoming fashionable throughout the country, and it is hard to estimate the importance of the exclusionary attitudes that provided the initial impetus for controls. But maintaining the character of neighborhoods and preventing intrusion by undesirable residents and workers were important motivations for the 1916 report, which became the basis for comprehensive zoning throughout the country.

Delafons reports that the number of U.S. cities with zoning ordinances grew from five in 1915 to thirty-five in 1920. By 1924 the national government had issued a standard state zoning enabling act, and by 1925 nearly five hundred cities had zoning codes. In 1926, the Supreme Court issued its classic ruling on zoning in *Village of Euclid* v. *Ambler Realty Co.* In it the Court ruled that zoning was a legitimate exercise of police power not requiring compensation of injured owners, even though it was agreed that zoning for residential development had reduced the value of the plaintiff's land to one-fourth its former value. By the end of the 1920s, three-fifth's of the urban population lived in zoned communities (Toll, 1969). Although most big cities had zoning, much of the most stringent zoning was found in suburbs and small towns even in the 1920s.

The *Euclid* decision contains the following remarkable sentences:

> The plain truth is that the true object of the ordinance in question is to place all the property in an undeveloped area of 16 square miles in a strait-jacket. The purpose to be accomplished is really to regulate the mode of living of persons who may hereafter inhabit it. In the last analysis, the result to be accomplished is to classify the population and segregate them according to their income or situation in life. The true reason why some persons live in a mansion and others in a shack, why some live in a single-family dwelling and others in a double-family dwelling, why some live in a two-family dwelling and others in an apartment, or why some live in a well-kept apartment and others in a tenement, is primarily economic.

Judge Westerhaver clearly perceived that the real purpose of the zoning under litigation was blatant exclusion, rather than legitimate protection against nuisances. Yet he felt unable to rule on the real motivations for the law.

Euclid was the liberating force for zoning advocates. Until then, experts had doubts about the constitutionality of zoning, and code provisions were somewhat timid. The most common provision was for a small number of cumulative districts in which single-family residences were the highest use, followed by multiple-family residences, commercial activities, and industrial activities. Land zoned for any use could also be used for higher uses, but not vice versa. Also common were setback requirements and height and bulk controls. The *Euclid* opinion not only legitimatized the fundamental concept of zoning but also contained obiter dicta that suggested that the Supreme Court would interpret police powers generously when land-use controls were instituted for an allegedly public purpose (Bosselman et al., 1973).

Euclid set off an explosion in the number and complexity of zoning ordinances. By the end of the 1930s virtually all large cities and many suburbs and small towns had zoning ordinances. Land-use categories became more numerous and complex. Fine classifications of types of residence and of commercial and industrial activities were introduced. Within residential categories, lot sizes and other density limits were established, bulk controls became widespread, and detailed requirements about construction, maintenance, and appearance of dwellings were introduced. Within commercial and industrial categories, the prohibitions of earlier laws were made to depend on a variety of details such as bulk, setback, and appearance of the structure.

Although the legal machinery for comprehensive zoning was in place in the 1920s and 1930s, its effects were not fully realized until after World War II. The depression of the 1930s slowed construction and urban migration and made communities that were desperate for homes and jobs loathe to enforce zoning requirements that might induce residents and employers to locate elsewhere. All this changed after World War II, when prosperity produced massive urbanization of the population, a construction boom in housing, offices, and factories, and a tendency for growth and decentralization of urban areas with its consequent spillover of people and jobs into surrounding suburbs that either had or could quickly institute stringent zoning controls. Although growth and decentralization of urban areas were not new, zoning provided a mechanism by which communities outside central cities could closely control their residential and nonresidential land uses. The rapid pace of urbanization and urban decentralization meant that many people and jobs located outside existing central city boundaries. Whereas the historical tendency had been to move boundaries outward to encompass newly settled suburbs, land-use controls provided a powerful incentive to suburbanites to resist inclusion in central cities so that they could have land-use controls and patterns of local public finance suited to their own situation. Thus, most postwar urban decentralization has been outside metropolitan central cities, and much of it has been in tightly zoned and exclusionary jurisdictions.

The postwar period also saw a rapid broadening of grounds for land-use controls that courts found constitutional. From an original concern with prevention of nuisances, goals of land-use controls spread to broad notions of preserving neighborhood character, of securing orderly urban development, and of preventing changes not wanted by politically influential groups. To achieve these broad ends new control devices were introduced, including architectural controls, building and housing codes and subdivision regulations. By the end of the 1960s many local governments could decide in great detail what kinds of people and economic activities to admit to the jurisdiction.

The period since 1970 has seen two new tendencies in land-use controls, one judicial and one legislative.

The new judicial tendency results from the questions that judges have finally begun to ask regarding the limits of the police power to control nuisances by means of land-use controls. Each time a local government improves the welfare of its constituents by preventing someone from entering, it impairs the welfare of the potential entrant. Furthermore, potential entrants are harmed by local government actions in which they have no say, since they are not voters in the community they wish to enter. This raises complex questions under the "equal protection of the laws" clause of the Fourteenth Amendment of the U.S. Constitution and similar provisions of state constitutions and laws. Most plaintiffs in key cases since 1970 have claimed that they have been deprived of equal access to the most important service provided by local government—education. The best-known case is *Serrano* v. *Priest,* in which the California State Supreme Court found the system of financing local public education mainly by property taxes to be unconstitutional. *Serrano* was overturned by the U.S. Supreme Court, but other cases tried under state laws, notably in New Jersey, have been allowed to stand. Similar issues have been raised in school busing cases.[1] In these cases, land-use controls are the lock on the door that keeps the poor, and especially the black poor, out of communities with high average incomes, high property values, and high quality school systems.

Serrano and related cases concern equal access to services of local governments. The most direct and comprehensive challenge to zoning is a New Jersey case, *Burlington NAACP* v. *Mt. Laurel Township.* Mount Laurel is a distant suburb of Philadelphia and a textbook case of exclusionary zoning. Its zoning code specifies minimum frontage and minimum dwelling floor area for single-family detached houses. Developers must dedicate 15 to 25 percent of development acreage for public use. There are severe limits on numbers of apartments with more than one bedroom, requirements of amenities such as air conditioning, and a requirement that a developer pay school expenses if there are more than 0.3 school age children per multi-family unit. The court ruled that such provisions have the intention and effect of excluding low income families from the community and hence of reducing the supply of housing to them. It ordered the community to devise a zoning plan that would enable a fair share of the region's poor to live in Mount Laurel, in small houses on small lots or in multi-family dwellings, unencumbered by requirements that would raise costs beyond their reach.

Most land-use controls retard growth of population and employment in communities. In recent years a tendency has developed to use land-use controls for the explicit purpose of slowing or stopping growth so as to preserve the community's character; much litigation has resulted, of which *Construction Industry Association of Sonoma* v. *City of Petaluma* is typical and the best known. Petaluma is a suburb of San Francisco, whose population grew rapidly in the 1960s. In 1971, it adopted a written policy to limit population growth to protect its small town character and open spaces. It drew an "urban extension line" beyond which development was not permitted. Within the area where development was permitted, zoning limited density. Prospective developers were put through a hazing to deter all but the most determined. The city limited its water supply contract to an amount sufficient for a population of only 55,000. Petaluma's slow growth policy was discriminatory against low income people, because development limitations were applicable only to contractors proposing to build four or more units, thus making life easier for the builder of a single, substantial unit.

The builders' association sued Petaluma in federal court. As in *Mt. Laurel,* the trial court showed great concern over the effect of slow growth policies on the price and availability of housing in the San Francisco area, especially for low-income residents. The court ruled against Petaluma on the ground that its policies interfered with citizens' rights to travel and reside in a place of their choice. Unfortunately, *Petaluma* was overturned on appeal on a technicality. The association had sued on behalf of potential residents, instead of on behalf of its members, and the appeals court ruled that the association had no standing to sue for potential residents.

Serrano and, especially, *Mt. Laurel* and *Petaluma* represent important judicial departures in that courts explicitly weighed the social implications of land-use controls. Although only *Mt. Laurel* survived appeal, all three trial courts found that the ostensible purposes of land-use controls to "ensure orderly growth" and "preserve community character" were outweighed by the harm done to excluded residents. Thus, the harm done to potential residents by exclusionary land-use controls has become an issue the courts are increasingly willing to face. The economic issues will be analyzed in a later section, but here it must be noted that the courts have only limited ability to provide remedies; about all they can do is tell communities that their land-use controls are excessively exclusionary and that they must devise new ones that obey broad guidelines set down by the court. If the community devises new controls, a new court case is required to ascertain their acceptability. Whether they are exclusionary by some new device, or can be made so by their administration, may not be easy for courts to discover. Land-use controls are a complex kit of tools, and communities have been ingenious in devising and bending them to accomplish their goals.

The legislative tendency of the 1970s has reflected society's broad concern with environmental protection. Local land-use controls have shown increasing concern with environmental issues. More important has been the realization that many environmental problems transcend local government boundaries. Open-space preservation, wetlands protection, and shoreline protection are examples. This realization has motivated states to formulate statewide land-use plans to complement state environmental protection plans. State plans tend to concentrate on protection of environmentally delicate areas such as shorelines and wetlands, but they may also be concerned with open-space preservation and with the overall character of state development. State governments invariably show fondness for preservation of agriculture against encroachment by urban and suburban developments. Some predominantly rural states have been blatantly exclusionary in their attitude toward land-use controls, but even highly urbanized states show an antiurban bias in statewide land-use control plans. The catchwords are *ecological protection, open-space preservation,* and *protection of farmland from urban growth.* States take little heed of the effect that preventing a person from living or working in one place has of forcing him to live or work in a less desirable place. State governments, like their local government creations, pay most attention to the damages from development to existing residents who can vote them out of office, and least attention to benefits from development to potential residents who cannot vote in their jurisdiction. Many state governments are beginning to apply exclusionary practices, long the province of local governments, at the state level. It will be more difficult for courts, both state and federal, to attack the exclusionary practices of state than of local governments, but it is not clear that the social damage from exclusionary actions by states will be less serious than those by local governments.

Recent indications are that the federal government may provide powerful incentives to states to undertake statewide land-use planning. In each recent Congress, land-use legislation has been introduced, and a bill sponsored by Senator Henry Jackson, the congressional leader in this area, was passed by the Senate in 1973. President Nixon advocated similar legislation. All the important bills that have been introduced provide federal funds and encouragement to states to undertake statewide land-use inventories, plans, and controls. The bills vary as to the funds and other incentives they would give states for these purposes and as to the penalties they would levy on states for failing to respond. All the bills state that their intention is to improve land-use controls and to make them more responsive to social needs, but not to interfere with property rights or state and local governments and not to establish national land-use policies, plans, or controls (*Congressional Digest,* 1973).

Most supporters of such federal legislation in and out of Congress do not hide their desire to limit urban and suburban growth. Few have made any effort at a coherent case for federal entrance into the land-use control arena. And none appears to have shown concern to help the courts in their efforts to prevent local governments from being excessively exclusionary in the formulation and administration of land-use controls.

The conclusion of this brief history of urban land-use controls is that they have been used much more for exclusionary purposes than to control what economists normally think of as external diseconomies. The ostensible legal purposes of land-use controls are to prevent such things as noise, air and water pollution, vibration, and traffic hazards in residential neighborhoods. Often such phenomena are a more or less important part of land-use controls, but almost always, the desire by a politically influential group to exclude a racial, ethnic, occupational, or income group from a community is part of the story. Often the exclusionary motivation is fuzzy, a desire to protect "neighborhood quality" or a familiar and customary residential composition, or merely a desire to prevent change. This conclusion is supported not only by the preceding history of land-use controls but also by an examination of administrative practices. Studies to estimate carefully the external damages that would be done by a particular proposed land use are rare in the administration of land-use controls. Much more common are studies of the relationship between dwelling value, number of children, tax yields, and school costs. Exclusion on racial grounds is of course illegal and is hence not an explicit consideration in land-use control administration, but there is no doubt that it is frequently among the real reasons for the ways controls are used.

The next three sections survey the analytical issues regarding land-use controls, all of which have arisen in the preceding historical survey: the first section starts with the easiest issue, external diseconomies from non-residential land uses; then the so-called neighborhood effect is analyzed as a justification for land-use controls on residences in a community; finally, the complex set of issues regarding exclusionary land-use controls is analyzed.

1. LAND-USE CONTROLS AND EXTERNAL EFFECTS OF INDUSTRIAL AND COMMERCIAL ACTIVITIES

It is probable that the most common popular association with land-use controls is zoning to keep such activities as factories, gasoline stations, and commercial laundries out of residential neighborhoods. The reasons for doing so fall into the category of external diseconomies imposed by non-residential activities on nearby residents. The most common such externalities are polluting discharges to air and water, noise, vibration, traffic congestion and hazards, and aesthetic disamenities. In fact, factory smoke that impairs the welfare of downwind residents is the most common example of an external diseconomy and was cited by Pigou and generations of welfare economists writing since his time. The purpose of this section is to analyze such externalities as they relate to land-use controls.

An externality is an effect of an activity on the welfare of people in ways that cannot be adequately compensated by private agreements. Adequate compensation refers to the ability to encourage or discourage the activity to the point at which marginal rates of transformation between it and other activities equal similar marginal rates of substitution or other measures of social benefits. Much has been written on the technological and other circumstances that might prevent adequate compensation by private agreements. There is still no agreement on the subject in the profession. Whatever causes the external effect, it means that resources are not allocated so as to satisfy conditions for Pareto-optimality. That in turn means that a set of private transactions exists that would be mutually beneficial to all parties. The question is, What prevents such transactions from being consummated?[2]

The answer given most frequently in the recent literature is that the under-utilized activity is a public good. Undoubtedly, the phenomena that are used to justify segregation of nonresidential activities are public goods or, more commonly, bads. If I live 500 yards from a noisy factory, my welfare is impaired to an extent that is independent of how many other people suffer from living a similar distance from the factory. The same is true of discharges of pollutants, of vibrations, and of visual disamenities. All such phenomena have the characteristic of being spatially localized, that is, their adverse effects fall off with distance from the source. If adverse effects of nonresidential activities were not spatially localized, it would not reduce the impact of such effects to segregate offending activities by land-use controls.

The usual argument that the private sector underproduces public goods stems from the assumption that it is costly or impossible to exclude people from consumption of the public good once it is produced, whether they agree to pay a share of its cost or not. If a private agreement is made between the factory management and downwind residents to abate discharges that pollute the air, I, as a downwind resident, cannot be prevented from enjoying the clean air just because I refuse to contribute to the cost of abating the discharges. Thus, it is claimed, the government must ensure adequate production of public goods by land-use controls or other means.

But the mere fact that clean air and a quiet neighborhood are public goods is not sufficient to prevent their production and compensation by private agreements. Suppose, for example, that a group of residents suffers from air pollution from a nearby factory. Using the principle that the optimum production of a public good is the level at which the sum over all consumers of the public good of their marginal rates of substitution between it and another good equals the marginal rate of transformation between the two goods, suppose also that optimum abatement costs $1000 and is worth $15 each to 100 families. Then a neighborhood organization can write a contract under which each family contributes $10 to pay for the abatement. The contract is conditional on all families signing it; otherwise it is void and no one pays. Each family's $15 benefit exceeds its $10 contribution and each family knows that the benefit will not be obtained if it does not sign, because the contract will be void. Thus, each family is motivated to sign the contract. By this procedure the public good can be produced in socially optimum quantity by private agreements.

Two reasons that this private procedure for optimizing public good production might not work are raised in the literature.

First, the neighborhood organization must know the benefit, as well as the cost, of abatement to each resident, and each citizen is motivated to understate his benefits. If I persuade the organization that the benefit to me of abatement is only $5, then it believes that that is all I am willing to contribute and others must pay more than $10. The problem of understating preference for public goods is real, but it is not solved by having government take responsibility for ensuring their optimum production. If a political candidate knows that each voter will benefit by $15 from cleaner air, he can run for office on a platform of a uniform tax of $10 per voter to pay for abatement, or he can submit the issue to referendum. Both will obtain unanimous support, as will the analogous private contract, but there is no advantage to government involvement. If the political candidate, or the government in general, does not know the magnitude of benefits, there is no apparent mechanism by which political processes can be more successful than private negotiation in inducing people to reveal their preferences for public goods.

Second, it is often claimed that the costs of arranging private compensation may be so great that public goods will be underproduced. There can be no doubt that the transaction costs of private contracts for public goods might be high. To return to the air pollution example, suppose there were several sources of discharges that affected many hundreds of families in varying amounts. The cost and difficulty of negotiating private contracts might be insurmountable. But, of course, the political process also involves transaction costs, which are by no means small even in an area such as land-use controls. The presumption that government transaction costs are less than private transaction costs in making public goods production decisions stems from the ability of government to use coercion. Most fundamentally, private groups can establish any procedures for making and executing public goods or other decisions that government can, but what they cannot do is coerce unwilling participants. Although coercion is an unpleasant notion, one should not underestimate how much cheaper it is to make public goods decisions using some coercion rather than none. Anyone familiar with committee decision-making knows there is an ignorant, unperceptive, or unreasonable minority on almost every issue. It seems certain that life would be impossible without some coercion in a complex society. Of course, its dangers are great, and keeping coercion within bounds is a key to the success of social organization.

In summary there are two considerations that together justify government intervention to prevent or limit external effects of nonresidential activities on nearby residents: the public good nature of the effects and the transaction costs of noncoercive private agreements to limit external effects to optimum levels. Having established this theoretical basis for government controls of external effects, we shall discuss two remaining questions: What is known about the nature and magnitude of the external effects? and are land-use controls the best government policy to deal with the important external effects?

Nature and Magnitude of External Effects on Nonresidential Land Uses

Many studies provide evidence on the magnitude of external effects of nonresidential land uses, but none provides strong evidence. The best studies of such external effects are studies of determinants of residential property values. There are now many such studies scattered through the technical literature Crecine et al. (1967); Kain and Quigley (1975), King and Mieszkowski (1973), and Reuter (1973) are among the best and most recent. A few studies, especially those related to air pollution,[3] focus on effects of externalities on property values, but most deal with broad property value determinants and include variables that only incidentally represent externalities.

If proximity to nonresidential activities causes a loss of welfare, it should be measured by the difference between actual land values and what they would be in the absence of the offensive activities. Markets value structures at replacement cost minus loss of value from depreciation. Only if the offensive activities damage the structure is its value affected; that can certainly happen, but is ignored here. Otherwise, external effects from nonresidential activities are measured by reduced land values. Some studies use land values as dependent variables, but most use total property values and include among the independent variables various physical characteristics of the structure.

When dependent variables are values of individual residential properties, external effects are usually represented by distance to nonresidential activities or by the traffic generated along the street on which the property fronts. When dependent variables are average property values in a neighborhood or census tract, external effects may be measured by numbers of nonresidential sites in the area.

A fair summary of available studies shows that external effects of nonresidential activities are unimportant or that they decline extremely rapidly with distance from the offending activity. Most nonresidential activities studied are relatively inoffensive. A shopping center half a mile away must be less offensive than a noisy factory at the same distance. But even allowing for the inoffensive nature of most nonresidential activities studied, the effects seem remarkably small. Coefficients are frequently insignificant and occasionally have the wrong sign. Even when significant, most effects are found to be small and decline rapidly with distance. Some support for this conclusion is found in studies of external effects that do not rely on property values. Tideman (1969) calculated percentages of residents who came from various distances to testify against proposed zoning exceptions and concluded that the probability of testifying declined by one-half for each 79 feet of distance between the site of the zoning issue and the residence. Two issues must be discussed regarding these studies.

First, the findings may be the result of good zoning practices rather than an argument against zoning. One purpose of zoning is to reduce external effects of nonresidential activities by segregating them. If zoning officials have done their jobs, it should not be surprising that observed nonresidential activities have small external effects. There is certainly something to this argument. With all the resources that have been devoted to zoning, it would be amazing if some of the most offensive nonresidential activities were not effectively segregated. But zoning laws and practices vary greatly from place to place, and in many places there are nonconforming uses that existed at the time the zoning codes were drawn up and that are still present. There is no reason to think that such "grandfather" activities should be particularly inoffensive. In addition, even relatively inoffensive activities should produce regression coefficients that suggest that larger or more offensive activities would have substantial effects. But it is certainly true that the effects of zoning place burdens on already inadequate sample sizes and data quality.

Second, and probably more important, the effect of distance to nonresidential sites on residential land values is theoretically ambiguous. Forget land-use controls for a moment. There are excellent reasons, aside from land-use controls, for a concentration of nonresidential land uses to be found in metropolitan central business districts (CBD). There are dozens of theoretical models, and overwhelming supporting empirical evidence,[4] that imply that land values fall with distance from CBDs. The reason is, of course, that people must travel to CBDs to work and shop, and land values close to the CBD are high because such sites provide cheap access to the CBD. The same is true, on a reduced scale, of any nonresidential land use anywhere in a metropolitan area. Every commercial and industrial site generates employment and/or shopping, and proximity to them is valuable. Thus, residential land values may even fall with distance from a nonresidential site; but that does not imply that there are no external diseconomies from the site, only that they are more than offset by the advantages of proximity. Future studies of externalities from nonresidential activities should take account of both the advantages and disadvantages of proximity to them.

The preceding paragraph implies that there are both costs and benefits of segregating nonresidential land uses. The benefit of segregation is that only few people suffer external diseconomies from proximate residences. Two factories of a given size have fewer residents within a mile of them if they are together than if they are separate. The cost of segregation is increased travel. At one extreme, if all nonresidential activities in a metropolitan area were in contiguous places, it would be an enormous CBD, and extensive travel to jobs and shops would be necessary. At the other extreme, very little travel would be required if nonresidential activities were scattered throughout the metropolitan area. Between these extremes is the ideal situation.

Two kinds of research are needed on this subject. First, we need to know more about private incentives for segregation of nonresidential activities. Most CBD firms are there because proximity to related activities is profitable, not because of land-use controls. Likewise, large suburban shopping centers result mainly from advantages to firms and customers of proximate locations of many retail activities, not from land-use controls. Indeed, Siegan (1972) suggests that clustering of land uses in Houston, where there is no zoning, differs little from that in other metropolitan areas. Second, we need to know more about optimum segregation. This requires calculation of benefits and costs of segregation and can be done only in a general equilibrium model of urban land use that includes both transportation and external diseconomies. It is certain that existing practices bear no relationship to a sensible calculation of optimum segregation of nonresidential activities. I know of no evidence that the question is even raised in zoning actions.

Land-Use Controls as Externalities Controls

It is striking that although land use controls are the basis of much government policy to control externalities, they hardly figure in the theoretical literature on externalities controls. Economists since Pigou have thought of taxes and subsidies for the purpose, whereas the political process hardly considers them. The paradox is the greater in that there are now direct controls on many externalities in the United States and elsewhere, yet no one appears to have asked whether land-use controls to segregate nonresidential activities have thereby been made redundant in whole or in part. The paradox is the greatest in regard to activities that discharge pollutants into the air and water. We have reams of regulations on such discharges; yet there are no studies of the need for land-use controls in addition to the direct controls on discharges.

Reflection shows that optimum direct controls on externalities make land-use controls redundant. To avoid circumlocution the argument will be placed in the context of polluting discharges, although it applies to any externality. Optimum direct controls—say, optimum effluent fees—can be varied by location and can therefore be set so as to induce an optimum locational pattern of polluting activities. They can also achieve optimum discharges at given locations. In principle, land-use controls can do the former but not the latter. In practice, U.S. pollution and land-use controls are hard to distinguish. Direct controls on polluting discharges in the form of standards, not effluent fees, are location-specific in some degree; and land-use controls in fact make permission to use land conditional on many details of the activity in question. Thus, in practice, the criticism is that we have saddled commercial and industrial activities with redundant and sometimes conflicting regulations.

Some segregation of nonresidential activities, whether voluntary or involuntary, is certainly justified. A little segregation almost certainly produces large benefits in the form of reduced external costs, and small costs in the form of increased travel. Suppose that each factory generates $5 worth of smoke damage to each resident within a mile of the factory, that population density is uniform, and that all land within one mile of the factory is required to house its workers. Then, if two factories were originally at least two miles apart, putting them next to each other would halve the number of residents damaged by smoke, but would increase average travel distance by only 40 percent, from 0.67 mile to 0.94 mile.[5]

Although some segregation is justified for externalities controls, it is not obvious that more is justified than is provided by private incentives. It has already been shown that private incentives provide considerable segregation of nonresidential activities in the absence of land-use controls. Siegen's study of Houston (1972), where there are no land use controls, suggests that private covenants there provide about the pattern of segregation that land-use controls provide elsewhere.

Of course, direct controls are not optimum. Even regarding polluting discharges, where the control apparatus is most elaborate, all economists who have studied existing direct control programs have concluded that they are gravely deficient.[6] It is hard to imagine that direct controls on noise, vibrations, and other external diseconomies are less defective than those on polluting discharges, to which so many government resources have been devoted.

The most basic evaluation of land-use controls to control externalities is that they are fundamentally defective for the simple reason that they control the wrong variable. The history of environmental controls is replete with examples of governmental attempts to control pollution by regulating the wrong variable. The most common such error is to regulate the output of a product whose production generates polluting discharges. Output regulation would be optimum government policy if polluting discharges were technically linked to output. But there is overwhelming evidence to the contrary. There are many processes that can produce given outputs, and each generates a different set of wastes. Even more important, there are many ways of returning waste to the environment, some of which are much more harmful than others. In this situation, standards or, better yet, fees on discharges are much better than controls on outputs, inputs, or other variables. This rationale applies with equal force to land-use controls. If noise is the offensive externality, it is much better to formulate government programs to control noise than to control land use. Land-use controls merely move the noise around. Although that may be better than nothing, it cannot be more than a peripheral contribution to solving the problem. This is especially true in an urban context, where most external diseconomies have substantial deleterious effects wherever they are located. A noisy factory may bother employees and/or customers in nearby nonresidential activities almost as much as it would bother nearby residents. Urban areas are inevitably and desirably high density areas for residences, employment, and shopping. Thus, wherever nuisances are put, they bother people. It is much better to control nuisances directly than to move them around.

2. THE NEIGHBORHOOD EFFECT

Neighborhood effect is interpreted somewhat narrowly in this section to refer to the effects of physical characteristics of one dwelling on the welfare or utility of nearby residents. The most likely objection to this narrow interpretation is that nearby residents' welfare is affected not only by physical characteristics of dwellings but also by the characteristics of the people who live in them, and that certain kinds of people tend to live in certain kinds of dwellings. For example, poor people may be objectionable as neighbors and they certainly tend to live in poor quality dwellings.

At the most basic level it is difficult to make a clear distinction between land-use controls whose motivation is to control externalities and those whose motivation is exclusionary. Analytically, a resident may receive disutility from a nearby smokestack, utility from a well-kept neighboring dwelling, or disutility from the fact that his neighbor is poor or black. If the motivation for exclusion is fiscal, it falls easily into the analysis in the next section; but if the motivation is skin color, or ethnic or religious affiliation, the situation is analytically similar to the smokestack case. In such cases the distinction between exclusion and externalities controls resides in the statement of the Constitution and of basic legislation that exclusion because of race or certain other characteristics is contrary to basic public policy and therefore not a legitimate exercise of police power.

The neighborhood effect to be discussed here rests on the simple assumption that residents of a given physical dwelling are better off the better the quality of nearby dwellings. It is hard to imagine that the assumption is false, although there may be strong disagreement about its importance. The direct implication of the assumption is that part of the return to investment in a dwelling by its owner accrues to residents or owners of nearby dwellings. This is true of investment in the dwelling when it is built, maintained, repaired, and improved. In what follows it is immaterial whether investment is understood to refer to construction of new dwellings or to maintenance and improvement of existing dwellings. All such investments improve the welfare of nearby residents. My neighbors are made better off if I paint my house or if I tear it down and replace it with a better one.

It is a sad commentary on the state of the theoretical analysis of land-use controls that the main theoretical tool used to analyze neighborhood effects is the prisoners' dilemma game. The prisoners' dilemma was first suggested as an analysis of land-use controls because of neighborhood effects by Davis and Winston (1964) and has been referred to in almost every subsequent work on the subject. Two suspects of a crime are separated and asked to confess. If neither confesses, both go free. Each is told that if he incriminates the other, he will be rewarded. If both confess, both go to jail. Plausible interpretations of these options imply that each will be made better off by confessing, given the unknown nature of the other's strategy. Thus, each confesses and both are worse off than if neither confessed.

The analogy relevant to land-use controls is that, because of the neighborhood effect, the owners of two proximate properties would both be better off if both maintained their properties than if neither did but, given the other's strategy, each is better off not to maintain his property. Thus, each ends up not maintaining his property, to the detriment of both. Land-use controls are viewed as a government mechanism to force each property owner to do what is in the collective interest of them both.

The prisoners' dilemma is a game of noncommunication. If the prisoners were allowed to communicate and sign binding agreements, they would agree not to confess and there would be no case. Property maintenance is certainly not a game of noncommunication. There is no physical or legal impediment to agreements by property owners about maintenance of their properties. In fact, private covenants to this effect are common. If communication is permitted, reasons for externalities from housing investment are those discussed in the previous section for other externalities. The public-good nature of benefits from housing investment and transaction costs of making agreements may be deterents to agreements to maintain property, but no light is shed on the problem by the prisoners' dilemma analysis.

Several characteristics of neighborhood effects seem obvious. First, only those characteristics of a property that are visible to neighbors, i.e., exterior condition of the structure, can have significant neighborhood effects. The interior of my house can hardly be of great concern to my neighbors. Second, the highly localized effect of nonresidential land uses referred to in the last section must also be typical of neighborhood effects. Although casual passers-by may receive some utility from an attractive house, most of the effect is presumably on those from whose residences the house is visible. Evidence cited in section 2 suggests that this is true of external effects of nonresidential land uses whose effects were mainly visual. Third, and almost a corollary, the neighborhood effect must be more important in high- than low-density neighborhoods, since such effects decay with distance. I am little affected by the condition of my neghbor's house if it is five miles away, but I may be much affected if it is attached to mine. Since there are more residents within a given distance of a property the higher the density of the neighborhood, it follows that the magnitude of the neighborhood effect is greater the higher the neighborhood density.

There is little direct evidence about the magnitude of the neighborhood effect. Many studies of the determinants of house values have included variables to represent average quality of neighboring dwellings, and most show significant effects (Crecine et al., 1967; Kain and Quigley, 1975; King and Mieszkowski, 1973). The most common such variable is a subjective index of neighborhood quality. This is of no help in estimating the return to neighboring residents from one dollar invested in a particular house. An excellent recent paper by Peterson (1974) uses data on single-family houses in suburban Boston to provide important quantitative evidence on the subject. Peterson estimates that the neighborhood effect is 13.2 percent of the internal effect of housing investment in his data.

Some limits can be placed on the magnitude of the neighborhood effect by indirect considerations. If the neighborhood effect were large, common ownership of neighboring dwellings would be the rule. An owner captures both the internal and external effects of painting his house if he also owns neighboring dwellings. In fact, common ownership is not uncommon among neighboring dwellings, especially in high density areas where the neighborhood effect is most important. The desire to internalize the neighborhood effect must be one reason for the predominance of rental apartments in high-density areas. And there is certainly a tendency for landlords to acquire several proximate properties in slums, although the evidence suggests that the tendency is slight (Sternlieb, 1966). As was mentioned, there are also many private agreements about development and maintenance of properties. The best-known example is the widespread use of covenants in Houston (Siegan, 1972).

It is sometimes claimed that desirable amounts of common ownership are inhibited by the capital required and by transaction costs. The former is certainly unimportant. Given that dwellings are excellent collateral, the equity required to acquire a few dozen dwellings is less than the assets of many small corporations. The latter is harder to deal with. Assume that the transaction cost of acquirng a house is 10 percent of its value. Transaction cost is important in that it gives power to a holdout. To take an extreme case, suppose I have acquired nine of ten houses I need in order to internalize a neighborhood effect. The owner of the tenth house can force me to split the benefit of internalizing the neighborhood effect with him by raising the price of his house above market value. There is a substantial benefit to me to acquire the tenth house. If I do not acquire it, I may have to sell the nine houses and try somewhere else. But the cost of unloading the nine houses may be as much as the value of the tenth, so he may be able to double the price of his house if the benefit from common ownership is great enough. He could not demand the higher price from me were it not for the high transaction cost of selling the nine houses. It is hard to know how much to make of this; there are many games realtors play to hide the identity of a buyer.

It is likely that the special federal income tax advantages to owner-occupiers are much more important deterents to common ownership of neighboring properties than are transaction costs. Owner-occupiers do not pay federal income tax on net imputed rent of their houses, whereas owners of rental housing do pay tax on net rent. Using Aaron's (1972) data it can be calculated that ownership is thereby made about 15 percent cheaper than rental for the average U.S. owner-occupier. This benefit is lost if neighboring dwellings are placed under common ownership and rented to occupants. Thus, only if the neighborhood effect exceeded 15 percent of housing costs would it make common ownership worthwhile for the typical U.S. owner-occupier. Roughly, the typical owner-occupier would be willing to change to rental status only if the benefit to him of the resulting improvement in the quality of neighboring houses was worth 15 percent of his housing costs. Peterson's estimates suggest that common ownership is worth less than 15 percent in neighborhoods where owner occupancy is typical.

For government policy the quantitative question is how far above the private marginal product is the social marginal produce of housing investments because of the neighborhood effect. Suppose the private return to housing investment is 10 percent per year. How much greater is the social return because of the neighborhood effect? My guess is that if the social marginal product exceeded the private marginal product by more than about 15 percent (that is, if the social rate of return were more than about 11.5 percent, given a private return of 10 percent), common ownership would be much more frequent than it is.

It is hard to imagine that there is no neighborhood effect or that it is greater than about 15 percent. If it is substantial, the classical remedy for the resulting resource misallocation is a subsidy for housing equal to the difference between the social and private marginal products of housing capital, evaluated at the equilibrium quantity of housing capital. If one is optimistic about the ability of the political process to solve such problems, one can conclude that the neighborhood effect has been perceived at 15 percent of housing costs and an equivalent subsidy has been introduced through the federal income tax. There are several objections to this conclusion. First, the neighborhood effect justifies a credit for housing costs, not a deduction. There is no reason related to social efficiency why a rich man should receive a bigger subsidy than a poor man whose housing circumstances are the same. Second, there is no net subsidy to owner-occupied housing. Unless one views them as benefit taxes,[7] real-estate taxes must be viewed as an offset against the deductability provisions, which are about half as large. Third, the subsidy is restricted to owner-occupiers. Renters certainly tend to live in denser areas than owner-occupiers, and the neighborhood effect is certainly greater in denser areas, yet there is no corresponding subsidy for renters.

The defects in federal tax treatment of housing as a policy to internalize neighborhood effects could be remedied easily; provided its magnitude were appropriate, its resource allocation effects could be made better if it were converted to a credit and applied to renters as well as to owner-occupiers. The law might simply permit 15 percent of housing costs to be subtracted from federal income tax regardless of whether the house were owned or rented by its occupant.

Whatever one's view of the neighborhood effect, it is hard to beleve that land-use controls are an effective way to deal with it. Density limits may reduce the neighborhood effect by reducing density, but that is a very inefficient method. The resource misallocation is underinvestment in housing, not excessive density; density controls govern a variable that is at best only peripherally related to the problem. Bulk controls are equally clumsy. The tendency in some communities is to introduce detailed physical requirements regarding external materials and appearance. These are justified only if uniformity rather than high quality is the goal. The basic problem is underinvestment, not excessive diversity. The right way to deal with the neighborhood effect, if it should be dealt with at all, is with housing subsidies, not land-use controls. More research is needed to estimate precisely the magnitude of the neighborhood effect.

3. LAND-USE CONTROLS
FOR FISCAL AND GROWTH CONTROL PURPOSES

This chapter has been primarily concerned with land-use controls to correct resource misallocations from externalities. In 1956 Tiebout published a paper in which he suggested that at least some land-use controls must be understood in the context of the exigencies of local-government finance instead of the context of externalities. The Tiebout model has since been formalized and extended;[8] it is described elsewhere in this volume and need not be repeated here. The emphasis in this section will be the relationship of that model to land-use controls, an aspect hardly mentioned by Tiebout.

The Tiebout model can be viewed as a positive or a normative theory of local-government organization and finance. The conclusion that a system of fragmented local governments in a metropolitan area can provide efficient resource allocation to local-government public service production follows from restrictions on the characteristics of the services in question. The primary restrictions are a limited magnitude of scale economies and a geographic limit to any publicness of the services. Practically, these restrictions require that nonconforming public services be produced by higher levels of government. They are at least approximately satisfied by education and other important services provided by local governments.

With such assumptions, the remarkable conclusion is that fragmented local governments can provide efficient menus of public services to constituents who are motivated to select among jurisdictions according to their demands for local-government services. The property tax is then a perfect benefit tax, entailing no deadweight loss. Carefully designed land-use controls are a key element in the scheme. They prevent people from living in a jurisdiction without paying local taxes equal to the cost of the local public services provided. The requirement that each household pay x dollars in local real estate taxes for the privilege of living in the community performs precisely the function of a price in a private market; it pays production costs and deters consumption by those to whom the product is worth less than production costs.

To evaluate the normative implication of Tiebout's model one must start with the assumption that for technological, constitutional, or social reasons everyone in a given jurisdiction is to have equal access to the local public services provided; otherwise, there would be little reason for the services to be provided publicly instead of by profit-seeking firms. With equal access, efficiency requires that each household in the jurisdiction make the same optimum payment to the local government for the services provided. In the absence of constraints on methods of raising revenue, a head tax would be best. Then, no land-use controls would be required to produce efficient resource allocation. If revenues are to be raised by a real-estate tax levied at the same rate on the market value of each dwelling, then land-use controls are required to ensure that each dwelling's market value is adequate to yield the appropriate tax payment. A simple land-use control that made illegal the construction of a dwelling whose market value was less than D dollars would be blatantly exclusionary and would presumably not get past the courts Instead, controls for fiscal purposes must bear some resemblance to controls for the constitutionally acceptable externalities basis for land-use controls. Much ingenuity has been employed by local zoners to devise controls that will be both adequately exclusionary and also acceptable to the courts. Throughout much of the post–World War II period, the courts have been extremely cooperative, as was shown in the historical survey. But recent court decisions threaten to make the rules of the exclusionary zoning game much more complex. Nevertheless, it is hard to imagine that the courts are yet a serious threat to the efforts of local governments to exclude "free riders" by land-use controls. There are too many ways to use too many land-use controls, each acceptable to the courts in some circumstances, for the cumbersome legal machinery to have much effect on efforts to exclude.

Thus, the essence of the Tiebout hypothesis is that each household in a jurisdiction must bear its share of the cost of the local public services it consumes. Land-use controls are necessary to exclude free riders only because of reliance on property taxes to finance local government. But the use of the property tax is costly in a Tiebout world. An efficent Tiebout world requires that a given jurisdiction contain only residents willing to pay for a given bundle of local public services; an efficient Tiebout world in which local government is financed by real-estate taxes requires that all residents of a jurisdiction not only demand the same bundle of local public services but also consume the same amount of housing. The latter constraint is necessitated by varying housing demands among people with the same local public service demands. Thus, many more jurisdictions are required in a metropolitan area if real-estate taxes are the source of local government revenues. But scale economies in local public service production and other considerations severely limit the number of jurisdictions in most metropolitan areas. Thus, real-estate tax financing greatly restricts the ability to match demand with supply of local public services.

A head tax is the ideal tax for efficient resource allocation in a Tiebout world, but most people, probably including many jurists, react violently against such a proposal. The reaction is, of course, on grounds of equity, not efficiency. A head tax is perfectly regressive, as any market price must be if it is to allocate resources efficiently. There is a lively debate in the literature as to how progressive or regressive the property tax is, but it is certainly not perfectly regressive. Nevertheless, the basic implication of the Tiebout model is that, in a world of fragmented local governments, local governments have no substantial ability to redistribute income. In practice, virtually all income redistribution by governments in the United States is carried out at the federal level. It is not obvious to me that financing local governments by a locally levied head tax, permitted in exchange for abolition of all exclusionary land-use controls, would lead to a less desirable world than the present one.

In fact, the trend in the United States has been in a quite different direction. Since World War II we have financed increasing fractions of local government expenditures by grants from higher levels of government. Since the piper calls the tune, local governments have inevitably been increasingly restricted in choosing the menu of local public services, and we are thus coming to approximate more closely a unitary form of government common elsewhere in the democratic world. Continuation of this trend will certainly remove the fiscal incentive for exclusionary land-use controls. Hamilton, Mills, and Puryear (Mills and Oates, 1975) presented evidence that there is a proportionally greater variety of income levels within jurisdictions with increased financing of local-government expenditures by grants from higher levels of government. But it will also end the tradition of local decision-making regarding local government service provision and finances.

Land-use controls to implement slow- and no-growth policies are in a sense extreme forms of those for exclusionary purposes. Exclusionary controls exclude those who would not pay their share of local public service costs, whereas slow- and no-growth policies exclude potential residents even if they would pay their share. The basic economic problem with slow-growth policies is obvious. Exclusionary policies exclude all who would not pay the cost of their local public services, and therein lies their claim to marketlike efficiency. Slow-growth policies exclude even those who would pay the opportunity cost of their local public services. Thus, they unduly restrict entry and local public service consumption in exactly the way a monopoly unduly restricts private goods consumption.

How can a fragmented local government, which competes with other local governments, exercise monopoly power? The answer lies in the coercive nature of the political process. Consider the following situation, which is typical of Petaluma and many other communities. Half the land in a suburban community has been developed. A few thousand voters live on the developed land. A much smaller group of farmers or developers owns the undeveloped land. It is in the interest of residents to restrict development of undeveloped land. Restriction will restrict housing supply, raising prices of existing units. Furthermore, it will preserve the character of the community, which may have been a reason they located there. Finally, in an era when courts and higher levels of government are insisting on low-income housing, it will help keep undesirable people out of the community.

Residents can easily outvote owners of undeveloped land, some of whom may not even live in the community. A large majority therefore votes for— or for elected officials who will institute—sewer bans, development boundaries, severe requirements on developers, time-consuming planning studies, ecological protection plans, delays in sewer and sewage treatment plant construction, open-space preservation or "green acre" plans, etc. The key to the success of such strategems is the ability of the majority of residents to coerce the minority of owners of undeveloped land.

Nobody knows the magnitude of the resulting resource misallocation. Newspaper and court accounts make clear that slow-growth policies are widespread among U.S. suburban communities. In several court cases there is undisputed testimony that slow-growth policies reduced prices of undeveloped land by 50 to 75 percent. The social cost of excessive slow-growth policies, including excessively high housing prices in both central cities and suburbs, inefficient locational patterns in metropolitan areas, and excessive commuting costs, must be substantial.

The basic reason for excessive restrictions on development is that the majority who benefit from slow growth can impose the cost on the minority of owners of undeveloped land. If the majority voted to tax themselves to buy undeveloped land at fair market prices for a park, there could be no objection. It is not the desire for slow or for no growth that is objectionable. Slow growth is excessive because the majority can obtain its benefits while imposing the costs on a minority who cannot prevent it. The majority of owner-occupant residents of many suburban communities thus have every incentive to interfere with community growth to an excessive extent through the political process.

There are basically two directions reforms can take to prevent excessive exclusionary and slow-growth policies in U.S. suburbs. First, the present trend toward state and federal financing and control over local-government services can continue. That trend would abolish a longstanding American tradition, and available evidence indicates that the resulting uniformity in local public services would lead to a large welfare loss.[9] Furthermore, as was suggested in the historical survey, higher levels of government may not prove much less exclusionary-minded than local governments have proven.

Second, the incentives that local governments have to control entry excessively can be removed. In principle, the solution is simply to require that local governments compensate property owners injured by exclusionary or slow-growth land-use controls. In a perceptive paper, Ellickson (1977) has analyzed the legal and economic issues involved. The difficulty with this solution is practical. Modern U.S. courts give local governments broad discretion to protect community character and to promote orderly growth with land-use controls. To ask courts to discriminate between such land-use controls, which do not require compensation, and exclusionary controls is to introduce chaos into the judicial process. Courts simply cannot function if they are forced to decide case by case whether controls are exclusionary, who was hurt, and by how much. Undoubtedly, judicial unwillingness to require compensation is based in part on judges' sense that to do so would flood their courts with litigation of a kind they are ill-equipped to handle.

My interpretation of the situation is based on two premises. First, exclusion is the overwhelming purpose of land-use controls other than those that segregate nonresidential activities. The only other justification for land-use controls on residential development is the neighborhood effect, and I have shown earlier that direct subsidization of housing is a more effective and simpler way to deal with that problem. Second, the notion of income redistribution by local governments is a phantom. Fragmented local governments mean that local taxes are approximately head taxes within a jurisdiction, and whatever redistribution results is arbitrary and unfocused. A modest adjustment of federal tax and expenditure policies could easily correct any worsening of income distribution that resulted from changes in methods of financing local governments.

The above two premises imply that it would be worthwhile to give up real-estate taxes in exchange for head taxes to finance local governments if at the same time land-use controls on residential development could be abolished. Specifically, my proposals for local government finance are:

1. Each community can choose its head tax, which must be paid by all residents, but no other local taxes are permitted.

2. No controls on residential development are permitted.

3. Any community can buy whatever land it wants to preserve for open space or any other purpose provided the land is bought at a fair market price.

Before these proposals are dismissed out-of-hand, consider the following:

1. The head tax and requirement for purchase of land at fair market price would provide communities with just the right incentive to exclude or slow development when benefits exceed costs of doing so.

2. Exclusion would be based on the correct criterion, namely, unwillingness to pay for the local menu of public services.

3. Metropolitan suburbs would be more integrated with respect to race, income, and ethnicity than they are now. At present, people excluded from suburbs live in central cities not mainly because local taxes per capita are lower there than in suburbs, but because they are "zoned out" of suburbs. In fact, local taxes per capita are at present higher in central cities than in suburbs.

4. The head tax would be deductible on federal income tax returns for renters as well as owner-occupiers, in contrast to present real-estate taxes.

5. Local governments would be free to engage in income redistribution if the local electorate wanted it. For example, the electorate could vote for a "head tax refund" for low-income residents if it wanted to.

6. The head tax would make the cost of local public services apparent to renters, thus improving their ability to vote rationally. It is impossible for renters to know how much real-estate tax they really pay.

CONCLUSION

The history and analysis of land-use controls can hardly be said to be one of the happier aspects of American life. They constitute an extraordinarily broad and powerful grant of authority to local governments to use for ill-defined purposes. When land-use controls are used to segregate non-residential activities, the analysis is straightforward. Some land-use controls are needed because direct controls on external diseconomies produced by nonresidential activities are imperfect at best. When land-use controls are used to control the amount and form of residential development, the analysis is more complex.

The easy analysis, on which this chapter has focused, is on controls to prevent free riders in a system of fragmented local governments. But it is a subtle distinction, not easily made in analysis or in court, between keeping out free riders and keeping out minorities, the poor, and almost everybody in general. My conclusion is that the combination of real-estate taxes as the main source of local government revenues and a laissez-faire attitude on the part of the courts toward local-government land-use controls guarantees that controls will be excessively exclusionary.

NOTES

1. On the subject of this paragraph, see Michelle White, "Fiscal Zoning in Fragmented Metropolitan Areas," in Mills and Oates (1973).

2. The common textbook statement that externalities are caused when one person's (or firm's) activities directly affect another's welfare, is certainly not sufficient, since that fact does not by itself prevent adequate compensation by voluntary agreement.

3. See Anderson (1974) and Stull (1975) and the references therein.

4. For a simple model that illustrates the relevant class of theoretical models see Mills (1972). Some evidence is in Mills (1969).

5. Within r miles of the factory there are $D\pi r^2$ residents, where D is density. If the factories are at least two miles apart, average commuting distance is $\int_0^1 2\pi r^2 dr/\pi \simeq 0.67$. If the factories are adjacent, average commuting distance is $\int_0^{\sqrt{2}} 2\pi r^2 dr/\pi = 0.94$.

6. See Kneese and Schultze (1975), for an excellent survey.

7. See section 3.

8. Henderson, J. Vernon, "The Theory of Jurisdiction and Group Life."

9. See Bradford and Oates (1974).

REFERENCES

Aaron, Henry. 1972. *Shelter and Subsidies*. Washington, D.C.: Brookings Institution.

Anderson, John. 1974. "Environmental Considerations: New Arguments for Large Lot Zoning." *Urban Law Annual* 7: 370.

Anderson, Robert. 1974. "Property Market Equilibria Model of Exchange and Some Empirical Results." February.

Babcock, Richard. 1966. *The Zoning Game: Municipal Practices and Policies*. Madison: University of Wisconsin Press.

Babcock, Richard, and Bosselman, Fred. 1973. *Exclusionary Zoning: Land Use Regulation and Housing in the 1970s*. New York: Praeger.

Bailey, Martin. 1959. "A Note on the Economics of Residential Zoning and Urban Renewal." *Land Economics* 35 (August): 288–92.

Bosselman, Fred. 1973. "Can the Town of Ramapo Pass a Law to Bind the Rights of the Whole World?" *Florida State Law Review* 1: 265.

Bosselman, Fred; Callies, David; and Banta, John. 1973. *The Taking Issue.* Washington, D.C.: Council on Environmental Quality.

Bradford, David, and Oates, Wallace. 1974. "Suburban Exploitation of Central Cities and Governmental Structure." In *Redistribution through Public Choice.* Edited by Harold Hochman and George Peterson. New York: Columbia University Press.

Branfman, Eric; Cohen, Benjamin; and Trubek, David. 1973. "Measuring the Invisible Wall: Land Use Controls and the Residential Pattern of the Poor." *Yale Law Journal* 82 (January): 483–508.

Brigham, Eugene. 1965. "The Determinants of Residential Land Value." *Land Economics* 41 (November): 325–34.

Chapin, Stuart. 1965. *Urban Land Use Planning.* Urbana: University of Illinois Press.

Clawson, Marion. 1973. *Modernizing Urban Land Policies.* Baltimore: Johns Hopkins University Press.

Clawson, Marion; and Hall, Peter. 1973. *Planning and Urban Growth: An Anglo-American Comparison.* Baltimore: Johns Hopkins University Press.

Congressional Digest. 1973. "Controversy over Proposed National Land Use Regulation." December.

Crecine, John; Davis, Otto; and Jackson, John. 1967. "Urban Property Markets: Some Empirical Results and Their Implication for Municipal Zoning." *Journal of Law and Economics* 10 (October): 79–99.

Davis, Otto. 1963. "Economic Elements of Municipal Zoning Decisions." *Land Economics* 39 (November): 375–86.

Davis, Otto, and Whinston, Andres. 1964. "The Economics of Complex Systems: The Case of Zoning." *Kyklos* 17: 419–46.

Delafons, John. 1969. *Land Use Controls in the United States.* Cambridge, Mass.: MIT Press.

Denman, D., and Prodano, S. 1972. *Land Use.* London: Allen and Unwin.

Downing, Paul. 1973. "Factors Affecting Commercial Land Values: An Empirical Study of Milwaukee, Wisconsin." *Land Economics* 49 (February): 44–56.

Downs, Anthony. 1973. *Opening Up the Suburbs.* New Haven: Yale University Press.

Durham, Allison. 1958. "A Legal and Economic Basis for City Planning." *Columbia Law Review* 58 (May): 650–71.

Ellickson, Robert. 1973. "Alternatives to Zoning: Covenants, Nuisance Rules, and Fines as Land Use Controls." *University of Chicago Law Review* 40 (Summer): 681–781.

―――. 1977. "Suburban Growth Controls: An Economic and Legal Analysis." *Yale Law Journal* 86 (January): 385–511.

Fielding, Richard. 1972. "The Right to Travel: Another Constitutional Standard for Local Land Use Regulations." *University of Chicago Law Review* 39: 612.

Finkler, Earl. 1973. "Nongrowth: A Review of the Literature." *Planning Association Service Report No. 289.* Chicago: American Society of Planning Officials.

Grether, David, and Mieszkowski, Peter. 1974. "Determinants of Real Estate Values." *Journal of Urban Economics* 1 (April): 127–46.

Haar, Charles, ed. 1964. *Law and Land*. Cambridge, Mass.: Harvard University Press.

Hamilton, Bruce. 1976. "Capitalization of Intrajurisdictional Differences in Local Tax Prices." *American Economic Review* 66 (December): 743–53.

Harris, R.; Tolley, G.; and Harrall, C. 1968. "The Residence Site Choice." *Review of Economics and Statistics* 50 (May): 241–47.

Henderson, J. V. 1974a. "Optimum City Size: The External Diseconomy Question." *Journal of Political Economy* 82 (March/April): 373–88.

———. 1974b. "The Size and Types of Cities." *American Economic Review* 64 (September): 640–56.

———. 1975. "Congestion and Optimum City Size." *Journal of Urban Economics* 2(January): 48–62.

Hirsch, Werner. 1973. *Urban Economic Analysis*. New York: McGraw-Hill.

———. 1977. "The Efficiency of Restrictive Land Use Instruments." *Land Economics* 52 (May): 145–56.

Hoch, Irving. In press. "Quality of Life Related to City Size." *Science*.

Jacobs, Jane. 1961. *The Death and Life of Great American Cities*. New York: Random House.

Kain, John, and Quigley, John. 1975. *Housing Markets and Racial Discrimination*. New York: National Bureau of Economic Research.

Karlin, Norman; Horton, Edward; and Polster, Lee. "Zoning Monopoly Effects and Judicial Abdication." *Southwestern Law Review* 4.

Keiper, Joseph; Kurnow, Ernest; Clark, Clifford; and Segal, Harvey. 1961. *Theory and Measurement of Rent*. Chicago: Chilton.

King, A. Thomas, and Mieszkowski, Peter. 1973. "Facial Discrimination, Segregation and the Price of Housing." *Journal of Political Economy* 81 (May/June): 590–606.

Kneese, Allen, and Schultze, Charles. 1975. *Pollution, Prices and Public Policy*. Washington, D.C.: Brookings Institution.

Mandelker, David. 1971. *The Zoning Dilemma*. New York: Bobbs-Merrill.

Marcus, Norman, and Graves, Marilyn. 1970. *The New Zoning: Legal, Administrative and Economic Concepts and Techniques*. New York: Praeger.

Maser, Steven; Riker, William; and Rosett, Richard. 1974. "The Effects of Zoning and Externalities on the Prices of Land in Monroe County, New York." April.

Mieszkowski, Peter. 1973. "Notes on the Economic Effects of Land Use Regulation." In *Issues in Urban Public Finance*, pp. 252–73. Paris: Institute Internationale de Finance Publiques.

Mills, Edwin. 1969. "The Value of Urban Land." In *The Quality of the Urban Environment*, pp. 231–56. Edited by Harvey Perloff. Baltimore: Johns Hopkins University Press.

———. 1972. *Urban Economics*. Glenview, Ill.: Scott, Foresman.

Mills, Edwin, and Oates, Wallace, eds., 1975. *Fiscal Zoning and Land Use Controls*. Lexington, Mass.: D.C. Heath.

Muth, Richard. 1969. *Cities and Housing*. Chicago: University of Chicago Press.

Natoli, S. 1971. "Zoning and the Development of Urban Land Patterns." *Eco-*

nomic Geography 47 (April) : 171–84.

Nourse, Hugh. 1977. "The Political Economy of Land Use Regulation." August.

Peterson, George. 1974. "The Influence of Zoning Regulations on Land and Housing Prices." Washington, D.C.: Urban Institute. July.

Rueter, Frederick. 1973. "Externalities in Urban Property Markets: An Empirical Test of the Zoning Ordinance of Pittsburgh." *Journal of Law and Economics* 16 (October) : 313–50.

Sagolyn, Lynne, and Sternlieb, George. 1972. *Zoning and Housing Costs: The Impact of Land Use Controls on Housing Prices.* New Brunswick, N.J.: Rutgers University, Center for Urban Policy Research.

Schafer, Robert. 1975. "Exclusionary Land Use Controls: Conceptual and Empirical Problems in Measuring the Invisible Wall." Department of City and Regional Planning, Harvard University. Discussion paper D 75-2. February.

Siegan, Bernard. 1972. *Land Use Without Zoning.* Lexington, Mass.: D.C. Heath and Co.

Sternlieb, George. 1966. *The Tenement Landlord.* New Brunswick, N.J.: Rutgers University Press.

Stull, William. 1974. "Land Use and Zoning in an Urban Economy." *American Economic Review* 64 (June) : 337–47.

———. 1975. "Community Environment, Zoning and the Market Value of Single-Family Homes." *Journal of Law and Economics* 18 (October) : 535–57.

Sundquist, James. 1975. *Dispersing Population.* Washington, D.C.: Brookings Institution.

Thompson, Wilbur. 1973. "Problems that Sprout in the Shadow of No-Growth." *American Institute of Architects Journal* 60: 30.

Tideman, T. N. 1969. "Three Approaches to Improving Urban Land Use." Ph.D. diss. University of Chicago.

Tiebout, Charles. 1956. "A Pure Theory of Local Expenditures." *Journal of Political Economy* 64 (October) : 416–24.

Toll, Seymour. 1969. *Zoned American.* New York: Grossman.

Tolley, George. 1974. "The Welfare Economics of City Bigness." *Journal of Urban Economics* 1 (July) : 324–45.

Ukeles, John. 1964. *Consequences of Municipal Zoning.* Washington, D.C.: Urban Land Institute.

United Nations. 1976. *Growth Role Strategy and Regional Development Planning in Asia.* Nagoza, Japan: United Nations Center for Regional Development.

White, Michelle. 1975. "The Effect of Zoning on the Size of Metropolitan Areas." *Journal of Urban Economics* 2 (October) : 279–90.

———. 1976. "Zoning for No Growth: A New Trend?" April.

Wilhelm, Sidney. 1962. *Urban Zoning and Land Use Theory.* New York: Free Press of Glencoe.

Yearwood, Richard. 1971. *Land Subdivision Regulation.* New York: Praeger.

Yeates, M. H. 1965. "Effects of Zoning on Land Values in American Cities: A Case Study." *Essays in Geography for Austin Miller.* Edited by R. Whitelaw. Reading, Pa.: University of Reading Press.

16

JUDICIAL APPROACHES
TO LOCAL PUBLIC-SECTOR EQUITY:
AN ECONOMIC ANALYSIS

DANIEL L. RUBINFELD

INTRODUCTION

During the past decade a vast number of legal actions have been taken against state and local governments in an attempt to bring about greater equality in the distribution of public services and taxes. From the point of view of an urban economist, the cases are relevant because they have important consequences for the analysis of expenditure, taxation, and land-use policies. This paper will analyze the likely economic impact of court originated or court ordered policies with income distribution implications. This analysis is relevant for economists (and lawyers) for two reasons: it suggests the kinds of institutional constraints that local public decision-makers are likely to face, and thus, which ought to be incorporated into models of urban fiscal behavior; and it suggests specific empirical policy questions that remain largely unanswered and that may provide fruitful grounds for future research.

The history of legal attempts to attain equity through the local public sector is a complex one. However, one might summarize the recent history by arguing that reformers have focused on the following four objectives: (1) equal provision of education and other public services within jurisdic-

Daniel L. Rubinfeld is associate professor, Department of Economics, and research associate, Institute of Public Policy Studies, University of Michigan.

Much of this paper's material is based upon research conducted jointly with Robert Inman. I wish to thank Gregory C. Staple for providing extensive and very capable assistance with the preparation of legal material. Robin Barlow, Harvey Brazer, Paul Courant, Paul Dimond, Robert Ellickson, William Fischel, Edward Gramlich, Robert Inman, Judith Lachman, Martin McGuire, Peter Mieszkowski, Susan Rose-Ackerman, Gregory Staple, John Weicher, and Michelle White made helpful comments on an early draft.

tions; (2) equal (effective) tax rates for all households within jurisdictions; (3) equal capacity (tax bases) among jurisdictions to finance education; and (4) the removal of minimum lot zoning and other land-use controls to open all jurisdictions to low-income housing. To some extent these objectives are consistent with a broad view of *horizontal* equity (equal treatment of equals) and are thus an end in themselves. What is of direct concern here, however, is that whether intended or not, the objectives can and will lead to a more *vertically* equitable distribution of income.

Much of the economic underpinning of my analysis lies in the recent (i.e., the past decade) literature of the urban and public economics disciplines. Part 1 of the paper describes some aspects of this literature that are pertinent to my discussion of the impact of the recent court decisions. Parts 2 and 3 consider the economic and legal issues surrounding the four equity objectives. In Part 2 the vertical equity and efficiency consequences associated with each of the two *intrajurisdictional* equity objectives are considered. I describe the existing case law and ask whether the courts are likely to be successful in bringing about either tax-rate or expenditure equality, whether the imposition of such constraints upon local governments is likely to increase or decrease efficiency, and whether there will be any improvement in the distribution of income.

Part 3 is concerned with the *interjurisdictional* equity objectives. I consider the legal history relating to the distribution of tax burdens and expenditures among jurisdictions within the metropolitan area, asking whether the courts have been or are likely to be successful in bringing about jurisdictional tax base equality or in removing zoning and other constraints that limit the supply of low-income suburban housing and the access of low-income households to suburban public services. In addition, I consider the efficiency and vertical equity implications of tax base equality and equal access. The final section contains a brief summary of the chapter and some tentative conclusions concerning the legal approach to local public-sector equity. I have attempted neither to survey all substantive areas relevant to the equity issue nor to exhaust the case law in the subject areas mentioned. Specifically, recent developments in the area of environmental law have been omitted, in part because the policy consequences apply more to state and regional than to local government. School desegregation cases are relevant; but, although school desegregation can help to achieve intrajurisdictional expenditure equity and improvements in access to public services among jurisdictions, the topic has been omitted, largely because of Clotfelter's treatment of school desegregation in chapter 11.

1. THE METROPOLITAN SYSTEM

The Model

The analysis of the impact of recent court opinions on the urban system requires an understanding of the motivations of households, firms, and governments viewed in the context of a metropolitan system of fragmented governments with a fixed total population.[1] I choose to distinguish between the motivations of central-city jurisdictions and suburban jurisdictions, in part because a substantial portion of the urban poor reside in the city center, and in part because the policy options available to central-city governments differ from those available to their suburban counterparts.[2] The court decisions are viewed as suggesting changes in the status quo. I then outline the likely responses of economic actors to the mandated changes, placing emphasis on the middle- and long-run impact of the legal attempts to attain equity. However, the courts are concerned with the short-run effect as well and are equipped to monitor the enforcement of decisions so that long-run and short-run impacts are not divergent.

Individual households are assumed to maximize utility subject to an income constraint. Assume first that the maximization process involves the household that chooses as its desired level the actual mean level of public spending in the community. This household calculates its desired level of public service expenditures, given its income (net of journey-to-work costs) and the "tax-price" that it faces.[3] The tax-price (defined as the added cost to the household of financing an extra dollar per household of public services in the community) implicitly defines the household's public-private budget line.[4] Given an exogenous set of matching and nonmatching grants and the assumption that all revenue is raised through the property tax, the tax-price will vary positively with the value of the house owned by the decisive voter, and inversely with the value of the per household fiscal base of the community.

If the decisive household chooses to remain in its present location, the analysis is complete. However, like all households, it has the option of relocating by calculating the desired public expenditure level, given the tax-price and income (net of transport costs) at alternative locations. The level of utility to be attained will be inversely related (other things being equal) to the tax-price that the household faces, and inversely related to the discrepancy between the household's desired level of public expenditure and the actual level of expenditure provided in each community. Only if the increased utility of a more desirable location outweighs the cost of moving will the household choose to relocate. If the household initially under consideration is not decisive, the previous analysis would be slightly more complex because the household suffers a loss in utility that depends on the difference between its desired expenditures and the level actually provided.

Firms are presumed to be profit-maximizers or at least to be locationally sensitive to profit incentives. As a consequence, an increase in the tax burden facing a firm without a concomitant increase in public services, or an adverse land-use policy change, will increase the probability that the firm will choose to leave the jurisdiction.[5] Governments are assumed to act as agents for the existing group of households and firms residing in that jurisdiction. Thus, each government will attempt to restrict immigration so that new households and firms will increase the utility of the decisive household. Making this objective operational is difficult (for one thing the decisive household may change as a result of any shift in public policy), and various authors have tried alternative approaches. Rothenberg, for example, assumes that the government attempts to maximize aggregate land value in the community; White suggests a number of objectives, including maximization of the total value of existing houses (a proxy for wealth).[6] Whatever the specific form of the objective function, I assume that governments are motivated to encourage immigration of those households that provide a nonnegative (positive) fiscal surplus and to discourage immigration of those with negative surpluses. The fiscal surplus is defined as the additional tax revenues generated minus the increased (marginal) cost of public services associated with the new immigrants. Similarly, the government is likely to encourage immigration of firms that add more to tax revenues than to public expenditures.[7]

The hypothesized governmental attitudes toward new entrants suggests the importance of obtaining empirical evidence concerning the fiscal motivations of local governments. It has usually been assumed that governments find higher-income households more desirable than lower-income households. On purely fiscal grounds, however, this need not always be true. On one hand, if single-family high-income households have several school-age children during their life cycle, the increased tax base may be more than counterbalanced by added expenditures. On the other hand, high-rise apartments with low-income households can be fiscally desirable, especially if the number of bedrooms is limited.[8] In fact, it is not inconceivable that severely limiting all future immigration may be optimal from the government's viewpoint. This suggests one explanation for the recent appearance of no-growth policies in newly developing suburban communities.

From the viewpoint of immigration by firms, two empirical issues seem relevant. First, to what extent do firms provide a fiscal residual that is available for allocation toward the provision of public expenditures to households? Second, how do available fiscal residuals compare to the environmental costs associated with firm location? If firms were mobile and there were no institutional constraints, communities might bid away much of the fiscal surplus associated with firm location. However, any fiscal surplus that remains is likely to serve as compensation for the undesirable external effects associated with the immigration of the firm. Preliminary evidence suggests that there are fiscal benefits, but that they are not large relative to other determinants of local expenditures and taxes; the fiscal benefits may balance the environmental costs.

The Policy Instruments

Consider the behavior of central-city governments, whose objective is to slow or stop the out-migration of both firms and high-income households. One obvious method is to use variations in assessment ratios to alter the economic incentives of potential out-migrants (hereafter called the *assessment-variation policy*). While the reasons for existing variations are not solely fiscal, some selected results are consistent with the view that assessors give tax breaks to the more mobile high-income households and the large industrial firms that represent a potentially major fiscal loss to the community.[9]

An analogous policy instrument is available on the expenditure side of the budget. Many local public services, such as sanitation, fire, and education, may differ in their provision by neighborhood and even by household. As a result, expenditures on inputs can be varied to provide better services to the more mobile households and firms, in particular to those whose out-migration would be likely to adversely affect the central city fiscal base (this is called the *expenditure-variation policy*).[10] I should note that both the assessment and expenditure variation policies typically involve differential treatment by neighborhood and by housing type and value. The impact of such policies on household income is more complex, depending upon the correlation between income and house value and the use of a current or permanent income measure.

Central city governments have the option of altering the mean quantity of public services provided as well as the geographical composition of those services. Higher expenditures are likely to be attractive to mobile high-income households but may involve a loss of consumer surplus for low- and middle-income households with low desired levels of public expenditures. From the point of view of suburban jurisdictions, a substantial increase in public expenditures, with a corresponding tax liability, will most probably diminish the utility to be gained by low-income households choosing to reside in the community, since the tax increases will be valued highly while the expenditure benefits will not. However, any loss in consumer surplus to high-income households is liable to be small. Thus, low-income residents can, in principle, be deterred (despite the low tax-prices), by being forced to consume a luxury level of public goods.

This effect on low-income households is strengthened substantially if potential residents are constrained by zoning to buy houses on a minimum-size lot. Zoning is a policy instrument most easily available to suburban governments in jurisdictions with available vacant land. While motivated in part for externality reasons, these minimum-lot regulations, bedroom requirements, and set-back restrictions, as well as land-use regulations controlling apartments and mobile homes, clearly allow governments to discourage low-income entrants. In effect, the government utilizes zoning to increase the tax-price of public services and the housing price-of-entry to suburban communities. Low-income households may also find zoned suburban locations undesirable because they do not place a high value on low-density housing and because the travel costs of commuting to central-city jobs may be substantial. Similar arguments can be applied to firm immigration, since land-use controls on the type and extent of commercial and industrial use provide a powerful policy tool for suburban governments.

The analysis of zoning changes is complex because of the impact of these changes on the fiscal base of the jurisdictions. Consider, for example, the impact of a zoning decision that allows a new industry to enter a community. Any fiscal surplus associated with the new entrant will improve the fiscal situation of the existing residents, but to the extent that there are externalities associated with the firm's location near residential areas, the market value of those single-family homes (and land) may fall. In fact, there is some evidence that there is capitalization of the externalities associated with residences located near firms.

The effects of minimum-lot residential zoning are also difficult to analyze. Theoretical models of residential zoning suggest that minimum-lot zoning is likely to cause an increase in housing prices in the community, but the impact on aggregate house and aggregate land value is theoretically indeterminate. The reasoning is quite straightforward. On the one hand, a binding zoning policy is likely to create an excess demand for housing and cause housing and land prices to rise. Lower population and housing density, however, are likely to be associated with lower housing prices, making the difference in property values unclear. In addition, a high minimum-lot zoning policy forces the production of houses that are more land intensive than optimal, given the original level of land prices. This housing production inefficiency will be borne in the long run by landowners, and a countervailing tendency to force land prices down will result.[11]

In this chapter I have chosen to stress the fiscal motives of households, firms, and governments, but I do not mean to imply that fiscal motives are necessarily of paramount importance in each and every instance. Zoning and land-use regulations have clearly been used to deal with many types of externalities, and zoning that is apparently fiscal in motivation may discriminate against racial, ethnic, or occupational groups, intentionally or not.[12]

Efficiency in the Metropolitan System

Prior to analyzing the judicial attempts to improve the distribution of household income within metropolitan areas, it is useful to consider what an "optimal" allocation of resources within an urban area might involve. I will use this normative discussion in the analysis of the consequences of the four equity objectives to point out the frequent conflict between equity norms and efficiency. The concept of optimality, or efficiency in resource allocation, has been described by a number of authors in the context of a somewhat distinct set of metropolitan models with varying assumptions and objectives. As a result, it is useful to distinguish among several ways in which inefficiencies might arise in a suboptimal system.

Consider a long-run Tiebout-like model of a system of local jurisdictions in which migration is costless and there are no interjurisdictional externalities and no biases in local budget determination. Assume also that public services can be provided at any level but must be available uniformly to all households within a jurisdiction. Then the efficient allocation of resources requires a varying pattern of public services among jurisdictions, with all households in each jurisdiction being satisfied in their public service demands. (I presume here that education is not a merit want, which society provides despite a lack of private demand.) Each household simply moves to the jurisdiction in which its preferred bundle of public service is provided, so that homogeneity of tastes for public services is a necessary condition for efficiency. With assessment rates assumed fixed, efficiency necessitates that all households live in identical houses, consume equal public services, and pay identical property tax bills.[13] For equilibrium to be maintained, any household paying more than it obtained in benefits could move to a more desirable community, while households wishing to purchase a small house and to pay less than their share would be excluded by a properly designed scheme, such as zoning. In effect, the zoning system is used to guarantee that all households consuming identical public services face the identical tax-price; and the property tax serves as a pure benefits tax, since the marginal benefit of public services just equals the marginal cost.[14]

Whenever the actual allocation of resources differs from the Tiebout allocation, inefficiencies can arise. It is difficult to fully characterize the sources of these inefficiencies, but for the present some illustrative examples should suffice. Tiebout presumed that his optimal allocation of resources would involve each community in the production of local public goods at a minimum average cost. Thus, to the extent that population and public services are otherwise allocated, a source of public-sector-production inefficiency is introduced. In addition, optimality requires that all households consume their desired public service bundles; the provision of service bundles at other than the desired level for all households results in inefficiency in consumption.

In his discussion of the optimality of group segregation, McGuire implies that when high- and low-income households are mixed in a community, house values will generally differ so that high-property-value households face higher tax prices than low-property-value households, even though both consume the identical level of public services.[15] McGuire illustrates quite clearly that both households could be made better off if the subsidy from high-income households to low-income households was a direct income transfer rather than a transfer involving distortions in tax-price. In effect, the tax-price distortion results from a property tax cum transfer-in-kind, which is clearly less efficient than an unconstrained income transfer.

Now consider a short-run model (without zoning) in which the housing stock is assumed to be fixed. Since house values vary within communities, tax prices also vary (assuming that all households face identical tax rates). As a result, low-income households with low demands for housing tend to migrate to communities in which they obtain positive fiscal residuals, and high-income households have an incentive to move from jurisdictions in which their fiscal residuals are negative. This creates a kind of inter-jurisdictional fiscal inefficiency in that, other things being equal, the distribution of the population among jurisdictions in the metropolitan area is not optimal. To see how the inefficiency is created, consider the impact on the metropolitan economy of a high-income household choosing to migrate from the central city to the suburbs. When the household leaves the central city, the fiscal base is likely to diminish, with relatively slight savings in public-service costs; the suburban community will gain in fiscal surplus as a result, but the members of the central city have no vote in the matter. In other words, in choosing to migrate to the suburbs, the high-income households ignore the costs imposed on the central city and the benefits conferred on the suburbs. Only if newcomers are taxed unequally to account for the social benefits and costs of a move can efficiency be achieved. This suggests that discriminatory taxation is a necessary condition for efficiency.[16]

To conclude the efficiency discussion, it is natural to ask to what extent the existing pattern of resources in most metropolitan areas approximates the efficient one; although such a question is clearly too complex to answer here, it is worthwhile to reflect briefly on some implications of our analysis. First, policies of assessment variation are likely to be necessary for efficiency, given the nature of fiscal externalities present in our metropolitan system. Second, zoning may be a useful fiscal tool for efficiency purposes, although there is no reason to believe that the existing zoning and land-use system is efficient. Third, a wide pattern of expenditure variation among jurisdictions is likely to be necessary for long-run efficiency.

2. INTRAJURISDICTIONAL EQUITY

The history of judicial involvement in the area of urban equity is long and involved. I have chosen to concentrate on the most recent developments, paying particular attention to the use of the equal protection doctrine of the Fourteenth Amendment as a basis for equity-oriented suits against states and local jurisdictions; focus will be on four objectives that are seen by some lawyers and commentators as means of improving the distribution of income within metropolitan areas and specifically of increasing the well-being of low-income households. In this section judicial attempts to achieve equity within jurisdictions are considered. First, each of the two intra-jurisdictional objectives, and the related case law, are discussed, and several questions are posed: (1) What are the objectives implicit in the court cases in each subject area? (2) Is the use of the equal protection doctrine likely to help in the attainment of those objectives? (3) Are other legal approaches to equity other than equal protection available? Second, I consider the efficiency consequences if the two objectives are met. Finally, I ask whether low-income households are likely to be helped or hurt by such reforms.

The Courts and Expenditure Equity

During the past decade a number of court cases, building on the equal protection clause of the Fourteenth Amendment, have served to define a set of equity requirements for the provision of local public services within each jurisdiction.[17] The present development of the law is far from requiring expenditure equality, and I believe that further legal attempts to attain intrajurisdictional equity will probably not be very successful. This conclusion, as well as some aspects of the analysis of the equal access (zoning) and equal tax-base (education) objectives, relies heavily on the interpretation of the role of the equal protection clause as an equity-oriented policy tool.

In the public service area, an equal protection suit may be brought if a local jurisdiction has provided its services so as to create a substantial disparity (in services) between identifiable classes of citizens in the community. If the government's action discriminates against a "suspect class" of citizens (such as blacks) or impairs a citizen's "fundamental interest" (such as the right to vote), the suit is very likely to be successful.[18] *Hawkins* v. *Town of Shaw*[19] is perhaps the best known of the suspect classification service equalization suits. In *Hawkins* a class action suit was brought on behalf of the black citizens of Shaw, Mississippi, which argued that blacks were receiving grossly unequal treatment in the provision of a number of public services, including lighting, water and sewers, and streets. As in many other service equalization cases, the plaintiffs relied entirely on the suspect classification aspect of equal protection; statistical evidence was presented to prove the existence of racial discrimination. Since courts generally defer to legislative judgments, the trial court ruled against the plaintiffs, holding that the actions of the local jurisdiction were not in violation of the law as long as they had a "rational basis." In reversing the trial court's decision, however, the U.S. Court of Appeals for the Fifth Circuit held that the statistical evidence made out a prima facie case of racial discrimination by Shaw. Since race is considered to be a suspect classification, Shaw was subjected to a stricter standard of review than the rational-basis standard.

The strict scrutiny standard was the more rigid alternative chosen by the appeals court. To survive the strict scrutiny test, a community must prove not only that a compelling interest justifies the treatment of the suspect group but also that such discrimination is necessary to achieve the community's objective.[20] If a compelling state interest cannot be demonstrated by the community, the court can order the locality to provide its services in a nondiscriminatory way. That is exactly what the appellate court ordered the town of Shaw to do. Thus, despite the "rational basis" for the current distribution of expenditures, the remedial action of equalizing service levels between the predominately black and the predominately white quarters of the town was required. By subjecting the actions of the local jurisdiction to this strict scrutiny analysis, *Hawkins* suggests that a court may order equality of service where discrimination has occurred with respect to members of a suspect class.[21]

Another case that was successfully litigated along lines somewhat similar to those in *Hawkins* was *Hobson* v. *Hansen*.[22] In *Hobson,* the court ruled that because of inequities in school spending, Washington, D.C., schools were depriving black and poor people of their right to equal educational opportunity. *Hobson* is interesting because of the remedy required by the court. Unable to deal with the problem of measuring educational output, the court required the removal of substantial disparities in average levels of per-pupil teaching expenditures between neighborhoods.[23] Clearly, the court set a precedent by relying on input measures rather than (or as a proxy for) output measures of equality. While there are exceptions, the usual stance of the court in service equality cases has been to avoid serious attempts to measure outputs.

In *Beal* v. *Lindsay*,[24] Puerto Rican residents of New York City brought a class-action suit claiming that their park had facilities, services, and repairs that were inferior to park facilities in white neighborhoods. In defense, the city did not attempt to argue that conditions in the parks were equal but provided evidence that inputs, or expenditures, had been equalized. The court, finding that output differences were related primarily to vandalism, ruled that equality of input was sufficient to satisfy the constitutional obligation of the jurisdiction; maintaining equality of output was held to be an unmanageable objective.

A related decision was handed down recently in *Burner* v. *Washington.*[25] In *Burner,* plaintiffs challenged racially discriminatory apportionment of police, recreation, and fire services, sidewalk maintenance, and refuse collection between two racially distinct Washington, D.C., neighborhoods. Placing heavy reliance on an Urban Institute study, the court ruled against the plaintiffs, holding that there was not substantially conclusive evidence of input differences between neighborhoods.[26]

While there have been some victories,[27] the suspect classification approach to equal service delivery has not been widely successful; in some cases, the plaintiffs were simply not able to prove that the municipal service at issue was allocated on the basis of race, while in others, the jurisdiction admitted past discrimination patterns but argued that it was presently acting to remedy the situation. Consider, for example, the case of *Hadnott* v. *City of Prattville.*[28] In *Hadnott,* the court agreed that general fund services had been allocated unfairly on the basis of race but found that a good-faith effort was being made to attain a more equitable distribution. However, the court declined to act against the city with respect to other services, because there was no evidence that blacks had been discriminated against in their right to petition for paving or water or sewage assessments. Of particular interest was the court's stance on the issue of whether equal protection can be applied when the services provided are allocated under a system of special assessments and user fees;[29] the implication was that equal protection was not relevant in *Hadnott,* because both black and white neighborhoods have the option of improving public services through the application of special assessments. Specifically, the court argued that when there was clear evidence of a difference in "ability and willingness to pay" for public services financed with special assessments or fees, expenditure equalization need not apply.

In *Hadnott* and other cases,[30] the court respected the right of the municipalities in question to provide services either through general funds or by special assessment. No attempt was made to decide what services might reasonably be provided by which method. As a result, municipalities may have the option of avoiding the requirements of the equal protection clause by using special assessments. An important instance of this possibility is *Citizens for Underground Equality* v. *City of Seattle.*[31] In that case, taxpayers in Seattle challenged a statute that authorized neighborhoods to form local improvement districts in order to collect special assessments for financing part of the cost of burying utility wires. The plaintiffs claimed that the statute was discriminatory against poor neighborhoods that might not be able to form improvement districts and take advantage of available matching funds. The court dismissed the taxpayers claim without mentioning *Hawkins* or *Hadnott*.[32] Given that the city did not abuse its discretion in determining the methods of financing the proposed improvement, the court was satisfied that each neighborhood had "an opportunity upon the same terms as all other areas of the city to underground its overhead utility writing."[33]

Citizens and *Hadnott* leave the legal limits of the use of special assessments open to question. Unless otherwise authorized by specific statute, a valid special assessment must be for the accommodation and convenience of inhabitants of an area, and must be of such a nature as to confer a special benefit upon the real property adjoining or near the improvement. One of the leading treatises on municipal corporation law,[34] asserts that it is reasonably clear that the following services can be provided by special assessment: street construction and repair; street sprinkling and cleaning; construction of sewers, ditches, and drains; street lighting; garbage collection; and provision of parking facilities. In contrast, construction and maintenance of municipal buildings and the cost of general education probably cannot be financed by special assessments.[35] The net result is that one of the consequences of continued equity attacks on the basis of suspect classification could be an expansion of the use of special assessments and fees as revenue raising devices.[36]

Equal protection analysis applies not only with respect to suspect classification but also when a pattern of discrimination is found with respect to a public service that the court considers to be a "fundamental interest." Just what constitutes a fundamental interest is a hotly debated topic, but traditionally only those interests expressly mentioned in the Constitution—such as the right to vote and the right to peacefully assemble—have qualified.

If a pattern of discrimination relates to a suspect classification, then, independently of the subject about which equal protection is sought, the court will apply the previously mentioned strict scrutiny standard. However, as the classification becomes less suspect, the court appears willing to apply the same strict scrutiny standard the more important the issue. In the extreme case of a fundamental interest like voting, strict review can be applied whether the pattern of discrimination is racially related or not. A number of court cases in the early 1970s involved attempts to extend the fundamental interest notion to public services such as education, welfare, housing, fire protection, and so on, but they were generally unsuccessful.[37]

The most significant case in this regard is *San Antonio Independent School District* v. *Rodriguez*,[38] in which the U.S. Supreme Court explicitly rejected the plaintiff's contention that public education could be raised to the level of a fundamental constitutional interest. In the words of Justice Powell, "the importance of a service performed by the State does not determine whether it must be regarded as fundamental for purposes of examination under the Equal Protection Clause . . . the key to discovering whether education is 'fundamental' . . . lies in assessing whether there is a right to education explicitly or implicitly guaranteed by the Constitution."[39] The Court also rejected the argument that a close relationship between education and the fundamental right to vote was sufficient to require strict judicial scrutiny of discrimination in service provision. Since *Rodriguez,* other cases have explicitly held that garbage collection, annexation, fire protection, and the right to live in a healthful environment are not fundamental interests.[40] I should point out, however, that Justice Powell also suggested (in dicta) that an absolute deprivation of educational benefits might lead the court to examine the actions of the jurisdiction more closely.[41] This appears to rule out the possibility of a school district closing its public facilities to avoid a desegregation order,[42] as Jackson, Mississippi, closed its swimming pools.[43]

While it is difficult to generalize or to forecast on the basis of a limited number of court cases, several tentative conclusions seem reasonable. First, the fundamental interest approach to local public service equity seems unlikely to win cases. Second, service equalization suits on the basis of "suspect class" are liable to be successful only when applied to services financed through general revenues that cannot be provided by special assessment. Third, the courts are inclined to rely on input measures of expenditure variation, rather than on output measures, as long as output measures remain elusive. Fourth, race appears to be the only suspect classification that the courts find relevant in service equalization suits. The fourth conclusion is especially important, because it suggests that successful service equalization suits will most probably concern jurisdictions with substantial black enclaves. Other legal or legislative approaches are necessary if intrajurisdictional expenditure equity is to be required of white jurisdictions and if poor white households are to benefit.

The Courts and Tax Equity

Because the property tax is the largest source of local revenue, attempts to improve tax equity within jurisdictions have concentrated on the property tax assessment process. As a rule, these attempts have focused on differential assessment practices and argued that intrajurisdictional variations in effective tax rates (the actual tax rates multiplied by the assessment-sales ratios) are inherently unfair. However, from a legal viewpoint, it is important to distinguish between two different types of tax "inequity": assessment rates (and thus effective tax rates) that vary within the same class of property; and different tax rates (or assessment practices) applied to each of various property classes.

Appeals based on the inequity within classes can be brought in a federal court, since the Supreme Court has held that the due process clause of the Fifth Amendment (as applied to the states under the Fourteenth Amendment) forbids a state from discriminating in its assessments within a given class of property.[44] Federal assessment suits by individual taxpayers, however, are unlikely to be successful unless the taxpayer can prove intentional and systematic discrimination by the local assessor.[45] Success requires either proof of overassessment relative to market value, or proof of assessment at full market value while other properties were intentionally underassessed.[46] Unfortunately, the latter is the more usual situation, and the more difficult to prove.

Appeals based on inequities between classes of property seem less likely to have a federal basis, since the Supreme Court has upheld the rights of states to classify property for the purpose of taxation and to assess various classes of property differently.[47] As a result, attempts to establish tax rate equality have proceeded and are likely to continue in the state courts. The reason is that many state constitutions require that all residential, commercial, and industrial property be taxed uniformly—a requirement that is not affected by the Supreme Court decisions just mentioned.[48] The greatest success has occurred in states with constitutional provisions that also require uniform full-market-value assessments;[49] proof of inequity is somewhat easier to demonstrate in such cases, and enforcement of full-market-value assessment leads to tax rate equality.

One of the important tax rate cases was *Hellerstein* v. *Assessor of the Town of Islip*.[50] Hellerstein, a property owner in the town, argued that the entire assessment roll was void because all assessments were based on a percentage of market value. The case is somewhat unusual because no attempt was made to claim that the plaintiff's individual property was treated unfairly relative to other properties in the community. The argument was simply that the assessments were not made in accordance with the property tax laws of the state of New York, which require full-value assessment. The New York Court of Appeals agreed that fractional assessment had long been a custom but was not satisfied with a defense so based. Rather, the court took into consideration the fact that (despite the existence of a State Equalization Board) fractional assessments make possible the receipt of proportionately more state aid by certain communities that intentionally underassess their property.[51] The court then directed the defendant township (Islip) to make all *future* assessments at full market value.

A more significant case, in terms of the magnitude of its impact, was *Sudbury* v. *Commissioner of Corp. and Tax*.[52] The case arose because, despite the Massachusetts State Tax Commission's responsibility to develop reasonable measures of fair market value as a basis for determining state aid allocations, substantial inequities remained. The plaintiffs, the town of

Sudbury and some of its officials, sought to clarify the role of the State Tax Commission and the commissioner of Corporations and Taxation in enforcing full-market-value assessments. The court ruled that the tax commission had the power and the duty to direct local assessors to take action to produce uniformity throughout the state. *Sudbury* thus d.ffers from *Hellerstein* by directly revising assessments for property in most jurisdictions throughout the state.

These cases suggest a possible trend toward substantial property-tax-assessment reform in many states. Whether such reform will actually occur on a large scale is not clear, however, since the decree in *Sudbury* is unusual. As a rule, courts seem reluctant to compel a state executive agency to reform its assessment practices and seem even more reluctant to supervise that reform. In addition, the ability of individuals to obtain assessment relief without attacking the tax system as a whole indicates the likelihood that cases such as *Sudbury* will occur infrequently.

A second issue that remains unresolved is whether the inequitable distributions of state aid resulting from fractional assessments are in violation of the Fourteenth Amendment. If such a decision were handed down, it would have a significant impact on tax and expenditure equity among—as well as within—jurisdictions. In *Levy* v. *Parker*,[53] the state's formula for providing property-tax relief to jurisdictions was overturned because the formula was sensitive to fractional assessments. In *Scarnato* v. *Parker*[54] the plaintiffs also argued that fractional assessments caused Louisiana's temporary state equalization plan for educational aid to be unconstitutional; but, citing *Rodriguez,* the district court held that the formula rationally furthered the state's purpose in reforming its system of financing schools.

Implications of the Equity-Oriented Objectives

The foregoing establishes that the courts are not likely to be fully successful in achieving each of the intrajurisdictional equity-oriented objectives of tax-rate and expenditure equality, but it is interesting to consider the implications of the successful enforcement of each of the objectives. If per-household public-service-expenditure equality were pursued by the courts or by the legislatures (which I view as unlikely), the end result would be the equality of input expenditures in many, if not all, public services (by neighborhood). The enforcement would most probably occur in the central city, where most low-income blacks reside, but intrajurisdictional expenditure equality could possibly be attained everywhere.

Equity considerations of the intrajurisdictional spending requirement were implicit in the point that, in some situations, equal expenditure inputs may well cause unequal and inequitable outputs. Clearly, compensatory spending programs must be kept intact if low-income households are to gain from the equal expenditure reform. However, the equity implications become more important when the probable responses of the economic actors in the system are taken into account. Consider the problem from the perspective of a central-city government in which the reform may be instituted; the change in expenditure distribution is liable to improve the well-being of the low-income population in the short run and to hurt those with high incomes (although the converse will be true if expenditures favor the poor to begin with). This will increase the probability of out-migration of high-income households and may well lead to a decline in the central-city fiscal base.[55] If the impact on the fiscal base is substantial, the long-run outcome could be a tangibly lower level of public service for most, or all, central-city residents.[56] Thus, the requirement of intrajurisdictional equity could hurt the central-city poor and increase interjurisdictional inequities.

One response of the central-city government (although unconstitutional) is to use its assessment-variation instrument to diminish the likelihood that high-fiscal-residual households will choose to migrate to the suburbs. However, further extensive use of assessment changes on either residential or commercial and industrial property will probably not be successful, since substantial use is already being made of the instrument. Other responses do not seem very promising; the initial conclusion appears likely to stand. In the long run, central-city expenditure equality requirements are liable to increase the rate of "flight" to the suburbs and may cause the income distribution of the metropolitan area to become more unequal.

If a suburban, within-jurisdiction policy of expenditure equality were pursued in isolation, it is doubtful that it would be effective, since suburban governments have more ways of avoiding the consequences of enforcement than do central-city governments. The issue is more interesting from the tax side, however, since there is good reason to expect assessment-ratio variations to be lessened in all metropolitan communities. Consider a policy of tax-rate equality and expenditure equality in the central city. If no strategic response occurs, the move toward equality of tax rates and expenditures in the central city may well improve the position of low-income households initially, but may make them worse-off in the long run if the rate of out-migration increases substantially. Of course, the result depends upon the extent to which assessments on all residential properties increase and on the assumptions one makes about the incidence of tax changes on commercial and industrial property. When tax-rate and expenditure equality policies are applied to suburbs, however, there are a number of responses or options available to avoid the equity consequences even when the expenditure-variation and tax-variation instruments are no longer in their control.

I have previously argued that a change (either up or down) in the level of expenditure may discourage the immigration of the poor, and that tighter fiscal zoning controls would presumably accomplish the same result. But it is important to realize that the community has important options available even if it decides to make no meaningful changes in the overall level of public services provided; the community can alter its revenue collection pattern, so as to rely more heavily on user charges and special assessments. Each of these revenue collection methods, although more efficient, approximates a benefits tax and is likely to be disadvantageous to low-income households when compared with the original property tax.

The difficulties of improving the distribution of real income through the local public sector are compounded by the direct conflict between equity and efficiency implicit in the tax-rate- and expenditure-equality objective. Consider the case in which all public services are homogeneous and all residents of a given community state their preferences for public services as a function of the level of expenditure in the community. Given that households in the community are inclined to vary in tastes and face different tax-prices, their demands for public expenditures will differ substantially. The legislation of expenditure equality clearly involves inefficiency in consumption, since most households will be forced to under- or overconsume public services. Likewise, inefficiency will result from the variance of tax-prices among households, even though public services are consumed equally. Assuming that governments have been concerned with the maximization of aggregate fiscal residuals, however, there is no reason to expect the actual behavior of governments prior to reform to coincide with the efficient solution. Recall that under the property tax system, an efficient outcome can only occur if, at the margin, the tax burden faced by a household just equals the marginal benefit to be obtained by consuming the public service (whether purely public or partly private). If locations are fixed, this necessary condition is equivalent to the condition that the *marginal* fiscal residual of all households is zero. Governments, however, are concerned with the total fiscal residual in the community and therefore will distribute expenditures, and tax burdens, so as to encourage households with high *average* fiscal residuals to remain in the community.

As a result of such government behavior in a world in which migration is costly, there is no reason to expect the actual distribution of expenditures to be efficient. This raises an interesting empirical issue: to what extent do public service demands deviate from the actual distribution of public services? In the absence of more extensive evidence, all that can be said is that the equalization of expenditures appears to introduce greater inefficiencies than exist under the present system. The problem is difficult from an empirical perspective, because an expenditure-equality reform is likely to bring about a change in tax-prices faced by households and thereby create a new optimal level of public services to be provided.

The conflict between efficiency and equity becomes especially clear when public services are recognized as nonhomogeneous and the courts are seen as willing to legislate expenditure equality for each public service rather than for the entire public service bundle. The problem is that households with different tastes may prefer to consume different mixes of public services. As a result, the requirement of expenditure equality in each service area *may* actually create inequities (and consumption inefficiencies) in situations that were at first equitable.

An additional source of inefficiency arises since, without further empirical evidence, the courts and the legislatures appear inclined to rely on expenditure variations (input measures) as evidence of inequalities, rather than seriously trying to deal with the problem of output measurement. The inefficiencies arise because, depending on the size of the community and the neighborhood environment, equal inputs may result in unequal outputs. For instance, if police output is measured by the probability of a crime being committed, higher inputs will probably be needed in the neighborhoods with the highest population densities.

A move to tax rate equality within the residential sector will be most likely to raise the tax-price of high-income households and lower the tax-price of low-income households. This will bring about a change in the desired level of consumption, and may, in fact, reduce the average discrepancy between desired and actual expenditures. However, nothing can be said with certainty about the efficiency change, because the actual level of public services provided may not be optimal. When the commercial and industrial tax base is taken into account, the analysis is even more complicated. Evidence from Massachusetts suggests that equal tax rates in most communities will increase the burden on residential property and decrease the burden on industrial property.[57] As a result, the tax-price facing most households may increase, lowering the public-service demands of many households, but again leaving the efficiency outcome in doubt. Finally, when we view the question from an interjurisdictional viewpoint, the equal-tax-rate solution looks clearly inefficient; given the presence of fiscal externalities in the system, the presence of varying effective tax rates in a community is a necessary prerequisite for interjurisdictional fiscal efficiency.

3. INTERJURISDICTIONAL EQUITY

A review of the recent history of school finance cases, comparing the impact of those cases whose decisions were based on either state constitutions or the United States Constitution, will introduce the discussion of the interjurisdictional equity objectives of equality of tax base and equality of access. Next, I will examine the use of state constitutions and the Fourteenth Amendment's equal protection clause in equal access cases. Third, I will analyze the income distributional consequences of both tax-base equality and equal access reforms, arguing that the responses of households and governments are likely to diminish the distributional impacts. Finally, the apparent conflict between the goal of equity and efficiency will be considered.

The Courts and Interjurisdictional Equity

The most important legal push toward interjurisdictional tax equity has concerned education. In the recent school finance cases, it is important to distinguish between suits brought in federal courts and those brought in state courts, since individual state suits cannot necessarily be generalized and may therefore not be relevant in other states.

Perhaps the best-known educational finance case is *Serrano* v. *Priest*.[58] In *Serrano,* the California Supreme Court responded to the inequality in levels of school spending that resulted from equal tax rates in jurisdictions having different property-tax bases. The court then invalidated the existing system of educational finance, in part because access to public education was deemed to be a "fundamental interest." The court held that the quality of a child's education should not be a function of the "wealth" (here considered to be a suspect classification) of his parents or of his community (unless there is a compelling state interest). The state was therefore required to restructure its school finance program so that communities with equal tax rates could raise equal school revenues. Equal expenditure per pupil was not required, nor was the state forced to eliminate the property tax as a means of financing school revenues.

As pointed out in section 2, some of the force of *Serrano* was taken away by the U.S. Supreme Court's decision in *Rodriguez. Rodriguez* is important not only because education was declared not to be a fundamental interest but also because the Court was unwilling to consider wealth as a suspect classification.[59] Thus, attempts (in the near future, at least) to argue for either intrajurisdictional or interjurisdictional equity using the Fourteenth Amendment in conjunction with reference to poverty, without explicit reference to race (an acknowledged suspect classification), seem likely to fail.

The obvious outcome of the Supreme Court's unwillingness to be flexible in its application of the equal protection argument is a substantial increase in the use of state courts to challenge the unequal provision of municipal services, within and among jurisdictions. One instructive case in the education area is *Robinson* v. *Cahill*.[60] In *Robinson,* the New Jersey Supreme Court struck down the existing means of school finance based on the state's constitutional requirement that "the Legislature shall provide for the maintenance and support of a thorough and efficient system of free public schools for the instruction of all children in this state between the ages of five and eighteen years."

It is difficult to predict the outcome of a state approach to interjurisdictional tax equity, but *Robinson* is not unique in this respect. A number of states have constitutional provisions that are similar to New Jersey's provision, while many others contain statements that have been or might be conducive to successful state suits. Thus, while it is unlikely that most states will explicitly follow New Jersey, it is conceivable that many states will strike down the existing finance system based solely on state constitutional grounds.[61]

Improvements in the welfare of low-income households can be achieved by expanding their opportunity to select among bundles of public services and taxes. In this sense, *Serrano* can be viewed as an equal access case as well as a school finance case, since *Serrano* requires school financing reforms that give citizens in low-wealth jurisdictions a greater opportunity to consume adequate levels of education. However, most access cases have concentrated on the ability of low-income households to obtain housing in high-income communities and on the constitutionality of minimum-lot zoning provisions.

In the housing area, the court has been willing to utilize the equal protection clause to regulate the use of building permits by local jurisdictions. *Gautreaux* v. *Chicago Housing Authority*[62] is especially pertinent because the defendants were found to have violated the plaintiffs' Fourteenth Amendment rights by selecting public housing sites and assigning tenants on the basis of race. In another case, the federal courts ruled against a municipality that refused a housing project permission to use municipal water and sewer systems.[63] Finally, the equal protection clause has been utilized in cases in which zoning ordinances were seen to be restrictive and racially motivated. For example, in *Kennedy Park Homes Ass'n.* v. *City of Lackawanna,*[64] the city council had adopted a moratorium on new subdivisions and had zoned certain acreage, including a proposed low-income housing project site, as open space and park area, despite a planning recommendation to the contrary. The court ruled for the plaintiff on equal protection grounds.

Despite these cases, the use of federal equal protection is limited, because for all practical purposes, an explicit proof of racial discrimination is needed. In fact, the difficulty of proving that local government decisions are racially motivated has been increased (although not to the point of impossibility) by recent Supreme Court decisions. In both *Washington* v. *Davis* and *Village of Arlington Heights* v. *Metropolitan Housing Development,*[65, 66] the court clearly indicated that the action of a community will not be held unconstitutional simply because the impact is racially disproportionate. Recall that in *Hawkins* v. *Shaw* it was sufficient, according to the appeals court, for the plaintiffs to prove that most blacks had received and were receiving unequal municipal services. In *Arlington Heights,* however, the fact that 40 percent of those eligible for a multifamily housing project were minorities did not lead the court to apply a stricter level of review.[67] As Justice Powell said, "Proof of racially discriminatory intent or purpose is required to show a violation of the Equal Protection Clause."[68]

In the zoning area, the Court has also shown a reluctance to utilize the equal protection clause. For example, in *Belle Terre* v. *Boraas* the U.S. Supreme Court upheld a local ordinance restricting land use to one-family dwellings.[69] Lower courts have generally been unwilling to overturn large-lot zoning, given the Supreme Court's rejection of wealth as a suspect classification and housing as a fundamental interest.[70]

As in the intrajurisdictional equity area, the natural consequence of the Supreme Court's position has been an increased use of the state courts in the struggle for equal access. Perhaps the best known of the equal-access zoning cases is *Southern Burlington County NAACP* v. *Mt. Laurel*.[71] In *Mt. Laurel,* the New Jersey Supreme Court affirmed a trial court recommendation that the community of Mt. Laurel be required to devise a zoning plan that would utilize undeveloped land in such a manner as to accommodate the community's "fair share" of the region's low- and moderate-income housing needs.[72] If enforced, the outcome of the *Mt. Laurel* decision would ensure that low-income households are not restricted in their access to low-income suburban housing and suburban public services because of exclusionary zoning. The fair-share housing plan is limited in its scope, however, because it applies only to communities with undeveloped land; many of the older suburban communities have little undeveloped land and may not be affected by the *Mt. Laurel* decision.

It is difficult to generalize about the likelihood of most states ruling against exclusionary zoning, because suitable cases have not been brought to the courts.[73] However, there is no reason that the decision in *Mt. Laurel* could not be extended to other jurisdictions. The New Jersey Constitution requires that zoning regulations (a use of police power) must promote the general welfare. The court simply ruled that zoning regulations restrict the options of low-income households and thereby hurt the general welfare. Since most state constitutions contain provisions concerning the relationship between the delegation of police power and the general welfare of the population, additional *Mt. Laurel*-like decisions seem possible.

Once again it is difficult to summarize the general trend in the courts, but several conclusions do seem clear. First, despite the U.S. Supreme Court's unwillingness to treat income as a suspect class or to declare education to be a fundamental interest, a strong stimulus for the reform of educational finance will probably be brought through the state courts. Whether based on equal protection grounds, as in *Serrano,* or on other state constitutional grounds, many state suits have been and are likely to be successful. Second, despite some successes, the use of the federal equal protection doctrine in equal-access cases is likely to be limited, because proof of intent to racially discriminate appears to be required for a successful suit. The present U.S.

Supreme Court seems unwilling (in these cases) to rely solely on statistical evidence to prove discrimination, since statistics themselves imply nothing about intent. Of course, the view of the Supreme Court could change over time, but for the present, the state courts appear to provide a more fruitful avenue for plaintiffs pursuing equal-access cases. However, present evidence suggests that equal-access cases such as *Mt. Laurel* are not liable to set a trend, despite the presence of a constitutional basis for similar actions in many state constitutions.

The Implications of Tax-base Equality

I argued previously that in *Serrano* (and in some of the other cases) the Court ruled that *if* property taxation is used to finance school expenditures, it must be done so that children in districts with low fiscal bases per pupil will have the same opportunity or access to tax bases (supplemented by state aid) that finance education as do children in high fiscal-base-per-pupil districts. I interpret this requirement to mean that, if the property tax remains the primary local revenue source, per pupil fiscal bases must be *equalized* across all jurisdictions in the state. There is some disagreement in the literature as to whether the courts implied other necessary conditions, but in my view, the equal per-pupil fiscal-base requirement is the only explicit requirement that follows from *Serrano* if one chooses to rely on the local property tax and maintain local fiscal autonomy.[74]

A number of fiscal-base equalizing schemes have been proposed, but the most widely discussed has been the district power equalizing scheme of Coons, Clune, and Sugarman.[75] In one version, the authors propose that the state allocate aid to local education in such a manner that each jurisdiction is guaranteed an identical *key* per-pupil fiscal base from which to raise school expenditures (this is often called the *district power equalizing plan*—DPE). As a result, a tax levy of one mill in each community will raise an identical amount of revenues per pupil. Communities that are lower in fiscal base per pupil than the key per-pupil fiscal-base level receive subsidies from the state, while those that are higher contribute funds. It is important to note that the *Serrano* decision did not imply equality of expenditures (nor does DPE); nor did it imply that after the reform, expenditures had to be uncorrelated with wealth (nor does DPE). Property tax bases may be equalized, but the choice of tax rate and thus total spending would remain under the control of local jurisdiction.

In my view, one major equity concern of reformers ought to be impact of DPE on low-income households, not on expenditures directly. In this case, equality of expenditures is not considered to be an end in itself, even though one might argue for such an objective on equal opportunity grounds. To clarify the discussion I will first describe the probable initial equity impact when the state aid system is altered to follow a DPE plan. Then I will consider the likely outcome when communities and households respond to the reform.

In terms of initial impact, DPE *may* cause the pattern of expenditures among jurisdictions to become more equal. This can best be seen by analyzing the effect of the reform on the tax price of education faced by the decisive household in each community. Recall that the tax-price of education is defined as the cost to the household of financing an extra dollar per pupil of local school expenditures. As a result, the tax-price varies directly with the value of the family's house, and inversely with the value of fiscal base per pupil and with the percentage of the tax base that is nonresidential. Initially, communities with low fiscal bases per pupil will receive additional aid, thus raising their effective fiscal base per pupil to the level of the key community. This implies a lower tax-price and a demand for more school expenditures. Analogously, decisive households in jurisdictions with high per-pupil fiscal bases will face an increased tax-price and will, other things being equal, demand a lower level of school expenditure. Thus, the extent to which expenditure patterns are equalized depends, of course, on the extent to which low-fiscal-base communities were originally spending less on schools than were high-fiscal-base communities and on the price elasticity of the demand for education.[76]

There are several reasons why the initial impact of such reforms on low-income households may be small and possibly inequitable. The primary reason is that low-fiscal-base communities are often middle- and high-income suburban communities, while central-city jurisdictions with substantial numbers of low-income households are often high in fiscal base because of the extensive commercial and industrial base. To the extent that low-fiscal-base communities actually spend more than central-city communities, the effect of the reforms may be increased inequality. Some corroborating evidence is provided by a comparison study of central cities in large metropolitan areas by Netzer.[77] Netzer found that central cities have lower per-pupil spending levels than suburban communities, but that fiscal base per pupil in central cities was *not* consistently lower than in other school districts. In fact, more than half of the central cities studied had higher than average levels of measured fiscal base per pupil.[78]

The distributional impact may be muted because fiscal base per pupil and income are not very highly correlated, making the link between base equalization and income equality a weak one at best. The correlations between income and fiscal base per pupil are likely to vary substantially among states, but recent evidence from Michigan is suggestive. For a sample of 177 school districts, high-income districts tended to be residential in nature (the correlation between the income variable and percentage residential was .43) so that the simple correlation between fiscal base per pupil and percent residential was actually negative (—.32).[79] As a result, the correlation between the fiscal base per pupil and the percentage of families with incomes above $15,000 was only .28.

However, the problem does not lie completely with the weak correlation between fiscal base and income. Since "wealth" is normally measured in terms of base per public-school pupil, the demographic and school attendance pattern of each jurisdiction is also important. Central-city jurisdictions often house an older population with fewer children; these jurisdictions may look quite "wealthy" when in fact they have lower than average incomes. This effect is compounded by the parochial school attendance of a substantial number of children in many central cities.[80]

Now consider the long-run implications of DPE reform, when households are presumed to respond to the changing aid structure. Initially, tax-prices will fall in those communities with low fiscal bases and rise in those communities with high fiscal bases. The long-run result will be a migration of families away from high-fiscal-base areas toward low-base areas. When account is taken of the effects of this migration on land values, DPE is likely to cause positive capitalization in low-fiscal-base areas (higher land prices), and vice versa. From the point of view of the average household in the low-fiscal-base community, the increased value of its house will tend to increase the tax-price that it faces (although it might lower the tax rate in the community). Likewise, the tax-price faced by the average household in the high base community will fall somewhat. At the least this will mitigate the previously described tendency toward expenditure equality, and if the capitalization effects are substantial, the DPE reform *might* tend to produce greater inequality in terms of expenditures, which is inequitable from the point of view of low-income households. Of course, to the extent that low-income households own houses in low-fiscal-base areas, they will enjoy a gain in wealth as a result of the capitalization process.

Finally, DPE is likely to increase the incentive of high-income households to send their children to private schools. To the extent that this outcome is important, the level of public education provided to poor families in those jurisdictions could fall, and although schools may be less crowded, greater income segregation of households could result.[81] The empirical evidence is not yet conclusive, but the previous analysis suggests that reforms promoting equal fiscal base per pupil may or may not tend to equalize expenditures and are likely to have a much less beneficial impact on low-income households than might have been expected. The benefits will be divided somewhat unequally, with low-income families residing in fiscally "poor" suburbs made better off, but with the outcome for center-city low-income families in doubt.[82]

To summarize, note that there are two "problems" that hinder the described DPE's effectiveness in redistributing income. First, there is a measurement problem that arises because fiscal base per pupil is not an appropriate base upon which to structure a wealth or income redistribution plan. This follows in part because the "benefits" of an industrial base may be more apparent than real and in part because adjustments for public school attendance tend to hurt those central city schools that are fiscally poor. Second, there is a conceptual problem that arises because the benefits of schooling are capitalized into land values. As a result, education is paid for by homeowners in two parts: the increased purchase price of their houses due to capitalization, and the direct property-tax payments. Thus, the equalization of fiscal base per pupil may unfairly penalize households in high-fiscal-base communities that have partially paid for their education in the purchase price of their homes.

Since a district power equalization scheme will have no direct impact on intrajurisdictional assessments and expenditures, the most important efficiency issues that arise concern interjurisdictional expenditure patterns. To the extent that a DPE plan does tend to equalize expenditures, the equity and efficiency goals are in conflict. Equalization of expenditures among districts involves a lesser breadth of public service choice for metropolitan households, and therefore of efficiency in Tiebout's sense. DPE also involves an intentional restructuring of state aid to school districts, and thus a restructuring of school subsidies. Since the objectives of such subsidies relate to equity and are not based on any technical externalities relating to the provision of education among districts, it is difficult to see how the restructuring of state aid in itself will affect the efficiency of the system.

The Implications of Improvements in Access

As described previously, there have been a number of cases in recent years in which the courts have struck down land-use plans and municipal ordinances that restricted the access of low-income families to suburban jurisdictions. While the motivations for restrictive land-use policies may vary, the fiscal advantage is to restrict the access of low-income families to the community's public services (unless adequate payment is made). A court-enforced or legislative end to minimum-lot zoning and other housing-related restrictions on migration is very likely to increase the opportunities for suburban migration with the net result of the increased income heterogeneity of suburbs being an increase in net fiscal benefits to the poor (although some high-income households will suffer windfall losses). With zoning and income homogeneity, no such redistribution is possible. From an empirical point of view, the magnitude of the income redistribution resulting from the zoning change is clearly an important issue.

One problem is that zoning may not be a binding constraint for most central-city low-income households choosing a housing location. This point can be seen more clearly in the context of a simple monocentric urban model in which all households are assumed to work in a central business district. With reasonable assumptions, the equilibrium outcome is for low-income households to reside in the central city and high-income households in the suburbs. In the context of such a model, it is entirely possible that suburban zoning will not be constraining. In a model with suburban jobs, however, the identical zoning ordinance may be severely constraining. The crucial issue relates, therefore, to the growth of suburban jobs in urban areas. To the extent that jobs suitable to low-income households move to the suburbs, zoning laws tend to become more exclusionary, and to the extent that they do, firms are likely to be discouraged from locating in the suburbs where a pool of unskilled labor is unavailable.[83] It is therefore extremely difficult to separate the impact of zoning on residential access of the poor from other access-restricting factors, such as lack of job opportunities, high transaction costs, and discrimination.

There is an additional reason why zoning might not be a binding constraint to low-income migrants. If zoning is binding, there will be market incentives to bring about zoning changes—most probably through the passage of amendments rather than the redrafting of ordinances. Maser, Riker, and Rosett argue that only if the political and economic power of those likely to gain by zoning outweighs the power of those likely to lose is zoning inclined to become constraining.[84] They present empirical evidence that is consistent with this view, arguing that in Monroe County, New York, zoning either has no effect or "it achieves its effect without significant distortion of the market allocation of land." Of course, there are arguments and evidence to the contrary.[85]

But in the end, the courts have been forced to base their decisions on rather flimsy statistical evidence; clearly, additional empirical research would be helpful.

Now, consider the response of suburban governments to the elimination of zoning as a policy instrument. To the extent that tax and expenditure variation instruments are not constrained by intrajurisdictional equity legislation or court enforcement, suburban governments will probably increase the use of both—to the disadvantage of low-income households that might potentially migrate into the community. If such options are no longer open, some of the other alternatives previously discussed might also come into play. As a result, the enforcement of exclusionary zoning cases is unlikely to improve the status of low-income households very much, unless some control is available over other suburban policy instruments, and the strategic fiscal-base oriented responses of the suburban communities can be limited.

Unlike the expenditure and tax cases, the enforcement of the court's new view on zoning involves the *removal* of a constraint. Whether the removal of the minimum-lot housing constraint actually leads to an improvement in efficiency depends very much on one's view of the existing zoning system.

There are a number of reasons why the actual system of zoning and land-use controls is not efficient. Most important are the existence of externalities and the lack of sufficient jurisdictions to provide "adequate" choice for the households determined to "vote with their feet." As a result, even among suburban jurisdictions, governments may well find it advantageous and feasible to *overuse* the minimum-lot-size requirement in order to increase the fiscal surplus obtained from new migrants.

The interesting empirical question is, To what extent does the existing zoning and land-use system deviate from the "efficient system"? From our point of view, the evidence is mixed and inconclusive. Evidence presented by Hamilton and Mills and Puryear provide some support for the Tiebout view by suggesting that a higher concentration of high-income households in suburban jurisdictions would be expected without the Tiebout-like incentives.[86, 87] Pack and Pack,[88] however, provide some evidence to suggest that suburban communities are much less homogeneous than would be expected from the purest form of the Tiebout model. The subject area is clearly an important one and needs further empirical study.

SUMMARY AND CONCLUSIONS

The major focus of this chapter has been whether the courts have been and are likely to be an effective force for bringing about a more equitable distribution of real household income within metropolitan areas. It is easy to argue that state and, particularly, federal levels of government are more appropriately equipped to handle income distribution. However, from a pragmatic point of view, it is understandable that reformers have attempted to achieve their desired equity norms through the local public sector. Unfortunately, my prognosis for the success of such legal attempts to attain equity is not favorable, for several reasons. First, the legal mandates for each of the four equity-oriented objectives (intrajurisdictional tax and expenditure equality, interjurisdictional tax-base equality, and equal access) are not strong. This is especially true of the intrajurisdictional-service-provision cases, in which the use of the Constitutional equal protection clause seems to offer a limited avenue for success. It is also true to a large extent in the equal access cases, in which the Supreme Court is requiring evidence of intent to discriminate on racial grounds rather than relying on statistical evidence of unequal access to low-income housing by race. Second, even if the courts were to intervene successfully to achieve each of the equity objectives, the long-term impact on the distribution of income is not likely to be substantial, primarily because suburban jurisdictions have a number of available policy options that will probably be used to mitigate the effect of the court-determined equity requirements. Finally, it is important to realize that there may be substantial efficiency costs if the equity norms are mandated. For example, in terms of allocative efficiency in the metropolitan system of government, a movement toward equality in service provision may limit the public-service-consumption choice of households. The inefficiency would arise even if all households had the same money income. In this case, different tastes might cause households to choose different bundles of public services. Court-mandated expenditure equality, while seemingly equitable, is in fact horizontally inequitable (and inefficient) since it forces households with identical money incomes (assuming costless mobility) to attain different levels of utility, or real income.

Are the courts really a useful vehicle for improving the distribution of income? My analysis suggests that the answer is a qualified no. To the extent that any of the equity norms have been partially achieved, legislative action (as in the school finance cases) has usually been responsible. It is simply extremely difficult to bring about a substantial improvement in the distribution of income without legislative intervention, either at the state or federal level. This is especially true when one considers the kinds of strategic response available to suburban jurisdictions faced with a court-ordered equity mandate. The legal approach is of necessity a piecemeal one (and the judicial process makes monitoring difficult), while, in principle, a legislative approach can deal simultaneously with a set of policy options.

Despite these arguments, I have qualified the answer to the question of the role of the courts for several reasons. First, legal mandates can and do change over time, so that the kinds of equity decisions made by the courts may look substantially different one or two decades from now. Second, even though the courts by themselves are not likely to achieve the equity norms, legal decisions can and do have an important impact on legislative policy—school finance is· a case in point. A number of states began to reform their school financial-aid systems before legal suits were brought, but in some of these cases, school-finance decisions in other states probably stimulated the reforms. Third, the negative forecast of the success of the four-equity objectives in redistributing income arose in part because the proposed reforms were not well thought out. Reform strategies that are more carefully designed to take account of potential responses of all metropolitan jurisdictions may be more successful. Finally, the legal approach to equity may be the proper one if one's objectives go beyond the goal of improving the distribution of income. For example, if equality of educational opportunity or, possibly, educational output were a goal in itself, the courts might be a promising arena for reform. Likewise, if the right of access to adequate housing is a goal in itself, direct legal attacks

may be successful, even though the overall distributional impact is small
or nonexistent.

NOTES

1. Allowing for the possibility of migration would probably strengthen the conclusions presented in sections 2 and 3, since the possibility of interurban migration of
high-income households makes intraurban income redistribution difficult.

2. In fact, a substantial number of low-income households reside outside the central city in many SMSAs, and suburban jurisdictions are not nearly as homogenous
in income as might be suggested by a strict interpretation of the Tiebout model of
metropolitan location. See, for example, H. Pack and J. R. Pack (1976), "Metropolitan Fragmentation and Suburban Homogeneity."

3. Output levels may differ among communities with identical input expenditures,
not only because input prices vary but also because the size of one community may
allow for economies of scale and more efficient production.

4. The tax-price is described in G. E. Peterson, "The Demand for Public Schooling," Urban Institute Working Paper no. 1207-28, 1973, and D. L. Rubinfeld,
"Voting in a Local School Election: A Micro Analysis," *Review of Economics and
Statistics* 59 (1977): 30–42. Other things being equal, a lower tax-price makes a
household better off, because it expands the household's budget set. Note, however,
that it is possible for households facing lower tax-prices to consume lower public
expenditures than households facing higher tax-prices. Expenditure levels are poor
measures of welfare because they vary with preferences for public goods as well as
budget opportunities.

5. Changes in tax burdens may arise either through increases in nominal tax rates
(without comparable benefits) or through increases in commercial and/or industrial
property tax assessment rates. Land-use changes may adversely affect the position of
existing firms by increasing the costs of expansion or of meeting existing statutory
requirements, but they are more likely to discourage the immigration of firms—either
by adding to development costs or simply by limiting the extent and type of new
commercial and industrial development.

6. J. Rothenberg, "Local Decentralization and the Theory of Optimal Government," in *The Analysis of Public Output,* ed. J. Margolis (New York: National
Bureau of Economic Research, 1970), pp. 31–64, and M. J. White, "Fiscal Zoning
in Fragmented Metropolitan Areas," in *Fiscal Zoning and Land Use Controls,* ed.
E. S. Mills and W. Oates (Lexington, Mass.: D. C. Heath, 1975).

7. The competing fiscal and environmental considerations involved with the loca-
tion of firms in suburban communities are described by W. A. Fischel, "Fiscal and
Environmental Considerations in the Location of Firms in Suburban Communities,"
Fiscal Zoning and Land Use Controls, ed. E. S. Mills and W. Oates, and M. J. White,
"Fiscal Zoning and Firm Location," in *Fiscal Zoning and Land Use Controls,* ed.
Mills and Oates. In the long run, competition among governments may bid away
some or all of these fiscal surpluses.

8. Using evidence provided in G. Sternlieb, *Housing Development and Municipal
Costs* (New Brunswick, N.J.: Center for Urban Policy Research, 1974), and L.
Sagalyn and G. Sternlieb, *Zoning and Housing Costs: The Impact of Land Use Controls on Housing Prices* (New Brunswick, N.J.: Center for Urban Policy Research,
1973), M. J. White, "Zoning for No Growth: A New Trend?" *Policy Analysis,* (in
press), provides an example in which high-rise apartments generate fiscal surpluses,
whereas single-family houses generate fiscal deficits.

9. For example, O. Oldman and H. Aaron ("Assessment Sales Ratios under the
Boston Property Tax," *National Tax Journal* 17 [1965]: 40) found that Boston

assessment ratios ranged from .341 for single-family houses to .650 for multi-family units in more than one structure (two-family houses or apartments were at .412, three- to five-family apartments at .520, and six- or more-family apartments at .579). D. M. Holland and O. Oldman ("Estimating the Impact of Full Value Assessment on Taxes and Values of Real Estate in Boston," in *Metropolitan Financing Principles and Practice,* ed. G. F. Break [Madison: University of Wisconsin Press, 1977]) used data for the state of Massachusetts and found current effective tax rates on new commercial property to be substantially lower (3.7%) than on old commercial property (10.6%). Residential properties faced an average effective property tax rate of 5.5%. The magnitude of the impact of such a policy depends upon the extent to which firms and households respond to tax incentives, but the potential for such a policy instrument seems clear. For details on this issue, see G. E. Peterson, A. P. Solomon, H. Madjid, and W. C. Apgar, Jr., *Property Taxes, Housing, and the Cities* (Lexington, Mass.: Lexington Books, 1973), and R. F. Engle, "De Facto Discrimination in Residential Assessments," *National Tax Journal* 28 (1975): 445–51.

10. The actual pattern of such expenditure variation is substantially more difficult to measure than assessment variation, and patterns are inclined to vary service by service. In the case of education, for example, the overall pattern of expenditure seems to favor high-income families, although the presence of compensatory educational spending tends to complicate matters. For partial support of this view, see M. T. Katzman, *The Political Economy of Urban Schools* (Cambridge, Mass.: Harvard University Press, 1971), P. C. Sexton, *Education and Income: The Inequality of Opportunity in Our Public Schools* (New York: Viking Press, 1971), A. A. Summers and B. L. Wolfe, "Intradistrict Distribution of School Resources to the Disadvantaged: Evidence for the Courts," (Philadelphia: Federal Reserve Bank Papers, July 1, 1976), and the evidence in *Hobson* v. *Hansen,* 269 F. Supp. 401 (D.D.C. 1967) aff'd sub. nom. *Smuck* v. *Hobson* 408 F.2d 175 (D.C. Cir. 1969), and *Brown* v. *Board of Education of City of Chicago,* 386 F. Supp. 110 (N.D. Ill, 1974). Other noneducational studies of interest include J. C. Weicher, "The Allocation of Police Protection by Income Class," *Urban Studies* 8 (1971): 207–20, and C. S. Benson and P. B. Lund, "Neighborhood Distribution of Local Public Services" (Berkeley: Institute of Government Studies, University of California, 1967). Some of the methodological issues involved in measuring the income-distribution impact of public-good provision are discussed in W. B. Neenan, *Political Economy of Urban Areas* (Chicago: Markham, 1972), and H. Aaron and M. McGuire, "Public Goods and Income Distribution," *Econometrica* 38 (1970): 908–20.

11. For evidence that proximity to industry lowers residential property values, see W. Stull, "Community Environment, Zoning, and the Market Value of Single-Family Homes," *Journal of Law and Economics* 18 (1975): 535–557. For a theoretical discussion of the link between zoning and labor markets, see D. L. Rubinfeld, "Suburban Zoning: A General Equilibrium Analysis," *Journal of Regional Science,* vol. 18 (1978). Zoning and housing market issues are discussed in various forms in White, "Fiscal Zoning in Fragmental Metropolitan Areas"; J. Ohls, R. C. Weisberg, and M. J. White, "The Effect of Zoning on Land Values," *Journal of Urban Economics* 1 (1974): 428–44, and P. N. Courant, "On the Effect of Fiscal Zoning on Land and Housing Values," *Journal of Urban Economics* 3 (1976): 88–94.

12. There remains considerable disagreement as to whether suburban zoning is motivated for fiscal or racial reasons. In one interesting analysis, E. J. Branfman, B. I. Cohen and D. M. Trubek ("Measuring the Invisible Wall: Land Use Controls and the Residential Pattern of the Poor," *Yale Law Journal* 82 [1973]: 483) provide some support for the view that zoning and other land-use controls do affect the income clustering of households and that the motivation for such controls is at least partially racial.

13. If tastes for housing differ, efficiency could arise with varying house sizes, but only if assessment rates vary to equate marginal benefits to marginal costs.

14. See B. W. Hamilton, "Zoning and Property Taxation in a System of Local Government," *Urban Studies* 12 (1975): 205–11. If there is exclusionary zoning, low-income (i.e., low-value) housing may be scarce and therefore capitalized upward in value, raising the tax-price, while the value of high-income housing might be capi-

talized downward. This issue is discussed in B. W. Hamilton, "Capitalization of Intra-jurisdictional Differences in Local Tax Prices," *American Economic Review* 66 (1976): 743–53.

15. M. McGuire, "Group Segregation and Optimal Jurisdictions," *Journal of Political Economy* 82 (1974): 112–132.

16. Interjurisdictional fiscal inefficiency is described in J. Buchanan and C. Goetz, "Efficiency Limits of Fiscal Mobility: An Assessment of the Tiebout Model," *Journal of Public Economy* 1 (1972): 25. Of course, fiscal inefficiency can occur when fiscal factors cause any distortion in the metropolitan land market. For example, suppose that, absent any fiscal factors, a firm chooses to locate in the central city. If a fiscal distortion causes the firm to move to a new urban location, the pattern of urban land prices will change, with, for example, suburban land prices rising and central-city land prices falling. This may increase the physical size of the urban area, adding to transportation costs and lowering the total social product.

17. Municipal corporations have long been subject to common-law rules concerning the equitable distribution of public services, which have been construed to require equal provision of services in certain cases: *Veach* v. *City of Phoenix*, 102 Ariz. 195, 427 P.2d 335 (1967), fire protection; *Travaine* v. *Maricopa Co.*, 9 Ariz. App. 228, 450 P.2d 1021 (1969), public sewers. In addition, there is some support for the public utility doctrine, which holds that a municipality providing services similar to those provided by privately owned utilities has a duty to serve all of the members within its territorial boundaries in an equal and nondiscriminatory manner. This doctrine has been limited to utility-oriented services such as telephone, water, gas, electricity, and transportation. See Abascal, "Municipal Services and Equal Protection. Variations on a Theme by *Griffin* v. *Illinois*," *Hastings Law Journal* 20 (1969): 1367.

18. For further details, see "Developments in the Law—Equal Protection," *Harvard Law Review* 82 (1969: 1065). Comment: "The Evolution of Equal Protection: Education, Municipal Service, and Wealth," *Harvard Civil Rights—Civil Liberties Law Review* 7 (1972): 103, and Fessler and May, "The Municipal Service Equalization Suit: A Case of Action in Quest of a Forum," in *Public Needs and Private Behavior in Metropolitan Areas,* ed. J. Jackson (Lexington, Mass.: Ballinger, 1975).

19. *Hawkins* v. *Town of Shaw* 303 F. Supp. 1162 (N.D. Miss. 1969), rev'd, 437 F.2d 1286 (5th Cir. 1971) aff'd en banc, 461 F.2d, 1171 (5th Cir. 1972).

20. In some cases the jurisdiction must also show that there are no reasonable alternative means of accomplishing the stated purpose without discriminating and that the classification of citizens (the suspect group) is neither impermissably broad nor underinclusive. See *Shapiro* v. *Thompson,* 394 U.S. 618 (1969), and "Developments in the Law—Equal Protection."

21. See *Nebbia* v. *New York,* 291 U.S. 502 (1934), *McGowan* v. *Maryland,* 366 U.S. 420 (1961), and *Williamson* v. *Lee Optical Co.* 348 U.S. 483 (1955).

22. *Hobson* v. *Hansen*. See also *Brown* v. *Board of Education*.

23. The remedy required that pupil expenditures be equalized within 5 percent of the average, with exceptions made for compensatory and special education programs. However, the court did not explicitly require equal spending for black and white students.

24. *Beal* v. *Lindsay,* 468 F.2d 287 (2d Cir. 1972).

25. *Burner* v. *Washington,* 399 F. Supp. 44 (D.D.C. 1975).

26. See P. B. Bloch, "Equality of Distribution of Police Services—A Case Study of Washington, D.C." (Washington, D.C.: Urban Institute, 1974). Another relevant case, as discussed by B. Ellickson ("Suburban Growth Controls: An Economic and Legal Analysis," *Yale Law Journal* 86 [1977]: 385), is *Manjares* v. *Newton,* 64 Cal. 2d 365, 411 P. 2d 901, 49 Cal. Rptr. 805 (1966), in which the Supreme Court of California regarded free school busing as a necessary requirement for equality of educational output.

27. See, for example, *Norwalk CORE* v. *Norwalk Redevelopment Agency,* 395 F.2d 920 (2d Cir. 1968), in which the court ruled that the defendants did not assure, or attempt to assure, relocation for Negro and Puerto Rican displacees to the same extent as they did for whites when planning and implementing an urban renewal project. In *Selma Improvement Assoc.* v. *Dallas County Commission,* 339 F. Supp.

477 (S.D. Ala. 1972), the court ordered the defendant to appropriate funds for planning and constructing paved streets in black residential areas. In *Franklin* v. *City of Marks,* 439 F. 2d 665 (5th Cir. 1971), *in dicta,* the court stated that the defendant could not avoid a discriminatory claim by deannexing an area.

28. *Hadnott* v. *City of Prattville,* 309 F. Supp. 967 (M.D. Ala. 1970).

29. See F. T. Goldberg, "Equalization of Municipal Services: The Economics and Serrano and Shaw," *Yale Law Journal* 82 (1972): 89; and Comment: "The Evolution of Equal Protection."

30. In *Fire* v. *City of Winner,* 352 F. Supp. 925 (D.S.D. 1972), the court refused to order the equalization of similar services between an Indian and a white portion of the community. During the lawsuit, the defendant began to remedy its discriminatory provision of surface water drainage ditches, fire hydrants, and street lights. The court found that the *remaining* improvements to which the plaintiff attached discrimination—street paving, sidewalks, and sewage facilities—were reasonable attributes of property ownership for which the plaintiff might pay by means of special assessment. According to the court, "the Equal Protection Clause was never intended to be a constitutional command forcing municipalities to assume the responsibilities of landowners for the development of their land." (Ibid., p. 928.)

31. *Citizens for Underground Equality* v. *City of Seattle,* 6 Wash. App. 338, 492 P. 2d 1071 (1972).

32. 51 ALR 3d 943, 945.

33. *Citizens for Underground Equality* v. *City of Seattle,* at 1075.

34. McQuillin, *Municipal Corporations,* 3rd ed (New York: Callaghan).

35. This should be contrasted with *Johnson* v. *N.Y.S. Ed. Dept.,* 449 F.2d 871 (2d Cir. 1971), cert. denied 405 U.S. 916 (1972), in which the court upheld a state law that required school boards to supply free textbooks to children in grades one through six only in the event of majority approval of tax assessments. The court held that the state was privileged to assign to the school district the task of financing textbooks used in the lower grades and that it was privileged to assign to the voters of that school district the task of deciding whether or not to supply the funds for such textbooks.

36. Of course, services have been provided by special assessment for a long time. Whether the court would respond similarly when the means of financing have been recently changed does not seem clear. Fessler and May, "The Municipal Service Equalization Suit," point out that one additional legal means of avoiding the consequences of equal protection decisions is the transfer of some public services to the private sector or to privately owned public utilities.

37. See, for example, *Dandridge* v. *Williams,* 397 U.S. 471 (1970), public welfare; and *Lindsey* v. *Normet,* 405 U.S. 56 (1972), housing.

38. *San Antonio Independent School District* v. *Rodriguez,* 411 U.S. 1 (1973).

39. *San Antonio Independent School District* v. *Rodriguez.* This should be compared to *Serrano* v. *Priest,* 5 Cal. 3d 584, 487 P.2d 1241 (1971), which found primary and secondary public education to be a fundamental interest under the equal protection clause of the California Constitution. See Marshall's dissent in *Rodriguez,* as well as comment: "Equal Protection in the Urban Environment: The Right to Municipal Services," *Tulane Law Review* 46 (1972): 513–16; "The Evolution of Equal Protection: Education, Municipal Service, and Wealth," pp. 115–21, 158–70; and Bond, "Toward Equal Delivery of Municipal Services in the Central Cities," *Fordham University Law Journal* 4 (1976): 263.

40. *Goldstein* v. *City of Chicago,* 504 F. 2d 989 (7th Cir. 1974), garbage collection; *Wilkerson* v. *City of Coralville,* 478 F.2d 709 (8th Cir. 1973), annexation; *Towns* v. *Beame,* 386 F. Supp. 470 (S.D.N.Y. 1974), fire protection; *Pinckney* v. *Ohio Environmental Protection Agency,* 375 F. Supp. 305 (N.D. Ohio, 1974), the right to live in a healthful environment.

41. *Rodriguez,* at 23.

42. *Bush* v. *Orleans Parrish School Bd.,* 187 F. Supp. 42 (E.D. La. 1960), invalidated a state law that authorized the governor to close all public schools if any were forced to desegregate. In *Griffin* v. *County Sch. Bd. of Prince Edward Cty.,* 377 U.S. 218 (1964), the court ruled that the closing of city public schools while

tuition grants and tax concessions were given to assist white children in private segregated schools violated the Fourteenth Amendment.

43. *Palmer* v. *Thompson,* 403 U.S. 217 (1971).

44. See *Township of Hillsborough* v. *Cromwell,* 326 U.S. 620 (1946); *Cumberland Coal Co.* v. *Board,* 284 U.S. 23 (1931); and *Sunday Lake Iron Co.* v. *Wakefield,* 247 U.S. 350 (1918).

45. *Charleston Federal Savings and Loan Association* v. *Alderson,* 324 U.S. 182 (1945).

46. *Southland Mall Inc.* v. *Gainer,* 455 F.2d 887 (6th Cir. 1972).

47. *Nashville, Chattanooga and St. Louis Railway* v. *Browning,* 310 U.S. 362 (1940). However, classifications of property must have some rational basis, and thus cannot be completely arbitrary.

48. See cases in 84 *C.J.S. Taxation,* sections 22–25, Welch, "The Way We Were: Four Decades of Change in the Property Tax," in U.S. Advisory Commission on Intergovernmental Relations, *The Property Tax in a Changing Environment* (Washington, D.C.: U.S. Government Printing Office, 1974), and comment: "The Road to Uniformity in Real Estate Taxation: Valuation and Appeal," *University of Pennsylvania Law Review* 124 (1976): 1418.

49. See, for example, *Merlin* v. *Tax Assessors for Town of North Providence,* 337 A.2d 796 (1975).

50. *Hellerstein* v. *Assessor of the Town of Islip,* 37 N.Y. 2d 1, 332 N.E.2d 279 (1975).

51. For commentary on this issue, see Zagarne, *"Hellerstein* v. *Assessor of the Town of Islip:* A Response to Inequities in Real Property Assessments in New York," 27 *Syracuse Law Review* 27 (1976): 1045.

52. *Sudbury* v. *Commissioner of Corp. and Tax.,* 321 N.E. 2d 641 (1974). Other tax equalization cases are *E. Ingraham* v. *Town and City of Bristol,* 144 Conn. 374, 132 A.2d 563 (1957), cert. denied 371 U.S. 929 (1960), Connecticut; *Bettigole* v. *Assessors of Springfield,* 343 Mass. 223, 178 N.E.2d 10 (1961), Massachusetts; *Walter* v. *Schuler,* 176 So. 2d 81 (1965), Florida; *Russman* v. *Luckett,* 391 S.W. 2d 694 (1965), Kentucky; *State ex. rel. Park Inv. Co.* v. *Board of Tax Appeals,* 175 Ohio St. 410, 195 N.E. 2d 908 (1964), cert. denied 379 U.S. 818 (1966), Ohio; *Southern Ry. Co.* v. *Clement,* 57 Tenn. App. 54, 415 S.W. 2d 146 (1967), Tennessee. Tennessee later held a constitutional convention to specifically provide for classification and fractional assessment. See "Equality in Property Taxation—the Law, Practice and Prospects," *New England Law Journal* 11 (1976); 617, as well as Comment: "The Road to Uniformity." For empirical evidence relevant to *Sudbury,* see D. L. Rubinfeld, "The Determination of Equalized Valuation: A Massachusetts Case Study," *Public Finance Quarterly* 3 (1975): 153–61.

53. *Levy* v. *Parker,* 346 F. Supp. 897 (E.D. La. 1972), aff'd 411 U.S. 978 (1973).

54. *Scarnato* v. *Parker,* 415 F Supp. 272 (M.D. La. 1976).

55. D. Bradford and H. Kelejian ("An Econometric Model of Flight to the Suburbs," *Journal of Political Economy* 81 [1973]: 566–89) present some interesting evidence on this issue.

56. The argument about the impact of public policy on fiscal base is clearly made by J. Buchanan, "Principles of Urban Fiscal Strategy," *Public Choice* 11 (1971): 2.

57. See Holland and Oldman, "Assessment Sales Ratios." Zagarne, "A Response," suggests the same, citing New York data.

58. *Serrano* v. *Priest.* See also *Van Dusartz* v. *Hatfield,* 334 F. Supp. 870 (D. Minn. 1971).

59. *Rodriguez,* p. 28. Cases following *Rodriguez* include *Citizens Committee for Faraday Wood* v. *Lindsay,* 507 F2d 1065 (2d Cir. 1974), cert. denied 421 U.S. 948 (1975); *Ybarra* v. *City of Town of Los Altos Hill,* 503 F. 2d 250 (9th Cir. 1974); *Brown* v. *Board of Education of City of Chicago;* and *Amen* v. *City of Dearborn,* 363 F. Supp. 1267 (E.D. Mich. 1973).

60. *Robinson* v. *Cahill,* 118 N.J. Super. 223 (1972) aff'd 62 N.J. 473, 303 A.2d 273 (1972), cert. denied 414 U.S. 976 (1973).

61. For details and commentary see U.S. Department of Health, Education, and Welfare, Office of Education, "State Constitutional Provisions and Selected Legal

Materials Relating to Public School Finance," H.E.W. Pubn. N. (PE) 73–00002, (1973); Levin, "Reform through the State Courts," *Law and Contemporary Problems* 38 (1974): 310–11; Trachtenberg, "Reforming School Finance through State Constitutions: *Robinson* v. *Cahill* Points the Way," *Rutgers Law Review* 27 (1974): 365; and Grubb, "The First-Round of Legislative Reforms in the Post-*Serrano* World," *Law and Contemporary Problems* 38 (1974): 485. One potentially far-reaching case is *Horton* v. *Meskill,* 31 Conn. Sup. 377, 332 A.2d 113 (1974), in which the court struck down the Connecticut system of school finance under the state's equal protection clause by finding that education was a fundamental interest under the state constitution. The decision was upheld by the state supreme court in April 1977.

62. *Gautreaux* v. *Chicago Housing Authority,* 296 F. Supp. 907 (N.D. I11, 1969); aff'd. *Hills* v. *Gautreaux* 425 U.S. 284 (1976). See also *Crow* v. *Brown,* 332 F. Supp. 382 (N.D. Ga. 1971) aff'd. 457 F. 2d 788 (5th Cir. 1972); *Banks* v. *Perk,* 341 F. Supp. 1175 (N.D. Ohio 1972); *Dailey* v. *City of Lawton,* 425 F. 2d 1037 (10th Cir. 1970).

63. *United Farm Workers of Florida Housing Project Inc.* v. *City of Delray Beach, Florida,* 493 F.2d 799 (5th Cir. 1974).

64. *Kennedy Park Homes Ass'n* v. *City of Lackawanna,* 436 F.2d 108 (2d Cir. 1970) cert. denied, 401 U.S. 1010 (1971). See, also, *United States* v. *City of Black Jack,* 508 F.2d 1179 (8th Cir. 1974) cert. denied, 422 U.S. 1042 (1975), *Joseph Skillken and Co.* v. *City of Toledo,* 380 F. Supp. 228 (N.D. Ohio 1974), and *Anderson* v. *Town of Forest Park, Oklahoma,* 239 F. Supp. 576 (W.D. Oklahoma, 1965).

65. *Washington* v. *Davis,* 427 U.S. 229 (1976).

66. *Village of Arlington Heights* v. *Metropolitan Housing Development Corp.,* 429 U.S. 252 (1977).

67. *Arlington Heights,* p. 4078.

68. Ibid., p. 4077. This should be contrasted with the earlier decision of *U.S.* v. *City of Black Jack,* which stated that once a prima facie case of a racially discriminatory effect had been made, the defendant must demonstrate a compelling state interest, or *Burton* v. *Wilmington Parking Authority,* 365 U.S. 715 (1961), in which the court stated that a good-faith denial of equal protection was of no consolation.

69. *Belle Terre* v. *Boraas,* 416 U.S. 1 (1974). See also *Usery* v. *National League of Cities,* 426 U.S. 833 (1976).

70. For commentary on the trend to reform through the state courts, see Ackerman, "The Mount Laurel Decision: Expanding the Boundaries of Zoning Reform," *University of Illinois Law Forum* 1 (1976): 1–73; and Payne, "Delegation Doctrine in the Reform of Local Government Law: The Case of Exclusionary Zoning," *Rutgers Law Review* 29 (1976): 803.

71. *Southern Burlington County NAACP* v. *Township of Mount Laurel,* 67 N.J. 151, 173, 336 A.2d 713, 724 (1975). See also *Berenson* v. *Town of New Castle,* 38 N.Y. 2d 102 (1975); *Town of Pompey* v. *Parker,* 385 N.Y.S. 2d 959 (1976); and *National Land and Investment Co.* v. *Easttown Twp. Board of Adjustment,* 419 Pa. 504, 215 A.2d 597 (1966).

72. For some problems raised by *Mt. Laurel* see "The Inadequacy of Judicial Remedies in Cases of Exclusionary Zoning," *Michigan Law Review* 74 (1976): 760, and Payne, "Delegation Doctrine."

73. Of course, the state constitution approach is not the only possible avenue to achieving equal access. A second approach may entail placing additional reliance on federal statutes. For example, in *Arlington Heights,* the U.S. Supreme Court remanded the case to the court of appeals to determine whether the refusal of Arlington Heights to rezone violated the Fair Housing Act. (42 U.S.C. 3601 et seq.)

74. Thus, M. S. Feldstein ("Wealth Neutrality and Local Choice in Public Education," *American Economic Review* 65 [1975]): 75–89 may be overstating the case when he argues that Serrano implied wealth neutrality, i.e., that fiscal base per pupil and expenditures be uncorrelated.

75. J. E. Coons, W. H. Clune, and S. D. Sugarman, *Private Wealth and Public Education* (Cambridge, Mass.: Harvard University Press, 1970).

76. Feldstein, "Wealth Neutrality," estimates low (.28) but positive wealth elasticities for educational spending, but since low-wealth communities often face lower prices for schooling (as defined by Feldstein), low-wealth communities may spend more than high-wealth communities. Feldstein points out, in fact, that his "adjusted wealth elasticity exceeds the price elasticity, DPE would still leave a positive elasticity with respect to wealth." (Ibid., p. 78.)

77. "State Education Aid and School Tax Efforts in Large Cities," by D. Netzer, in *Selected Papers in School Finance* (Washington, D.C.: Government Printing Office, 1974), U.S. Department of Health, Education, and Welfare, Office of Education.

78. R. D. Reischauer and R. W. Hartman (*Reforming School Finance* [Washington, D.C.: Brookings Institution, 1973], p. 67) also conclude that "central cities exhibit property values per pupil well above the average for their states, and in many instances property values per pupil are higher in central cities than in their suburbs."

79. H. E. Brazer and A. P. Anderson, "Adjusting for Differences among School Districts in the Costs of Educational Inputs: A Feasibility Report," in *Selected Papers in School Finance*.

80. Empirical evidence on these issues for the Commonwealth of Massachusetts are described in D. L. Rubinfeld, "Property Taxation, Full Valuation, and the Reform of Educational Finance in Massachusetts," in *Property Taxation and the Finance of Education* (ed. R. W. Lindholm) (Madison: University of Wisconsin Press, 1974).

81. This point is made more extensively in R. P. Inman, "Optimal Fiscal Reform of Metropolitan Schools: Some Simulation Results with a General Equilibrium Model," *American Economic Review* 68 (1978): 107–22.

82. The potentially progressive consequences of many statewide equalization programs is often blunted, because little money is actually contributed by wealthy districts and the range of expenditures that is subsidized is often severely limited.

83. For some preliminary evidence on the location and movement of jobs in metropolitan areas, see J. Kain, "Housing Segregation, Negro Employment, and Metropolitan Decentralization," *Quarterly Journal of Economics* 82 (1968): 175, 197, and "The Distribution and Movement of Jobs and Industry," in *The Metropolitan Enigma*, ed. J. Q. Wilson pp. 1–33 (Cambridge, Mass.: Harvard University Press, 1968).

84. R. Maser, W. Riker, and R. Rosett (1974), "The Effects of Zoning and Externalities on the Prices of Land in Monroe County, New York," University of Rochester, p. 12.

85. See Branfman, Cohen, and Trubek, "Measuring the Invisible Wall," and G. E. Peterson, "Land Prices and Factor Substitution in the Metropolitan Housing Market," *American Economic Review* (in press).

86. B. W. Hamilton, E. S. Mills and D. Puryear, "The Tiebout Hypothesis and Residential Income Segregation," in *Fiscal Zoning and Land Use Controls*.

87. B. W. Hamilton, "Property Taxes and the Tiebout Hypothesis: Some Empirical Evidence," in *Fiscal Zoning and Land Use Controls*.

88. H. Pack and J. R. Pack, "Metropolitan Fragmentation and Suburban Homogeneity."

NAME INDEX

SUBJECT INDEX

THE JOHNS HOPKINS UNIVERSITY PRESS
This book was composed in Linotype Times Roman text and Ultra Bodoni Italic display type by the Maryland Linotype Composition Co., Inc., from a design by Charles West. It was printed on 50-lb. Publishers Eggshell Wove and bound by Universal Lithographers, Inc.

Library of Congress Cataloging in Publication Data
Main entry under title:

Current issues in urban economics.

Includes index.
1. Cities and towns—United States—Addresses,
essays, lectures. 2. Urban economics—Addresses,
essays, lectures. I. Mieszkowski, Peter M., 1936–
II. Straszheim, Mahlon R., 1939–
HT151.C87   330.9′173′2   78–14947
ISBN 0–8018–2109–6
ISBN 0–8018–2184–3 pbk.